P9-CDH-014

Guides to Information Sources

Information Sources in

Law

Guides to Information Sources

A series under the General Editorship of
Ia C. McIlwaine,
M.W. Hill and
Nancy J. Williamson

This series was known previously as 'Butterworths Guides to Information Sources'.

Other titles available include:

Information Sources in Environmental Protection
edited by Selwyn Eagle and Judith Deschamps
Information Sources in Official Publications
edited by Valerie J. Nurcombe
Information Sources in Architecture and Construction (Second edition)
edited by Valerie J. Nurcombe
Information Sources in Chemistry (Fourth edition)
edited by R.T. Bottle and J.F.B. Rowland
Information Sources in Physics (Third edition)
edited by Dennis F. Shaw
Information Sources in Engineering
edited by Ken Mildren and Peter Hicks
Information Sources in Finance and Banking
by Ray Lester
Information Sources in Grey Literature (Third edition)
C.P. Auger
Information Sources in the Life Sciences (Fourth edition)
edited by H.V. Wyatt
Information Sources in Sport and Leisure
edited by Michele Shoebridge
Information Sources in Patents
edited by C.P. Auger
Information Sources for the Press and Broadcast Media
edited by Selwyn Eagle
Information Sources in Information Technology
edited by David Haynes
Information Sources in Pharmaceuticals
edited by W.R. Pickering
Information Sources in Metallic Materials
edited by M.N. Patten
Information Sources in the Earth Sciences (Second edition)
edited by David N. Wood, Joan E. Hardy and Anthony P. Harvey
Information Sources in Cartography
edited by C.R. Perkins and R.B. Barry
Information Sources in Polymers and Plastics
edited by R.T. Adkins

Guides to Information Sources

Information Sources in

Law

Second Edition

Edited by
Jules Winterton
and
Elizabeth M. Moys

London • Melbourne • Munich • New Providence, N.J.

British Library Cataloguing in Publication Data
A catalogue record for this title is available from the British Library

Library of Congress Cataloging-in-Publication Data
Information sources in law / edited by Jules Winterton and Elizabeth M. Moys. -- 2nd ed.
p. cm. -- (Guides to information sources)
Includes bibliographical references and index.
ISBN 1-85739-041-5
1. Legal research--Europe. 2. Law--Europe--Bibliography.
I. Winterton, Jules. II. Moys, Elizabeth M. III. Series: Guides to information sources (London, England)
KJC76.I54 1997
340′.07204--dc21 97-1205
CIP

Published by Bowker-Saur, Maypole House, Maypole Road,
East Grinstead, West Sussex RH19 1HU, UK
Tel: +44(0)1342 330100 Fax: +44(0)1342 330191
E-mail: lis@bowker-saur.com
Internet Website: http://www.bowker-saur.com/service/
Bowker-Saur is part of REED BUSINESS INFORMATION.

ISBN 1-85739-041-5

Cover design by Calverts Press
Typesetting by The Castlefield Press, Kettering, Northants
Printed on acid-free paper
Printed and bound in Great Britain by Antony Rowe Ltd, Chippenham

Series editors' foreword

The second half of the 20th century has been characterized by the recognition that our style of life depends on acquiring and using information effectively. It has always been so, but only in the information society has the extent of the dependence been recognized and the development of technologies for handling information become a priority. These modern technologies enable us to store more information, to select and process parts of the store more skilfully and transmit the product more rapidly than we would have dreamt possible only 40 years ago. Yet the irony still exists that, while we are able to do all this and are assailed from all sides by great masses of information, ensuring that one has what one needs just when one wants it is frequently just as difficult as ever. Knowledge may, as Johnson said in the well known quotation, be of two kinds, but information, in contrast, is of many kinds and most of it is, for each individual, knowable only after much patient searching.

The aim of each Guide in this series is simple. It is to reduce the time which needs to be spent on that patient searching; to recommend the best starting point and sources mostly likely to yield the desired information. Like all subject guides, the sources discussed have had to be selected, and the criteria for selection will be given by the individual editors and will differ from subject to subject. However, the overall objective is constant; that of providing a way into a subject to those new to the field or to identify major new or possibly unexplored sources to those already familiar with it.

The great increase in new sources of information and the overwhelming input of new information from the media, advertising, meetings and conferences, letters, internal reports, office memoranda, magazines, junk mail, electronic mail, fax, bulletin boards etc. inevitably tend to make one reluctant to add to the load on the mind and memory by consulting books and journals. Yet they, and the other traditional types of printed material, remain for many purposes the most reliable sources of information. Despite all the information that is instantly accessible via the new technologies one still has to look things up in databooks, monographs, journals, patent specifications, standards, reports both official and commercial, and on maps and in atlases. Permanent recording of facts, theories and opinions is still carried out primarily by publishing in printed form. Musicians still work from printed scores even though they are helped by sound recordings. Sailors still use printed charts and tide tables even though they have radar and sonar equipment.

However, thanks to computerized indexes, online and CD-ROM, searching the huge bulk of technical literature to draw up a list of references can can be undertaken reasonably quickly. The result, all too often, can still be a formidably long list, of which a knowledge of the nature and structure of information sources in that field can be used to put in order of likely value.

It is rarely necessary to consult everything that has been published on the topic of a search. When attempting to prove that an invention is genuinely novel, a complete search may seem necessary, but even then it is common to search only obvious sources and leave it to anyone wishing to oppose the grant of a patent to bear the cost of hunting for a prior disclosure in some obscure journal. Usually, much proves to be irrelevant to the particular aspect of our interest and whatever is relevant may be unsound. Some publications are sadly lacking in important detail and present broad generalizations flimsily bridged with arches of waffle. In any academic field there is a 'pecking order' of journals so that articles in one journal may be assumed to be of a higher or lower calibre than those in another. Those experienced in the field know these things. The research scientist soon learns, as it is part of his training, the degree of reliance he can place on information from co-workers elsewhere, on reports of research by new and (to him) unknown researchers, on data compilations and on manufacturers of equipment. The information worker, particularly when working in a field other than his own, faces very serious problems as he tries to compile, probably from several sources, a report on which his client may base important actions. Even the librarian, faced only with recommending two or three books or journal articles, meets the same problem though less acutely.

In the Bowker-Saur Guides to Information Sources we aim to bring you the knowledge and experience of specialists in the field. Each author regularly uses the information sources and services described and any tricks of the trade that the author has learnt are passed on.

Nowadays, two major problems face those who are embarking upon research or who are in charge of collections of information of every kind. One is the increasingly specialized knowledge of the user and the concomitant ignorance of other potentially useful disciplines. The second problem is the trend towards cross-disciplinary studies. This has led to a great mixing of academic programmes – and a number of imprecisely defined fields of study. Courses are offered in Environmental Studies, Women's Studies, Communication Studies or Area Studies, and these are the forcing ground for research. The editors are only too aware of the difficulties raised by those requiring information from such hybrid subject fields and this approach, too, is being handled in the series alongside the traditional 'hard disciplines'.

Guides to the literature have a long and honoured history. Marion Spicer of SRIS recently drew to our attention a guide written in 1891 for engineers. No doubt there are even earlier ones. Nowadays, with the information and even the publishing fields changing quite frequently, it is necessary to update guides every few years and this we do in this present Series.

Michael Hill
Ia McIlwaine
Nancy Williamson

About the contributors

Pal A. Bertnes is the Law Librarian at the Law School Library, University of Oslo. After graduating as a lawyer in 1972, he has worked mostly in law librarianship. Since 1983 he has been the director of the Law School Library in Oslo. He is also a well known author and editor in the field of methodology and tools concerning legal sources and scientific librarianship and has lectured to law students on these topics for the past twelve years. He has also developed Bibjure, an electronic library system and database for private law firms and governmental legal institutions in Norway.

Peter Blume is Professor of Legal Informatics at the Faculty of Law, University of Copenhagen. Having graduated from the university in 1974 he obtained his PhD in 1981 and his LLD in 1989. He has written several books including a book on retrieval of legal information in Danish law, *Juridisk informationssøgning*, 5th ed., 1997.

William E. Butler is Professor of Comparative Law in the University of London, Academician of the Russian Academy of Natural Sciences and of the Academy of Sciences of Ukraine, Director of the Vinogradoff Institute, University College London, and Professor of International and Comparative Law and Dean of the Faculty of Law, Moscow Higher School of Social and Economic Sciences. He read law at Harvard University, where he has been Visiting Professor of Law, and holds higher doctorates from The Johns Hopkins University (PhD) and the University of London (LLD). He served as a member of the EC/IS Joint Task Force on Law Reform in the Independent States and has advised The World Bank, the European Bank for Reconstruction and Development, the European Commission, the United Kingdom Know-How Fund, and specialized agencies of the United Nations on law reform in the Independent States.

Eugene Buttigieg is a lecturer in European Community law in the Department of European and Comparative Law at the University of Malta. Prior to his university appointment, he was a Senior Legal Officer at the EU Directorate within the Ministry of Foreign Affairs where his main areas of responsibility included competition policy, consumer protection and intellectual property. Dr. Buttigieg has published widely on European Community law.

Mário Bigotte Chorão is a Professor in the Faculty of Law of the Catholic University of Portugal in Lisbon, where he teaches Introduction to the Study of Law. His published works include: *Probation. Alguns aspectos juridícos, criminologicos e sociais* (*Probation. Some legal, criminological and social aspects*), Coimbra, 1959; *Introdução ao Direito I. O conceito de direito* (*Introduction to law. I. The concept of law*), Coimbra, repr. 1994; and *Temas fundamentais de direito* (*Fundamental themes of law*), Coimbra, repr. 1991. He is a director of the editorial team for the encyclopedias *Verbo. Enciclopédia Luso-Brasileira de Cultura*, Lisboa, 1963, 23 vols., and *Polis, Enciclopédia Verbo da Sociedade e do Estado*, Lisboa, 1983–87, 5 vols.

Peter Clinch is Information Specialist – Law at the University of Wales, Cardiff. He graduated in law in 1968 and completed a PhD on law reporting in 1989. He has devised and led legal research skills courses for undergraduates, postgraduates and staff from public sector organisations and has written several books, the latest being *Legal information: what it is and where to find it*, Aslib 1995. He is also a regular contributor to journals on law, teaching and librarianship.

Ettore S. D'Elia took his degree in law at the University of Bari where he then became Assistant Professor in Commercial Law. He has also practised law as an attorney in the fields of civil and administrative law. He is currently a Research Fellow at the Istituto per la Documentazione Giuridica (Institute for Legal Documentation) of the Italian National Research Council in Florence. He has written widely on leasing, software protection, administrative courts, legal promulgation and the theory of legal information.

Osman Doğru is an Associate Professor at the Law Faculty of Marmara University, Istanbul. After graduating from the Law Faculty of Istanbul University, he completed a PhD there. He currently lectures on International Human Rights Law at Marmara. He has published two books and is involved with research projects in the field of human rights law.

Ilse Dosoudil is Director of the University Library, Vienna. She is Chairman of the Commission of Law Problems in Vereinigung Osterreichischer Bibliothekare/innen, Chairman of the Arbeitsgemeinschaft der Bibliotheksdirektoren/innen (Ministry of Science, Research and Arts), member of the Arbeitsgemeinschaft für juristisches Bibliotheks- und Dokumentationswesen, Regensburg (the German section of the International Association of Law Libraries).

Joanna Drake is a lecturer in European Community law in the Department of European and Comparative Law at the University of Malta. Prior to her university appointment, she was a Legal Research Officer at the Embassy of Malta in Brussels and subsequently for five years, a Senior Legal Officer at the EU Directorate within the Ministry of Foreign Affairs, where her main areas of responsibility were competition policy, trade, external relations and internal market. Dr. Drake has published widely on European Community law.

Maria Manuela Farrajota is a lawyer practising in a law firm in Lisbon. She has a law degree from the Faculty of Law of the Catholic University of Portugal in Lisbon, and a post-graduate Diploma in European Community Law from the Centre for European Studies from the same university.

John Furlong is Information Manager with William Fry, Solicitors, one of Ireland's largest law firms. He worked for many years as a manager in a number of legal departments within the Irish Civil Service. He has contributed a number of articles on legal issues and technology matters to Irish legal journals and periodicals.

Claire M. Germain is currently the Edward Cornell Law Librarian and Professor of Law at Cornell University, New York. She was born and raised in France where she received her Lic. Lettres from Paris III-Sorbonne, and Lic. Droit from Paris XII. She has a MCL from Louisiana State University and a Masters in Law Librarianship from the University of Denver, and was a research scholar at the Max-Planck-Institute, Hamburg, Germany. Her publications include *Germain's transnational law research: a guide for attorneys*, looseleaf, (1991) and *Guide to foreign legal materials: French*, with C. Szladits, 1985, as well as many articles in comparative law and legal research topics. She teaches a seminar in French law. She is actively involved in all aspects of legal information from rare books to the use of computer technologies for research and teaching.

David R. Hart studied history at the University of Glasgow and librarianship at the University of Sheffield. Specializing initially in European Communities information, he was appointed Law Librarian at the University of Dundee in 1986. He is presently Chair of the British and Irish Association of Law Librarians.

Guy Holborn, MA, LLB, ALA has been Librarian of Lincoln's Inn Library since 1985, having previously held posts at the House of Lords Library and the Institute of Advanced Legal Studies. He is author of *Butterworths Legal Research Guide* (1993) and is currently Honorary Secretary of the British and Irish Association of Law Librarians.

Gunnel Jarbrant is law librarian at the Stockholm University Library. She is the head of its department of law.

Giina Kaskla has been Head of the Law Literature Section of the Reference and Information Analysis Centre of the National Library of Estonia since 1995. She holds a degree in Estonian philology from the University of Tartu.

Holger Knudsen is Deputy Librarian at the Max-Planck-Institute for Foreign Private Law and Private International Law in Hamburg, Germany. He has degrees in law and library information science and has worked in Cologne, Florence, Lausanne and Bonn. Dr. Knudsen is an honorary professor of law, Chairman of the Board of Legal Advisers of the German Librarians' Association and member of the Board of Directors of the International Association of Law Libraries.

Halvor Kongshavn is the Law Librarian at Bergen University Library, Norway. He has a law degree (cand. jur.) and an MA in criminology both from the University of Oslo. He has written several books and articles on legal research, legal bibliographies and other topics.

Jarmila Looks is lawyer-librarian at the Swiss Institute of Comparative Law, a federal research institute with an important library of foreign, international and comparative law literature, situated in Lausanne, Switzerland. She has a degree in Arts from Brno, Czech Republic, and is a graduate of the Lausanne Law School. In addition, she has a librarianship diploma from the Swiss Association of Librarians.

Küllike Maurer has been the Legal Adviser to the Estonian Translation and Legislative Support Centre since 1995. She holds a degree in law from the University of Tartu. Her publications include: *Sources of legal information in the Baltic States* in *Central- och Osteuropas juridiska informationskällor: Rapport från det tredje nordiska juridiska biblioteksmötet in Helsingfors, 8–11 juni 1994* (*Report of the Third Conference of Law Librarians of the Nordic Countries*) (1995) Helsinki University Institute of International Economic Law, and *Bibliographia juridica Estonica, 1918–1940: legal literature of Estonia* (1994) National Library of Estonia.

Elizabeth M. Moys, BA, FLA, Registered Indexer, retired from librarianship in 1989, after twenty-one years as College Librarian of Goldsmiths' College in the University of London, to become a free-lance indexer. She started her professional career with seven years at the Institute of Advanced Legal Studies in London. She was a founder member of the British and Irish Association of Law Librarians, and was the Editor and Chair of the Publications Committee, 1970–7, Vice-President 1987–90 and was President for the term 1990–3. Member of the Board of the International Association of Law Libraries, 1965–8. Winner of the Library Association Wheatley Medal for an outstanding index in 1991. Publications include: *European Law Libraries Guide, 1971; Manual of Law Librarianship*, 1976 and 2nd ed. 1987; editorship of *The Law Librarian*, 1970–7; articles in various journals.

Anne Pries (Anne P. Pries-Heijke) is the Librarian at the Institute of East European Law and Russian Studies at the University of Leiden. After graduating from Leiden University in 1978, where she studied Slavonic Languages and Literature, she started to work at the then named Documentation Office for East European Law. She wrote her doctoral thesis on a legal subject in Russian literature and defended it in the Leiden Law Faculty in 1988. She participates regularly in international juridical and Slavonic librarian conferences. Since 1990 she has been a member of the Leiden University Council.

Mario Ragona took his degree in Law from the University of Florence and is currently a Senior Research Fellow at the Istituto per la Documentazione Giuridica (Institute for Legal Documentation) of the Italian National Research Council. His fields of special interest are legal information technology and the construction of legal data banks. He has collaborated in building data banks related to Italian law journals, the press and the law, and environmental law.

Sami Sarvilinna is a graduate of the University of Helsinki Law School and St. Edmund Hall, Oxford. He is a licensed translator and has worked in the Finnish Ministry of Justice as editor of the series *Translations of Finnish Legislation* and information officer for the Ministry's European Law Unit. He is now a trainee at Helsinki District Court, expecting to receive his qualification as a judge in 1998.

Frances Shipsey has been European Documentation Centre Librarian at the British Library of Political & Economic Science, London School of Economics & Political Science since 1990. Before that she worked at the Institute of Advanced Legal Studies Library and at the Law Commission.

Maria I. Smolka-Day is Associate Director for Foreign and International Law and Lecturer at the Biddle Law Library, University of Pennsylvania Law School. She earned an LLM there in 1983. Before moving to the United States, she earned an SJD from Marie Curie-Sklodowska University in Lublin, Poland, where she was an Assistant Professor of Law for several years. With a background in both law and library science, she has published legal and bibliographic articles in both Poland and the United States.

Heather Thrift is Law Librarian at the University of Sheffield. After graduating from The University of London Goldsmiths College with a degree in music and the University of Sheffield with a Masters degree in Librarianship, she worked first in public libraries before moving to Baker & McKenzie as Assistant Librarian in 1987. In 1989 she moved to Lancaster University where she was Subject Librarian for Law, Official Publications, the EDC and Women's Studies. She joined the University of Sheffield in 1993.

Christian F. Verbeke is a freelance law bibliographer and author of several legal bibliographies including *Belgian law: an annotated bibliographic guide* *to reference materials* (1994). He read law in Boston in the 1950's and is the founder of Droit Ancien & Moderne, a firm specialising in law collections development, for whom he has edited some 25 annotated catalogues of early law books. A member of CEJA, Belgium's professional association of expert witnesses and arbitration specialists, he is also editor of the Belgian Bibliographical Commission's *Bibliographia Belgica* series.

Derek Way has recently retired after 28 years as law librarian at the University of Liverpool. He is also a founder member of BIALL (the British and Irish Association of Law Librarians), and has contributed to the *Law Librarian* and to the *Manual of law librarianship*.

Jules Winterton is Librarian of the Institute of Advanced Legal Studies, University of London, and before that worked at the Institute of Classical Studies and as European Documentation Centre Librarian and Law Librarian at Queen Mary and Westfield College. He has a degree in English and Latin from the University of Kent at Canterbury, a diploma in library and information studies from Manchester Polytechnic and a law degree from the University of London. He has contributed to the *Manual of law librarianship 2nd edn.* (1987) and the *Bibliography of Commonwealth law reports* (1991) and to various journals. He is a visiting research fellow at the Max-Planck-Institute in Hamburg in June 1997. He was Chair of the British and Irish Association of Law Librarians 1994/95 and is a member of the Board of Directors of the International Association of Law Libraries and the Libraries Committee of the Society of Public Teachers of Law.

George D. Woodman has been Librarian of the Northern Ireland Assembly Library in Belfast since 1981. He has written articles on Northern Ireland legislation for *Law Librarian* and is a regular reviewer for *Reference Reviews*.

Peter G. Xuereb is Head of Department of European and Comparative Law and Chairman of the European Documentation and Research Centre of the University of Malta. Professor Xuereb was previously Senior Lecturer at Queen Mary and Westfield College, University of London and has published widely in EC and Comparative Company Law and in European Law.

Georgios Yannopoulos, LLB, PhD is a qualified lawyer and has qualifications in computer programming and systems analysis. He was awarded his PhD at Queen Mary and Westfield College, University of London, for a thesis on Modelling the Legal Decision Process for Information Technology Applications in Law. He is currently the European Union Postdoctoral Research Fellow examining the legal issues of electronic patient cards. His research interests include the use of IT for legal applications as well as aspects of substantive computer law. His most recent publications concern software protection in Greece.

Contents

Introduction

This is a practical book for practical people, both for those in the commercial world and for other researchers. We also hope it will assist those developing services and collections relating to the law of European countries, wherever they are based. We have tried to ensure that there is never a dead end and always a further source of information whether printed, electronic or direct to an organization.

When first asked to compile this volume, we had to decide what limits should be set to its jurisdictional coverage. Clearly world coverage would be impossible within the time and space limits set by the Series Editors. On the other hand, restriction to the legal systems of the United Kingdom would have been too narrow, ignoring the steadily increasing influence of European legal systems on each other and the expansion of the European market. We decided that the most useful arrangement would be to include as many individual countries as possible in the geographical area of Europe, regardless of any regional groupings to which they might or might not belong, since sources in many of those countries were insufficiently documented in English. We had hoped to indicate the coverage of this book in the title by calling it 'Information sources in law in Europe' but this did not prove possible because of the requirements of the series to which it belongs.

We are very grateful to the authors from so many countries who have contributed chapters on their own and other national legal systems, helping to fill a serious gap in the literature in English. We should have liked to include chapters on several other European countries and in particular we expected a chapter on Hungary but, at a late stage, illness prevented the chapter being delivered.

We have included the European Union itself because its law becomes part of the law of its member states in a much more immediate way than is the case with other sources of law outside the jurisdictions themselves.

Otherwise we have not attempted to document sources of public international law such as international organizations based in Europe, except basic treaty sources, because this would require and deserve another volume.

The previous edition of this work was devoted almost entirely to English-speaking jurisdictions, including some in other continents. Since that book was written, further guides to legal research in those countries have appeared, so that it seemed to us that it would be invidious to attempt to improve on their excellent reference publications.

This volume covers selected sources of information for law both in the original language and in other languages, mainly in English. Of necessity sources specific to particular branches of law are not covered, although the most important codes, treatises and leading journals in the main areas of law are mentioned in many of the chapters; the book concentrates on general sources and the research tools which will provide further specialist sources if required.

This book differs considerably from some other volumes in the series because of the nature of law and legal information. First, law is usually tied to territory and is therefore highly jurisdictional, unlike some other subjects which are not likely to vary in their basics from country to country. Each legal jurisdiction has its own legal system and, although some systems may bear a family resemblance, each one is different in detail.

Second, the laws applying in any jurisdiction are in a continual state of flux. New legislation is constantly being produced, some existing laws are revoked and, at least in common law jurisdictions, decisions in the superior courts from day to day make varying degrees of change to the application of law. Therefore, a considerable proportion of legal information must be sought in serial publications: legislation, law reports, government gazettes, etc.

The text is up to date generally to December 1996 with some amendments at the proof stage in early 1997. In our attempt to make this volume of direct use, we have included information which can be more subject to change than bibliographic references, in particular telephone and fax numbers and notoriously Internet addresses. For any changes which affect you, we apologise, and we should be glad to receive new or corrected information (Elizabeth Moys was responsible for the European Union, Ireland, Malta and United Kingdom chapters and the index, Jules Winterton for the remaining chapters).

We should like to thank all the authors for their care and dedication and their colleagues who participated in whatever way in gathering the information. We should also like to thank our own friends and colleagues for their support and encouragement and tolerance, particularly the staff of the Institute of Advanced Legal Studies Library and Bowker-Saur.

Jules Winterton
Elizabeth M. Moys

Notes on the arrangement of materials

The author of each chapter has followed a general framework and order of presentation provided by the Editors and used a common but flexible set of sections which is described below. Each jurisdiction and its literature will of course have its own particular nature and features which its chapter reflects and so sections will differ in prominence in each chapter, being expanded or omitted as appropriate.

Chapters covering several jurisdictions may additionally contain a general section at the start which describes historical material or current general material relevant to all the jurisdictions. The first chapter is on general sources which may supplement the other chapters.

The general framework for each jurisdiction is as follows:

Introduction to the legal system with attention to the constitution, law-making bodies and the sources of law;

Introductory works on the legal system and legal research includes introductory works in English and works on the legal literature of the country and how to perform legal research.

Legislation mentions the up to date sources for legislation, often the official gazette, and any other major official or commercial series or collections of legislation. Notes on when legislation normally comes into force and the form of citation also appear here. Preparatory materials including draft legislation and parliamentary proceedings are mentioned here.

Codes and commentaries contains reference to the major codes with dates, plain and annotated editions and major commentaries, which in some jurisdictions include the major treatises for some areas of law.

Treaties mentions the source of treaty-making power, the publication of single treaties and compilations and any source of information on the current status of treaties.

Law reports, judgments deals with reports of judgments of courts and administrative tribunals with some mention of the court system and the importance of judicial decisions in the legal system. Digests or compilations of summaries of judgments are included where available. Periodicals in several jurisdictions contain law reports but also legislation and scholarly articles and do not fall neatly into our categories.

Computer-based systems focuses on databases of primary materials in various formats, including those available on Internet sites, other systems and relevant Internet addresses are mentioned in the appropriate section.

Other government documents is occasionally used for official publications, not included elsewhere, which are important to the practice or study of law.

Encyclopedias, large collections describes legal encyclopedias of major significance across the whole field of law, not in particular subject areas.

Directories

Bibliographies include legal bibliographies, current and older, bibliographies of official publications and, particularly in the absence of specialized works, general or national bibliographies in which legal works may be found.

Dictionaries, concentrating on legal dictionaries where available.

Other reference books has been used in some chapters to mention some of the major handbooks of law in particular subject areas and works about the legal profession.

Current information sources:

- **Journals**, frequent journals for the practitioner and outstanding scholarly journals;
- **News information**
- **Business and financial information**, selected basic sources;
- **Statistics**, standard collections of statistics of relevance to law and to general business giving basic economic and trade indicators.

Useful addresses for each jurisdiction:

(Telephone numbers are given in their international form with the country code prefix instead of the leading '0'.)

- **Associations of lawyers**
- **Government organizations**
- **Courts**
- **Education and training**, leading law schools, professional training centres;
- **Research institutions**
- **Libraries**
- **Publishers and booksellers**, including suppliers of databases.

List of works cited at the end of the chapter, lists all the works cited in the chapter even if it covers several jurisdictions, except for the United Kingdom chapter which has a list at the end of each jurisdiction.

CHAPTER ONE

General sources

JULES WINTERTON

This chapter is a brief guide to a range of sources of legal information in English which may be useful for European jurisdictions and may be more easily available or accessible than jurisdiction-specific sources for some readers. The sources are mainly encyclopedic or multi-jurisdictional compilations of national materials rather than true comparative studies. Individual contents of some of these works are cited selectively in the following chapters.

It is not possible in the space available to mention more than a very small proportion of the large number of sources which might be relevant. General legal reference sources have been selected which give direct answers but also form starting points for further research. The arrangement below is the same as in the following chapters (described in **Notes on the arrangement of materials**) but exceptionally there is no 'List of useful addresses' since they all appear in the appropriate country chapter.

Legal systems

The legal systems or legal families to which the countries of Europe belong and the other systems by which they have been influenced are described in the comparative studies *Major legal systems of the world today* (David and Brierley, 1985) and 'The legal systems of the world, their comparison and unification: structure and the divisions of law' (*International Encyclopedia of Comparative Law*, 1971–, volume 2, chapter 2). Although each country in Europe displays unique characteristics, the large majority belong in general terms to the 'the civil law system' family, while Ireland and the jurisdictions of the United Kingdom belong to the 'common law system' family, the majority of whose members are outside Europe. The civil law system is described in Szladits ([1974]) and the common law system in Weir ([1974]), and David and Brierley (1985) describe both with extensive bibliographical information. Many of the country chapters which follow make reference in their introductory sections to this basic distinction.

The chapters each provide their own brief description of the legal system of the individual country and its constitution. *Constitutions of the countries of the world* (1971–), a monumental work at present in 21 looseleaf volumes, contains constitutions, and sometimes related legislation, in both English and the original language. It also contains helpful chronologies of relevant events and select bibliographies with emphasis on the political as well as legal aspects of the constitution and its making. Although the latest amendments may not be included, the work is regularly updated and assiduous in giving the date of applicability of the text and the work often has translations not easily obtained elsewhere. Until recently this work was edited by Blaustein and Flanz, and is still known informally as 'Blaustein'; we cite it with both editors although the looseleaf title pages now show Gisbert Flanz only, following the death of Albert Blaustein. The volume numbers cited may change as material expands and is moved into different binders. As with other looseleaf works, the dates of the contents cited in the following chapters will change as they are updated.

The International Constitutional Law server (ICL) at the University of Würzburg, http://www.uni-wuerzburg.de/law/home.html, also contains a wide selection of translations of constitutions with brief related information.

The opportunity in each of the following chapters to describe the legislature of each country was extremely limited. Two recent books offer analysis of major issues affecting the role of the legislature in Europe, *The new parliaments of Central and Eastern Europe* (Olson and Norton, 1996) and *National parliaments and the European Union* (Norton, 1996). While addressing particular issues, they give a great deal of information about the structure and procedure of the parliaments as well as references to further literature.

Information about the legal professions in Europe is vital to an understanding of the legal systems. *The legal professions in the new Europe* (Tyrrell and Yaqub, 1996) describes in detail the various professions, including their names and functions, training and qualification, rights and codes of conduct. There are chapters by local experts on each of the member states of the European Union, on Iceland, Norway, and Switzerland, and a chapter on the Channel Islands and the Isle of Man. The book also gathers together the provisions of Community law and issues in its development which are directly relevant to the practice of law and the provision of legal services.

Introductory works on legal systems and legal research

Introductory works to law in each jurisdiction are noted in all chapters although for some countries there is no recent book in English.

The *International encyclopedia of comparative law* began publication in 1971 and is not yet completed. The national reports which comprise volume one, which is almost complete, represent excellent examples of concise and helpful introductions, often with extensive selected bibliographies, by leading local scholars. They were issued in paperback parts covering letters of the alphabet, so the pagination consists of letters as well as numbers. Many of the national reports, mostly written in the 1970s, are now very dated but remain of value if used with care.

The *Modern legal systems cyclopedia* (1984–) also contains descriptions of the legal systems of each country with some additional essays on particular topics of relevance to the jurisdiction. There are volumes for 'Western Europe EEC': 3 and 3A, for 'Western Europe non-EEC': 4 and 4A, and for 'Eastern Europe': 8 and 8A. Recent developments in membership of the EU and elsewhere in Europe have yet to be fully taken into account and the arrangement of the work can be confusing. Although more up to date than the *International encyclopedia of comparative law* and containing some valuable commentaries, this looseleaf work is varied in content and quality and it is often difficult to ascertain the date of composition of the chapters or the extent of revision. The annual *Martindale-Hubbell international law digest* (1993–), companion to the multi-volume *Martindale-Hubbell law directory* (1868–) from the United States, provides brief introductions and summaries of the laws of foreign legal systems which are quite highly regarded and relatively up to date.

Among the works on legal literature and guides to legal research, the work which should be highlighted is *Foreign law: current sources of codes and legislation in jurisdictions of the world* (Reynolds and Flores, 1989–). Volumes 2 and 2A of this major looseleaf work cover Europe as a whole, a-z by country. The main part of the text for each country is an index to legislation described below under **legislation**. It also provides scholarly introductions to the legal system of each country with references to introductory works. There is extensive bibliographic detail of major primary legal publications such as official gazettes, other publications of laws, and law reports.

Germain's transnational law research (Germain, 1991–) is a guide to legal research in a single looseleaf volume which focuses on Europe and contains advice and commentary as well as extremely useful annotated bibliographies on matters of transnational concern, for example commercial law, environmental law, taxation, or trade. It also has brief country sections for most west European countries. There is extensive treatment of general and comparative works and all the international bodies, outside the scope of this book, are covered by Germain. The sub-title is 'a guide for attorneys' and the work pays particular attention to practical and procedural issues such as transnational litigation, discovery, recognition and enforcement of judgments, etc.

Both country and regional sources for central and eastern Europe are documented in the individual chapters which follow but the article by Kiszely (1994), 'Central and Eastern Europe and the republics of the former Soviet Union: guide to current sources of laws and other documents in English' in the *International Journal of Legal Information*, may be particularly useful and covers a wide range of sources which may be of use throughout Europe.

Legislation, codes and commentaries

Various forms of legislation are produced in the legal systems of each of the countries of Europe. They and their publication are described in the individual chapters. In the countries with a civil law system a frequent official gazette is often the first published source for pieces of legislation. In those countries the main statement of law is commonly in the form of codes supplemented by specific legislation on other topics. This is not the case in the common law countries of Ireland and the UK. In the UK codification has commanded enthusiastic support in some quarters, and has the official attention of the Law Commissions, but little progress has been made.

Codes are comprehensive and systematic statements of major areas of law such as the civil law, civil procedure, criminal law, criminal procedure, and commercial law and some countries have several more specialized codes. The codes are normally available in commercially published editions with annotations indicating related legislation, points clarified in judicial decisions and important scholarly contributions to interpretation. Some editions may be convenient single volumes or even pocket editions, whereas major multi-volume editions with annotations and extensive commentary are major scholarly works which appear in many editions over a very long period of time.

Foreign law: current sources of codes and legislation in jurisdictions of the world, (Reynolds and Flores, 1989–), as its name suggests, is primarily an index to legislation. For each country, it identifies the major codes and contains a standard alphabetical list of subjects citing the specific provisions not only in the country's own legislation and codes but also, importantly, any translation available in secondary sources. Translations include both stand-alone translations and those in any one of a long list of multi-jurisdictional and encyclopedic works, both general and subject specific.

European Current Law (1992–) appears in monthly parts and an annual cumulation containing digests of important legislation and cases in Community law and in the national law of over thirty legal systems of the EU member states, Central and Eastern Europe and the CIS. The digests often extend to a long paragraph but the full text is not included; they all have a citation to the original source publication and are arranged by subject heading with a detailed index. There is a list of legislation by country and a list of legislation recently passed so it is possible to research the law of particular countries and to monitor recent developments. The work is necessarily very selective but can be extremely useful both as an alerting service and as an index from which to approach the original sources.

Commercial Laws of Europe (1978–) publishes a selection of important national legislation, mainly from EU member states, relating to commercial law. There are two sections to each monthly issue, one reproducing laws in the original language and the other giving translations of laws which have normally appeared in the original language in an earlier issue.

There is a great variety of other compilations of translated laws or digests of laws or commentaries on laws, some covering Europe, some with a broader international coverage. *Martindale-Hubbell international law digest* (1993–), mentioned above, is both general and international in coverage. *Central and East European legal materials* (Pechota, 1990–) is regional in coverage and a companion to *Russia and the Republics legal materials* mentioned in the chapter on Russia. There are many works in the broad field of commercial law such as, for example, the *Digest of commercial laws of the world* (1981–) and *Commercial laws of the world* (1972–) and many others in other subject areas. The list of works indexed in the process of maintaining the references to translated laws in *Foreign law* (Reynolds and Flores, 1989–), under the 'materials indexed' tab in volume 2 covering Europe, is itself a useful checklist of multi-jurisdictional subject compilations and Germain is also useful in identifying works in these categories.

International Legal Materials (1962–) published by the American Society of International Law reproduces many important documents from individual countries in the area of international law and relations, and the selection now extends on occasion to legislation relating to foreign economic activity. Various journals, often from international organizations, also regularly reproduce legislation in their field of interest, for example *Copyright* (1965–) and *Industrial Property* (1962–) both from the World Intellectual Property Organization, the *Nuclear Law Bulletin* (1968–) from the OECD and *Labour Law Documents* (1990–95) from the International Labour Office.

Electronic sources of primary materials are dealt with below under **Computer-based systems**.

Treaties

The chapters on individual countries refer to the publication of treaties which they have concluded, although it should be noted that the publications of the other signatory, or one of the other signatories, to a treaty might offer easier access.

There are, of course, major series of multilateral and bilateral treaties: *League of Nations Treaty Series* (1920–46), *United Nations Treaty Series* (1947–) and the collection of earlier treaties under the editorship of Clive Parry, the *Consolidated Treaty Series, 1648–1918* (1969–86). *Multilateral treaties deposited with the Secretary-General; status at [year]* (1949–) gives status information including accessions, ratifications, etc. However the sources of information on public international law require a whole book to themselves and treaty research itself requires considerable expertise in the relevant materials, see Beyerley (1991) at pp. 46–56 for treaties and generally for a wide-ranging guide to public international law sources with helpful annotations. A 'Bibliographic checklist on international law research: eastern European countries' appears in *International Journal of Legal Information* (Popa, 1994) and pays particular attention to treaty research with an annotated list of relevant computer files, looseleaf services and journals as well as original sources; many of the sources are equally relevant to all European countries.

There is a range of international organizations which publish conventions, not least the Council of Europe whose *European Treaty Series* (1949–) should not be confused with publications of the European Union or thought to be a general compilation of treaties in Europe. Many international organizations are described and their publications listed in Germain (1991–) and Beyerley (1991).

The Library of Congress 'Guide to Law Online: Collections of Multinational Conventions' at http://lcweb2.loc.gov/glin/x-treaty.html gives access to full-text collections of multinational treaties in English on the Internet including intellectual property, environment, and trade. The US House of Representatives 'Internet Law Library' also has a section for treaties at http://law.house.gov/89.htm which contains the text of a large number of treaties and related secondary materials; it also has links to sites such as the collection on the gopher service at Cornell Law School, the treaty section on the extraordinarily miscellaneous gopher service at gopher://wiretap.spies.com/11/Gov/Treaties and the web server maintained by the Ministry of Foreign Affairs in Turkey which contains a range of treaty texts in English at http://www.mfa.gov.tr/GRUPI/i2i.htm

The bimonthly *International Legal Materials* (1962–) is an excellent current source which contains a range of treaties and agreements including major multilateral treaties and bilateral agreements. Other international law journals carry documents sections, such as *Journal du Droit International* (1874–), known informally as 'Clunet'.

There are subject compilations which contain relevant international agreements; these are often the same compilations which contain legislation on the subject, see above. One example is *European Taxation* (1961–) from the International Bureau of Fiscal Documentation which is a slim monthly journal but whose 'supplementary service' is a large multi-volume looseleaf reference work which contains among other materials both multilateral and bilateral tax treaties.

Law reports, judgments

The term law reports is used for reports of cases heard in courts of law, usually containing the text of the judgment or opinion and sometimes considerably more detail, and reports of decisions in administrative and other tribunals; despite its formulation, the term does not refer to the publication of reports of laws or legislation. The French term for judicial decisions, *jurisprudence*, can be a source of confusion for English speakers who commonly use the word to denote the philosophy of law.

The relative lack of prominence of the sections on law reports in many of the following chapters points up the different status of court decisions as a source of law in civil law jurisdictions in comparison with common law jurisdictions. The doctrine of binding precedent in the common law countries of Ireland and the UK does not exist in other countries of Europe where judicial decisions are generally considered to occupy a less central place. However this should not suggest that earlier decisions in similar legal situations are not significant and the practical importance of reported decisions of the courts to practising lawyers throughout Europe should not be underestimated.

Citation of reported decisions in many parts of Europe apart from Ireland and the UK places very little emphasis on the names of the parties; the citation often consists of the court and the date and a reference number. Where specific reference to a publication is given, most countries adopt very abbreviated forms of the title and sources to assist in the interpretation of legal abbreviations are mentioned in many of the chapters below or reference may be made to Kavass and Prince (1991–).

There are few Europe-wide series of law reports. *European Current Law* (1992–), mentioned above in relation to legislation, contains digests of selected important cases arranged by subject from the national courts of EU member states, Central and Eastern Europe countries and the CIS. The digests often run to 20 lines or so.

European Commercial Cases (1978–) contains selected judgments of national courts of European countries, translated into English, on commercial and business matters. *Common Market Law Reports* (1962–), although primarily publishing judgments of the courts of the European Union, also includes some judgments from national courts of member states in matters relating to European law. The scope of the 'European Court Reports' is explained by their full title *Reports of cases before the European Court of Justice and the Court of First Instance of the European Communities*; they are the official reports of those courts and do not include decisions of national courts.

International Law Reports (1950–) include a considerable number of decisions of municipal courts applying rules of international law, as well as decisions of international tribunals. Although the decisions of international tribunals are outside the scope of this book, a valuable guide to research on the subject is in Popa (1994), 'Bibliographic checklist on international law research: eastern European countries', whose value is by no means limited to Eastern Europe.

It should be remembered that journals covering Europe as a whole in a particular area of law often carry case notes and sometimes quite extensive court reports, for example *European Transport Law* (1966–) contains reasonably lengthy reports in the original languages of the decision and *International Litigation Procedure* (1990–) carries many reports from European courts.

Computer-based systems

This section concentrates on primary materials. Most of the electronic legal information systems in Europe for legislation and court decisions are jurisdiction-specific and are described in the following chapters. Regional resources for Central and Eastern Europe as a whole are given particular attention in Kiszely (1994). Germain (1991–) at the head of each of her country sections gives advice on the coverage of LEXIS and WESTLAW which are both based in the USA but are major multinational systems.

LEXIS has extensive materials from the European Union itself, including the CELEX database, from jurisdictions of the United Kingdom and from France. Both LEXIS and WESTLAW have international agreements not confined to those concluded by the USA, see the databases' own guides for up to date details of coverage and Popa (1994) for an annotated list of files. They both also have selected translated laws, mainly in the broad commercial and business-related field, from Central and Eastern Europe. These two massive databases cover a very wide range of secondary materials, see below.

Internet

Useful materials for legal research on the Internet are now proliferating rapidly. Readers will be aware that there are outstanding problems regarding authentication and citation for materials obtained from the Internet. Whatever is written here about specific materials will be overtaken as sites develop and more are established. Addresses tend to change as sites expand and are reorganized or projects move. Some projects represent models of distributed cooperative electronic publishing radically different from the massive commercial databases.

Certain major sites are making a consistent effort to document and provide gateways to resources on the Internet and some are relevant here. Many sites are jurisdiction-specific in Europe and are mentioned in the following chapters; many of these which have been available in the past only in the language of the jurisdiction are adding English pages.

The ICL server for constitutions is mentioned above (under **Legal systems**). The Internet Law Library at the U.S. House of Representatives offers an a-z list of countries in its 'Laws of other countries' section at http://law.house.gov/52.htm with a range of documents including constitutions, some laws in English and various reports from, for example, the Department of State and the World Trade Organization and many links to other servers; it is a well-maintained and useful first stop. Likewise the Library of Congress Guide to law online has a 'Nations of the world' section at http://lcweb2.loc.gov/glin/x-nation.html with numerous links arranged a-z by country. The Legal Information Institute at Cornell Law School, http://www.law.cornell.edu, also maintains a large gopher and web site.

There is an extensive listing of links to judicial institutions with the function of constitutional review in Europe and elsewhere on CourtNet maintained at http://www.sigov.si/us/eus-ds.html on the server of the Slovenian Constitutional Court. There is also a project, CoCoNet, organized by the University of Chicago Law School's Center for the Study of Constitutionalism in Eastern Europe to establish Internet servers at the constitutional courts of countries of Central and Eastern Europe. The description of the project is at http://www.sanet.sk/court/project.html on the server of the Constitutional Court of the Slovak Republic with links to a small but growing number of other courts. Each Court will provide information regarding their activities but particularly their decisions and opinions in at least the original and English languages.

National government and associated servers on the Internet are making increasing amounts of primary legal materials available, particularly constitutional materials and legislation. National servers are mentioned in the following chapters and many can be accessed via the European Union Server at http://europa.eu.int/en/gonline.html and other governmental institutions with a web presence are listed at http://home.pages.de/~anzinger/govt/europa.html, see **Directories** below for more detail.

Encyclopedias

The *International encyclopedia of comparative law* (1971–) covers a range of subjects, in addition to the national reports in volume 1 mentioned above: the legal systems of the world, private international law, persons and family, succession, property and trust, contracts in general, specific contracts, commercial transactions and institutions, quasi-contracts, torts, and law of transport.

There are many multi-jurisdictional works and encyclopedias which go further than general introductions to the legal system and describe the law in detail, often with translated texts. Germain (1991–) lists and provides commentary on many of the major works in this category in chapters devoted to different branches of transnational law. The list of works indexed in the process of maintaining the entries for translated laws in *Foreign law* (Reynolds and Flores, 1989–) is itself a useful checklist of multi-jurisdictional subject encyclopedias. See also **Bibliographies** below.

Some encyclopedias in specific areas of law are massive publishing initiatives. One well-known example in a subject area is the *International encyclopaedia for labour law and industrial relations* (1977–) which contains extensive chapters for each of a large range of countries and translated laws and case reports in appendix volumes.

The same publisher now issues an *International encyclopaedia of laws* (1991–) reproducing the successful format for various other areas of law and several series of looseleaf volumes have appeared. It should be noted that these series contain 'monographs' for each jurisdiction so far covered which may also be published separately. Some recent monographs in English which are cited for individual countries were originally published as chapters in the encyclopedia.

Two particular works among many in the area of practice and procedure may be valuable. *European civil practice* (O'Malley and Layton, 1989) deals with practice at the European Court of Justice but also includes introductions to the practice and procedure in the civil courts of the member states of the European Union; membership is as at the time of publication since this is not a looseleaf publication. The *Encyclopedia of international commercial litigation* (1991–) is a looseleaf arranged by country and gives similar information on practice and procedure, the courts and the practising profession. The *European litigation handbook* (Taylor and Cooper, 1995) covers most western European countries in a much slimmer volume.

After the boom in publication of works on the European Union, many legal reference works boast European in their title but this often indicates that they deal with the home jurisdiction and the relevant European Union provisions not with the legal systems of other states of Europe.

Directories

Individual law firms in the various countries or major law firms with offices in various cities across Europe are obviously themselves major sources of information and increasingly international firms publish valuable material on the law of countries and specialist branches of law in which they operate. Each chapter gives references to local directories of lawyers where available. There are also several international law directories which may be consulted. The *Martindale-Hubbell international law directory* (1992–) is the most extensive listing of practising lawyers outside the USA arranged by country in 3 volumes. *Kime's international law directory* reached its 103rd year of publication in 1996; it lists both local and foreign firms and has a very brief introduction to legal practice and enforcement of foreign judgments, it also cites the occasional introductory publication but many are very dated.

The *Guide to legal studies in Europe* (1996) compiled by the European Law Students' Association aims to be the most extensive source of information available on legal studies and opportunities to study law in Europe. It gives considerable detail on law schools and the curriculum of each, together with background information and contact names and addresses in particular for students from other countries. ELSA International's site is at http://www.jus.uio.no/elsa/homepage.html which has links to sites in various member countries.

More general reference publications include the *World of learning* (1947–) which is exceptionally useful for both institutions of higher education and also cultural institutions such as libraries and scholarly associations. From the same publisher, the *Europa world year book* (1989–) is an annual two volume work covering in one volume a large number of international organizations with descriptive and contact information and, in the other, country surveys with recent political, social and economic history, a brief statistical survey and a directory of names and addresses in government, politics, diplomatic service, judicial system, press and broadcasting and other areas of institutional and economic life. The *Directory of European professional and learned societies* (1995) has more than 80 entries under the heading for law and a broad coverage of other professional bodies.

The Europa server of the European Union gives access to national government servers on the Internet at http://europa.eu.int/en/gonline.html including not only EU member states but also a growing number of other European governments, for example Croatia, Malta and Turkey. There is naturally a range of presence on the Internet from national governments, and their nature derives from the arm of government initially responsible, but their scope is expanding quickly as is provision of English language materials. An extensive list of most governmental institutions at national, regional and municipal level in Europe which provide information on the Internet is at http://home.pages.de/~anzinger/govt/europa.html. The list includes parliaments, executive institutions (such as ministries), law courts, embassies, and also public broadcasting companies, although it does not include educational and cultural institutions (such as libraries). Shipsey's article on 'European information on the Internet' in *EIA Review* concentrates mainly on EU information but also lists a range of sources for national jurisdictions (Shipsey, 1996).

Bibliographies

The individual chapters cite the classic works of legal bibliography for their jurisdictions and also more general bibliographies such as, in some cases, the national bibliography. It is beyond the scope of this chapter to cover all the other major legal bibliographies which might be consulted in research on European law, however *International legal bibliographies: a worldwide guide and critique* (Goedan, 1992) covers the major works in considerable depth and Germain (1991–) makes extensive reference to international bibliographies and research guides both general and subject-specific.

The outstanding bibliography for English speaking researchers of European law is *Szladits' bibliography on foreign and comparative law: books and articles in English*, originally compiled by Charles Szladits in 1955 covering the period from 1790 to 1953 and continued by him in a further five editions covering 1953 to 1983. Three further editions have appeared so far under the editorship of Vratislav Pechota taking coverage up to and including 1990. The comprehensive work arranges under subject both books, with some annotation, and articles from a huge range of periodicals worldwide which deal in English with foreign law and with subjects bearing on the comparative study of law. Foreign law was originally limited to non-common law countries and so would always have covered most European countries but from the 1978–83 edition also covers common law countries outside the USA. There is, not surprisingly, a considerable delay between publication of an item and the publication of the edition which indexes it.

Foreign law (Reynolds and Flores, 1989–) can be used as a bibliography for introductory works and for a large range of primary legal publications. Guides in the 'Information sources in . . .' series, to which this book belongs, may well be of use, particularly *Information sources in official publications* (Nurcombe, 1997) which has direct relevance to some of the ground covered by this volume and covers more recent materials than Johansson (1988) for Western Europe and Walker (1982) for Eastern Europe.

It should not be forgotten that library catalogues, particularly those of the great research libraries, contain a vast bibliographical treasure house.

Many national and university libraries have automated systems which offer sophisticated searching over the Internet. Major legal libraries are mentioned in each chapter below with contact details. However there are gateway sites which try to simplify the process of connecting to large numbers of libraries worldwide. Many universities have built up gateway services to the Internet and one well-known example specific to library catalogues is Hytelnet at http://www.cam.ac.uk/Hytelnet/ and another is gopher://libgopher.yale.edu:70/1 The Gabriel site has been established as a 'Gateway to Europe's National Libraries' at http://portico.bl.uk/gabriel/en/welcome.html with a mirror in the Hague at http://www.konbib.nl/gabriel/en/welcome.html and in Helsinki at http://renki.helsinki.fi/gabriel/en/welcome.html (Jefcoate, 1996). It is available in English, French and German at present. The wealth of material to which this organized list provides access should not be underestimated. It covers national libraries of countries alphabetically from Austria, Belgium, Bulgaria, Czech Republic, Denmark, Estonia, Finland, France, Germany, Greece, Hungary, Iceland and many others through to Turkey, United Kingdom and Vatican City, with more being added. It has more than just links by telnet session to the automated catalogues of these libraries, it also includes links to a variety of national bibliographies, national union catalogues, indexes to the contents of periodicals and to the national libraries' web and gopher servers.

Indexing and abstracting services

Commonly in many countries of Europe there are publications which perform the functions of both bibliographies of books and indexes of articles in periodicals; these appear in a single section for bibliographies in the chapters for those countries. *Szladits' bibliography on foreign and comparative law* itself covers both books and articles in periodicals.

Goedan (1992) discusses in detail the major indexes to legal periodicals in his work on international legal bibliographies. They are also the focus for Reynolds (1992) in 'Secondary sources for research in European law'.

The major source to discover articles in periodicals from non-English speaking jurisdictions is the *Index to Foreign Legal Periodicals* (1960–) which indexes a large selection of periodicals from around the world, the majority from Europe. Periodicals are selected which deal with the municipal law of countries other than those whose legal systems have a common law basis. It also indexes private and public international law and comparative law periodicals and the number of English language periodicals in the area of comparative and international law has increased in recent years. It would not normally be a tool for legal researchers within their own jurisdiction and each chapter suggests the local tools which are used.

The *Index to Legal Periodicals* (1908–), *Current Law Index*/LEGALTRAC/LEGAL RESOURCE INDEX (1980–), and *Legal Journals Index* (1986–) are useful for English-speaking researchers to find articles in their own language on the legal systems of Europe, and each is available in electronic formats. They are by design much more up to date than *Szladits* and pick up articles in journals not normally associated with civil law jurisdictions. The *Legal Journals Index* is the pre-eminent index for the UK itself and is complemented by the *European Legal Journals Index* (1993–) which indexes articles in legal periodicals published in English in Europe relating to the law of the European Union or its member states.

Dictionaries

There are a few established multilingual legal dictionaries: *Dictionnaire de termes juridiques en quatre langues* covering French, Spanish, English and German (Le Docte, 1987) and the earlier work covering French, Dutch, English, German (Le Docte, 1982); *Law and commercial dictionary in five languages: definitions of the legal and commercial terms and phrases in American, English and civil law jurisdictions: English to German, Spanish, French, Italian* (1985) and *Elsevier's dictionary of commercial terms and phrases in five languages: English, German, Spanish, French and Swedish* (Appleby, 1984).

Current information sources

Journals

Articles on foreign law or particular foreign laws can appear in almost any journal and the indexing services mentioned above give access to the major journals and include listings of the journals indexed and their publishers. There are some journals dedicated to foreign law and comparative law and these were listed and described in David and Brierley (1985, pp. 578–580). The major titles in English are the *American Journal of Comparative Law* (1952–) and *International and Comparative Law Quarterly* (1952–) and important titles in other languages include *Revue internationale de droit comparé* (1949–) and *Rabels Zeitschrift für ausländisches und internationales Privatrecht* (1927–). The *International Journal of Legal Information* (1982–) contains descriptions of the legal literature, bibliographies and reviews and research guides for countries around the world and for international law.

There is now a range of journals in English from the major European legal publishers whose intention is to cover some or all of the national jurisdictions of Europe for a particular branch of law, and this area is a particular growth area for publishing, for example *European Public Law* (1995–) and *European Review of Private Law* (1993–). The *European Legal Journals Index* (1993–) adds such titles to their list of periodicals indexed as they appear.

There is an excellent selection of the journals which concentrate on Central and Eastern Europe cited in several of the relevant chapters (see, for example, the **Czech Republic**).

News information

The *Bulletin of Legal Developments* (1966–) is a fortnightly newsletter with worldwide coverage which acts as a valuable alerting service; it is drawn from other published sources. There are many specialist newsletters and a range of other legal publications which carry news as well as articles, either general such as the *European Legal Developments Bulletin* (1989–) from Baker & McKenzie, or devoted to specialist areas such as the monthly *European Business Law Review* (1990–).

LEXIS and WESTLAW have already been mentioned above for their legal content. They both allow access to a huge amount of news, business, and financial information contained in news wire services such as UPI, AP and Reuters, newspapers, weeklies and other periodicals. NEXIS is the news database offered in association with LEXIS and WESTLAW offers access, using its own interface to the vast resources of DIALOG databases. These database services continually augment their coverage and the contents descriptions issued by their suppliers should be checked for the services and titles included.

The press and broadcast news scanning services, for example *Summary of World Broadcasts* (1947–) published by the British Broadcasting Corporation in regional sections, and available on LEXIS-NEXIS from 1979 onwards, provide timely information. The Eurojournalism site at http://www.demon.co.uk/eurojournalism has links to many news and current affairs sources including newspaper and magazine sites across Europe. The International Business Network at http://www1.usa1.com/~ibnet/index.html is also a useful gateway to a range of newswire and research tools which usually give selected information with details of further services available to subscribers; they include the *Financial Times* (1888–), the *Economist* (1843–), *Business Week* (1929–), and national news agencies such as the Czech News Agency, the Romanian Press Review and many others.

Business and financial information

Sources of European economic and business information produced by the British Library Business Information Service (1995) is a valuable guide and also emphasises the value of their information service. The

International directory of business information sources and services (1996) has wider international coverage. *International business information: how to find it, how to use it* (Pagell and Halperin, 1994), published in the USA, cites more American sources; it was well reviewed for law librarians who need to tackle this specialized area. The recent *Information sources in finance and banking* (Lester, 1996) lists and evaluates a vast range of sources.

Publications which deal with 'doing business in . . .' are innumerable. The looseleaf *Doing business in Europe* (1972–) from CCH Editions is up to date and has a legal slant. The *CBI European Business Handbook 1997* (Jolly, 1997) includes analysis of commercial factors affecting business across Europe, information on business practices and analysis of business prospects in individual countries and essays on major issues of concern for those trading or investing in Europe. Its publisher Kogan Page also produce guides to doing business in various countries of Europe east and west in conjunction with the CBI and national chambers of commerce.

The European Network of Chambers of Commerce and Industry at http://www1.usa1.com/~ibnet/eurocham.html has links to many national, regional, and local chambers of commerce in European countries. These organizations are indispensable for business information and their web sites give an indication of their extensive resources, published and in-house, and contact details. This page is part of the International Business Network at http://www1.usa1.com/~ibnet/index.html which gives access to the International Chamber of Commerce, a global business opportunity exchange database, and verified lists of finance and economic service providers, merchants and commercial service providers, trade and related international organizations.

The daily *Financial Times* (1888–), with its associated information databases, is one of the most important sources of financial and business information. The Financial Times site at http://www.ft.com/ requires online registration but is not fee-based; the information is selective and details of the range of products and services are given. FT PROFILE or one of the other FT databases, which are available from a range of hosts on a fee basis, is required for access to the mass of accumulated data.

The weekly *Economist* (1843–) is a consistently informative and reliable source of business, financial and economic news, analysis and commentary. The Economist site, still fairly recent at the time of writing, at http://www.economist.com offers selected articles from the current issue but more materials from past issues are on Enews, the electronic magazine stand, at http://www.enews.com/magazines/economist/.

The European Business Directory site, English version at http://www.europages.com/, lists a large selection of European companies with a sophisticated search mechanism and also has information about European chambers of commerce, standards institutions, patent offices, a directory of business product catalogues and forthcoming trade fairs and exhibitions.

Statistics

Many of the statistics available at a supra-national level are compiled by international organizations such as the United Nations, the Organization for Economic Cooperation and Development, and the World Bank. *Statistics Europe: a guide to sources of statistical information* (1996) is a commercial directory with broad coverage of national and international sources. *European official statistics: sources of information* (1994) is a free booklet which lists the addresses of about 250 bodies including statistical offices of international and supra-national organizations, national and regional statistical institutes, and national ministries and central banks which publish statistics. Eurostat, the statistical office of the European Union, publishes a huge range of statistics covering the member states of Europe, see the European Union chapter and Thomson (1996) *Bibliographic snapshot: European Union information sources for business*. The Eurostat home page is at http://europa.eu.int/en/comm/eurostat/eurostat.html. The site at http://www.europages.com/ carries European macro-economic analysis and economic sectoral indicators.

List of works cited

American Journal of Comparative Law. (1952–) Ann Arbor, Mich.: American Association for the Comparative Study of Law.

Appleby, B.L. (1984) (comp.) *Elsevier's dictionary of commercial terms and phrases in five languages: English, German, Spanish, French and Swedish*. Amsterdam & London: Elsevier.

Beyerley, Elizabeth. (1991) *Public international law: a guide to information sources*. London: Mansell.

British Library Business Information Service. (1995) (ed.) *Sources of European economic and business information*. 6th edn. Aldershot: Gower.

Bulletin of Legal Developments. (1966–) London: British Institute of International and Comparative Law.

Business Week. (1929–) New York: McGraw-Hill.

Commercial Laws of Europe. (1978–) London: Sweet & Maxwell. 12 p.a.

Commercial laws of the world. (1972–) Ormond Beach, Fla.: Foreign Tax Law Association. Looseleaf.

Common Market Law Reports. (1962–) London: Sweet & Maxwell.

Consolidated Treaty Series, 1648–1918. (1969–86) Ed. Clive Parry. Dobbs Ferry, NY: Oceana. 231 vols and 12 vols of index-guides.

Constitutions of the countries of the world. (1971–) Ed. A.P.Blaustein and G.H.Flanz. Dobbs Ferry, NY: Oceana. Looseleaf. 20 vols.

Copyright. (1965–) Geneva: WIPO.

Current Law Index. (1980–) Belmont, Cal.: Information Access Corporation. Sponsored by the American Association of Law Libraries. Also available on CD-ROM as LEGALTRAC and online as LEGAL RESOURCE INDEX via several hosts including LEXIS and WESTLAW.

CURRENT LEGAL INFORMATION. (1996–) London: Sweet & Maxwell. CD-ROM and on the Internet at http://www.smlawpub.co.uk/

David, R. and Brierley, J.E.C. (1985) *Major legal systems of the world today*. London: Stevens.

Digest of commercial laws of the world. (1981–) Ed. L.Nelson. Dobbs Ferry, NY: Oceana. Looseleaf. 15 vols.

Directory of European professional and learned societies. (1995) Ed. S.Greenslade. 5th edn. Beckenham: CBD Research.

Doing business in Europe. (1972–) Bicester: CCH Editions. Looseleaf. 2 vols.

Economist. (1843–) London: Economist.

Encyclopedia of international commercial litigation. (1991–) Ed. A.D.Coleman. London: Graham & Trotman. Looseleaf.

Europa world year book. (1989–) London: Europa Publications.

European Business Law Review. (1990–) The Hague & London: Kluwer Law International.

European Commercial Cases. (1978–) London: Sweet & Maxwell. 6 issues p.a.

European Current Law. (1992–) London: Sweet & Maxwell. 12 issues p.a. and annual cumulative volume.

European Legal Developments Bulletin. (1989–) London: Baker & McKenzie.

European Legal Journals Index. (1993–) Hebden Bridge: Legal Information Resources, Sweet & Maxwell. Also available on CD-ROM and the Internet as part of CURRENT LEGAL INFORMATION and as a tape service.

European official statistics: sources of information. (1994) Luxembourg: Eurostat.

European Public Law. (1995–) The Hague & London: Kluwer Law International.

European Review of Private Law. (1993–) The Hague & London: Kluwer Law International.

European Taxation. (1961–) Amsterdam: International Bureau of Fiscal Documentation. Also *Supplementary service to European Taxation*. Looseleaf. 16 vols.

European Transport Law. (1966–) Antwerp: European Transport Law.

European Treaty Series. (1949–) Strasbourg: Council of Europe.

Financial Times. (1888–) London: Financial Times.

FT PROFILE. (available from FT Information. Tel: +44 171 825 7905. Email ftprofile@ft.com and from a range of hosts).

Germain, Claire M. (1991–) *Germain's transnational law research: a guide for attorneys*. Ardsley-on-Hudson, NY: Transnational Juris Publications. Looseleaf.

Goedan, J.C. (1992) *International legal bibliographies – a worldwide guide and critique*. Ardsley-on-Hudson, NY: Transnational Juris Publications.

Guide to legal studies in Europe 1996–1997. (1996) Comp. European Law Students' Association. Ed. Erik Vrij. Brussels: Law Books in Europe.

Index to Foreign Legal Periodicals. (1960–) Berkeley, Cal.: University of California Press for the American Association of Law Libraries. Also available on CD-ROM and online.

Index to Legal Periodicals. (1909–) New York: Wilson. Also available on CD-ROM and online (for example via LEXIS, WESTLAW and WILSONLINE).

Industrial Property. (1962–) Geneva: WIPO.

International and Comparative Law Quarterly. (1952–) London: British Institute of International and Comparative Law.

International directory of business information sources and services. (1996) 2nd edn. London: Europa.

International encyclopaedia for labour law and industrial relations. (1977–) Ed. R.Blanpain. The Hague & London: Kluwer Law International. Looseleaf. 23 vols.: 12 vols text, 2 vols codex, 4 vols case law, 5 vols legislation.

International encyclopaedia of laws. (1991–) Gen. ed. R.Blanpain. The Hague & London: Kluwer Law International. This title incorporates *International encyclopaedia for labour law and industrial relations* and a range of looseleaf 'international encyclopaedia of . . .' in other branches of law which are being published.

International encyclopedia of comparative law. (1971–) Tübingen: J.C.B. Mohr. 12 vols being issued in fascicules. Different editor for each volume, under the general editorship of K. Zweigert.

International Journal of Legal Information. (1982–) Washington, DC: International Association of Law Libraries. Continues *International Journal of Law Libraries* 1973–1981.

International Law Reports. (1950–) Ed. by E.Lauterpacht, C.J.Greenwood and A.G.Oppenheimer. Cambridge: Grotius Publications, Cambridge University Press. Entitled *Annual digest and reports of public international law cases* 1919/22–1949.

International Legal Materials. (1962–) Washington, DC: American Society of International Law. 6 p.a.

International Litigation Procedure. (1990–) London: Sweet & Maxwell.

Jefcoate, Graham. (1996) Gabriel: gateway to Europe's national libraries. *Program*, **30**, 229–238.

Johansson, Eve. (1988) (ed.) *Official publications of western Europe.* London: Mansell.

Jolly, Adam. (1997) (ed.) *CBI European business handbook 1997.* London: Kogan Page.

Journal du Droit International (1874–) Paris: Éditions Techniques. Vols.1–41, 1874–1914 entitled: *Journal du Droit International Privé.*

Kavass, Igor I and Prince, Mary Miles. (1991–) (eds) *World dictionary of legal abbreviations.* Buffalo, NY: Hein. Looseleaf.

Kime's international law directory. (1892–) London: FT Law & Tax. Annual.

Kiszely, M. (1994) Central and eastern Europe and the republics of the former Soviet Union: guide to current sources of laws and other documents in English. *International Journal of Legal Information*, **22**, 141–190.

Labour Law Documents. (1990–95) Geneva: International Labour Office. Previously entitled *Legislative Series* 1919–1989.

Law and commercial dictionary in five languages: definitions of the legal and commercial terms and phrases in American, English and civil law jurisdictions: English to German, Spanish, French, Italian. (1985) Munich: Beck; Paris: Éditions Techniques; St.Paul, Minn.: West. 2 vols.

Le Docte, Edgard. (1982) *Dictionnaire de termes juridiques en quatre langues = Viertalig juridisch woordenboek = Legal dictionary in four languages = Rechtsworterbuch in vier Sprachen.* 3rd edn. London: Sweet & Maxwell; Antwerp: Maklu. French, Dutch, English, German.

Le Docte, Edgard. (1987) *Dictionnaire de termes juridiques en quatre langues = Diccionario juridico en cuatro idiomas = Legal dictionary in four languages = Rechtsworterbuch in vier Sprachen.* London: Sweet & Maxwell; Antwerp: Maklu. French, Spanish, English, German.

League of Nations Treaty Series = Recueil des traités de la Sociétés des Nations. (1920–1946) Geneva: League of Nations. 205 vols and general index 9 vols.

Legal Journals Index. (1986–) Hebden Bridge: Legal Information Resources, Sweet & Maxwell. Also available on CD-ROM and the Internet as part of CURRENT LEGAL INFORMATION and as a tape service.

Lester, Ray. (1996) *Information sources in finance and banking.* London: Bowker-Saur.

LEXIS-NEXIS (available from Lexis-Nexis Inc. Dayton Headquarters: 9443 Springboro Pike B4F2, Miamisburg, OH 45342, USA. Tel: +1 513 865 1446. Fax: +1 513 865 6949. Internet: http://www.lexis-nexis.com/. In the UK: Lexis-Nexis Europe Ltd, International House, 1 St. Katharine's Way, London E1 9UN, UK. Tel: +44 171 464 1300. Fax: +44 171 464 1399. Elsewhere in Europe: Lexis-Nexis Information Services GmbH, Lindenstrasse 37, 60325 Frankfurt-am-Main, Germany. Tel: +49 69 9740170. Fax: +49 69 740638.)

Martindale-Hubbell international law digest. (1993–) New Providence, NJ: Martindale-Hubbell. Annual. Also available with the main directory on CD-ROM. Originally in *Martindale-Hubbell law directory.* Entitled *Martindale-Hubbell law digest* 1991–1992.

Martindale-Hubbell international law directory. (1992–) New Providence, NJ: Martindale-Hubbell. Annual. 3 vols. Also available with the main directory on LEXIS and on CD-ROM. Originally in *Martindale-Hubbell law directory*.

Martindale-Hubbell law directory. (1868–) New Providence, NJ: Martindale-Hubbell. Annual. 17 vols. Also available on LEXIS and on CD-ROM. Title varies before 1931.

Modern legal systems cyclopedia. (1984–) Ed. K.R.Redden. Buffalo, NY: Hein. Looseleaf. 21 vols.

Multilateral treaties deposited with the Secretary-General; status at [year] = Traités multilatéraux déposés auprès du Secrétaire-Général; état [année]. (1949–) New York: United Nations. Title varies. Updated by a monthly *Statement of treaties and international agreements registered or filed and recorded with the Secretariat of the United Nations = Relevé des traités et accords internationaux*. . . . (1947–) New York: United Nations.

NEXIS. See LEXIS-NEXIS.

Norton, Philip (1996) (ed.) *National parliaments and the European Union*. London & Portland, Oreg.: Frank Cass. First appeared as a special issue of *Journal of Legislative Studies* vol.1, no.3 (Autumn 1995).

Nuclear Law Bulletin. (1968–) Paris: OECD Nuclear Energy Agency.

Nurcombe, Valerie. (1997) *Information sources in official publications*. London: Bowker-Saur.

O'Malley, S. and Layton, A. (1989) *European civil practice*. London: Sweet & Maxwell.

Olson, David M. and Norton, Philip (1996) (eds) *The new parliaments of Central and Eastern Europe*. London & Portland, Oreg.: Frank Cass. First appeared as a special issue of *Journal of Legislative Studies* vol.2, no.1 (Spring 1996).

Pagell, R.A. and Halperin, M. (1994) *International business information: how to find it, how to use it*. Phoenix, Ariz.: Oryx.

Pechota, Vratislav. (1990–) *Central and East European legal materials*. Ardsley-on-Hudson, NY: Transnational Juris. Looseleaf.

Popa, R. (1994) Bibliographic checklist on international law research: eastern European countries. *International Journal of Legal Information*, **22**, 119–140.

Rabels Zeitschrift für ausländisches und internationales Privatrecht. (1927–) Berlin: Rabels Zeitschrift.

Revue internationale de droit comparé. (1949–) Paris: LGDJ for Société de Législation Comparé.

Reynolds, T.H. (1992) Secondary sources for research in European law. *International Journal of Legal Information*, **20**, 41–53.

Reynolds, T.H. and Flores, A.A. (1989–) *Foreign law: current sources of codes and legislation in jurisdictions of the world*. AALL Publications Series, no.33. Littleton, Col.: Rothman. Looseleaf. 5 vols.

Shipsey, F. (1996) European information on the Internet. *EIA Review*, **8**, 9–19.

Statistics Europe: a guide to sources of statistical information. (1996) 6th edn. Beckenham, Kent: CBD Research Ltd.

Summary of World Broadcasts. (1947–) London: British Broadcasting Corporation. Available on LEXIS-NEXIS from 1979.

Szladits, Charles. ([1974]) The civil law system. In *International encyclopedia of comparative law*, ed. R.David, vol.2, chapter 2, pp. 15–76. Writing completed July 1969.

Szladits' bibliography on foreign and comparative law: books and articles in English. (1955–) Dobbs Ferry, NY: Oceana. Editions covering the following periods: 1790–1953, 1953–59, 1960–65, 1966–71, 1972–77, 1978–83 under the editorship of Charles Szladits; and under the editorship of Vratislav Pechota: 1984–86, 1987–88, 1989–90.

Taylor, Tim and Cooper, Nigel. (1995) *European litigation handbook*. London: Sweet & Maxwell.

Thomson, Ian. (1996) Bibliographic snapshot: European Union information sources for business. *European Access*, April 1996, 37–47.

Tyrrell, Alan and Yaqub, Zahd. (1996) (eds) *The legal professions in the new Europe: a handbook for practitioners*. 2nd edn. London: Cavendish.

United Nations Treaty Series: treaties and agreements registered or filed and recorded with the Secretariat of the United Nations = Recueil des traités. Traités et accords . . . (1947–) New York: United Nations. Covers 1946/47–.

Walker, Gregory. (1982) (ed.) *Official publications of the Soviet Union and eastern Europe 1945–1980: a select bibliography*. London: Mansell.

Weir, Tony. ([1974]) The common law system. In *International Encyclopedia of Comparative Law*, ed. R.David, vol.2, chapter 2, pp. 77–114. Writing completed December 1971.

WESTLAW. (available from West Information Publishing Group, 620 Opperman Drive, Eagan, MN 55123, USA. Tel: +1 612 687 4064. Email: westmedia@westpub.com Internet: http://www.westpub.com London office: West Publishing UK Ltd., 2 London Wall Buildings, London Wall, London EC2M 5PP, UK. Tel: +44 171 638 9997. Fax: +44 171 638 9908).

World of learning. (1947–) London: Europa Publications.

CHAPTER TWO

European Union

FRANCES SHIPSEY

The legal system of the European Union (EU) is unique. It is made up of the supranational law of the EU, the national laws of each member state, and intergovernmental law. This chapter is restricted to a description of the main EU legal sources and to selected UK sources relating to the EU.

The European Communities were established by three treaties, the European Coal and Steel Community (ECSC) in Paris in 1951, the European Economic Community (EEC) and the European Atomic Energy Community (EAEC or Euratom) both in Rome in 1957. These were the founding treaties of the European Communities. Amending treaties have been signed over the years, including the Single European Act (SEA) which was signed in 1986 with the aim of achieving a Single European Market by the end of 1992, and the Treaty on European Union (TEU), also known as the Maastricht Treaty. The TEU was signed in 1992, came into force on 1 November 1993 and thereby established the European Union. The TEU established three 'pillars' of activity for the European Union: first, European Community, based on existing Community law; second, a Common Foreign and Security Policy (CFSP); and third, Cooperation in Justice and Home Affairs (JHA). The second and third pillar activities are carried out largely at intergovernmental level by the Council of the European Union and the European Council. The Commission and the Parliament have very limited roles here, while the Court of Justice has no jurisdiction over second and third pillar activities. The TEU also amended and renamed the original EEC Treaty (Treaty of Rome) as the European Community Treaty. The founding treaties together with the amending treaties make up the Constitution of the European Union today. They are considered the primary legislation of the EU.

Terminological uncertainty followed the creation of the European Union. To summarize, European Union (EU) is the general term commonly used now to refer to all the institutions, policies and activities encompassed by the TEU. European Community (EC) has taken on a narrower more legal sense than it had previously. EC is now an appropriate term for legislation and case law arising from the European Community Treaty and for first pillar activities, but is not synonymous with European Union or EU. The Commission of the European Communities is now known simply as the European Commission. The Council of the European Communities formally changed its name to Council of the European Union. The Court of Justice of the European Communities retained its name, indicating its lack of jurisdiction over second and third pillar EU activities.

There are currently fifteen member states of the EU. Further enlargement to the European Union will be considered after the 1996 Intergovernmental Conference. Applications for membership are pending from more than ten countries. Up-to-date information about membership of the EU, including applications for membership, is available from EUROPA, the EU's official Internet World Wide Web server at http://europa.eu.int.

The text of the treaties is published in an official collected edition by the EU publisher, the Office for Official Publications of the European Communities (OOPEC). OOPEC is also known as EUR-OP. The latest version *European Union: selected instruments taken from the treaties* (1995) is in two books, each of which is in two volumes. Book 1 contains the Treaty on European Union and the European Community Treaty in consolidated form, plus the ECSC and Euratom treaties and other important treaties and instruments. Book 2 (in preparation at the time of writing) will contain the whole collection of founding treaties, amending treaties and acts of accession in their original versions. Individual treaties are often published by OOPEC as monographs, for example *Treaty on European Union* (1992).

The text of treaties is generally also published in the *Official Journal of the European Communities* (see below), though this is not always the most convenient or rapidly available source. EU treaties can also be found in the United Kingdom *Treaty series* (1892–), published by HMSO as Command Papers (see page 522).

Commercially published versions of the treaties are included in looseleaf works such as *Encyclopedia of European Community law* (looseleaf) and in volumes of basic materials for EU law, such as Rudden and Wyatt (1996) or *Blackstone's EC legislation* (1996). Both of these contain the treaties and a selection of important secondary legislation. There are several versions of the Treaty on European Union on the Internet. Addresses for these are listed at the end of the chapter. EU treaties are eventually included in CELEX, the EU official online legal database.

Introductory works on legal system and legal research

There is no shortage of student textbooks and standard works in English on EC law. Weatherill and Beaumont (1995) and *Lasok and Bridge: law and institutions of the European Union* (1994) are comprehensive and well established. Hartley (1994) is extremely clear. Steiner (1996) is an example of a shorter introductory textbook.

Borchardt (1994), a free publication, and Louis (1990) are useful publications from OOPEC. Church and Phinnemore (1994) provides a detailed analysis of the TEU and fuller treatment of the second and third pillars than the other books. It includes a comprehensive bibliography. Nugent (1994) is an excellent and highly readable introduction to the EU institutions and policies.

Legal research

Zolynski (1996) covers European Community law clearly and concisely. The chapter describes how legislation and judgments are made, and how to trace and cite legal sources. Holborn (1993) takes a different approach by integrating UK and EU legal research. The first part of the book explains legal research methods clearly and illustrates this by examples. The second part is a quick reference guide. Holborn and Zolynski together offer an excellent set of research guides.

Thomson (1989) is still very useful, although it is important to remember that it predates the European Union and the European Economic Area. The European Information Association publishes a range of good value guides on sources of EU legal information and official publications.

Legislation

The legislation enacted by the EU institutions is referred to as secondary legislation. Its authority derives from the treaties. The vast majority of secondary legislation (Regulations, Directives, Decisions, Recommendations and Opinions) has its legal basis in the European Community Treaty, although the Euratom and ECSC treaties also provide for secondary legislation. Recently, EU (as opposed to EC) legislation in the form of Joint Actions and Joint Positions relating to CFSP and JHA and having their legal basis in the Treaty on European Union, have been adopted by the Council.

The Official Journal of the European Communities

Individual acts are published in the *Official Journal of the European Communities: L series* (1973–) (*OJ*), which is the authoritative text in eleven official languages. The *OJ* is similar to a government gazette. It is published in several series, including three main ones:

- *L series*: Legislation (includes all secondary legislation and the budget).
- *C series*: Information and Notices (Information: exchange rate of the Ecu, announcements of applications to the Courts and the operative part of judgments, notifications of competition cases, the annual report of the Court of Auditors; Preparatory Acts: Commission proposals, Economic and Social Committee and Committee of the Regions opinions, European Parliament minutes and resolutions; Notices: calls for proposals for research and development contracts;).
- *S series*: Supplement (contains calls for tender for public contracts).

Official Journal of the European Communities: English special edition (1972), containing secondary legislation still in force in 1973 was published by OOPEC in two series. For pre-1973 legislation the French edition of the *OJ* should be quoted as the authentic text, with a reference to the English Special Edition if it is available.

The *OJ* is published almost every day and is received by UK subscribers on or just after the publication date. Legislation can take several weeks after the date of enactment to appear in the *OJ*. Information about when the act comes into force is provided in one of the final articles of the act. Subscriptions to the *OJ* are handled by OOPEC's sales agents, which include the Stationery Office in the UK. The *OJ* is available in print or on microfiche. The *S series* is available on CD-ROM from 1997. The text of legislation is also made available on the EU legal database CELEX, but after a further delay.

Citations

Citations to secondary legislation include: the name of the institution(s) adopting the act, such as Council, Commission, or European Parliament and Council; the form of legal act, such as regulation or directive; a running number followed by the year for regulations, or the year followed by a running number for directives and decisions; the treaty which provides the legal basis for the act, such as EC; the date of adoption; and the title. The *OJ* reference should follow, as it forms part of the official citation, including *OJ* and the series; issue number; date; page number. Example:

> European Parliament and Council Directive 95/62/EC of 13 December 1995 on the application of open network provision (ONP) to voice telephony, *OJ* L 321, 30.12.95, p. 6.

If a full citation is given it is possible to go straight to the *OJ* and find the act. However, if the *OJ* reference has been omitted, as frequently happens, there is a range of indexes to legislation.

Indexes

The *Index to the Official Journal of the European Communities* (1978–) is published monthly in two parts: an Alphabetical index arranged by subject and a Methodological index arranged by act number. There is an annual cumulation. The Index is published in arrears so its main use is for older legislation of which one is certain of the year. The *Official Journal of the European Communities: Directory of Community legislation in force* (1984–), gives a snapshot of current legislation every six months. The electronic sources described on pages 32–3 also serve as powerful indexes to the legislation.

European Communities legislation: current status (1988–) is an excellent research tool containing references to all secondary legislation in force in 1973 and all secondary legislation adopted since then. It is published annually in two volumes with a comprehensive subject index. The main sequence is chronological. For each year entries are listed by type of act and then in numerical order. Amending legislation is listed for each entry. Interim updating is provided by three cumulative supplements, a fortnightly newsletter and a telephone enquiry line for subscribers.

Individual acts can be purchased from the Stationery Office fax delivery service SCANFAX. Many European Documentation Centres, Euro Info Centres and other libraries and information relays can provide access to copies of acts. Directories of these sources are listed on pages 35–6.

Commercial sources

Encyclopedia of European Community law (looseleaf) is the best known and most comprehensive commercial collection of EC law in the UK. It contains texts of the treaties and secondary legislation with annotations. At the time of writing, this encyclopedia was undergoing a major restructuring. Volume A which covers United Kingdom Sources has been discontinued and is to be replaced by a new completely separate publication. Volume B, European Community Treaties and Volume C, Community Secondary Legislation will be merged as *Encyclopedia of European Union law*. The replacement for Volume B was published first, with the subtitle *Constitutional texts*. The replacement for Volume C was due to be published in early 1997. This service is by no means cheap, but if the *OJ* is not available it is probably the most comprehensive alternative.

Consolidations

There is no official comprehensive consolidated edition of EC secondary legislation. The Commission has begun work on consolidation at the request of the Edinburgh European Council of December 1992. Five hundred Acts which have been modified over five times have been identified. To date approximately 140 of these have been consolidated. References to consolidated texts are indicated in CELEX and individual 'provisional unrevised texts' are published by OOPEC as *Collection of consolidated texts* (1996–).

Implementation of secondary legislation

Directives must be implemented into the national laws of member states. *Butterworths EC legislation implementator* (1992–) contains a basic list of directives in force, in number order, with the target date for implementation and a reference to UK implementing legislation. CELEX, INFO 92 and SPEARHEAD databases all provide information about implementation.

Documents in the legislative process

Several important series of documents are produced as part of the legislative process. The Commission has the right of initiative, i.e. the authority to propose new legislation. Texts of proposals are published in the *Official Journal of the European Communities: C series* (1973–) and in a series known as Commission documents or *COM documents* (1983–). These documents are cited by their document numbers, e.g. COM(95) 482 final. The word 'final' indicates that the document has been approved by the Commission as a whole. Proposals can bear an extra reference indicating the legislative procedure being followed. For example, COD stands for Codecision procedure and SYN for Cooperation procedure. Proposals are accompanied by an Explanatory Memorandum in the COM final version but not in the version published in the *OJ* C series.

COM documents are available on subscription (paper or microfiche) from OOPEC sales agents. It is possible to subscribe to the entire series or to one or more broad subject categories. Documents are generally received by UK subscribers about six weeks after their issue date. Individual documents may be purchased in the UK from the sources mentioned above for legislation.

Commission proposals are considered by the European Parliament, the Economic and Social Committee and the Committee of the Regions. European Parliament *Reports* (1985–) and the Economic and Social Committe of the European Communities *Opinions* (1984–) are published by OOPEC as series, the former on microfiche only. ESC and Committee of the Regions *Opinions* are published in the *Official Journal of the European Communities: C series* (1973–). The debates of the European Parliament plenary sittings and oral questions are published in *Official Journal of the European Communities: Annex: debates of the European Parliament* (1973–). Answers to written questions and the minutes of the plenary sittings are published in the *OJ* C series. Proceedings of the Committees of the EP are not published.

The deliberations of the Commission and of the Council are held in private so there is no publicly available record of proceedings. Council and Commission decisions aimed at improving public access to documents led to publication of a *Code of Conduct concerning public access to Council and Commission documents* (1993). The Commission also sets out its procedure for requesting documents in the booklet *Access to Commission documents: users' guide* (1994).

Treaties and agreements

Established by treaty itself, the European Community has the power (in the EC Treaty) to make treaties or agreements with third countries or other intergovernmental organizations. Agreements are generally negotiated by the Commission and concluded by the Council. Commercial agreements are simple trade agreements and are numerous. The Commission negotiates these under mandate from and in consultation with the Council. Cooperation agreements are further reaching and the European Parliament must be consulted before the Council concludes this type of agreement. Association agreements provide for even closer contact and are sometimes intended as a precursor to membership of the EU. Examples of association agreements include: the 'Europe Agreements' with Central and Eastern European countries; agreements with Mediterranean and Middle Eastern countries; the Lomé Conventions with African, Caribbean and Pacific (ACP) states; and the Agreement on the European Economic Area. Association agreements require the assent of the European Parliament before the Council concludes them.

Agreements are published in the *Official Journal of the European Communities: L series* and on CELEX. An alternative source in English is the *European Communities* series of the UK *Treaty series* (1892–). The *Agreement on the European Economic Area* (1992) is available from OOPEC as a monograph. Various collections of agreements have been issued by the Council and published by OOPEC.

Information about the current status of agreements is to be found in *Annotated summary of agreements linking the Communities with non-member countries (as at [. . .])* (1992–) compiled by the European Commission's DG for External Political Relations and available from their Secretariat. This is updated frequently but irregularly and is arranged by country in regional groupings. Tables give *OJ* references, legal basis, period of validity and remarks.

Law reports, judgments, digests

Official sources

The Court of Justice of the European Communities (ECJ) consists of 15 Judges, assisted by 9 Advocates General. It hears direct actions, references for preliminary rulings from national courts, and appeals from the Court of First Instance (CFI), which became operational in 1989. The CFI hears cases relating to competition, anti-dumping, intellectual property, and staff cases. The decisions of the European Commission relating to competition policy, although technically classed as secondary legislation, have a quasi-judicial status.

All Judgments of the Court and Opinions of the Advocates General are published formally in *Reports of cases before the Court* (1973–). This is the official series and it should be cited in preference to commercially published series. The Reports are translated into all official languages, but the authentic text is the version in the language of the case. The series is referred to as the European Court Reports (ECR). Since 1990 it is in two sections, I for Court of Justice and II for Court of First Instance. Since 1995, staff cases have been published in a separate sequence of reports, ECR-SC. This is available as a joint subscription with ECR. The arrangement of cases in each volume is chronological in order of the date of judgment.

Citations should include: case number, names of the parties in the form used in the heading of the pages of the Reports, the year in square brackets, abbreviated title of the reports (ECR), page number preceded by the numeral 'I' for cases before the Court of Justice and by numeral 'II' for cases before the Court of First Instance. The name of the court is also given in the case number, C for Court of Justice and T for Court of First Instance, e.g.: C-348/93 *Commission v. Italy* [1995] ECR, I-673.

By the early 1990s a severe delay in publication of the Reports had built up, largely owing to translation backlogs. A catching up exercise took place by moving straight on to publication of the 1994 reports. At the time of writing the 1993 Reports were still incomplete in English.

The reports for the Hearings (or the report of the Judge Rapporteur) are not published or translated. However, these reports of the early stages of the case are available in the language of the case, outside the Court on the day of the hearing, or on request from the Registry. On the day of the judgment transcripts are available in the language of the case and in French. Transcripts are translated into the other official languages soon after the date of the judgment and are available from the court free of charge on the day, or by subscription. They are known as *Judgments or Orders of the Court and Opinions of the Advocates-General*). Transcripts are also on LEXIS. The 'operative part' of the judgment is published in the *OJ* C series.

Commercial sources

Common Market law reports (1962–)(CMLR), publishes reports in English more rapidly than the ECR. It is not an official source however. All significant cases are reported, both cases before the ECJ and CFI and cases from national courts relating to the application of EU law. *All England law reports: European cases* (1995–), is cited as *All ER (EC)*. It reports cases of relevance to the EU from the ECJ and from the English courts. *European Community cases* (1989–)(CEC), is available on its own or as part of the *Common market reporter* (1962–). Selected cases before the ECJ and CFI and certain Commission decisions are included. This looseleaf work is accompanied by annual bound volumes, starting with 1989.

Competition cases

Commission Decisions relating to competition are published in the *OJ* L series. The Commission has issued its competition Decisions, reproduced from the *OJ*, *Reports of Commission decisions relating to competition: articles 85, 86 and 90 of the EEC Treaty* (1992–). Volumes published so far cover 1973–1992. Commission merger decisions are announced in the *OJ* C series. The text of the decisions has recently been added to CELEX with coverage back to 1990. *CMLR antitrust reports* (1988–) includes Commission Decisions, competition cases before the Courts, and other official documents on competition policy. Information about competition cases is available on the Directorate-General for Competition's Internet home page on EUROPA.

Indexes

The Court of Justice produces a comprehensive *Index A–Z: numerical and alphabetical index of cases before the Court of Justice of the European Communities since 1953* (cumulative), updated annually. This gives references to the ECR for all cases. Indexes are provided to case numbers, names of parties, and by country to all the questions referred to the ECJ for a preliminary ruling by national courts. The Court's Research and Documentation Division can carry out searches on its internal database of national court judgments.

Butterworths EC case citator and service (1991–) indexes the majority of EC cases from 1954, with indexes to parties, subjects, legislation and names in common usage. Updating is twice a year with interim updates by fortnightly newsletter. References are given not only to the ECR, but to CMLR, to the *OJ* C series, or to a transcript if the case has not yet been published.

Gazetteer of European law: case search: European Community law, 1953–1983 (1983) is useful for older cases. It covers the first thirty years of the Court, 1953–1983 and two years 1989 and 1990. References to key national cases relating to EC law are also given. Indexes to parties, case numbers, and subjects are provided. CELEX (see below) also offers powerful indexes to EC case law.

Digests

European current law: monthly digest (1992–) digests selected cases from the European Courts and from national courts throughout Europe. References are given to commercially published series of law reports as well as to ECR. The Court's weekly summary of the judgments and of the opinions of the Advocates General is called *Proceedings of the Court of Justice of the European Communities*. Since 1994 this series has been available on RAPID, the EU's press release database and since 1996 on the Court's Internet home page.

The Court publishes an official looseleaf digest in two series. *Digest of case-law relating to the European Communities: A series* (looseleaf) digests ECJ judgments on EC law and *Digest of case-law relating to the European Communities: D series* (looseleaf) covers ECJ and selected national judgments on the Brussels Convention. This series is very behind in publication.

Computer-based systems of basic legal texts

CELEX, the official legal database of the European Union is produced by the Commission's online host Eurobases. It is available to most subscribers through a national gateway host, Context Ltd for UK subscribers. CELEX is currently available in all the official languages except Finnish, Greek and Swedish.

Broadly speaking, the treaties, the *OJ* L series and the ECR are available in full text on CELEX, while analytical references are given to items in the Preparatory acts section of the *OJ* C series. In 1996 Eurobases announced their intention to extend full text coverage in the database to the *OJ* C series and to fill other existing gaps. Another category of information recently added in full text is the merger decisions of the Commission, back to 1990.

Not all parts or 'sectors' of the database are equally up to date. Online information about full text availability and currency of the different sectors is available. Material from the *OJ* L and C series appears on CELEX several days after publication. Analytical entries for judgments are added within a few weeks. The full text of the opinion of the Advocate General and the judgment follows much later. As a rule the French version of case law is more up to date than the English. The gaps in the printed series of law reports, mentioned above, also affect the coverage on CELEX. Transcripts of cases may be requested from the court itself.

CELEX is a highly analytical database with information about legislative amendments, national implementation and so on. It allows for powerful searches. A set of excellent user manuals is available to support searching. There is also a simple menu interface for novice users. Developments planned for 1997 include a Web interface for CELEX with a link to EUDOR, a document delivery service.

Alternatives to CELEX

LEXIS contains EC case law and legislation in its EURCOM library. Case law includes the text of judgments as reported in the ECR in English and French; transcripts of judgments and opinions of the Advocates General, and Commission decisions in competition cases. The legislation section includes secondary legislation from 1980, and in French from 1993, the SPICERS CENTRE FOR EUROPE database (a digest of *OJ* references) from 1989, treaties from 1979, and references to preparatory acts from 1984. FT-PROFILE contains parts of the secondary legislation from CELEX.

There are various CD-ROM versions of CELEX. The two most popular in English are JUSTIS CELEX and EUROLAW. The JUSTIS title has a link to CELEX online and to other JUSTIS online products for subscribers. Both EUROLAW and JUSTIS CELEX include the SPEARHEAD database which is described below.

Other legal databases

Pending developments to CELEX mentioned above, the only full text electronic version of the *OJ* C series to date is the non-official JUSTIS OFFICIAL JOURNAL C SERIES CD-ROM, which has coverage from 1990.

APC provides references to proposals in progress. ECOSOC includes the full text of *Economic and Social Committee Opinions* (1994–). EPOQUE indexes all the main documents of the European Parliament.

INFO 92 contains information about Single Market legislation and its national implementation. The UK Department of Trade and Industry's SPEARHEAD gives details of UK government contacts for single market legislation in progress and information about national implementation.

Since January 1994, the *Proceedings of the Court of Justice of the European Communities* have been included in full text on RAPID, which is described below. The Law Society Library in London maintains a database of the progress of cases since 1991 which is available to Law Society members in person or by phone.

Other important official documents

The *COM documents* (1983–) series, mentioned in the context of proposed legislation, also contains a wide range of important material, including Green and White papers, and annual reports. SEC documents from the Secretariat-General of the Commission, are more difficult to trace and obtain but many documents in this series are significant. The House of Commons *Weekly information bulletin* (1978–) lists SEC and COM documents received during the week.

General report on the activities of the European Union (1995–) and *Bulletin of the European Union* (1994–) are authoritative sources of information from the European Commission for activities and decisions taken by the EU. The *General report* gives a narrative account of all policy areas during the year with tables of legislation indicating full *OJ* references for each stage in the legislative process. The Commission's *Report on competition policy* (1972–) is published annually in conjunction with the *General report*. It includes main developments in policy with detailed notes and tables of competition decisions and cases. The Commission's *Annual report on the monitoring of the application of Community law* (1984–) includes a survey of progress towards the Single European Market followed by statistical annexes on implementation of each directive, and on ECJ judgments not yet implemented, by country. It is also partly reproduced in *Butterworths EC legislation implementator* (1992–).

To follow closely very recent activities of the Council and other institutions, the best approach is to use one of the news or current awareness sources noted below.

Each of the institutions of the EU issues rules of procedure which are published in the *OJ* L series. From time to time the Court of Justice publishes *Selected instruments relating to the organization, jurisdiction, and procedure of the Court* (1993), which includes the rules of procedure.

National parliamentary scrutiny of European legislation in progress is an important source of information. The [UK] House of Commons Select Committee on European Legislation *Reports* (1973–) give a brief weekly summary of the examination of every proposal coming before the committee. The House of Lords Select Committee on the European Communities *Reports* (1974–) demonstrates a different approach by sifting the proposals and scrutinizing only the most important. It also reports on broad policy areas. Its *Reports* (1974–) are published with evidence.

Encyclopedias, large collections and services

Encyclopedia of European Community law (looseleaf) was described above and is about to be relaunched as *Encyclopedia of European Union laws*. *Vaughan : law of the European Communities service* (looseleaf) was originally reprinted from volumes 51 and 52 of *Halsbury's Laws of England*, 4th edition in 1986 (for details see the chapter on England and

Wales). It covers institutional and substantive EC law. It has now been published as a looseleaf service in its own right and is updated along with the relevant volumes in Halsbury's.

Two looseleaf works offer texts and commentary on European Community law. Smit and Herzog (looseleaf) in six volumes is arranged to mirror the format of the EC Treaty. The text of each article is accompanied by a bibliography, details of implementing measures and Court decisions, and often substantial background sections. *Common market reporter* (1962–) is also structured article by article around the EC Treaty. The text of articles, some full text secondary legislation, passages of editorial explanation and commentary, and digests of decisions and rulings are provided. Other important EU treaties are included in both these works.

Many of the specialist looseleaf services and handbooks now contain a substantial proportion of European law. In the area of competition law, for example, *Butterworths competition law* (looseleaf) or *Encyclopedia of competition law* (looseleaf) may be the most convenient sources.

Directories

The European Commission coordinates the production of *Interinstitutional directory: European Union* (1995–) which covers all the EU institutions and gives telephone extension numbers. The directory is available on EUROPA as a database called IDEA.

Vacher's European companion and consultants' register (1972–) is a convenient source updated quarterly. It lists names and addresses, and personnel for each of the institutions and for some other non-EU organizations in Europe. The *European public affairs directory* (1991–) contains sections on large companies, trade associations and professional organizations including law firms, media, EU institutions, and other practical information.

For comprehensive coverage of information sources in the UK, the *European Union information: directory of UK sources* (1995) is a useful recent addition which lists libraries and other information sources by region. The exhaustive *Directory of EU information sources* (1989–) covers EU institutions, press agencies, consultants, trade and professional organizations, postgraduate studies in European integration, EU grants and loans, and lawyers specializing in EU questions. There are indexes for each section and a general index. The law section is arranged by country, and the section on Belgium also includes the Brussels offices of firms from other countries.

Law firms in Europe: the guide to Europe's commercial law firms (1996) is arranged by country. Specialization in EC and competition law is noted. Once again the section on Belgium is relevant because it lists the Brussels offices of non-indigenous firms specializing in EC law. *Kime's international law directory* (1892–) and *Martindale-Hubbell international law directory* (1892–) both include subject indexes through which it is possible to trace law firms practising EC law.

Directory of higher education institutions in the European Community: 1992 (1993) lists universities by country with very brief details of courses offered and student numbers. The subject index includes an entry for EC law.

Bibliographies

The Court of Justice publishes two complementary legal bibliographies. *Legal bibliography of European integration* (1990–) covers all aspects of European Union law except case law. *Notes: références des notes de doctrine aux arrêts de la Cour de justice et du Tribunal de première instance des Communautés européennes* (cumulative) contains references to articles on all the judgments of the Court of Justice and the Court of First Instance. The work is arranged in case number order, with a chronological list at the end by date of judgment.

The Office for Official Publications of the European Communities produces two main catalogues. *Publications* (1992–) lists monographs and periodicals, both priced and free. The latest cumulation covers the years 1985–1995. *Documents* (1988–) lists COM documents, Reports of the European Parliament, and Opinions of the Economic and Social Committee. These two catalogues are subject to publication delay, so are most useful for retrospective searches. *EUR-OP news* (1992–), OOPEC's free newsletter, includes abstracts of new publications. The Stationery Office is the UK sales agent for OOPEC, so the value of its catalogues for tracing EU publications should not be overlooked.

European access: the current awareness bulletin to the policies and activities of the European Union (1989–) is published six times a year and is invaluable for the regular bibliographic review essays, often on legal topics, and for the recent references section which lists official and non-official publications of significance arranged in a consistent subject classification.

Indexing and abstracting services

The European Commission's SCAD database is an excellent starting-point for literature searches. Although not specifically a legal bibliography it abstracts a wide range of EU official publications, including individual acts and proposals in the *OJ* L and C series and over 2000 journals, including all the main EU law journals. SCAD is available online, but is more user-friendly on CD-ROM as EC INFODISK or as JUSTIS EC REFERENCES. The latter also includes the SPICERS CENTRE FOR EUROPE database.

European legal journals index (1993–) provides excellent monthly coverage of articles and book reviews on EC law. Before 1993 articles were indexed in *Legal journals index* (1986–). Arrangement is by subject, with indexes to authors, cases, and legislation, both UK and EU. Around 300 journals, including newsletters from professional firms, are indexed with the focus on English language journals published in Europe. The index is also on a monthly CD-ROM as part of CURRENT LEGAL INFORMATION, which includes *Current law* (for details see the England and Wales chapter) and the other LIR indexes. This database is also available by fortnightly tape service.

Current and completed theses are indexed and abstracted in *Recherches universitaires sur l'integration européenne = University research on European integration: EURISTOTE* (1982–), which is also available on the Internet as EURISTOTE.

Dictionaries

The European Union's eleven official working languages, its enthusiasm for acronyms, and the unique legal system make dictionaries and glossaries of EU terms and acronyms an essential tool for legal research.

The Council compiles and revises authoritative bilingual glossaries of European Union terms in the official languages. Details of volumes published are available from OOPEC or from the Council's Library. The European Commission Translation Service's online database EURODICAUTOM includes 4.5 million terms and 180,000 abbreviations in all EU languages and Latin. De Foulay (1992) is a handy one-volume dictionary and glossary including words, phrases and abbreviations and their equivalents in English, French, German, Italian and Spanish.

The Penguin companion to European Union (1995) is a welcome reference work. It is more than a dictionary but is included here because it defines many EU terms succinctly. Cross-referencing and citations to official and secondary sources are given throughout. The focus is on the EU, but entries relating to other European organizations are included where this illuminates a point of confusion, or where there is an overlap of activities. *The Oxford encyclopaedia of European Community law* (1990) is to be a three volume work. Only Volume 1, covering institutional matters, has appeared to date. The entries for selected words and phrases are clear and detailed. Full references are given to official documents and to further reading.

Ramsay (1994) lists full names and some contact addresses. The Council has produced an authoritative work in *Multilingual glossary of abbreviations* (1994), intended for use by translators working in EU institutions. It covers all official languages and contains 6400 entries, which are arranged by index numbers with one index for Roman alphabet languages and another for Greek.

Current Information sources

Journals, research reports

There is a wide range of journals on EU law. *Common market law review* (1963–) and *European law review* (1975–) are published six times a year and aimed at both academics and practitioners. In addition to articles, *Common market law review* includes lengthy case notes and literature surveys. *European law review* features include a regular survey of legal developments in the EU, Council of Europe and European countries and a separate annual *Competition law checklist* (1990–). The *Journal of Common Market studies* (1962–) focuses on the economics and politics of the European Union, but articles on legal aspects are also included. Its annual review, published since 1993 as a separate supplement, *The European Union [. . .]: annual review of activities* (1992–) has a useful section on EU official documentation.

Two important yearbooks are published in English. *Yearbook of European law* (1981–) contains substantial articles, annual surveys on topics such as competition law and CFSP. It has an index and tables of cases and legislation. *Annuaire européen = European yearbook* (1956–) covers the EU and other European intergovernmental organizations. Several articles are included but the main part is a documentary section on each organization, and an extensive bibliography.

European competition law review (1980) is practitioner orientated. Published eight times a year it includes articles and news of competition decisions and activities in the Commission, the ECJ, and the national competition authorities. DGIV publishes a free newsletter, *Competition policy newsletter: published quarterly* by *the Competition Directorate-General of the European Commission* (1996–). This contains articles, commentary and press releases and a well-sourced information section.

News information

Two briefing services *Europe* (1952–) and *European report* (1972–) produced in Brussels are widely used by journalists, lobbyists and EU officials. *Europe*, often known as *Agence Europe* after the name of its publisher, is published daily on pink paper. The Europe documents series issued with it is a particularly useful and sometimes unique source for the text of many important documents. *European report* is published twice a week. Various subsets of *European report* are available if the full service is not required, e.g. the monthly *European intelligence* which covers EU company law, tax, competition and intellectual property. These services are expensive and it may be more cost effective to use them online if they are only needed occasionally. *Agence Europe* is on REUTER BUSINESS BRIEFING, while *European Report* is available via FT-PROFILE and LEXIS-NEXIS. Of the UK daily newspapers the *Financial Times* has the fullest coverage of EU matters. It publishes regular law reports of European cases.

The EU institutions' press releases are available online in the official press release database RAPID. The database began in the early 1980s as a Commission service. More recent additions to the database since 1994 are *Proceedings of the Court of Justice of the European Communities*, and more recently, press releases from the Committee of the Regions and the Economic and Social Committee, Information Notes from the Court of Auditors, European Council Conclusions of the Presidency, and Common Foreign and Security Policy Declarations by the European Union. RAPID is available on EUROPA and also as part of REUTER BUSINESS BRIEFING and LEXIS-NEXIS.

The Internet is an increasingly important source of current information from the EU institutions and agencies. A selected list of the main addresses is given at the end of the chapter.

The weekly newsletter on legislation and case law *Butterworths EC brief* (1989–) provides current awareness of legal developments. The free information sheets *The week in Europe* and *Background report* available on paper or via the Internet from the Representation of the European Commission in the United Kingdom, are also useful for keeping track of recent events.

Business and financial information

The daily exchange rate for the ECU is published in *Official journal of the European Communities: C series* (1973–). Calls for tender for public contracts are published in the *Supplement to the Official journal of the European Communities: [S series]* (1978–) and also online as TED (Tenders Electronic Daily). Details of research, technology and development contracts are available from the Commission database CORDIS. Hopkins (1995) is a convenient free publication from the European Commission Representation in the United Kingdom. It provides an overview with both EU and UK government contacts.

The European Commission's *European economy* (1978–) carries substantial articles and surveys of the economic situation and comes with three supplements: *European economy: supplement A: economic trends* (1984–) describes the main trends in the economy and includes tables of interest rates and consumer price indices; *European economy: supplement B: business and consumer survey results* (1985–) includes tables of confidence indicators from manufacturing, construction and consumers, and the results of business surveys. *European economy: supplement C: economic reform monitor* (1996–) provides overviews of economic reforms in Central and Eastern European countries.

Panorama of EU industry (1994–), jointly produced by the Commission DG for Industry and Eurostat, the Statistical Office of the European Communities, is a comprehensive annual survey of trends and developments in industry and services. The arrangement is by sector, using a standard EU classification of industry. Although there is no index, there is a detailed table of contents. The chapter on business services includes a section on legal services. *Panorama of EU industry: short-term supplement* (1994–) provides bi-monthly updates.

Statistics

The Court of Justice produces an annual report, *Report of proceedings [. . .]: synopsis of the work of the Court of Justice and of the Court of First Instance of the European Communities* (1995–). The title was formerly *Synopsis of the work of the Court of Justice*. The report includes statistics of cases heard by the Court during the year under review and also some historical statistical tables, such as the number of references for preliminary rulings from each country.

Eurostat publishes a range of datasets, printed statistical yearbooks and monthly and quarterly publications. Their annual catalogue *Eurostat catalogue: publications and electronic services* (1988–) lists printed and electronic sources. The recent *Eurostat yearbook* (1995–) contains general economic and social statistics aimed at the non-specialist.

Useful addresses

Lawyers associations

Council of the Bars and Law Societies of the European Community (CCBE), rue Washington 40, B-1050 Brussels, Belgium. Tel: +32 2 640 42 74. Fax: +32 2 647 79 41. Represents the legal profession at European Union level

Official organizations

Committee of the Regions, rue Belliard 79, B-1040 Brussels, Belgium. Tel: +32 2 282 22 11. Fax: +32 2 282 28 96

Council of the European Union, General Secretariat, rue de La Loi 175, B-1048, Brussels, Belgium. Tel: +32 2 285 61 11. Fax: +32 2 285 73 81

Court of Auditors of the European Communities, rue Alcide de Gasperi 12, L-1615 Luxembourg. Tel: +352 43 98 1. Fax: +352 43 98 430

Economic and Social Committee, rue Ravenstein 2, B-1000 Brussels, Belgium. Tel: +32 2 546 90 11. Fax: +32 2 513 48 93

European Commission, rue de la Loi 200, B-1049 Brussels, Belgium. Tel: +32 2 299 11 11.

European Commission, Directorate-General for External Political Relations (DG1A), Secretariat. Tel: +32 2 295 15 55. Fax: +32 2 295 80 82. Legal officer: Tel: +32 2 295 61 62

European Commission, Directorate General for Competition (DGIV), Cellule Information. Tel: +32 2 299 11 11. Fax: +32 2 295 54 37. e-mail: info4@dg4.cec.be

European Commission Representation in the United Kingdom, Jean Monnet House, 8 Storey's Gate, London SW1P 3AT, UK. Tel: +44 (0)171-973 1992. Fax: +44 (0)171-973 1900/1910. There are also offices in Belfast, Cardiff and Edinburgh

European Parliament, Secretariat, Centre européen, Plateau de Kirchberg, L-2929 Luxembourg. Tel: +352 43 001. Fax: + 352 43 48 42

European Parliament, Information Office, 2 Queen Anne's Gate, London SW1H 9AA, UK. Tel: +44 (0)171-227 4300. Fax: +44 (0)171-227 4302

Courts

Court of Justice of the European Communities, Palais de la Cour de Justice, L-2925 Luxembourg. Tel: +352 430 31. Fax: +352 43 03 26 00. Information Service: Tel: +352 430 333 66. Fax: +352 430 325 00. Registry: Tel: +352 430 322 96. Fax: +352 430 337 66

Court of First Instance, Registry. Tel: +352 430 335 87. Fax: +352 4303 2100

Research institutions

These institutions have close links with the EU and offer postgraduate studies and research in EU law:

College of Europe, Dyver 11, B-8000 Bruges, Belgium. Tel: +32 5 033 53 34. Fax: +32 5 033 64 27

European University Institute, Badia Fiesolana, I-50016 San Domenico di Fiesole (FI), Italy. Tel: +39 55 50 921. Fax: +39 55 46 85 636

European University Institute, Academy of European Law, Villa Schifanoia, via Boccaccio 121, I-50133 Firenze, Italy. Tel: +39 55 4685 725. Fax: +39 55 4685 717

Libraries

See the Directories listed above for a list of:

1. European Documentation Centres (for the academic sector and local community).
2. European Depository Libraries and Public Information Relays (for the general public).
3. Euro Info Centres (for the business sector) .

Council of the European Union, Library/Documentation, rue de La Loi 175, B-1048 Brussels, Belgium. Tel: +32 2 285 65 23. Fax: +32 2 285 81 74

Court of Justice of the European Communities, Library, Kirchberg, Boulevard Adenauer, L-2926 Luxembourg. Tel: +352 4303 2681. Fax: +352 4303 2424

European Commission, Central Library, ave de Cortenberg 1, B-1040 Brussels, Belgium. Tel: +32 2 295 29 76. Fax: +32 2 296 1149

European Information Association, Central Library, St Peter's Square, Manchester, M2 5PD, UK. Tel: +44 (0)161-228 3691. Fax: +44 (0)161-236 6547. e-mail: eia@cityscape.co.uk (International body of information specialists concerned with improving provision of information on the EU).

Publishers and booksellers

Office for Official Publications of the European Communities (EUR-OP), rue Mercier 2, L-2925 Luxembourg. Tel: +352 499 281. Fax: +352 495 719

Butterworths EC Legislation Service, 35 Chancery Lane, London WC2A 1EL, UK. Tel: +44 (0)171-400 2555.

Context Ltd, Grand Union House, 20 Kentish Town Road, London NW1 9NR, UK. Tel:

+44 (0)171-267 8989. Fax: +44 (0)171-267 1133. e-mail: sales@context.co.uk; and support@context.co.uk

ECHO, European Commission Host Organization, BP 1078, L-1010 Luxembourg. Tel: +352 401 162 200. Fax: +352 34981 234. e-mail: echo@echo.lu

EPOQUE, Documentary Databases, European Parliament, Bâtiment Schuman, 3/73, L-2929 Luxembourg. Fax: +352 43 93 17

Eurobases, Help Desk. Tel: +352 2929 42001. Fax: +352 2929 42700. e-mail: helpdesk.eurobases@opoce.cec.be. UK subscribers should contact Context Ltd, the national gateway for Eurobases

ILI, Index House, Ascot, Berks SL5 7EU, UK. Tel: +44 (0)1344 874343. Fax: +44 (0)1344 291194

LEXIS-NEXIS, PO Box 933, Dayton, Ohio 45401-0933, USA. Tel: +1 937 859 1608. Internet: http//www.lexis-nexis.com/. In the UK, Butterworths, 35 Chancery Lane, London WC2A 1EL, UK. Tel: +44 171 400 2500. Fax: +44 171 400 2842. In France, Tel: +33 1 44 72 12 12. In Germany, Tel: +49 6997 40170

Reuters Business Information, 85 Fleet Street, London EC4P 4AJ, UK. Tel: +44 (0)171-250 1122. Fax: +44 (0)171-955 0011. Tel: 0800 010 701 (UK Helpline)

Stationery Office Publications Centre, PO Box 276, London SW8 5DT, UK. Tel: +44 (0)171-873 9090 (general telephone orders). Tel: +44 (0)171-873 8372 (enquiries about EU publications and SCANFAX orders). Fax: +44 (0)171-873 8416 (EU publications and SCANFAX orders)

Selected Internet addresses

Europa (the main official EU server) http://europa.eu.int/

Britain in the European Union (UK Foreign and Commonwealth Office EU information) http://www.fco.gov.uk/europe/index.html

Court of Justice of the European Communities http://europa.eu.int/cj/index.htm

EURISTOTE http://www.epms.nl/www/ecsa/euristot.htm

European Commission Representation in the United Kingdom http://www.cec.org.uk/

European Information Association (information specialists on EU publications, with links to European Documentation Centre pages) http://www.hull.ac.uk/php/lbsebd/index.html

European Law Students Association (ELSA) UK Section (information about the aims and activities of ELSA, local contacts and forthcoming events) http://www.dur.ac.uk/~dla0www/elsa/elsa.html

European University Institute (information about the EUI and the Academy of European Law) http://www.iue.it/

I'm Europe (European Commission DGXIII information, also provides public access to ECHO services) http://www2.echo.lu

RAPID (EU press release database) http://europa.eu.int/en/comm/spp/rapid.html

Treaty on European Union (two sites offering the full text of the Treaty on European Union) http://www2.echo.lu/eudocs/en/maastricht *and* gopher://wiretap. spies.com/11/Gov/Maast

List of works cited

EU official publications

Notes

i) Unless otherwise indicated all the EU publications listed below are published in Luxembourg by the Office for Official Publications of the European Communities.

ii) ECHO databases apart from TED are free of charge.

ABEL (available from Eurobases).

Access to Commission documents: users' guide (1994).

Agreement on the European Economic Area (1992).

Annotated summary of agreements linking the Communities with non-member countries (as at [. . .]) (1992–) Brussels: European Commission, Directorate-General for External Political Relations. Formerly: *Agreements and other bilateral commitments linking the Communities with non-member countries* (1982–1991).

Annual report on the monitoring of the application of Community law. 1st, 1983– (1984–).

APC (available from Eurobases).

Borchardt, K.-D. (1994) *The ABC of community law* 4th ed.

Bulletin of the European Union (1994–). Formerly: *Bulletin of the European Communities* (1968–1993); published in French (1958–).

CELEX (available from Eurobases or via Context Ltd for UK subscribers).

Code of Conduct concerning public access to Council and Commission documents (1993) *OJ* L 340, 31.12.93, p. 41.

Collection of consolidated texts = Recueil de textes consolidés (1996–).

COM documents (1983–). Formerly internal documents; available to European Documentation Centres (1974–).

Competition policy newsletter: published quarterly by the Competition Directorate-General of the European Commission (1996–). Formerly: *Competition policy newsletter: the quarterly publication of the Competition Directorate of the European Commission* (1994–1995).

CORDIS (available from ECHO).

Directory of higher education institutions in the European Community: 1992 (1993) 2nd edn. (also published in London by Kogan Page).

Economic and Social Committee of the European Communities (1984–) *Opinions.* Formerly distributed by the Committee.

ECOSOC (available from ECHO).

EPOQUE (available from European Parliament).

EURODICAUTOM (available from ECHO).

European economy (1978–).

European economy: supplement A: economic trends (August/September 1994–). Formerly: *European economy: supplement A: recent economic trends* (1979–July 1994).

European economy: supplement B: business and consumer survey results (March 1985–). Formerly: *European economy: supplement B: economic prospects: business survey results.* (1979–1982); *European economy: supplement B: business survey results* (1983–February 1985).

European economy: supplement C: economic reform monitor (1996–). Formerly: *European economy: supplement C: economic prospects: consumer survey results* (1979–1982); *European economy: supplement C: consumer survey results* (1983–July 1984).

European Parliament. 1985/86– (1985–) *Reports (Session documents: series A).* Formerly: *Working documents: reports.* 1972/73–1984/85 (1973–1984). Published in French (1958–).

European Union: selected instruments taken from the treaties (1995) Book I, 2 vols in 1.

Eurostat catalogue: publications and electronic services (1988–). Formerly: *Catalogue of Eurostat publications* (1986).

Eurostat yearbook (1995–).

General report on the activities of the European Union 1994– (1995–). Formerly: *General report on the activities of the Communities.* 1967–1972 (1968–1973); *General report on the activities of the European Communities.* 1973–1993 (1974–1994).

IDEA (available from EUROPA).

Index to the official journal of the European Communities (1978–). Formerly: *Supplement to the official journal of the European Communities: annual alphabetical and methodological index.* (1973–1977). Published in French (1964–).

INFO 92 (available on Eurobases).

Interinstitutional directory: European Union. Oct. 1994– (1995–).

Louis, J.-V. (1990) *The Community legal order* 2nd comp. rev edn.
Multilingual glossary of abbreviations (1994) [2nd] edn.
Office for Official Publications of the European Communities. *Documents*. 1987– (1988–). Formerly: *Catalogue [. . .]: part B: documents*. 1985–1986. (1987).
Office for Official Publications of the European Communities. *EUR-OP news* (1992–).
Office for Official Publications of the European Communities. *Publications*. 1985/1991– (1992–). Formerly: *Catalogue of the publications of the European Community institutions, 1972–1973*. (1974); *Publications of the European Communities: catalogue [. . .]*. 1974–1984 (1975–1985); *Catalogue [. . .]: part A: publications*. 1985–1996 (1986–1987); *Publications of the European Communities*. 1987–1990 (1988–1990).
Official journal of the European Communities: annex: debates of the European Parliament (1973–). Published in French (1958–).
Official journal of the European Communities: information and notices: ['C' series] (1973–). Published in French (1968–). *Journal officiel des Communautés européennes* (1958–1967) split into 'L' and 'C' series in 1968.
Official journal of the European Communities: Directory of Community legislation in force. 5th ed. (1984–). Formerly: *Register of current Community legal instruments*. 1st–4th ed. (1980–1983).
Official journal of the European Communities: English special edition (1972); Second series (1974–76).
Official journal of the European Communities: legislation ['L' series] (1973–). Published in French (1968–). *Journal officiel des Communautés européennes* (1958–1967) split into L and C series in 1968.
Panorama of EU industry (1994–). Formerly: *Panorama of EC industry* (1988–1993).
Panorama of EU industry: short-term supplement (no. 5, 1994–). Formerly: *Panorama of EC industry: short-term supplement* (1993– no. 4, 1994).
RAPID (available on EUROPA).
Recherches universitaires sur l'integration européenne = University research on European integration: EURISTOTE. 12 (1982). Formerly: *Etudes universitaires sur l'integration européenne = University studies on European integration*. 1–11 (1963–1980).
Report on competition policy. 1st– (1972–).
Reports of Commission decisions relating to competition: articles 85, 86 and 90 of the EEC Treaty (1992–).
SCAD (available on EUROPA).
Supplement to the official journal of the European Communities ['S' series] (1978–).
TED (available from ECHO).
Treaty on European Union (1992).

Court of Justice material

All these items are published by the Court of Justice of the European Communities in Luxembourg or by OOPEC.

Digest of case-law relating to the European Communities: A series (looseleaf) OOPEC.
Digest of case-law relating to the European Communities: D series (looseleaf) OOPEC.
Index A-Z: numerical and alphabetical index of cases before the Court of Justice of the European Communities since 1953 (cumulative) OOPEC.
Judgments or Orders of the Court and Opinions of the Advocates-General.
Legal bibliography of European integration. 10– (1990–). Vols 1–9 (1981–89) issued as internal publications of the Court.
Notes: références des notes de doctrine aux arrêts de la Cour de justice et du Tribunal de première instance des Communautés européennes (cumulative).
Proceedings of the Court of Justice and of the Court of First Instance of the European Communities (1990–). Formerly: *Proceedings of the Court of Justice of the European Communities*.

Report of proceedings [. . .]: synopsis of the work of the Court of Justice and of the Court of First Instance of the European Communities 1992/1994 (1995–). Formerly: *Review of cases heard by the Court of Justice of the European Communities in [. . .].* 1969–1970 (1970–1971); *Synopsis of the work of the Court of Justice of the European Communities in [. . .]* 1971–1982 (1972–1983); *Synopsis of the work of the Court of Justice of the European Communities in [. . .] and record of formal sittings in [. . .]* 1984 and 1985, 1986 and 1987 (1986, 1988); *Synopsis of the work of the Court of Justice and the Court of First Instance of the European Communities in [. . .] and record of formal sittings in [. . .]* 1988 and 1989, 1990 (1990, 1991).

Reports of cases before the Court. 1954– (1973–). 1954–1972 volumes published in English (1975–1979).

Selected instruments relating to the organization, jurisdiction, and procedure of the Court (1993) OOPEC.

Other sources

All England law reports: European cases (1995–) London: Butterworths.

Annuaire européen = European yearbook (1956–) Dordrecht: Martinus Nijhoff.

Background report (1976–) London: Representation of the European Commission in the United Kingdom.

Blackstone's EC legislation (1996) 7th edn. London: Blackstone.

Butterworths competition law (looseleaf) London: Butterworths.

Butterworths EC brief (1989–) London: Butterworths.

Butterworths EC case citator and service (1991–) London: Butterworths.

Butterworths EC legislation implementator (1992–) London: Butterworths.

Church, C. H. and Phinnemore, D. (1994) *European Union and European Community: a handbook and commentary on the post-Maastricht treaties* London: Harvester Wheatsheaf.

CMLR antitrust reports (1988–) London: European Law Centre at Sweet & Maxwell.

Common market law reports (1962–) London: European Law Centre at Sweet & Maxwell.

Common market law review (1963–) London: Stevens; Leiden: Sijthoff.

Common market reporter (1962–) Bicester: CCH Editions Ltd.

CURRENT LEGAL INFORMATION (available from Legal Information Resources Ltd).

De Foulay, C. (1992) *Glossary of EC terms and acronyms.* London: Butterworths.

Directory of EU information sources (1989–) Rixsensart (Belgium): Euroconfidential.

EC INFODISK (available from ILI).

Encyclopedia of competition law (looseleaf) London: Sweet & Maxwell.

Encyclopedia of European Community law (looseleaf) London: Sweet & Maxwell.

EUROLAW (available from ILI).

Europe (1952–) Brussels: Agence Europe.

European access: the current awareness bulletin to the policies and activities of the European Union (1989–) Cambridge: Chadwyck-Healey.

European Communities legislation: current status (1988–) London: Butterworths.

European Community cases (1989–) Bicester: CCH Editions Ltd.

European competition law review (1980–) Oxford: Sweet & Maxwell/ESC Publishing.

European current law: monthly digest (1992–) London: European Law Centre at Sweet & Maxwell.

European law review (1975–) London: Sweet & Maxwell.

European legal journals index (1993–) Hebden Bridge: Legal Information Resources Ltd.

European public affairs directory (1991–) Brussels: Landmarks.

European report (1972–) Brussels: Europe Information Service.

FT-PROFILE (available from Financial Times Information).

Gazetteer of European law: case search: European Community law, 1953–1983 (1983) London: European Law Centre. With 1989 and 1990 supplements.

Hartley, T.C. (1994) *The foundations of European Community law: an introduction to the constitutional and administrative law of the European Community* 3rd edn. Oxford: Clarendon Press.

Holborn, G. (1993) *Butterworths legal research guide.* London: Butterworths.

Hopkins, M. (1995) *Finance from Europe: a guide to grants and loans from the European Union.* London: Representation of the European Commission in the United Kingdom.

House of Commons (1978–) *Weekly information bulletin.* London: HMSO.

House of Commons Select Committee on European Legislation (1973–) *Reports.* London: HMSO.

House of Lords Select Committee on the European Communities (1974–) *Reports.* London: HMSO.

Journal of Common Market studies (1962–) Oxford: Blackwell.

JUSTIS CELEX (availabe from Context Ltd).

JUSTIS EC REFERENCES (available from Context Ltd).

JUSTIS OFFICIAL JOURNALS C SERIES (available from Context Ltd).

Kime's international law directory (1892–) London: FT Law & Tax.

Lasok and Bridge: law and institutions of the European Union (1994) 6th edn. London: Butterworths.

Law firms in Europe: the guide to Europe's commercial law firms (1996) 6th edn. London: Legalease.

Legal journals index (1986–) Hebden Bridge: Legal Information Resources Ltd.

LEXIS-NEXIS (available from LEXIS-NEXIS).

Martindale-Hubbell international law directory (1992–) New Providence, N.J.: Martindale-Hubbell. Originally part of Martindale-Hubbell Law Directory (1868–).

National Coordinating Committee of the Network of European Relays (1995) *European Union information: directory of UK sources.* London: Representation of the European Commission in the United Kingdom.

Nugent, N. (1994) *The government and politics of the European Union* 3rd edn. Basingstoke: Macmillan.

The Oxford encyclopaedia of European Community law (1990) Vol.1: Institutional law. Oxford: Clarendon Press.

The Penguin companion to European Union (1995) London: Penguin.

Ramsay, A. (1994) *Eurojargon: a dictionary of European Union acronyms, abbreviations and sobriquets* 4th edn. Stamford: Capital Planning Information.

REUTER BUSINESS BRIEFING (available from Reuters Business Information).

Rudden, B. and Wyatt, D. (1996) *Basic Community laws* 6th edn. Oxford: Clarendon Press.

Smit, H. and Herzog, P. E. (looseleaf) *The law of the European Economic Community: a commentary on the EEC treaty.* New York: Bender.

SPEARHEAD (available from FT-PROFILE, and available with EUROLAW and JUSTIS CELEX).

SPICERS CENTRE FOR EUROPE (with FT-PROFILE, JUSTIS EC REFERENCES, LEXIS-NEXIS, REUTER BUSINESS BRIEFING).

Steiner, J. (1996) *Textbook on EC law* 5th edn. London: Blackstone.

Thomson, I. (1989) *The documentation of the European Communities: a guide.* London: Mansell.

United Kingdom *Treaty series* (1892–) London: HMSO.

Vacher's European companion and consultants' register (1972–) London: Parliamentary Monitoring Services.

Vaughan: law of the European Communities service (looseleaf) London: Butterworths.

Weatherill, S. and Beaumont, P. (1995) *EC law* 2nd rev. edn. London: Penguin.

The week in Europe. London: Representation of the European Commission in the United Kingdom.

Yearbook of European law (1981–) Oxford: Clarendon Press.

Zolynski, B. (1996) European Community law. In *How to use a law library: an introduction to legal skills*, by P.A. Thomas and C. Cope, pp. 198–220. London: Sweet & Maxwell.

CHAPTER THREE

Albania

ANNE PRIES

Introduction to the legal system

Historial and legal background

The basis for the Albanian state was laid in November 1912 in the city of Vlora, with the proclamation of the Independence of Albania from the decaying Ottoman Empire and the formation of a provisional government. Up to that time, apart from Ottoman law, local customary law formed an important source (Hasluck, 1954); a recent translation into English of one collection of customary laws is Fox (1989).

After the first Balkan war, which lasted from October 1912 until May 1913, the six Great Powers organized the London Conference of Ambassadors in order to control the post-war settlement of the countries of South-East Europe following the disintegration of the Ottoman Empire. The Conference ignored the decisions of the Assembly of Vlora and did not recognize the provisional government of Albania. A far from complete Albanian State was founded on 29 July 1913; its borders were the result of a compromise between Greece and Serbia on the one hand and Austria and Italy on the other and its constitution of 1914 was effectively imposed by the more powerful states.

After occupation by several powers during World War I, Albanians rejected proposals for a form of protectorate status or further partition and demanded a sovereign Albanian state. They held a conference in Lushnja and subsequently elected a parliament and a government. The country's first National Council, consisting of 37 members, was elected in January 1920 and a new constitution was put in place in 1920. The first parliament, consisting of 78 members, was assembled on 21 April 1921 in Tirana. Ahmet Zogu, a member of one of the leading families of central Albania became Minister of Internal Affairs and in 1922, with the support of the large landowners, he became Prime Minister.

The 'revolution' of 10 June 1924 forced the landowning aristocracy to withdraw from their position of power and Zogu fled into Yugoslavia. Before the end of that year, direct intervention from Yugoslavia had overthrown the new democratic government under Fan Noli and Zogu returned to power. A republic was established in January 1925, with Zogu as President. A new constitution was written using the US constitution as a model.

The question of the borders underwent several examinations and re-examinations at various international levels. The Border Protocol between Albania and Yugoslavia was finally established in 1926.

In 1928 Albania underwent another constitutional change: having consolidated his power, Zogu proclaimed Albania a parliamentary and hereditary monarchy, with himself as Zog I, 'King of the Albanians'. An Italian–Albanian pact of 27 November 1926, signed in Tirana, had made Albania almost completely subservient to Italy. When Zogu refused to renew the pact in 1939, the Italians occupied the country. Zogu and his family escaped to Greece. State affairs were taken over by a puppet administrative committee which convoked a constituent assembly. This assembly offered the Albanian crown to the Italian King and Albania fell under the jurisdiction of the Italian government. After the defeat of Italy, Germany placed the country under military government.

Albanian wartime resistance was largely dominated by the communists, supported by Tito. His wartime friend Hoxha established an 'independent' Albania in 1944, dominated by Yugoslavia. The elections of 1945 were won by the communists. In January 1946 Albania was declared a People's Republic and on 14 March 1946 it ratified the first constitution of the communist regime, based on the Soviet Constitution of 1936 and began the task of constructing a socialist legal system. An English translation of the Albanian communist constitution can be found in *The constitutions of the communist world* (Simons, 1980, pp. 8–31).

Hoxha broke with Tito in 1948. Albania's open break with the Soviet Union came in 1961, followed by its withdrawal from the CMEA and the Warsaw Pact in 1968. Albania shifted its foreign policy toward a firm alignment with China and adopted Maoist principles. After the break-up with China in 1978, Albania was completely isolated. Hoxha died in 1985; his memoirs are available in English (Halliday, 1986). For a modern history of the Albanians see Vickers (1995) which has references to books covering the specific periods mentioned above.

Recent constitutional developments

In December 1990 the democratic transformation of Albania and the rewriting of its legal system started. The most important changes took place when, by Law Nr.7381 of 5 May 1990, the Albanian parliament re-established both the position of the private lawyer and the Ministry of Justice. The statute was followed by significant legal changes, especially in the Civil and Criminal Procedure Codes.

The new Law Nr.7491 On the Major Constitutional Provisions must be seen as a transitional constitution, replacing the communist constitution of 28 December 1976. It was adopted on 29 April 1991 and published in the Official Gazette 1991, Nr.4, pp. 145–160; it has been amended several times. An unofficial English translation of the *Law on major constitutional provisions* (1991) was published in Tirana, a German translation can be found in *Osteuropa-Recht* (1991, pp. 286–296). In 1994 the Bureau of Liaison of the Republic of Albania at the Council of Europe in Strasbourg published *Constitutional laws of the Republic of Albania*. A translation up to date to May 1995 is available in *Constitutions of the countries of the world* together with a description of constitutional progress from 1990 to 1995 (Flanz, 1995).

Under the new transitional constitution the judiciary in Albania has been reorganized. The system includes the Courts of Cassation, the Courts of Appeal, the Courts of First Instance and Military Courts. The Constitutional Court is the highest authority that protects and guarantees the constitution and legislation. The chapter on the Constitutional Court can be found in the Law on Major Constitutional Provisions, art.17–28. The professional status of judges and public prosecutors, guaranteed by the constitution, is to be secured by an administrative body, the Supreme Council of Justice, which may nominate and discharge judges of first instance and appeal and public prosecutors.

The Law on the Organization of the Judiciary and on Changes in Criminal and Civil Procedure Codes, Nr.7574, 24 June 1992 was amended by Law Nr.7919, published in the *Fletorja Zyrtare e Republikës së Shqipërisë* [Official Gazette of the Republic of Albania] 11/95, p. 451.

A draft of a new constitution *Projekti i Kushtetutës së Republikës të Shqipërisë*, prepared with intensive advice from the Council of Europe, was published in October 1994, but after a referendum, it was vetoed by the Albanian president. A complete new constitution should be expected in the near future. In the draft it is stated that legislative power belongs to the People's Assembly of the Republic of Albania. The Head of State is the President of the Republic, elected by the People's Assembly, and the Supreme Organ of the Executive Power is the Council of Ministers and the rights and duties attached to those organs of government are defined by law. Judicial power is exercised by independent courts.

Introductory works on the legal system and legal research

The legal system of Albania has been changing fundamentally during the last few years and introductory works to the new law and order have not yet been published. However, mention should be made here of the publications of Ajani (1993), Nagan, Hoxha and Dirks (1994) and, for historical aspects, the chapter on Albania in Gsovski and Grzybovski (1959). The chapter on Albania in the looseleaf *Modern legal systems cyclopedia* in its present form precedes the recent legal developments but gives a brief history of the legal system (Ford, 1991).

The most important guide in English to earlier material is Gregory Walker's chapter on Albania in *Official publications of the Soviet Union and Eastern Europe 1945–1980: a select annotated bibliography* (Walker, 1982). Another useful source is the publication of the German specialist in Albanian law, Wolfgang Stoppel (1985).

Legislation

The first non-communist government was elected on 13 April 1992. The Assembly is a unicameral parliament [Kuvendi Popullor i Republikës së Shqipërisë], consisting of 140 elected members with a term of four years.

The official gazette, published from 1923 onwards, has had the same title since 1992 as it had before 1944: *Fletorja Zyrtare e Republikës së Shqipërisë* [Official Gazette of the Republic of Albania]. It carries those laws [ligji], decrees [dekrets] and other formal legislation from the People's Assembly and the government and regulations of the Council of Ministers, which are intended for public consultation. International treaties are also published in the *Fletorja Zyrtare*. Due to lack of paper the official gazette was not published in the period starting mid-December 1991, when the last issue under the previous title of *Gazeta Zyrtare* was published, until April 1992 when the new title began. During that period about 30 laws had been promulgated including a new law on wages and salaries, tax laws, laws on joint ventures, a law on adoption, and others. As daily newspapers also did not appear, information about new laws could scarcely be found.

Authoritative commentary on legislation is given in *Drejtësia popullore* [People's justice], an organ of the Supreme Court and Procuracy-General, published from 1948; it includes a French translation of its contents page.

In the past many official documents were not published for political reasons and the official gazette was a very incomplete record. A general collection of the legislation currently in force did not exist. Occasionally books with a selected collection of laws were published but from 1979 these books were available only under very restricted conditions. For example, the collection of laws published in two volumes in 1986 in Tirana, *Përmbledhëse e përgjithshme e legjislacionit në fuqi të RPSSH 1945–1985* [General collection of legislation in force of the People's Republic of Albania 1945–1985] were 'only for officials'. Since mid-1990 the situation is far better; new normative acts and new drafts of laws are even published in the daily newspapers. Due to lack of paper the official gazette is published and distributed with great delay.

Albanian legislation is not translated systematically. In the soviet-communist years some of the laws were published in Russian. The Bureau of Liaison of the Republic of Albania in the Council of Europe in Strasbourg regularly distributes English translations of Albanian legislation. German translations of the constitution and other documents are to be found in a looseleaf work by Brunner, Schmidt and Westen (1992–), *Wirtschaftsrecht der osteuropäischen Staaten.*

Current information on legislative developments can best be found in English and German language journals, see **Journals** below. A survey of the most important laws adopted in Albania and the other countries of Central and Eastern Europe published in their official gazettes and of international agreements made by those countries is given in *WGO: Monatshefte für Osteuropäisches Recht,* which also contains German translations of the full text of some laws.

Codes and commentaries

Although Albania adopted codifications of law in the period preceding World War II, during the period 1945 to 1981 Albanian civil legislation was enacted in the form of separate statutes. Several new codes have been drawn up as part of the recent task of reconstructing the legal system and published in the official gazette, but have not yet been published separately.

In the major enterprise of preparing a new civil code, those of 1928 and 1981 were considered as models for the new one. A workshop on civil law, organized by the International Development Law Institute (IDLI), an international intergovernmental organization with its headquarters in Rome, was held in Tirana in June 1992. The new Albanian Civil Code, *Kodi Civil i Republikës së Shqipërisë*, Ligj Nr.7850, was ready at the end of June 1994 and came into force at the start of 1995. It has been published in issues 11–14 of the *Fletorja Zyrtare*. It replaces the Communist Civil Code of 1981 (with a few exceptions). It is, in a way, the successor of the first Albanian Civil Code of 1928, that was based upon the French Code Civil of 1804 and the Italian Codice Civile of 1865. The new Civil Code is subdivided into five books: General Part, Ownership and Property, Law of Inheritance, Obligations, Agreements. An unofficial English translation is available at the Library of the Institute of East European Law and Russian Studies of Leiden University. A new Code of Civil Procedure, *Kodi i procedurës civile*, appeared in May 1996 in *Fletorja Zyrtare* 1996 nos. 9–11.

Transitional arrangements for commercial enterprises are included in a Law on the Introductory Part of a Commercial Code, Nr.7632 of 4 November 1992, published in *Fletorja Zyrtare* 8/92. A German translation of that law appears in *Wirtschaft und Recht in Osteuropa* (1994, **3**, pp. 350). An English translation of the Law on Foreign Investments, made public by Decree Nr.280 of 11 August 1992, can be found in *Review of Central and East European Law* (1993, pp. 561–567).

With the help of the Council of Europe the new Criminal Code, *Kodi Penal i Republikës së Shqipërisë*, Ligj Nr.7895 of 27 January 1995, was adopted and published in issues 2 and 3/95 of the *Fletorja Zyrtare.* It replaces the Albanian Criminal Code of 1 October 1977 which was translated in *Jahrbuch für Ostrecht* (1979, pp. 231).

The new Code of Criminal Procedure, *Kodi i Procedurës Penale i Republikës së Shqipërisë*, Ligj Nr.7905 of 21 March 1995, was published in issues 5–7/95 of the *Fletorja Zyrtare.* It replaces Law Nr.6069 of 25 December 1979. A German translation of Albanian criminal legislation was published by Stoppel (1990).

The Labour Code of October 1981 was replaced by the new Albanian Labour Code, *Kodi i Punës i Republikës së Shqipërisë*, Ligj Nr.7961 of 12 July 1995, published in issue 16/95 of the *Fletorja Zyrtare.*

The State Budget for 1995 was published in issues 8–10/95 of the *Fletorja Zyrtare.*

Treaties

International treaties concluded by Albania are published in the *Fletorja Zyrtare.*

Law reports, judgments

The decisions of the Constitutional Court are published in the *Fletorja Zyrtare. Udhëzime e vendime të Gykatës së Lartë te RSPH* is a series of collections of court decisions published at intervals; collections have been published in 1965, 1972 and 1975 and probably at later dates but recent information is not available.

Drejtësia popullore [People's justice] (1948–) includes some law reports. The *OMRI Daily Digest* published in electronic form by the Open Media Research Institute includes English summaries of several court decisions. *East European Case Reporter of Constitutional Law* (1994–) may also be useful.

Computer-based systems

Albanian computer-based systems of legal texts are not available. The Albanian *Parliamentary Library* was founded in January 1992 and with the help of the US Congress automation was started and CD-ROMs have been introduced. There are no external databases. Analytical data on Albanian legislation have been loaded on to the library's databases. The information is accessible for members of the parliament only. Useful information on Albanian legislation can be found in LEXIS-NEXIS and general information is given on the *Albanian Home Page* on Internet, http://www.ios.com/%7Eulpiana/Albanian/index.html which contains links to a large number of other sites.

Other important government documents

Many of the ministries and other organs of central government used to publish material within their own spheres of responsibility. The Presidium of the People's Assembly, the Prime Minister's Office, the Ministry of Justice and the Statistical Directorate used to publish their own documents.

A few examples are: *Mbrojtja*, military and cultural journal, published by the Ministry of Defence; *Ushtria dhe Koha*, newspaper, the main periodical published by the Ministry of Defence; *Policia sot*, journal published by the Ministry of the Interior; *Mesuesi*, newspaper, published by the Ministry of Education; *Vjetar Kulturor*, cultural annual, published by the Ministry of Culture, Sport and Youth. No detailed bibliographic information can be given for any of these periodicals.

Encyclopedias, large collections

An encyclopaedia covering the legal system has not been published. For research on legal subjects one has to consult publications on the legal systems of Central and Eastern Europe as a whole mentioned elsewhere in this chapter and general works of comparative law.

Bibliographies

There is no specialist comprehensive bibliography of Albanian legal publications. The National Library in Tirana publishes a national bibliography of Albanian books, quarterly, and a national bibliography of Albanian periodicals, monthly. The volume of the World Bibliographical Series on Albania appeared in 1988 (Bland). The bibliographies of Hetzer (1980), and Hetzer and Roman (1983), although overtaken by events, deserve mention.

Dictionaries

Since a legal dictionary has not yet appeared in Albania, the titles of recent general Albanian dictionaries might be useful: *Albanian–English dictionary* (Hysa, 1993) originally published in Tirana, paperback edition printed in New York, and *Fjalor Anglisht–Shqip* [English-Albanian dictionary] (1992).

Other reference books

Doing business in Eastern Europe (1992–), a looseleaf compilation, may be of use. Useful background information on Albania can be found in Hall (1994), Grothusen (1991, 1993), Brown (1994) and in *Country profile: annual survey of political and economic background* from Economist Publications; since 1992 several series have been published including one on Albania.

Current information sources

Journals

Journals for general legal practice published in Albania are not known. In about 1992 two periodicals relating to economic law were founded: *Lajme Tregtare* and *Tribuna Ekonomike Shqiptare* but detailed information about them is not available.

Developments in Albanian law are covered by journals published abroad devoted to Central and Eastern Europe. These include major scholarly journals such as the *Review of Central and East European Law* (1992–) published in cooperation with the Institute of East European Law and Russian Studies of Leiden University, *Jahrbuch für Ostrecht* (1960–) which contains an overview of the legal changes in Albania and the other Central and East European states, *Parker School Journal of East European Law* (1994–), *Recht in Ost und West* (1957–), *WGO: Monatshefte für Osteuropäisches Recht* (1959–).

The Bureau of National Affairs in Washington publishes information about Albania in *BNA's Eastern Europe Reporter* (1991–). Other information on legal issues can be found in the publication of the Center for the Study of Constitutionalism in Eastern Europe at the University of Chicago Law School, *East European Constitutional Review* (1992–); *Journal of Constitutional Law in Eastern and Central Europe* (1994–); in the *Eastern European Forum Newsletter*, a publication of the London International Bar Association; in KPMG's international newsletter *Image on Central + Eastern Europe* (1991–) and in *Law in Transition: A*

Newsletter on Legal Cooperation & Training from the European Bank for Reconstruction and Development (1993–). Some law firms produce up-to-date newsletters of relevance including *Central Europe Newsletter* (1992–) from Clifford Chance and *Central European and CIS Legal Update* (1993–) from Baker & McKenzie.

News information

The electronic periodical *OMRI Daily Digest* (1994–) gives political, economic and legal information; Part II covers Central, Eastern and South Eastern Europe. Besides the *OMRI Daily Digest*, the Open Media Research Institute in Prague publishes the journal *Transition: Events and Issues in the Former Soviet Union and East Central and Southeastern Europe*, weekly from July 1995, formerly biweekly, covering analyses and news focusing on the political, social, economic, legal and other affairs. Political and economic information on the country can be found in *SWB: summary of world broadcasts* (1993–) from BBC Monitoring; Part 2 covers Central Europe, The Balkans.

Useful addresses

Associations of lawyers

Albanian Lawyers' Association, No.44, Pallati Nr.38, Hyrja 4, Rruga Frosina Plaku, Tirana, Albania. Tel/Fax: +355 42 27971

General Assembly of the Albanian Colleges of Advocates, c/o Ministry of Justice (see below)

Government organizations

Bureau of Liaison of the Republic of Albania, Bureau 5096, Council of Europe, Strasbourg, France. Permanent Secretariat of the Albanian National Representatives to the Council of Europe, People's Assembly, Tirana, Albania. Tel: +355 42 62003. Fax: +355 42 27949

Chamber of Commerce, Konferenca e Pezeës 6 Street, Tirana, Albania. Tel: +355 42 27997

Ministry of Justice, Bulevardi Deshmoret e Kombit D5, Tirana, Albania. Tel/Fax: +355 42 28378

National Bank of Albania, Sheshi Skeënderbej 1, Tirana, Albania. Tel: +355 42 28315

Education and training

University of Tirana, Universiteti i Tiranës, Tirana, Albania. Tel: +355 28258. Telex: 2211

Research institutions

Center for the Study of Constitutionalism in Eastern Europe, University of Chicago Law School, 1121 E. 60th Street, Chicago, IL 60637, USA. Tel: +1 312 702 9494. Fax: +1 312 702 0356

Institute of East European Law and Russian Studies, Faculty of Law, Leiden University, Hugo de Grootstraat 32, 2311 XK Leiden, Netherlands. Tel: +31 71 5277818. Fax: +31 71 5277732

Institute of International Relations, Instituti i Studimeve të Marrëdhënieve Ndërkombëtare, Tirana, Albania. Tel: +355 29521. Fax: +255 32970

Open Media Research Institute (OMRI), 140 62 Prague 4. Motokov Building. Na Strzi 63, Prague, Czech Republic. Tel: +42 2 6114 2114; Fax +42 2 6114 3323. Internet: http://www.omri.cz/Publications/Digests/DigestIndex.html

Libraries

National Library, Biblioteka Kombëtare, Tirana, Albania. Tel/Fax: +355 42 23843. Founded in 1922.

Parliamentary Library, Tirana, Albania. Tel: +355 42 32003. Fax: +355 42 27949. Founded in 1992.

Publishers and booksellers

Kubon & Sagner Buchexport-Import GmbH, PO Box 340108, D-80328 Munich, Germany. Tel: +49 89 54 218130. Fax: +49 89 54 218218. Telex: 5 216 711 kusa d. A specialized vendor of Eastern European books and periodicals.

General

Albanian Home Page on the Internet: http://www.ios.com/%7Eulpiana/Albanian/index.html

Anglo-Albanian Association, 6/38 Holland Park, London W11 3RP, UK. Tel: +44 171 727 0287. Fax: +44 171 262 7664

List of works cited

Ajani, G. (1993) Die Kodifikation des Zivilrechts in Albanien. *Recht in Ost und West*, **9**, 257–260.

Bland, William B. (1988) *Albania*. World Bibliographical Series, no.94. Oxford: Clio.

BNA's Eastern Europe Reporter. (1991–) Washington, DC: Bureau of National Affairs.

Brown, J.F. (1994) *Hopes and shadows: Eastern Europe after communism*. Durham, NC: Duke University Press.

Brunner, G., Schmidt, K. and Westen, K. (1992–) *Wirtschaftsrecht der osteuropäischen Staaten*. Baden-Baden: Nomos. Looseleaf.

Central Europe Newsletter. (1992–) London: Clifford Chance.

Central European and CIS Legal Update. (1993–) London: Baker & McKenzie.

Constitutional laws of the Republic of Albania. (1994) Strasbourg: Council of Europe.

Country profile: annual survey of political and economic background. (1992–) London: Economist Publications.

Doing business in Eastern Europe. (1992–) Bicester: CCH Editions.

Drejtësia popullore [People's justice]. (1948–) Tirana.

East European Case Reporter of Constitutional Law. (1994–) Den Bosch: Bookworld.

East European Constitutional Review. (1992–) Chicago, Ill.: Center for the Study of Constitutionalism in Eastern Europe at the University of Chicago Law School in partnership with the Central European University.

Eastern European Forum Newsletter. (1993–) London: International Bar Association.

Fjalor Anglisht–Shqip [English–Albanian dictionary]. (1992) New Delhi: J.R. Printing Press.

Flanz, Gisbert H. (1995) Republic of Albania. In *Constitutions of the countries of the world*, ed. A.P. Blaustein and G.H. Flanz, vol.I. Dobbs Ferry, NY: Oceana.

Fletorja Zyrtare e Republikës së Shqipërisë [Official Gazette of the Republic of Albania]. (1923–) Tirana. Published as *Fletorja Zyrtare e Republikës së Shqipërisë* (1922–1942); *Gazeta Zyrtare e RPS të Shqipërisë* (1944–1991); this title from 1992.

Ford, Donald Lehman (1991) The legal system of Albania. In *Modern legal systems cyclopedia*, ed. K.R. Reddy, vol.8, pp. 8.10.1–28. Buffalo, NY: Hein. Date taken from title page of volume.

Fox, Leonard (1989) *Kanuni i Leké = The Code of Leké Dukagini: Albanian text collected and edited by Shtjefén Gjeçov*. New York: Gjonlekaj. Parallel Albanian and English, translation and introduction by Fox.

Grothusen, K. (1991) (ed.) *Albanien in Vergangenheit und Gegenwart: internationales Symposium der Südosteuropa-Gesellschaft in zusammenarbeit mit der Albanischen Akademie der Wissenschaften, Wintersheide bei Bonn, 12–15 September 1989*. Südosteuropa-Studien, Bd. 48. Munich: Südosteuropa Gesellschaft.

Grothusen, K. (1993) *Albanien = Albania*. Südosteuropa-Handbuch, Bd. 7 = Handbook on South Eastern Europe, vol.7. Göttingen: Vandenhoeck & Ruprecht.

Gsovski, V. and Grzybovski, K. (1959) (eds) *Government, law and courts in the Soviet Union and eastern Europe*. London: Stevens & Sons; The Hague: Mouton & Co. 2 vols.

Hall, D. (1994) *Albania and the Albanians*. London & New York: Pinter.

Halliday, Jon (1986) (ed.) *The artful Albanian: the memoirs of Enver Hoxha*. London: Chatto and Windus.

Hasluck, Margaret H. (1954) *The unwritten law in Albania*. Cambridge: Cambridge University Press.

Hetzer, Armin. (1980) *Arbeitsmaterialien zu einer Landesbibliographie Albanien* [Material for a bibliography of Albania]. Bremen: Bremen University. 6 vols. On cover: *Albanien Bibliographie*. Vol.4 is devoted to law. Gives German translations of Albanian titles.

Hetzer, Armin and Roman, Viorel S. (1983) *Albanien: ein bibliographischer Forshungsbericht = Albania: a bibliographic research survey*. Bibliographien zur regionalen Geographie und Landeskunde. Munich: K.G. Saur.

Hysa, Ramazan (1993) *Albanian–English dictionary*. New York: Hippocrene Books.

Image on Central + Eastern Europe: the International KPMG Newsletter. (1991–) Brussels: KPMG.

Jahrbuch für Ostrecht. (1960–) Munich: Beck.

Journal of Constitutional Law in Eastern and Central Europe. (1994–) Den Bosch: Bookworld.

Kodi Civil i Republikës së Shqipërisë [Civil Code of Albania]. (1994) *Fletorja Zyrtare*, 1994, nos. 11–14.

Kodi i Procedurës Penale i Republikës së Shqipërisë [Code of Criminal Procedure of Albania] (1995) *Fletorja Zyrtare*, 1995, Nos. 5–7.

Kodi i Punës i Republikës së Shqipërisë [Labour code of Albania]. (1995) *Fletorja Zyrtare*, 1995, No. 16.

Kodi Penal i Republikës së Shqipërisë [Penal code of Albania]. (1995) *Fletorja Zyrtare*, 1995, nos. 2–3.

Law in Transition: a newsletter on legal cooperation & training from the European Bank for Reconstruction and Development. (1993–) London: European Bank for Reconstruction and Development.

Law on Major Constitutional Provisions. (1991) Tirana. Unofficial translation.

Nagan, W.P, Hoxha, A. and Dirks, P.J. (1994) Strengthening the rule of law in Albania: impartiality, independence, and the transformation of the legal profession. *Review of Central and East European Law*, **6**, 677–698.

OMRI Daily Digest. (1994–) Prague: Open Media Research Institute. Electronic periodical (available at Listserv@ubvm.cc.Buffalo.edu).

Osteuropa-Recht (1955–) Stuttgart: Gesellschaft für Osteuropakunde.
Parker School Journal of East European Law. (1994–) New York: Parker School of Foreign and Comparative Law, Columbia University School of Law.
Përmbledhëse e përgjithshme e legjislacionit në fuqi të RPSSH 1945–1985 [General collection of legislation in force of the People's Republic of Albania 1945–1985]. (1986) Tirana. 2 vols.
Projekti i Kushtetutës së Republikës të Shqipërisë [Draft of the Constitution of Albania]. *Rilindja Demokratike*, 9 October 1994.
Recht in Ost und West. (1957–) Berlin: Arno Spitz.
Review of Central and East European Law. (1992–) Dordrecht: Kluwer. Published in cooperation with the Institute of East European Law and Russian Studies of Leiden University. Formerly *Review of Socialist Law*.
Review of Socialist Law. (1975–1991) Dordrecht: Nijhoff. Published in cooperation with the Institute of East European Law and Russian Studies of Leiden University. Superseded by *Review of Central and East European Law* (1992–).
Simons, William B. (1980) *The constitutions of the communist world*. Alphen aan den Rijn: Sijthoff & Noordhoff.
Stoppel, Wolfgang (1985) Die Rechtsquellen und juristischen Publikationsorgane in Albanien. *Jahrbuch für Ostrecht*, 409–426.
Stoppel, Wolfgang (1990) *Albanische Strafgesetze*. Sammlung ausserdeutsche Strafgesetzbücher in deutscher Übesetzung, no.105. Berlin & New York: de Gruyter.
SWB: summary of world broadcasts. (1993–) London: BBC Monitoring. Part 2, Central Europe, the Balkans.
Transition: Events and Issues in the Former Soviet Union and East Central and Southeastern Europe. (1995–) Prague: OMRI.
Udhëzime e vendime të Gykatës së Lartë te RSPH. (1958–) Tirana.
Vickers, Miranda (1995) *The Albanians: a modern history*. London: Tauris.
Walker, G. (1982) (ed.) *Official publications of the Soviet Union and Eastern Europe 1945–1980: a select annotated bibliography*. London: Mansell.
WGO: Monatshefte für Osteuropäisches Recht. (1959–) Heidelberg: Müller.
WiRO: Wirtschaft und Recht in Osteuropa. (1992–) Munich: Beck.

CHAPTER FOUR

Austria

ILSE DOSOUDIL

Introduction to the legal system

In the middle of the 19th century Austria was transformed from an absolute monarchy to a constitutional monarchy. The constitutions of 1848 and 1849 were formal, containing some few civil rights. From 1852 to 1867 a number of reform bills were issued, aiming to shift the sovereignty from the monarch to the representatives of the people. This development concluded with the *Dezemberverfassung* [December Constitution] of 1867, which was not a unified constitution, but rather a compilation of several *Staatsgrundgesetzen* [basic constitutional laws].

Following the end of World War I and the fixing of the frontiers of the state of Austria by the Treaty of St Germain, a constitution for the Republic of Austria was formulated in 1920. This constitution of the first Austrian Republic was subsequently amended in 1925 and 1929. The Republic of Austria was integrated into Germany in 1938 and downgraded to the status of an administrative territory. After the end of World War II and the restoration of the state of Austria the Constitution of 1920 in its 1929 version was re-enacted in 1945. Together with the *Staatsvertrag* [State Treaty] of 1955 and the declaration of Austrian neutrality this forms the legal basis of the second Austrian Republic.

Austria joined the European Union as a full member on 1 January 1995.

Austria is a federal state comprising nine Länder [member states or provinces]. The functions of legislation and administration are divided between the member states and the federation. There are legislative bodies for the federation and also for each of the Länder. Legislative power at federal level is exercised by the *Nationalrat* [chamber of the people] and by the *Bundesrat* [chamber of the member states]. Each of the member states also has its own parliament, a *Landtag*. Member states are relatively autonomous in local matters and within the framework of administration delegated from the federal executive. The agencies for provincial legislation, their procedure and the organization of provincial administration are established in the constitutions of the individual member states. However the extent of their jurisdiction rests with the competence of the federation.

The Constitution, Bundes-Verfassungsrecht or B-VG, was first published in the *Bundesgesetzblatt der Republik Österreich* [Federal Law Gazette of the Republic of Austria] in 1920 and published in its revised form in 1929 (BGBl.nr.1/1930). Das *Österreichische Bundes-Verfassungsrecht* (Mayer, 1994) is a collection of all federal constitutional statutes and citations to provincial constitutional statutes with a commentary concerning the doctrine and jurisdiction of constitutional law; it is widely used in the legal profession. A compilation of the texts of constitutional law was recently published in a seventh edition by Klecatsky and Morscher (1995). An unofficial English translation appears in Flanz and Knize (1985) incorporating amendments to the end of 1984. The most popular textbook of Austrian constitutional law is *Grundriß des österreichischen Bundesverfassungsrechts* (Walter and Mayer, 1995). A short book in English, *Outline of Austrian constitutional law*, gives an introduction to the relatively complicated subject (Heller, 1989).

Article 149 of the Constitution assimilates various 19th century laws including provisions on personal liberty and fundamental rights appearing in other statutes. A collection of the sources of human rights in Austrian law with a systematic description is entitled *Grundriß der Menschenrechte in Österreich* (Ermacora, 1988); an English version appeared as *International human rights* (Ermacora, Nowak and Tretter, 1993). All international treaties of human rights to which Austria is a party appeared in English, entitled *Human rights in international law* (Berchtold, 1978). A short introduction to the rule of law was published in 1994 entitled *Austrian contributions to the rule of law* by Machacek.

In accordance with the Constitution, the government and its subordinate bodies have to execute and administer the federal laws. In Austria administration has a long tradition and therefore there is extensive administrative law and procedure. The general statute of administrative procedure [Allgemeines Verwaltungsverfahrensgesetz] was published in 1925 and again in BGBl.nr.172 Anlage 2 of 1950. A handy text edition is *Verwaltungsverfahren* (List, 1995). The amendments of the statutes of administrative procedure of 1995 appeared in a separate volume entitled *Die Verwaltungsverfahrensnovellen 1995* (Walter and Thienel, 1995) and is very useful for all administrative officials. The major commentary is *Die österreichischen Verwaltungsverfahrensgesetze* by Ringhofer (1987–1992) and is often used by practitioners.

An introduction and systematic description of the law of administrative procedure for students and lawyers is *Grundriß des österreichischen Verwaltungsverfahrensrechts* (Walter and Mayer, 1995) and by the same authors *Grundriß des besonderen Verwaltungsrechts* (Walter and Mayer, 1987).

Introductory works on the legal system and legal research

It should be emphasized that Austrian legal literature is mostly published only in German. Therefore lawyers from abroad without a knowledge of German will find it difficult to search for information on Austrian law. Few translations into English are published.

A comprehensive introduction to the legal system of Austria has not yet been produced. A short but very clear introduction to Austrian law entitled *Einführung in das österreichische Recht* by Posch (1985), with a short bibliography of legal literature, is used by students and foreign lawyers. A short description of the legal systems of Austria and Germany was published in 1993, *Einführung in das deutsche und österreichische Rechtssystem und in die deutsche Rechtssprache* (Heidinger, Abel, and Hochleitner, 1993).

In English, volume 1 of the *International encyclopedia of comparative law* contains a concise article on the Austrian legal system which is dated but still useful (Schwind and Zeman, 1972). A more recent chapter on the legal system of the Republic of Austria appears in the *Modern legal systems cyclopedia* (Kantner, 1989). *Austrian business law* (Heller *et al.*, 1992) has a narrower focus and much more detail.

A helpful guide for law students, showing them how to use legal literature and write dissertations is *Wissenschaftliche Arbeitstechnik und -methodik für Juristen* (Kerschner, 1993). Another basic textbook for students is *Einführung in die Rechtswissenschaft und ihre Methoden* (Schnorr, 1988). A guide to Austrian legal research in English appeared in the *Law Library Journal* (Fox, 1988).

Legislation

In Austria, all legislation including statutes, amended and repromulgated statutes, international treaties signed by the Federal Republic, treaties between the provinces, decrees as well as announcements and orders of the ministers must be published in the *Bundesgesetzblatt für die Republik Österreich* [Federal Law Gazette of the Republic of Austria] (1945–) and attain the full force of law on the day of publication unless a different date has been determined by the parliament or the relevant minister.

The *Bundesgesetzblatt* is issued by the Bundeskanzleramt [Federal Chancellor's Office] in accordance with a special federal law and published by a private publishing house, the Österreichische Staatsdruckerei in Vienna. Individual issues [Stücke] appear when required, normally at weekly intervals and contain several statutes, regulations, etc., which are identified by running numbers within each annual series [Jahrgang]. The issues are also identified by running numbers within each annual series. A typical citation of the *Bundesgesetzblatt* refers to the number of the particular statute, decree, etc. (not the number of the issue) and the year, for example BGBl.Nr.519/1995 (part of issue 169 dated 8 August 1995). The table of contents of each annual series consists of two parts: part 1 contains a numerical list of legislation, part 2 a keyword index. The *Bundesgesetzblatt* is available either by subscription or in individual parts from the Österreichische Staatsdruckerei.

The Bundeskanzleramt issues an annual subject index of the entire federal law announced in the Bundesgesetzblatt, in force on 1 January of the year of publication, entitled *Index 1996*, and published by the Österreichische Staatsdruckerei. The Index has a systematic subject and a chronological register and also a keyword register. It is kept up to date in *JUS-EXTRA* (1985–) published in monthly looseleaf form by the Österreichische Staatsdruckerei.

Another index, *BGBl-Index: Wegweiser durch Österreichs Bundesgesetzgebung* (1995) is a privately published annual collection of federal law in force. It also includes an index of abrogated statutes and a short-title list of statutes. This work is very useful for anyone who wants to find a particular statute.

A privately published looseleaf collection, *Das österreichische Recht* (Heinl, Loebenstein and Verosta, 1948–), covers the complete Austrian law since 1945 in full text with annotations and is continually updated. It is a very extensive work with a keyword register and a chronological index. It is generally considered an essential work used in courts, at universities and by lawyers.

The work of the legislative bodies, *Nationalrat* and *Bundesrat*, is set down in the *Stenographische Protokolle des Nationalrates* and . . . *des Bundesrates* [proceedings of the chambers of parliament] (1945–), together with supplements, including the debates on new laws, reports of the various committees, etc. The proceedings appear regularly under the number of the legislative period and the year and can be purchased by subscription from the official publisher.

The laws and regulations issued by the Austrian provinces are published in the respective provincial law gazettes *Landesgesetzblatt für das Land*. . .. The legislative body of each province's *Landtag* publishes the proceedings of its sessions and resolutions as *Protokolle*. Each provincial government publishes also a weekly official gazette.

Codes and commentaries

In Austria all important statutes are federal statutes. On principle, they have to be published in the *Bundesgesetzblatt* and are available back to 1946 from the Österreichische Staatsdruckerei, Vienna.

The commercial editions of the codes are very important for the practical work of lawyers because they contain amendments, annotations, other relevant statutes and bibliographical references. This helps to avoid the difficulties of searching in the great number of volumes of the *Bundesgesetzblatt*. Revised commercial editions appear at irregular intervals. Systematic descriptions of the codes, which are equally used by students and lawyers, are also published.

Civil Code

The Civil Code [Allgemeines Bürgerliches Gesetzbuch or BGB] entered into force in 1812. The code as a whole has not been rewritten since, only some parts revised such as the family law, the law of inheritance. The recently published annotated edition is *Das Allgemeine bürgerliche Gesetzbuch* (Dittrich and Tades, 1994). The text of the Civil Code is also available on floppy disk for MS Windows.

An extensive commentary to the Civil Code was published in two volumes by Rummel (1990). A textbook compiled for students but often used by lawyers is *Grundriß des Bürgerlichen Rechts* in two volumes, tenth edition recently published (Koziol and Welser, 1995). For further reference to the system of civil law the six books by Gschnitzer (1979, 1984, 1985, 1988, 1991 and 1992) should be used.

Commercial Code

The Commercial Code [*Handelsgesetzbuch* or HGB] was derived from German law and came into force in 1897. *Das Handelsgesetzbuch* (Nitsche, Nowotny and Zetter, 1994) contains the text and the relevant specific commercial law. A convenient edition of commercial law especially used by students was edited by List (1994) entitled *Handelsrecht*. As an important comprehensive commentary one can recommend *Kommentar zum Handelsgesetzbuch* in two volumes by Straube *et al.* (1992–1995). An English translation of the Austrian Commercial Code was edited by Andréewitch *et al.* (1987).

Systematic descriptions of the commercial law are published as *Grundriß des Handelsrechts* (Krejci, 1995) and *Grundriß des österreichischen Gesellschaftsrechts* (Kastner, Doralt and Nowotny, 1990).

Important special statutes of commercial law are *Wechselgesetz* [law of bills of exchange] and *Scheckgesetz* [law concerning cheques]. An annotated edition of these laws in one volume was edited by Pimmer (1992). Company law was recently published in an English translation entitled *Company law and accounting in Austria* by Andréewitch *et al.* (1995) in looseleaf form.

Labour and social law

In the field of labour and social law the most important statute is *Arbeitsverfassungsgesetz* [Labour Relations Law]. An annotated edition by Floretta and Strasser (1988–1993) entitled *Arbeitsverfassungsgesetz* appeared in 1988, with supplements 1990 and 1993. All statutes and regulations concerning labour law, with annotations and judgments, have been collected in *Arbeitsrecht* by Dittrich and Tades (1963–1995) in a looseleaf edition. Students and lawyers use the systematic descriptions *Arbeitsrecht* (Floretta, Spielbüchler and Strasser, 1988–1990) in two volumes and *Grundriß des österreichischen Sozialrechts* (Tomandl, 1992).

Code of Civil Procedure

The Zivilprozeßordnung [Code of Civil Procedure] with its introductory statute originates from 1895. A private edition entitled *Zivilprozeßgesetze* was published in 1995 (Stohanzl, 1995). The most widely used comprehensive commentary is by Fasching (1971–1974) entitled *Kommentar zu den Zivilprozeßgesetzen*. A more recent annotated edition of the jurisdictional norms and the Code of Civil Procedure is entitled *Jurisdiktionsnorm und Zivilprozeßordnung* with annotations by Stohanzl (1990). The *Exekutionsordnung* [Code on enforcement of judgments] was promulgated in 1895 and the *Ausgleichsordnung* [Statute of arrangements] in 1914. There is an annotated edition of the Code on enforcement of judgments by Angst, Jakusch and Primmer (1995) and of the Statute of arrangements in *Konkurs-, Ausgleichs- und Anfechtungsordnung* by Mohr (1995).

In the field of the law of civil procedure and the insolvency law several systematic descriptions have been compiled, for example, *Grundriß des österreichischen Zivilprozeßrechtes* (Rechberger and Simotta, 1994), *Österreichisches Zwangsvollstreckungsrecht* (Holzhammer, 1993) and *Österreichisches Insolvenzrecht* (Holzhammer, 1994).

Penal Code and Code of Criminal Procedure

The *Strafgesetzbuch* [Penal Code] came into force in 1852 and was newly codified in 1974 together with the Code of Criminal Procedure. A former Minister of Justice, E. Foregger, published several editions of the Penal Code, the last one in 1991, with a supplement 1993 (Foregger and Kodek, 1991). An annotated edition, used by students and lawyers, was recently edited in its twelfth edition (Foregger, 1995). The most important comprehensive commentary, entitled *Wiener Kommentar zum Strafgesetzbuch*, is currently appearing in looseleaf form (Foregger and Nowakowski,

1979–). A dated translation is available (West and Shuman, 1966). The Code of Criminal Procedure was published as *Die österreichische Strafprozeßordnung* (Foregger and Kodek, 1994). This edition contains annotations and judgments. The introductory works to the penal law, *Österreichisches Strafrecht, allgemeiner Teil* (Triffterer, 1994) and *Grundzüge des österreichischen Strafverfahrens* (Platzgummer, 1994) should also be mentioned.

Treaties

In Austria treaties are concluded by the president and the relevant minister with the approval of the parliament and a bill has to be brought in by the federal government or a minister. Treaties between the member states or treaties which concern a member state have to be approved by that province's *Landtag*. All treaties are published in the *Bundesgesetzblatt* in their various original languages with a translation into German. A list of all treaties can be found in the annually published *Index [year]*, issued by the Federal Chancellor's Office. A list of multilateral treaties arranged by subject and a list of bilateral treaties arranged by countries can be found in *BGBl-Index*.

Law reports, judgments

The execution of law is by judicial bodies which are independent from the administrative bodies. The ordinary courts exercise civil and criminal jurisdiction. The highest authority is the Oberster Gerichtshof [Supreme Court]. The courts of public law are the Verwaltungsgerichtshof [Court of Administration] and the Verfassungsgerichtshof [Constitutional Court].

Entscheidungen des österreichischen Obersten Gerichtshofes in Zivilsachen [decisions of the Supreme Court in civil cases] (1922–) have been published annually covering the years since 1919. The annual collections of the rulings are available back to 1959 from the Österreichische Staatsdruckerei and also two general indices covering the years 1919 to 1967. *Entscheidungen des österreichischen Obersten Gerichtshofes in Strafsachen* [rulings of the Supreme Court in criminal cases] (1920–) also covering the years from 1919 are available from 1949 with general index for 1919–1959.

Both collections contain a comprehensive subject index, a table of materials and a table of statutory provisions. Law reports with index volumes have been published for special areas such as family law, commercial law, real property law, labour law, insurance law, law of trade marks and law of patents.

Important judgments in specialist areas can also be found in the Austrian law journals such as *Juristische Blätter* (1872–), *Österreichische Juristenzeitung* (1946–), *JUS extra* (1985–). The *Österreichische Juristenzeitung* also contains Leitsatzkartei [heading note documentation] of all the judgments on cards for filing by the subscriber; it is also available on floppy disk.

The decisions of the supreme courts of public law in fundamental questions, especially of the Court of Constitution, are important sources of law. The official collection of the decisions of the Constitutional Court has been appearing annually since 1919, entitled *Erkenntnisse und Beschlüsse des Verfassungsgerichtshofes*. From volume 12 (1946) they are available from the Österreichische Staatsdruckerei. The collection is arranged chronologically by the date of decision and has an index. In addition, the Constitutional Court issues a cumulative selection of its most important judgments, which is available as a printed edition and also on CD-ROM (see below).

The decisions of the Administrative Court appear in two parts entitled *Erkenntnisse und Beschlüsse des Verwaltungsgerichtshofes*, divided into *Administrativrecht* [administrative] and *Finanzrecht* [financial law] volumes, published annually since 1948, covering the years from 1946. This official collection contains a systematic index, an index of statutory provisions and an index by decision number. For the administrative law part, a general index was published covering the period from 1946 to 1974. A CD-ROM version is published twice a year (see below).

Important decisions of the courts are also published and annotated in the commercially published journals.

Computer-based systems

Most electronic information products are produced by commercial publishers using a variety of formats. For instance, the Viennese publishing houses Manz and Orac since 1994 have been issuing a series of law texts on floppy disks, for MS Windows, entitled MODAT-RECHTSTEXTE. Paragraphs, headings and a hierarchical content list are searchable on these disks. So far the following have been published in this series: *Allgemeines bürgerliches Gesetzbuch* [Civil Code] 1994, *Einkommensteuergesetz* [income tax law] 1994, *GmbH-Gesetz* [limited liability company law] 1994, *Mietrechtsgesetz* [real property law], 1994, *Steuer-Index* [taxation index] 1994, *Umsatzsteuergesetz* [sales tax] 1995, *Wohnungseigentumsgesetz* [condominium law] 1994, and *Straßenverkehrsordnung* [rules of the road] 1995.

The floppy disks can be purchased at a price range (at the time of writing) between Sch280.-- and Sch480.--. They are very useful and cheap instruments for lawyers and attorneys. A subseries, MODAT-CD-ROM contains law texts on CD-ROM also for MS-DOS based personal computers. The first publication in this series is *Arbeitsrecht* [Labour law] 1994 at Sch26.400.--.

The publishing house Österreichische Staatsdruckerei, Vienna, produces a number of legal databases on CD-ROM. ZIVILRECHT COMPACT is a full-text database of the civil law in force, judgments of the courts from 1946 to 1991 and since 1991 original judgments of the Supreme Court in civil law. The database is updated twice a year and costs Sch24.000.-- plus Sch6.000.-- per update. STRAFRECHT COMPACT is the full text database of penal law and the judgments of the Supreme Court since 1975. It is available at a price of Sch24.000,-- plus Sch6.000,-- per update twice a year. Equally priced and arranged is STEUERRECHT COMPACT, the database of taxation laws and the relevant judgments of the Court of Administration. VfGH=VERFASSUNGSGERICHTSHOF [Constitutional Court] and VwGH=VERWALTUNGSGERICHTSCHOF, ADMINISTRATIVRECHT [Court of Administration, administrative law] are full-text databases of the judgments of those courts since 1919 and 1950 respectively. They are updated twice a year and cost, at the time of writing as a guide, Sch9.000.-- plus Sch3.200.-- per update and Sch18.000.-- plus Sch3.600.-- respectively.

The Office of the Federal Chancellor, Vienna, has built up an online legal information system RECHTSINFORMATIONSSYSTEM DES BUNDES (RIS). This federal law information system is used in the federal and provincial public administration. It contains three databases: federal law in force since 1983, judgments of the courts and supreme courts, provincial law. Private users in Austria and other countries can access RIS via Radio Austria after obtaining permission from the Office of the Federal Chancellor.

The government web site is at http://gov.austria.info.at/ForeignAffairs which gives information on Austrian foreign policy and has links to various other government ministries and public organizations, mainly in German.

Other important government documents

The federal ministries and important administrative authorities issue official journals in which regulations, decrees, announcements, etc. are published, for example, *Amtsblatt der Österreichischen Justizverwaltung* [Official Gazette of the Austrian Judicature] (1945–). Criminal law problems, questions of procedure and proposals for reform are covered in a large series, edited by the Ministry of Justice in Vienna, entitled *Schriftenreihe des Bundesministeriums für Justiz* (1982–). These volumes are summaries of reports of courses and congresses for judges and appear once or twice a year.

Encyclopedias, large collections and services

The largest collection of the entire body of Austrian law is *Das österreichische Recht* published as a looseleaf edition (Heinl, Loebenstein, and Verosta, 1948–). Also in looseleaf form is *Österreichische Gesetze*, a collection of civil law, commercial law, penal law and law of procedure by Bydlinski (1980–1995) in cooperation with a German publisher.

The series *KODEX des österreichischen Rechts* at present comprises 24 volumes of the texts of Austrian statutes in force. These volumes are reissued if amendments of statutes are made. A supplementary series, *Mini-KODEX*, contains the text of special statutes.

Some years ago a keyword dictionary of the whole law was compiled in eight volumes, entitled *Rechtslexikon*, by Maultaschl (1959–1971).

Directories

A very useful reference work is *Österreichischer Amtskalender*, published from official sources since 1922 by Österreichische Staatsdruckerei. It lists all Austrian federal and provincial authorities with their departments and areas of responsibility, their officials and the addresses of the individual offices. Ecclesiastical authorities, bodies representing sectional interests and commercial bodies are also included. The courts, judges and attorneys of each Austrian member state are listed, as well as the law faculties of the universities. Since 1994 this publication is also available on CD-ROM.

The *Österreichischer Rechtsanwaltskammertag* [Austrian Bar Association] publishes an annual compilation of courts, bar associations of the member states and attorneys. This volume is available from the Bar Association.

Bibliographies

There is no recent bibliography of Austrian legal literature. In 1978 a law bibliography was published entitled *Rechtsbibliographie 1977* by Cerutti. A selective compilation of basic literature on Austrian law in German and English entitled *Grundliteratur zum österreichischen Recht* was made by Dosoudil (1988).

Legal literature is selectively listed in several journals and databases. Austrian legal literature can also be found in the German *Karlsruher Juristische Bibliographie.*

The Austrian national bibliography, *Österreichische Bibliographie* (1945–), lists legal works published in Austria in section 4. In series B, Österreichische Hochschulschriften [Austrian dissertations] of this bibliography juridical dissertations can be found. The Austrian bibliography is edited by Österreichische Nationalbibliothek [the Austrian National Library].

Legal works are also listed in the catalogues of specialized publishing houses such as Manz, Orac, Österreichische Staatsdruckerei.

Indexing and abstracting services

The most important index to judgments, articles in journals and *Festschriften* is the *Hohenecker Index* which has appeared annually since 1946. *JUS-Extra* (1985–) contains information on judgments, statutes, articles and monographs. It is also available as a CD-ROM updated twice a year.

The online database RECHTSDATENBANK-RDB contains full-text articles and judgments published in Austrian law journals. It is a commercially produced database with monthly updating. The publisher Österreichische Staatsdruckerei also produces the CD-ROM databases RIDA PLUS and RIDA PLUS 2. They contain decisions of the Supreme Courts, judgments and legal literature in full text covering the whole area of law. RZL STEUERRECHT PLUS contains abstracts of articles in journals and the decisions of the Supreme Courts in the area of taxation law.

Dissertations in law with abstracts can be found in the OSTERREICHISCHE DISSERTATIONSDATENBANK [Austrian dissertation database]. This is on the Internet at http://s1.uibk.ac.at/ddb/ and covers all Austrian dissertations since 1990.

Dictionaries

A single language dictionary explaining Austrian legal terms, *Österreichisches Rechtswörterbuch*, by Russwurm was published in 1988. Austrian lawyers also use the *Rechtswörterbuch* by Creifelds *et al.* (1996) published in Munich. Latin legal terms used in Austrian law are explained in *Juristenlatein* (Luggauer, 1979). The most frequently used bilingual law dictionary is *Law dictionary* (Beseler and Jacobs-Wüstefeld, 1991). Another widely used volume is *PONS Fachwörterbuch Recht* (Collin *et al.*, 1990).

Austrian legal abbreviations and their rules are collected in *Abkürzungs- und Zitierregeln der österreichischen Rechtssprache (AZR) samt Abkürzungsverzeichnis* (Friedl and Loebenstein, 1994). This dictionary of abbreviations is also available on floppy disk for MS Windows in the series MODAT.

Other reference books

As reference books for the legal profession, the following should be mentioned: *Cross border practice compendium* by Donald-Little (1991–) in looseleaf form and the rules for Austrian attorneys entitled *Rechtsanwaltsordnung* (Schuppich and Tades, 1994). The publication *Guide to legal studies in Europe 1996–97* also covers information about Austria.

Current information sources

Journals, research reports

The most essential journals for practising lawyers are issued by commercial publishers. The most important titles include the following:

Juristische Blätter, published monthly since 1872, contains both scholarly essays and articles on practical problems over the whole field of law, as well as a regular bibliography. A detailed summary of decisions demonstrates the development of the jurisdiction of the supreme courts.

Österreichische Juristenzeitung, published twice per month since 1946, contains articles, recent judgments and decisions of the supreme courts and headnote documentation forming a subject index to judgments. The wide area of administrative law is covered by *Zeitschrift für Verwaltung* (1976–) which contains articles on the development of administrative law as well as the decisions of the Court of Administration and of the Constitutional Court in cases of administrative law.

The journal of the Bar Association *Österreichisches Anwaltsblatt* (1946–) is published monthly by a commercial publisher. It contains articles, news of the Association, judgments and a bibliography. The Austrian Association of Judges also publishes a journal, *Österreichische Richterzeitung* (1907–), which contains articles, judgments, bibliographical references and news.

Especially for students, but also useful for lawyers, is the journal *Juristische Ausbildung und Praxis Vorbereitung* (1988–), abbreviated to JAP. This has been published quarterly since 1988 and contains essays, cases, legislation and literature over the whole field of law.

In addition to the journals above there is a number of journals devoted to special fields of law, for example taxation law or business law. A series of proceedings of the annual congresses of lawyers entitled *Österreichischer Juristentag* (1961–) contains essays and papers dealing with current law problems. The Ludwig Boltzmann-Institut publishes a series of monographs written by teachers of the law faculties of the Austrian universities.

The *Austrian Journal of Public and International Law* (1946–) publishes articles on problems of public international law and on constitutional and administrative law. It contains an annual survey of Austrian practice and cases on international law.

In 1963 the Österreichische Juristenkommission-ÖJK [Austrian Commission of Jurists], a section of the International Commission of Jurists, was founded. Proceedings of this committee are published in several series, for example, *Schriftenreihe des Bundesministeriums für Justiz*.

News information

Information on recent legal developments and public affairs can be found in the *Wiener Zeitung*, a daily newspaper, edited by the Österreichische Staatsdruckerei, Vienna, since the 18th century. Until 1982 it was a governmental newspaper. It contains the Amtsblatt [official gazette] where official announcements, calls for tender, entries to public registers etc. are published. A private newspaper, *Die Presse* (1848–), publishes a weekly news section information on law [Rechtspanorama] and business [Economics].

Business and financial information

Business life in Austria is affected by a broad range of regulation. Two English language reference books appearing in looseleaf form are: *Austrian business law* (Heller *et al.*, 1992–) and *Austrian business taxation* (Polak and Gröhs, 1992–). A recently published guide to economic law is *Wirtschaftsrecht in Österreich* (Graf *et al.*, 1995). For information on taxation it is useful to consult the English language publication *Austrian tax guide 1995* (Prachner and Schuster, 1995).

All companies in Austria have to be registered with the *Handelsregister* [trade register] at the Handelsgericht [Trade Court] in Vienna; entries in this *Firmenbuch* [companies book] have to be published additionally in the *Amtsblatt* [official gazette] of the *Wiener Zeitung*. The trade register as well as the *Grundbuch* [Register of landed property] are public, which means that the entries are made by officials of courts and everybody is allowed to use these books for information and to make photocopies of individual entries.

Recent developments in economic and business law and in banking are documented in the monthly journals *Österreichisches Recht der Wirtschaft* (1983–), *Ecolex* (1990–) and *Bankarchiv* (1953–).

Statistics

Official statistics are compiled and published by the Österreichisches Statistische Zentralamt [Austrian Central Statistical Office], for example in the annual *Statistisches Jahrbuch für die Republik Österreich* [Statistical yearbook of the Republic of Austria] (1993). Specialized statistics appear in a large series; in particular to be mentioned are the *Statistik der Rechtspflege* [statistic of jurisdiction] (1994) and *Gerichtliche Kriminalstatistik* [judicial criminal statistics] (1994). The Ministry of Home Affairs publishes yearly statistics of criminal affairs compiled by the police.

A private editor publishes a short survey of the Austrian economy and its international position in German and in English entitled *Survey of the Austrian economy 95/96* (1995).

Useful addresses

Associations of lawyers

Juristenverband [Association of Legal Experts], 1016 Wien, Museumstr. 12, Austria. Tel: +43 222 521 52 882

Österreichische Notariatskammer [Austrian Association of Notaries], 1010 Wien, Landesgerichtsstr. 20, Austria. Tel: +43 222 402 45 09

Österreichische Patentanwaltskammer [Austrian Chamber of Patent Attorneys], 1070 Wien, Museumstr. 3, Austria. Tel: +43 222 523 43 82

Österreichischer Rechtsanwaltskammertag [Austrian Bar Association], 1010 Wien, Rotenturmstr. 13, Austria. Tel: +43 222 535 12 65. Internet: http://www2.telecom.at/jusline

Vereinigung der österreichischen Richter [Association of Austrian Judges], 1016 Wien, Justizpalast, Austria. Tel: +43 222 521 52 644

Government organizations

Bundeskanzleramt [Federal Chancellery], 1014 Wien, Ballhausplatz 2, Austria. Tel: +43 222 531 15-0. Fax: +43 222 5350 338

Bundesministerium für Inneres [Ministry of the Interior], 1014 Wien, Herreng. 7, Austria. Tel: +43 222 531 26

Bundesministerium für Justiz [Ministry of Justice], 1070 Wien, Museumstr. 7, Austria. Tel: +43 222 521 52-0

Courts

Arbeits-und Sozialgericht Wien [Employment and Social Court], 1080 Wien, Wickenburgg. 8–10, Austria. Tel: +43 222 401 27-0. Fax: +43 222 401 27 2666

Generalprokuratur beim Obersten Gerichtshof [Office of the Attorney General at the Supreme Court], 1016 Wien, Justizpalast, Museumstr. 12, Austria. Tel: +43 222 521 52-0. Fax: +43 222 521 52 313

Handelsgericht Wien [Commercial Court], 1010 Wien, Riemerg. 7, Austria. Tel: +43 222 515 28-0. Fax: +43 222 515 28 576

Oberster Gerichtshof [Supreme Court], 1016 Wien, Schmerlingplatz 10–11, Museumstr. 12, Austria. Tel: +43 222 521 52-0. Fax: +43 222 521 52 310

Verfassungsgerichtshof [Constitutional Court], 1010 Wien, Judenplatz 11, Austria. Tel: +43 222 531 22. Fax: +43 222 531 22 499

Verwaltungsgerichtshof [Administrative Court], 1010 Wien, Judenplatz 11, Austria. Tel: +43 222 531 11-0. Fax: +43 222 532 89 21

Wirtschaftskammer Österreich [Austrian Economic Chamber Courts], 1045 Wien, Wiedner Hauptstr. 63, Austria. Tel: +43 222 501 05-0. Fax: +43 222 50206 250

Education and training

Johannes Kepler Universität Linz, Fakultät für Rechtswissenschaften, 4040 Linz-Auhof, Austria. Tel: +43 732 25 68-0

Karl-Franzens-Universität Graz, Rechtswisssenschaftliche Fakultät, 8010 Graz, Universitätsplatz 3, Austria. Tel: +43 316 380-0

Leopold-Franzens-Universität Innsbruck, Fakultät für Rechtswissenschaften, 6020 Innsbruck, Innrain 52, Austria. Tel: +43 512 507-0

Universität Salzburg, Fakultät für Rechtswissenschaften, 5020 Salzburg, Churfürststr. 1, Austria. Tel: +43 662 80 44-0

Universität Wien, Fakultät für Rechtswissenschaften, 1010 Wien, Schottenbastei 10–16, Austria. Tel: +43 222 40 103-0

Research institutes

Hans Kelsen Institut, 1190 Wien, Gymnasiumstr. 79, Austria. Tel: +43 222 34 63 17

Institut für Menschenrechte, 1070 Wien, Berggasse 7, Austria. Tel: +43 222 317 40 20

Institut für Rechtsvorsorge und Urkundenwesen, 1010 Wien, Rathausstr. 19, Austria. Tel: +43 222 408 26 28

Ludwig Boltzmann Gesellschaft: Forschungsstelle für Gesetzgebungspraxis und Rechtsanwendung, 1010 Wien, Rotenturmstr. 13, Austria. Tel: +43 222 535 12 75

Libraries

Fakultätsbibliothek für Rechtswissenschaften, 1010 Wien, Schottenbastei 10–16, Austria. Tel: +43 222 40103 3315

Fakultätsbibliothek für Rechtswissenschaften, 8010 Graz, Universitätsplatz 3, Austria. Tel: +43 316 380 3240. Fax: +43 316 394987

Parlamentsbibliothek, 1017 Wien, Dr. Karl Renner-Ring 3, Austria. Tel: +43 222 40110. Fax: +43 222 40110 2825

Rechtsanwaltskammer, Bibliothek, 1011 Wien, Rotenturmstr. 13, Austria. Tel: +43 222 535 12 35

Universitätsbibliothek Graz, 8010 Graz,Universitätsplatz 3, Austria. Tel: +43 316 380 3100. Internet: http://www-ub.kfunigraz.ac.at

Universitätsbibliothek Innsbruck, 6010 Innsbruck, Innrain 50, Austria. Tel: +43 512 507 2415. Fax: +43 512 507 2893. Internet: http://info.uibk.ac.at.c108

Universitätsbibliothek Linz, 4040 Linz-Auhof, Austria. Tel: +43 732 2468. Fax: +43 732 2468 680. Internet: http://www.ubl.uni-linz.ac.at

Universitätsbibliothek Salzburg, 5010 Salzburg, Hofstallg. 2–4, Austria. Tel: +43 662 8044. Fax: +43 662 8044 214. Internet: http://dbibs2.edvz.sbg.ac.at/bibhaupt/home.html

Universitätsbibliothek Wien, 1010 Wien, Dr. Karl-Lueger Ring 1, Austria. Tel: +43 222 40103 2376. Internet: http://www.univie.ac.at/UB-WIEN/biblio.htm

Verwaltungsgerichtshof, Bibliothek, 1010 Wien, Judenplatz 11, Austria. Tel: +43 222 5311 408. Fax: +43 222 5328921

Publishers and booksellers

Manz Verlag und Buchhandlung, 1014 Wien, Kohlmarkt 16, Austria. Tel: +43 222 531 61 100. Fax: +43 222 531 61 167. Internet: http://www.manz.co.at/manz/

ORAC Verlag und Buchhandlung, 1010 Wien, Graben 17, Austria. Tel: +43 222 546 21-0. Fax: +43 222 546 21 96

Österreichische Staatsdruckerei, 1037 Wien, Rennweg 12 a, Austria. Tel: +43 222 797 89 295. Fax: +43 222 797 89 455

RDB Rechtsdatenbank Ges.m.b.H & Co KG, 1040 Wien, Wiedner Hauptstr. 18/14, Austria. Tel: +43 222 587 36 20-0/586 52 50-0. Fax: +43 222 587 36 20 34. e-mail: martin.tesar@rdb.co.at

List of works cited

Allgemeines bürgerliches Gesetzbuch. (1994) MODAT-RECHTSTEXTE. Vienna: Manz.

Amtsblatt der Österreichischen Justizverwaltung. (1945–) Vienna: Bundesministerium für Justiz.

Andréewitch, M. (1987) *The Austrian Commercial Code*. Manz. Taschenausgaben, no.27. Vienna: Manz.

Andréewitch, M. *et al.* (1995) *Company law and accounting in Austria*. Austrian Law & International Business, no.2. Vienna: Manz. Looseleaf.

Angst, P., Jakusch, W. and Primmer, H. (1995) (eds) *Die Exekutionsordnung*. 13th edn. Manz. Große Gesetzesausgaben, no.7. Vienna: Manz.

Arbeitsrecht. (1994) MODAT-CD-ROM. Vienna: Manz.

Austrian Journal of Public and International Law. (1946–) Vienna: Springer.

Bankarchiv. (1953–) Vienna: Orac.

Berchtold, K. (1978) *Human rights in international law*. Vienna: Österreichische Staatsdruckerei.

Beseler D. v. and Jacobs-Wüstefeld, B. (1991) *Law dictionary* 4th edn. Berlin: Walter de Gruyter.

BGBl-Index: Wegweiser durch Österreichs Bundesgesetzgebung. (1995) 45th edn. Vienna: Manz.

Bundesgesetzblatt für die Republik Österreich. (1945–) Vienna: Österreichische Staatsdruckerei. Originally published from 1780–, title and place of publication varies, publication suspended 1939–44.

Bydlinski, F. (1980–1995) *Österreichische Gesetze*. Vienna: Manz; Munich: Beck.

Cerutti, N.M. (1978) *Rechtsbibliographie 1977*. Zürich: Studio-Verlag.

Collin, P.H. *et al.* (1990) *PONS Fachwörterbuch Recht*. Stuttgart: Klett.

Creifelds, C. *et al.* (1996) *Rechtswörterbuch* 13th edn. Munich: Beck.

Dittrich, R. and Tades, H. (1963–1995) *Arbeitsrecht*. Manz. Große Gesetzesausgaben, no.10. Vienna: Manz.

Dittrich, R. and Tades, H. (1994) *Das Allgemeine bürgerliche Gesetzbuch* 34th edn. Manz. Große Gesetzesausgaben, no.2. Vienna: Manz.

Donald-Little, D.M. (1991–) (ed.) *Cross border practice compendium*. London: Sweet & Maxwell; Vienna: Manz. Looseleaf.

Dosoudil, I. (1988) *Grundliteratur zum österreichischen Recht*. Arbeitshefte der Arbeitsgemeinschaft für juristisches Bibliotheks- und Dokumentationswesen, no.12. Hamburg: AjBD.

Ecolex: fachzeitschrift für Wirtschaftsrecht. (1990–) Vienna: Manz.

Einkommensteuergesetz. (1994) MODAT-RECHTSTEXTE. Vienna: Manz.

Entscheidungen des österreichischen Obersten Gerichtshofes in Strafsachen. (1920–) Vienna: Österreichische Staatsdruckerei. Covering 1919–. General index 1919–1959.

Entscheidungen des österreichischen Obersten Gerichtshofes in Zivilsachen. (1922–) Vienna: Österreichische Staatsdruckerei. Covering 1919–. General indices 1919–1967. Earlier series date from 1853.

Erkenntnisse und Beschlüsse des Verfassungsgerichtshofes. (1919–) Vienna: Österreichische Staatsdruckerei. Title varies prior to 1969.

Erkenntnisse und Beschlüsse des Verwaltungsgerichtshofes Administrativrecht. (1948–) Vienna: Österreichische Staatsdruckerei. Covers 1946–. General index 1946–1974. Earlier series date from 1867. CD-ROM version available.

Erkenntnisse und Beschlüsse des Verwaltungsgerichtshofes Finanzrecht. (1946–) Vienna: Österreichische Staatsdruckerei. Covers 1946–. General index 1946–1974. Earlier series date from 1867. CD-ROM version available.

Ermacora, F. (1988) *Grundriß der Menschenrechte in Österreich*. Manz. Kurzlehrbuchreihe, no.14. Vienna: Manz.

Ermacora, F., Nowak, M. and Tretter, H. (1993) *International human rights*. Manz.

Taschenausgaben, no.39. Vienna: Manz.
Fasching, H. (1971–1974) *Kommentar zu den Zivilprozeßgesetzen*. Manz. Großkommentare, no.4. Vienna: Manz.
Flanz, Gisbert H. and Knize, Peter (1985) Austria. In *Constitutions of the countries of the world*, ed. A.P. Blaustein and G.H. Flanz, vol.I. Dobbs Ferry, NY: Oceana.
Floretta, H., Spielbüchler, K. and Strasser, R. (1988–1990) *Arbeitsrecht* 3rd edn. Manz. Kurzlehrbücher, no.5. Vienna: Manz. 2 vols.
Floretta, H. and Strasser, R. (1988–1993) *Arbeitsverfassungsgesetz* 2nd edn. Manz. Kurzkommentare zum Arbeits- und Sozialrecht, no.1. Vienna: Manz.
Foregger, E. (1995) (ed.) *Strafgesetzbuch (StGB)* 12th edn. Manz. Taschenausgaben, no.10. Vienna: Manz.
Foregger, E. and Kodek, G. (1991) *Strafgesetzbuch (StGB)*. Manz. Kurzkommentare, no.1. Vienna: Manz. Supplement 1993.
Foregger, E. and Kodek, G. (1994) *Die österreichische Strafprozeßordnung* 6th edn. Manz. Kurzkommentare, no.2. Vienna: Manz.
Foregger, E. and Nowakowski, F. (1979–) (eds.) *Wiener Kommentar zum Strafgesetzbuch*. Manz. Großkommentare, no.2. Vienna: Manz. Looseleaf.
Fox, James R. (1988) A guide to Austrian legal research. *Law Library Journal*, **80**, pp. 99–113.
Friedl, G. and Loebenstein, H. (1994) (eds) *Abkürzungs- und Zitierregeln der österreichischen Rechtssprache (AZR) samt Abkürzungsverzeichnis* 3rd edn. Vienna: Manz.
Gerichtliche Kriminalstatistik 1993. (1994) Vienna: Österreichische Staatsdruckerei.
GmbH-Gesetz. (1994) MODAT-RECHTSTEXTE. Vienna: Manz.
Graf, F. *et al.* (1995) *Wirtschaftsrecht in Österreich*. Vienna: Orac.
Gschnitzer, F. (1979) *Österreichisches Familienrecht* 2nd edn. Springers Kurzlehrbücher der Rechtswissenschaft. Vienna: Springer.
Gschnitzer, F. (1984) *Österreichisches Erbrecht* 2nd edn. Springers Kurzlehrbücher der Rechtswissenschaft. Vienna: Springer.
Gschnitzer, F. (1985) *Österreichisches Sachenrecht* 2nd edn. Springers Kurzlehrbücher der Rechtswissenschaft. Vienna: Springer.
Gschnitzer, F. (1988) *Österreichisches Schuldrecht. Besonderer Teil und Schadenersatz* 2nd edn. Springers Kurzlehrbücher der Rechtswissenschaft. Vienna: Springer.
Gschnitzer, F. (1991) *Österreichisches Schuldrecht. Allgemeiner Teil* 2nd edn. Springers Kurzlehrbücher der Rechtswissenschaft. Vienna: Springer.
Gschnitzer, F. (1992) *Allgemeiner Teil des bürgerlichen Rechts* 2nd edn. Springers Kurzlehrbücher der Rechtswissenschaft. Vienna: Springer.
Guide to legal studies in Europe 1996–97. (1996) Brussels: Law Books in Europe.
Heidinger, F.J., Abel, N. and Hochleitner, M. (1993) *Einführung in das deutsche und österreichische Rechtssystem und in die deutsche Rechtssprache*. Vienna: Orac.
Heinl, A., Loebenstein, E. and Verosta, S. (1948–) *Das österreichische Recht*. Vienna: Last. Looseleaf.
Heller, K. (1989) *An outline of Austrian constitutional law*. Deventer: Kluwer.
Heller, K. *et al.* (1992–) *Austrian business law* 2nd edn. Vienna: Manz. Looseleaf.
Hohenecker Index '93. (1994) Vienna: Manz.
Holzhammer, R. (1993) *Österreichisches Zwangsvollstreckungsrecht* 4th edn. Springers Kurzlehrbücher der Rechtswissenschaft. Vienna: Springer.
Holzhammer, R. (1994) *Österreichisches Insolvenzrecht* 3rd edn. Springers Kurzlehrbücher der Rechtswissenschaft. Vienna: Springer.
Index 1996. (1996) Vienna: Österreichische Staatsdruckerei. Annual.
Juristische Ausbildung und Praxis Vorbereitung (JAP). (1988–) Vienna: Manz.
Juristische Blätter. (1872–) Vienna: Springer.
JUS-EXTRA. (1985–) Vienna: Österreichische Staatsdruckerei.
Kantner, H.-G. (1989) The legal system of the Republic of Austria (Republik Österreich). In *Modern legal systems cyclopedia*, ed. K.R. Redden, vol.4, pp. 4.3.1–4.30.57.

Buffalo, NY: Hein. The title page of the volume gives 1989, the chapter was partly revised in 1993.
Karlsruher Juristische Bibliographie. (1965-) Munich: Beck.
Kastner, W., Doralt, P., and Nowotny, Ch. (1990) *Grundriß des österreichischen Gesellschaftsrechts* 5th edn. Manz. Kurzlehrbücher, no.2. Vienna: Manz.
Kerschner, F. (1993) *Wissenschaftliche Arbeitstechnik und -methodik für Juristen* 3rd edn. Vienna: WUV, Univ. Verl.
Klecatsky, H.R. and Morscher, S. (1995) *Die österreichische Bundesverfassung* 7th edn. Manz. Taschenausgaben, no.2. Vienna: Manz.
KODEX des österreichischen Rechts. (in progress) Vienna: Orac.
Koziol, H. and Welser, R. (1995) *Grundriß des bürgerlichen Rechts* 10th edn. Manz. Kurzlehrbücher, no.1. Vienna: Manz.
Krejci, H. (1995) *Grundriß des Handelsrechts.* Manz. Kurzlehrbücher, no.19. Vienna: Manz.
List, W. (1994) (ed.) *Handelsrecht* 3rd edn. Vienna: Manz.
List, W. (1995) *Verwaltungsverfahren* 4th edn. Vienna: Manz.
Luggauer, K. (1979) *Juristenlatein* 3rd edn. Juridica-Nachschlagewerke. Vienna: Juridica-Verl.
Machacek, R. (1994) *Austrian contributions to the rule of law.* Kehl: Engel.
Maultaschl, F. (1959–1971) (ed.) *Rechtslexikon.* Vienna: Hollinnek. 8 vols.
Mayer, H. (1994) *Das österreichische Bundes-Verfassungsrecht.* Manz. Kurzkommentare, no.7. Vienna: Manz.
Mietrechtsgesetz. (1994) MODAT-RECHTSTEXTE. Vienna: Manz.
MODAT-CD-ROM (available from Manz).
MODAT-RECHTSTEXTE (available from Manz).
Mohr, F. (1995) (ed.) *Die Konkurs-, Ausgleichs- und Anfechtungsordnung* 8th edn. Manz. Große Gesetzausgaben, no.29. Vienna: Manz.
Nitsche, G., Nowotny, Ch. and Zetter, P. (1994) *Handelsgesetzbuch* 13th edn. Manz. Taschenausgaben, no.23. Vienna: Manz.
Österreichische Bibliographie (1945–). Vienna: Österreichische Nationalbibliothek.
ÖSTERREICHISCHE DISSERTATIONSDATENBANK (available from Seibersdorf).
Österreichische Juristenzeitung. (1946–) Vienna: Manz.
Österreichische Richterzeitung. (1907–) Vienna: Motopress.
Österreichischer Amtskalender. (1995–96) Vienna: Österreichische Staatsdruckerei. Also available on CD-ROM.
Österreichischer Juristentag. (1961–) Vienna: Manz.
Österreichisches Anwaltsblatt. (1946–) Vienna: Manz.
Österreichisches Recht der Wirtschaft. (1983–) Vienna: Manz.
Pimmer, H. (1992) (ed.) *Wechselgesetz und Scheckgesetz* 9th edn. Manz. Große Gesetzausgaben, no.13. Vienna: Manz.
Platzgummer, W. (1994) *Grundzüge des österreichischen Strafverfahrens* 6th edn. Springers Kurzlehrbücher der Rechtswissenschaft. Vienna: Springer.
Polak, P. and Gröhs, B. (1992–) *Austrian business taxation.* Austrian Law & International Business, no.1. Vienna: Manz. Looseleaf.
Posch, W. (1985) *Einführung in das österreische Recht.* Einführungen in das fremdländische Recht. Darmstadt: Wissenschaftliche Buchgesellschaft.
Prachner, D. and Schuster, B. (1995) *Austrian Tax Guide.* Vienna: Manz.
Die Presse. (1848–) Vienna: Die Presse.
Rechberger, W. and Simotta, D. (1994) *Grundriß des Österreichischen Zivilprozeßrechts* 4th edn. Manz. Kurzlehrbücher, no.18. Vienna: Manz.
RECHTSDATENBANK-RDB (available from Österreichische Staatsdruckerei).
RECHTSINFORMATIONSSYSTEM DES BUNDES (RIS) (available from RDB Rechtsdatenbank GesmbH & Co KG).
RIDA PLUS (available from Österreichische Staatsdruckerei).
RIDA PLUS 2 (available from Österreichische Staatsdruckerei).

Ringhofer, K. (1987–1992) *Die österreichischen Verwaltungsverfahrensgesetze*. Manz. Große Gesetzausgaben, no.5. Vienna: Manz.

Rummel, P. (1990) (ed.) *Kommentar zum Allgemeinen bürgerlichen Gesetzbuch* 2nd edn. Manz. Großkommentare, no.3. Vienna: Manz.

Russwurm, H.G. (1988) *Österreichisches Rechtswörterbuch*. Juridica-Nachschlagewerke. Vienna: Juridica-Verl.

RZL STEUERRECHT PLUS (available from Österreichische Staatsdruckerei).

Schnorr, G. (1988) *Einführung in die Rechtswissenschaft und ihre Methoden*. Vienna: Orac.

Schriftenreihe des Bundesministeriums für Justiz. (1982–) Vienna: Bundesministerium für Justiz.

Schuppich, W. and Tades, H. (1994) *Rechtsanwaltsordnung* 5th edn. Manz. Sonderausgaben, no.34. Vienna: Manz.

Schwind, F. and Zemen, H. (1972) Austria. In *International encyclopedia of comparative law*, ed. V. Knapp, vol.1, pp. A67–A87. Tübingen: J.C.B. Mohr.

Statistik der Rechtspflege 1992. (1994) Vienna: Österreichische Staatsdruckerei.

Statistisches Jahrbuch für die Republik Österreich. (1993) Vienna: Österreichische Staatsdruckerei.

Stenographische Protokolle des Bundesrates. (1945–) Vienna: Österreichische Staatsdruckerei.

Stenographische Protokolle des Nationalrates. (1945–) Vienna: Österreichische Staatsdruckerei.

STEUERRECHT COMPACT (available from Österreichische Staatsdruckerei).

Steuer-Index. (1994) MODAT-RECHTSTEXTE. Vienna: Manz.

Stohanzl, R. (1990) *Jurisdiktionsnorm und Zivilprozeßordnung* 14th edn. Manz. Große Gesetzesausgaben, no.6. Vienna: Manz.

Stohanzl, R. (1995) (ed.) *Zivilprozeßgesetze* 7th edn. Manz. Taschenausgaben, no.16. Vienna: Manz.

STRAFRECHT COMPACT (available from Österreichische Staatsdruckerei).

Straßenverkehrsordnung. (1995) MODAT-RECHTSTEXTE. Vienna: Manz.

Straube, M. *et al.* (1992–1995) (eds.) *Kommentar zum Handelsgesetzbuch* 2nd edn. Manz. Großkommentare, nos 8 and 9. Vienna: Manz.

Survey of the Austrian economy 95/96. (1995) Vienna: Orac.

Tomandl, T. (1992) *Grundriß des österreichischen Sozialrechts* 4th edn. Manz. Kurzlehrbücher, no.3. Vienna: Manz.

Triffterer, O. (1994) *Österreichisches Strafrecht. Allgemeiner Teil* 2nd edn. Springers Kurzlehrbücher der Rechtswissenschaft. Vienna: Springer.

Umsatzsteuergesetz. (1995) MODAT-RECHTSTEXTE. Vienna: Manz.

VFGH=VERFASSUNGSGERICHTSHOF (available from Österreichische Staatsdruckerei).

VWGH=VERWALTUNGSGERICHTSHOF, ADMINISTRATIVRECHT (available from Österreichische Staatsdruckerei).

Walter, R. and Mayer, H. (1987) *Grundriß des besonderen Verwaltungsrechts* 2nd edn. Manz. Kurzlehrbuchreihe, no.9. Vienna: Manz.

Walter, R. and Mayer, H. (1995) *Grundriß des österreichischen Bundesverfassungsrechts* 8th edn. Manz. Kurzlehrbuchreihe, no.8. Vienna: Manz.

Walter, R. and Mayer, H. (1995) *Grundriß des österreichischen Verwaltungsverfahrensrechts* 6th edn. Manz. Kurzlehrbuchreihe, no.7. Vienna: Manz.

Walter, R. and Thienel, R. (1995) *Die Verwaltungsverfahrens-Novellen 1995*. Vienna: Manz.

West, Norbert D. and Shuman, Samuel I. (1966) *The Austrian Penal Act*. American Series of Foreign Penal Codes, no.12. South Hackensack, NJ: Rothman; London: Sweet & Maxwell.

Wiener Zeitung. (1780–) Vienna: Österreichische Staatsdruckerei.

Wohnungseigentumsgesetz. (1994) MODAT-RECHTSTEXTE. Vienna: Manz.

Zeitschrift für Verwaltung. (1976–) Vienna: Orac.

ZIVILRECHT COMPACT (available from Österreichische Staatsdruckerei).

CHAPTER FIVE

Baltic States

GIINA KASKLA and KÜLLIKE MAURER

General introduction

Estonia, Latvia and Lithuania are three independent states on the coast of the Baltic Sea. The three states have much in common: geographic location, they are all very small with unique languages and they share the same history in the 20th century. They became independent states at the end of World War I in 1918, yet were occupied and forcibly annexed by the Soviet Union in 1940 as a direct result of the Nazi–Soviet Pact and its secret agreements. The Baltic States remained annexed to the Soviet Union until 1991, which was crucial to all three Baltic States, marking the collapse of the Soviet Union and the restoration of their independence. Lithuania was proclaimed independent on 11 March 1990, Estonia on 20 August 1991, Latvia on 21 August 1991.

Historically their legal system is a civil law system, being under the influence of German law. Historical background is given in the following articles: 'Russian and Baltic peasant laws before 1917 as an aid to historical interpretations of subsequent events' (Beermann, 1987) and 'The USSR's basic legislation: legislative authority of the Baltic Republic' (Uibopuu, 1988).

An introductory work dealing with all the three states is *International legal status of Lithuania, Latvia and Estonia in the years 1918–1994* (Sozanski, 1995). In 1994 a collection of articles, *The Baltic path to independence,* was published (Sprudzs, 1994). It contains scholarly writings in English, French and German. The book is divided into two sections: I. The struggle for independence and, II. International law and the Baltic independence. It contains such articles as: 'The achievement of independence in the Baltic States and its justifications' by Susan E. Himmer and 'Die baltischen Staaten vor völkerrechtlichen Problemen' by Dietrich A. Loeber. For other material in English, 'Sources for post-Soviet law in Russia and the other republics: an annotated bibliography of books and articles in English, 1992' (Kavass, 1993) contains material relating to the Baltic States.

A general overview of sources of legal information in the Baltic States by Maurer has been published in the collection of papers including several in English presented at the Third Conference of Law Librarians of the Nordic Countries (Maurer, 1995b). An article on 'The Baltic Republics and their legal information systems' by Bing (1994), based on a study trip in 1993, concentrates on computer-based systems both for producing and retrieving laws.

The Baltic States started to participate in international relations, including legal ones, in 1988–1989. In the period between August 1991 to mid-1994, Lithuania, Latvia and Estonia concluded in total about 420 international treaties (Sozanski, 1995: p. 139). The UN Charter can be assumed to be the most important universal agreement joined by the Baltic States after restoring full sovereignty. The Baltic States have acceded the Council of Europe and adopted its documents. Specific information about the agreements signed with the United Nations or the Council of Europe can be found in *International human rights norms in the Nordic and Baltic countries* (Scheinin, 1996). All three Baltic States signed association agreements with the European Union in 1995 and have submitted applications for membership of the EU to the Council of Ministers.

There are several sources covering news information about all the three states. *The Baltic Times* (1996–) is a successor of two newspapers: *Baltic Observer* (1992–1996) and *Baltic Independent* (1991–1996). The newspaper also contains news on legislation in the Baltic States. The quarterly *Baltic Review* (1992–) contains both business and financial overviews and legal questions concerning the three states. *Baltic Business News* is published twice a month and covers politics, economics, finance, business and law. *A foreign investor in the Baltics* by Sorainen (1993) is written for foreign business people entering the Baltic markets.

An electronic journal, EAST EUROPEAN LEGISLATIVE MONITOR, is a free, monthly publication of the Constitutional and Legislative Policy Institute; its subscription address is taylorj@osi.hu. The Baltic News Service delivers news in English on all three countries in a variety of forms, by computer feed, online connection, fax, e-mail and mail; the *Baltic Business Weekly* (1995–) covers company news, taxes, finance, trade, statistics and there is also BNS Daily News and BNS Business News (all are available to subscribers at the BNS site: http://www.bns.ee/). The *Baltic Information: Business Directory 1994/95* (1994) can be contacted on the Internet (http://www.massoc.com/bbd/). Vilnius University operates a useful gateway page (http://www.vu.lt/index_baltic.html) for sites in all the countries including new services, a list of libraries and the Latvian and Estonian home pages.

Estonia

Introduction to the legal system

During the first period of Estonian independence three constitutions were adopted: in 1920, 1933 and 1937. The development of the constitutional system of Estonia is analysed in the article 'The Constitutional Development of Estonian Republic' (Uibopuu, 1973).

The Constitution [*põhiseadus*] of the Republic of Estonia was adopted on 28 June 1992 by a referendum; the text is available as *Eesti Vabariigi põhiseadus* (1994). Estonia is a parliamentary republic. The parliament [*Riigikogu*] has one chamber and 101 members. The head of the state is the president who is elected by the *Riigikogu* for a period of five years.

The preamble of the Constitution states that it was adopted 'on the basis of article 1 of the Constitution which entered into force in 1938 . . .' Art.1 of the 1992 Constitution states the following: 'Estonia is an independent and sovereign democratic republic wherein the supreme power is vested in the people'. Art.3 states the principle of separation and balance of powers.

Laws [*seadus*] are adopted by the *Riigikogu* in accordance with the Constitution. There are two kinds of laws: the so-called constitutional laws that are listed in article 104 in the Constitution that may be adopted or amended only by a majority of the members of the *Riigikogu*, and the 'ordinary' laws that are adopted if the majority of the *Riigikogu* members participating in the sitting vote in favour thereof. Laws are proclaimed by the president and they enter into force ten days after their publication, if no other term is fixed. The president issues decrees [*seadlus*] countersigned by the prime minister and subsequently approved by the *Riigikogu* if it is unable to convene.

Regulations [*määrus*] may be issued in accordance with the law and for the fulfilment of the law (regulations *intra legem*) by government and by ministers. The right to issue a regulation must be delegated to the executive by a law. Regulations are subordinate to laws and it is not possible to amend a law or to replace a law with a regulation. The local municipalities also have the right to adopt regulations. The orders [*korraldus*] of the government are also issued in accordance with the law and for fulfilment of the law. The order is an individual act of the government by which the government is carrying out executive power.

Foreign agreements [*välislepingud*] signed by Republic of Estonia are also sources of law. Article 123 of the Constitution states as follows: 'If Estonian laws or other acts contradict foreign treaties ratified by the Riigikogu, the provisions of the foreign treaty shall be applied.'

The latest publication of the Estonian Constitution is a bilingual edition in the periodical *Estonian legislation in translation* (The Constitution of the Republic of Estonia, 1996). This is a new translation replacing the earlier version which had appeared in a bilingual publication, *Eesti Vabariigi põhiseadus* (1993) and in collections of constitutions such as Ruchti (1994a) in *Constitutions of the countries of the world* and in *Rebirth of democracy* (1995). The Constitution has been published in German as *Verfassung für die Republik Estland* (1993).

Introductory works on the legal system and legal research

The collection of scholarly writings in English, French and German *The Baltic path to independence* (Sprudzs 1994) was mentioned in the **General introduction** above. In 1994 a survey *Current developments in the Estonian law* (1994) was published by the Law Office Lepik & Luhaäär; it contains a short overview of Estonian legal system and an introduction to property law and competition law. An article in English by Daimar Liiv about the renewal of the legal system in Estonia has appeared in the periodical *The Baltics* (Liiv, 1994). An introduction to the Estonian legal system is also provided by *English for lawyers* (Grant, Kostabi and Soobik, 1994) which contains chapters on the history of the Faculty of Law at Tartu University and on different branches of Estonian law.

Legislation

The State Gazette [*Riigi Teataja*] issued by the State Chancellery [*Riigikantselei*] is the official publication in which all legislation should be published. Art.3 of the Constitution states that only published laws have obligatory force. The State Gazette appears irregularly, according to necessity, usually three or four times a week. The publication of legal acts in the State Gazette is regulated by the State Gazette Act; the law requires the issuing of the four series:

- *Riigi Teataja*. Part 1: Legal acts passed by the *Riigikogu*, president and government (abbreviated to RT I).
- *Riigi Teataja*. Part 2: Foreign Agreements. (In Estonian and in English) (RT II).
- *Riigi Teataja*. Part 3: Rulings of the National Court (RT III).
- *Riigi Teataja Lisa* (Supplement). Regulations of ministers, the Bank of Estonia and local governments are published here, and also announcements (RTL).

The law states that laws must be published within a week of being proclaimed by the president. Other acts of the *Riigikogu* must be published within a week of being signed. All other acts must be published within ten days of being handed over to the State Chancellery.

It is stated in the law that laws come into force on the tenth day after they have been published in the State Gazette if no other term is fixed in the law itself. Regulations of the government and president's decisions on appointments or dismissals come into force on the day they are signed. The decisions of the National Court come into force as is stated in the law on constitutional supervision and international treaties come into force as is stipulated in the treaties. All other acts come into force the next day after publication in the State Gazette.

It is also provided in the law that the State Gazette is published in Estonian and the selective translation of acts and publication of official and unofficial translations is organized by the State Chancellery.

There are currently two series of State Gazette being published containing translations of legal acts. The series in Russian is *Pravovyje akty Estoni* (1993–) which contains about 95 per cent of the acts originally published in Estonian in *Riigi Teataja*; all the acts of the *Riigikogu* and the government regulations have been translated. The English version of the State Gazette is the monthly *Estonian Legislation in Translation* (1996–), formerly *Legal Acts of Estonia* (1993–1995); a selection of laws has been published there. Since 1996 it has been published by the Eesti Õigustõlke Keskus [Estonian Translation and Legislative Support Centre] (address below) which was founded in 1995 to translate Estonian legislation into English and EU legislation into Estonian.

An unofficial looseleaf publication of current Estonian laws *Eesti Seadus* (1992–) is published by the initiative of the Estonian Association of Lawyers. It is updated twice a year but it is not very widely used by lawyers as legislation is changing rapidly and lawyers need actual information faster.

Translations of main legislative documents can be found at the site: http://www.ibs.ee/law/transl.html on the Internet. A full-text database of Estonian legislation 1988–1993 with interface in Estonian is at the site: http://www.ibs.ee/seadus/index.html which contains selected legislation from this period.

Codes and commentaries

The Civil Code of Estonia, *Tsiviilseadustik*, is currently being drafted and some parts of it have been adopted. Property Law [*Asjaõigusseadus*] was published in *Riigi Teataja I* 1993, no.39, p. 590 and entered into force on 1 December 1993; an English translation will be published in *Estonian Legislation in Translation*. The Law on the General Principles of the Civil Code [*Tsiviilseadustiku üldosa seadus*] was published in *Riigi Teataja I* 1994, no.53, p. 889 and entered into force on 1 September 1994; the English translation is in *Legal Acts of Estonia* 1995, no.2. The Family Law [*Perekonnaseadus*] was published in *Riigi Teataja I*

1994, no.75, p. 1326) and entered into force on 1 January 1995. The Inheritance Law [*Pärimisseadus*] was adopted on 15 May 1996 and it will enter into force on 1 January 1997. The Law on Obligations [*Võlaõigusseadus*] is still in drafting stage and it will probably enter into force by the end of 1997; until it is adopted, the part of the 1964 Civil Code [*Eesti NSV tsiviilkoodeks*] on obligations still applies.

The Commercial Code [*Äriseadustik*] of Estonia published in *Riigi Teataja I* 1995, nos. 26–28, p. 355, came into force on 1 September 1995. It has been translated into English and has appeared in *Estonian Legislation in Translation* 1996, nos. 4–6. The Estonian text can be found at the site: http://www.ibs.ee/law/arisds/index.html and an English summary at the site: http://www.vm.ee/eia/9510claw.html on the Internet.

The Criminal Code of Estonia [*Kriminaalkoodeks*] which was published in *Riigi Teataja* 1992, no.20, p. 288, was adopted in 1992. It is a slightly modified version of the old Soviet Criminal Code of 1961. A new Criminal Code is currently being drafted.

The Law on Civil Procedure [*Tsiviilkohtupidamise seadustik*] which was published in *Riigi Teataja I* 1993, nos. 31/32, p. 528, was adopted in 1993.

Treaties

Treaty-making power rests with the *Riigikogu* which ratifies and renounces international treaties as provided in art.121 of the Constitution. The government may conclude agreements that do not require ratification as is regulated in the Foreign Relations Act of 28 October 1993 (RT I 1993, 72, 1020). Information on the current status of treaties is maintained by the Ministry of Foreign Affairs (address below). The Ministry of Foreign Affairs also administers publication of treaties which appear in *Riigi Teataja,* part 2 and selected translations into English on their Internet site (http://www.vm.ee/laws/).

Law reports, judgments

The judgments of the National Court of Estonia are published in the State Gazette, *Riigi Teataja*, Part 3. A cumulative volume for 1993 and 1994 with indexes has been published (*Riigikohtu lahendid*, 1995).

Computer-based systems

The full-text database of Estonian legal acts is ESTLEX which is a state register of legal acts founded by the *Justiitsministeerium* [Ministry of

Justice] and maintained by the *Riigiarvutuskeskus* [State Computing Centre]. The register is in Estonian and it contains legal acts adopted since 16 November 1988. The texts of the acts are kept in up to date version with all the amendments that have been passed.

The database is offline at present. The clients receive the updates twice a month on diskettes or by modem. The preparation work is now going on to make the database usable online with free text search possibilities.

The State Computing Centre has created also a Russian version of the database which is similar to the database in Estonian (the homepage of ESTLEX is at http://www.rak.ee/ESTLEX/).

A great deal of useful information may be found via Internet at the Foreign Ministry homepage (http://www.vm.ee/) and at the Estonian Government homepage (http://www.rk.ee/) and also at the Office of the President of the Republic of Estonia homepage (http://www.ee/president/).

Directories

The *University of Tartu Faculty of Law directory* (Liin, 1994) provides an overview of the history of the faculty, its institutes and degree programmes and also a biographical directory of professors and lecturers.

The *Riigikogu directory* (1993–) is an annual directory of the Republic of Estonia Parliament. The Foreign Ministry homepage at http://www.vm.ee/ contains an online directory of Parliament. A directory of the judges of Estonia has been published (*Eesti kohtunikud*, 1996) with general data about courts in Estonia and personal data on all the judges, including the National Court Justices.

Bibliographies

A bibliography concerning Estonian legal literature in the years 1918–1940 has been published by the National Library of Estonia, *Bibliographia iuridica Estonica, 1918–1940* (Maurer, 1994). Current legal bibliography, also entitled *Bibliographia iuridica Estonica*, is being compiled at the National Library of Estonia, starting with a volume for 1994 (Maurer, 1995a). A retrospective bibliography for the years 1988–1993 was published in 1996. A bibliography of works published by Estonian lawyers in exile in the years 1942–1976 forms a part of a larger work *Folia bibliographica* (Arens, 1977).

Current analytical bibliography covering law articles in periodicals and newspapers has appeared regularly in *Juridica* since August 1993; it is compiled in the National Library.

A bibliography covering official publications from 1993 has been compiled in the National Library of Estonia (Hillermaa, 1994–).

Bibliographical databases

Bibliographical databases on Estonian legislation and legal literature are compiled and held at the National Library of Estonia. The database SEADUS contains bibliographical data about legislation in Estonian, Russian or English published in the State Gazette, periodicals or collections. The database ÕIGUS contains citations of books and articles in Estonian and other languages, published since 1993. Database IURIDICA contains citations of books and articles in Estonian and other languages, published in Estonia or abroad since 1918 until June 1940. The databases are maintained with the bibliographical software package ProCite and they are offline at present.

Dictionaries

There are two main general dictionaries: the *English–Estonian dictionary* (Silvet, 1995) is based on the *Concise Oxford dictionary*. The *Estonian–English dictionary* was first printed by Yale University Press in 1982 and is now in its second edition (Saagpakk, 1992). A small English–Estonian law dictionary has been published by the University of Tartu (Grant and Soobik, 1993). A Finnish–Estonian Law Dictionary has been compiled in co-operation with the Finnish Lawyers Society (Kull and Vettik, 1993). Company TEA has published an *English–Estonian & Estonian–English business dictionary* (Aule, Jõgi and Toompere, 1993) and an *English–Estonian dictionary of economics* (Raid, 1995) which also contain some legal terminology.

Current information sources

Journals

In 1993 the Faculty of Law of the University of Tartu started issuing the law journal *Juridica* with financial support from the Scottish Law Society. In 1995 *Juridica* joined with the other law journal in Estonia, *Eesti Jurist* (1990–1994) which was issued by the Estonian Association of Lawyers, and *Juridica* is now the only law journal in Estonia.

News information

A weekly review of Estonian news, *Eesti Ringvaade*, is compiled from local news services by the Press and Information Department of the Ministry of Foreign Affairs both in English and in Estonian and is freely available on the Estonian Foreign Ministry WWW site (http://www.vm.ee).

Business and financial information

For information about the legal framework for the activities of banks in Estonia, and also a list of laws and major regulations see the Central Bank–Bank of Estonia homepage (http://www.ee/epbe). The Estonian Chamber of Commerce and Industry can be found at http://sun.nlib.ee/ESTCG/Eandt/ECCI.html on the Internet.

Statistics

An annual statistical yearbook, *Statistika aastaraamat* (1995), which includes statistics on the administration of justice is published by Eesti Statistikaamet [Statistical Office of Estonia] whose address appears below. Criminal statistics have been published by the Estonian State Police in English (Leps, 1992).

Useful addresses for Estonia

Associations of lawyers

Advokatuur [Estonian Bar Association], Viru 19, Tallinn EE0001, Estonia. Tel: +372 2 449180, 442673. Fax: +372 2 440298

Eesti Akadeemiline Õigusteaduse Selts [Estonian Academic Law Society], Lossi 17, Tartu EE2400, Estonia. Tel: +372 7 441411. Fax: +372 7 441433

Eesti Juristide Liit [Estonian Association of Lawyers], 19 Viru, Tallinn EE0001, Estonia. Tel/Fax: +372 2 449501

Government organizations

Eesti Pank [Bank of Estonia], Estonia pst 13, Tallinn EE0100, Estonia. Tel: +372 6310900, 6310911. Fax: +372 6310954. E-mail: info@epbe.ee Internet: http://www.ee/epbe/

Justiitsministeerium [Ministry of Justice], Suur-Karja 19, Tallinn EE0104, Estonia. Tel: +372 6282601. Fax: +372 6282609. Internet: http://www.just.ee/

Majandusministeerium [Ministry of the Economics Affairs], Harju 11, Tallinn EE0100, Estonia. Tel: +372 2 440577. Fax: +372 6313660. Internet: http://www.online.ee/mineco/

Rahandusministeerium [Ministry of Finance], Suur-Ameerika 1, Tallinn EE0100, Estonia. Tel: +372 6317808. Fax: +372 6317810. Internet: http://www.netexpress.ee/rahmin/

Välisministeerium [Ministry of Foreign Affairs], Rävala pst 9, Tallinn EE0100, Estonia. Tel: +372 6317600, 6317091. Fax: +372 6317099. E-mail: vminfo@vm1.vm.ee Internet: http://www.vm.ee/

Courts

Riigikohus [National Court of the Republic of Estonia], Lossi 17, Tartu EE2400, Estonia. Tel: +372 7 441411. Fax: +372 7 441433. E-mail: nc@nc.ee Internet: http://www.nc.ee

Education and training

Juristide Täienduskoolitukeskus [Lawyers' Training Centre], Ülikooli 18, Tartu EE2400, Estonia. Tel/Fax: +372 7 432 072. E-mail: meris@ut.ee

Õiguskeskus [Estonian Law Centre], Lossi 17, Tartu EE2400, Estonia. Tel: +372 7 441411. Fax: +372 7 441433. E-mail: akaine@lc.ee

Õigusteaduskond [Faculty of Law], University of Tartu, Ülikooli 18, Tartu EE2400, Estonia. Tel: +372 7 432571. Fax: +372 7 431119. E-mail: juura@ut.ee Internet: http://www.ut.ee/teaduskond/oigus/

Libraries

Eesti Rahvusraamatukogu [National Library of Estonia], Reference and Information Analysis Centre, Tõnismägi 2, Tallinn EE0100, Estonia. Tel: +372 6307386. Fax: +372 6311417. E-mail: iuridica@venus.nlib.ee Internet: http://www.nlib.ee

Tartu Ülikooli Raamatukogu [Tartu University Library], Struve 1, Tartu EE2400, Estonia. Tel: +372 7 465700. Fax: +372 7 465701. E-mail: library@utlib.ee Internet: http://utlib.ee/~ingrid

Publishers and booksellers

Eesti Õigustõlke Keskus [Estonian Translation and Legislative Support Centre], Tõnismägi 8, Tallinn EE0001, Estonia. Tel: +372 6316136. Fax: +372 6461075. E-mail: etlc@legaltext.rk.ee

Eesti Statistikaamet [Statistical Office of Estonia], Endla 15, Tallinn EE0100, Estonia. Tel: +372 2 451821

Õigusteabe AS Juura [Legal Information Ltd], Kentmanni 13, Tallinn EE0001, Estonia. Tel: +372 2 445 172

Riigiarvutuskeskus [State Computing Centre], Suur-Ameerika 1, Tallinn EE0001, Estonia. Tel: +372 6308666. E-mail: estlex@rak.ee Internet: http://www.rak.ee/ESTLEX/

Latvia

Introduction to the legal system

In Latvia the pre-war constitution has been re-enacted. It was originally adopted by the Constituent Assembly at its meeting on 15 February 1922 and the Constitution [*satversme*] was restored upon the proclamation of independence in August 1991. The Constitution of Latvia is available through Internet (http://latvia.vernet.lv/satversme.htm/). The official English translation of the Constitution with the amendments of 1993 has been published in a collection of constitutions of East European countries issued by the Council of Europe, *The rebirth of democracy* (1995) and the official translations with amendments to October 1992 and a detailed chronology is in Ruchti (1994b). An English translation of the 1922 Constitution is on the International Constitutional Law server (http://www.uni-wverzburg.de/law/). For historical material on the development of the Constitution see: 'Perspectives on the Constitution of the Republic of Latvia of 1922' by Zile (1989) in a multi-lingual volume, *Constitution of the Republic of Latvia. . . .* (1989).

Latvia is a parliamentary republic. The Latvian Parliament, the *Saeima*, has a one-chamber system and consists of 100 elected representatives. The head of state is the president who is elected by the *Saeima* for a period of three years.

The right of legislation belongs to both the *Saeima* and the people. Bills may be presented to the *Saeima* by the president, the cabinet, the committees of the *Saeima*, not less than five members of the *Saeima* or by one-tenth of the electors. Laws are promulgated by the president between the seventh and twenty-first day after their adoption. If no other term is fixed, the laws come into force fourteen days after their promulgation.

The president has the right to postpone promulgation of a law for a period of two months and that law shall be submitted to a referendum, if at least one-tenth of the electors so desire. Should such request not be formulated within the period of two months, the law shall be promulgated at the expiration of that period. The referendum shall not be taken if the *Saeima* put this law to the vote once more and if then at least three-quarters of all the members are in favour of its adoption.

In cases of urgent necessity between sessions, the Cabinet has the right to issue regulations which have the force of Law.

Legislation

Laws (*likums*), government orders (*lēmums*), and so forth, are published in *Latvijas Respublikas Saeimas un Ministru Kabineta Ziņotâjs* (1993–), entitled *Latvijas Respublikas Augstâkâs Padomes un Valdîbas Ziņotâjs* until July 1993. It is issued twice per month and contains all government laws, decisions, regulations, official announcements, and information about state accession to international agreements and conventions. Until July 1993 it was published in parallel Latvian and Russian languages but subsequently only in Latvian.

Official texts of legal acts appear in the following publications:

Government documents come into force after their publication in the newspaper *Latvijas Vēstnesis* [The Latvian Herald] (1993–) which is the sole state gazette; it began publication in July 1993 and is issued five times per week. *Latvijas Vēstnesis* continues the traditions of the pre-war official newspaper *Valdîbas Vēstnesis* [The Government Herald] (1919–1940). *Latvijas Vēstnesis* has 3 supplements:

a. *Latvijas Vēstnesis. Dokumenti* (1994–); a monthly supplement which includes the official texts of legal acts published in the previous month in chronological order;
b. The Russian version – *Latvijas Vēstnesis. Dokumenty* (1995–); an irregular supplement containing the translation of all state laws and more important decisions;

c. The *Zemes Reformas Vēstnesis* contains legislation about land (agrarian) reform.

The newspaper *Diena* formerly held the status of official government publisher. Its supplement *AP. MP* was published from August 1991 and was renamed *Saeima. Ministru Kabineta* at the commencement of the 5th Saeima. This supplement also appears in a Russian translation – *V Saeime i Kabinete Ministrov*; this text is unofficial and rather differs from original texts. Both supplements appear weekly.

Rîgas Balss is the only newspaper which publishes documents of the Rîga Council.

A three volume official collection of Latvian economic legislation, *Economic legislation of the Republic of Latvia in English* (1991–1992) has been published. A private organization, the Latvia Law Institute was formed in March 1996 to translate Latvia's laws into English.

Codes and commentaries

The Civil Code, available as *Civillikums* (1993) was promulgated on 28 January 1937. On September 1, 1992 two parts of it were re-enacted: inheritance law [*mantošanas tiesîbas*] and property law [*lietu tiesîbas*]. Contract law [*saistîbu tiesîbas*] came into force on 1 March 1993, family law [*gimenes tiesîbas*] on 1 September 1993.

The Criminal Code (*Latvijas Kriminâlkodekss*, 1994) and Criminal Procedure Code (*Latvijas Kriminâlprocesa Kodekss*, 1995) were adopted on 6 January 1961. The Civil Procedure Code (*Latvijas Civilprocesa Kodekss*, 1995) was adopted on 27 December 1963. These codes are still in force and recent editions are cited above.

There are three laws regulating business in Latvia: the Law On Entrepreneurial Activity of 26 September 1990, the Law On Limited Liability Companies of 23 January 1991 and the Law on Joint-Stock Companies of 18 May 1993.

Law reports, judgments

The documents of the Supreme Court are published in the journal *Juristu Žurnâls* (1994–) issued by the Latvian Judicial Training Centre six times per year.

Computer-based systems

The full text-database of legal acts, NAIS (Normativo aktu informacijas sistema) has been developed since 1991 by a private company, Software

House, which is maintaining it in co-operation with the Cabinet of Ministers and the Ministry of Justice. The database contains almost all legal acts adopted by the *Saeima* (and its predecessor, the Supreme Council) and the Cabinet of Ministers (and its predecessor, the Council of Ministers), the Ministry of Finance, Rîga Council and other executive bodies after the restoration of independence on 5 May 1990. The acts published in the pre-war State Gazette (1922–1940) have also been registered. The database also contains international agreements.

The database is in Latvian but some acts have been translated into English or Russian. The texts are kept in their current version. Updating takes place every week by mailing diskettes to subscribers. Those customers who have modems receive updates online. It is also possible to receive single documents via modem.

The Latvian homepage at http://www.latnet.lv/ gives access to a wide range of information.

Bibliographies

The monthly *Latvian Press Chronicle* (1949–) compiled by the National Library of Latvia forms the Latvian national bibliography and includes legal works.

Dictionaries

Recently two legal dictionaries have been published: Latvian–Russian, *Juridisko terminu vârdnîca: Latviešu krievu, krievu latviešu* (1994) and Latvian–English, *Latviešu–anglu–latviešu juridisko terminu vârdnîca* (1993). There is also a *Dictionary of Legal Synonyms Latvian–English–Latvian* (1993) published by the American Bar Association.

Current information sources

Journals

The journal of the Latvian Ministry of Justice, *Temîda*, was published six times per year from 1990 until 1993. *Juristu Žurnâls* [The Law Journal] (1994–), mentioned above, is the only periodical which contains documents of the Supreme Court.

Nekustamais îpašums Latviju [Real Property in Latvia] appears monthly since 1995; some materials are translated into English. *Cilvēktiesîbu Žurnâls* [Human Rights Journal] (1996–) is published quarterly by the Latvian Human Rights Institute. *Latvijas Jurists* [The Latvian Lawyer] was a newspaper of the Latvian Lawyers Association which appeared monthly from 1989 to 1994. *Kriminâlvēstnesis* is a supplement to the newspaper *Likuma Vârdâ* (1992–) which newspaper was formerly entitled *Kaujas Posteni.*

Business and financial information

Legal information in the entrepreneurial sphere is given by the weekly supplement *Gramatvedibas ABC* of the newspaper *Dienas Bizness* (1992–); similar information in Russian is published weekly by the newspaper *Biznes & Baltiya*. The Latvian Development Agency publishes a monthly journal *Business with Latvia* (1996–).

Statistics

The *Statistical Yearbook of Latvia/Latvijas statistikas gadagrâmata* is published every year by the Central Statistical Bureau of Latvia and criminal statistics are included in it.

Useful addresses for Latvia

Association of lawyers

Council of Sworn Advocates, Brîvîbas bulv. 34, Rîga LV1535, Latvia. Tel: +371 2 283358. Fax: +371 2 282277

Government organizations

Bank of Latvia, K. Valdemâra iela 2a, Rîga LV 1050, Latvia. Tel: +371 7022260. Fax: +371 7820168

Ministry of Foreign Affairs, Brîvîbas iela 36, Rîga LV 1395, Latvia. Tel: +371 7223307. Fax: +371 7227755

Ministry of Justice, Brîvîbas iela 34, Rîga LV 1536, Latvia. Tel: +371 7282607. Fax: +371 7331920

Ministry of the Economy, Brîvîbas iela 55, Rîga LV 1050, Latvia. Tel: +371 7013101

Courts

Supreme Court, Brîvîbas iela 34, Rîga LV 1511, Latvia. Tel: +371 7289434

Education and training

Latvian Judicial Training Centre, Miesnieku iela 11, Rîga LV 1903, Latvia. Tel: +371 7227864. Fax: +371 829 340170

University of Latvia, Faculty of Law, Raina iela 19, Rîga LV 1098, Latvia. Tel: +371 2 224721. Fax: +371 2 223996

Libraries

National Library of Latvia, Parliamentary Information Department, K. Barona iela 14, Rîga LV 1423, Latvia. Tel: +371 2 7287221. Fax: +371 2 7280851. E-mail: icielava@ezis.lnb.lv

Latvian Academic Library, Rupniecības iela 10, Rīga LV 1235, Latvia. Tel: +371 2 7323649/7323976. Fax: +371 2 7321421. E-mail: acadlib@mii.lu.lv Internet: http://www.acadlib.lv/katalogs

University of Latvia Library, Kalpaka bulv. 4, Rīga LV 1820, Latvia. Tel: +371 2 7223984/7220087. Fax: +371 2 7225039. Internet: http://iko.telekom.lv:8080/alise/brief.htm

Law Library, University of Latvia, Jūrmalas gatve 74/76, Rīga LV 1083, Latvia

Information Department of the *Saeima* of the Republic of Latvia, Library of *Saeima*, Jēkaba iela 11, Rīga LV 1811, Latvia. Tel: + 371 7325434

Publishers, booksellers, database suppliers

Latvia Law Institute, M. Pils iela 2, Rīga LV 1050, Latvia. Tel: +371 7326418

Legal Information Centre, Brīvības bulv. 21, Rīga LV 1050, Latvia. Tel: +371 7220422

Software House Rīga Kommerccentrs, K. Barona iela 4, Rīga LV 1050, Latvia. Tel: +371 7221278

State Institution 'Latvijas Vēstnesis' ['The Latvia Herald'], Brušinieku iela 36–2, Rīga LV 1001, Latvia. Tel: +371 7298833

Lithuania

Introduction to the legal system

The Constitution [*konstitucija*] of Lithuania was adopted in the referendum of 25 October 1992. Lithuania is a parliamentary republic. The Parliament [*Seimas*] has a one chamber system and consists of 141 members who are elected for a four-year term. The head of state is the president who is elected by the citizens of the Republic for a term of five years.

Laws (*istatymas*) are enacted by the Seimas. There are two kinds of laws. The Seimas enacts amendments to the constitution: constitutional laws are deemed adopted if more than half of all the members vote in the affirmative; constitutional laws can be amended by at least a three-fifths majority vote of all the Seimas members. Ordinary laws are deemed adopted if the majority of the Seimas members participating in the sitting vote in favour. Laws may also be adopted by referendum.

The right of legislative initiative belongs to the members of the Seimas, the President of the Republic, and the Government. A draft law may be submitted to the Seimas by 50 000 citizens.

Laws are promulgated by the President within ten days of receiving a law passed by the Seimas. The President has the right to withhold from promulgation and refer the law back to the Seimas together with relevant reasons for reconsideration. The laws come into force after the signing and official promulgation of the President unless the laws themselves establish a later date.

The President may issue acts-decrees (*aktas-dekretas*). The Government issues directives (*nutarimas*) which must be passed by a majority vote of all members of the government.

The courts have the exclusive right to administer justice. Judges may not apply laws which contradict the Constitution. In cases where there are grounds to believe that the law or other legal act applicable in a certain case contradicts the Constitution, the judge shall suspend the investigation and shall appeal to the Constitutional Court to decide whether the law or other legal act in question complies with the Constitution. Rulings adopted by the Constitutional Court shall have the power of law.

Art.150 of the Constitution identifies two other documents as 'constituent parts' of the Constitution: the Constitutional Law on the State of Lithuania of 11 February 1991 and the Constitutional Act on the Non-Alignment of the Republic of Lithuania with Post-Soviet Eastern Alliances of 8 June 1992.

The Constitution was published as at 1992 by the parliament, *Constitution of the Republic of Lithuania* (1993) and also appears in *Constitutions of the countries of the world,* together with a detailed chronology with a supplement containing the two laws mentioned above (Ruchti, 1994c). An English translation of the 1992 Constitution is also on the International Constitutional Law server (http://www.uni-wverzburg.de/law/). The role of the court is described in *The Constitutional Court of the Republic of Lithuania* (1995).

Legislation

Legal acts are published in the State Gazette, *Valstybes zinios* (1990–), which is issued twice a week. There is also the Russian version: *Vedomosti Litovskoi Respubliki* (1990–) and also since 1990 monthly unofficial English translations are published in *Parliamentary Record.* See also **Computer-based systems** below.

The Bank of Lithuania issues *Acts of Law Regulating the Activities of the Banks of Lithuania* (1993–) in English. A *Selected anthology of economic and financial legislation* (1994) has been published in English by the Seimas. The State Patent Bureau has published a bilingual edition of *Industrial property protection in Lithuania: laws* (1996).

Codes and commentaries

The Civil Code [*civilinis kodeksas*] was adopted in 1964 and an edition has recently been published: *Lietuvos Respublikos civilinis kodeksas* (1995). The Company Law was adopted on 5 July 1994; it has been translated into English and has been published in the *Parliamentary Record* (Company Law, 1994). The Criminal Code [*baudžiamasis kodeksas*] was adopted in 1961 and a recent edition is *Lietuvos*

Respublikos baudžiamasis kodeksas (1994). Civil Procedure [*civilinio proceso kodeksas*] was adopted in 1964 (*Lietuvos Respublikos civilinio proceso kodeksas*, 1994). The main publisher of the official texts, including those above is the Legal Information Centre of the Ministry of Justice.

Law reports, judgments

Rulings and decisions of the Constitutional Court are published officially in a separate chapter of *Parliamentary Record.* A special collection, *Rulings and Decisions of the Constitutional Court of the Republic of Lithuania* (1994–), is published both in Lithuanian and English by the Constitutional Court of Lithuania and appears periodically, once or twice a year.

Computer-based systems

The full-text database of legal acts is LITLAKS which has been developed at the Legal Information Centre of the Ministry of Justice. The database contains legal acts of the *Seimas*, the government and other executive bodies. Texts are in their current version and the database will be updated once a month. The database is in Lithuanian but preparations are being made to include translations now available in print. The database will be made available to subscribers.

Some most important laws of Lithuania are available through the Internet at the Centre of Legal Information of the Ministry of Justice site (http://www.tm.lt/Englpage.htm).

There is a gateway to many of the networked resources of Lithuania at http://www.ciesin.ee/LITHUANIA/ and many of the links are reproduced on the 'Mirror of Lithuania' which may provide a faster connection (http://www.mcs.com/~thomas/www/lt/).

Directories

A short handbook *Official Vilnius* (1993–) about the Lithuanian presidency, the *Seimas* [Parliament], government, ministries, banks, associations and local administration of Vilnius is published annually. *Lietuvos Respublikos Seimas: 1992–1996 = The Seimas of the Republic of Lithuania 1992–1996: directory* (1995) is a reference book, in both English and in Lithuanian, reflecting the activities of the Seimas and including statistical data and biographies of the members of the parliament.

Bibliographies

The Centre of Bibliography and Book Science of the National Library of Lithuania compiles the *Lithuanian national bibliographical index* in Lithuanian. There are four series: *Books* (1947–), *Periodicals* (1949–), *Journal and newspaper articles* (1949–) and *Reviews* (1947–). This is a general index that includes law publications and articles.

Dictionaries

A general Lithuanian–English, English–Lithuanian dictionary was published in 1994 (Piesarskas and Svecevicius, 1994). Some legal terms can be found in a dictionary of business, banking, stock exchange terms: *Biznio, banku, birzos terminu zodynas–zinynas* (Buracas and Svecevicius, 1994) and an economic terms dictionary (Austrevicius, Pupkevicius and Treigiene, 1991).

Current information sources

Journals

The Law Institute publishes a quarterly, *Teisës problemos* (1993–). *Teisë* (1957–) contains research reports from Vilnius University.

Business and financial information

A directory of the companies of Lithuania is published by the Lithuanian Information Institute, revised yearly, *LITCOM'95* (1995). The Bank of Lithuania has issued from 1993 the *Bulletin of the Bank of Lithuania*. Specialist collections of legislation relating to business and finance are mentioned under **Legislation** above.

Verslo zinios [Business news] appears twice per week in Lithuanian; a summary in English can be reached online via http://www.omnitel.net/vz/.

Statistics

The Lithuanian Department of Statistics compiles the *Statistical yearbook of Lithuania* (1994). Department of Statistics to the Government of the Republic of Lithuania issues a monthly bulletin *Economic and Social Development in Lithuania*.

Useful addresses for Lithuania

Association of lawyers

Lithuanian Bar Association, Jogailos 11, Vilnius LT 2600, Lithuania. Tel: +370 2 624546

Government organizations

Bank of Lithuania, Gedimino 6, Vilnius LT 2600, Lithuania. Tel: +370 2 224008. Fax: +370 2 628124

Ministry of Economy, Gedimino pr.38/2, Vilnius LT 2600, Lithuania. Tel: +370 2 622416. Fax: +370 2 625604

Ministry of Foreign Affairs, J.Tumo-Vaizganto 2, Vilnius LT 2600, Lithuania. Tel: +370 2 618337. Fax: +370 2 618689

Ministry of Justice, Gedimino pr.30/1, Vilnius LT 2600, Lithuania. Tel: +370 2 624670. Fax: +370 2 625940

Courts

Constitutional Court of the Republic of Lithuania, Gedimino pr.53, Vilnius LT 2039, Lithuania. Tel: +370 2 226398. Fax: +370 2 227975

Supreme Court of the Republic of Lithuania, Gyneju 6, Vilnius LT 2755, Lithuania. Tel: +370 2 610560

Education and training

Institute of Philosophy, Sociology and Law, Saltoniskiu 58, Vilnius LT 2600, Lithuania. Tel: +370 2 751898. Fax: +370 2 751898

Law Institute, Guneju 6, Vilnius LT 2600, Lithuania. Tel: +370 2 616665. Fax: +370 2 223591

Lithuanian Information Institute, Kalvariju 3, Vilnius LT 2659, Lithuania. Tel: +370 2 753590. Fax: +370 2 353017

Vilnius University Faculty of Law, Saulėtekio 9, Vilnius LT 2054, Lithuania. Tel: +370 2 769509. Fax: +370 2 223563. Internet (main University site): http://www.vu.lt/

Libraries

Information Analysis Department of the Seimas, Gedimino 53, Vilnius LT 2002, Lithuania. Tel: +370 2 626680. Fax: +370 2 614544. E-mail: reblag@rc.lrs.lt

Lithuanian Academy of Sciences Library, Zigimantu 1/8, Vilnius LT 2632, Lithuania. Tel: +370 2 629537. Fax: +370 2 221324. E-mail: Root@liblas.aiva.lt

Martynas Mažvydas National Library of Lithuania, Gedimino 51, Vilnius LT 2635, Lithuania. Tel: +370 2 629023. Fax: +370 2 627129. Internet: http://lnb.lrs.lt/

Vilnius University Library, Universiteto 3, Vilnius LT 2633, Lithuania. Tel: +370 2 610616. Fax: +370 2 223563. E-mail: MB@Vu.Lt

Publishers, booksellers and database suppliers

Centre of Legal Information of the Ministry of Justice [Teis. informacijos centras], Gedimino 30/1, Vilnius LT 2695, Lithuania. Tel: +370 2 615282/623650. Fax: +370 1 621523. Internet: http://www.tm.lt/Info.htm

List of works cited for the Baltic States

Acts of Law Regulating the Activities of the Banks of Lithuania. (1993–) Vilnius: Bank of Lithuania.

Arens, E. (1977) *Folia bibliographica: a bibliography of works published by Estonian scholars in exile: jurisprudence, sociology, economy 1942–1976.* Stockholm: Institutum Litterarum Estonicum.

Aule, A., Jõgi, E. and Toompere, H. (1993) *English–Estonian & Estonian–English business dictionary.* Tallinn: TEA.

Austrevicius, P., Pupkevicius, D. and Treigiene, D. (1991) *Siuolaikiniu ekonomikos terminu enciklopedinis zodynas.* Vilnius: Lietuvos laisvosios rinkos institutas.

Baltic Business News. (1995–) Vilnius: Baltijos Naujienos. Continues: *Baltic News.*

Baltic Business Weekly. (1995–) Rîga: Baltic News Ltd. Also available online from Baltic News Service in Estonia.

Baltic Independent. (1991–1996) Tallinn: Estonian News Agency. Formerly: *The Estonian Independent.* Continued by: *Baltic Times.*

Baltic information: Business directory 1994/95. (1994) Centerport: New Horizons Trading Network.

Baltic News. (1992–1995) Vilnius: Baltijos Naujienos. Continued by: *Baltic Business News.*

Baltic Observer. (1992–1996) Rîga: Baltic News Ltd. Continued by: *Baltic Times.*

Baltic Review. (1992–) Tallinn: Pilt & Sõna Ltd.

Baltic Times. (1996–) Rîga: Baltic News Ltd. Continues: *The Baltic Observer* and *The Baltic Independent.*

Beermann, R. (1987) Russian and Baltic peasant laws before 1917 as an aid to historical interpretations of subsequent events. *Journal of Baltic Studies*, **4**, 375–388.

Bing, Jon (1994) The Baltic Republics and their legal information systems. *International Journal of Law and Information Technology*, **2**, 32–63.

Biznes & Baltiya. (no start date known) Rîga: Biznes & Baltiya.

Bulletin of the Bank of Lithuania. (1993–) Vilnius: Bank of Lithuania.

Buracas, A. and Svecevicius, B. (1994) *Biznio, banku, birzos terminu zodynas–zinynas.* Vilnius: Zodynas.

Business with Latvia. (1996–) Rîga: Latvian Development Agency.

Cilvēktiesîbu Žurnâls. (1996–) Rîga: Latvian Human Rights Institute.

Civillikums. (1994) Rîga: TIC.

Commercial Code = Äriseadustik. (1996) In *Estonian Legislation in Translation*, nos. 4–6.

Company Law of the Republic of Lithuania, 5 July 1994, no.I-528. (1994) *Parliamentary Record of the Seimas of the Republic of Lithuania*, **11**, 2–35.

Constitution of the Republic of Estonia; The Constitution of the Republic of Estonia Implementation Act = Eesti Vabariigi põhiseadus; Eesti Vabariigi põhiseaduse rakendamise seadus. (1996) *Estonian Legislation in Translation*, **1**.

Constitution of the Republic of Latvia = Die Verfassung der Republik Lettland = Constitution de la République de Lettinie = Konstitutsija Latviiskoi Respubliki (Latvijas Republikas Satversme). (1989) Stockholm: The Latvian National Foundation.

Constitution of the Republic of Lithuania 1992. (1993) Vilnius: Publishing House of the Seimas.

The Constitutional Court of the Republic of Lithuania. (1995) Vilnius: Viltis.

Current developments in the Estonian law. (1994) Tallinn: Lepik & Luhaäär.

Dictionary of Legal Synonyms Latvian-English-Latvian. (1993) Rîga: American Bar Association.

Diena. (no start date known) Rîga: Diena. Has supplements: *AP. MP* (1991–1995?) continued by *Saeima. Ministru Kabineta* (1995?–), in Russian *V Saeime i Kabinete Ministrov* (1995–).

EAST EUROPEAN LEGISLATIVE MONITOR. (available from the Constitutional and Legislative Policy Institute; subscription address: taylorj@osi.hu).

Economic and social development in Lithuania. (1995–) Vilnius: Department of Statistics, Government of Lithuania.

Economic legislation of the Republic of Latvia in English. (1991–1992) Rîga: Council of Ministers. 3 vols.

Eesti Jurist. (1990–1994) Tallinn: Eesti Juristide Liit. Absorbed by: *Juridica.* (1993–).

Eesti kohtunikud. (1996) Tartu: Atlex.

Eesti seadus. (1992–) Tallinn: Õigusteabe AS Juura. 5 vols, looseleaf.

Eesti Vabariigi põhiseadus = Republic of Estonia Constitution. (1993) Tallinn: Eesti Vabariigi Riigikantselei.

Eesti Vabariigi põhiseadus. (1994) Tallinn: Riigi Teataja.

English–Estonian & Estonian–English business dictionary. (1993) Tallinn: TEA.

ESTLEX: a register of legal acts of the Republic of Estonia (available from the Riigiarvutuskeskus [State Computing Centre] of Estonia).

Estonian Legislation in Translation. (1996–) Tallinn: Estonian Translation and Legislative Support Centre. Formerly: *Legal Acts of Estonia.*

Gramatvedibas ABC. (1992?–) Rîga: Dienas Bizness. Supplement to *Dienas Bizness* (1992–).

Grant, J.P. and Soobik, L. (1993) *Inglise–eesti juriidiline sõnastik = English–Estonian law glossary.* Tartu: TÜ õigusteaduskond.

Grant, J.P., Kostabi, L. and Soobik, L. (1994) *English for lawyers.* Tartu: University of Tartu.

Hillermaa, R. (1994–) (comp.) *Eesti ametlikud väljaanded = Official Publications of Estonia, 1993–.* Tallinn: Eesti Rahvusraamatukogu.

Industrial property protection in Lithuania: laws = Pramoninës nuosavybës apsauga Lietuvoje: Istatymai. (1996) Vilnius: State Patent Bureau.

Juridica. (1993–) Tallinn: Õigusteaduskond [Faculty of Law], University of Tartu/Eesti Juristide Liit. Absorbed: *Eesti Jurist* (1990–1994).

Juridisko terminu vârdnîca: Latviešu–krievu, krievu–latviešu. (1994) Rîga: no publisher information.

Juristu Žurnâls. (1994–) Rîga: Latvian Judicial Training Centre.

Kavass, Igor I. (1993) Sources for post-Soviet law in Russia and the other republics: an annotated bibliography of books and articles in English, 1992. *International Journal of Legal Information,* **21**, 211–319.

Kriminâlvēstnesis (start date not known) Rîga: Likuma Vârdâ. Supplement to *Likuma Vârdâ* (1992–) formerly entitled *Kaujas Posteni.*

Kull, R. and Vettik, A. (1993) (eds) *Suomalais-virolainen lakikielen sanakirja.* Helsinki: Lakimiesliiton Kustannus; Tallinn: Õigusteabe AS Juura.

Latvian Press Chronicle. (1949–) Rîga: National Library of Latvia.

Latviešu–anglu–latviešu juridisko terminu vârdnîca = Dictionary of legal synonyms Latvian–English–Latvian. (1993) Rîga.

Latvijas Civilprocesa Kodekss. (1995) Rîga: TIC.

Latvijas Jurists. (1989–1994) Rîga: Latvian Lawyers Association.

Latvijas Kriminâlkodekss. (1994) Rîga: TIC.

Latvijas Kriminâlprocesa Kodekss. (1995) Rîga: TIC.

Latvijas Respublikas Saeimas un Ministru Kabineta Zinotâjs. (1993–) Rîga: Legal Information Centre. Entitled *Latvijas Respublikas Augstâkâs Padomes un Valdîbas Zinotâjs* until July 1993.

Latvijas Vēstnesis [The Latvian Herald]. (1993–) Rîga: State Institution 'Latvijas Vēstnesis'. Has supplements: *Dokumenti* (1994–); *Dokumenty* (1995–); *Zemes Reformas Vēstnesis.*

Legal Acts of Estonia. (1993–1995) Tallinn: State Chancellery.

Leps, A. (1992) *A brief survey of the criminogenic situation in the Republic of Estonia, 1945–1992.* Tallinn: Estonian State Police.

Lietuvos Respublikos baudžiamasis kodeksas. (1994) Vilnius: Teis. informacijos centras.

Lietuvos Respublikos civilinio proceso kodeksas. (1994) Vilnius: Teis. informacijos centras.

Lietuvos Respublikos civilinis kodeksas. (1995) Vilnius: Teis. informacijas centras.

Lietuvos Respublikos Seimas: 1992–1996 = The Seimas of the Republic of Lithuania 1992–1996: directory. (1995) Vilnius: Danelius.

Liin, U. (1994) (comp.) *University of Tartu Faculty of Law directory.* Tartu: The University.

Liiv, D. (1994) The renewal of legal system in Estonia. *The Baltics*, **2**, 33–34.

LITCOM '95. (1995) Vilnius: Lithuanian Information Institute.

Lithuanian national bibliographical index. Vilnius: National Library of Lithuania. In 4 series: *Books* (1947–), *Periodicals* (1949–), *Journal and newspaper articles* (1949–) and *Reviews* (1947–). In Lithuanian.

LITLAKS: Legal acts of Lithuania (available from the Legal Centre of the Ministry of Justice).

Maurer, K. (1994) (comp.) *Bibliographia iuridica Estonica, 1918–1940: legal literature of Estonia.* Tallinn: National Library of Estonia.

Maurer, K. (1995a) (comp.) *Bibliographia iuridica Estonica, 1994: legal literature of Estonia.* Tallinn: National Library of Estonia.

Maurer, K. (1995b) Sources of legal information in the Baltic States. In *Central- och Östeuropas juridiska informationskällor: Rapport från det tredje nordiska juridiska biblioteksmötet in Helsingfors, 8–11 juni 1994*, ed. Gunilla Häkli and Kaarina Puttonen. Publikationer utgivna av Institutet för internationall ekonomisk rätt vid Helsingfors universitet, B:5, pp. 35–58. Helsinki: Institute of International Economic Law, Helsinki University.

NAIS: Normativo aktu informacijas sistema. (available from Software House Rîga, Latvia).

Nekustamais îpašums Latvija. (1995–) Rîga: no publisher information.

Official Vilnius. (1993–) Vilnius: Lithuanian Information Institute. Annual.

Parliamentary Record of the Seimas of the Republic of Lithuania. (1990–) Vilnius: Publishing House of the Seimas. Unofficial English translations of texts from *Valstybes zinios* (1990–).

Piesarskas, B. and Svecevicius, B. (1994) *Lietuviu–anglu, anglu–lietuviu kalbu žodynas = Lithuanian–English, English–Lithuanian dictionary.* Vilnius: Žodynas.

Pravovye akty Estonii. (1993–) Tallinn: Riigikantselei.

Raid, V. (1995) *English–Estonian dictionary of economics.* Tallinn: TEA.

Rebirth of democracy: 12 constitutions of Central and Eastern Europe. (1995) Strasbourg: Council of Europe.

Rîgas Balss. (no start date known) Rîga: Rîgas Balss.

Riigi Teataja. Tallinn: Riigikantselei. In four series: *I osa: Riigikogu, Vabariigi Presidendi ja Vabariigi Valitsuse õigusaktid.* (1990–); *II osa: Välislepingud.* (1993–); *III osa: Riigikohtu lahendid.* (1995–); *Riigi Teataja Lisa* (1991–).

Riigikogu directory [Republic of Estonia Parliament directory]. (1993–) Tallinn: National Library of Estonia. Annual.

Riigikohtu lahendid 1993/1994. (1995) Tallinn: Õigusteabe AS Juura.

Ruchti, J.J. (1994a) Estonia. In *Constitutions of the countries of the world*, eds A.P. Blaustein and G.H. Flanz, vol.VI. Dobbs Ferry, NY: Oceana.

Ruchti, J.J. (1994b) Latvia. In *Constitutions of the countries of the world*, eds A.P. Blaustein and G.H. Flanz, vol.X. Dobbs Ferry, NY: Oceana.

Ruchti, J.J. (1994c) Lithuania. In *Constitutions of the countries of the world*, eds A.P. Blaustein and G.H. Flanz, vol.XI. Dobbs Ferry, NY: Oceana. Also Supplement, August 1994.

Rulings and Decisions of the Constitutional Court of the Republic of Lithuania. (1994–) Vilnius: The Constitutional Court.

Saagpakk, P. (1992) *Estonian–English dictionary* 2nd edn. Tallinn: Koolibri.

Scheinin, M. (1996) (ed.) *International human rights norms in the Nordic and Baltic countries.* The Hague & London & Boston: Martinus Nijhoff.

Selected anthology of economic and financial legislation. (1994) Vilnius: Publishing House of the Seimas.
Silvet, J. (1995) *English–Estonian dictionary.* 6th edn. Tallinn: Valgus.
Sorainen, A. (1993) *A foreign investor in the Baltics: a legal study about the possibilities of a foreign investor to begin business activity and obtain real estate in the Baltics.* Helsinki: Lakimiesliiton Kustannus.
Sozanski, J. (1995) *International legal status of Lithuania, Latvia and Estonia in the years 1918–1994.* Rîga: no publisher information.
Sprudzs, A. (1994) (ed.) *The Baltic path to independence: an international reader of selected articles.* Buffalo, NY: Hein.
Statistical Yearbook of Latvia/Latvijas statistikas gadagrâmata. (1995) Rîga: Central Statistical Bureau of Latvia.
Statistical Yearbook of Lithuania/Lietuvos statistikos metraštis 1993. (1994) Vilnius: Methodical Publishing Centre for the Lithuanian Department of Statistics.
Statistika aastaraamat = Statistical Yearbook. (1995) Tallinn: Eesti Statistikaamet.
Teisë. (1957–) Vilnius: Vilnius University.
Teisës problemos. (1993–) Vilnius: The Law Institute.
Temîda. (1990–1993) Rîga: Ministry of Justice.
Uibopuu, H.J. (1973) The constitutional development of the Estonian Republic. *Journal of Baltic Studies*, **1**, 11–35.
Uibopuu, H.J. (1988) The USSR's basic legislation: legislative authority of the Baltic Republics. *Journal of Baltic Studies*, **2**, 117–128.
Valdîbas Vestnesis [The Government Herald]. (1919–1940) Rîga.
Valstybes zinios. (1990–) Vilnius: Publishing House of the Seimas.
Vedomosti Litovskoi Respubliki. (1990–) Vilnius: Publishing House of the Seimas. Russian language version of *Valstybes zinios* (1990–).
Verfassung für die Republik Estland. (1993) Tallinn: Miniplast.
Verslo zinios [Business news]. (1996–) Vilnius: Verslo zinios.
Zile, Zigurds L. (1989) Perspectives on the Constitution of the Republic of Latvia of 1922: an introduction. In *Constitution of the Republic of Latvia = Die Verfassung der . . .* (1989).

Acknowledgements

The authors would like to express their thanks to Danute Vabalaite from the Parliamentary Information Department of the Seimas of the Republic of Lithuania and Ieva Cielava, Head of the Information Analysis Department at the National Library of Lithuania for their assistance.

CHAPTER SIX

Belgium

CHRISTIAN F. VERBEKE

Introduction to the legal system

No unified or codified system of law existed in Belgium before the French Revolution, as each county, province, principality or region had its own set of customary laws, (*la coutume*), some going back to the 12th century. Authoritative historical writings on the subject include Britz (1847), *Code de l'ancien droit belgique*, also Defacqz (1846–73), *Ancien droit belgique*. Both works are dated and are superseded by Godding's definitive *Le droit privé dans les Pays-Bas méridionaux du 12e au 18e siècle* (Godding, 1991). Customary laws had as major drawbacks the uncertainty resulting from not being written law and their lack of uniformity from one jurisdiction to another, a phenomenon prevalent in Belgium. The drafting and influence of customary laws in Belgium are described in Gilissen (1962), *Rédaction des coutumes*.

The Décret of 9 vendémiaire, an IV (1 October 1795) of the Convention, ratified by the Treaty of Campo-Formio of 17 October 1797 and the subsequent Treaty of Lunéville (1801), annexed the Belgian provinces and the Pays de Liège to France, resulting in the repeal of the earlier laws, customs and institutions of the *ancien régime*. French law was imposed and the transitional revolutionary laws and décrets were succeeded by Napoleonic law which remained in force after 1815 and even after 1830. The standard reference work on the subject is Poulet (1907), *Les Institutions françaises de 1795 à 1814*.

After the fall of Napoléon, article 6 of the Treaty of Paris of 30 May 1814, confirmed by the Act of 21 July 1814 (William I of Orange-Nassau), united Belgium with Holland, and the new state was called the Netherlands. In 1830 Belgium seceded from the Netherlands and became independent. An essential reference work of comparative civil law of Belgium and Holland is Van Dievoet (1948), *Le droit civil en Belgique et en Hollande*. Modern Belgian law is thus derived from early French law (droit écrit, droit coutumier) modified by the laws of the Revolutionary and Imperial periods, with an addition of residual vestiges of Dutch, Austrian and Spanish laws of earlier centuries.

Belgium is a limited constitutional monarchy with a parliamentary system of government which now functions in a federal structure of régions. The Constitution of Belgium of 1831 was influenced by earlier French constitutions, as well as by the Fundamental Law of the Netherlands [Grondwet] of 1815. An authoritative 19th century commentary on the Belgian Constitution is Beltjens (1894). Major revisions of the Belgian Constitution took effect in 1893 introducing universal suffrage with pluralistic vote; in 1920–21 establishing universal suffrage with total franchise; the third phase of fundamental revisions, 1954 to 1970, and finally the major 1993 structural revision introducing federalization.

The standard trilingual text of the new Constitution is Dujardin *et al.* (1994), *Constitution coordonnée*, whereas the full implications of the revised Constitution of 17 February 1994 are amply documented in *La Belgique fédérale,* edited by Delpérée (1994) to be consulted jointly with the official and integral text *La Constitution de la Belgique du 17 février 1994* [*Constitution* . . ., 1994]. The text of the Constitution in English appears up to date to 17 February 1994 in Flanz (1994) together with the Dutch, French and German texts; the English translation in Taeymans (1984) is now outdated. For constitutional law practice the most frequently cited work is Delpérée (1986–89), *Droit constitutionnel.* Access in English is available with Alen (1992), *Treatise on Belgian constitutional law*, now somewhat dated because of the accelerated developments in Belgium's constitutional landscape.

The new federal system ensures autonomy of the Flemish [Vlaamse Gemeenschap], Walloon [Communauté française], and German-speaking 'Deutschsprachigen Gemeinschaft' communities. Each region has its own parliamentary structures (i.e. Conseil région wallon, Vlaamse Raad, Rat der Deutschsprachigen Gemeinschaft) and the concomitant right to make laws and decrees in increasingly large areas of responsibility. Brussels (region) has its own council, known as the Conseil de la Région de Bruxelles-Capitale.

Belgium's legal materials are published either in the French or the Dutch language (the written Flemish language, 'Vlaams', is variously known as Nederlands, Néerlandais, Netherlandish, Dutch). French legal publications are however historically predominant, and to this day form the majority of Belgian legal literature. Numerous legal materials, including all official publications, are available in German translations for use in the German-speaking so-called Ostkantone of Belgium (Deutschsprachigen Gemeinschaft). The juridical status of the German language in Belgium is documented by Bergmans (1988), *Le statut juridique de la lange allemande.*

Increasing numbers of Flemish jurists do publish their legal treatises in their own language, Dutch, and this is also true of all collections of court decisions of the Flanders jurisdictions. The result is an increasingly large body of jurisprudence, case law, commentaries, and doctrine published in the Dutch language. This subject has been competently explored in Herbots (1973), *Meertalig rechtswoord*. The foreign practitioner or student of Belgian law must take into account the existence of these texts and of a number of important law periodicals published only in the Dutch language.

Introductory works on the legal system and legal research

The first introductory work to Belgian law history to take fully into account the country's federalization is Cerexhe (1991), *Introduction à l'étude du droit*. The best all-round manual on legal research and an essential reference work in French is *Documentation et methodologie juridiques* (Leurquin-De Visscher and Simonart, 1980) which is out of print but not superseded. A new and vastly expanded manual on the subject is *Précis de méthodologie juridique* (De Theux and Kovalovszky, 1995). For style of citations, notes, and abbreviations, *Guides des citations et abbréviations* (Ingber, 1994) is a very handy reference work.

Although treating a particular area of law, *Business law guide to Belgium* (Van Bael and Bellis, 1992) gives a fairly broad introduction for foreign lawyers. Older general introductions are in a chapter concentrating on constitution, government, court system and legal profession by Taeymans (1984) and a concise and still valuable chapter by Limpens and Schrans (1972). Although dated, Graulich *et al.* (1968) has considerable explanation of the legal system in English in addition to its value as a legal bibliography.

Legislation

The official record of Belgium's laws and statutes is the bilingual *Moniteur belge*, *Belgisch Staatsblad* (Flemish), a single edition in which the full text appears in both languages. Laws become effective ten days after publication, which is mandatory pursuant to article 190 of the Constitution. The *Moniteur belge* has been published since 1845, daily since 1898. Bulk and storage problems of this comprehensive publication, comprising almost 30 000 pages in 1993, have been solved by a microfilm and microfiche system MICROBIBLEX published by the legal database service CREDOC. A typical form of citation is L. or Loi du 22 déc. 1986 relatives aux intercommunales, M.B. 16 juin 1987, p. 9909.

The series *Documents parlementaires* (1844–) is a bilingual publication containing essential legislative history, travaux préparatoires, including the draft legislation itself, accompanying documents explaining the intentions and meaning of the authors of the draft, the advice of the Council of State on the draft and a committee stage where the draft is examined. Belgium's equivalent of Hansard or the Congressional Record containing the debates is the *Annales parlementaires* (1844–) complemented by the *Bulletin des questions et réponses* (1845–), the weekly record of parliamentary questions and answers.

The major unofficial law series covering 1830 onwards is the *Pasinomie* (abbreviated Pasin.), a monthly publication in French, produced some time after original publication in the *Moniteur belge*. It is the principal chronological collection and an indispensable reference work and it provides useful references to the legislative history of the laws it records. Two earlier series of the *Pasinomie* cover 1788–1830. Other unofficial law series include the *Bulletin législatif belge* (1931–), a weekly compilation of materials of general interest from the *Moniteur belge* of the previous week, completed by ten complete cumulative chronological and alphabetical indexes per year; the publication updates the *Codes Larcier* (see below). The *Bulletin usuel des lois et arrêtés* (1851–), bi-monthly, records in French retrospective laws back to 1539, and is accompanied by a cumulative chronological table. Other major reference series include the bilingual monthly *Omnilégie* (1952–). Provincial decisions are published in the 'Mémorial administratif' published for each province.

The legislative council of the Ministry of Justice has edited the *Recueil de la législation générale en vigueur en Belgique* (1932–59). This important series, retrospective from 1487 to 1921 gives all laws still effective on 31 December 1959, when publication halted; it remains uncompleted after that date. This work is still of use for older legislative texts particularly the pre-1830 texts in the first two volumes of the set.

Codes and commentaries

The Napoleonic codes exercised a strong influence on Belgian law-making. A certain number of Belgian codes have basically retained to this day the elements of these earlier French codes. The French Code pénal of 1810 was replaced without major changes by the Belgian penal code of 1867. The French Code de commerce of 1807 was entirely reworked between 1851 and 1879 without however altering its basic structure. The Belgian Judicial Code of 1967 effective in 1970, replaced the French Code de procedure civile of 1806 and also the numerous laws on the administration of justice particularly the French law of 1869. The Belgian code of criminal procedure is a revised version of the French Code d'instruction criminelle of 1808. Over the years approximately one sixth of the French Code civil of 1804 has been modified by specific Belgian laws, without alteration of its basic structure however.

In general use by the legal profession are the privately published and regularly updated collections of codes: Servais and Mechelynck, *Les Codes et les lois spéciales*, (*Codes Bruylant*), published since 1913, after 1975 published as a looseleaf collection in five volumes; looseleaf supplements appear three times per year. The *Codes Larcier* (1857–) in five volumes are republished every five years and are updated by cumulative supplementary booklets twice per year; relevant page numbers also appear in the *Bulletin législatif belge* which serves to bring the set up to date. A large number of collections of codes in particular areas of law and individual codes, often in paperback and republished regularly, are available from various publishers.

A representative selection of the leading commentaries on the codes and case law follows. A much cited work of transcendental importance on the civil law is De Page and Dekkers (1949–90), *Traité élémentaire de droit civil belge*. Of the highest authority on commercial law are Fredericq (1950–55), *Traité de droit commercial belge* and Van Ryn and Heenen (1965–88), *Principes de droit commercial*. The latest addition to commercial law is *Code de commerce et lois particulières* (Buyle, 1995).

Standard manuals of practice in the administration of justice and civil procedure are *Droit judiciaire civil* (Cambier, 1974–81) and *Manuel de procédure civile* (Fettweis, 1987) also the latter's *Précis de droit judiciaire* (Fettweis *et al.*, 1971–74), a vastly more complex and all-encompassing work. As a simplified current practice manual on the same subject Leclercq (1993), *Éléments pratiques de procédure civile* is worth considering. The latest addition to the subject is Kohl and Block (1995), *Code judiciaire*, a text which includes international conventions.

Indispensable in penal law and procedure are *Éléments de droit de la procédure pénale*, (Bosly, 1995), and the great classic of criminal practice *Les crimes et les délits du Code pénal*, the 'Rigaux and Trousse' as the work is familiarly known (Rigaux and Trousse, 1950–68). Penal case law is extensively covered by Hennau and Verhaegen (1991) with *Droit pénal général*, as it analyses some 500 decisions of the last decade, with details of 60 leading cases.

Treaties

International treaty making powers are vested in the king whose government communicates them to the houses of parliament (article 68 of the Constitution). Treaties become effective after approval, ratification, publication and recording. Important treaty collections include *Recueil des traités . . . concernant le royaume de Belgique* (De Garcia De La Vega, 1850–1914). An indispensable tool is *Répertoire des traités conclus par la Belgique* (De Troyer, 1973–88) which catalogues some 6300 bilateral and multilateral treaties concluded by Belgium and is the only complete record from 1830 to 1986.

Treaties concluded by Belgium to 1921 can also be located in the *Recueil de la législation générale en vigueur en Belgique*. Current treaties are generally published in the *Moniteur belge/Belgisch Staatsblad*.

Law reports, judgments

In Belgian legal science, jurisprudence (case law) is not a binding or compulsory source of Belgian positive law. It can only be considered a source in the sense that it reflects the evolution of legal thought in the courts of the various jurisdictions at any given moment in time.

Belgian case law is found in the monthly *Pasicrisie belge* (1838–) covering 1791 onwards, the most popularly used collection (abbreviated Pas.). A collection used in parallel was *Répertoire général de la jurisprudence belge* (Jamar *et al.*, 1882) covering 1814–1880 continued until 1975 by the *Répertoire décennal de la jurisprudence belge*. Detailed yearly summaries are found in *Recueil annuel de jurisprudence belge* (1949–) arranged by subject. The past fifteen years are available on disk from the publisher as mentioned below.

From a legal history point of view *La Belgique judiciaire* (1842–1939) remains important as it combines law bibliography, legislation, case law, doctrine, book reviews and special studies.

Higher jurisdictions' collections include the *Bulletin des arrêts de la Cour de cassation* (1928–), the separate edition in Flemish is *Arresten van het Hof van Cassatie*, records Cassation court decisions, the highest court of civil and criminal appeal in Belgium with the power to break (*casser*) decisions of lower courts. Of central importance is the *Recueil des arrêts et avis du Conseil d'État* (1948–) which records the decisions of the Conseil d'État (the Council of State), the highest administrative authority acting as a tribunal. Jurisdictional case law collections include: *Revue de Jurisprudence de Liège, Mons et Bruxelles* (1888–) which records cases and decisions of the Liège appeals court and other French-speaking jurisdictions.

Decisions of the justices of the peace are found in the *Journal des juges de paix et de police* (1890–). *Revue de droit commercial belge* (1980–) preceded by *Jurisprudence commerciale de Belgique* (1968–) and before that by *Jurisprudence commerciale de Bruxelles* (1903–1967), reports on commercial cases in all Belgian jurisdictions and also includes scholarly articles. *Jurisprudence du port d'Anvers* (1856–) is a rich source of maritime and commercial law cases heard in the Antwerp courts.

Computer-based systems

CREDOC

CREDOC (Credoc asbl-vzw: Documentation juridique, rechtsdocumentatie), founded in 1968, is the oldest continuously functioning electronic juridical information service in Europe. This comprehensive online service was organized by a group of Belgian jurists as a collective information centre to provide access to legal documentary sources in legislation, doctrine and case law. CREDOC databases include:

BJUS: a bibliographical database of Belgian doctrine and case law;
BLEX: current and new Belgian legislation based on the *Moniteur belge*;
ORBI: bibliographical database on international legal doctrine;
CAPA: a factual record of bankruptcies and interdictions;
NAME: a descriptive index of Belgian jurists;
LJUS: a database of Luxembourg (Grand Duchy) case law.

CREDOC can be consulted via the BISTEL network and is also available on the BELINDIS mainframe, server for the Ministry of Economic Affairs.

JUDIT

Rechtsdocumentatie – Rechtsgids – Databank, published in 1988, JUDIT is the first Dutch language database on CD-ROM. It is based on *Tijdschrift Rechtsdocumentatie* [Review for legal documentation], a Dutch language law journal covering legal materials published since 1980. JUDIT can run on any standard (HS) CD-ROM player under the so-called ASTRO retrieval software.

RAJBI

The database RAJBI (Recueil annuel de jurisprudence belge informatisé) covers the last 15 years, 1979 to 1993, of the *Recueil annuel de jurisprudence belge*. It is delivered on disk for uploading to personal computer. The retrieval software runs under Windows. Subscription can be obtained, either independently for the database only or at reduced rates for existing subscribers of the printed book version, from the law publishers Larcier.

JUSTEL

JUSTEL, the user-friendly Ministry of Justice legal information database, a superb work instrument, is available through the awkward VIDEOTEX, a service provided by BELGACOM, Belgium's problem-ridden privatized telephone company. Individual databases include:

INTITULES: 218 000 entries from the *Moniteur belge*;

LEGISLATION & ARCHIVES: 24 000 legislative integral texts;
JURISPRUDENCE: 100 000 decisions in case law;
BIBLIOTHÈQUE: a law book catalogue, principally of the Ministry of Justice collection, some 94 000 entries.

Internet

The government web site is at http://www.fgov.be/ and offers general government information, in English as well as Dutch, French and German. The Moniteur belge is available from April 1996 onwards, French version at http://belgium.fgov.be/staat/inhoudfr.htm. The legal pages of Matthias E. Storme at http://www.vfsia.ac.be/~estorme/belius.html have a wealth of case and statute law. Also useful are the legal information pages of the Faculty of Law at the University of Louvain at http://www.drt.vcl.ac.be/Faculte/pointeurs/SignetsLawInt.html.

Other government documents

Civil procedure reform, one of the major law reforms of this century, is published by the Ministry of Justice as *Rapport sur la réforme judiciaire*, popularly known as the 'Van Reepinghen report' after the name of its compiler. The work remains a major reference work for magistrates and civil procedure specialists (Van Reepinghen, 1964).

Encyclopedias

The major Belgian law encyclopedia *Les Pandectes belges* ceased publication in 1949 after publication of 152 volumes (*Pandectes* . . ., 1878–1949). It was succeeded by the indispensable *Les Novelles. Corpus juris belgici* which comprises about 50 volumes published thus far, some now rather dated (*Novelles* . . ., 1931–). The collection contains studies of all areas of law and covers legislation, case law, doctrine and legal bibliography in all areas of the law.

The most ambitious commentary of the Civil Code ever undertaken is F. Laurent, *Principes de droit civil*, 1869–78 with a *Supplément*, 1889–1903; the treatment of the subject is encyclopedic.

Another indispensable work is *Répertoire pratique du droit belge* (1930–) as it provides instantaneous access to all subjects covered by Belgian law. It is said that, if one were entitled to only one reference work, this would be the choice. For the historical context the *Encyclopédies* (Beltjens, 1905–08) are noteworthy.

For notarial law Gougnard (1908–33), *Nouveau dictionnaire, ou Encyclopédie du Notariat*, is recommended when used in conjunction with the newest collection *Répertoire notarial* (1966–).

Directories

Administrative and judicial Belgium is detailed in *Annuaire administratif et judiciaire de Belgique* (1994–95), a 1400–page manual which provides information on the constitutional, executive, and judicial powers, with names, addresses, telephone and fax numbers. It also covers the regional, provincial and municipal authorities, tax-exempt institutions, foundations, trusts, higher education institutions, museums. Names of magistrates, lawyers, notaries and bailiffs are recorded in the greatest detail under each jurisdiction, as well as the different courts and tribunals and local bar associations. A more compact and limited, but considerably less expensive directory is *Répertoire de l'information* (Service Fédéral d'Information, 1995). Information on Belgium's institutions appears in a comprehensive guide, *Mémento des institutions* (Service Fédéral d'Information, 1995).

Bibliographies

The major general Belgian law bibliographies for the period 1800 to date are: Picard and Larcier (1882–1890), *Bibliographie générale du droit belge . . . 1814–1889*; this landmark in legal bibliography was continued by Van Arenbergh (1906) covering 1889–1903.

A serious gap in Belgian law bibliography for the years 1800 to 1813 and 1903 to 1919, not yet covered by a Belgian bibliography, is filled by the general French law bibliography *Bibliographie générale des sciences juridiques, 1800 à 1925* (Grandin, 1926) and also by the selective bibliographies in *Pandectes belges* and *Belgique judiciaire*.

The post-World War I cycle of legal bibliography is completed with *Répertoire bibliographique du droit belge, 1919–1970* (Bosly, Del Marmol and Goossens, 1947–72). The effort continues in periodical format in 'Documentation juridique belge' which appears from 1973 in *Actualités de droit: revue de la Faculté de Droit de Liège* (1956–). A periodical bibliography of Flemish legal literature, *Tijdschrift Rechtsdocumentatie* (1980–) records an average of 6000 titles yearly.

In English a dated but still useful reference work is *Guide to foreign legal materials: Belgium, Luxembourg, Netherlands* (Graulich *et al.*, 1968). Also in English and extending the period covered by Graulich from 1803 to 1993 is Verbeke (1994), *Belgian law: an annotated bibliographic guide* and an abridged version in *International Journal of Legal Information* (Verbeke, 1992).

Specialized and subject law bibliographies include *Elementaire bibliografie van het strafrecht* (Arnou, 1981–82) for Belgian penal law and procedure. Social law is covered by Dekeersmaker and Van Steenberge (1980–), *Bibliografie van het belgisch sociaal recht. Bibliographie du droit social belge.* Of central historical importance is

Gilissen (1986), *Bibliographie de l'histoire du droit des provinces belges*, of which *Introduction bibliographique à l'histoire du droit, C/3 Belgique et Nord de la France* (Gilissen, 1970) is an abridgement. In Dutch and within the limitations of that language, Belgian legal literature is covered by Malliet (1995), *Elementaire bibliografie Belgisch recht*, an abridgement which suffers from lack of an index. Also in Dutch is Velle (1994), *Recht en gerecht*, a general bibliography of Belgian law noteworthy for its comprehensiveness and excellent index.

An important bibliographic tool for Belgian and foreign insurance and insurance law is *International Insurance Library Louvain: catalogue* (ABB Insurance, 1984) with introductions and access apparatus in Dutch, French, German and English which records 24 000 titles.

Dictionaries

French legal terms are covered in *Vocabulaire juridique* (Cornu, 1990), a comprehensive compilation of 9078 words in public and private law. Latin remains inextricably linked with the legal literature of most continental law systems and an excellent manual is *Expressions et proverbes latins* (Merminod, 1993).

While Le Docte's *Dictionnaire des termes juridiques en quatre langues* (Le Docte, 1988) might suffice in some instances, if a French–Dutch and Dutch–French law dictionary is essential, this need is filled by *Dictionnaire juridique Français–Néerlandais, Néerlandais–Français* (Moors, 1991).

Other reference books

The rules and customs of the Brussels Bar, which serves as a model for other Bar associations in Belgium, have been brought up to date by Lambert (1994) in *Règles & usages*.

Other important reference books and commentaries include: *Traité théorique et pratique des marchés publics* (Flamme, 1969), an essential manual on access to the labyrinthine legislation and procedure of public markets and contracts. *Procédure fiscale contentieuse* (Cardyn and Depret, 1987–92) is an essential treatise on recourse and procedure in contested fiscal cases at all levels of jurisdiction. Leading commentaries on intellectual property are *Droit d'auteur* (Berenboom, 1985) and *Brevets d'invention* (Van Reepinghen and De Brabanter, 1987).

Notarial law and its intricacies have been skilfully unravelled by De Valkeneer (1988), *Précis du notariat*. A reliable treatise on social law is *Droit de la sécurité sociale* (Denis, 1986–89). Town planning and building permits in the widely divergent legislation of the Wallon and Flemish regions has been covered by De Suray (1989–91), *Droit de l'urbanisme*.

For a wide-ranging number of real estate laws consult the various treatises by A. Hilbert. Standard works on Belgium's international law are *Sources du droit international privé belge* (Erauw and Watté, 1993) and *Droit international privé belge* (Vander Elst and Weser, 1983–85).

In English, *Belgian company law* (Warendorf, Thomas and Wymeersch, 1996) provides a translation of the Belgian Coordinated Acts on Commercial Companies, the only current text of its kind. An earlier and more general work is *Belgium and Luxembourg: practical commercial law* (Van Crombrugghe and Arendt, 1992). Also in English the latest provisions of Belgium's contract law are covered by *Contract law in Belgium* (Herbots, 1995).

Current information sources

Journals, research reports

The *Journal des Tribunaux* (1881–) is the oldest and most prestigious continuously published Belgian legal periodical; this weekly covers legislation, case law, doctrine, law bibliography and book reviews. The Flemish-language weekly *Rechtskundig Weekblad* (1931–) publishes on average double the number of decisions of *Journal des Tribunaux* but presents the language barrier of Flemish use.

News information

The federal government issues the weekly newsletter *Faits* (1994–) which records decisions taken by the Council of Minsters and information campaigns conducted by the federal government and its different departments. The *Catalogue 1995* of publications of the Centre d'Information du Service Fédéral d'Information, abbreviated to SFI, is available on request (Service Fédéral d'Information, 1995).

Business and financial information

A wide range of economic and financial information is available from the Bureau du Plan, Services du Premier Ministre, Ministère des Affaires économiques. A daily source giving basic economic and trade indicators is *L'Écho, le quotidien de l'économie et de la finance*.

Statistics

The central source of statistics concerning Belgium is the Institut national de Statistique. Leading trade and economic indicators are also available from the Service de l'Indice. A comprehensive statistical survey of Belgium is *Mémento statistique de la Belgique* (Service Fédéral d'Information, 1994).

Useful addresses

Associations of lawyers

Belgian Bar Association, Ordre National des Avocats de Belgique (also Flemish Order), Secrétariat, avenue de la Toison d'Or 65, 1060 Bruxelles, Belgium. Tel: +32 2 534 6773. Fax: +32 2 539 3920

Brussels Bar Association, Ordre français des avocats du barreau de Bruxelles, place Poelaert, 1000 Bruxelles, Belgium

National Chamber of Bailiffs at Law, Chambre nationale des Huissiers de Justice de Belgique, Nationale Kamer van Gerechtsdeurwaarders van België, avenue Henri Jaspar 93, 1060 Bruxelles, Belgium. Tel: +32 2 538 0092. Fax: +32 2 539 4111

Royal Association of Notaries (conveyancers and drafters of wills), Fédération Royale des Notaires de Belgique, Koninklijke Federatie van Belgische Notarissen, rue de la Montagne 30–32, 1000 Bruxelles, Belgium. Tel: +32 2 505 0811. Fax: +32 2 514 1448

Government organizations

Banque nationale de Belgique, boulevard de Berlaimont 14, 1000 Bruxelles, Belgium. Tel: +32 2 221 2111

Bureau du Plan, Services du Premier Ministre, Ministère des Affaires économiques, avenue des Arts 47–49, 1040 Bruxelles, Belgium. Tel: +32 2 507 7311

Commission bancaire et financière, avenue Louise 99, 1050 Bruxelles, Belgium. Tel: +32 2 535 2211. Fax: +32 2 535 2323 (Belgium's banking commission controls all financial institutions, the stock market, investment vehicles, brokerage houses and financial information generally.)

Institut national de Statistique, Renseignements et Service de Documentation, rue de Louvain 44, 1000 Bruxelles, Belgium. Tel: +32 2 548 6211. Fax: +32 2 548 6262

Ministère de la Justice, boulevard de Waterloo 115, 1000 Bruxelles, Belgium. Secrétaire général or the Agent d'Information, Mr P. Baudewijn. Tel: +32 2 542 7911. Fax: +32 2 538 0767

Ministère des Affaires étrangères, du Commerce extérieur et de la Coopération au Développement, rue Quatre Bras 2, 1000 Bruxelles, Belgium. Tel: +32 2 516 8111. Fax: +32 2 514 3067

Service de l'Indice, rue J.A. De Mot 26, 1040 Bruxelles, Belgium. Tel: +32 2 233 6111

Service Fédéral d'Information, Centre d'Information, 54 boulevard du Régent, 1000 Bruxelles, Belgium. Tel: +32 2 514 0800. Fax: +32 2 512 5125

Trade and Commerce. Office Belge du Commerce Extérieur, World Trade Center – Tour 1, boulevard Émile Jacqmain 162, Bte 26, 1210 Bruxelles, Belgium. Tel: +32 2 209 3511. Fax: +32 2 217 6123

Law reform

Commission de la Révision de la Constitution et Réforme des Institutions, Sénat, Palais de la Nation, place de la Nation 1, 1009 Bruxelles, Belgium. Tel: +32 2 515 8211. Fax: +32 2 514 0685. The leading institutional and constitutional reform body; a Senate Commission.

Courts

Conseil d'État, rue de la Science 33, 1040 Bruxelles, Belgium. Tel: +32 2 234 9611

Cour de Cassation, Palais de Justice, rue aux Laines, 1000 Bruxelles, Belgium. Tel: +32 2 508 6111. Fax: +32 2 508 6273

Education and training

Katholieke Universiteit Leuven, Faculteit Rechtsgeleerdheid, Tiensestraat 41, 3000 Leuven, Belgium. Tel: +32 16 285101. Fax: +32 16 325103

Université catholique de Louvain, Faculté de Droit, Collège Thomas More, place Montesqiueu 2, 1348 Louvain-la-Neuve, Belgium. Tel: +32 10 474626

Université libre de Bruxelles, Faculté de Droit, avenue F.D. Roosevelt 50, 1050 Bruxelles, Belgium. Tel: +32 2 650 3935. Fax: +32 2 650 4074

Vrije Universiteit Brussel, Faculteit Rechtsgeleerdheid, Pleinlaan 2, 1050 Bruxelles, Belgium. Tel: +32 2 641 2540. Fax: +32 2 629 2282

Research institutions

Institut de Sociologie, Université libre de Bruxelles, avenue Jeanne 44, 1050 Bruxelles, Belgium. Tel: +32 2 650 2111. This leading research institution houses the collections and files of the Centre d'Histoire et d'Ethnographie juridiques, publishers of the ambitious law bibliography project *Introduction bibliographique l'histoire du droit et à l'ethnologie juridique* directed by the late John Gilissen.

Libraries

The law schools mentioned above have extensive libraries. See LIBIS-NET below.

Bibliothèque du Parlement, Palais de la Nation, place de la Nation, 1008 Bruxelles, Belgium. Tel: +32 2 519 8111

Ministère de La Justice, Bibliothèque, boulevard de Waterloo 115, 1000 Bruxelles, Belgium. Tel: +32 2 542 6900/05. Fax: +32 2 542 7003

Publishers and booksellers

Etablissements Emile Bruylant, rue de la Régence 67, 1000 Bruxelles, Belgium. Tel: +32 2 512 9845. Fax: +32 2 511 7202

CREDOC. Credoc asbl-vzw: Documentation juridique, rechtsdocumentatie, rue de la Montagne 34, Box 11, B-1000 Bruxelles, Belgium. Tel: +32 2 511 6941. Fax: +32 2 513 3195

L'Écho, le quotidien de l'économie et de la finance, 131 rue de Birmingham, 1070 Bruxelles, Belgium. Tel: +32 2 526 5511. Fax: +32 2 526 5526

JUDIT. Kluwer rechtswetenschappen, Santvoortbeeklaan 21–25, B-2100 Antwerp, Belgium. Tel: +32 3 360 0211. Fax: +32 3 360 0467

JUSTEL. Ministère de la Justice, Service d'information juridique, boulevard de Waterloo 115, B-1000 Bruxelles, Belgium. Tel: +32 2 542 6900/05. Fax: +32 2 542 7003

LIBIS-NET (Bibliotheek Automatisering), Mgr Ladeuseplein 21, 3000 Leuven, Belgium. Tel: +32 16 324619. Internet access at http://www.libis.kuleuven.ac.be/libis/ General cooperative OPAC which includes access to the extensive law collections of the Katholieke Universiteit Leuven.

Maison Larcier, rue des Minimes 39, 1000 Bruxelles, Belgium. Tel: +32 2 512 4712/9679. Fax: +32 2 513 9009

Moniteur belge (official publishers), rue de Louvain 40, B-1000 Bruxelles, Belgium. Tel: +32 2 512 0026

Service Fédéral d'Information, Subscriptions, rue de la Loi 155, B-1040 Bruxelles, Belgium. Tel: +32 2 287 4111. Fax: +32 2 287 4100

List of works cited

ABB Insurance. (1984) *International insurance library Louvain: catalogue* 4th edn. Louvain: ABB. 5 vols.

Actualités de droit: revue de la Faculté de Droit de Liège. (1956–) Liège: Story-Scientia. From 1956–75 entitled *Annales de la Faculté de Droit de Liège*. From 1975–82 entitled *Annales de la Faculté de droit, d'économie et de sciences sociales de Liège*. From 1983–90 entitled *Annales de droit de Liège*. From 1973 includes Documentation juridique belge which updates Bosly, Del Marmol and Goossens (1947–72).

Alen, A. (1992) (ed.) *Treatise on Belgian constitutional law*. Deventer: Kluwer Law and Taxation. Originally published in *International encyclopedia of laws: constitutional law*.

Annales parlementaires. (1844–) Annales de la Chambre des Représentants; Annales du Sénat de Belgique. Brussels: Moniteur belge.

Annuaire administratif et judiciaire de Belgique, 1994–1995. (1995) 112th edn. Brussels: Bruylant.

Arnou, P. (1981–82) *Elementaire bibliografie van het strafrecht. Deel 1: Materieel strafrecht. . . . Deel 2: Formeel strafrecht*. Louvain: Uitgeverij Acco. 2 vols.

Arresten van het Hof van Cassatie. (1937–) Brussels: Moniteur belge. The Flemish version of *Bulletin des arrêts de la Cour de cassation*, see below.

La Belgique judiciaire. (1842–1939) Brussels: Alliance typographique. 97 vols.

Beltjens, Gustave (1894) *La Constitution belge révisée*. Liège: J. Godenne.

Beltjens, Gustave (1905–7) *Encyclopédies: Droit civil belge. I. Code civil* 3rd edn. Brussels: Bruylant-Christophe. 6 vols; (1908) *II. Code de procédure civile* 2nd edn. Brussels: Bruylant. 2 vols.

Berenboom, Alain (1985) *Le droit d'auteur*. Brussels: F. Larcier.

Bergmans, Bernhard (1988) *Le statut juridique de la lange allemande en Belgique*. Brussels: Bruylant.

Bosly, H., Del Marmol, C. and Goossens, C. (1947–72) *Répertoire bibliographique du droit belge, 1919–1970*. Liège: Université de Liège, Faculté de Droit. 4 vols.

Bosly, Henri D. (1995) *Eléments de droit de la procédure pénale*. Brussels: Bruylant.

Britz, Jacques (1847) *Code de l'ancien droit Belgique, ou histoire de la jurisprudence et de la législation, suivie de l'exposé du droit civil des provinces Belgiques*. Brussels: A. Van Daele. 2 vols.

Bulletin des arrêts de la Cour de cassation [in Brussels]. (1928–) Brussels: Moniteur belge.

Bulletin des questions et réponses (1845–) Brussels: Moniteur belge. Official weekly, bound each session, for both houses with a general alphabetical index.

Bulletin législatif belge. (1931–) Brussels: F. Larcier.

Bulletin usuel des lois et arrêtés. (1851–) Brussels: Bruylant.

Buyle, Jean-Pierre (1995) *Code de commerce et lois particulières, textes en vigueur au 1er janvier 1995*. Brussels: Bruylant.

Cambier, Cyr (1974–81) *Droit judiciaire civil. I. Fonction et organisation judiciaires. II. La compétence*. Brussels: F. Larcier. 2 vols.

Cardyn, Charles and Depret, Henri R. (1987–92) *Procédure fiscale contentieuse. Réclamations et recours, recouvrements et poursuites en matière d'impôts directs et indirects de l'État et des pouvoirs locaux, de conventions internationales et de droit communautaire*. Brussels: Bruylant. 2 vols.

Cerexhe, Etienne (1991) *Introduction à l'étude du droit. Les institutions et les sources du droit*. Brussels: Bruylant.

Codes Larcier. (1857–) Brussels: F. Larcier. 5 vols. Latest reissue 1995.

Constitution de la Belgique du 17 février 1994. (1994) Brussels: Bruylant.

Cornu, Gérard (1990) *Vocabulaire juridique* 2nd edn. Paris: Presses Universitaires de France.

CREDOC (available from Credoc asbl-vzw: Documentation juridique, rechtsdocumentatie).

De Garcia De La Vega, D. (1850–1914) *Recueil des traités et conventions concernant le royaume de Belgique*. Brussels: J. Lebègue. 21 vols.

De Page, Henri and Dekkers, R. (1949–90) *Traité élémentaire de droit civil belge* 3rd edn. Brussels: Bruylant. 16 vols and 4 *Complément* [supplement] vols.

De Suray, Jacques (1989–91) *Droit de l'urbanisme et de l'environnement*. Brussels: Bruylant. 3 vols. to date.

De Theux, Axel and Kovalovszky, Imre (1995) *Précis de méthodologie juridique: les sources documentaires du droit*. Brussels: Publications des Facultés Universitaires Saint-Louis.

De Troyer, Ignace (1973–88) *Répertoire des traités conclus par la Belgique. I. 1830–1940. II. 1941–1986*. Brussels: J. Goemaere. 2 vols.

De Valkeneer, R. (1988) *Précis du notariat*. Brussels: Bruylant.

Defacqz, Henri E.M. (1846–73) *Ancien droit Belgique; ou précis analytique des lois et coutumes observées en Belgique avant le Code Civil*. Brussels: Bruylant-Christophe. 2 vols.

Dekeersmaker, J.F. and Van Steenberge, J. (1981–) *Bibliografie van het belgisch sociaal recht. Bibliographie du droit social belge*. Antwerp: Kluwer.

Delpérée, Francis (1986–89) *Droit constitutionnel* 2nd edn. Brussels: F. Larcier. 4 vols.

Delpérée, Francis (1994) (ed.) *La Belgique fédérale*, Brussels: Centre d'Études constitutionelles et administratives, U.L.B.

Denis, Pierre (1986–89) *Droit de la sécurité sociale*. Brussels: F. Larcier. 2 vols.

Documents parlementaires. (1844–) Brussels: Moniteur belge.

Droit commercial belge. (1910–27) 2nd edn. Brussels: Bruylant. 4 vols.

Droit criminel belge. (1901) Part I. *Code pénal et les lois pénales spéciales*. Brussels: Bruylant-Christophe. 1 vol. (1903) Part II. *Code d'instruction criminelle*. Brussels: Bruylant-Christophe. 2 vols.

Dujardin, J. *et al*. (1994) *Constitution coordonnée*. Brussels: La Charte.

L'Écho: le quotidien de l'économie et de la finance. (1881–) Brussels: L'Écho.

Erauw, Johan and Watté, Nadine (1993) *Les sources du droit international privé belge et communautaire*. Brussels: Bruylant.

Faits. (1994–) Brussels: Service Fédéral d'Information.

Fettweis, Albert (1987) *Manuel de procédure civile* 2nd edn. Brussels: Bruylant.

Fettweis, Albert *et al*. (1971–74) *Précis de droit judiciaire*. Brussels: Larcier. 6 vols.

Flamme, Maurice-Aandré (1969) *Traité théorique et pratique des marchés publics, précédé d'un Essai de théorie générale des contrats de l'administration en droit belge et droit comparé*. Brussels: Bruylant. 2 vols.

Flanz, Gisbert H. (1994) Belgium. In *Constitutions of the countries of the world*, eds A.P. Blaustein and G.H. Flanz, vol.II. Dobbs Ferry, NY: Oceana.

Fredericq, (Baron) Louis (1950–55) *Traité de droit commercial belge*. Brussels: Bruylant. 11 vols including index.

Gilissen, John (1962) La rédaction des coutumes dans le passé et dans le présent and La rédaction des coutumes en Belgique aux XVIe et XVIIe siècles. In *La rédaction des coutumes dans le passé et dans le présent*, ed. J. Gilissen, pp. 15–61; 87–111. Brussels: Institut de Sociologie (ULB).

Gilissen, J. (1965, [i.e. 1986]) (ed.) *Bibliographie de l'histoire du droit des provinces belges*. s.l.: s.n. Tirage limité.

Gilissen, J. (1970) *Introduction bibliographique à l'histoire du droit et à l'ethnologie juridique: C/3 Belgique et Nord de la France*. Brussels: ULB.

Godding, Philippe (1991) *Le droit privé dans les Pays-Bas méridionaux du 12e au 18e siècle* 2nd edn. Brussels: Palais des Académies.

Gougnard, D. (1908–33) *Nouveau dictionnaire, ou Encyclopédie du Notariat*. Brussels: priv. publ. 24 vols.

Grandin, A. (1926) *Bibliographie générale des sciences juridiques, politiques, économiques et sociales de 1800 à 1925*. Paris: Recueil Sirey. 3 vols.

Graulich, Paul *et al*. (1968) *Guide to foreign legal materials: Belgium, Luxembourg, Netherlands*. Dobbs Ferry, NY: Oceana.

Hennau, Christiane and Verhaegen, J. (1991) *Droit pénal général*. Brussels: Bruylant. [Faculté de droit de l'Université catholique de Louvain].

Herbots, Jacques (1973) *Meertalig rechtswoord, rijkere rechtsvinding* [On the interpretation of multilingual legal texts by the means of compared versions]. Ghent: Story-Scientia.

Herbots, Jacques H. (1995) *Contract law in Belgium*. The Hague: Kluwer Law International.

Ingber, Léon (1994) (ed.) *Guide des citations, références et abbréviations juridiques*. New edn. Brussels: Kluwer and Bruylant.

Jamar, Lucien *et al.* (1882) (eds) *Répertoire général de la jurisprudence belge, contenant l'analyse de toutes les décisions rendues en Belgique depuis 1814 jusqu'en 1880. . .* . Brussels: Bruylant. Continued as *Répertoire décennal de la jurisprudence belge* covering 1880–1975. Brussels: Bruylant.

Journal des juges de paix et de police. (1890–) Brussels: La Charte.

Journal des Tribunaux. (1881–) Brussels: F. Larcier.

JUDIT (available from Kluwer Rechtswetenschappen).

Jurisprudence commerciale de Belgique – Belgische rechtspraak in handelszaken formerly *Jurisprudence commerciale de Bruxelles*. See *Revue de droit commercial belge*.

Jurisprudence du port d'Anvers. (1856–) Antwerp: Lloyd anversois.

JUSTEL (available from the Ministère de la Justice, Service d'information juridique).

Kohl, Alphonse and Block, G. (1995) *Code judiciaire, conventions internationales*, Brussels: Bruylant.

Lambert, Pierre (1994) *Règles et usages de la profession d'avocat du Barreau de Bruxelles*. 3rd edn. Brussels: Bruylant.

Laurent, François (1869–78) *Principes de droit civil*. Brussels: Bruylant. 33 vols. *Supplément*. (1889–1903) Léon Siville *et al.* (eds) Brussels: Bruylant. 8 vols.

Le Docte, Edgard (1988) *Dictionaire de termes juridiques en quatre langues* [French, Dutch, English, German]. Antwerp-Apeldoorn: Maklu.

Leclercq, Cléo (1993) *Éléments pratiques de procédure civile et modèle d'actes* 2nd edn. Brussels: Bruylant.

Leurquin-De Visscher, F. and Simonart, H. (1980) Documentation et methodologie juridiques. Brussels: Bruylant.

Limpens, Jan and Schrans, Guy (1972) Belgium. In *International encyclopedia of comparative law*, ed. V. Knapp, vol.1, B11–B25. Tübingen: J.C.B. Mohr.

Malliet, Christoph (1995) *Elementaire bibliografie Belgisch recht*. Ghent: Mys & Breesch.

Merminod, Y. (1993) *Expressions et proverbes latins, adages juridiques*. Neuchâtel: Duchemin, Paris distr.

MICROBIBLEX (available from Moniteur belge).

Moniteur belge – Belgisch Staatsblad. (1845–) Brussels: Moniteur belge. Bilingual edition.

Moors, J. (1991) *Dictionnaire juridique Français–Néerlandais, Néerlandais–Français*. New edn. Brussels: Bruylant.

Les Novelles. Corpus juris belgici. (1931–) Brussels: F. Larcier.

Omnilégie, collection complète des lois. . . . (1952–) Bruges: La Charte.

Les Pandectes belges: corpus juris belgici. Inventaire du droit. . . . (1878–1949) Brussels: F. Larcier. 136 volumes in 152, including an index and concordance volume. Founded by E. Picard, continued by L. Hennebicq *et al.* Earlier subititle: *Encyclopédie de législation, de doctrine et de jurisprudence belges*.

Pasicrisie belge: recueil général de la jurisprudence des Cours et tribunaux et du Conseil d'État de Belgique. (1838–) Brussels: Bruylant. 300 vols. to date. Coverage: 1st series, 1791–1814; 2nd series, 1814–1840; 3rd series 1841–1903; new series 1904 to date.

Pasinomie collection complète des lois, décrets, arrêtés et règlements généraux qui peuvent être invoqués en Belgique. (1833–) Brussels: Bruylant. Two earlier series covered 1788–1814 in 16 vols, and 1815–1830 in 9 vols.

Picard, Edmond and Larcier, F. (1882–1890) *Bibliographie générale et raisonnée du droit belge . . . 1814–1889*. Brussels: F. Larcier. 2 vols.

Poulet, Prosper (1907) *Les Institutions françaises de 1795 à 1814, essai sur les origines des Institutions belges contemporaines*. Brussels: A. Dewit.

RABJI (available from Larcier).

Rechtskundig Weekblad. (1931–) Antwerp: Kluwer, for Rechtskundig Weekblad v.z.w.

Recueil annuel de jurisprudence belge. (1949–) Brussels: F. Larcier.

Recueil de la législation générale en vigueur en Belgique. (1932–59) Brussels: Bruylant. 13 vols.

Recueil des arrêts et avis du Conseil d'Etat. (1948–) Brussels: UGA.

Recueil des lois et arrêtés – Verzameling der wetten en besluiten. Brussels: Moniteur belge, published since March 1845.

Répertoire décennal de la jurisprudence belge. See Jamar *et al*. (1882).

Répertoire notarial. (1966–) Brussels: F. Larcier. 16 vols published to date.

Répertoire pratique du droit belge. Législation, doctrine et jurisprudence. (1930–) Brussels: Bruylant. 17 vols published 1930–61 and 6 Supplement vols 1964 to date.

Revue de droit commercial belge. (1980–) Brussels: Jurisdiction commerciale de Belgique, a.s.b.l. Formerly *Jurisprudence commerciale de Belgique – Belgische rechtspraak in handelszaken* (1968–1979) which was preceded by *Jurisprudence commerciale de Bruxelles* (1903–1967).

Revue de jurisprudence de Liège, Mons et Bruxelles. (1888–) Brussels: Story-Scientia. Formerly *Jurisprudence de la Cour d'appel de Liège* and published in Liège by Imprimerie liègeoise.

Rigaux, Marcel and Trousse, P.É. (1950–68) *Les crimes et les délits du Code Pénal*. Brussels: Bruylant. 5 vols.

Servais, Jean F. and Mechelynck, E. (1913–) *Les Codes et les lois spéciales les plus usuelles en vigueur en Belgique avec les arrêtés royaux*. Brussels: Bruylant. 5 vols. 'Les Codes Bruylant'.

Service Fédéral d'Information (1994) *Mémento statistique de la Belgique*. Brussels: S.F.I. Ref.: ES/06.

Service Fédéral d'Information (1995) *Catalogue 1995*. Brussels: S.F.I.

Service Fédéral d'Information (1995) *Mémento des Institutions*. Brussels: S.F.I. Ref.: AA/32.

Service Fédéral d'Information (1995) *Répertoire de l'Information*. Brussels: S.F.I. Ref.: AA/36.

Taeymans, Marc J. (1984) The legal system of Belgium. In *Modern legal systems cyclopedia*, ed. K.R. Redden, vol.3, pp. 3.20.1–78. Buffalo, NY: Hein. Supplemented by some new pages in 1994.

Tijdschrift Rechtsdocumentatie. (1980–) Antwerp: Kluwer Rechtswetenschappen.

Van Arenbergh, É. (1906) *Bibliographie générale et raisonnée du droit belge. Tome II (1889–1903), Fascicules I-IV, Supplément, Tables générales, Notices N° 9518 to 21335*. Brussels: F. Larcier.

Van Bael, Ivo and Bellis, Jean-Francois (1992) *Business law guide to Belgium*. Bicester: CCH Europe.

Van Crombrugghe, Nicole and Arendt, Guy (1992) *Belgium and Luxembourg: practical commercial law*. European commercial law series. London: Longman.

Van Dievoet, Émile (1948) *Le droit civil en Belgique et en Hollande de 1800 à 1940, les sources du droit*. Brussels: Bruylant.

Van Reepinghen, B. and De Brabanter, M. (1987) *Les brevets d'invention, la loi belge du 28 mars 1984*. Brussels: F. Larcier.

Van Reepinghen, Charles (1964) *Rapport sur la réforme judiciaire. I. Code judiciaire. II. Projet de Code judiciaire*. Brussels: Moniteur belge for the Ministère de la Justice. 2 vols.

Van Ryn, Jean and Heenen, J. (1965–88) *Principes de droit commercial* 2nd edn. Brussels: Bruylant. 6 vols including index vol. New eds of some vols in preparation.

Vander Elst, R. and Weser, M. (1983–85) *Droit international privé belge et droit conventionnel international*. Brussels: Bruylant. 2 vols.

Velle, Karel (1994) *Recht en gerecht: bibliografische inleiding tot het institutioneel onderzoek van de gerechtelijke macht (1796–1994)*. Brussels: Algemeen Rijksarchief.

Verbeke, Christian F. (1992) Belgian law: a bibliographic guide to reference materials, 1830–1990. In *International Journal of Legal Information*, **20**, 133–154.

Verbeke, Christian F. (1994) *Belgian law: an annotated bibliographic guide to reference materials, 1803–1993*. Bibliographia Belgica, no.144. Brussels: Commission Belge de Bibliographie.

Warendorf, H.C.S., Thomas, R.L. and Wymeersch, E. (1996) *Belgian company law: a trilingual edition with an English translation of the Coordinated Acts on Commercial Companies as amended and in effect from 1 July 1996*. Brussels: Bruylant; The Hague: Kluwer International Law.

CHAPTER SEVEN

Bulgaria

ANNE PRIES

Introduction to the legal system

After Bulgaria's conquest by the Ottoman Turks in 1393, it became a part of the Turkish Empire and therefore subject to its laws. Turkish rule over Bulgaria was terminated by the Russo-Turkish war of 1877–1878. Soon after the Treaty of Berlin, which marked the end of the war, a constitutional assembly was convoked in the former capital Veliko Tirnovo. The so-called Constitution of Tirnovo was adopted on 16 April 1879 and it was valid until 1947. Even after the adoption of the Constitution, Bulgaria continued to apply some of the basic Ottoman laws, until they were replaced by its own laws. However, in general, the legal system of Bulgaria followed the Western European pattern.

On 8 September 1944 the Soviet Union declared war on Bulgaria and a communist regime was established during the Soviet military occupation. After the referendum of 8 September 1946 the monarchy was abolished and a People's republic was proclaimed. The first communist constitution of 1947, published in the *Dŭrzaven vestnik* [State gazette] no.284/1947, called the Dimitrov Constitution, replaced the Tirnovo Constitution of 1879 and was closely modelled on Stalin's Soviet Constitution of 1936. Although the Bulgarian Communist Party at its VIIth Congress held in 1958 decided to write a new constitution, it took several years and three Constitutional Commissions to realize the project. Amendments to the 1947 constitution appeared in 1961, 1965 and 1969. The second Constitution was adopted by a national referendum on May 16, 1971 and published in the *Dŭrzaven vestnik* no.39/1971. An English translation of the communist constitution can be found in *The constitutions of the communist world* (Simons, 1980).

In less than a year after the 1989 collapse of communism, the communist constitution of 1971 was amended twice. The new Bulgarian Constitution, replacing the Constitution of 1971, was adopted in 1991 by the Grand National Assembly after more than twenty drafts were introduced. It was published in the *Dŭrzaven vestnik* no.56/1991. A collection of constitutional laws has been compiled by Botusharova (1993).

An English translation of the new constitution of Bulgaria can be found in *The rebirth of democracy* (1995, pp. 11–64) edited by the International Institute for Democracy in Strasbourg, in *The constitutions of new democracies in Europe* (Raina, 1995) and in the *Constitutions of central and eastern Europe* (Flanz, 1995) a looseleaf volume from Oceana Publishers. German translations of the Constitution and other documents are to be found in a looseleaf work by Brunner, Schmidt and Westen (1992–), *Wirtschaftsrecht der osteuropäischen Staaten.*

Bulgaria became a democratic republic based on the doctrine of the separation of powers. Any reference to the communist ideology was abolished. The legislative body, the unicameral National Assembly [Narodno Sŭbranie na Republika Bŭlgariya] has 240 members; the term is four years. Head of state is the president, elected for a period of five years. The *Rules on the organisation and procedure of the National Assembly*, promulgated in *Dŭrzaven vestnik* no.13/1995, amended in no.10/1996, are available in English in the series *Bulgarian Law* (1995–, no.68).

The executive body consists of the Council of Ministers, chaired by the Prime Minister who is appointed by the President. Pursuant to and in implementation of the laws, the Council of Ministers adopts decrees, ordinances and resolutions. The Council of Ministers promulgates rules and regulations by decree.

The judicial system is independent and has an independent budget. The supreme judicial function is administered by the Supreme Court of Cassation and the Supreme Administrative Court. The professional status of judges and public prosecutors, guaranteed by the Constitution, is to be secured by an administrative body, the Supreme Judicial Court. Judges, prosecutors and investigators are to be elected, promoted, demoted, reassigned and dismissed by this Court consisting of 25 members, of which eleven must be elected by the National Assembly, eleven by the bodies of the judicial branch and ex officio the Chairmen of The Supreme Court of Cassation, of the Supreme Administrative Court and the Chief Prosecutor. The members are elected for terms of five years. The new law on the judicial system, *Zakon za sŭdebnata vlast*, enacted 23 July 1994, has been promulgated in the *Dŭrzaven vestnik* no.59/1994. An English translation, the *Judicial System Act* has been published in 1995 in the series *Bulgarian Law* (1995–, no.128).

Introductory works on the legal system and legal research

Because of the fundamental changes in the Bulgarian legal system, introductory works summarizing Bulgarian laws are not yet available. The article by Reynolds (1992) on socialist legal systems gives useful background information, as does the chapter on Bulgaria in Michta (1994). The chapters by Sipkov (1991 and 1992) in the *Modern legal systems cyclopedia* are sufficiently recent still to be of practical use. The section in Gsovski and Grzybovski (1959) deals with an earlier period.

A guide to earlier material is the chapter on Bulgaria (Terry, 1982) in *Official publications of the Soviet Union and eastern Europe 1945–1980* and the work of Sipkov (1959) *Legal sources and bibliography of Bulgaria*

Legislation

The State Gazette, *Dŭrzaven vestnik*, has been published in Sofia since 1879 under more or less the same name, except for the period 1950–1962 when it appeared under the title: *Izvestiya na presidyuma na Narodnoto Sŭbranie* [News of the Presidium of the National Assembly]. It has an annual cumulative index, arranged by subject and governmental agency. It is the source for all laws, statutes and decrees, treaties and other official notices to be published by law, including the annual budget and development plans. It is also the official organ of the National Assembly. It is issued twice a week. The *Stenografski Dnevnitsi* [Stenographic Journal] of the National Assembly has been published from 1944 onwards; a similar journal was published in the period 1879–1944.

The *Sbornik postanovleniya i razporezhdaniya na Ministerskiya Sŭvet na Narodna Republika Bŭlgariya* [Collection of decisions and directives of the Council of Ministers] was issued monthly in Sofia in the period 1951–1972. Since 1973 it has been continued under the title *Normativni Aktove*, a looseleaf edition, published since 1990 by the National Assembly and the Council of Ministers. A chronological and alphabetical register of Bulgarian legislative acts for the period 1944–1984 can be found in the *Zakonodatelni aktove: Spravochnik* compiled by Zlatanova (1984).

Under the communist regime the printing and sale of books was a monopoly of the state and social organs. At present quite an amount of juridical materials, especially translations of laws, are being published by private publishing houses. A good collection of laws in Bulgarian is published by APIS from 1991 onwards entitled *Sbornik zakoni: zakoni i drugi normativni aktove* [Collection of laws: laws and other normative acts].

There is no single source which includes all Bulgarian acts in translation. 'Sofita-Inter, private agency' has recently published the series of full-text translations in English of individual Bulgarian acts, decrees and regulations entitled *Bulgarian Law* (1995–). English translations of Bulgarian laws, mainly of a commercial nature, can be found in the *Collection of Bulgarian laws* (Katzarsky, 1993–) published irregularly by 168 Hours BBN. Full-text translations of some laws in English can be found in the *Review of Central and East European Law* and in the LEXIS-NEXIS and WESTLAW databases. A survey of the most important laws published in the official gazettes of Bulgaria and the other countries of Central and Eastern Europe and of the international agreements made by those countries is given in *WGO: Monatshefte für Osteuropäisches Recht* (1959–) which also contains German translations of the full text of some laws.

Codes and commentaries

After World War II Bulgarian civil legislation was enacted in the form of separate statutes for every field of civil law. A civil code as such does not exist. The Code of Civil Procedure was promulgated in *Izvestiya na presidyuma na Narodnoto Sŭbranie* no.12/1952 of 8 February 1952 and amended several times. It is still in force; the latest amendment was promulgated in *Dŭrzaven vestnik* no.87/1995.

Recent publications on civil law with commentaries include Srefanov (1995) and Dzherov (1994). The *Zakon za sobstvenostta* [Ownership Act] was promulgated in *Dŭrzaven vestnik* no.92/1951 and amended several times. The latest amendment was promulgated in the *Dŭrzaven vestnik* no.77/1991. The Copyright and Neighbouring Right Acts promulgated in no.56/1993, amended in *Dŭrzaven vestnik* no.63/1994, has been translated in the series *Bulgarian Law* (1995, no.91). The Family Code of 1985 was amended in 1992 and promulgated in *Dŭrzaven vestnik* no.11/1992 and no.15/1992. The text has been published in book form together with related material: *Semeen kodeks: tekst, sŭdebna praktika (1968–1992), bibliografiya po semeĭno pravo (1945–1992) i normativni aktove* [Family Code: text, court practice (1968–1992) bibliography of family law (1945–1992) and normative acts] (1993). The Labour Code of 1986 has been amended several times, the last amendment was promulgated in *Dŭrzaven vestnik* no.87/1995.

After 1944 the whole existing system of commercial law collapsed and the market economy was replaced by a centrally planned economy. During the 1980s efforts were made to restore the market economy, culminating in the adoption of the Decree no.56 'On Economic Activity' in 1989. Finally, in 1991 the Bulgarian Tŭrgovski zakon [Commercial law] was adopted and published in *Dŭrzaven vestnik* no.48/1991 and subsequently amended four times, the last amendment was promulgated in *Dŭrzaven vestnik* no.63/1995. An English translation can be found in *Collection of Bulgarian laws* (Katzarsky, 1993–, vol.1, pp. 46–100). In the series *Bulgarian Law* a translation appeared under the title 'Commerce Act' (1995–, no.8). Foreign investments laws can be found in *Izbrani normativni i drugi aktove po vŭnshnoikonomicheskite otnosheniya na NR Bŭlgariya* [Selected normative and other acts on foreign economic relations] (Ivantsev, 1986–) .

Nakazatelen Kodeks [the Criminal Code] of Bulgaria was enacted in 1968 and published in *Dŭrzaven vestnik* no.26/1968. It is still in force although amended more than twenty times. The most recent revision was promulgated in the *Dŭrzaven vestnik* no.10/1993. A separate edition by Gruev was published in 1993, *Nakazatelen Kodeks na Republika Bŭlgariya*. The Code of Criminal Procedure was amended twice in 1993 (*Dŭrzaven vestnik* no.39/1993 and no.110/1993). A separate edition was edited by Tredafilova (1993): *Nakazatelno protsesualen Kodeks na Republika Bŭlgariya* [Code of Criminal Procedure of the Bulgarian Republic]. A combined edition of the Criminal Code and the Code of Criminal Procedure has been published in 1991: *Nakazatelen Kodeks. Nakazatelno protsesualen kodeks. Zakon za izpŭlnenie na nakazaniyata* [Criminal Code. Code of Criminal Procedure. Law on the Execution of Penalties].

Treaties

The President of Bulgaria has the right to conclude international treaties in circumstances established by the law and the Council of Ministers confirms them. International treaties concluded by Bulgaria are published in the *Dŭurzaven vestnik*

Law reports, judgments

During the period of the People's Republic no official collection of court decisions was published. The only official source was the legal periodical *Sotsialistichesko Pravo* [Socialist Law] issued by the Ministry of Justice and the Chief Government Attorney's Office in the period 1952–1987 and in the period 1946–1951 under the title *Yuridicheska misŭl* [Legal thought]. It has an annual cumulative table of contents which also appears in Russian and French. In 1988 it was renamed in *Dŭrzhava i Pravo* and issued as a co-publication of the Ministry of Justice, the Supreme Court, the Chief Government Attorney's Office, the Union of Jurists and other juridical institutions.

Since 1985 the Vŭrkhoven Sŭd [Supreme Court] has promulgated its decisions in a monthly bulletin: *Byuletin na Vŭrkhovniya Sŭd na RB. Sŭdebna Praktika* [Bulletin of the Supreme Court of the Bulgarian Republic. Court Practice], in 1993 renamed in *Sŭdebna Praktika na Vŭrkhovniya Sŭd na Republika Bŭlgariya* [Court Practice of the Supreme Court of the Republic of Bulgaria], with a section for civil cases and one for criminal cases. Decisions on labour law taken by the Supreme Court in the period 1987–1994 have been collected by Mikhaĭlov (1995).

Since the fall of the communist system a constitutional court has been established in Bulgaria, as in other countries of Central and Eastern Europe, as a result of the new constitutional order. A description of the development of a constitutional judiciary in Eastern Europe is given by Brunner. Legislation on the Bulgarian Constitutional Court is given in art.147–152 of the Constitution of the Republic of Bulgaria of 12 July 1991, *Dŭrzaven vestnik* no.56/1991 and in the Act on the Constitutional Court of 9 August 1991, *Dŭrzaven vestnik* no.67/1991. The *Konstitutsionen Sŭd* [Constitutional Court] was established at the end of 1991. Its first decisions concerned the validity of presidential and parliamentary mandates. The decisions of the Constitutional Court are published in *Dŭrzaven vestnik* and its activities may be reported in *East European Case Reporter of Constitutional Law* (1994–). The Rules on the Organization of the Activities of the Constitutional Court are available in the series *Bulgarian Law* (1995–, no.71A). As to the selection of constitutional judges, the three branches of government are given equal rights: the Parliament, the President and the Supreme Judiciary each appoint one-third of the judges.

The *OMRI Daily Digest* from the Open Media Research Institute in Prague publishes English summaries of court decisions.

Computer-based systems

The Library of the National Assembly, situated in the Parliament building since 1884–5, is mainly meant for deputies and parliamentary committees and groups. The library carries out indexing of periodicals and other sources. Automation was started in 1988 by using the MICRO CDS/ISIS system. The information, such as new books, publications covering the activities of the National Assembly, bills, acts, foreign legislation, etc., is stored in computer databases. There is no public access to this system.

Full-text translations of some laws into English can be found in the database LEXIS-NEXIS and WESTLAW, mentioned above.

Bibliographies

A comprehensive bibliography of Bulgarian legal publications is *Bibliografiya na bŭlgarskata pravna literatura* (1970–1977) prepared by the state university 'Kliment Okhridski'. An updated version of this title was prepared in 1989 by Iolova *et al.*, *Bibliografiya na bŭlgarskata pravna literatura 1944–1984*, an edition of the Bulgarian Academy of Sciences, BAN. A continuation of this bibliography has been published irregularly in *Dŭrzhava i Pravo* starting with no.6 of 1988.

A bibliography on electoral law has been compiled by Angelova (1994), Librarian at the National Assembly. A retrospective bibliography on civil law was prepared by Boncheva in 1974.

Indexing services

A retrospective index of Bulgarian legislation *Zakonodatelstvo na Narodna Republika Bŭlgariya, 1944–1986: spravochnik* [Legislation of the People's Republic of Bulgaria 1944–1986: handbook] has been compiled by Iolova (1988). A previous edition of 1982, covering the period 1944–1981 is by the same author. Earlier editions are of 1955, 1969, 1974 and 1978, edited by Yanakiev.

A separate annual index to governmental publications is published as an annex to the National Bibliography, series 2: official publications and dissertations, published by the National Library in Sofia, *Natsionalna Bibliografiya na Bŭlgariya: seriya 2, Bŭlgarski knigopis: sluzhebni izdaniya i disertatsiĭ* (1974–).

Dictionaries

A special Bulgarian legal dictionary covering labour law, constitutional law, international law, the judiciary and civil procedure was compiled by Georgiev and Velinov (1995). A recent general *Bulgarian–English, English–Bulgarian dictionary* has been published in New York (Tchomakov, 1992).

Other reference books

Useful background information on the country can be found in Grothusen (1990) and in the annual survey by Economist Publications, *Country profile: annual survey of political and economic background*. The dissertation of Verheijen (1995) and the work of Brown (1994) should also be mentioned in this context.

Current information sources

Journals, research reports

The most important journal for legal practice published in Bulgaria is *Sŭvremenno pravo* [Contemporary law] (1990–), issued by the Faculty of Law of the University of Sofia; it has a table of contents in English. The same Faculty of Law publishes a yearbook *Godishnik na Sofiĭskiya universitet 'Sv. Kliment Okhridski', Yuridicheski fakultet* ([1907–]). *Dŭrzhava i Pravo* (1988–) is mentioned above under **Law reports**. A popular legal periodical issued by the Ministry of Justice and the Union of Jurists is *Obshtestvo i pravo* [Society and law] (1980–1994). *Pravna Misŭl* [Legal thought] (1975–) is a publication of the Institute of Legal Sciences of the Academy of Sciences. *Problemi na morskoto pravo* [Problems in maritime law] (1977–) is issued by the Bulgarian Association of Maritime Law.

Developments in Bulgarian law are covered more and more frequently by journals published abroad devoted to Central and Eastern Europe. These include: the *Review of Central and East European Law* (1992–) published in cooperation with the Institute of East European Law and Russian Studies of Leiden University and the *Parker School Journal of East European Law* (1994–). The Bureau of National Affairs in Washington publishes information about Bulgaria in the *BNA's Eastern Europe Reporter* (1991–). Other information on legal issues can be found in the publication of the Center for the Study of Constitutionalism in Eastern Europe in Chicago, *East European Constitutional Review* (1992–) as well as in the *Journal of Constitutional Law in Eastern and Central Europe* (1994–) published in the Netherlands and in the *Eastern European Forum Newsletter* (1993–), a publication of the London International Bar Association. Newsletters of law firms such as *Central Europe Newsletter* (1992–) and *Central European and CIS Legal Update* (1993–) can be extremely helpful. *Recht in Ost und West* (1957–) gives legal information in German as does *Osteuropa-Recht* (1955–). An overview of the legal changes in Bulgaria and the other central and east European states can be found in the *Jahrbuch für Ostrecht* (1960–).

News information

General information about Bulgaria is also given on a home page on the Internet at http://199.17.131.45/inter/pub/bulgaria/index.html. The Library of the National Assembly issues a daily bulletin *Publikatsiĭ za Narodnoto Sŭbranie* [Publications for the National Assembly] (1990–).

Besides the *OMRI Daily Digest* mentioned above, the Open Media Research Institute in Prague publishes *Transition: Events and Issues in the Former Soviet Union and East Central and Southeastern Europe*, a weekly from July 1995, formerly biweekly, containing analyses and news covering political, social, economic, legal and other affairs.

Business and financial information

Basic business information on Bulgaria can be found in the publications of 168 Hours BBN. Many foreign periodicals are also focused on Bulgarian economic activities and business including: *Image on Central + Eastern Europe* (1991–), KPMG's international newsletter; *Law in Transition*, a newsletter on legal cooperation and training from the European Bank for Reconstruction and Development (1994–); *Doing business in eastern Europe* (1992–). A German periodical devoted to legal aspects of commercial activities in Eastern Europe is *WiRO: Wirtschaft und Recht in Osteuropa* (1992–).

The electronic periodical *OMRI Daily Digest* (1994–) gives political, economic and legal information; part II covers Central, Eastern and Southeastern Europe. Political and economic information on the country can also be found in the *SWB: Summary of world broadcasts* (1993–), Part 2: Central Europe, the Balkans.

Statistics

The *Statisticheski spravochnik na Narodna Republika Bŭlgariya* [Statistical handbook of the People's Republic of Bulgaria] was published in the period 1958–1992. Earlier editions are known under various titles. Since 1993 the new series is published by the National Statistical Institute under the title: *Statisticheski spravochnik*. The current law on statistics, *Zakon za Statistikata*, has been promulgated in the *Dŭrzaven vestnik* no.25/1991; an amendment was promulgated in no.64/1991.

Useful addresses

Associations of lawyers

Bulgarian Bar Association, Vish Advocatski Svet, Blvd. Vitosha 1A, 2nd floor, Sofia 1000, Bulgaria. Tel: +359 2 875513. Fax: +359 2 87651

Government organizations

Ministry of Justice, 1 Slavyanska St., 1000 Sofia, Bulgaria. Tel: +359 2 873576. Fax: +359 2 8673231; 8673226

National Statistical Institute, Information Service and Publications Division, 10 6th September Street, 1000 Sofia, Bulgaria. Tel: +359 2 879638. Fax: +359 2 877825

Courts

Vŭrkhoven Sŭd [Supreme Court], Blvd. Vitosha 2, 1000 Sofia, Bulgaria. Tel: +359 2 8571

Education and training

Faculty of Law, Free University of Burgas, 101 Alexandrowska St., 8000 Burgas, Bulgaria. Tel: +359 56 23279

Faculty of Law, St. Kliment Ohridsky University of Sofia, Tsar Osvoboditel 15, 1504 Sofia, Bulgaria. Tel: +359 2 873634

Research institutes

Center for the Study of Constitutionalism in Eastern Europe, University of Chicago Law School, 1121 E. 60th Street, Chicago, IL 60637, USA. Tel: +1 312 702 9494. Fax: +1 312 702 0356

Institute of East European Law and Russian Studies, Faculty of Law, Leiden University, Hugo de Grootstraat 32, 2311 XK Leiden, Netherlands. Tel: +31 71 277818. Fax: +31 71 277732

Law Institute, Bulgarian Academy of Science, G.Benkovsky 3, Sofia 1000, Bulgaria. Bulgaria Association of International Law at the same address. Tel: +359 2 871548

Open Media Research Institute (OMRI), 140 62 Prague 4. Motokov Building. Na Strzi 63, Prague, Czech Republic. Tel: +42 2 6114 2114. Fax: +42 2 6114 3323. Internet: http://www.omri.cz/Publications/Digests/DigestIndex.html

Libraries

Library of the National Assembly, Narodno Sŭbranie Sq. 2, 1169 Sofia, Bulgaria. Tel: +359 2 8872357. Fax: +359 2 803346

St Cyril and St Methodius National Library, Vassil Levski 88, 1504 Sofia, Bulgaria. Tel: +359 2 882811. Fax: +359 2 881600

St Kliment Ohridsky University of Sofia Library, Tsar Osvoboditel 15, 1504 Sofia, Bulgaria. Tel: +359 2 443719. Fax: +359 2 467170

Publishers and booksellers

168 Hours BBN (Bulgarian Business News), Tsarigradsko Chausse Blvd. 47, 1504 Sofia, Bulgaria. Tel: +359 2 443477/4339249/4339264. Fax: +359 2 443477

Kubon & Sagner Buchexport-Import GmbH, PO Box 340108, D-80328 Munich, Germany. Tel: +49 89 54 218130. Fax: +49 89 54 218218. Telex: 5 216 711 kusa d. A specialized vendor of Eastern European books and periodicals.

Sofita-Inter Private Agency, Nishava St. bl.133, entrance A, 1612 Sofia, Bulgaria. Tel: +359 2 599337; 599120. Fax: +359 2 581055

General

Bulgarian home page. Internet: http://199.17.131.45/inter/pub/bulgaria/index.html

Bulgarian Chamber of Commerce and Industry, Blvd. A. Stamboliiski 11A, 1040 Sofia, Bulgaria. Tel: +359 2 872631. Fax: +359 2 873209. Telex: 22374

List of works cited

Angelova, M. *et al.* (1994) *Bŭlgarski zakoni za izbirane na Narodno Sŭbranie 1879–1991: Sb. tekstove* [Bulgarian laws on parliamentary elections 1879–1981: collection of texts]. Sofia: Narodno Sŭbranie.

Bibliografiya na bŭlgarskata pravna literatura. (1970–1977) Sofia: State University 'Kliment Okhridski'. 5 vols.

BNA's Eastern Europe Reporter. (1991–) Washington, DC: Bureau of National Affairs.

Boncheva, K. *et al.* (1974) *Trideset godini grazhdansko pravo (bibliografiya)* [Thirty years of civil law (a bibliography)]. Sofia: University 'Kliment Okhridski', Faculty of Law.

Botusharova, S. (1993) (ed.) *Konstitutsionno pravo: Konstitutsiya na Republika Bŭlgaria i aktove po prilaganeto ì* [Constitutional law: the Constitution of the Republic of Bulgaria and related acts]. Sofia: 'KA-LKA'-OOD.

Brown, J.F. (1994) *Hopes and shadows: eastern Europe after communism.* Durham, NC: Duke University Press.

Brunner, G. (1992) Development of a constitutional judiciary in eastern Europe. *Review of Central and East European Law* 1992, no.6, pp. 535–553.

Brunner, G., Schmidt, K. and Westen, K. (1992–) *Wirtschaftsrecht der osteuropäischen Staaten.* Baden-Baden: Nomos. Looseleaf.

Bulgarian Law. (1995–) Sofia: Sofita-Inter.

Byuletin na Vŭrkhovniya Sŭd na RB. Sŭdebna Praktika [Bulletin of the Supreme Court of the Bulgarian Republic. Court Practice]. (1985–1992) Sofia: Vŭrkhoven Sŭd.

Central Europe Newsletter. (1992–) London: Clifford Chance.

Central European and CIS Legal Update. (1993–) London: Baker & McKenzie.

Country profile: annual survey of political and economic background [Bulgaria]. (1992–) London: Economist Publications.

Doing business in eastern Europe. (1992–) Bicester CCH Editions Ltd.

Dŭrzhava i Pravo [State and law]. (1988–) Sofia: [Ministry of Justice and other institutions].

Dŭrzaven vestnik [State gazette]. (1879–1949; 1963–) Sofia. During the intervening years 1950–1962 *Izvestiya na presidyuma na Narodnoto Sŭbranie* [News of the Presidium of the National Assembly] served as a gazette.

Dzherov, A. (1994) *Grazhdansko pravo: obshta chast: kniga pŭrva* [Civil law: general part: book one]. Sofia: Ak. izd. prof. Marin Drinov.

East European Case Reporter of Constitutional Law. (1994–) Den Bosch: Bookworld.

East European Constitutional Review. (1992–) Chicago, Ill.: Center for the Study of Constitutionalism in Eastern Europe at the University of Chicago Law School in partnership with the Central European University.

Eastern European Forum Newsletter. (1993–) London: International Bar Association.

Flanz, Gisbert H. (1995) *Constitutions of central and eastern Europe.* Dobbs Ferry, NY: Oceana. Looseleaf.

Georgiev, G.Ch. and Velinov, L. St. (1995) *Yuridicheski rechnik* [Juridical dictionary]. Sofia: Izd. Otechestvo, cop.

Godishnik na Sofiĭskiya universitet 'Sv. Kliment Okhridski', Yuridicheski fakultet [Yearbook of the law. Faculty of Law of the University of Sofia]. (1907–) Sofia.

Grothusen, K. (1990) (ed.) *Bulgarien = Bulgaria.* Südosteuropa-Handbuch Bd.6 = Handbook on South Eastern Europe; vol.6. Göttingen: Vandenhoeck & Ruprecht.

Gruev, L. (1993) (ed.) *Nakazatelen Kodeks na Republika Bŭlgariya* [Criminal Code of the Bulgarian Republic]. Sofia: Sofi-R.

Gsovski, V. and Grzybovski, K. (1959) (eds) *Government, law and courts in the Soviet Union and eastern Europe.* London: Stevens & Sons; The Hague: Mouton & Co. 2 vols.

Image on Central + Eastern Europe: the International KPMG Newsletter. (1991–) Brussels: KPMG.

Iolova, G.N. (1982) *Spravochnik po zakonodatelstvoto na Narodna Republika Bŭlgariya 1944–1981* [Handbook of legislation of the PR of Bulgaria 1944–1981]. Sofia: Nauka i izkustvo.
Iolova, G.N. (1988) *Zakonodatelstvo na Narodna Republika Bŭlgariya, 1944–1986: spravochnik* [Legislation of the People's Republic of Bulgaria, 1944–1986: handbook]. Sofia: Nauka i izkustvo.
Iolova, G.N. *et al.*. (1989) *Bibliografiya na bŭlgarskata pravna literatura 1944–1984.* Sofia: Bulgarian Ak. of Sciences.
Ivantsev, B. (1986–) (ed.) *Izbrani normativni i drugi aktove po vŭnshnoikonomicheskite otnosheniya na NR Bŭlgariya* [Selected normative and other acts on foreign economic relations]. Sofia: Chamber of Commerce.
Izvestiya na presidyuma na Narodnoto Sŭbranie [News of the Presidium of the National Assembly]. Sofia, 1950–1962..
Jahrbuch für Ostrecht. (1960–) Munich: Beck.
Journal of Constitutional Law in Eastern and Central Europe. (1994–) Den Bosch: Bookworld.
Katzarsky, Alexander (1993–) (ed.) *Collection of Bulgarian laws.* Sofia: 168 Hours BBN.
Law in Transition: a Newsletter on Legal Cooperation & Training from the European Bank for Reconstruction and Development. (1994–) London: European Bank for Reconstruction and Development.
Mikhaĭlov, B. (1995) *Resheniya po trudovite dela na Vŭrkhovniya sŭd na Republika Bŭlgariya 1987–1994 g.* [Decisions of the Supreme Court of the Republic of Bulgaria on labour law 1987–1994]. Sofia: Perfekt Konsult.
Michta, A. (1994) *The government and politics of postcommunist Europe.* Westport, Conn. [etc.]: Praeger.
Nakazatelen Kodeks. Nakazatelno protsesualen kodeks. Zakon za izpŭlnenie na nakazaniyata [Criminal Code. Code of Criminal Procedure. Law on the execution of penalties]. (1991) Sofia: University Press.
Natsionalna Bibliografiya na Bŭlgariya: seriya 2, Bŭlgarski knigopis: sluzhebni izdaniya i disertatsiĭ [National Bibliography of Bulgaria, series 2: official publications and dissertations]. (1974–) Sofia: National Library.
Normativni Aktove izd. na Narodnoto Sŭbranie i Ministerskiya Sŭvet na Republika Bŭlgariya [Normative acts/published by the National Assembly and the Council of Ministers of the Republik of Bulgaria, with register]. (1973–) Sofia. Looseleaf.
Obshtestvo i pravo: mesechno [Society and Law: monthly]. (1980–1994) Sofia: Ministerstvoto na pravosŭdieto i Sŭyuza na yuristite v Bŭlgariya [Ministry of Justice and Union of Jurists].
OMRI Daily Digest. (1994–) Prague: Open Media Research Institute. Electronic periodical (available at Listserv@ubvm.cc.Buffalo.edu.).
Osteuropa-Recht (1955–) Stuttgart: Gesellschaft für Osteuropakunde.
Parker School Journal of East European Law. (1994–) New York: Parker School of Foreign and Comparative Law, Columbia University School of Law.
Pravna Misŭl [Legal thought]. (1975–) Sofia: instituta za pravni nauki pri BAN. Quarterly.
Problemi na morskoto pravo/Bŭlgarska asotsiatsiya po Morsko pravo [Problems in maritime law/Bulgarian Association of Maritime Law]. (1977–) Sofia: Chamber of Commerce.
Publikatsi ĭ za Narodnoto Sŭbranie [Publications for the National Assembly]. (1990–) Sofia: Library of the National Assembly.
Raina, P. (1995) (ed.) *The constitutions of new democracies in Europe.* Cambridge: Merlin Books .
The rebirth of democracy: 12 constitutions of central and eastern Europe. (1995) Edited by The International Institute for Democracy. Strasbourg: Council of Europe Press.
Recht in Ost und West. (1957–) Berlin: Arno Spitz.
Review of Central and East European Law. (1992–) Dordrecht: Kluwer. Published in cooperation with the Institute of East European Law and Russian Studies of Leiden

University. Formerly *Review of Socialist Law.*

Review of Socialist Law. (1975–1991) Dordrecht: Nijhoff. Published in cooperation with the Institute of East European Law and Russian Studies of Leiden University. Superseded by *Review of Central and East European Law* (1992–).

Reynolds, T.H. (1992) Socialist legal systems: reflections on their emergence and demise. *International Journal of Legal Information*, **20**, pp. 215–237.

Sbornik postanovleniya i razporezhdaniya na Ministerskiya Sŭvet na Narodna Republika Bŭlgariya [Collection of decisions and directives of the Council of Ministers of the People's Republic of Bulgaria]. (1951–1972) Sofia.

Sbornik zakoni i drugi normativni aktove [Collection of laws and other normative acts]. (1991–) Sofia: Apis.

Semeen kodeks: tekst, sŭdebna praktika (1968–1992), bibliografiya po semeĭno pravo (1945–1992) i normativni aktove [Family Code: text, court practice (1968–1992) bibliography of family law (1945–1992) and normative acts]. (1993) Sofia: Sibi.

Simons, William B. (1980) *The constitutions of the communist world.* Alphen aan den Rijn etc.: Sijthoff & Noordhoff.

Sipkov, I. (1959) *Legal sources and bibliography of Bulgaria.* Praeger Publications in Russian History and World Communism, no.18. New York: Praeger.

Sipkov, Ivan (1991) The legal system of Bulgaria. In *Modern legal systems cyclopedia*, ed. K.R.Redden, vol.8, pp. 8.30.1–8.30.46. Buffalo, NY: Hein. Date taken from volume title page. Looseleaf.

Sipkov, Ivan (1992) Bulgaria: period of democratization. In *Modern legal systems cyclopedia*, ed. K.R.Redden, vol.8, pp. 8.35.1–8.35.18. Buffalo, NY: Hein. Looseleaf.

Sotsialisticheskо Pravo [Socialist law]. (1952–1987) Sofia: Ministry of Justice and Chief Government Attorney's Office.

Srefanov, G. (1995) *Grazhdansko pravo: obshta chast: yuridicheski litsa* [Civil law: general part: juridical persons]. Sofia: Sofi-R.

Statesticheski spravochnik. (1993–) Sofia: National Statistical Institute. Formerly *Statisticheski spravochnik na Narodna Republika Bŭlgariya* [Statistical handbook of the People's Republic of Bulgaria] 1958–1992.

Stenografski Dnevnitsi [Stenographic minutes of the sessions of the Parliament]. (1944–) Sofia.

Sŭdebna Praktika na Vŭrkhovniya Sŭd na Republika Bŭlgariya [Court Practice of the Supreme Court of the Republic of Bulgaria]. (1993–) Sofia: Vurkhoven Sŭd .

Sŭvremenno pravo [Contemporary Law]. (1990–) Sofia: SIBI.

SWB: Summary of World Broadcasts: part 2, Central Europe, the Balkans. (1993–) Reading: BBC Monitoring.

Tchomakov, Ivan (1992) *Bulgarian–English, English–Bulgarian dictionary.* New York, NY: Hippocrene Books.

Terry, G.M. (1982) Bulgaria. In *Official publications of the Soviet Union and eastern Europe 1945–1980: a select annotated bibliography*, ed. Gregory Walker, pp. 17–41. London: Mansell.

Transition: Events and Issues in the Former Soviet Union and East Central and Southeastern Europe. (1995–) Prague: OMRI.

Tredafilova, E. (1993) (ed.) *Nakazatelno protsesualen Kodeks na Republika Bŭlgariya* [Code of Criminal Procedure of the Bulgarian Republic]. Sofia: Sofi-R.

Verheijen, A.T.G. (1995) *Constitutional pillars for new democracies: the cases of Bulgaria and Romania.* Leiden: DSWO Press.

WGO: Monatshefte für Osteuropäisches Recht. (1959–) Heidelberg: Müller.

WiRO: Wirtschaft und Recht in Osteuropa. (1992–) Munich: Beck.

Yuridicheska misŭl [Legal thought]. (1946–1951) Sofia: Ministry of Justice and Chief Government Attorney's Office.

Zlatanova, Chr. (1984) *Zakonodatelni aktove 1944–1984: Spravochnik* [Legislative acts: handbook]. Sofia: Library of the Parliament and the State Council.

CHAPTER EIGHT

Czech Republic

ANNE PRIES

Introduction to the legal system

The historical background: Czechoslovakia

In 1918 Czechoslovakia was founded as a democracy based on Austrian laws for Bohemia, Moravia and Silesia and Hungarian laws for Slovakia and Subcarpathian Ruthenia. As a result two jurisdictions existed in Czechoslovakia. In the first thirty years after the unification comparatively few new laws covered the whole territory of Czechoslovakia.

In 1939 Czech lands were incorporated into the German Reich as the Bohemian–Moravian Protectorate, while Slovakia became a German puppet state which ceased to exist in its own right with the expulsion of the German armies from its territory in the spring of 1945. The acts of the Provisional Government of the Czechoslovak Republic in exile in London were ratified by the parliament and promulgated in the Official Gazette of the Czechoslovak Republic after the end of World War II. However, there was no return to the pre-war constitution and an 'asymmetric system' was devised under which the Slovak National Council received some autonomous powers to administer the interests of Slovakia. The Czechoslovak national government and parliament held the legislative, administrative and executive powers for the country as a whole and for the regional interests of Bohemia and Moravia.

In 1948 when the Czechoslovak Communist Party came to power several fields of law were uniformly regulated by communist legislation and the former legal systems were almost entirely replaced within a relatively short period. In 1949 the country's administration was divided into regions, replacing the old lands of Bohemia, Moravia and Slovakia.

Almost twenty years later the national government started to prepare legislation for the establishment of a federal system and other political initiatives which culminated in the 'Prague Spring' of 1968. The constitutional laws of 1968 which did come into force on 1 January 1969 established two independent national republics of equal rights: the Czech Socialist Republic and the Slovak Socialist Republic, which voluntarily participated in the Federal Czech and Slovak Socialist Republic. The Czech and Slovak Federal Republic was a federal state that guaranteed the equal rights of the Czech and Slovak nations. Its basic principles included voluntary participation and respect for the sovereignty of each republic and for the federation as a whole. There were governments and assemblies for the federation and both the individual republics.

In November 1989 the 'President-for-life' Husak was forced to resign and on 29 December 1989 Vaclav Havel was unanimously elected Czechoslovakia's President. The non-violent upheaval earned the name of 'Velvet Revolution'. The first democratic elections were held in June 1990 at which 58 political parties were registered. The new Federal Assembly, consisting of 300 members, was elected for a two-year term, with the principal task of drafting a new constitution. The Federal Assembly passed a considerable number of measures including Constitutional Acts, for example the Constitutional Act no.23/1991 instituting a Charter of Fundamental Rights and Freedoms. An English translation of the Charter with a brief commentary appears in *Bulletin of Czechoslovak law* (Azud, 1991) and several other constitutional measures are translated in the same volume.

A strong separatist sentiment in Slovakia was represented by the militant separatist Slovak National Party and fuelled by the remoteness of federal authorities in Prague and the dominance of the Czech Republic in the federation. Discussions on the constitutional future culminated during the electoral campaign for parliament. After the elections of June 1992 it became clear that the Federal Republic was about to disintegrate. Slovakia adopted a new constitution as an independent state on 3 September 1992, the Czech Republic adopted its new constitution on 16 December 1992. On 1 January 1993, after 74 years, the federation was formally dissolved. It was succeeded by the Czech Republic (see below) and Slovakia or the Slovak Republic (see the chapter on the **Slovak Republic**).

The legal system of the Czech Republic

In practice the Czech Republic [Ceská Republika] is Czechoslovakia minus Slovakia. The main institutions and organizations in Prague, formerly operating at a federal level for both republics, continued their work as Czech institutions after the divorce. In many cases Slovakia had to start from the beginning.

The Czech Republic has a two-chamber parliament. The lower house, the Chamber of Deputies [*Poslanecká sněmovna*], consists of 200 members, elected for a four-year term. The Senate [*Senát*] has 81 members, elected for a six year term, with one-third of the senators elected every two years. The president, elected by the parliament at a joint session of both chambers, appoints and dismisses the prime minister and his government. The government is the supreme executive authority of the state. The constitutionality of legislation and government action is guarded by the Constitutional Court (art.83–89 of the Constitution) consisting of 15 judges appointed by the President for a ten-year term. The Constitution also provides for an independent judiciary consisting of the Supreme Court, the Supreme Administrative Court and high, regional and district courts (art.91).

The original text of the constitution of the Czech Republic was published in 1992: *Ústava České republiky a listina základních práv a svobod z dne 16 prosince 1992*; an extensive edition with commentary has been edited by Pavlíček (1994). An English translation of the new Constitution can be found in *The rebirth of democracy: 12 constitutions of central and eastern Europe* (1995, pp. 115–152), in *The constitutions of new democracies in Europe* (Raina, 1995) and in *Constitutions of central and eastern Europe* (Flanz, 1995). An English translation of the communist constitution was published in *The constitutions of the communist world* (Simons, 1980). German translations of the Constitution and other documents are to be found in the looseleaf *Wirtschaftsrecht der osteuropäischen Staaten* (Brunner, Schmidt and Westen, 1992–).

Introductory works on the legal system and legal research

Introductory works to the current Czech legislation are not yet available. The article by Reynolds (1992) on socialist legal systems gives useful background information as does the chapter on Czechoslovakia in Michta (1994). Glos (1992) in *Modern legal systems cyclopedia* is sufficiently up to be of direct use; Knapp (1979) in the *International encyclopedia of comparative law* is now outdated but still interesting.

The chapter on Czechoslovakia in the work of Gsovski and Grzybovski (1959) deals with an earlier period. A good guide to earlier material is the chapter on Czechoslovakia (Chrástek, 1982) in *Official publications of the Soviet Union and eastern Europe 1945–1980* and the basic work of Bohmer (1959).

Legislation

It must be assumed for the purposes of this chapter that there is some continuity between the existing legislation of the federal republic of

Czechoslovakia and the legislation of the new Czech Republic, although it is not clear how far federal legislation has been adopted.

Official gazette

The official gazette of the Czech Republic is the *Sbírka zákonů České republiky* [Collection of laws of the Czech Republic] issued by the Ministry of Internal Affairs since late 1992. It is partly a continuation of *Sbírka zákonů republiky Československé* [Collection of laws of the Czechoslovak Republic], issued from 1918–1992; the title varied with the nomenclature of the state.

The *Sbírka zákonů* contains full texts of all the laws issued by the Czech parliament, formerly by the federal parliaments and the parliaments of each republic. It was published in Slovak and until 1945 in German.

The following acts are promulgated in *Sbírka zákonů* : 1. Laws passed by the legislature; 2. Resolutions of the Presidium of the National Assembly; 3. Decrees issued by the Cabinet of Ministers, by individual Ministers and other central authorities; 4. Proclamations of the Cabinet of Ministers and of individual Ministers concerning international treaties; 5. Other legal provisions, if required by law or by the nature of the subject.

The *Bulletin of Czechoslovak Law* (1960–), published by the Association of Lawyers of the Czech and Slovak Federal Republic up to 1992 (no later issues seen at time of writing) has been devoted particularly in recent years to the publication of translations of new legislation with brief commentary; a French-language edition was also published between 1925 and 1990 and a Russian version from 1951 to 1990. A survey of the most important laws and international agreements published in the official gazette of the Czech Republic is given in *WGO: Monatshefte für Osteuropäisches Recht*. It contains German translations of the full text of some laws.

Parliamentary proceedings

In the federal republic of Czechoslovakia the minutes of the joint sessions of the People's Assembly and the Assembly of Nations *Zpráva o schůzi Sněmovny lidu a Sněmovny Národú* were published 1970–1990. The minutes of the separate sessions of the People's Assembly *Zpráva o schůzi Sněmovny lidu* and those of the sessions of the Assembly of Nations *Zpráva o schůzi Sněmovny Národú* were published 1969–1990. The proceedings of the federal parliament in the period between the Velvet Revolution and the break-up of the federation were published in Prague: *Zpráva o . . . samostatne schůzi Sněmovny lidu: . . . volebni obdobi* [Minutes of the . . . session of the Assembly] until 1993.

The current stenographic reports of sessions of the Chamber of Deputies of the Czech Republic are entitled *Tesnopisecké zprávy o schůzi Poslanecké snemovny* (1993).

Codes and commentaries

The Czechoslovak Civil Code adopted in 1918 had its roots in the Austrian Civil Code of 1811. The 1918 Civil Code remained in force until 1950 when the communist government introduced a new one modelled on Soviet law, replaced by another in 1964. Since the beginning of the reform process in Czechoslovakia, the Civil Code has been substantially amended several times. The Czech Civil Code is now based on the consolidated text published in *Sbírka zákonů* no.47 of 1992 amended in no.264 of 1992. The *Občanský zákonik* [Civil Code] has been published in 1993 followed by the Code of Civil Procedure with commentary edited by Bureš and Drápal (1994). The Czech firm Trade Links in Prague has been publishing English translations of current Czech and Slovak laws, mainly in the field of commercial and economic law, since 1990. The *Civil Code* (1995) has been published including amendments in early 1995.

A new Commercial Code was promulgated as Act 513/1991 in *Sbírka zákonů* no.98 of 1991. A translation appears in the *Bulletin of Czechoslovak law* by Pelikánová (1992) whose textbook on commercial law appeared in 1994. Trade Links has published the *Commercial Code* (1995) in English including amendments in early 1995. A translation of other trade-related legislation (amended Procurement Act, Act on Protection of Economic Competition, Bankruptcy and Composition Act, and the Copyright Act) was published in 1996. The textbook in English on *Czechoslovakian business law* by Heller Löber Bahn and Partners (1992) takes account of the new Code as well as addressing wider business law concerns.

The current Criminal Code is based upon the Czechoslovak Criminal Code of 29 November 1961, that has since been amended several times, notably in *Sbírka zákonů* no.65 of 1994. A compilation of current legislation on criminal law and procedure is to be found in Jelínek and Sovák (1995).

The German publisher Beck has compiled very good looseleaf editions of current Czech legislation in Czech. The general collection is entitled *České zákony* [Czech laws], formerly *Československé zákony* [Czechoslovak laws], in which constitutional law, civil law, criminal law, labour law, etc., can be found. The binders *Ústavní a správní zákony* [Constitutional and administrative laws] and *Pracovní a sociální zákony* [Labour and social laws] have more specific coverage. Beck also publishes separate editions of several codes with commentaries, for example the Civil Code and the Code of Civil Procedure mentioned above.

Treaties

International treaties are promulgated in an appendix to the *Sbírka zákonů*. It is, as yet, unclear how far treaties made by the federal republic have been adopted by the new Czech Republic.

Law reports, judgments

Starting with 1994 the *Sbírka soudních rozhodnutí a stanovisek* [Collection of decisions and opinions of the courts] publishes the decisions of the Supreme Court of the Czech Republic. It has a table of contents in English and in German. In the period 1948–1993 it contained the decisions of the Supreme Court of Czechoslovakia. It gives the complete text of Supreme Court decisions and has annual indexes by subject, title and statute number. Selected decisions also appear in major Czech law journals (see below).

In the course of 1991, Czechoslovakia passed the necessary legislation to establish a constitutional court. The Constitutional Act on the Constitutional Court of the Czech and Slovak Federal Republic of 27 February 1991 was published in the *Sbírka zákonů* 1991, no.91 and translated in *Bulletin of Czechoslovak Law* (1991, **30**, pp. 29–34); the Act on the Organization of the Constitutional Court of the Czech and Slovak Federal Republic of 7 November 1991 can be found in the *Sbírka zákonů* 1991, no.491; the Organizational and Procedural Statute of the Constitutional Court of the Czech and Slovak Federative Republic of 26 March 1992 can be found in the *Sbírka zákonů* 1992, no.51. A description of the development of a constitutional judiciary in Eastern Europe has been given by Brunner (1992). Selected decisions may appear in *East European Case Reporter of Constitutional Law* (1994–).

The *OMRI Daily Digest* (1994–) published by the Open Media Research Institute (see below) contains English summaries of selected court decisions.

Encyclopedias

A small legal encyclopedia has recently been compiled by Fiala (1994).

Bibliographies

The *Bibliography of Czechoslovak legal literature 1945–1958* was compiled by Knapp (1959). For a later period the *Normotvorba vo federativnej ČSSR 1969–1979* [Legislation in Federal Czechoslovakia 1969–1979] compiled by Czafik and Virsík (1980) is useful.

Currently the Národní knihovna v Praze [National Library in Prague] (address below) publishes the national bibliography consisting of eight series which gives information on legal publications. Recently the National Library founded the National Centre of Bibliographic Information (NBCI) that carries out searches in several databases at the library and on CD-ROMs.

Dictionaries

A recent English–Czech dictionary has been compiled by Chromá (1995). A specialized English–Czech, Czech–English dictionary in the field of economy, finance and law is *Odborný slovník česko-anglický, anglicko-čueský z oblasti ekonomiké, finanční a právní* (1994). An English–Czech Dictionary of the Czech Republic's business law and economy, including a Czech–English index and explanations of terms using quotations from Czech laws, was published by Trade Links (address below) in 1996.

Current information sources

Journals, research reports

The Ministry of Internal Affairs of the Czech Republic publishes *Správní právo* [Administrative law]; it has been published since 1968, applying to Czechoslovakia in its early years. The Ministry of Justice issues *Právni Praxe* [Law practice], formerly *Právo a zákonost.*

The Institute of State and Law of the Czech (formerly Czechoslovak) Academy of Sciences [Ústav státu a práva AV ČR] publishes *Právník. Teoretický časopis pro otázku státu a práva* [The lawyer. Review of problems of state and law] (1956–). The Academy started a series of articles on state and law in 1956: *Stát a právo* [State and law] but this series ended with volume 28 in 1990.

The Law Faculty of the Charles University in Prague issues the juridical series of the *Acta Universitatis Carolinae. Iuridica* (1963–) and a monograph series under the same name, both with summaries in English. In 1971 the Law Faculty of the University of Brno started the juridical series of the *Acta Universitatis Brunensis.*

Developments in Czech and Slovak law are covered more and more frequently by journals published abroad devoted to Central and Eastern Europe such as the *Review of Central and East European Law* (1992–), published in cooperation with the Institute of East European Law and Russian Studies of Leiden University and the *Parker School Journal of East European Law* (1994–). Information about legal issues in the Czech Republic can be found in *BNA's Eastern Europe Reporter* (1991–), in the publication of the Center for the Study of Constitutionalism in Eastern Europe at the University of Chicago Law School *East European Constitutional Review* (1992–), in the *Journal of Constitutional Law in Eastern and Central Europe* (1994–) and in the *Eastern European Forum Newsletter* (1993–), a publication of the London International Bar Association. Law firms active in the area may include valuable information in their newsletters, for example, among others: *Central Europe Newsletter* (1992–) and *Central European and CIS Legal Update* (1993–).

Recht in Ost und West (1957–), published in Berlin, gives legal information in German as does *Osteuropa-Recht* (1955–) published in Stuttgart. An overview of the legal changes in the Czech Republic and other Central and East European states can be found in the *Jahrbuch für Ostrecht* (1960–).

News information

The Open Media Research Institute, OMRI, (address below) was founded in 1994 with its research offices in Prague and home offices in the USA, as a non-profit, public service research enterprise dedicated to the study of the former Soviet Union and East, Central and Southeastern Europe. It gives information about regional affairs through regular publication of analysis and news concerning the region and makes accessible the extensive Radio Free Europe/Radio Liberty Archives. The electronic periodical *OMRI Daily Digest* (1994–) gives political, economic and legal information; part II covers Central, Eastern and Southeastern Europe.

Besides the *OMRI Daily Digest* OMRI in Prague publishes *Transition: Events and Issues in the Former Soviet Union and East Central and Southeastern Europe* (1995–), a weekly, originally a biweekly, journal of analysis and news of political, social, economic, legal and other affairs. Political and economic information on the country can also be found in the *SWB: Summary of world broadcasts*, (1993–), part 2: Central Europe, the Balkans.

Business and financial information

The Ministry of Internal Affairs publishes an illustrated periodical containing legal information, *Státní správa a samospráva: týdeník vlády České republiky* [State management and self-management: weekly of the government of the Czech Republic], (1990–) with an annual index. A periodical devoted to commercial law and practice is *Obchodní právo* [Commercial law], formerly *Arbitrážni praxe*. A monthly for economic questions and economic arbitrage published since 1967 in Prague *Hospodářské právo* [Economic law], renamed *Hospodářství a právo* [Economy and law] in 1991, seems to have ceased publication.

The weekly electronic periodical: *OMRI Economic Digest* (1995–97) carried reports on recent economic and business developments in all the countries of Eastern Europe and the former Soviet Union and is in part continued by *Transition.*

Many foreign periodicals are also focused on Czech and Slovak economic activities and business such as: *Image on Central + Eastern Europe* (1991–), KPMG's international newsletter, and *Law in Transition* (1994–), a newsletter on legal cooperation and training from the European Bank for Reconstruction and Development; *Doing business in eastern Europe* (1992–) and in the *Parker School Journal of East*

European Law (1994–). A German periodical devoted to legal aspects of commercial activities in Eastern Europe is *WiRO: Wirtschaft und Recht in Osteuropa* (1992–). Useful background information on the country can be found in the annual survey of Economist Publications, *Country profile: annual survey of political and economic background*; since 1992 several series have been published, including one on Czechoslovakia.

Statistics

The most important official statistical series *Československá statistica* has been published in Prague by the Federal Statistical Office since 1922, with some interruptions during World War II. The first series, in 18 subseries, was issued until 1949; the new series started in the early 1950s.

The *Statistická ročenka Československé Republiky* [Statistical yearbook of the Czechoslovak Republic] was published in Prague from 1934–1992 under slightly varying titles; publication was suspended 1939–1956. Before and during the federal period statistics were also issued under similar titles for the Czech region, later Czech Republic. Since 1993 Statistical Office in Prague (address below) issues statistics for the Czech Republic only, *Česká statistica* (1993–).

Useful addresses

Associations of lawyers

Česká Advokátní Komora [Czech Bar Association], Národní Trída 16, 110 00 Prague 1, Czech Republic. Tel: +42 2 2491 3606. Fax: +42 2 2491 0162

Government organizations

Czech Statistical Office, Sokolovská 142, 186 04 Prague 8, Czech Republic. Tel: +42 2 814 2451. Fax: +42 2 683 4830

Ministry of Justice, Vysehradská 16, 12810 Prague 2, Czech Republic. Tel: +42 2 2491 1465/2491 5228. Fax: +42 2 2491 1365

Courts

Nejvyšši Soud CR [Czech Supreme Court], Buresova 20, 65737 Brno, Czech Republic. Tel: +42 5 4132 1237. Fax: +42 5 4121 3493

Ústavní Soud CR [Czech Constitutional Court], Jostova 8, 66083 Brno 2, Czech Republic. Tel: +42 5 4216 1111. Fax: +42 5 758 825

Education and training

Univerzita Karlova, Právnická fakulta UK [Charles University, Faculty of Law], nám. Curieov'ych 7, 116 40 Prague 1, Czech Republic. Tel: +42 2 232 8024

Univerzita Masarykova, Právnická fakulta MU [Masaryk University, Faculty of Law], Zelný trh 2, 657 90 Brno 2, Czech Republic. Tel: +42 5 753750

Univerzita Palackého v Olomouci, Právnická fakulta [Palacký University, Faculty of Law], Křížkovského 8, 771 47 Olomouc, Czech Republic. Tel: +42 68 522 3494. Fax +42 68 26476

Research institutes

Open Media Research Institute (OMRI), 140 62 Prague 4. Motokov Building. Na Strzi 63., Prague, Czech Republic. Tel: +42 2 6114 2114. Fax +42 2 6114 3323. Internet: http://www.omri.cz/Publications/Digests/DigestIndex.html

Ústav státu práva AV ČR [Institute of State and Law, Academy of Sciences of the Czech Republic], Národní 18, 110 00 Prague 1, Czech Republic. Tel +42 2 2491 2002. Fax: +42 2 2491 0495

Libraries

Czech Parliamentary Library, Snemovní 4, 118 26 Prague 1, Czech Republic. Tel: +42 2 539411. Fax: +42 2 539406. Founded in 1857

Národní knihovna v Praze [National Library in Prague], Klementinum 190, 11001 Prague 1, Czech Republic. Tel: +42 2 2422 9500. Fax: +42 2 2422 7796. Founded in 1366 as a university library and central research library of Bohemia and Moravia

Publishers and booksellers

Trade Links, POB 131, Opletalova 4, 11001 Prague 1, Czech Republic. Tel: +42 2 2424 1535/2424 1536. Fax: +42 2 2421 0692/2421 0897

General

Czech Republic home page. Internet: http://www.czech.cz/

Czech Chamber of Commerce, Argentinska 38, 170 00 Prague 7, Czech Republic. Tel: +42 2 872 4111. Fax: +42 2 879134

List of works cited

Acta Universitatis Brunensis. Iuridica = Spisy právnické fakulty univerzita Masarykova v Brně. (1971–) Brno: Univerzita Masarykova, Právnická fakulta MU [Masaryk University, Faculty of Law].

Acta Universitatis Carolinae. Iuridica. (1963–) Prague: Univerzita Karlova, Právnická fakulta UK [Charles University, Faculty of Law].

Azud, Ján (1991) The Charter of Fundamental Rights and Freedoms. *Bulletin of Czechoslovak Law*, **30**, pp. 5–23.

BNA's Eastern Europe Reporter. (1991–) Washington, DC: Bureau of National Affairs.

Bohmer, A. *et al.* (1959) *Legal sources and bibliography of Czechoslovakia.* Praeger Publications in Russian History and World Communism, No.19. New York: Praeger.

Brunner, G. (1992–) Development of a constitutional judiciary in eastern Europe. *Review of Central and East European Law* 1992, no.6, pp. 535–553.

Brunner, G., Schmidt, K. and Westen, K. (1992–) *Wirtschaftsrecht der osteuropäischen Staaten.* Baden-Baden: Nomos. Looseleaf.

Bulletin of Czechoslovak Law. (1960–) Prague: Association of Lawyers of the Czech and Slovak Federal Republic.

Bureš, J. and Drápal, L. (1994) *Občanský soudní řád. Komentár* [Code of Civil Procedure. Commentary]. Prague: Beck.

Central Europe Newsletter. (1992–) London: Clifford Chance.

Central European and CIS Legal Update. (1993–) London: Baker & McKenzie.
Česká statistica [Czech statistics]. (1993–) Prague: Czech Statistical Office.
České zakony [Czech laws]. (1993–) Prague: Beck. Looseleaf. Formerly *Československé zakony* [Czechoslovak laws].
Československá statistica [Czechoslovak statistics]. (1922–1992) Prague: Federal Statistical Office.
Chrástek, D. (1982) Czechoslovakia. In *Official publications of the Soviet Union and eastern Europe 1945–1980: a select annotated bibliography*, ed. Gregory Walker, pp. 43–64. London: Mansell.
Chromá, Marta (1995) *Anglicko-české právnický slovnik*. Prague: LEDA.
Civil Code [Czech Republic]. (1995) Prague: Trade Links.
Commercial Code [Czech Republic]. (1995) Prague: Trade Links.
Country profile: annual survey of political and economic background [Czech Republic]. (1992–) London: Economist Publications.
Czafik, J. and Virsík, A. (1980) *Normotvorba vo federativnej ČSSR 1969–1979* [Legislation in Federal Czechoslovakia 1969–1979]. Prague: Obzor. 2 vols.
Doing business in eastern Europe. (1992–) Bicester: CCH Editions Ltd.
East European Case Reporter of Constitutional Law. (1994–) Den Bosch: Bookworld.
East European Constitutional Review. (1992–) Chicago, Il.: Center for the Study of Constitutionalism in Eastern Europe at the University of Chicago Law School in partnership with the Central European University.
Eastern European Forum Newsletter. (1993–) London: International Bar Association.
Fiala, J. (1994) (ed.) *Malá právnická encyklopedie* [Small legal encyclopedia]. Prague: Linde.
Flanz, Gisbert H. (1995) *Constitutions of central and eastern Europe*. Dobbs Ferry, NY: Oceana. Looseleaf.
Glos, G. (1992) The legal system of Czechoslovakia. In *Modern legal systems cyclopedia*, ed K.R. Redden, vol.8, pp. 8.40.1–8.40.40. Buffalo, NY: Hein.
Gsovski, V. and Grzybovski, K. (1959) (eds) *Government, law and courts in the Soviet Union and eastern Europe*. London: Stevens & Sons;The Hague: Mouton & Co. 2 vols.
Heller Löber Bahn and Partners (1992) *Czechoslovakian business law*. Deventer: Kluwer.
Hospodářské právo [Economic law]. (1967–1990) Prague: SNTL.
Hospodářství a právo [Economy and law]. (1991–92) Prague: SNTL.
Image on Central + Eastern Europe: the International KPMG Newsletter. (1991–) Brussels: KPMG.
Jahrbuch für Ostrecht. (1960–) Munich: Beck.
Jelínek, J. and Sovák, Z. (1995) *Trestní zákon a trestní řád* [Criminal law and criminal procedure]. Prague: Linde.
Journal of Constitutional Law in Eastern and Central Europe. (1994–) Den Bosch: Bookworld.
Knapp, Viktor (1959) (ed.) *Bibliography of Czechoslovak legal literature 1945–1958*. Prague: Publishing House of the Academy of Sciences.
Knapp, Viktor (1979) Czechoslovakia. In *International encyclopedia of comparative law*, ed. V. Knapp, vol.1, pp. C111–C126. Tübingen: J.C.B. Mohr.
Law in Transition: a Newsletter on Legal Cooperation & Training from the European Bank for Reconstruction and Development. (1994–) London: European Bank for Reconstruction and Development.
Michta, A. (1994) *The government and politics of postcommunist Europe*. Westport, Conn. [etc.]: Praeger.
Občanský zákonik [Civil code]. (1993) Munich/Prague: Beck.
Obchodní právo [Commercial law]. (1992–) Prague: Prospektrum. Formerly *Arbitrazni praxe*.
Odborný slovník česko-anglický, anglcko-český z oblasti ekonomiké, finanční a právní

[Specialized English–Czech, Czech–English dictionary in the field of economy, finance and law]. (1994) Prague: Linde.
OMRI Daily Digest. (1994–) Prague: Open Media Research Institute. Electronic periodical (available at Listserv@ubvm.cc.Buffalo.edu.).
OMRI Economic Digest. (1995–97) Prague: Open Media Research Institute. Electronic periodical (available at Listserv@ubvm.cc.Buffalo.edu.).
Osteuropa-Recht (1955–) Stuttgart: Gesellschaft für Osteuropakunde.
Parker School Journal of East European Law. (1994–) New York: Parker School of Foreign and Comparative Law, Columbia University School of Law.
Pavlíček, V and Hřebejk, J. (1994) *Ústava České republiky* [Constitution of the Czech Republic]. Prague: Linde.
Pelikánová, I. (1992) The Czechoslovak Commercial Code. *Bulletin of Czechoslovak Law*, **31**, pp. 3–152 and 4 unnumbered index pages. The brief commentary and translation of the extensive text forms the whole of volume 31.
Pelikánová, I. (1994) *Obchodní právo I a II* [Commercial law I and II]. Prague: Codex.
Pracovní a sociální zákony [Labour and social laws]. (1994–) Prague: Beck. Looseleaf.
Právní Praxe [Law practice]. Prague: Ministry of Justice. Formerly *Právo a zákonost.*
Právník. Teoretický časopis pro otázku státu a práva [The lawyer. Review of problems of state and law]. (1956–) Prague: Institute of State and Law, Academy of Sciences of the Czech Republic [Ústav státu a práva AV ČR].
Raina, P. (1995) (ed.) *The constitutions of new democracies in Europe*. Cambridge: Merlin Books.
The rebirth of democracy: 12 constitutions of central and eastern Europe. (1995) Edited by The International Institute for Democracy. Strasbourg: Council of Europe Press.
Recht in Ost und West. (1957–) Berlin: Arno Spitz.
Review of Central and East European Law. (1992–) Dordrecht: Kluwer. Published in cooperation with the Institute of East European Law and Russian Studies of Leiden University. Formerly *Review of Socialist Law.*
Review of Socialist Law. (1975–1991) Dordrecht: Nijhoff. Published in cooperation with the Institute of East European Law and Russian Studies of Leiden University. Superseded by *Review of Central and East European Law* (1992–).
Reynolds, T.H. (1992) Socialist legal systems: reflections on their emergence and demise. *International Journal of Legal Information*, **20,** pp. 215–237.
Sbírka soudních rozhodnutí a stanovisek [Collection of court decisions and determinations]. (1948–1993) Prague: Supreme Court [Nejvyšš soud]. Czech and Slovak Federal Republic.
Sbírka soudních rozhodnutí a stanovisek [Collection of court decisions and determinations]. (1993–) Prague: Supreme Court [Nejvyšš soud]. Czech Republic.
Sbírka zákonů České Republiky [Collection of laws of the Czech Republic]. (1992–) Prague: Ministry of Internal Affairs. First issue dated 28 December 1992.
Sbírka zákonů Republiky Československé [Collection of laws of the Czechoslovak Republic]. (1918–1992) Prague: Statistické a evidenčni vydavatelstvi tiskopisů.
Simons, William B. (1980) *The constitutions of the communist world.* Alphen aan den Rijn: Sijthoff & Noordhoff.
Správní právo. Odborný časopis pro oblast státní správy a správnígo práva [Administrative law]. (1968–) Prague: Ministry of Internal Affairs.
Stát a právo [State and law]. (1959–1990) Prague: Institute of State and Law, Academy of Sciences of the Czech Republic [Ústav státu a práva AV ČR].
Statistická ročenka Československé Republiky [Statistical yearbook of the Czechoslovak Republic]. (1934–1992) Prague: Federal Statistical Office. Title varies.
Státní správa a samospráva: týdeník vlády České republiky [State management and self-management: weekly of the government of the Czech Republic]. (1990–) Prague: Ministry of Internal Affairs.
SWB: summary of World Broadcasts: part 2, Central Europe, the Balkans. (1993–) Reading: BBC Monitoring.

Tesnopisecké zprávy o schůzi Poslanecké sněmovny [Stenographic reports of the sessions of the Chamber of Deputies]. (1993–) Prague: Kancelář Federálního shromáždění ČSFR.

Transition: Events and Issues in the Former Soviet Union and East Central and Southeastern Europe. (1995–) Prague: OMRI.

Ústava České republiky a listina základních práv a svobod z dne 16 prosince 1992 [Constitution of the Czech Republic . . .]. (1992) Ostrava: Aries.

Ústavní a správní zákony [Constitutional and administrative laws]. (1994–) Prague: Beck. Looseleaf.

WGO: Monatshefte für Osteuropäisches Recht. (1959–) Heidelberg: Müller.

WiRO: Wirtschaft und Recht in Osteuropa. (1992–) Munich: Beck.

Zpráva o . . . samostatne schůzi Sněmovny lidu : . . . volebni obdobi. [Minutes of the . . . session of the Assembly]. (1990?-1993) Prague: Kancelář České Národní rady.

Zpráva o schůzi Sněmovny lidu a Sněmovny Národů [Minutes of the joint sessions of the People's Assembly and the Assembly of Nations]. (1970–1990) Prague: Kancelář České Národní rady.

Zpráva o schůzi Sněmovny lidu [Minutes of the sessions of People's Assembly]. (1969–1990) Prague: Kancelář České Národní rady.

Zpráva o schůzi Sněmovny Národů [Minutes of the sessions of the Assembly of Nations]. (1969–1990) Prague: Kancelář České Národní rady.

CHAPTER NINE

Denmark

PETER BLUME

Introduction to the legal system

Early Danish Law was based on regional laws and until the 17th century there was no legal unity. The most important regional law was the Law of Jutland 1241 [*Jyske Lov*] which in its preface states several general principles of law. This preface is often viewed as the first constitution.

Danish law has never been deeply influenced by Roman law and after the Reformation 1536 when Lutheran doctrine was acknowledged, a new legal development started, independent of church influence. In 1660 absolute rule was instigated and in the Royal Act of 1661 the basic rules of the king's government were stated. Legal unity was mainly promoted through the Danish Code of 1683 [*Danske Lov*] which is the first European codification in a national language. The Code which was renowned as a masterpiece of legislation and of which a few sections are still in force today was the basic lawbook until the second half of the 19th century.

Danish law mainly developed through supplementary royal decrees and the decisions of the courts. In 1661 the Supreme Court was established and in 1736 a law degree was introduced at the University of Copenhagen. From the end of the 18th century professional jurists in general acted as judges and occupied the leading positions in public administration. In a decree of 26 January 1821 it was stated that certain positions presupposed a law degree. Today only the position of judge and the right to act as a lawyer are reserved for people with a law degree.

A major development was the first free Constitution of 5 June 1849 [*Danmarks Riges Grundlov*] when a democratic mode of government was introduced. In the first years after the Constitution the king still maintained a fairly strong position and it was not until 1901 that the principle of cabinet responsibility was recognized. The Constitution has only been amended a few times since 1849, most recently in 1953. This is because the amendment conditions outlined in section 88 are very demanding, including a general election and a referendum. In the Constitution the basic formal rules concerning parliament, the courts and public administration are stated at the same time as the traditional human rights are protected.

The present Constitution, [*Danmarks Riges Grundlov*], is Law no.169 of 5 June 1953. Together with all the previous constitutional laws from the Royal Law of 1665 it can be found in *Dansk Forfatningslove, 1665–1953* (Himmelstrup and Møller, 1958). An official translation of the 1953 Constitution together with the Danish text, an extensive chronology and a bibliography appear in Henry and Miller (1985). A leading treatise on constitutional law is *Dansk forfatningsret* by Zahle (1995–96).

In 1972 Denmark became a member of the European Union and since then Danish law has been strongly influenced by EU law both with respect to EU legislation and decisions from the European Court of Justice. The extensive character of EU legislation creates many problems for the enactment of national laws and for the ability of parliament to control government. A special committee in parliament discusses all future EU legislation and determines which position the government shall take in negotiations, but the extent of the proposed legislation rarely makes in-depth consideration possible. In this connection it is important to mention that a Danish government normally only represents a minority of the parties represented in parliament and accordingly each piece of legislation has to be discussed with other parties. This fact has a major practical impact on the legislation process and the development of Danish law in general.

Introductory works on the legal system and legal research

An introduction to and general survey of the basic principles of Danish law written in English is given in *Danish law in the European perspective* (Dahl, 1996). A dated work but still of some use is *Danish law: a general survey*, a comprehensive collection of essays (Gammeltoft-Hansen, Gomard and Philip, 1982). More dated is the concise introduction in the *International encyclopedia of comparative law* (Koktvedgaard, 1972). There are no other introductory works except in Danish where the following should be mentioned. In Dübeck (1994) the basic rules of Danish law are described. A similar book by Peter Blume (1995) is focused on the legal fields taught within the compulsory part of the law curriculum. Retrieval of legal information both in printed and electronic form is described in *Juridisk Informationssøgning* (Blume, 1997).

Legislation

Lovtidende and *Ministerialtidende*, the Official Gazettes

Acts of Parliament are promulgated in *Lovtidende for Kongeriget Danmark* (1871–) generally known as *Lovtidende*, the Official Gazette, which is published by the Ministry of Justice every Tuesday and Friday and if necessary more frequently. Publication in the Gazette is legally necessary for the application of an act (section 22 of the Constitution and the Gazette Act, consolidated no.842 of 16 December 1991). Statutes normally come into force eight days after their publication unless an earlier or later date has been stated. There is no prohibition in Danish law against legislation with retroactive force and such rules occur in particular within tax law.

Acts are published in *Lovtidende* section A. Consolidated acts providing an up-to-date text incorporating all amendments are also published here and it should be mentioned that most acts are frequently consolidated. The ministry responsible for the act makes the consolidation. Statutory instruments are also published in section A of the Gazette. It is possible by royal decree to exempt certain instruments from publication in the Gazette and a list of exempted instruments indicating where they can be obtained is printed once a year as part of the index to the Gazette.

Every three months an index to the Gazette section A is issued and a consolidated index is issued each year. In the index acts and other instruments can be retrieved both chronologically and by subject.

Section B of the Gazette, normally published twice a year, contains fiscal acts, mainly the state budget. Section C contains treaties and international agreements (see below).

Administrative circulars and guidances, such as statements of practice and interpretation, are published in *Ministerialtidende for Kongeriget Danmark* (1798–) generally known as *Ministerialtidende*, the administrative gazette, published normally once a week. Not all circulars and guidances are published; a selection is made with the purpose that only rules of legal or general interest appear. Every three months an index is issued and a consolidated index is published each year. There is a systematic subject as well as a chronological index.

The indexes of the two gazettes are only useful if it is known in which year the rules have been published.

Indexing services for the gazettes

There are two main commercially published indexes covering current legislation which are both used by many lawyers. First, *Dansk Lovregister*, published annually with a systematic index to all current (published) acts, statutory instruments and circulars/guidances. Thirty-two main subject groups are used and in addition there is an extensive list of individual subjects, useful to locate the relevant main group. Second, *Lovnøglen*, a looseleaf service, updated four times per year, covering all legislation including those rules not published in the gazettes. This index provides information on legislative history and is the best if it is necessary to trace amendment acts.

Karnovs Lovsamling

However, the essential source to current legislation, used by all lawyers, is *Karnovs Lovsamling* (1995–) which is an annotated compilation of all current acts (except fiscal statutes) and the main statutory instruments, printed in full text. Each act is annotated in great detail. References are given to preparatory material, including parliamentary proceedings, judicial and administrative decisions and legal literature. Furthermore, advice as to how the single sections should be interpreted is included in the annotation. *Karnov* is very thoroughly indexed: there is an alphabetical index, a chronological index, and most usefully a very detailed systematic index with references to the individual sections of the different acts and instruments. *Karnov* is updated each month by a supplementary booklet and every year a volume containing all new and amended legislation is published. A new edition of the whole work is issued every four years and it is also available on CD-ROM (see below). *Karnov* is an outstanding work and the basic reference tool to current Danish legislation.

Citation

All acts, statutory instruments, and circulars/guidances published in the gazettes are given a number, sequentially on publication. It should be noticed that the number of a bill and of the enacted statute are not the same. The normal citation is number and date, e.g. Lov 395 of 14 June 1995 on copyright. If there is a consolidated act it is normal practice to cite this act and not the original statute or the single amendment acts.

Legislative history

In Danish legal theory preparatory material to acts of parliament is recognized as an important legal source. Courts and other decision-making bodies often refer to preparatory material when interpreting statutory rules.

Comprehensive or complex new legislation is often prepared in committees and their results and suggestions are published in reports which are normally printed in serial order. These reports can be obtained from the official publishers, Schultz Information A/S. In the bibliography *Danske Kommissionsbetænkninger* (Svennevig, 1972–1992) currently in five volumes covering 1859–1990, all reports are listed systematically by subject. There is an extensive index, making it quite easily possible to locate a report. As for new reports the journal *Status* can be used (see below).

Proceedings of parliament are documented in *Folketingstidende* (1953–), the parliamentary gazette. The gazette was originally entitled *Rigsdagstidende* (1849–1953) but changed its name in connection with a constitutional reform in 1953. *Folketingstidende* consists of different sections covering the debates, proposed bills, committee reports and the enacted legislation. Of legal interest in particular is section A containing bills and section B with reports from the different committees of parliament (see also below).

Until the session 1986–87 there were two reference works to *Folketingstidende*; these were special parts of the Gazette: Oversigtsbindet and Folketingets Årbog. From session 1986–87 these two have been merged into *Årbog og Registre til Folketingstidende* which covers one parliamentary session (October–June). In this part of the gazette there are several lists, including both voted bills and those bills that have not been passed. There are two indexes systematically arranged for each ministry and for each bill. It is also possible to find proceedings on a bill by using the number of the promulgated act.

However, it is not always clear in which session a certain act has been debated. The best way to locate proceedings is accordingly via the annotation to the act in *Karnovs Lovsamling*.

Besides *Folketingstidende*, the parliamentary gazette, there is a looseleaf service entitled *Spørgsmål og Svar fra Folketingets udvalg* containing questions to and answers from ministers, raised during the deliberations in the committees. There are no indexes to this vast material, but using the number of the bill it is possible to retrieve relevant data quite easily.

Codes and commentaries

In Danish law there is no tradition of compiling legislation in codes as, for example, in French law. The basic statutes mentioned below function as codes.

Two acts are the basic private law codes in Danish law. The law of contracts [*Lov om aftaler og andre retshandler på formuerettens område*] was enacted in 1917. The current consolidated act is no.600 of 8 June 1986. There is one basic commentary, *Aftaleloven*, by Andersen and Nørgaard (1993). The *Lov om køb* [Sale of Goods Act] was enacted in 1906 and the current consolidated act is no.28 of 21 January 1980. The basic commentary is *Købeloven* by Nørager-Nielsen and Theilgaard (1993).

Two books in English may be mentioned in passing here: *Corporations and partnerships in Denmark* (Ebeling and Gomard, 1993) and *Danish insurance law* (Lyngsø, 1992).

Within public law the basic acts are *Forvaltningsloven* [the Administration Act] no.571 of 19 December 1985 with the commentary by Vogter (1992a), and *Lov om offentlighed i forvaltningen* [the Publicity Act] no.572 of 19 December 1985, with the commentary *Offentlighedsloven* (Vogter, 1992b).

The *Retsplejeloven* [Administration of Justice Act] was originally enacted in 1916 and the current consolidated act is no.905 of 10 November 1992. An extensive commentary is given by Gomard and Møller (1994). The *Straffeloven* [Penal Code] was enacted in 1930 and the current consolidated act is no.886 of 30 October 1992; there is an English translation, *The Danish criminal code* (Spencer and Høyer, 1987). The commentary is in two works by Greve, in 1993 and 1994.

Treaties

Treaty-making power is vested in the parliament and ratified treaties are published in *Lovtidende* section C which has been published since 1936. Before that date ratified treaties can be found in the work *Danmarks traktater og aftaler med fremmede magter 1814–1935* (1918–1951). The Ministry of Foreign Affairs maintains a register of ratification.

Law reports, judgments

Danish legal theory recognizes precedents as a legal source in the determination of current law. The main legal source is however statutory law and the importance of precedents is widely divergent within the different fields of law. It is in particular the decisions of the Supreme Court that can determine the outcome of future similar cases. In this respect it should be noticed that Danish courts traditionally only offer fairly brief arguments for their decisions.

The Danish judicial system consists of the *Højesteret* [Supreme Court], two high courts: *Østre og Vestre Landsret*, the *Sø- og Handelsretten* [maritime and commercial court] and the *byretterne* [lower courts]. The vast majority of cases is decided in the lower courts.

There is only one general series of law reports, *Ugeskrift for Retsvæsen* (1867–) which is issued every week. *Ugeskrift for Retsvæsen* publishes in section A all supreme court decisions, a selection (approximately 20 per cent) of high court and maritime and commercial court decisions while no cases decided in the lower courts are included.

However, reports of cases decided in the higher courts also include the decisions of the previous courts. Each reported case is published with an abstract written by the editors who are acting judges. Cases are normally reported approximately six months after they have been decided. There is no standard procedure for obtaining more recent cases or unreported cases. Such cases are registered by the individual courts and can be accessed if a legal interest in the particular case can be documented (section 41 of the Administration of Justice Act).

The annual edition of *Ugeskrift for Retsvæsen* has two indexes. First, there is a subject index which consists of 40 main topics subdivided into special topics; a new improved subject index was introduced in 1988 to coincide with the CD-ROM version (see below). Second, there is an index where cases can be retrieved with respect to the statutory rule under consideration. Every five years the index is consolidated for civil cases and a special book, *Realregister*, is published; criminal cases are covered in the same way by consolidated indexes, *Systematisk oversigt over domme i kriminelle sager.*

There are a few special journals reporting cases within individual fields of law. All cases within tax law are reported in *Tidsskrift for skatter og afgifter* (1994–) and the decisions of the labour courts are reported in *Arbejdsretligt Tidsskrift* (1980–). It should also be mentioned that the associations of judges issue a looseleaf service, *Domsoversigter*, with cases from selected areas.

In general *Ugeskrift for Retsvæsen* is, as mentioned, the only series of law reports and the normal mode of citation is the reference to this journal, e.g. U.1992 p. 762H (the 'H' refers to *Højesteret* and indicates it is a Supreme Court decision).

In many areas of law administrative decisions play an important role in the determination of current law. This is because there are only few judicial decisions. There is no common publication of these decisions but several administrative bodies issue annual reports in which they publish their most important decisions. Each year the Royal Library publishes *Impressa Publica Regni Danici* (1949–), a catalogue of official publications, in which it is possible to discover if a certain authority published a report. This work is fairly easy to use as publications are listed for each ministry.

Some administrative decisions are also published as circulars in *Ministerialtidende* (see above). According to the Gazette Act these should be decisions which have an interest for the general public. It is doubtful to what extent such decisions are actually published in the gazette but there has been an increase in the volume of published decisions in recent years.

With respect to administrative law an especially important work is the *Folketingets Ombundsmands Beretning* [annual report of the Parliamentary Ombudsman] which has been published since 1955. The reported cases are very extensively documented. Although the

Ombudsman cannot decide cases but only state his opinion, the reported cases are considered a basic source of administrative law. In each report there is an index which also covers previous reports. A new indexing system was started in 1989 implying that the index of report 1988 covers the reports back to 1955 and that the last published report covers the reports from 1989.

Computer-based systems

The primary legal sources are also accessible electronically. In 1985 the Ministry of Justice started the online database, RETSINFORMATION, which from 1989 has contained all current Danish legislation in full text. This means that all Acts, all statutory instruments (including also those which are not printed in *Lovtidende*), and all circulars (including those not printed in *Ministerialtidende*) can be retrieved in RETSINFORMATION. A special feature is that Acts which are not consolidated in the Gazette are consolidated in the database. This is accordingly the most comprehensive documentation of Danish legislation.

Legislation is located in separate databases according to which ministry is responsible but it is possible to retrieve them by using general search commands covering all the sub-databases. It is possible to retrieve information using free text or by use of designated keywords. The information is updated constantly. Acts can be retrieved as soon as they appear in the Official Gazette, and instruments and circulars shortly after they have been issued.

Use of RETSINFORMATION has been considered difficult by lawyers and the system has not been a great success, but from the beginning of 1996 a new more user-friendly interface has been introduced. It is likely that the system will be used more frequently in the future. This is also because the system of payment has been changed from a search-time fee system to an annual payment of DKr6150 (approximately £500) at the time of writing.

In RETSINFORMATION proceedings of parliament dating back to the session 1983–84 can also be retrieved in full text. The proceedings are updated each day and can normally be retrieved a few hours after the actual debate. Administrative decisions can also be retrieved in RETSINFORMATION. RETSINFORMATION also hosts commercial databases and today there is a database consisting of tax legislation and cases.

While RETSINFORMATION is the only online database there are several commercial CD-ROM systems available. *Ugeskrift for Retsvæsen* from 1960 is published on CD-ROM under the name JURIDISC and is updated every three months. The system initially costs DKr12 000 (approximately £1100) and there is an annual fee of DKr3000 (approximately £250) for a one-user licence. The CD-ROM does not contain more cases than reported in the printed edition and the newest reported cases are accordingly in the printed version. However, use of free text retrieval means that cases of interest can be more quickly and precisely retrieved in the electronic version.

Karnovs Lovsamling is also issued as CD-ROM updated twice a year. The system initially costs DKr9000 (approximately £750) and DKr6000 (approximately £500) for the annual fee.

The search system of these two CD-ROMs and the electronic editions of the leading commentaries (see under **Codes and commentaries** above) is the same so that it is very easy to combine the systems. A statutory rule mentioned in a court decision can be quickly studied in the commentary or in Karnov.

The official presence on the Internet, the Statens Datanet provided by the Danish State Information Service (address below), is at http://www.sdn.dk which contains government information, addresses of ministries and related organizations and some official documents in Danish with some English content which is increasing.

Encyclopedias

There is no general law encyclopedia in Denmark.

Directories

In *Labor Kontor Dagbog*, published annually, there is a list of all practising lawyers with their addresses, phone and fax numbers. In the same work there are lists of the courts, the prosecution and the police authorities. In *Ministeriernes Telefonbog*, issued once a year, there are lists of all ministries with phone numbers for all departments and the employees. *Kommunal Håndbog* provides a list with addresses and phone numbers of all the municipalities.

In the work *Dansk Juridisk Stat*, most recently published in 1995, there are biographical notes for all living persons with a Danish law degree.

Bibliographies and indexing services

Danish legal literature is well documented. Older literature from 1900 to 1949 can be found in *Juridiske litteraturhenvisninger* by Lund (1950). Literature after 1950 can be retrieved in *Dansk Juridisk Bibliografi*, produced at the Royal Library under the editorship of Jens Søndergaard, whose four printed volumes cover the period 1950–1987 (Søndergaard, 1973–1990). A fifth volume edited by Lotte Jacobsen covers 1988–89. The works include both monographs and articles in journals and can be searched both under authors and subjects. The newest literature is not covered by a printed bibliography as *Dansk Juridisk Bibliografi* is now only available as one of the databases included on the MAGNUS CD-ROM available from Skattekartoteket, appearing as two files: 1981–1987 and 1988–.

In the first four volumes of *Dansk Juridisk Bibliografi* covering 1950–87 publications in English, French and German on Danish law, including translations of Danish legislation, are listed in a separate section of each volume. Lists covering such works for the periods 1920–62 (Søndergaard, 1963) and 1963–74 (Søndergaard, 1976) are published in *Scandinavian Studies in Law*.

Dictionaries

In *Juridisk Ordbog* (von Eyben, 1987) legal terms are explained. A multilingual legal dictionary does not exist.

Current information sources

Journals

The main law journals are the following:

Juristen (1919–). This journal contains articles concerning all fields of law but with emphasis on public law. A special feature is that significant new legislation is often described in articles written by civil servants from the responsible ministry.

Ugeskrift for Retsvæsen, Section B (1867–). This part of the series of law reports (see above under **Law reports, judgments**) contains articles on a varied number of legal subjects with some emphasis on private and procedural law. A special feature is that important new Supreme Court decisions are commented on by one of the participating judges. It should also be mentioned that new books are frequently briefly reviewed.

Advokaten (1922–). This is the journal of the association of advocates containing articles dealing with practical legal subjects and new legislation of particular interest for practising lawyers.

Tidsskrift for Rettsvitenskap (1888–). This is a Nordic journal containing mainly scholarly articles, normally of high standard.

News information

The best source for information about new proposed legislation, new legislation itself and new reports from public bodies is the journal *Status*, produced by Statens Information [Danish State Information Service] and issued every second week. In this journal developments are briefly described and it is indicated where further information can be obtained. *Status* (1983–96) is also available on the MAGNUS CD-ROM.

In *DJØF-bladet*, the monthly journal of the lawyers' association, developments of legal interest are described and legal policy issues are debated.

Business and financial information

The Erhvervsministeriet [Ministry of Commerce] has the main responsibility for legislation with respect to private business and finance (see below). Denmark has very well-developed public files in this respect. Information on all companies can be retrieved in Det Centrale Virksomhedsregister [Central Business Register] (Act no.417 of 22 May 1996), and information on limited companies in the online database of Erhvervs-og Selskabsstyrelsen [Danish Commerce and Companies Agency] according to the rules in Statutory Instrument no.98 of 4 March 1993. Financial transactions are supervised by Finanstilsynet [Danish Financial Supervisory Authority].

Statistics

Main statistical information of relevance to both law and general business is published in the *Statistical yearbook*, published by Danmarks Statistik [Statistics Denmark]. In the yearbook and as a separate work crime statistics are published containing information on convictions, etc. In the section, Social Security and Justice, the number of cases disposed in the courts is given. Some statistical information is provided in the *Politiets Årsberetning* [Police Annual Report] including the number of convictions with respect to the Penal Code and the Traffic Code.

Useful addresses

Associations of lawyers

Advokatsamfundet [Association of Advocates], Kronprinsessegade 28, DK 1306 København K, Denmark. Tel: +45 33 96 97 98. Fax: +45 33 32 18 31

DJØF [Association of Danish Lawyers and Economists], Gothersgade 133, DK 1123 København K, Denmark. Tel: +45 33 95 97 99. Fax: +45 33 95 99 99

Government organizations

Det Centrale Virksomhedsregister [Central Business Register], Sejrøgade 11, DK 2100 København Ø, Denmark. Tel: +45 39 17 31 20. Fax: +45 31 18 48 01

Danmarks Statistik [Statistics Denmark], Sejrøgade 11, DK 2100 København Ø, Denmark. Tel: +45 39 17 39 17. Fax: +45 31 18 48 01

Erhvervs-og Selskabsstyrelsen [Danish Commerce and Companies Agency], Kampmannsgade 1, DK 1604 København V, Denmark. Tel: +45 33 12 42 80. Fax: +45 33 32 44 80

Erhvervsministeriet [Ministry of Commerce], Slotsholmsgade 12, DK 1216 København K, Denmark. Tel: +45 33 92 33 50. Fax: +45 33 12 37 78

Finanstilsynet [Danish Financial Supervisory Authority], Gammel Kongevej 74 A, DK 1850 Frederiksberg C, Denmark. Tel: +45 33 55 82 82. Fax: +45 33 55 82 00

Justitsministeriet [Ministry of Justice], Slotsholmsgade 10, DK 1216 København K, Denmark. Tel: +45 33 92 33 40. Fax: +45 33 93 35 10

Sekretariatet for Retsinformation [Legal Information Secretariat], Vægtergaarden, Axeltorv 6, 5., DK 1609 København V, Denmark. Tel: +45 33 32 52 22. Fax: +45 33 91 28 01

Statens Information [Danish State Information Service], Nørre Farimagsgade 65, DK 1364 København K, Denmark. Tel: +45 33 37 92 00. Fax: +45 33 37 92 99. E-mail: si@si.dk Internet: http://www.sdn.dk

Udenrigsministeriet [Royal Danish Ministry of Foreign Affairs], Asiatisk Plads 2, DK 1448 København K, Denmark. Tel: +45 33 92 00 00. Fax: +45 31 54 05 33

Courts

Højesteret [Supreme Court], Prins Jørgens Gaard 13, DK 1218 København K, Denmark. Tel: +45 33 15 66 50. Fax: +45 33 15 00 10

Østre Landsret [High Court East], Bredgade 59, DK 1260 København K, Denmark. Tel: +45 33 97 02 00. Fax: +45 33 14 58 22

Sø- og Handelsretten i København [Maritime and Commercial Court], Bredgade 70, DK 1260 København K, Denmark. Tel: +45 33 47 92 22. Fax: +45 33 14 56 77

Vestre Landsret [High Court West], Gråbrødre Kirkestræde 3, DK 8800 Viborg, Denmark. Tel: +45 86 62 62 00. Fax: +45 86 62 63 65

Education, training and research institutions

Juridisk Institut, Aarhus Universitet [Legal Institute, University of Aarhus], Bygn. 430, DK 8000 Århus C, Denmark. Tel: +45 89 42 11 33. Fax: +45 86 20 27 21

Juridisk Institut, Handelshøjskolen i København [Legal Institute, Copenhagen Business School], Nansensgade 19, 2., DK 2200 København N, Denmark. Tel: +45 38 15 26 26. Fax: +45 38 15 26 10

Det juridiske Fakultet, Københavns Universitet [Faculty of Law, University of Copenhagen], Store Kannikestræde 11, 1., DK 1169 København K, Denmark. Tel: +45 35 32 32 22. Fax: +45 35 32 35 86. E-mail: pia@adm.ku.dk

Libraries

Juridisk Institutbibliotek [Law Library, University of Copenhagen], Studiegården, Studiestræde 6, DK 1455 København K, Denmark. Tel: +45 35 32 31 30. Fax: +45 35 32 32 03

Det kongelige Bibliotek [Royal Library], Slotsholmen, P.O. Box 2149, DK 1016 København K, Denmark. Tel: +45 33 93 01 11. Fax: +45 33 93 22 18

Publishers and booksellers

DJØF Forlag [Association of Danish Lawyers and Economists, Publishers], Gothersgade 133, DK 1123 København K, Denmark. Tel: +45 33 95 97 99. Fax: +45 33 95 99 99

Gad Jura [Gad Legal Publishers], Nytorv 19, DK 1450 København K, Denmark. Tel: +45 33 12 16 33. Fax: +45 33 12 16 36

Schultz Information A/S [Government Publishers: Schultz], Herstedvang 14, DK 2620 Albertslund, Denmark. Tel: +45 43 63 23 00. Fax: +45 43 63 19 49

Skattekartoteket A/S, Palægade 4, DK 1261 København K, Denmark. Tel: +45 33 11 04 31. Fax: +43 33 93 80 09

List of works cited

Advokaten. (1922–) Copenhagen: Advokatsamfundet.

Andersen, Lennart Lynge and Nørgaard, Jørgen (1993) *Aftaleloven* 2nd edn. Copenhagen: DJØF Forlag.

Arbejdsretligt Tidsskrift. (1980–) Copenhagen: DJØF Forlag.

Blume, Peter (1995) (ed.) *Introduktion til Jura*. Copenhagen: Akademisk Forlag.

Blume, Peter (1997) *Juridisk Informationssøgning* 5th edn. Copenhagen: Akademisk Forlag.

Dahl, Børge (1996) (ed.) *Danish law in the European perspective*. Copenhagen: Gad Jura.

Danmarks Statistik (1995) *Statistical yearbook*. Copenhagen: Danmarks Statistik.

Danmarks traktater og aftaler med fremmede magter 1814–1935. (1918–1951) Copenhagen: Nordisk Forlag.

Dansk Juridisk Stat. (1995) Copenhagen: DJØF Forlag.

Dansk Lovregister. (1928–) Copenhagen: Gad Jura.

DJØF-bladet. (1982–) Copenhagen: DJØF Forlag. Monthly.

Domsoversigter. (1979–) Copenhagen: DJØF Forlag. Looseleaf.

Dübeck, Inger (1994) *Introduktion til dansk ret*. Baden-Baden: Nomos Verlagsgesellschaft.

Ebeling, Mogens and Gomard, Bernhard (1993) *Corporations and partnerships in Denmark*. Deventer: Kluwer Law and Taxation.

Folketingets Ombundsmand. [Parliamentary Ombudsman]. (1955–) *Beretning* [annual report]. Copenhagen: Schultz.

Folketingstidende. (1953–) Copenhagen: Schultz. Originally entitled *Rigsdagstidende* (1849–1952).

Gammeltoft-Hansen, Hans, Gomard, Bernhard and Philip, Allan (1982) (eds) *Danish law: a general survey*. Copenhagen: G.E.C. Gads.

Gomard, Bernhard and Møller, Jens (1994) *Retsplejeloven* 5th edn. Copenhagen: DJØF Forlag.

Greve, Vagn (1993) *Straffelovens Almindelige Del* 5th edn. Copenhagen: DJØF Forlag.

Greve, Vagn (1994) *Straffelovens Specielle Del* 5th edn. Copenhagen: DJØF Forlag.

Henry, Roxanne E. and Miller, Kenneth E. (1985) Denmark including Greenland and the Faroes. In *Constitutions of the countries of the world*, ed. A.P. Blaustein and G.H. Flanz, vol.V. Dobbs Ferry, NY: Oceana.

Himmelstrup, Jens and Møller, Jens (1958) *Dansk Forfatningslove, 1665–1953*. Copenhagen: Schultz.

Impressa Publica Regni Danici. (1949–) Copenhagen: Royal Library of Denmark.

Jacobsen, Lotte. See Søndergaard, Jens (1973–1990).

JURIDISC (available from Gad Jura).

Juristen. (1919–) Copenhagen: DJØF Forlag. Entitled *Juristen og Oekonomen* 1974–1981.

Karnovs Lovsamling. (1995–) 14th edn. Copenhagen: Karnov. Updated by supplements. First edition published 1924.

Koktvedgaard, Mogens (1972) Denmark. In *International encyclopedia of comparative law*, ed. V. Knapp, vol.1, pp. D23–D35. Tübingen: J.C.B. Mohr.

Kommunal Håndbog. (1970–) Copenhagen: Mostrup.

Labor Kontor Dagbog. (1928–) Copenhagen: Wrollenski. Annual.

Lovnøglen. (1977–) Copenhagen: Schultz. Looseleaf.

Lovtidende for Kongeriget Danmark. (1871–) Copenhagen: Schultz.

Lund, Torben (1950) *Juridiske litteraturhenvisninger*. Copenhagen: Nyt Nordisk Forlag. Covers 1900–1949.

Lyngsø, Preben (1992) *Danish insurance law*. Deventer: Kluwer Law and Taxation.

MAGNUS (available from Skattekartoteket).

Ministerialtidende for Kongeriget Danmark. (1798–) Copenhagen: Schultz.

Ministeriernes Telefonbog. (1971–) Copenhagen: Schultz. Annual.

Nørager-Nielsen, Jacob and Theilgaard, Søren (1993) *Købeloven* 2nd edn. Copenhagen: Gad Jura.

Politiets Årsberetning [Police annual report]. (1995) Copenhagen: Rigspolitichefen.

Realregister. (1877–) Copenhagen: Gad Jura. Every five years.

RETSINFORMATION (available from the Ministry of Justice).

Søndergaard, Jens (1963) Danish legal publications in English, French and German. *Scandinavian Studies in Law*, **7**, 167–254. Covers 1920–1962. Reprinted as a booklet by Almqvist & Wiksell International, Stockholm.

Søndergaard, Jens (1976) Danish legal publications in English, French and German 1963–74. *Scandinavian Studies in Law*, **20**, 267–337. Reprinted as a booklet by Almqvist & Wiksell, Stockholm.

Søndergaard, Jens (1973–1990) *Dansk Juridisk Bibliografi*. Copenhagen: DJØF Forlag. 5 vols covering 1950–1989: 1950–71, 1972–1980, 1981–84, 1985–87, 1988–89. Continued on CD-ROM. 1988–89 volume edited by Lotte Jacobsen.

Spencer, Martin and Høyer, Gitte (1987) The Danish criminal code. (Kriminalistisk Institut Series, no.39) Copenhagen: Kriminalistisk Institut.

Spørgsmål og Svar fra Folketingets udvalg. (1984–) Copenhagen: Schultz. Looseleaf.

Status. (1983–) Copenhagen: Statens Information. Every two weeks.

Svennevig, Palle (1972–1992) *Danske Kommissionsbetænkninger 1850–1990*. Vols.1–4: Copenhagen: Folketingets Bibliotek. Vol.5: Århus: Statsbiblioteket.

Systematisk oversigt over domme i kriminelle sager. (1976–) Copenhagen: Gad Jura. Every five years.

Tidsskrift for Rettsvitenskap. (1888–) Oslo: Scandinavian University Press.

Tidsskrift for skatter og afgifter. (1994–) Copenhagen: Skattekartoteket.

Ugeskrift for Retsvæsen. (1867–) Copenhagen: Gad Jura. Section A contains law reports, section B contains scholarly articles.

Vogter, John (1992a) *Forvaltningsloven*. Copenhagen: DJØF Forlag.

Vogter, John (1992b) *Offentlighedsloven*. Copenhagen: DJØF Forlag.

von Eyben, W.E. (1987) *Juridisk Ordbog* 7th edn. Copenhagen: Gad Jura.

Zahle, Henrik (1995–6) *Dansk forfatningsret* 2nd edn. Copenhagen: Christian Ejlers.

CHAPTER TEN

Finland

SAMI SARVILINNA

Introduction to the legal system

The legal system of Finland is characterized by its long history as a part of the Kingdom of Sweden, dating from the 13th and 14th centuries. The Swedish legislation in force at the time when Finland was ceded to the Russian Empire in the early 19th century continued to be applied in the new political situation, and a small part of that legislation is in force even now. During Russian rule, the status of Finland as an autonomous Grand Duchy allowed also for legislative self-determination, with the result that Western influences, especially from Germany, play a much larger role than the Eastern ones in Finnish legal history.

As a matter of historical interest, one should note that it was only in the early 20th century that legislation which was to be applied in Finland was also drafted in Finnish. Swedish was for centuries the language of the educated classes and of the administration. Even today Finland is officially a bilingual country where all official documents are available in both languages. In addition, the documents directly concerning the Sámi minority in the north of Finland must be available in the Sámi language as well. In this chapter the titles of most publications are given in both language versions, first in Finnish and then in Swedish; an English translation of a title is provided in parentheses.

Independence, in 1917, brought about the need for Finland's own constitution. The constitutional provisions have since the beginning been divided into four separate documents, the *Suomen hallitusmuoto/ Regeringsform för Finland* [Finnish Constitution Act], the *Valtiopäiväjärjestys/ Riksdagsordning* [Parliament Act], the *Ministerivastuulaki/Minister-ansvarighetslagen* [Ministerial Responsibility Act] and the *Laki valtakunnanoikeudesta/Lag om riksrätten* [Act on the High Court of Impeachment].

The latest published English translation of these constitutional texts, an official translation published by the Finnish Parliament, the Foreign Ministry and the Ministry of Justice (*Constitutional laws of Finland & procedure of Parliament*, 1996) is up to date at the time of writing. The official Finnish text and an unofficial English translation appear in Scheinin (1996), which includes the constitutional amendments relating to the accession of Finland to the European Union and the recent basic right reform. A new reform project was set up in 1995 to revise thoroughly the constitutional legislation and to produce a draft for a single constitutional act incorporating all of it. The deadline set for the project is the year 2000.

A special case is the autonomous province of Åland. Åland's right of self-determination has been laid down in the *Ahvenanmaan itsehallintolaki/Självstyrelselag för Åland* [Act on the Autonomy of Åland] which is considered to have the same legal status as the constitutional acts mentioned above, even if it is not formally a part of the Finnish Constitution. The Åland authorities have published the Act as a translation into English and German, *Act on the autonomy of Åland* (Åland Legislative Assembly and the Government of Åland, 1993).

Since the beginning of 1995 Finland has been a member of the European Union.

Introductory works on the legal system and legal research

The basic introductory work on the Finnish legal system is the *Johdatus Suomen oikeusjärjestelmään/Inledning till Finlands rättsordning* which appears in two volumes (Timonen, 1996a–d). It is the set book for the entrance examinations in Finnish law schools and new editions of it appear at commendable intervals. An English equivalent, *An introduction to Finnish law* (Pöyhönen, 1993), is also available. This extensive collection of essays is not identical to Timonen's book as the aim has been to concentrate on subjects considered to be of topical interest to foreign readers. An earlier collection of essays in English is dated but may be available to foreign readers, *The Finnish legal system* (Uotila, 1985). A briefer general overview by the same author, *The legal system of Finland* can be found as a chapter in the *Modern legal system cyclopedia* (Uotila, 1989). A short article *Sources of legal information in Finland* describes a selection of legal literature and databases (Tolvanen, 1994).

Legislation

Finland has a statutory law system. There is a hierarchy of statutes with the *laki/lag* [Act] enacted by parliament on the highest level. Acts need to be ratified by the president of the republic in order to enter into force. The date of the entry into force of an Act is usually specified therein. The president is competent to issue lower level statutes, called *asetus/förordning* [Decree] for the implementation of Acts. Also a number of other authorities have been empowered to issue lower level regulations in their own administrative fields.

The only official publication channel for all Finnish legislation, from constitutional amendments, regular parliamentary Acts and presidential Decrees to certain decisions of the Council of State, the Ministries and some other authorities, is the *Suomen säädöskokoelma* (1981–)/ *Finlands författningssamling* (1860–) [The Statutes of Finland] published by Edita Oy. It is first available in leaflet format, with new leaflets coming out almost daily, and later as a bound volume. It should be noted that the Finnish and the Swedish versions are two separate series, even though the format and the publication timetables are identical. Orders are accepted for both annual subscriptions and single leaflets. Monthly and annual indexes, both alphabetical and chronological, are also available. In addition to this general source, many Ministries have their own series for the publication of lower level regulations.

The established manner of amending legislation in Finland is to publish only the amendments with references as to which Act and which part thereof is affected. In some cases the current text can only be compiled by hand, adding amendment after amendment to the original version. This may result in some confusion especially with those pieces of legislation that have been amended dozens of times.

The most widely used solution to the problem of finding current versions of Finnish legislation is a commercial collection, the *Suomen laki/Finlands lag* [The Finnish law]. It is edited by prominent Finnish lawyers and published by the Finnish Lawyers' Publishing Co. This publication, which comes out annually in two volumes in Finnish and also in Swedish, contains the consolidated version of almost every Finnish statute that is of more general interest, together with references to the official publication and to relevant case law. It does not, however, include tax law, which is published as separate annual volumes, the *Verolait/Skatteförfattningarna.*

The *Suomen laki/Finlands lag* is arranged systematically by subject with each statute appearing under a general heading (for example, commercial law, criminal law) and bearing a signum (classification number) for easier cross-reference. The old system of headings and signums, from 1955, was completely reformed for the 1995 edition, but the publisher provides a booklet which contains a signum cross-index between it and the 1994 edition. The *Suomen laki/Finlands lag* is the de facto official source of Finnish law in virtually all circumstances, including the courts of law.

Legislation in translation

As regards the availability of Finnish legislation in other European languages, two projects merit a special mention.

First, the Finnish Ministry of the Environment has compiled a folder called *Finnish environmental legislation*, which contains fairly up-to-date English translations of the legislation in the ambit of that Ministry (Ministry of the Environment, 1992).

The other noteworthy translation project is the Ministry of Justice's *Translations of Finnish legislation*. This series, which comes out in the format of single booklets, covers those aspects of Finnish legislation that traditionally belong to the ambit of the Ministry of Justice. These include criminal and procedural law, basic civil law (for example, contract, property), administrative law, etc. Three to four new booklets are published annually, mainly in English, but occasionally also in German or Spanish. In August 1995 the series contained twenty English, four German and one Spanish title. Unfortunately some of the older publications in the series are already quite dated. Both the products of the Ministry for the Environment and the Ministry of Justice are available from Edita Oy. Other Finnish authorities also produce translations of the legislation pertinent to their operations, albeit somewhat more sporadically.

The Terminology Service of the Prime Minister's Office, whose primary task is to assist in problems relating to the translation of Finnish political and legal concepts into other languages, also has a considerable collection of translated legislation. The reliability or even the availability of any given translation cannot, unfortunately, be guaranteed.

Legislative history

Virtually all legislation enacted by the Finnish Parliament is based on Bills submitted to it by the government. A *hallituksen esitys/regeringens proposition*, as such Bills are called in Finnish and Swedish, contains a statement on the aims of the proposal, some comparative analysis and other relevant information, as well as a detailed explanation on each proposed provision. The Bills and the pertinent parliamentary committee reports, which are acknowledged as authoritative sources for purposes of interpretation, are published by Edita Oy. They are not available in foreign languages.

Preliminary drafting of legislation in the government is often conducted by committee. While the Committee reports [komiteanmietintö/

kommittébetänkande] are not available, for example, in English, they usually contain English summaries of the main points of the draft. The reports are available from Edita Oy. The reports are listed in an annual directory published by the Library of Parliament, *Valtion komiteanmietinnöt = Statens kommittébetänkanden* (1930–).

Codes

One should note that while a number of Finnish Acts, for historical reasons, still carry as a part of their titles the suffix *-kaari/-balk*, which is most often translated into English as 'code', Finland does not have codes in the sense the word is used in for example Germany or France.

Treaties

Treaty-making power is vested in parliament and the president of the republic. All treaties concluded by Finland are published in two dedicated series, the *Suomen säädöskokoelman sopimussarja/Finlands författningssamlings fördragsserie* [The Treaty series of the statutes of Finland] (1917–). For a foreign reader the publication format is quite convenient as the treaty texts are arranged side by side in different languages. Where appropriate, the most common practice is to print the English text along with the Finnish and the French along with the Swedish.

The Finnish Ministry for Foreign Affairs maintains a treaty register and from time to time publishes a printed catalogue of the treaties in force.

Law reports, judgments

The Supreme Court and the Supreme Administrative Court, as well as certain special courts, all publish their most significant decisions in yearbooks: *Korkeimman Oikeuden ratkaisuja/Avgöranden av Högsta domstolen* (1987–) and *Korkeimman hallinto-oikeuden vuosikirja/Högsta förvaltningsdomstolens årsbok* (1963–) respectively. Publication does not have an effect as regards the finality or the validity of the decisions, nor do the decisions constitute 'judge-made law'. They are merely authoritative interpretations of existing legislation and as such can be used as precedents in later trials of a similar nature. Multiyear indexes are available for each yearbook series. Reports and commentaries also appear in the major law journals and in particular in the frequent *Oikeuskehitys* (see below). As already noted, *Suomen laki/Finlands lag* contains references to relevant judgments.

Transcripts of the judgments of the lower courts are kept in the court in question.

Computer-based systems

FINLEX

The main online source for legal information in Finland is the FINLEX data bank. Its databases contain court decisions, current and repealed legislation, an index of legislative amendments, information on the legislative processes in parliament, treaties, references to legal literature, etc. The Ministry of Justice is responsible for the maintenance of the greater part of the data bank. Recent additions to the database array include information relating to the EEA and the accession of Finland to the European Union. The query language used with FINLEX online is Minttu v4.01, which can be switched to respond to English commands. Unfortunately for foreign readers, virtually the entire contents of the data bank are available only in Finnish and/or in Swedish. However, there have been some preliminary plans to make the legislation published in the Ministry of Justice translation series available also in FINLEX.

Some of the most significant FINLEX databases relating to Finnish legislation are FSLV (legislation in force, in Finnish), FLAG (legislation in force, in Swedish) and FSLH (index to the legislation in force). The contents of these databases correspond to *Suomen laki/Finlands lag*; they are not a comprehensive collection, but merely a selection of Finnish legislation. Updates are loaded at two-week intervals.

A comprehensive index of all Finnish legislation does exist in the database SMUR which is produced by Edita Oy, the official government publisher. SMUR is basically a list of the statutes published in *Suomen säädöskokoelma/Finlands författningssamling* with references to the subsequent amendments. It is intended to be used in conjunction with the paper edition of the series.

Furthermore, the Ministry for Foreign Affairs maintains a separate file within FINLEX on the treaties concluded by Finland. This database, FSOP, contains only the Finnish texts of the treaties, and therefore falls somewhat short of the convenience level of the paper edition of *Suomen säädöskokoelman sopimussarja/Finlands författningssamlings fördragsserie* with its multilingual format.

FINLEX also contains a number of case law databases. These include FKKO (the Supreme Court), FHDR (the Supreme Court, in Swedish), FKHO (the Supreme Administrative Court), FEIT (the European Court for Human Rights), FETS (the Court of Justice of the European Communities), as well as several special court databases. Unless otherwise indicated, the contents of these databases are available in the Finnish language only. Updates of, for example, FKKO and FKHO are loaded twice a month.

Other noteworthy databases in FINLEX are FVPA and FLEK, which contain references to the legislative processes in the Finnish Parliament; VIRA, which contains references to Finnish official publications; FBIF, the Finnish legal bibliography; and FOKI, a reference database on case commentaries in Finnish legal literature.

Other online systems

The Finnish state government has recently entered the Internet age. The Prime Minister's Office maintains an experimental WWW server with a multilingual home page (http://www.vn.fi), which contains information on political decision-making and current issues in the government. There are also links to the home pages of various ministries. It is to be assumed that the service will later expand so that practical legal information is also available.

The official government publisher, Edita Oy, also offers a WWW service (http://www.edita.fi). The service contains references to recent legislation and Bills, parliamentary and government journals, etc.

CD-ROMs

There are two competing CD-ROM products containing information on Finnish legislation in force. One is the SUOMEN LAKI CD-ROM, which is a computerized version of *Suomen laki/Finlands lag* [The Finnish law]. It includes the tax law collection of the Finnish Lawyers' Publishing Co, published separately in the paper version. The other is YRITYKSEN LAKIKANTA CD-ROM, published by Edita Oy and containing material edited from the various specialized legislative collections of that publisher. Both products have been released relatively recently and are currently available in the Finnish language only. The former is updated three times a year and the latter twice a year.

Other important government documents

For the purpose of dissemination of miscellaneous official information the government of Finland publishes the *Virallinen lehti/Officiella tidningen* [official gazette] (1917–). This bilingual (Finnish and Swedish in the same issue) gazette is published three times per week and contains, for example, references to newly enacted legislation and new Bills submitted to Parliament, public notices and advertisements for vacant posts in the civil service. Weekly journals of parliamentary and governmental affairs are published as supplements.

Encyclopedias

Until recent times Finland has lacked a definitive legal encyclopedia, even if some popular legal guidebooks in encyclopedia format have been available. The situation has now improved because the first volumes of a new work, the *Encyclopedia iuridica fennica*, have been completed. This Finnish-language encyclopedia is an ambitious effort to collect into one work all the permanent and fundamental aspects of the Finnish legal culture. The complete encyclopedia will include seven volumes, each of which is to provide a comprehensive insight to a field of law. The four volumes already out concern property and commercial law, land, water and environmental law, family and labour law, as well as criminal and procedural law.

Directories

The latest extensive handbook on State authorities and institutions, the *Valtion virastot ja laitokset*, was published in 1989 and is already somewhat out of date. Edita Oy publishes also the annual *Valtiokalenteri/ Statskalender* [State Almanac] and *Valtionhallinnon puhelinluettelo* [State Telephone Directory]; the latter especially can be deemed a useful tool in information work.

The Finnish Bar Association publishes an annual directory of its members, *Suomen asianajajaliiton toimistoluettelo = Finlands advokatförbunds byråförteckning*. In addition to the contact information, this bilingual (Finnish-Swedish) directory contains the Act governing the operations of advocates and the by-laws of the Bar Association. The Act has been published in English in the Ministry of Justice translation series; the by-laws are available in English in the office of the Bar Association.

Bibliographies

The *Bibliographia iuridica fennica* is no doubt the most useful source of references to Finnish legal literature, covering both books and articles in journals. The first five volumes, covering the years 1809 to 1981, were published by the Finnish Lawyers' Association, but the Library of Parliament has since then assumed the responsibility of editing and publishing the bibliography. From 1982 onwards it has been published annually. The similarity of the title with that of the *Encyclopedia iuridica fennica* does not imply any affiliation between the two works.

The bibliography covers legal literature published in Finland, as well as that published abroad, in so far as it concerns Finland or is written by

Finnish authors. It does not include government publications. As noted above, the bibliography is accessible also through FINLEX in the database FBIF.

Of particular interest to foreign readers is a special edition of the main bibliography titled *Bibliographia iuridica fennica: literature in foreign languages 1982–1992.*

The Library of Parliament produces an annual catalogue of Finnish official publications, *Valtion virallisjulkaisut = Statens officiella publikationer* (1961–); at the moment the catalogues cover the period 1859–1992.

Dictionaries

There are two legal dictionaries featuring both Finnish and English terminology. The more comprehensive of the two is the *Lakikielen sanakirja suomi-englanti* [Finnish–English Legal Dictionary] by Joutsen (1995). It includes also a reverse index (i.e. English–Finnish). The intention behind the work has been to provide a tool for the translation of Finnish legal concepts into English. As the legal system of Finland differs considerably from that of the Anglo-Saxon tradition, some compromises as to the accuracy and the brevity of the linguistic equivalents have been inevitable. The other dictionary is the *Suomi–englanti–suomi lakikielen perussanakirja* [Finnish–English–Finnish basic legal dictionary] by Eriksson (1995). This two-way work has, naturally, a somewhat more limited scope than that of Joutsen's dictionary.

The *English–Finnish general dictionary* (Hurme, Pesonen, and Syväoja, 1990) and the *Finnish–English general dictionary* (Hurme, Malin, and Syväoja, 1984), both published by WSOY, constitute the essential tool for more general purposes of translation between the two languages.

Current information sources

Journals

Almost every field of law in Finland is covered by one or more journals, but there is also a number of periodicals that are more general in orientation. The most essential of these include *Defensor legis* (1920–), which is published by the Finnish Bar Association; *Lakimies* (1903–); *Oikeus* (1972–) and *Tidskrift utgiven av Juridiska Föreningen i Finland* (1865–), abbreviated to *JFT*. The format of all of the above publications is similar: the main emphasis is on articles, but shorter notices, case commentaries and book reviews are also included. *JFT* is published in the Swedish language, while the others are in Finnish. Short summaries in English or German are sometimes provided.

News information

Lakimiesuutiset (1945–), the monthly newsletter of the Finnish Lawyers' Association, is a good source for current information in the legal field. It contains material both in Finnish and in Swedish, with occasional English articles included.

In September 1995 the Finnish Lawyers' Publishing Co. launched a new publication, the *Oikeuskehitys* [Legal developments]. This Finnish-language current affairs periodical, which comes out 21 times per year, covers the recent judgments of the Supreme Court and the Supreme Administrative Court and the pending legislative projects in Finland. It contains also longer articles on topical issues. The orientation of the periodical is towards civil and commercial law.

As already noted, *Virallinen lehti/Officiella tidningen* [the official gazette] (1917–) contains more up-to-date information on government affairs. In particular, the weekly supplement, *Valtioneuvoston viikko* [The week in government], provides an insight into new projects, appointments and decisions.

Business and financial information

The easiest access to general business information in Finland is provided by the weekly *Talouselämä* (1938–) and the daily *Kauppalehti* (1898–) newspapers; both are in Finnish. The business and financial pages of the main daily newspaper, *Helsingin Sanomat* (1889–), also carry useful material. The Bank of Finland and the Ministry for Finance also publish material relating to the Finnish economy.

The company register, as well as a number of other registers relating to commerce in Finland, is maintained by the National Board of Patents and Registration. The Helsinki Stock Exchange is another source of financial information; its publications include the recent title *The Securities Markets Act and other securities legislation* (Stock Exchange, 1994), a translation of the most essential Finnish statutes governing the operations of the Stock Exchange. The publications are available from Edita Oy.

A volume titled *Listed companies in Finland 1995* from the Finnish Lawyers' Publishing Co. contains analyses of the financial statements of a number of Finnish companies, as well as other information on Finnish business life.

Statistics

The Statistics Finland service produces *Suomen virallinen tilasto = Finlands officiella statistik = The official statistics of Finland*, a series of statistics publications, most of which are trilingual (Finnish–Swedish–English). There is a sub-series called *Justice*, with some half a dozen issues per year on various aspects of law and justice. A legal statistics yearbook is also published as a part of the sub-series.

The trilingual *Suomen tilastollinen vuosikirja – Finlands statistisk årsbok = Statistical yearbook of Finland* is the general source for those with a more varied interest in Finnish statistics.

Useful addresses

Associations of lawyers

Suomen asianajajaliitto/Finlands advokatförbund [Finnish Bar Association], Simonkatu 12 b, FIN-00100 Helsinki, Finland. Tel: +358 9 694 2744. Fax: +358 9 694 8237

Suomen lakimiesliitto/Finlands juristförbund [Finnish Lawyers' Association], Uudenmaankatu 4–6 b, FIN-00120 Helsinki, Finland. Tel: +358 9 680 3450. Fax: +358 9 602 139

Government organizations

Oikeusministeriö/Justitieministeriet [Ministry of Justice], Eteläesplanadi 10, FIN-00130 Helsinki, Finland. Tel: +358 9 182 51. Fax: +358 9 182 577 30

Patentti- ja rekisterihallitus/Patent- och registerstyrelsen [National Board of Patents and Registration], Arkadiankatu 62, FIN-00100 Helsinki, Finland. Tel: +358 9 693 9500

Ulkoasiainministeriö/Utrikesministeriet [Ministry for Foreign Affairs], Merikasarmi, FIN-00160 Helsinki, Finland. Tel: +358 9 134 151

Valtioneuvoston kanslia/Statsrådets kansli [Prime Minister's Office], Terminology Service, Snellmaninkatu 1a, FIN-00170 Helsinki, Finland. Tel: +358 9 160 2058. Fax: +358 9 160 2163

Courts

Korkein hallinto-oikeus/Högsta förvaltningsdomstolen [Supreme Administrative Court], Unioninkatu 16, FIN-00130 Helsinki, Finland. Tel: +358 9 185 31. Fax: +358 9 185 3382

Korkein oikeus/Högsta domstolen [Supreme Court], Pohjoisesplanadi 3, FIN-00170 Helsinki, Finland. Tel: +358 9 123 81. Fax: +358 9 123 8354

Education and training

Helsingin yliopisto/Helsingfors universitet [University of Helsinki], Faculty of Law, Porthania, Hallituskatu 11, FIN-00100 Helsinki, Finland. Tel: +358 9 191 1. Fax: +358 9 191 221 52

Lapin yliopisto/Lappland universitet [University of Lapland], Faculty of Law, Yliopistonkatu 8, FIN-96100 Rovaniemi, Finland. Tel: +358 16 324 520. Fax: +358 16 324 500

Turun yliopisto/Åbo universitet [University of Turku], Faculty of Law, Calonia, Vänrikinkatu 2, FIN-20500 Turku, Finland. Tel: +358 2 633 5502. Fax: +358 2 633 6363

Libraries

Eduskunnan kirjasto/Riksdagsbibliotek [Library of Parliament], Aurorankatu 6, FIN-00100 Helsinki, Finland. Tel: +358 9 432 3432. Fax: +358 9 432 3495

Publishers and booksellers

Finnish Lawyers' Publishing Co, Uudenmaankatu 4–6, FIN-00120 Helsinki, Finland. Tel: +358 9 601 236. Fax: +358 9 611 230

Edita Oy [official publisher], Hakuninmaantie 2, FIN-00430 Helsinki, Finland. Tel: +358 9 566 01. Fax: +358 9 566 0374

Tilastokeskus/Statistikcentralen [Statistics Finland], Työpajakatu 13, FIN-00580 Helsinki, Finland. Tel: +358 9 17 341. Fax: +358 9 173 2279

VTKK-Tietopalvelu Oy, Espoontori B, FIN-02100 Espoo, Finland. Tel: +358 9 457 1. Fax: +358 9 457 3620

Commercial institutions

Helsingin arvopaperipörssi/Helsingfors fondbörs [Helsinki Stock Exchange], Fabianinkatu 14, FIN-00130 Helsinki, Finland. Tel: +358 9 1733 01. Fax: +358 9 1733 0399

Suomen pankki/Finlands Bank [Bank of Finland], Snellmaninaukio, S-00170 Helsinki, Finland. Tel: +358 9 183 1. Fax: +358 9 174 872

List of works cited

Åland Legislative Assembly and the Government of Åland. (1993) *Act on the Autonomy of Åland*. Mariehamn: Åland Legislative Assembly and the Government of Åland.

Avgöranden av Högsta domstolen. (1987–) Helsinki: Högsta domstolen. Earlier titles: *Högsta domstolens utslag och domar* (1918–1925); *Redogörelser och meddelanden angående Högsta domstolens avgöranden* (1926–1986).

Bibliographia iuridica fennica. Helsinki: Finnish Lawyers' Association to 1981, Library of Parliament from 1982. Coverage 1809–1981 in 5 vols. Annual from 1982.

Bibliographia iuridica fennica 1982–1992: littérature en langues étrangères = literature in foreign languages. (1994) Helsinki: Library of Parliament.

Constitutional laws of Finland & procedure of Parliament. (1996) Helsinki: Finnish Parliament, the Foreign Ministry and the Ministry of Justice.

Defensor legis. (1920–) Helsinki: Finnish Bar Association.

Encyclopedia iuridica fennica: Suomalainen oikeustietosanakirja. (1994–) Helsinki: Suomalainen Lakimiesyhdistys. In progress. 7 vols when complete.

Eriksson, J. (1995) (ed.) *Suomi–englanti–suomi lakikielen perussanakirja*. Helsinki: Finnish Lawyers' Publishing Co.

Finlands författningssamling. (1860–) Helsinki: Edita Oy. Earlier title: *Samling of placater førordninger, manifester och påbud*, 1808/12–1857/59.

Finlands författningssamlings fördragsserie: Överenskommelser med främmande makter. (1917–) Helsinki: Edita Oy.

Finlands lag. (annual) Helsinki: Finnish Lawyers' Publishing Co. 2 vols.

FINLEX (available from VTKK-Tietopalvelu Oy).

Helsingin Sanomat. (1889–) Helsinki: Sanoma Oy.

Högsta förvaltningsdomstolens årsbok. (1963–) Helsinki: Edita Oy.

Hurme, R., Malin, R.-L. and Syväoja, O. (1984) (eds) *Uusi suomi–englanti suursanakirja = Finnish–English general dictionary*. Porvoo: WSOY.

Hurme, R., Pesonen, M. and Syväoja, O. (1990) (eds) *Englanti–suomi suursanakirja = English–Finnish general dictionary*. Porvoo: WSOY.

Joutsen, M. (1995) (ed.) *Lakikielen sanakirja: suomi–englanti* 2nd edn. Porvoo: WSOY.

Kauppalehti. (1898–) Helsinki: Kustannusosakeyhtiö Kauppalehti. Newspaper.

Korkeimman hallinto-oikeuden vuosikirja (1963–) Helsinki: Edita Oy.

Korkeimman Oikeuden ratkaisuja (1987–) Helsinki: Korkein Oikeus. Earlier titles: *Kort redogörelse for kejserliga senatens justitiedepartments utslag och domar* (1894–1915); *Suomen senaatin oikeusosaston päätokset ja tuomiot* (1916–1917); *Korkeimman oikeuden päätokset ja tuomiot* (1918–1925); *Selostuksia ja tiedonantoja korkeimman oikeuden päätoksista* (1926–1986).

Lakimies. (1903–) Helsinki: Suomalainen Lakimiesyhdistys.

Lakimiesuutiset. (1945–) Helsinki: Finnish Lawyers' Association.

Listed companies in Finland 1995. (1995) Helsinki: Finnish Lawyers' Publishing Co.

Ministry of Justice. *Translations of Finnish legislation*. Helsinki: Ministry of Justice. Series of booklets.

Ministry of the Environment (1992) *Finnish environmental legislation*. Helsinki: Ministry of the Environment.

Oikeus. (1972–) Helsinki: Demla.

Oikeuskehitys. (1995–) Helsinki: Finnish Lawyers' Publishing Co.

Pöyhönen, J. (1993) (ed.) *An introduction to Finnish law*. Helsinki: Finnish Lawyers' Publishing Co.

Scheinin, Martin (1996) Finland. In *Constitutions of the countries of the world*, ed. A.P. Blaustein and G.H. Flanz, vol.VII. Dobbs Ferry, NY: Oceana.

Skatteförfattningarna. (annual) Helsinki: Finnish Lawyers' Publishing Co.

Statskalender. (annual) Helsinki: Edita Oy.

Stock Exchange (1994) *The Securities Markets Act and other securities legislation*. Helsinki: the Stock Exchange.

Suomen asianajajaliiton toimistoluettelo = Finlands advokatförbunds byråförteckning. (annual) Helsinki: Finnish Bar Association.

Suomen laki. (annual) Helsinki: Finnish Lawyers' Publishing Co. 2 vols.

SUOMEN LAKI CD-ROM (available from the Finnish Lawyers' Publishing Co.).

Suomen säädöskokoelma. (1981–) Helsinki: Edita Oy. Earlier titles: *Samling of placater førordninger, manifester och påbud*, 1808/12–1857/59 and *Suomen asetuskokoelma*, 1860–1980.

Suomen säädöskokoelman sopimussarja: ulkovaltain kanssa tehdyt sopimukset. (1917–) Helsinki: Edita Oy.

Suomen tilastollinen vuosikirja = Finlands statistisk årsbok = Statistical yearbook of Finland. (annual) Helsinki: Statistics Finland.

Suomen valtiokalenteri = Finlands statskalender. Helsinki: University of Helsinki (annual).

Suomen virallinen tilasto = Finlands officiella statistik = Official statistics of Finland. Helsinki: Statistics Finland (series).

Talouselämä. (1938–) Helsinki: Talentum. Newspaper.

Tidskrift utgiven av Juridiska Föreningen i Finland. Helsinki: Juridiska Föreningen i Finland (series).

Timonen, P. (1996a) (ed.) *Inledning till Finlands rättsordning I: privaträtt* 3rd edn. Helsinki: Finnish Lawyers' Publishing Co.

Timonen, P. (1996b) (ed.) *Inledning till Finlands rättsordning II: straff- och processrätt samt offentlig rätt* 3rd edn. Helsinki: Finnish Lawyers' Publishing Co.

Timonen, P. (1996c) (ed.) *Johdatus Suomen oikeusjärjestelmään I: yksityisoikeus* 3rd edn. Helsinki: Finnish Lawyers' Publishing Co.

Timonen, P. (1996d) (ed.) *Johdatus Suomen oikeusjärjestelmään II: rikos- ja prosessioikeus sekä julkisoikeus* 3rd edn. Helsinki: Finnish Lawyers' Publishing Co.

Tolvanen, Marjo (1994) Sources of legal information in Finland. *International Journal of Legal Information*, **22**, 191–8.

Uotila, J. (1985) *The Finnish legal system* 2nd edn. Helsinki: Finnish Lawyers' Publishing Co.

Uotila, J. (1989) The legal system of Finland. In *Modern legal systems cyclopedia*, ed. K.R. Redden, vol.4, pp. 4.40.5–4.40.26. Buffalo, NY: Hein.

Valtiokalenteri. (annual) Helsinki: Edita Oy.

Valtion komiteanmietinnöt = Statens kommittébetänkanden (1930–) Helsinki: Eduskunnan kirjasto/Riksdagsbibliotek. Earlier title: *Luettelo komiteain mietinnöistä ja ehdotuksista* (1859–1929).
Valtion virallisjulkaisut = Statens officiella publikationer. (1961–) Helsinki: Eduskunnan kirjasto, Riksdagsbibliotek. The catalogues cover the period 1859–1992.
Valtion virastot ja laitokset. (1989) Helsinki: Edita Oy.
Valtionhallinnon puhelinluettelo. (annual) Helsinki: Edita Oy.
Verolait. (annual) Helsinki: Finnish Lawyers' Publishing Co.
Virallinen lehti = Officiella tidningen. (1917–) Helsinki: Edita Oy.
YRITYKSEN LAKIKANTA CD-ROM (available from Edita Oy).

CHAPTER ELEVEN

France

CLAIRE M. GERMAIN

Introduction to the legal system

The French legal system belongs to the civil law tradition, like most continental European countries, and is often classified as part of the Romano-Germanic family of law, because of its historical links with both Roman law, revived in the universities since the 12th century, and Germanic customary law. From the 13th century on, the northern part of France was under the influence of *droit coutumier* (Germanic tribe customs) and the southern part was controlled by *droit écrit* (Roman law influence). During the period from the 16th century to the Revolution, known as the *ancien régime* (*ancien droit*), France emerged as a nation-state, under the strong centralization of royal authority. The sources of law of that period included *coutumes locales* [local customs], Roman law, canon law, royal ordinances, the case law of the parliaments, and doctrinal writings [*doctrine*]. Law was taught in the universities. Academic writers exercised an important influence on the development of a *droit commun* (*jus commune*) through systematic expositions of the law. Charles Dumoulin wrote an influential commentary on the Custom of Paris in 1559 and synthesized Roman law with contemporary practice. In the 17th century, Jean Domat, in his seminal work *Les lois civiles dans leur ordre naturel* (1689) systematically expounded principles of Roman law, holding them out as a coherent body of legal rules in accordance to principles of natural law. Robert Joseph Pothier wrote several treatises on the whole of private law, and exercised an immense influence on the drafters of the civil code especially in the area of obligations. The natural law movement of the 17th and 18th centuries led to the concept of law as systematized and founded on reason. These influences led to the codification movement.

The period of the *Droit intermédiaire* (1789–1803, between the Revolution and Napoleon), saw a period of tumultuous and violent alteration to the social order. In the midst of much bloodshed, it abolished ancient privileges, established equality before the law, the guarantee of individual liberties, and the protection of private property. It introduced a fundamental break with regard to constitutional law, with the introduction of a written constitution separating legislative, executive and judicial powers, and establishing a dual court structure, regular and administrative courts. Napoleon's major achievement was the drafting of the *Code civil des français*, as well as four other codes which unified private law, while public law (administrative and constitutional law) developed in the 19th century. On French legal history see *Histoire des institutions* (Ellul, 1992–) and *Histoire du droit français, des origines à la révolution* (Olivier-Martin, 1948, 1992 reprint).

France is a republic and a unitary state, with a tradition of strong centralized government. Decentralization laws in the 1980s have introduced true local government structures, with a transfer of power from centrally appointed government representatives to locally elected representatives of the people, within the 26 regions (22 metropolitan and 4 overseas ones: Martinique, Guadeloupe, Réunion and French Guyana), 100 departments, overseas territories (New Caledonia, French Polynesia, Wallis, and Futuna) and territorial collectivities (Mayotte, in the Comoro group, and St Pierre and Miquelon, in the Gulf of St Lawrence).

Constitution

France has had fifteen different constitutions since the first one of 1791. The current one is the Gaullist Constitution of 1958, adopted by the referendum of 28 September, 1958 and promulgated on 4 October, 1958. It provides for a strong executive to share power with a bicameral legislature. The parliament consists of the directly elected National Assembly [*Assemblée nationale*] and the Senate, elected by indirect suffrage. The Constitution can be amended by the legislature, subject to special majority and other rules, set out in art.89 (1958 Constitution). A recent development is the constitutionalization of French law, and a developing body of case law from the Conseil constitutionnel since 1971. Current constitutional law is actually composed of four sources, and referred to by the courts as the *bloc de constitutionalité*, as follows:

1. The text of the 1958 Constitution itself.
2. Its Preamble, which refers to the French commitment to the Rights of Man and principles of national sovereignty enshrined in the 1789

Declaration, reaffirmed and complemented by the Preamble of the Constitution of 1946.

3. The Preamble to the 1946 Constitution itself which contains a long list of political, economic and social principles.
4. The 1946 Preamble itself refers not only to the 1789 Declaration, but to *Les principes fondamentaux reconnus par les lois de la République*.

Two looseleaf services offer an English translation of the 1958 Constitution and the other documents mentioned above: *French law: constitution and selective legislation* (Bermann, De Vries and Galston, 1981–) and Spitzer (1988) in *Constitutions of the countries of the world*. The text of earlier French constitutions can be found in *Les constitutions et les principales lois politiques de la France depuis 1789* (1979), and in Debbasch and Pontier (1989). The text of the current constitution can be found in Avril and Conac (1996). The first edition of the *Code constitutionnel* (1995) contains an annotated version of the text of the Constitution of 1958, the *Declaration* of 1789, and of the *Préambule* of 1946, as well as other relevant texts. The text of the constitution and other documents can also be found on various Internet Web sites (see below for the addresses of some sites).

Useful books on constitutional law include *The birth of judicial politics in France* (Stone, 1992), *French constitutional law* (Bell, 1992), *Institutions politiques et droit constitutionnel* (Prélot, 1990), *Le droit constitutionnel de la Ve République* (Lavroff, 1995), and also Colliard (1995) and Lebreton (1995).

Introductory works on the legal system and legal research

There are several recent English-language introductions, including *The French legal system: an introduction* (West *et al.*, 1992), *The French legal system* (Dadomo and Farran, 1996), *Introduction to French law* (Dickson, 1994), *Sourcebook on French law* (Kahn-Freund, Levy and Rudden, 1991), and under a similar title by Pollard (1996), *Introduction to French law* (Cairns and McKeon, 1995), and *An English reader's guide to the French legal system* (Weston, 1991), the latter two with a special focus on linguistic problems. Business law guides include *Doing business in France* (1983–) and *French tax and business law guide* (1983–) published by Éditions Francis Lefèbvre which publish many useful business publications, and the chapter on France in *Investing, licensing and trading conditions abroad*.

Older works include the excellent chapter by Blanc-Jouvan and Boulouis (1972) in the *International encyclopedia of comparative law*, and such classics as *English law and French law* (David, 1980), *Introduction to French law* (Amos and Walton, 1967), *The French legal system* (David and De Vries, 1958), *French law: its structure, sources, and methodology* (David, 1972), and *English law and French law* (René, 1980). These older books contain much of historical interest and expound the principles of French law. They are to be used with caution because they can be misleading as to contemporary French law.

For an overall panorama of French law, *Introduction au droit français* (Guimezanes, 1995) is very good and current. Other excellent French introductions include *Droit civil. Introduction générale* (Terré, 1994), explaining the structure of French law, as well as *Institutions judiciaires* (Perrot, 1995), and *La justice et ses institutions* (Vincent *et al.*, 1991), both dealing with the administration of justice, the courts, and the legal professions in France, including statistics and charts. Introductions to French law can also be found as part of more general works on comparative law, treatises and casebooks, including such classics as *Major legal systems in the world today* (David and Brierley, 1985), *Introduction to comparative law* (Zweigert and Kötz, 1993), *A common lawyer looks at the civil law* (Lawson, 1953), *Comparative law: cases, texts and materials* (Schlesinger, 1988), and *Comparative legal traditions: text, materials, and cases* (Glendon, Gordon and Osakwe, 1994). Useful information on French law can also be found in books dealing with various legal subjects on a multi-jurisdictional basis, see the subject part of *Germain's transnational law research* (Germain, 1991–) for specific information.

Among the works focusing on French legal research, Szladits and Germain (1985), *Guide to foreign legal materials: French*, explains how to understand and do research in French law; *Germain's transnational law research: a guide for attorneys* (Germain, 1991–), includes a section on France; Tanguy (1991), *La recherche documentaire en droit*, is an excellent guide to French legal research written for French law students and researchers and Dunes (1977), *La documentation juridique*, is an interesting guide to read, but more difficult to use as a learning tool. Buffelan-Lanore (1991), *Informatique juridique documentaire*, focuses on computerized legal research and contains useful information on legal databases and thoughtful remarks on the various categories of legal research tools. A more general guide, Reynolds and Flores (1989–) *Foreign law: current sources of codes and basic legislation in jurisdictions of the world* contains excellent information on France.

Legislation

Legislation in France in its broad meaning consists of the treaties, Constitution, codes, statutes and regulations. Since the Constitution of 1958, the domain of parliamentary statutes [*lois*] (legislation in its narrow meaning) is restricted to a limited number of matters, as set out in art.34 of the 1958 Constitution; for example, 'Parliamentary laws shall establish the rules concerning civil rights, nationality, status and capacity of persons, inheritance, crimes and criminal procedure, taxes and currency. They shall also determine the fundamental principles of education, property rights, labour law, and social security'. All other legislation can be enacted by the executive by means of regulations [*règlements*] which can be autonomous (art.37) or taken to implement a statute (art.21). In addition, the government can legislate within the legislative field of competence via ordinances [*ordonnances*] (art.38, *lois d'habilitation* that authorize the measures for a limited time, to be ratified by parliament) and presidential decisions (art.16 on emergency powers).

Regulations are called a *décret* (if taken by the president or the prime minister) (*autonome* or *d'application*), *arrêté* (*ministériel, préfectoral* or *municipal* if taken by a minister, a prefect or a mayor), or *circulaire* (no force of law but can be reviewed by administrative courts).

Because of the long tradition of the pre-eminence of legislation as the legislative expression of the will of the people, before 1958 French courts could not question or review the constitutionality of a duly enacted and published act. Since the Constitution of 1958, and the creation of the *Conseil constitutionnel,* the constitutionality of parliamentary statutes can be reviewed before they are enacted, but not a posteriori. The *Conseil constitutionnel*, however, has now developed a growing body of constitutional cases, which has led to the 'constitutionalization' of French law. This marks a fundamental change in French law, which is accompanied by the 'Europeanization' of French law, since European Union law is immediately applicable in French law.

Journal Officiel

Statutes and regulations are published and come into force upon publication in the *Journal Officiel de la République Française* (1869–), the official gazette, cited as JO, which appears daily. Unless otherwise provided, a *loi* or *décret* will come into force in Paris one clear day after publication, and in the provinces one clear day after the arrival of the *Journal Officiel.* The *Lois et Décrets de la République Française* part of the JO is the official gazette in the proper sense of the word and contains the text of statutes, decrees, circulars and notices. The electronic version of the JO, Lois et Décrets, JOURNAL OFFICIEL. LOIS ET DÉCRETS. DISQUE OPTIQUE COMPACT (1994–) from the publisher also called Journal Officiel, provides digital images of the JO on CD-ROM.

Commercial collections

New laws and regulations are also available in commercial publications, particularly the three legal reviews, which contain a separate part on legislation, the *Recueil Dalloz Sirey* (1945–), the *Gazette du Palais* (1881–), as well as the *Semaine juridique: juris classeur périodique* (1927–) (JCP).

For comprehensive access to all the laws in force, the looseleaf *Juris Classeur Codes et Lois* contains both private and public laws, codified and uncodified, with good indexes, including a 'Fichier législatif et règlementaire' which provides subject access to the laws and regulations. *Juris Classeur Codes et Lois* (*Droit Public-Droit Privé*) contains in chronological order all public and private laws legislation in ten volumes except taxation; *Juris Classeur Codes et Lois* (*Droit Fiscal*) in four volumes on tax laws; and some supplementary series, such as *Juris Classeur Agricole* in four volumes.

There are now several CD-ROM legislative series, including Legisoft's LEGI-CD collection (*Civil, Sociétés, Commercial, Travail, Pénal, Administratif,* and *Fiscal*) which contains the relevant code or codes for a particular field, for example, the commercial CD-ROM contains the Commercial Code, Code of Intellectual Property, Code of Consumers [Consommation], Insurance, etc., as well as the Cour de cassation and Conseil d'État decisions in full text. CD-INFOCODES (see below) covers the 55 codes published by the Journal Officiel, together with relevant case law in full text.

Citation

Statutes and regulations are cited by date and numbered, for example *Loi 96–516 du 14 juin 1996* (Law number 516 of 1996 dated 14 June, 1996); numbering by year and serial number within year began in 1945. Codes are cited by indicating the number of the article followed by the abbreviated title of the code, for example art.2101 C.Civ. The newer codes have separately numbered parts according to the nature of the texts, parliamentary laws (Art . . . ., or Art.L. . .), *décrets* (Art.D. . .), and *règlements* (Art.R. . .). These parts may be followed by a list of non-codified related texts in chronological order.

Preparatory materials

Bills and parliamentary debates and documents can be found in the *Journal Officiel*. Since 4 June, 1996, the Senate publishes the verbatim text of its debates on its web site (http://www.senat.fr/). The National Assembly does the same (http://www.assemblee-nat.fr/). Both sites provide useful information and pictures on the two legislative bodies and are bound to grow.

Codes and commentaries

The commentaries and treatises mentioned in this section are extremely selective and emphasize comprehensive works, rather than the more specialized ones. The selection does not do justice to the richness of French legal treatise literature.

In spite of the great mass of special statutes and regulations, the codes are still the basis of the French legal system. The five original Napoleonic codes were the Civil Code, Code of Civil Procedure, Code of Commerce, Criminal Code, and Code of Criminal Procedure [*instruction criminelle*]. The most eminent code is the *Code civil*, called the *Code civil des français*, or later, the *Code Napoléon*. English-language translations of selected provisions of the various codes can be found in Bermann, De Vries and Galston (1981–) as well as in general translation services such as *Commercial laws of Europe* (1978–) and *Commercial laws of the world: France* (1970–). *European current law* (1992–) is a useful abstracting service for European legislation and case law. The *Martindale-Hubbell international law digest* (1993–), accompanying its law directory, provides a useful digest of the laws of France with citations to primary sources.

Civil Code

There is a current translation of the Civil Code (CC or C.Civ.) by Crabb (1995) and several French language editions. These include the new *Mégacode civil Dalloz*, which, in addition to the information contained in the regular 'red' codes (see below), has additional annotations from various databases. Among the many works on civil law the following stand out: *The French law of contract* (Nicholas, 1992), *Droit civil* (Carbonnier, 1995), *Leçons de droit civil* (Mazeaud, 1989–), Marty and Raynaud (1986–), Ghestin (1994), and Weill (1996). A good book on intellectual property is Colombet (1994).

Code of Civil Procedure

The Code of Civil Procedure [*Code de procédure civile*] (CPC) of 1806 was replaced by the New Code of Civil Procedure [*Nouveau code de procédure civile*] (NCPC) in 1976. It is supplemented by related laws, such as the law on court organization and the status of judges and the Code of Judicial Organization (*Code de l'organisation judiciaire*). Selected English-language translations are available in Bermann, De Vries and Galston (1981–) and de Kertstrat and Crawford (1978), *New Code of Civil Procedure in France* which is somewhat out of date. Herzog (1967), *Civil procedure in France*, is now out of date but presents a good discussion of the principles of French civil procedure. The standard treatise by Solus and Perrot (1961), *Droit judiciaire privé*, is dated.

Shorter standard textbooks include Vincent and Guinchard (1994), Cadiet (1996), Héron (1995), and Couchez (1994).

Commercial Code

The Commercial Code [*Code de commerce*] of 1807 (C.Com.) has not survived well. Most of the provisions affecting commercial law are outside of the code (e.g. law of 1966 on commercial corporations [*sociétés*], of 1967 on bankruptcy, 1978 on protection of consumers). The major commercial law treatises, which also cover corporation law, competition law, banking and stock exchange, as well as bankruptcy, include: *Manuel de droit commercial* (Jauffret and Mestre, 1995), *Traité de droit commercial* (De Juglart and Ippolito, 1992–), *Traité élémentaire de droit commercial* (Ripert, 1991–), *Droit commercial* (Pedamon and Merle, 1994), and *Droit commercial* (Dekeuwer-Defossez, 1995). Practitioner-oriented texts include the Collection of 'mémentos pratiques' by Francis Lefèbvre updated frequently, as well as the series *Joly sociétés* (1993–), and the *Encyclopédie Delmas des affaires*.

Penal Code and Code of Criminal Procedure

The Penal Code of 1810 [*Code pénal*] (C.Pen.) was replaced by a new Code in 1994. A new Code of Criminal Procedure [*Code de procédure pénale*] (C.Proc.Pén.) of 1959 replaced the Code of Criminal Procedure of 1810. Important criminal law texts include: *Droit pénal* (Pradel, 1995), *Droit pénal comparé* also by Pradel (1995), and Stefani, Levasseur and Bouloc, *Droit pénal général* (1994) and also their *Procédure pénale* (1996).

Other codes

In addition to the five codes, there are other more specialized codes, for example, the forestry and rural code.

Beside these true codes, other codes represent the official or unofficial consolidation of diverse statutes and regulations concerning one subject matter. Among the more important of these consolidated 'codes' are the *Code du travail* [labour], *Code général des impôts* [tax], *Code des douanes* [customs], *Code du blé* [wheat], *Code du vin* [wine], *Code de la santé publique* [public health], and Code de la sécurité sociale [social security]. There are also unofficial collections of various laws concerning one subject, like the *Code administratif* [administrative], *Code des sociétés* [corporations], *Code de la copropriété* [co-ownership], and *Code de l'environnement* [environment].

On French public law, the *Code administratif* is an unofficial compilation of statutes. English language texts include Bell (1992) *French constitutional law*, Brown and Bell (1993) *French administrative law,* and the classic Schwartz (1954) *French administrative law and the common law world.* Laubadère (1993–), *Traité de droit administratif*, is the standard text. Private international law leading texts are Batiffol and Lagarde (1994), Loussouarn and Bourel (1993), and Mayer (1994). A good book on French labour law is Lyon-Caen, Pélissier and Supiot (1994).

Collections of codes

The 30 official codes published by Journal Officiel are not used much because they only contain the plain text of the law. The annotated, red *Petits Codes Dalloz* published since 1902 on the major subjects and sold individually in compact portable softbound form are very popular and many are updated annually. They contain digests of leading decisions and case notes and occasional bibliographic references to doctrinal writings in law reviews, and a cross-reference to the place where the provision is discussed in the *Répertoire Dalloz*. They also include the text of statutes and decrees. A newer competitor, Éditions Litec, produces a series of annotated codes, *Codes bleus*, annotated and with cross-references to sister publications, and *Codes oranges,* annotated and commented. Not all the laws are inserted in the codes. If not in the codes, legislation can be found in the *Journal Officiel* or the legal reviews (*Recueil Dalloz Sirey, Gazette du Palais* and *Semaine juridique*). *Actualité Législative Dalloz* (ALD) (1983–) is a convenient monthly compendium of new legislation, together with useful commentaries. LEXIS has the text of the *Journal Officiel* and the codes. Legislation on certain specific subjects, for example tax, can be found in print or CD-ROM through the publisher Lamy which specializes in taxation and other fiscal matters, for example, LAMY FISCAL, or other publishers.

Treaties

Article 55 of the 1958 Constitution states that duly ratified or approved treaties and agreements have an authority superior to that of parliamentary statute. Treaties are first published in the *Journal Officiel, Lois et décrets* edition. Surbiguet and Wibaux (1982) *Liste des traités et accords de la France en force au ler Janvier 1982* allows researchers to find out treaties in force up to 1982. *Recueil général des traités de la France* (Pinto and Rollet, 1976–) is an extremely valuable publication, also available on LEXIS. For recent treaties, the *Recueil des traités et accords de la France* (1981–) is published fortnightly and cumulates annually. New treaties can also be found in *Journal de droit international* (1874–), often known as *Clunet.* For information on older treaties, the two important collections are De Clercq (1864–1917), *Recueil des traités de la France*, covering the period from 1713 to 1906; and

Basdevant (1918–22), *Traités et conventions en vigueur entre la France et les puissances étrangères,* which covers treaties in force in 1918.

Law reports, judgments

In theory, case law is not an authoritative source of law and judges are prohibited from setting precedents (art.5 Civil Code). In reality, case law exercises an important influence on the development of law. Another fundamental tenet of the French judicial system lies in the duality of the court system. Judicial civil and criminal courts (also referred to as ordinary or regular courts) govern disputes among private individuals. Administrative courts govern disputes whenever the state is involved. Each court system has its own hierarchy and judges and applies its own law. The *Cour de cassation* is the highest judicial court, and the *Conseil d'État* the highest administrative court.

Generally speaking, there is no comprehensive official system of reports of judicial decisions. *Cour de cassation* cases are reported in an official set, *Bulletin des arrêts de la Cour de cassation* in two series, civil (Bull. Civ.) (1947–) and criminal (Bull. Crim.) (1954–). About two-thirds of the *Cour de cassation* decisions are reported. The *Conseil d'État* (CE) decisions are published in a semi-official, private publication under the sponsorship of the *Conseil d'État, Recueil des décisions du Conseil d'État . . .* (1821–), also known as *Recueil Lebon*; Tribunal des conflits (TC) decisions are included. Conseil constitutionnel (CC) decisions are published in *Recueil des décisions du Conseil Constitutionnel.*

The most frequently used collections of reports are the well-indexed legal reviews, which appear frequently and contain a large selection of decisions of all courts, civil, criminal, and administrative, the *Recueil Dalloz Sirey* (D), now available in CD-ROM, *Semaine Juridique* (JCP), and *Gazette du Palais* (GP). Many decisions in special fields of the law can be found in the specialized periodicals. LEXIS has an extensive library which, however, includes the text only, and does not provide access to the case notes written by learned commentators that are essential to the understanding of the impact of a particular decision.

Computer-based systems

ORT-Journal Officiel

Pursuant to an exclusive contract with the French government for the dissemination of public texts (the contract came up for renewal in 1996), ORT-Journal Officiel publish CD INFOCODES which provide the text of the 30 official codes and applicable case law in full text.

Lexis

LEXIS has very useful libraries and files of French law. In the LOIREG library, it includes the full text of the *Journal Officiel. Edition des lois et décrets* (JO), all the codes (CODES) and other materials. In the INTNAT library, one can find treaties, conventions and other international agreements (ACCORD). LEXIS has very good files of French case law. In the PRIVE library, it has the *Cour de cassation* decisions (CASSCI, civil since 1959, CASSCR criminal since 1970). The *Cour d'appel* file (APPEL) goes back to 1983, but has not been updated since 1988. The PUBLIC library contains the *Conseil Constitutionnel* decisions back to 1958, the *Tribunal des Conflits* decisions (CONFL) back to 1964 and the *Conseil d'État* (CONSET) decisions back to 1966.

Juris-data

JURIS-DATA contains an extensive database of case law, including all officially published *Cour de cassation* decisions (civil since 1960 and criminal since 1975); selected *Conseil d'État* decisions since 1980, and selected administrative courts of appeal decisions since 1990.

Since 1985, JURIS-DATA contracted with the Ministry of Justice, under the auspices of the *Secrétariat général du gouvernement*, to publish a *fichier national de la jurisprudence des cours d'appel*. 15,000 'inédites' [unpublished] court of appeals and lower court decisions are indexed every year, under the auspices of the *ateliers régionaux de jurisprudence* (going back to 1980).

Others

LEXILASER CD-ROMs include *Conseil d'État & cours administratives* (June 1993–), *Cour de cassation* (1984–), *Lois et règlements* (1980–) which contain the full text of all decisions of the *Conseil d'État*, five administrative appeals courts, *Cour de cassation* (with hypertext links to legislative texts), and all laws and regulations published in the JO

The TRANSPOSIAL CD-ROM includes full text of all of the directives adopted by the European Union and their transposition into French law.

Internet

France has embraced the Internet and is in the process of switching from Minitel to the Internet. Internet Web sites are developing rapidly. Among the official Web sites, the Web site of the French Ministry of Foreign Affairs (http://www.france.diplomatie.fr/) available in French, English and Spanish, contains much useful information on the French government, including constitutional and other texts, biographies and photographs of government figures, on the economy, legal system and social affairs. It also contains headlines of French newspapers. The

Web sites of the National Assembly and of the Senate are mentioned under **Legislation** above.

Among the unofficial French Web sites, two private initiatives are particularly noteworthy: a French engineer, Mr Scherrer, has created a comprehensive Web site for French law (http://www.ensmp.fr/ ~ scherer/ adminet/) which sometimes runs into trouble with the French government which maintains a tight control over official publications. It is still hard to find free electronic version of French official publications because the government has given an exclusive contract to a private publisher for the publication of its official documents. The exclusive contract is up for renewal in 1996. Many legal researchers argue that French official documents should be in the public domain.

For a combination mail-group and a database of archival texts, http://www.liber.net/law-france/ is excellent. Initiated by Mr Wiesenbach (e-mail: roger@amgot.org), it is an open but moderated mailing list for the exchange of information on the practice of law in France.

A useful gateway to French sources is the Web site of the Law Library of Congress in Washington, DC, (http://lcweb2.loc.gov/glin/ france.html) because it not only points to useful links, but evaluates them (pointing out that the text of the Constitution may not be up to date, etc.).

Other government documents

Many French government documents are distributed by the Documentation française. Examples are *Conditions juridiques et culturelles de l'intégration. Rapport au Premier ministre, Haut Conseil de l'Intégration* (1992), and *Commission nationale de l'informatique et des libertés. 15e rapport d'activité* (1995).

Encyclopedias

The major encyclopedias are the *Encyclopédie juridique Dalloz. Répertoires* and *Juris classeurs: encyclopédie juridique.* The *Dalloz Répertoires* form a comprehensive encyclopedia, divided according to the main fields of law, as follows: *Répertoire de droit civil* (Rép. Civ.); *Répertoire de droit commercial* (Rép. Com.); *Répertoire des sociétés* (Rép. Soc.); *Répertoire de droit pénal et de procédure pénale* (Rép. Pén.); *Répertoire de droit du travail* (Rép. Trav.); *Répertoire de procedure civile*; *Répertoire de contentieux administratif*; *Répertoire de la Responsabilité de la puissance publique*; *Répertoire de droit communautaire.* It contains a lucid presentation of the law on a high scholarly and a practical level. Each volume is updated in autumn and spring, with a cumulative yearly supplement [*mise à jour*], with cross-references and further updates found in the weekly *Recueil Dalloz Sirey*. The *Juris classeurs* series consists of over 200 binders, on many different subjects, which can be acquired separately. It is the most comprehensive encyclopedia, eminently useful for practitioners, because it is always up to date, through fascicle updating. Because of its bulk and filing difficulties, few libraries abroad keep a complete set of it.

Directories

An excellent directory of legal professions, *Guide des professions juridiques* (1994), lists members of the various courts, professional organizations, and legal personnel (judges, lawyers, notaires and huissiers), and provides useful information on the courts and various texts. Volume 2 provides directory-type information on how to get administrative, fiscal or judicial information in all the 'communes'. A smaller annual version, *Le petit G.P.J. Guide des professions juridiques* lists all avocats, avoués, notaires, huissiers, arranged by department. *Quo juris: guide des juristes d'affaires* (annual) is also useful. The annual *Bottin administratif* (1989–) is useful for information on the administration and universities. The French administration is covered in *Répertoire de l'Administration française* (1995), which contains names of 13 000 civil servants in 10 500 public services, ministries, etablissements publics nationaux, préfectures and sous-préfectures, etc. It can be updated continuously via Minitel. The *Répertoire des guides 'droits et démarches'* (Édition 1994) is a handy guide for laypeople to find out about their rights and where to go. Meyronneinc et Vital-Mareille (1991), *Droit. Guide des formations supérieures à débouches professionnels*, describes various legal professions, programmes of legal studies, and study programmes abroad in a useful and practical way. Magliulo (1990) *Les 3es cycles et la recherche* is devoted to graduate studies in law and other fields.

Bibliographies

The *Bibliographie nationale française: BNF* (1970–) provides author, subject, and title access to all legal deposit books in France since 1970. The online catalogue of the Bibliothèque Nationale, BN Opale, can be accessed by telnet either through the library's web site (http://www.bnf.fr) or by direct telnet to Opale02.bnf.fr (login:Opale). CD QUARTIER LATIN is a biannual union catalogue of the libraries of the Sorbonne, Cujas (the largest law library in France) and Sainte Geneviève on CD-ROM. ELECTRE is a database on monthly CD-ROM for French-language books in print, by title or subject, with a list of publishers and vendors. *Les livres disponibles* (1977–) is a traditional catalogue of books in the French language in print; there are weekly lists of books published in *Livres hebdo*. MYRIADE is a biannual CD-ROM version of the national union catalogue of over 220 000 serial publications, including locations in over 2800 libraries and documentation centres. The classic bibliography for law is Grandin (1926, 1984 reprint), *Bibliographie générale des sciences juridiques, politiques, économiques et sociales, 1800–1926* and *Suppléments, 1926–1951*.

Indexing and abstracting services

DOCTRINAL (1993–) is an excellent and comprehensive new monthly CD-ROM index to over 130 French legal publications. The *Index to Foreign Legal Periodicals* (1960–) is worldwide in scope, but picks up most major French law reviews.

JURIS-DATA's 'Jurinfo' provides a computerized subject and keyword index of eight major legal reviews, with bibliographical references and summaries of documents found, since 1990. Almost all subjects provide a cross-reference to commentary in one of the *Juris-Classeurs* encyclopedias. It also includes abstracts of over 60 reviews (back to 1972); decisions and doctrinal articles (back to 1970). This index is produced at the IRETIJ (Université de Montpellier 1, Institut de Recherche et d'Etudes pour le Traitement de l'Information Juridique) of Montpellier. Access is online and via Minitel.

GPDOC INFOBASES: GAZETTE DU PALAIS provides summaries of cases published in the GP, since 1980, and bibliographic references to the doctrinal articles and legislation published since 1986.

Dictionaries

Baleyte *et al.* (1995), *Dictionnaire économique et juridique français/anglais – English/French* (now also on CD-ROM) and *Dahl's law dictionary: French to English/English to French* (1995) are the standard legal dictionaries. *West's law and commercial dictionary in five languages* (1985) is also useful. Roland and Boyer (1991), Cornu (1994), Guillien and Vincent (1995), and Guinchard and Montagnier (1995) are compendia of legal terms. Gendrel (1980) *Dictionnaire des principaux sigles utilisés dans le monde juridique de A à Z* explains abbreviations. More specialized are Roland and Boyer (1992), *Adages du droit français* and their *Locutions latines du droit français* (1993).

Other reference books

The *Préparation au CRFPA* (*Centre Régional de Formation Professionnelle d'Avocats*), under the direction of Serge Guinchard and Michèle Harichaux, provides students with practical guides on how to prepare for the various parts of the bar examination, for example Guinchard (1995) *Comment devenir avocat?* The rules regarding the legal profession can be found in *Les règles de la profession d'avocat* (Hamelin and Damien, 1995).

Current information sources

Journals

There are over 130 law reviews and legal periodicals. Leading law reviews include *Revue trimestriellee de droit civil* (1902–), *Revue trimestrielle de droit commercial et de droit économique* (1948–), *Revue critique de droit international privé* (1946–), *Journal du droit international* (1874–), *Revue de science criminelle et de droit pénal comparé* (1936–), and *Revue trimestrielle de droit européen* (1965–). This highly selective listing does not include many more specialized reviews.

News information

The three major legal reviews are excellent sources of information on legal developments. They each also contain sections of legislation, law reports and doctrine (scholarly articles) and have been mentioned in the appropriate sections above. The weekly *Semaine juridique: Juris classeur périodique* (JCP) (1927–) is often known by the second part of its title only. *Recueil Dalloz Sirey* (1945–) has since 1983, a green page called 'Flash Dalloz' which highlights the most important developments of the week. The *Gazette du Palais* (1881–) is published three times a week. A new Internet listserv is becoming an excellent source of information and networking, Law-France@amgot.org (http://www.liber.net/law-france/).

Statistics

The *Annuaire statistique de la justice 1988–92* (1995) provides useful information. For criminal justice information *Administration pénitentiaire: Rapport annuel d'activité 1994* (1995) is good. The annual reports of the *Cour de cassation, Rapport de la Cour de cassation* (1970–) and the *Conseil d'État, Rapport public*, part of the *Conseil d'État, Etudes et documents* series (1947–) yield much useful information, since they review the activities and major decisions of each body and include statistical data, together with other studies. *La justice administrative en pratique* (1994) is also useful.

For more general statistics, the well-established INSEE, Institut national de la statistique et des études économiques (address below) publishes useful demographical, economic and social statistics on France. The *Annuaire statistique de la France* (available on CD-ROM) contains a wide range of statistics including business and financial information, and a chapter on justice and law enforcement. The *Dictionnaire des sources statistiques* (1988) is useful for further research. The popular *Quid* (1963–) might come in handy for quick reference.

Acknowledgements

The author would like to thank Mademoiselle Carpentier, the Director of the Bibliothèque Cujas and its staff, in particular Mesdames Fischer, Le Coz and Maximin, and Monsieur Chardon, for their precious help in writing this chapter.

Useful addresses

Associations of lawyers

Association Française des Avocats Conseils d'Entreprises (ACE), 23/25 avenue MacMahon, 75017 Paris, France. Tel: +33 1 47 66 30 07. Fax: +33 1 47 63 35 78

Chambre des Avoués près les Cours d'Appel, 4 boulevard du Palais, 75001 Paris, France. Tel: +33 1 43 54 18 44

Chambre Nationale des Commissaires-priseurs, 13 rue de la Grange-Batelière, 75009 Paris, France. Tel: +33 1 47 70 89 33. Fax: +33 1 48 00 06 83

Chambre Nationale des Huissiers de Justice, 79 rue Monceau, 75008 Paris, France. Tel: +33 1 49 70 12 90

Conseil de l'Ordre des Avocats à la Cour de Paris, 2 boulevard du Palais, 75001 Paris, France. Tel: +33 1 44 32 48 48. Fax: +33 1 46 34 77 65

Conseil National des Administrateurs Judiciaires et des Mandataires Judiciaires à la liquidation des entreprises, 25 avenue de l'Opéra, 75001 Paris, France. Tel: +33 1 42 61 77 44

Conseil National des Barreaux (CNB), 67 rue du Rocher, 75008 Paris, France. Tel: +33 1 42 93 72 15

Conseil Supérieur du Notariat, 31 rue du Général-Foy, 75008 Paris, France. Tel: +33 1 44 90 30 00

Ordre des Avocats au Conseil d'État et à la Cour de Cassation, 5 quai de l'Horloge, 75001 Paris, France. Tel: +33 1 43 29 36 80

Government organizations

Assemblée Nationale, 126 rue de l'Université, 75355 Paris 07 SP, France. Tel: +33 1 40 63 60 00. Fax: +33 1 42 60 99 03. Information: +33 1 40 63 99 99

Commission Supérieure de Codification, 72 rue de Varenne, 75700 Paris, France. Tel: +33 1 42 75 85 83. Fax: +33 1 42 75 72 06

Ministère de la Justice, 13 place Vendôme, 75042 Paris Cedex 01, France. Tel: +33 1 44 77 60 60. Fax: +33 1 42 96 50 96

Ministère des Affaires Étrangères, 37 quai d'Orsay, 75007 Paris, France. Tel: +33 1 43 17 53 53

Sénat, Palais du Luxembourg, 15 rue de Vaugirard, 75291 Paris Cedex 06, France. Tel: +33 1 42 34 20 00

Courts

Conseil Constitutionnel, 2 rue de Montpensier, 75001 Paris, France. Tel: +33 1 40 15 30 00

Conseil d'État, Palais Royal, 75100 Paris RP, France. Tel: +33 1 40 20 80 00

Conseil Supérieur de la Magistrature, 15 quai Branly, 75007 Paris, France. Tel: +33 1 42 92 82 00

Cour de Cassation, 5 quai de l'Horloge, 75055 Paris RP, France. Tel: +33 1 44 32 50 50

Tribunal des Conflits, Palais Royal, 75001 Paris, France. Tel: +33 1 40 20 80 00

Education and training

Ecole Nationale de la Magistrature – ENM, 9 rue Maréchal-Joffre, 33080 Bordeaux Cedex, France. Tel: +33 56 00 10 10. Fax: +33 56 00 10 99

There are many universities in most large cities with law schools and law libraries. For further information, the researcher can consult *World of Learning* and *Annuaire national des universités, 1996.*

Libraries

The largest law library in France is the Bibliothèque inter-universitaire Cujas, 2 rue Cujas, 75006 Paris, France. Tel: +33 1 46 34 99 72. Fax: +33 1 46 34 98 32

Publishers and booksellers

La Documentation Française (official bookseller/publisher), 29 quai Voltaire, 75344 Paris Cedex 07, France. Tel: +33 1 40 15 70 00. Fax: +33 1 40 15 72 30

Éditions Dalloz Sirey, 35 rue Tournefort, 75240 Paris Cedex 05, France. Tel: +33 1 40 51 54 54. Fax: +33 1 45 87 37 48

Éditions du Juris Classeur (Éditions Techniques), 141 rue de Javel, 75747 Paris Cedex 15, France. Fax: +33 1 45 58 94 00

Éditions Francis Lefèbvre, 42 rue de Villiers, 92532 Levallois Cedex, France. Tel: +33 1 41 05 22 00. Fax: +33 1 41 05 22 30

Éditions Juridiques Associées (EJA), 14 rue Pierre et Marie Curie, 75005 Paris, France. Tel: +33 1 44 41 97 10. Fax: +33 1 43 54 78 21. Results from the association between Librarie Générale de Droit et Jurisprudence (LGDJ) and Montchrestien; also includes Jupiter, Navarre dictionaries, etc.

Éditions Techniques. See Éditions du Juris Classeur

GLN Joly Éditions, 1 avenue Franklin-D-Roosevelt, 75008 Paris, France. Tel: +33 1 44 95 16 20. Fax: +33 1 45 63 89 39

INSEE Info Service, Tour Gamma A, 195 rue de Bercy, 75582 Paris Cedex 12, France. Tel: +33 1 41 17 66 11. Fax: +33 1 53 17 88 09

Journal Officiel, 26 rue Desaix, Paris 75727 France. Fax: +33 1 45 79 17 84

Lamy, 187–188 quai de Valmy, 75480 Paris Cedex 10, France. Tel: +33 1 44 72 12 12. Fax: +33 1 44 72 13 65

Legisoft, 4 bis rue de l'Assomption, 75016 Paris. Tel: +33 1 45 25 13 12. Fax: +33 1 45 25 25 94

LEXIS-NEXIS. See the addresses given on page 19 in the **General sources** chapter. In France see also Lamy above.

Librairie Duchemin, 18 rue Soufflot, 75005 Paris, France. Tel: +33 1 43 54 79 16. Fax: +33 1 46 34 17 43. Bookseller and subscription agent.

Litec (service commercial), 6 rue Victor-Cousin, 75005 Paris, France. Fax: +33 1 46 33 50 32

Les Petites Affiches, Les Journaux judiciaires associés, 2 rue Montesquieu, 75001 Paris, France. Tel: +33 1 42 61 56 14/42 61 56 15. Fax: +33 1 42 86 09 37

ORT: Journal officiel. l'Européenne de Données, 12 villa de Lourcine, 16–24 rue Cabanis, 75014 Paris, France. Tel: +33 1 53 62 63 64. Fax: +33 1 53 62 63 63

PUF (Presses Universitaires de France), 108 bd Saint-Germain, 75006 Paris, France. Tel: +33 1 46 34 12 01. Fax: +33 1 46 34 65 41 (Direction de la communication)

List of works cited

Actualité législative Dalloz. (1983–) Paris: Dalloz.

Administration pénitentiaire. Rapport annuel d'activité 1994. (1995) Paris: Ministère de la Justice. Documentation française.

Amos, M.S. and Walton, F.P. (1967) *Introduction to French law* 3rd edn. Oxford: Clarendon Press.

Annuaire national des universités, 1995. (1995) Paris: L'Etudiant.

Annuaire statistique de la France. Edition 1996. (1996) 99th edn. Paris: INSEE.

Annuaire statistique de la justice, 1988–92. (1995) Paris: Documentation française.

Avril, P. and Conac, G. (1996) *La Constitution de la République Française. Textes et revisions*. Paris: LGDJ.

Baleyte, J. *et al.* (1995) *Dictionnaire économique et juridique français/anglais – English/ French* 4th edn. Paris: LGDJ.

Basdevant, J. (1918–22) *Traités et conventions en vigueur entre la France et les puissances étrangères*. Paris: Imprimerie Nationale. 4 vols.

Batiffol, H. and Lagarde, P. (1994) *Traité élémentaire de droit international privé*. Paris: LGDJ 2 vols.

Bell, J. (1992) *French constitutional law*. Oxford: Clarendon Press; New York: Oxford University Press.

Bermann, G., De Vries, H., and Galston, N. (1981–) *French law: constitution and selective legislation*. Ardsley-on-Hudson, NY: Transnational Juris. Looseleaf.

Bibliographie de la France. (1811–1971) Bibliographie officielle. Paris: Cercle de la librairie. Continued by *Bibliographie de la France: Biblio*. (1972–1989) Paris: Cercle de la librairie.

Bibliographie nationale française: BNF. (1970–) Paris: Chadwyck-Healey France. Bi-annual. CD-ROM.

Bibliographie nationale française. Livres. (1990–) Paris: Bibliothèque nationale, Office général du livre. Also *Supplément I, Publications en série*. (1990–) and *Supplément II, Publications officielles*. (1991–). Continues *Bibliographie de la France*.

Blanc-Jouvan, Xavier and Boulouis, Jean (1972) France. In *International encyclopedia of comparative law*, ed. V. Knapp, vol.1, pp. F47–F87. Tübingen: J.C.B. Mohr.

Bottin administratif. (1989–) Paris: Éditions Bottin. Annual.

Brown, L. and Bell, J. (1993) *French administrative law* 4th edn. Oxford: Clarendon Press.

Buffelan-Lanore, J.-P. (1991) *Informatique juridique documentaire*. Paris: Éditions de l'Espace européen.

Bulletin des arrêts de la Cour de cassation: Chambre criminelle. (1954–) Paris: Imprimerie des Journaux officiels. Monthly.

Bulletin des arrêts de la Cour de cassation: Chambres civiles. (1947–) Paris: Imprimerie des Journaux officiels. Monthly.

Cadiet, L. (1996) *Droit judiciaire privé* 2nd edn. Paris: LITEC.

Cairns, W. and McKeon, R. (1995) *Introduction to French law*. London: Cavendish.

Carbonnier, J. (1995) *Droit civil. Introduction* 23rd edn; (1994) *Droit civil. Les personnes. Tome 1* 19th edn; (1993) *Droit civil. La famille. Les incapacités. Tome 2* 16th edn; (1995) *Droit civil. Les biens. Tome 3* 16th edn; (1994) *Droit civil. Les obligations. Tome 4* 18th edn. Paris: PUF.

CD INFOCODES. (1995–) Paris: ORT-Journal Officiel. Bi-annual. CD-ROM.

CD QUARTIER LATIN. (1988–) Paris: Cujas. Union catalogue of the libraries of the Sorbonne, Cujas and Sainte Geneviève. Available from Bureau Van Dijk. 2 p.a.

Code constitutionnel. (1995) Paris: Dalloz.

Colliard, C.A. (1995) *Libertés publiques*. Paris: Dalloz.

Colombet, C. (1994) *Propriété littéraire et artistique et droits voisins* 7th edn. Paris: Dalloz.

Commercial laws of Europe. (1978–) London: European Law Centre, Sweet & Maxwell. Monthly.

Commercial laws of the world: France. (1970–) Gainesville, Fla.: Foreign Tax Law Association. Looseleaf.

Commission nationale de l'informatique et des libertés. 15è rapport d'activité. (1995) Paris: Documentation française.

Conditions juridiques et culturelles de l'intégration. Rapport au Premier ministre, Haut Conseil de l'Intégration. (1992) Paris: Documentation française.

Conseil d'État. Études et documents. (1947–) Paris: Documentation française. Annual.

Conseil d'État. Rapport Public. (Annual) Coll. Études et documents. Paris: Documentation française.

Les constitutions de la France depuis 1789. (1979, reprint 1993) Garnier-Flammarion texte intégral, 228. Paris: Garnier-Flammarion.

Les constitutions et les principales lois politiques de la France depuis 1789. (1988) 2nd edn. Paris: LGDJ. Originally compiled by L. Duguit *et al.*

Cornu, G. (1994) *Vocabulaire juridique* 4th edn. Paris: PUF.

Couchez, G. (1994) *Procédure civile*. 8th edn. Paris: Dalloz-Sirey.

Crabb, John H. (1995) (trans.) *French Civil Code*. Translated with an introduction. Littleton, Colo.: Rothman; Deventer: Kluwer Law and Taxation.

Dadomo, C. and Farran, S. (1996) *The French legal system* 2nd edn. London: Sweet & Maxwell.

Dahl, H. S. (1995) *Dahl's law dictionary: French to English/English to French: an annotated legal dictionary, including authoritative definitions from Codes, case law, statutes and legal writing = Dictionnaire juridique Dahl*. Buffalo, NY: Hein; Paris: Dalloz.

David, R. (1972) *French law: its structure, sources, and methodology*. Baton Rouge, La.: Louisiana State University Press.

David, R. (1980) *English law and French law*. London: Stevens.

David, R. and Brierley, J. (1985) *Major legal systems in the world today* 3rd edn. London: Stevens.

David, R. and De Vries, H.P. (1958) *The French legal system*. Dobbs Ferry, NY: Oceana.

Debbasch, C. and Pontier, J.-M. (1989) *Les Constitutions de la France* 2nd edn. Paris: Dalloz-Sirey.

De Clercq, A. and J. (1864–1917) *Recueil des traités de la France*. Paris: Amyot/Pedone. 23 vols. Published under the auspices of the Ministry of Foreign Affairs.

Dekeuwer-Defossez, Fr. (1995) *Droit commercial* 4th edn. Paris: Domat.

Dickson, Brice (1994) *Introduction to French law*. London: Pitman.

Dictionnaire des sources statistiques. (1988) Paris: Institut national de la statistique et des études économiques. 3 vols: vol.1, *Présentation et index*; vol.2, *Statistiques démographiques et sociales*; vol.3, *Statistiques du système productif, statistiques monétaires et financières*.

DOCTRINAL. (1993–) Paris: Transactive. Monthly. CD-ROM.

Doing business in France. (1983–) By the law firm of Siméon Moquet Borde & Associés. New York: Matthew Bender. 2 vols. Looseleaf.

Domat, Jean (1689) *Les lois civiles dans leur ordre naturel*. Paris. Edition of 1713, Paris: Gosselin in 2 vols. Edition of 1835 by J. Remy, Paris: Gobelet in 4 vols. English translation: (1850) *Civil law in its natural order* trans. W. Strahan from the 2nd London edition. Boston, Mass: Little and Brown.

Dunes, A. (1977) *La Documentation juridique*. Paris: Dalloz.

ELECTRE. (available from Chadwyck Healey France).

Ellul, J. (1992–1994) *Histoire des institutions*. Paris: PUF. 5 vols: (1992) *L'Antiquité. Tome 1–2* 8th edn; (1992) *Le Moyen Age. Tome 3* 12th edn; (1994) *XVI-XVIII siècles. Tome 4* 12th edn; (1992) *Le XIX siècle. Tome 5* 10th edn.

Encyclopédie Delmas des affaires. Paris: Delmas.

Encyclopédie juridique Dalloz. Répertoires. (1951–) 2nd edn. Paris: Dalloz. Looseleaf. Includes: *Répertoire de droit civil* (Rép. Civ.) 9 vols; *Répertoire de droit commercial* (Rép. Com.) 6 vols, incl. formbook; *Répertoire des sociétés* (Rép. Soc.) 5 vols, incl. formbook; *Répertoire de droit pénal et de procédure pénale* (Rép. pén.) 5 vols; *Répertoire de droit du travail* (Rép. Trav.) 4 vols; *Répertoire de procedure civile*, 6 vols incl. formbook in 2 vols; *Répertoire de contentieux administratif*, 2 vols; *Répertoire de la Responsabilité de la puissance publique*, 1 vol.; *Répertoire de droit communautaire*, 3 vols.

European current law. (1992–) London: European Law Centre, Sweet & Maxwell. Monthly.

French tax and business law guide. (1983–) Paris: Éditions Francis Lefèbvre; Chicago, Ill: CCH. Looseleaf.

Gazette du Palais. (1881–) Paris: Gazette du Palais. 3 times a week.

Gendrel, M. (1980) *Dictionnaire des principaux sigles utilisés dans le monde juridique de A à Z*. Paris: Montchrestien.

Germain, C. (1991–) *Germain's transnational law research: a guide for attorneys*. Ardsley-on-Hudson, NY: Transnational Juris. Looseleaf.

Ghestin, Jacques (1994) *Traité de droit civil* 4th edn. Paris: LGDJ.

Glendon, M.A., Gordon, M.W. and Osakwe, C. (1994) *Comparative legal traditions: text, materials, and cases on the civil and common law traditions, with special reference to French, German, English, and European law* 2nd edn. St. Paul, Minn.: West.

GPDOC INFOBASES: GAZETTE DU PALAIS. (1980–) Paris: Gazette des Palais. Annual. CD-ROM.

Grandin, A. (1926, reprint 1984) *Bibliographie générale des sciences juridiques, politiques, économiques et sociales, 1800–1926*. Vaduz, Liechtenstein: Topos. 3 vols. Supplements 1–19, 1926–1951.

Guide des professions juridiques. (1994) Paris: Éditions J.N.A. Société du journal des notaires et des avocats. 2 vols.

Guillien, R. and Vincent, J. (1995) *Termes juridiques* 10th edn. Paris: Dalloz.

Guimezanes, N. (1995) *Introduction au droit français*. Baden-Baden: Nomos.

Guinchard, S. (1995) *Comment devenir avocat?* 2nd edn. Paris: Monchrestien.

Guinchard, S. and Montagnier, G. (1995) *Lexique des termes juridiques* 10th edn. Paris: Dalloz.

Hamelin, J. and Damien, A. (1995) *Les règles de la profession d'avocat* 8th edn. Paris: Dalloz.

Héron, J. (1995) *Droit judiciaire privé* 2nd edn. Paris: Domat.

Herzog, P. (1967) *Civil procedure in France*. The Hague: Nijhoff.

Index to Foreign Legal Periodicals. (1960–) Berkeley, Cal.: University of California Press Quarterly. Available in print, CD-ROM and online formats.

Investing, licensing and trading conditions abroad. (Current) New York: Business International. Also available on LEXIS and WESTLAW.

Jauffret, A. and Mestre, J. (1995) *Manuel de droit commercial* 22th edn. Paris: LGDJ/Montchrestien.

Joly Sociétés under the direction of Daniel Lepeltier. (1993–) Paris: GLN Joly Éditions. Comprises: *Dictionnaire Joly* on CD-ROM. 2 p.a.; *Bulletin Joly*. Annual.

Journal du droit international. (1874–) Paris: LGDJ. Quarterly.

Journal officiel. (1869–) Paris: Imprimerie Nationale. Six series [*sections*] and some annexes, as follows: *Lois et Décrets, Débats de l'Assemblée Nationale, Débats du Sénat, Avis et Rapports du Conseil Economique et Social, Impressions, Documents Administratifs*. Formerly *Le moniteur universel* (1789–1868).

JOURNAL OFFICIEL. LOIS ET DÉCRETS. DISQUE OPTIQUE COMPACT. (1994–) Paris: Journal Officiel. Digital images of *Journal Officiel, Lois et Décrets* on CD-ROM.

Juglart, M. de and Ippolito, B. (1992, 1995) *Cours de droit commercial*. Paris: Montchrestien. Tome 1: (1995) *Actes de commerce. Commerçants. Fonds de commerce et effets de commerce* 11th edn; Tome 2: (1992) *Les sociétés commerciales* 9th edn.

Juris Classeur Codes et Lois. Comprises several parts: *Juris Classeur Codes et Lois* (*Droit Public-Droit Privé*) 10 vols; *Juris Classeur Codes et Lois* (*Droit Fiscal*) 4 vols; *Juris Classeur Agricole*. 4 vols. Paris: Éditions Techniques. Looseleaf.

Juris classeurs: encyclopédie juridique. (1901–) Paris: Éditions Techniques. Approx. 200 vols. Looseleaf.

Juris classeur périodique. See *Semaine juridique*.

JURIS-DATA. (available from Éditions du Juris Classeur).

La justice administrative en pratique. (1994). Paris: Documentation française.

Kahn-Freund, O., Lévy, C. and Rudden, B. (1991) *A source-book on French law: public law: constitutional and administrative law; private law: structure, contract*. Oxford: Clarendon Press; New York: Oxford University Press.

Kertstrat, F.G. de and Crawford, W. (1978) *New Code of Civil Procedure in France, Book 1/Nouveau code de procédure civile, livre 1*. Dobbs Ferry, NY: Oceana.

LAMY FISCAL. (1993–) Paris: Lamy. 2 p.a. CD-ROM version of the *Code général des impôts* and related tax documents and case law.

LAMY SOCIAL. (1993–) Paris: Lamy. 2 p.a. CD-ROM.

Laubadère, A. de (1993–) *Traité de droit administratif*. Paris: LGDJ. Comprises: vol.1, J.-C. Venezia and Y. Gaudemet (1994) *Organisation administrative, jurisdiction administrative, actes et objet de l'action administrative, responsabilité de l'administration*. 13th edn; vol.2, J.-C. Venezia et Y. Gaudemet (1995) *Fonction publique, domaines administratifs, expropriation, réquisition, travaux publics, urbanisme, aménagement du territoire* 10th edn; vol.3, J.-C. Venezia (1993–) *Les grands services publics administratifs* 5th edn; vol.4 (1996?) *L'administration de l'économie* 4th edn.

Lavroff, D.G. (1995) *Le droit constitutionnel de la Ve République*. Paris: Dalloz.

Lawson, F.H. (1953) *A common lawyer looks at the civil law*. Ann Arbor, Mich: University of Michigan Law School.

Lebreton, G. (1995) *Libertés publiques et droits de l'homme*. Paris: Armand Colin 'U Droit'.

Lefèbvre, F. (1995) Collection of '*mémentos pratiques*'. Paris: Lefèbvre. e.g. *Droit des affaires* (1995), *Sociétés commerciales* (1996). Updated frequently.

LEGI-CD COLLECTION. (available from Legisoft).

LEXILASER. *Conseil d'État & cours administratives* (1993–) 2 p.a.; *Cour de cassation* (1984–) 2 p.a.; *Lois et règlements* (1980–) 2 p.a. Paris: Téléconsulte-Lamy and Bureau Van Dijk. CD-ROM.

LEXIS. (available from Lamy in France and from LEXIS-NEXIS).

Les livres disponibles: la liste des ouvrages disponibles publiés en langue française dans le monde [French books in print]. (1977–) Paris: Service Bibliographique du Cercle de la Librairie. *Livres hebdo* weekly from the same publisher.

Loussouarn, Y. and Bourel, P. (1993) *Droit international privé* 4th edn. Paris: Dalloz.

Lyon-Caen, G., Pélissier, J, and Supiot, A. (1994) *Droit du travail* 17th edn Paris: Dalloz.

Magliulo, B. (1990) *Les 3es cycles et la recherche* 4th edn. Paris: Bordas.

Martindale-Hubbell international law digest. (1993–) New Providence, NJ: Martindale Hubbell. Annual. Also available on LEXIS.

Marty, Gabriel and Raynaud, Pierre (1986–) *Traité de droit civil*. Paris: Sirey. Comprises: Jestaz, Ph. (in preparation) *Introduction générale à l'étude du droit* 3rd edn; Jestaz,

Ph. (1989) *Les obligations: tome 1, les sources; tome 2, le régime* 2nd edn; Jestaz, Ph. (1987) *Les suretés: la publication foncière* 2nd. edn; (1986) *Les régimes matrimoniaux* 2nd edn.

Mayer, P. (1994) *Droit international privé* 5th edn. Paris: Domat.

Mazeaud, Henri (1989–) *Leçons de droit civil* 9th edn. Paris: Montchrestien.

Mégacode civil Dalloz. (1996) Paris: Dalloz.

Meyronneinc, J.-P. and Vital-Mareille, C. (1991) *Droit. Guide des formations supérieures à débouchés professionnels*. Paris: Le Monde-Éditions.

MYRIADE. CCN/Ministère de l'éducation nationale. Paris: Chadwyck Healey France. 2 p.a.

Nicholas, B. (1992) *The French law of contract*. Oxford: Clarendon Press.

Olivier-Martin, F. (1948) *Histoire du droit français, des origines à la révolution*. Paris: Montchrestien, Éditions Domat. Reprinted 1984 by Éditions CNRS.

Pédamon, M. and Merle, P. (1994) *Droit commercial*. Paris: Dalloz. Comprises: Pédamon, M. *Commerçants et entreprises commerciales. Concurrence et contrats du commerce* 10th edn; Merle, P. *Sociétés commerciales* 4th edn.

Perrot, R. (1995) *Institutions judiciaires* 7th edn. Paris: Montchrestien.

Le petit G.P.J.: guide des professions juridiques. (1994) Paris: Éditions JNA. Société du journal des notaires et des avocats.

Pinto, R. and Rollet, H. (1976–) *Recueil général des traités de la France*. Paris: Documentation française.

Pollard, David (1996) Sourcebook on French law. London: Cavendish.

Pradel, J. (1995) *Droit pénal*. Paris: Éditions Cujas. 2 vols: vol.1 (1995) *Introduction, Droit pénal général* 10th edn; vol.2, (1995) *Procédure pénale* 8th edn.

Pradel, J. (1995) *Droit pénal comparé*. Paris: Dalloz.

Prélot, Marcel (1990) *Institutions politiques et droit constitutionnel* 11th edn. by J. Boulouis. Paris: Dalloz.

Quid. (1963–) Paris: Laffont. Annual.

Quo juris: guide des juristes d'affaires. (1995) 4th edn. Paris: MM Éditions.

Rapport de la Cour de cassation. (1970–) Paris: Documentation française. Annual.

Recueil Dalloz Sirey. (1945–) Paris: Jurisprudence générale Dalloz. Weekly.

Recueil des décisions du Conseil Constitutionnel. (1958–) Paris: Imprimerie Nationale.

Recueil des décisions du Conseil d'État statuant au contentieux du Tribunal des conflits et des jugements des tribunaux administratifs. (1821–) Paris: Sirey. Bimonthly. Also known as *Recueil Lebon*.

Recueil des traités et accords de la France. (1981–) Paris: Imprimerie des Journaux Officiels. Fortnightly, cumulates annually.

René, D. (1980) *English law and French law: a comparison in substance*. London: Stevens; Calcutta: Eastern Law House.

Répertoire de l'administration française. (1995) 53rd edn. Paris: La Documentation française. Annual. Permanent update via Minitel. Continues: *Répertoire permanent de l'administration française*.

Répertoire des guides 'droits et démarches'. (1994) Paris: Documentation française.

Répertoire des publications en série de l'administration française (périodiques et collections). (1991) 5th edn. Paris: Commission de coordination de la documentation administrative.

Répertoires livres hebdo. (1980–) Paris: Éditions professionnelles du livre.

Revue critique de droit international privé. (1946–) Paris: Sirey. Quarterly.

Revue de science criminelle et de droit pénal comparé. (1936–) Paris: Institut de Droit Comparé.

Revue trimestrielle de droit civil. (1902–) Paris: Sirey. Quarterly.

Revue trimestrielle de droit commercial et du droit économique. (1948–) Paris: Sirey. Quarterly.

Revue trimestrielle de droit européen. (1965–) Paris: Sirey.

Reynolds, T. and Flores, A. (1989–) *Foreign law: current sources of codes and basic legislation in jurisdictions of the world*. Littleton, Colo.: Rothman. Looseleaf.

Ripert, Georges (1991–) *Traité élémentaire de droit commercial*. Paris: LGDJ. Vol.1 (1991), 14th edn. by R. Roblot; Vol.2 (1992), 13th edn. by R. Roblot; Vol.3 (1992), 2nd cdn. by. P. Serlooten.

Roland, H. and Boyer, L. (1991) *Dictionnaire des expressions juridiques* 2nd edn. Lyon: L'Hermés.

Roland, H. and Boyer, L. (1992) *Adages du droit français* 3rd edn. Paris: LITEC.

Roland, H. and Boyer, L. (1993) *Locutions latines du droit français*. 3rd edn. Paris: LITEC.

Royer, J.-P. (1995) *Histoire de la justice en France. De la monarchie absolue à la République*. Paris: PUF.

Schlesinger, R.B. (1988) *Comparative law: cases, text, materials*. Mineola, NY: Foundation Press.

Schwartz, B. (1954) *French administrative law and the common law world*. New York: New York University Press.

Semaine juridique: juris classeur périodique. (1927–) Paris: Éditions Techniques.

Solus, H. and Perrot, R. (1961–) *Droit judiciaire privé*. Paris: Sirey. 3 vols: vol.1 (1961) *Introduction. Notions fondamentales (action en justice, formes et délais, acte juridictionnel). Organisation judictionnelle*; vol.2 (1973) *La compétence*; vol.3 (1991) *Procédure de première instance*.

Spitzer, Vlad G. (1988) France. In *Constitutions of the countries of the world*, eds A.P. Blaustein and G.H. Flanz, vol.VII. Dobbs Ferry, NY: Oceana. Supplements by G.H. Flanz in September 1994 and December 1995. Looseleaf.

Stéfani, G., Levasseur, G. and Bouloc, B. (1994) *Droit pénal général* 15th edn. Paris: Dalloz.

Stéfani, G., Levasseur, G. and Bouloc, B. (1996) *Procédure pénale* 16th edn. Paris: Dalloz.

Stone, A. (1992) *The birth of judicial politics in France*. Oxford & New York: Oxford University Press.

Surbiguet, M. and Wibaux, D. (1982) (eds) *Liste des Traités et Accords de la France en Force au. . . .* Paris: Imprimerie Nationale.

Szladits, C. and Germain, C. (1985) *Guide to foreign legal materials: French* 2nd edn. Dobbs Ferry, NY: Oceana.

Tanguy, Y. (1991) *La recherche documentaire en droit*. Paris: PUF.

Terré, F. (1994) *Droit civil. Introduction générale* 2nd edn. Paris: Dalloz.

TRANSPOSIAL. (1995–) Paris: Transactive. CD-ROM. 2 p.a.

Vincent, J. *et al.* (1991) *La justice et ses institutions* 3rd edn. Paris: Dalloz.

Vincent, J. and Guinchard, S. (1994) *Procédure civile* 23rd edn. Paris: Dalloz.

Weill, Alex (1996) *Droit civil: Les personnes, la famille, les incapacités* 6th edn. Paris: Dalloz.

West, A. *et al.* (1992) *The French legal system: an introduction*. London: Fourmat.

West's Law and commercial dictionary in five languages: definitions of the legal and commercial terms and phrases of American, English, and civil law jurisdictions. Law and commercial dictionary in five languages. (1985) St. Paul, Minn.: West.

Weston, M. (1991) *An English reader's guide to the French legal system*. New York & Oxford: Berg.

World of learning. (1947–) London: Europa Pubs. Annual.

Zweigert, K. and Kötz, H. (1993) *Introduction to comparative law* 2nd rev. ed Oxford: Clarendon Press; New York: Oxford University Press.

CHAPTER TWELVE

Germany

HOLGER KNUDSEN

Introduction to the legal system

The German state has evolved over the last 1000 years from early Germanic roots to the present-day federal republic. This evolution was in the beginning characterized by an ever-growing strength, first of the tribal dukes, then of the princes, and, consequently, a weak position of the ruling monarch. From the 13th century onwards, the king was elected by the seven most powerful princes and bishops, the 'Electors', and then anointed Emperor by the Pope.

The 'Holy Roman Empire of the German Nation' was further weakened by religious confrontations following Luther's Reformation and the subsequent Counter-Reformation, and social unrest which manifested itself in the Peasants' Wars. All this culminated in the Thirty Years' War which widely devastated the country and during which an estimated one third of the population was killed. After the peace treaty of 1648 the Empire continued to exist *de jure*, but it disintegrated *de facto* into some 1300 principalities, dominions, and free cities, ranging from the two predominant powers, Austria and Prussia, down to rather tiny and insignificant territories.

The Empire was finally smashed by Napoleon in 1806, and the number of German states diminished considerably. After the Congress of Vienna, only 39 of them had survived. They formed a confederation [Deutscher Bund], from which Austria was forced to withdraw in 1866. The remaining 25 states founded the German Empire [Deutsches Reich] under Prussian leadership in 1871. Thus only in 1871 did Germany finally acquire its national unity – the starting point of the contemporary legal development.

The following years, 1871 to 1897, saw the enactment of the major

German codes which replaced one by one the individual codes of the German states. They are still in force today, though having undergone numerous changes. The codes will be explained in more detail below. Whereas the first all-German codes can be considered modern and efficient masterpieces of legislation, by contrast the Empire's Constitution of 1871 consisted of rather backward provisions. This radically changed, however, when Germany became a republic after World War I. The Constitution of 1919 granted all the rights which characterize a modern liberal democracy, and tried (in vain, as is known) to stabilize the political life through the introduction of a constitutional system of checks and balances. Historians disagree whether, perhaps, the Weimar Republic of 1919 was doomed to failure from the beginning. It is, however, true that the abuse of the constitutional freedoms so abundantly granted was one of the main reasons for her collapse.

The darkest years of German history with Hitler's 'Third Reich', 1933 to 1945, were, after World War II, followed by an interregnum during which the four Allied Powers exerted the supreme legislative authority, 1945 to 1949. Both periods can be ignored here since few laws from that time remain in force and consequently their traces are only indirectly perceptible.

Two books in English on the more recent German legal history can be particularly recommended, namely Holborn, Carter and Herz (1970) and Hucko (1989).

In 1949 two states emerged from the ruins of the Reich: the Bundesrepublik Deutschland [Federal Republic of Germany, or FRG], and the Deutsche Demokratische Republik [German Democratic Republic, or GDR], the former being an amalgamation of the three Western zones, the latter replacing the Soviet occupation zone.

The GDR ceased to exist on 3 October 1990 when Germany was reunified. This happened following a general gradual decline of communist rule in the Eastern bloc, which did not leave the GDR untouched and finally led to public demonstrations against the government. On 9 November 1989, the Berlin Wall came down, and on 18 March 1990, the first free elections ever took place in the GDR. The main task of the government so elected was to abolish the country. This was achieved by several treaties between the FRG and the GDR. The most important of these treaties was the Unification Treaty of 31 August 1990. According to this treaty West German law was to be applied in Eastern Germany after accession except as otherwise stated in the treaty. Since the exceptions relate to questions of domestic law which are of little general interest for the comparative lawyer, the law of the former GDR will not be dealt with here.

The events that eventually led to the disintegration of the former German Democratic Republic were described by Pond (1993). This book, though not strictly legal, compels admiration for its scholarly, yet easily readable way of making complicated matters understandable. The Unification Treaty has been translated and reproduced by Wegen and Crosswhite (1990).

The Constitution of the present German state is the *Grundgesetz* [Basic Law] of May 23, 1949. The *Grundgesetz* is divided into two parts, one section on constitutional civic and human rights (articles 1 to 19), and 13 sections on the political system and the organization of the state (articles 20 to 146). An excellent and most scholarly textbook about the Basic Law is Currie (1994). The text of the Constitution is reproduced in English in *Basic Law for the Federal Republic of Germany – official translation* (1995), a free booklet from the Press and Information Office of the federal government which is also reproduced in Flanz (1994) with the German text.

Because of its history, the Bundesrepublik Deutschland [Federal Republic of Germany] is a state which is strictly organized according to federalist principles, composed of the federation [Bund] and 16 states [Land, plural: Länder]. Bund and Länder are each vested with their own legislative powers. On a third level of government there are municipal units. The FRG is a state with a parliamentary system on all three levels.

The FRG was in 1957 one of the six founding members of the European Economic Community, and since 1973 it has been member of the United Nations.

Introductory works on the legal system and legal research

There is no legal system, outside the English-speaking world, about which there is such a great variety of texts in English than that of Germany. A recent bibliography, *German law in English* (Radke *et al.*, 1993), provides access to some 1400 books and articles published during the last 25 years. As the subtitle indicates, it is only conceived as a 'select bibliography' and, as a matter of fact, it is far from being complete. Yet it is an excellent tool for anyone interested in the German legal system. In recent years, probably due to a revived interest in Germany after the fall of the Berlin Wall, many more books and articles on the German legal system have been published. It therefore seems appropriate to concentrate here on texts of recent date, in English whenever possible.

Four excellent introductory works merit special mention in this section: *Sourcebook on German law* (Youngs, 1994); *German legal system and laws* (Foster, 1996); *Guide to foreign legal materials: German* (Kearley and Fischer, 1990); and *Introduction to German law* (Ebke and Finkin, 1996).

Whereas the first book offers access to the German legal system through carefully and judiciously chosen annotated documents and thus may be considered a kind of casebook in the common law tradition, the second is a well-written and very knowledgeable treatise by an obviously well-versed expert and is particularly good for those readers who have little or no knowledge of the German legal system. The third book, however, can best be compared to readers on 'how to find the law' in the Anglo-American tradition which are otherwise not known in Germany. It enumerates the main legal literature of Germany for the non-German reader and explains how to use it. Regrettably, it contains little evaluation of the practical usefulness of the literature so presented. Nevertheless, it is an excellent guide on how to perform research in Germany. Kearley and Fischer also provide an introduction of about forty pages to the legal system which is, however, partially dated because it describes the state of affairs existing before reunification. Last but not least, the *Introduction to German law* is a joint work written by 20 German experts. It is of high quality but, as a rule, readers are required to have a basic understanding of the civil law system already.

Since the four books look at the German legal system from different points of view, they should be used in conjunction with one another. As a general recommendation, the bibliography *German law in English*, as well as the books of Youngs, Foster, Kearley and Fischer, and Ebke and Finkin would be the ideal stock for the German bookshelf of libraries with some interest in, but no particular emphasis on, foreign and comparative law. Libraries with a particular interest in foreign private law might consider adding the well-written introduction of Dannemann (1993) and some of the codes recommended below.

A recently published book on the *German legal system and legal language* (Fisher, 1996) is a primer of some 180 pages, to which is added a bilingual legal dictionary. It is useful for the beginner looking for a first overview, but seems to be designed for legal translators rather than for practical lawyers. However, since it has a different approach to the German legal system, it can be recommended.

Since abbreviations are abundantly used in the German legal system, Kirchner's directory of abbreviations (1993) is indispensable and must be added to this basic list. This selection may be complemented by Oeckl's directory (1996) and by Creifelds' encyclopedia (1996), both discussed under the appropriate sections below.

Legislation

Official texts

The official record of Germany's laws and ordinances on the federal level is the *Bundesgesetzblatt* [Federal Gazette] (1949–). It is issued according to need, normally once or twice per week and consists of two parts: Teil I [part one] contains domestic laws and ordinances, Teil II [part two] contains international treaties and agreements to which the FRG has become a party. Both parts are accessible through two annual indexes: *Fundstellennachweis A* for the *Bundesgesetzblatt* Teil I; *Fundstellennachweis B* for the *Bundesgesetzblatt* Teil II. Amended laws are reproduced in a consolidated version whenever considerable changes have taken place. There are no determined intervals for such revisions. According to article 82 of the Basic Law, legislation comes into force 14 days after its publication in the *Bundesgesetzblatt* unless otherwise stated in the respective law or ordinance itself.

In 1963 an official consolidated collection of the federal laws in force at that time was completed, which is known as *Bundesgesetzblatt* Teil III. It has not been continued since but retains its value whenever it is questionable whether a law enacted between 1867 and 1958 is still in force. The *Bundesgesetzblatt* Teil III is not widely used among the profession and is now out of print; in any case it is of such a particularly poor paper quality that in the foreseeable future there will only be a few copies left.

Subsidiary legislation, administrative regulations, important legal notices, and official court announcements relating to the registration of enterprises and bankruptcy proceedings can be found in the *Bundesanzeiger* [Federal Bulletin] (1949–). It is published several times per week and can only be recommended to institutions with profound interest in German legal affairs owing to its considerable size and growth rate. Both the *Bundesanzeiger* and the *Bundesgesetzblatt* are available in microfiche editions.

Commercial collections

There are three widely used and up-to-date commercial looseleaf collections of federal statutes in force: the very comprehensive *Das Deutsche Bundesrecht*; Schönfelder, *Deutsche Gesetze*, which contains the most frequently used laws, complemented by Sartorius, *Verfassungs- und Verwaltungsgesetze der Bundesrepublik Deutschland* for the most frequently used constitutional and administrative laws.

All three collections are held in high esteem for both their immediate updates and their reliability, but whereas *Das Deutsche Bundesrecht* can only be used in libraries owing to its size, the two latter collections (known among German lawyers simply as 'Schönfelder' and 'Sartorius') are easy to handle and to carry. Use in court is not only acceptable but customary. Whereas there is as yet no complete edition of the *Bundesgesetzblatt* on CD-ROM, the three commercial collections have recently been published as CD-ROM editions and been regularly updated since. This option seems to be particularly attractive to foreign lawyers.

In addition to federal legislation, every German Land provides for its own official journal, and for every Land there are commercially produced loose leaf collections of the law in force. The legislation of 12 of the 16 German states is published in that form by the publisher Beck-Verlag of Munich.

Both the majority of the federal laws and the most important state laws are covered by the commercial *Sammelblatt* (1950–), where they are reprinted shortly after their official publication. The *Sammelblatt* has good standing as a reliable source.

Citation

A citation of a federal law or ordinance would typically look like this: name of the legislative text, abbreviation of that name where applicable, date of publication, abbreviation of *Bundesgesetzblatt*, volume, first page: Pflichtstückverordnung (PflStVO) vom 14.12.1982 (BGBl I, 1739). An international treaty would be cited as follows: Einigungsvertrag vom 31.8.1990 (BGBl II, 889).

By analogy, a typical Land statute would be cited as: Thüringer Hochschulgesetz (ThürHG) vom 7.7.1992 (GVBl 1992, 315). GVBl is the standard abbreviation for most, but not all, of the Land gazettes: Gesetz- und Verordnungsblatt.

Even though German lawyers normally use commercial editions for their work, this standardized citation form according to the official sources always has to be (and by custom always is) applied. The only exception would be the aforementioned *Sammelblatt* which is, although commercial, considered to be fully citable for formal purposes, e.g.: Bayerische Gemeindeordnung (BayGO) vom 5.12.1973 (SaBl 1974, 166).

Preparatory texts

Proceedings in the federal parliament, including debates on new laws, are contained in *Verhandlungen des Deutschen Bundestages: Stenographische Berichte* (1950–), whereas draft legislation is published in *Verhandlungen des Deutschen Bundestages: Drucksachen* (1950–). Both parts of the Verhandlungen are also available on microfiche. Both editions, microfiche or hardcover, are provided with an excellent index. *Bundesgesetzblatt*, *Bundesanzeiger*, and *Verhandlungen des Deutschen Bundestages* are all published by, and available through, the Bundesanzeiger Verlagsgesellschaft.

Codes and commentaries

The German legal system is characterized by the widespread existence and use of sophisticated commentaries. Commentaries cite the law article by article and, for each article, name the relevant general literature followed by an explanatory section in which legal problems and questions of the precise meaning and interpretation of individual notions are defined and illustrated by the aid of suitable doctrinal writings and court decisions.

As a rule, for every law of some significance there is a commentary. The more important and frequently needed laws are often explained by several competing commentaries. For example, Germany's most important law, the Civil Code, can be interpreted by means of no less than nine commentaries (to which can be added several older commentaries which have not been brought up to date). Unfortunately the one-volume commentaries, which are the more frequently used ones, employ abbreviations to a very large extent. This makes them difficult to read even for the German lawyer and almost incomprehensible to non-lawyers or foreigners. By contrast, access to the multi-volume commentaries is difficult owing to the sheer extent of information and they are not widely available outside Germany because of their tremendous acquisition costs.

The most frequently used commentaries for major laws are as follows.

Federal Constitution [*Grundgesetz*] of 23 May 1949:
- Schmidt-Bleibtreu and Klein (1995) *Kommentar zum Grundgesetz.*

Civil Code [*Bürgerliches Gesetzbuch*] of 18 August 1896 (in force 1 January 1900):
- Palandt *et al.* (1997) *Bürgerliches Gesetzbuch.*
- Erman *et al.* (1993) *Handkommentar zum Bürgerlichen Gesetzbuch.*
- *Münchener Kommentar zum Bürgerlichen Gesetzbuch.* (1992–).
- Soergel and Siebert (1987–) *Bürgerliches Gesetzbuch.*
- Staudinger *et al.* (1995–) *Kommentar zum Bürgerlichen Recht.*

Commercial Code [*Handelsgesetzbuch*] of 10 May 1897:
- Baumbach and Hopt (1995) *Handelsgesetzbuch.*

Code of Civil Procedure [*Zivilprozessordnung*] of 30 January 1877:
- Thomas and Putzo (1997) *Zivilprozessordnung.*
- Baumbach *et al.* (1997) *Zivilprozessordnung.*
- *Münchener Kommentar zur Zivilprozessordnung.* (1992).

Criminal Code [*Strafgesetzbuch*] of 15 May 1871:
- Lackner and Kühl (1995) *Strafgesetzbuch mit Erläuterungen.*
- Dreher and Tröndle (1995) *Strafgesetzbuch.*
- Schönke *et al.* (1997) *Strafgesetzbuch: Kommentar.*

Code of Criminal Procedure [*Strafprozessordnung*] of 1 February 1877:
- Kleinknecht *et al.* (1995) *Strafprozessordnung.*

Code of Administrative Procedure [*Verwaltungsgerichtsordnung*] of 21 January 1960:
- Redeker and von Oertzen (1994) *Verwaltungsgerichtsordnung: Kommentar.*
- Kopp *et al.* (1994) *Verwaltungsgerichtsordnung.*

These commentaries are not necessarily the most scholarly or voluminous ones but simply the most frequently used and cited commentaries. Some important commentaries, although none of them is mentioned above, are published in looseleaf format.

English translations

Whereas there is no commentary on German law in English with the exception of Currie (1994) *The Constitution of the Federal Republic of Germany*, all important German codes have been translated into the English language:

Civil Code: Goren (1994b).
Private International Law Code: Wegen (1988).
Commercial Code: Peltzer (1995).
Code of Civil Procedure: Goren (1990).
Criminal Code: Darby (1987).
Code of Criminal Procedure: Niebler (1965).

Other important, but less general, codes have also been translated into English and can be found in the bibliography 'German Law in English' (1993). Translations after that date include: *German industrial property laws* (Beier *et al.* 1996), *Law of reorganizations – Reorganization tax law* (Benkert and Bürkle, 1996), *Asylum Procedure Act* (Born, 1994a), *Environmental legislation* (Born, 1995), *Federal electoral law* (Born, 1993), *Law on political parties* (Born,1994c), *Press laws* (Born, 1994b), *German accounting legislation* (Brooks and Mertin, 1996), *The condominium property law of the FRG* (Goren, 1994a), *German Trade Mark Act and Regulation* (Kuhnen and Wacker, 1995), *German insider and stock exchange law* (Mohr, 1994), *German law pertaining to companies with limited liability* (Peltzer, Brooks and Hopcroft, 1995), *German Securities Trade Act* (Peltzer and Scesniak, 1995), *Labor Management Relations Act* (Peltzer and Stewart, 1995), *German insurance laws* (Pfennigstorf, 1995), *German environmental law* (Schlemminger and Wissel, 1996), *German Stock Corporation Act* (Schneider and Heidenhain, 1996), and *Banking Act* (Zerwas, 1996).

Up-to-date information about the German legal system can also be found in a number of valuable looseleaf collections which have, however, a comparative approach and therefore their coverage of Germany is by necessity limited. The only looseleaf services written in English which exclusively cover Germany are *Business transactions in Germany* (Rüster *et al.*, 1983–), and *German tax and business law guide* (1995–). Whereas the first collection is well established and enjoys a good reputation for both its texts, all written by professionals, and its far-reaching provision of translated business related statutory materials, the second collection is relatively new on the market. The first impression is good, however, and it is equipped with accurate and recent information.

Treaties

According to article 59 of the Basic Law, treaty-making power is vested in the Deutscher Bundestag [Federal Parliament], though it is the Bundespräsident [Federal President] who represents Germany in her diplomatic relations. The relevant government department is the Auswärtiges Amt [Ministry of Foreign Affairs]. Treaties, once ratified, appear in the *Bundesgesetzblatt* Teil II (see above). The treaties to which the FRG is a party, including those concluded before 1949 but still in force, are accessible through the Fundstellenverzeichnis B which is published yearly as an annex to the *Bundesgesetzblatt* Teil II. It offers threefold access: by reference to the contracting party or parties, chronological, and by subject. For multilateral treaties in force to which Germany is a party there is a semi-official collection *Verträge der Bundesrepublik Deutschland* produced by the Ministry of Foreign Affairs (1955–). There is no such collection for bilateral treaties yet.

Law reports, judgments

In Germany case law is *de jure* not a primary source of law since the courts do not create law and since there is no rule of *stare decisis*. Nevertheless, judicial decisions *de facto* do have a considerable binding effect. This is particularly true for the judgments of the different high courts which are generally followed by other courts. Thus judgments, though they are not formally binding, are considered to have a certain authority and German courts on all levels frequently refer to previous court decisions.

The administration of justice in Germany is characterized by a complex system of distribution of responsibilities among different courts, each of them being the decision-making body for a particular field of law: constitutional, civil, criminal, administrative, labour, social, tax, patent, disciplinary affairs of civil servants. There is no supreme court as an overall judicial institution.

As a rule (with numerous exceptions) the court system in each field of law is also horizontally divided into courts of first instance, courts of appeals, and high courts. The German names for these courts vary. In the most important field of civil and criminal matters, ordinary jurisdiction [ordentliche Gerichtsbarkeit], the names are Landgericht (abbreviation: LG), Oberlandesgericht (OLG), and Bundesgerichtshof (BGH). For historical reasons, the name of the Oberlandesgericht Berlin is Kammergericht (KG). Within the ordinary jurisdiction, there are also lower courts for small claims litigation in civil matters and minor criminal cases [Amtsgericht, or AG].

Owing to Germany's federal tradition, the high courts are not centred in the capital, but seated in different cities all over the country. The Bundesverfassungsgericht [Constitutional Court] and the Bundesgerichtshof [High Court for Civil and Criminal Matters] are both seated in Karlsruhe, in the South-Western part of Germany.

A recent description of the German court system, which takes into account the changes after the German unification, can be found in Heyde (1994).

There is no overall collection of court decisions in Germany because of the nature of the court system. Decisions of courts of lower instance remain unpublished for all practical purposes with some rare exceptions, for example, new legal issues or spectacular cases. Many but not all decisions of the Constitutional Court and the different high courts are, as a rule, published firstly with minimum delay in one or several of the general or specialized law reviews and then in one of the semi-official collections published by members of the individual courts.

Since the publication of judgments in law reviews is often confined to their more important parts and since publication in the semi-official collections may take some time, those interested in a particular judgment can obtain it from the court concerned by indicating the respective file number [*Aktenzeichen*] which is always given when judgments are published. However, the fees charged by the courts for such a service may be very high.

The important semi-official collections of the high courts, with the standard abbreviations, are:

Constitutional Court:
Entscheidungen des Bundesverfassungsgerichts, BVerfGE, (1952–).

Federal High Court for Civil Matters:
Entscheidungen des Bundesgerichtshofes in Zivilsachen, BGHZ, (1951–), also available on CD-ROM.

Federal High Court for Criminal Matters:
Entscheidungen des Bundesgerichtshofes in Strafsachen (1951–), BGHSt, also available on CD-ROM.

Imperial High Court for Civil Matters:
Entscheidungen des Reichsgerichts in Zivilsachen, RGZ, (1880–1945).

Imperial High Court for Criminal Matters:
Entscheidungen des Reichsgerichts in Strafsachen, RGSt, (1880–1944).

Federal High Court for Labour Matters:
Entscheidungen des Bundesarbeitsgerichts, BAGE, (1955–).

Federal High Court for Social Matters:
Entscheidungen des Bundessozialgerichts, BSGE, (1956–).

Federal High Court for Administrative Matters:
Entscheidungen des Bundesverwaltungsgerichts, BVerwGE, (1955–).

There is a number of commercial reporting services, but they are either not widely used by the profession or in looseleaf format and rather expensive. All sources, whether semi-official or unofficial, may be cited in court, but if a case has been reported in parallel locations it is customary though not absolutely imperative to cite the semi-official sources above.

It is a generally accepted standard to abbreviate citations to a densely concise format. A typical citation according to one of the semi-official collections of court decisions would take the following form (abbreviation of the collection's name, volume, first page, relevant page): BGHZ 8, 72 (75). The citation for the same judgment, as reported by the country's leading law journal *Neue Juristische Wochenschrift* would take the form (abbreviation of the court's name, abbreviation of the journal's name, year of publication, first page, relevant page): BGH NJW 1953, 420 (422). Contrary to the tradition in the common law countries, cases do not carry names of the parties involved and therefore name tables or the like are unknown in Germany.

Owing to the sophisticated system of commentaries (see above) there are no digests in the common law tradition in Germany. A German lawyer would identify the judgments relevant to a case by consulting a commentary on the respective law. Recently the sometimes tedious research in commentaries has been partially superseded by the growing impact of legal databases (see below).

There are, with one exception, no collections in English dedicated to German court decisions. This exception is *Decisions of the Bundesverfassungsgericht, Federal Constitutional Court* .... (1992–). A good selection of translated court decisions can also be found in Youngs (1994).

Computer-based systems

The major computer-based system for German law is the semi-official JURISTISCHES INFORMATIONSSYSTEM – JURIS, which has been publicly available on line since 1986. It consists of several databases, the most important ones offering access to the complete German legislative texts in force, some 400 000 court decisions, as well as some 350 000 bibliographic records of law books and articles in about 450 law reviews. JURIS is rapidly growing and up to date. Connections to JURIS from outside Germany are possible, including via Internet, subject to a prior subscription contract. JURIS is accessible through its own command language which is very sophisticated and so might be difficult to handle without training and without basic notions of the German language and legal terminology.

The contents of the JURIS databases are also available on CD-ROM. JURIS thus competes with the commercial suppliers of legislative texts and court decisions on a fast-growing market (see above under **Legislation** and **Law reports, judgments** where publications available on CD-ROM are noted). Whereas JURIS is the leading supplier of computer-based general legal information in Germany, other databases offer access to parts of the law, for example, tax law. The number of legal CD-ROMs has rapidly grown in recent times and there are now more than 200 different titles on the market, but the majority of them cover either specialist fields of law, are designed for teaching purposes, or reproduce the more recent volumes of long established law journals. This does not, however, seem to exploit the medium to its best advantage and can only be considered a first step towards complete full text CD-ROM editions.

The government Internet site is at http://www.auswaertiges-amt.government.de but it contains little information with a directly legal content at present and mainly deals with foreign policy but a general federal server is under construction.

Encyclopedias

Probably owing to the predominant position of commentaries within the legal system of Germany, the country has by contrast no tradition of overall multi-volume encyclopedias. There is one vast encyclopedia *Deutsches Rechts-Lexikon* (1992), which is, however, very expensive. Widely used is *Rechtswörterbuch* (Creifelds *et al.*, 1996), an excellent and comprehensive one-volume encyclopedia of legal terms. Because of Creifelds' extremely plain and concise language, non-native speakers may find it difficult to use the *Rechtswörterbuch*. It is still an absolute must for every German law collection. Creifelds' successors also publish regularly an introduction into the German legal system for non-lawyers, *Staatsbürger-Taschenbuch* (Creifelds *et al.*, 1995). It is easy to read and yet a truly excellent source of information.

Directories

The following list of research tools contains material for a basic reference collection. The best directory with virtually all important German addresses is Oeckl (1996), *Taschenbuch des öffentlichen Lebens*. It is published yearly and is a concise, up-to-date and reliable directory which contains some 14 000 addresses. It is particularly good for research into government departments on both the federal and the state level but also contains addresses of public, private, research related and business related institutions and organizations. The best nationwide directory of practising lawyers is *Anwalts- und Notarverzeichnis* (1996). Courts and judges can best be found in *Handbuch der Justiz* (1996).

Whereas a general directory of universities can be found in the aforementioned book by Oeckl, there is as yet no directory of law schools which would take into account the changes which have occurred since reunification, including the reopening of nine law schools in Eastern Germany. A good alternative is the German section in *Guide to legal studies in Europe* (1996). A very good directory of all German libraries holding more than 50 000 law books is Lansky (1993).

Bibliographies and indexing services

The country's leading legal bibliography is the *Karlsruher Juristische Bibliographie*, abbreviated to *KJB* (1965–). It is a monthly publication and includes references to articles from some 700 law journals, and to books, both commercially and non-commercially published. The non-commercially published books embodied in the *KJB* are often doctoral dissertations which play an important role in the German legal system, though the better ones are normally published by publishing houses. Literature within the *KJB* is arranged in systematic subject order. Each issue has an author's index, there are cumulative indexes annually and every five years. The *KJB* includes literature in foreign languages. Goedan (1992) describes the *KJB* in more detail.

It might suffice to point out here that while the *KJB* remains unmatched as to reliability and coverage, the database JURIS (see above) has recently gained more acceptance within the profession, due to the speed at which items are included.

There is no predecessor to the *KJB* worth mentioning. Kearley and Fischer (1990) offer a comprehensive list of all sources which might be useful to this end on pp. 41–47, but the normal German lawyer would not know, let alone use them.

Of importance is, however, the *Union list of legal serials-VRZS* (1990). It contains both German and foreign legal periodical titles subscribed to by German libraries, with the holding libraries specified, and it is extremely useful for bibliographical purposes and interlibrary loan. The *VRZS* is a printed excerpt from the 'Zeitschriften-Datenbank', Germany's nationwide database for the holdings of periodicals on all subjects of all German libraries of some importance.

This section is the right place to focus attention again on *German law in English* (Radke *et al.*, 1993) (see above under **Introductory works**).

The German legal system is characterized by one further particularity which over the years has become a tradition: the bountiful dedication of commemorative books [Festschrift, plural: Festschriften]. Since Festschriften are often rather arbitrarily composed, they are justly regarded as graves of knowledge and access to their contents is considered to be difficult. Dau (1962–1995), *Bibliography of legal festschriften 1864–1993*, lists and indexes virtually every German (as well as Swiss and Austrian) legal Festschrift. It is a truly unique and unprecedented tool of great value which eases reference work considerably.

Dictionaries

The most commonly used German legal dictionary is Creifelds *Rechtswörterbuch* (Creifelds *et al.*, 1996), described above under **Encyclopedias**. There are two English–German/German–English law dictionaries of good quality, Romain (1989/1994), and Dietl *et al.* (1990/1992). For style of abbreviations Kirchner (1993), *Abkürzungsverzeichnis der Rechtssprache*, is the most widely used and a reference work of authority. Abbreviations are regularly and methodologically employed in the German legal system, and it is therefore impossible to oversee it without this indispensable tool. Not quite as good and complete, but perhaps more easily accessible to foreign readers is Kavass and Prince (1991–).

Current information sources

Journals, research reports

There are some 800 law journals in Germany, many of them highly esteemed but with a very special coverage. Owing to the general character of this outline it must suffice to name the two most important: *Neue Juristische Wochenschrift* (1947–), abbreviated to *NJW*, and *Juristenzeitung* (1946–), abbreviated to *JZ*. Their layout is quite typical: they contain news information, scholarly articles, and court decisions. They do not, however, reprint legislative texts.

News information

It is customary that German law reviews offer news information, often specialized, in a separate section. Particularly good for information about new legislative projects is the newsletter of the Ministry of Justice, *Recht* (1970–).

Business and financial information

Business information can be found in Rüster *et al.*(1983–) and in *German tax and business law guide* (1995–). For an evaluation of these two important loose leaf collections see above at the end of the section on **Codes and commentaries**.

Recent treatises on the topic include: Mergers and acquisitions in Germany (1995), *German capital market law* (Siebel, Löwenstein and Finney, 1995), *Protection of technical innovations and designs in Germany* (Stockmair, 1994), *Transactions in real property* (1994), *Starting business operations in Germany* (Jung, 1993), and *Germany: practical commercial law* (1992).

Germany's leading commercial daily newspaper is *Handelsblatt* (1946–).

Useful addresses

Associations of lawyers

Bundesrechtsanwaltskammer, Joachimstr. 1, D-53113 Bonn, Germany. Tel: +49 228 911860. Fax: +49 228 261538

Bundesnotarkammer, Burgmauer 53, D-50667 Köln, Germany. Tel: +49 221 256823. Fax: +49 221 256808

Government organizations

Auswärtiges Amt [Ministry of Foreign Affairs], Adenauerallee 99–103, D-53113 Bonn, Germany. Tel: +49 228 170. Fax: +49 228 173402

Bundesministerium der Justiz [Ministry of Justice], Heinemannstr. 6, D-53175 Bonn, Germany. Tel: +49 228 580. Fax: +49 228 584525

Deutscher Akademischer Austauschdienst, Kennedyallee 50, D-53175 Bonn, Germany. Tel: +49 228 8820. Fax: +49 228 882444

Inter Nationes, Kennedyallee 91–103, D-53175 Bonn, Germany. Tel: +49 228 8800. Fax: +49 228 880457

Presse- und Informationsamt der Bundesregierung [Press and Information Office of the Federal Government], Welckerstr. 11, D-53113 Bonn, Germany. Tel: +49 228 2080. Fax: +49 228 2082555

Courts

Bundesverfassungsgericht [Federal Constitutional Court], Schlossbezirk 3, D-76131 Karlsruhe, Germany. Tel: +49 721 91010. Fax: +49 721 9101382

Bundesgerichtshof [Federal High Court for Civil and Criminal Matters], Herrenstr. 45a, D-76131 Karlsruhe, Germany. Tel: +49 721 1590. Fax: +49 721 159830

Education and training

All law schools are parts of universities which are run by the state under identical schemes for admission, curricula and examination. There is no 'leading' or 'elite' law school. For more details see above **Directories.**

Research institutions

Max-Planck-Institut für ausländisches öffentliches Recht und Völkerrecht [Max-Planck Institute for Foreign Public Law and Public International Law], Im Neuenheimer Feld 535, D-69120 Heidelberg, Germany. Tel: +49 6221 4821. Fax: +49 621 482288

Max-Planck-Institut für ausländisches und internationales Strafrecht [Max-Planck Institute for Foreign and International Criminal Law], Günterstalstr. 73, D-79100 Freiburg im Breisgau, Germany. Tel: +49 761 70811. Fax: +49 761 7081294

Max-Planck-Institut für ausländisches und internationales Privatrecht [Max-Planck Institute for Foreign Private Law and Private International Law, Mittelweg 187, D-20148 Hamburg, Germany. Tel: +49 40 419000. Fax: +49 40 41900288

Libraries

The Max-Planck Institutes listed above all contain major research libraries at the same addresses.

Bibliothek des Deutschen Bundestages [Library of the German Federal Parliament], Bundeshaus, D 53113 Bonn, Germany. Tel: +49 228 163073. Fax: +49 228 1686037

Staatsbibliothek zu Berlin [State Library in Berlin], Potsdamer Str. 33, D-10772 Berlin, Germany. Tel: +49 30 2661. Fax: +49 30 2662814

Access to these five libraries is granted subject to prior arrangement.

Publishers and booksellers

Juristisches Informationssystem – JURIS, Gutenbergstr. 23, D-66117 Saarbrücken, Germany. Tel: +49 681 58660. Fax: +49 681 5866239

Verlag C.H. Beck, Wilhelmstr. 9, D-80801 München, Germany. Tel: +49 89 381890. Fax: +49 89 38189547

Bundesanzeiger Verlagsgesellschaft, Postfach 1320, D-53003 Bonn, Germany. Tel: +49 228 382080. Fax: +49 228 3820836

Carl Heymanns Verlag, Luxemburger Str. 449, D-50939 Köln, Germany. Tel: +49 221 943730. Fax: +49 221 94373901

Nomos Verlagsgesellschaft, Waldseestr. 3–5, D-76530 Baden-Baden, Germany. Tel: +49 7221 21040. Fax: +49 7221 210427

List of works cited

(Only the English version of bilingual titles is given.)

Anwalts- und Notarverzeichnis. (1996) 21st edn. Cologne: Schmidt.

Aufenanger, M. (1996) *German Trade Mark Act*. Weinheim: VCH.

Basic Law for the Federal Republic of Germany – official translation. (1995) Bonn: Press and Information Office of the Federal Government. Free of charge.

Baumbach, A. and Hopt, K. (1995) *Handelsgesetzbuch* 29th edn. Munich: Beck.

Baumbach, A. *et al.* (1997) *Zivilprozessordnung* 55th edn. Munich: Beck.

Beier, F.K. *et al.* (1996) *German industrial property, copyright and antitrust laws* 3rd edn. Weinheim: VCH.

Benkert, M. and Bürkle, A. (1996) *Law of reorganizations – Reorganization tax law*. Cologne: RWS.

Born, S. (1993) *Federal electoral law*. Bonn: Inter Nationes. Free of charge.

Born, S. (1994a) *Asylum Procedure Act*. Bonn: Inter Nationes. Free of charge.

Born, S. (1994b) *Press laws*. Bonn: Inter Nationes. Free of charge.

Born, S. (1994c) *Law on political parties*. Bonn: Inter Nationes. Free of charge.

Born, S. (1995) *Environmental legislation*. Bonn: Inter Nationes. Free of charge.

Brooks, F.P. and Mertin, D. (1996) *German accounting legislation*. 3rd edn. Dusseldorf: IDW.

Bundesanzeiger. (1949–) Bonn: Bundesanzeiger Verlagsgesellschaft. Also available in a microfiche edition.

Bundesgesetzblatt. (1949–) Bonn: Bundesanzeiger Verlagsgesellschaft. Also available in a microfiche edition.

Creifelds, C. *et al.* (1995) *Staatsbürger-Taschenbuch* 28th edn. Munich: Beck.

Creifelds, C. *et al.* (1996) *Rechtswörterbuch* 13th edn. Munich: Beck.

Currie, D.P. (1994) *The Constitution of the Federal Republic of Germany*. Chicago Ill: University of Chicago Press.

Dannemann, G. (1993) *Introduction to German civil and commercial law*. London: British Institute of International and Comparative Law.

Darby, J.H. (1987) *Penal Code of the Federal Republic of Germany. English translation with an introduction*. Littleton, Colo.: Rothman.

Dau, H. (1962–1995) *Bibliography of legal festschriften 1864–1993*. Berlin: Berlin-Verlag. 9 vols.

Decisions of the Bundesverfassungsgericht, Federal Constitutional Court, published by the members of the Court. (1992–) Baden-Baden: Nomos.

Das Deutsche Bundesrecht: Systematishe Sammlung der Gesetze und Verordnungen. (1949–) Baden-Baden: Nomos. Looseleaf. 31 vols. Also available as CD-ROM edition.

Deutsches Rechts-Lexikon. (1992) Munich: Beck. 3 vols.

Dietl, C.E. *et al.* (1990/1992) *Dictionary of legal, commercial, and political terms* 4th/5th edn. Munich: Beck. 2 vols.

Dreher, E. and Tröndle, H. (1995) *Strafgesetzbuch und Nebengesetze* 47th edn. Munich: Beck.

Ebke, W.F. and Finkin, M.W. (1996) *Introduction to German law.* The Hague: Kluwer.

Entscheidungen des Bundesarbeitsgerichts (1955–) Berlin: de Gruyter.

Entscheidungen des Bundesgerichtshofes in Strafsachen. (1951–) Cologne: Heymann. Also available on CD-ROM.

Entscheidungen des Bundesgerichtshofes in Zivilsachen. (1951–) Cologne: Heymann. Also available on CD-ROM.

Entscheidungen des Bundessozialgerichts. (1956–) Cologne: Heymann.

Entscheidungen des Bundesverfassungsgerichts. (1952–) Tübingen: Mohr.

Entscheidungen des Bundesverwaltungsgerichts. (1955–) Cologne: Heymann.

Entscheidungen des Reichsgerichts in Strafsachen. (1880–1944) Berlin: de Gruyter.

Entscheidungen des Reichsgerichts in Zivilsachen. (1880–1945) Berlin: de Gruyter.

Erman, W. *et al.* (1993) *Handkommentar zum Bürgerlichen Gesetzbuch* 9th edn. Münster: Aschendorff. 2 vols.

Fisher, H.D. (1996) *German legal system and legal language.* London: Cavendish.

Flanz, G.H. (1994) Germany. In *Constitutions of the countries of the world,* ed. A.P. Blaustein and G.H. Flanz, vol.VII. Dobbs Ferry, NY: Oceana.

Foster, N.G. (1996) *German legal system and laws* 2nd edn. London: Blackstone.

German law in English. See Radke, K. *et al.*

German tax and business law guide. (1995–) Bicester: CCH. Looseleaf.

Germany: practical commercial law. (1992) London: Longman.

Goedan, J.C. (1992) *International legal bibliographies – a worldwide guide and critique.* Ardsley-on-Hudson, NY: Transnational Juris Publishers.

Goren, S.L. (1990) *The Code of Civil Procedure rules of the Federal Republic of Germany.* Littleton, Colo.: Rothman.

Goren, S.L. (1994a) *The condominium property law of the FRG.* Littleton, Colo.: Rothman.

Goren, S.L. (1994b) *The German Civil Code* 2nd edn. Littleton, Colo.: Rothman.

Guide to legal studies in Europe. (1996) Brussels: Bruylant.

Handbuch der Justiz. (1996) 23rd edn. Hamburg: v.Decker.

Handelsblatt. (1946–) Düsseldorf: Handelsblatt.

Heyde, W. (1994) *Justice and the law in the Federal Republic of Germany.* Heidelberg: Müller.

Holborn, L.W., Carter, G. and Herz, J. (1970) (eds) *German constitutional documents since 1871 – selected texts and commentary.* London: Pall Mall.

Hucko, E.M. (1989) (ed.) *The democratic tradition – four German constitutions.* Oxford: Berg.

Jung, H. (1993) *Starting business operations in Germany* 2nd edn. Neuwied: Luchterhand.

JURISTISCHES INFORMATIONSSYSTEM – JURIS (available from the company of the same name, Juristisches Informationssystem – JURIS).

Juristenzeitung. (1946–) Tübingen: Mohr.

Karlsruher Juristische Bibliographie. (1965–) Munich: Beck.

Kavass, I.I. and Prince M.M. (1991–) (eds) *World dictionary of legal abbreviations.* Buffalo, NY: Hein. Looseleaf.

Kearley, T. and Fischer, W. (1990) *Charles Szladits' guide to foreign legal materials: German.* Dobbs Ferry, NY: Oceana.

Kirchner, H. (1993) *Abkürzungsverzeichnis der Rechtssprache.* 4th edn. Berlin: de Gruyter.

Kleinknecht, T. *et al.* (1995) *Strafprozessordnung* 42nd edn. Munich: Beck.
Kopp, F. *et al.* (1994) *Verwaltungsgerichtsordnung* 10th edn. Munich: Beck.
Kuhnen, R.A. and Wacker, P.A. (1995) *German Trade Mark Act and Regulation*. Cologne: Heymann.
Lackner, K. and Kühl, K. (1995) *Strafgesetzbuch mit Erläuterungen* 21st edn. Munich: Beck.
Lansky, R. (1993) *Handbook of law libraries*. Berlin: Deutsches Bibliotheksinstitut.
Mergers and acquisitions in Germany. (1995) Bicester: CCH.
Mohr, K. (1994) *German insider and stock exchange law: an introduction with synoptic English translation*. Frankfurt: Knapp.
Münchener Kommentar zum Bürgerlichen Gesetzbuch. (1992–) 3rd edn. Munich: Beck. 10 vols.
Münchener Kommentar zur Zivilprozessordnung. (1992) Munich: Beck. 3 vols.
Neue Juristische Wochenschrift. (1947–) Munich: Beck.
Niebler, H. (1965) *The German Code of Criminal Procedure*. South Hackensack, NY: Rothman.
Oeckl, A. (1996) (ed.) *Taschenbuch des öffentlichen Lebens* 46th edn. Bonn: Festland.
Palandt, O. *et al.* (1997) *Bürgerliches Gesetzbuch* 56th edn. Munich: Beck.
Peltzer, M. *et al.* (1995) *German Commercial Code* 3rd edn. Cologne: Schmidt.
Peltzer, M., Brooks, J.P. and Hopcroft, T. (1996) *German law pertaining to companies with limited liability* 3rd edn. Cologne: Schmidt.
Peltzer, M. and Scesniak, P. (1995) *German Securities Trade Act*. Cologne: Schmidt.
Peltzer, M. and Stewart, C. (1995) *Labor Management Relations Act* 4th edn. Frankfurt: Knapp.
Pfennigstorf, W. (1995) *German insurance laws* 3rd edn. Karlsruhe: Versicherungswirtschaft.
Pond, E. (1993) *Beyond the Wall – Germany's road to unification*. Washington, DC: The Brookings Institution.
Radke, K. *et al.* (1993) *German law in English: a select bibliography* 2nd edn. Bonn: Deutscher Akademischer Austauschdienst. Free of charge.
Recht – Informationen des Bundesministers der Justiz. (1970–) Bonn: Deutscher Bundesverlag. Free of charge.
Redeker, K. and von Oertzen, H.J. (1994) *Verwaltungsgerichtsordnung: Kommentar* 11th edn. Stuttgart: Kohlhammer.
Romain, A. (1989/1994) *Dictionary of legal and commercial terms* 3rd/4th edn. Munich: Beck. 2 vols.
Rüster, B. *et al.* (1983–) *Business transactions in Germany*. New York: Matthew Bender. Looseleaf. 5 vols.
Sammelblatt für Rechtsvorschriften des Bundes und der Länder. (1950–) Wiesbaden: Engel.
Sartorius, C. *Verfassungs- und Verwaltungsgesetze der Bundesrepublik Deutschland*. Munich: Beck. Looseleaf. Also available as CD-ROM edition under the title SARTORIUS PLUS.
Schlemminger, H. and Wissel, H. (1996) *German environmental law*. The Hague: Kluwer.
Schmidt-Bleibtreu, B. and Klein F. (1995) *Kommentar zum Grundgesetz* 8th edn. Neuwied: Luchterhand.
Schneider, H. and Heidenhain, M. (1996) *The German Stock Corporation Act*. Munich: Beck.
Schönfelder, H. *Deutsche Gesetze: Sammlung des Zivil-, Straf- und Verfahrensrechts*. Munich: Beck. Looseleaf. Also available as CD-ROM edition under the title SCHÖNFELDER PLUS.
Schönke, A. *et al.* (1997) *Strafgesetzbuch: Kommentar* 25th edn. Munich: Beck.
Siebel, U.R., Löwenstein, M. and Finney, R. (1995) (eds) *German capital market law*. Munich: Beck.
Soergel, H.T. and Siebert, W. (1987–) (eds) *Bürgerliches Gesetzbuch* 12th edn. Stuttgart: Kohlhammer. 10 vols.

Staudinger, J. von. (1995–) (ed.) *Kommentar zum Bürgerlichen Gesetzbuch* 13th edn. Berlin: Sellier, de Gruyter. 39 vols published so far.

Stockmair, W. (1994) *Protection of technical innovations and designs in Germany*. Weinheim: VCH.

Thomas, H. and Putzo, H. (1997) *Zivilprozessordnung* 20th edn. Munich: Beck.

Transactions in real property in Germany. (1994) Bicester: CCH.

Union list of legal serials – VRZS. (1990) 3rd edn. Munich: Saur.

Verhandlungen des Deutschen Bundestages: Drucksachen [draft legislation]; *Stenographische Berichte* [proceedings]. (1950–) Bonn: Bundesanzeiger. Microfiche edition Munich: Beck.

Verträge der Bundesrepublik Deutschland – Serie A: Multilaterale Verträge. (1995–) Cologne: Heymann.

Wegen, G. and Crosswhite, C. (1990) Text of the Treaty establishing a Monetary, Economic, and Social Union between the FRG and the GDR. *International Legal Materials*, **29**, 1108–85.

Wegen, G. (1988) Act on the Revision of the German Private International Law. *International Legal Materials*, **27**, 1–36.

Youngs, R. (1994) *Sourcebook on German law*. London: Cavendish.

Zerwas, H. (1996) *Banking Act*. Düsseldorf: IDW.

CHAPTER THIRTEEN

Greece

GEORGIOS N. YANNOPOULOS

Introduction to the legal system

Law and legal thought in Greece have a history of 3000 years. Ancient Greek law, classical law, Hellenistic and Byzantine law have generated a long legal tradition. Greek legal history is described in English in *Historical development* by Yiannopoulos (1993). However, the Greek revolution of 1821 (the Greek War of Independence) marks the beginning of modern Greek law, which is mainly influenced by the Roman–Byzantine tradition as well as by the German, French and Swiss codifications of the 19th century.

The three revolutionary Constitutions adopted by the assemblies of Epidaurus in 1822, of Astros in 1823 and of Troezene in 1827, presented a liberal and democratic character influenced by the Declaration of the French Revolution and several ideas of Jeremy Bentham. The first governor of Greece, Ioannis Capodistrias, a former minister of the Tsar of Russia, dissolved the parliament and governed Greece with the assistance of an appointed senate until his assassination in 1831. Law and order were re-established when the young King Otho arrived in Greece in 1833. Initially a regency and then the king himself ruled the country as an absolute monarch.

A successful revolution on 3 September 1843 compelled the king to grant a constitution and Greece was made a constitutional monarchy. Otho was overthrown by a another revolution in 1862 and the crown was offered by the protecting powers to Prince William of Denmark. Prince William assumed the title 'King George I of the Hellenes' and proclaimed a new Constitution which vested all legislative power in the parliament and the king. This Constitution, which introduced universal male suffrage, came into force in 1864 and was revised in 1911. In 1875 the principle of parliamentary government was introduced. The revised Constitution was suspended a number of times and finally in 1927 was replaced by a Constitution which abolished the monarchy. The 1911 Constitution was reintroduced after the restoration of the monarchy in 1935 but was inoperative during the Metaxas dictatorship (1936–1940).

After World War II a new revision of the 1911 Constitution resulted in the adoption of the 1952 Constitution. In 1967 a coup d'état resulted in the establishment of a military regime. After the fall of the dictatorship in 1974 and a national plebiscite, Greece was proclaimed a parliamentary republic and the parliament voted on a new constitution. The 1975 Constitution (Syntagma) is still in force. On 1 January 1981 Greece became a member of the European Communities and since then EC and now EU law has become part of the legal system. A constitutional revision, reducing the powers of the president, became effective in 1986. A parliamentary committee was in session in 1996 in order to revise a number of articles of the constitution. The revision was to have taken place after the general election scheduled for 1997, but because of an early election in September 1996, the whole procedure was cancelled.

For the texts of the Greek constitutions see Mavrias and Pantelis (1990) *Syntagmatika keimena* [Constitutional texts]. The English text, including a very comprehensive constitutional chronology, can be found in the encyclopedia *Constitutions of the countries of the world* (Flanz, 1988). For a monograph, in French, see Pantelis (1979) *Les grands problèmes de la nouvelle constitution hellénique* and for a recent work in English see the monograph of Spyropoulos (1995) *Constitutional law in Hellas*. Greek constitutional history is covered in Alivizatos (1981) *Isagogi stin Elliniki Syntagmatiki Istoria 1821–1941* [Introduction to the Greek constitutional history 1821–1941], and in French in Alivizatos (1979) *Les institutions politiques de la Grèce travers les crises 1922–1974*. For administrative law in French see the treatise of Spiliotopoulos (1991) *Droit administratif Hellénique*.

Under the 1975/86 Constitution, Greece is a presidential parliamentary republic (art.1). The *Vouli* [Parliament] or in full *Vouli ton Ellinon* [Parliament of the Hellenes] of 300 representatives is the main legislative body producing formal laws [*Nomos*] with no constraints regarding its power. Greek law follows a hierarchy on the top of which stands the Constitution, whose provisions take precedence over all other laws, and next comes ordinary legislation in the form of codifications or statutes. Executive power is exercised by the president and the government and they may enact legal rules only on the basis of statutory delegation, the most important being the *proedriko diatagma* [presidential decree] and *ypourgiki apofasi* [decisions from cabinet ministers].

Judicial power is exercised by the courts of law (civil, criminal and administrative) and their decisions must contain a statement of their reasons. Judicial decisions, although the courts are not bound by judicial precedent, are always taken into consideration, especially in the case of interpretation of legislation, by lower rank courts and by lawyers. It is not formally admitted but the decisions of judges usually conform to the decisions of higher courts and especially to those of the *Areios Pagos* [Supreme Court]. Doctrine is not a formal source of law but often the opinions of legal scholars are taken into consideration and cited in decisions. For the sources of law in general see Grammaticaki-Alexiou (1993) *Sources and materials*.

Introductory works on the legal system and legal research

Introduction to Greek law edited by Kerameus and Kozyris (1993) is the only comprehensive work on modern Greek law in English. Professor Fragistas (1978) has written a comprehensive but outdated national report on Greece in the *International encyclopedia of comparative law*. In Greek, the treatise of the co-ordinator of the Civil Code drafting committee, G. Balis (1961), *Genikes arches astikou dikeou* [General principles of civil law], is recommended, as well as volume I, on general principles, of the commentary on the Civil Code by Georgiadis and Stathopoulos (1978–93), and the treatises by Papantoniou (1983) and Simantiras (1988) both entitled *Genikes arches astikou dikaiou* [General principles of civil law].

Legislation

According to the Constitution (art.42.1) statutory law must be published in Part A [*Teuxos A*] of the Official Gazette of the Greek Republic [*Efimeris tis Kyverniseos tis Ellinikis Dimokratias*]. Laws become effective ten days after publication. Statutes and other legislative instruments are known by their number and the year of publication, e.g. N.1329/1983. The letter N. stands for the Greek word *Nomos* [Law]. The *Efimeris tis Kyverniseos* has been published since about 1833 under different names by the Ethniko Typografeio [State Printers] and individual laws can be purchased. Statutory law is also published in a number of private collections which sometimes include cases as well. To cover wide areas of law one could select:

Kodikas Nomikou Vimatos [Code of the Law Tribune] edited by the Athens Bar Association and the one most frequently used.

Raptarchis – Diarkis kodikas ischyousas nomothesias [Permanent code of the legislation in force] is a widely used looseleaf encyclopedia, named also simply *Raptarchis* after the lawyer who initiated it in the 1930s. After his death the whole collection and the copyright was donated to the Greek state. *Raptarchis* since 1979 has been a government publication edited by the Ypourgeio Esoterikon, Apokentrosis kai Dimosias Dioikisis [Ministry of Public Administration] according to N. 805/78

Diarki evretiria nomologias kai nomothesias [Permanent indexes of cases and legislation] from the publishers Zacharopoulos-Daidalos.

Deltion ergatikis nomothesias [Bulletin of labour legislation].

Forologiki epitheorisi [Tax review] edited by employees of the internal revenue service.

The *Praktika tis Voulis* [Proceedings of the Parliament] including debates on new laws and preparatory works can be obtained from a special service at the Parliament (see the Library of the Parliament under 'Libraries' in the section of **Useful addresses** below).

Codes and commentaries

Civil Code [*Astikos Kodikas*]

It was not until 1940 that the final text of the Greek Civil Code [*Astikos Kodix*], ordered by an 1835 Royal Decree, was delivered. However, due to World War II and the occupation of Greece, this Code was only put into effect on 23 February 1946. It was amended by Law 1250/1982 and, in the light of a constitutional mandate for equality of sexes, a number of provisions were amended by Law 1329/1983. In 1984 the Civil Code was recast into demotic Greek. For an English translation see Taliadoros (1982), *Greek Civil Code* and Iatrou (1986) *An outline of the Greek Civil Code.* A French translation was published in 1982 by Mamopoulos.

A modern commentary is by Georgiadis and Stathopoulos (1978–93) in eight volumes, *Astikos Kodix, erminia kat'arthro* [Civil Code, article-by-article commentary]. There is a recent work in English on Greek contract law by Stathopoulos (1995).

Commercial Code [*Emporikos Nomos*]

The Napoleonic Code of Commerce of 1807 was adopted in 1828 to regulate commercial relations. Since then many amendments have taken place so only a few articles of the original text remain in force. The draft of a new code has been prepared but has not yet been enacted by the Parliament. An English translation of the Commercial Code has been made by Taliadoros (1983) *Greek commercial law*; see also Taliadoros (1985) *Business and trade laws of Greece*. Especially for company law the commentary in six volumes by Levantis (1985–1991) *Dikaion emporikon etairion* [Law of commercial companies] is the one mostly used by practitioners. In English see Rokas (1992) *Greece: practical commercial law*, and Kotsiris (1993) *Greek company law* and the periodical sections on Greece in the *International Business Lawyer* (1973–). See also Kozyris (1993) *Business associations*, Anastassopoulou (1993) *Corporations and partnerships in Hellas,* and Rokas (1993) *Hellenic insurance law*. In French see Gofas (1992) *Loi codifiée 2190/1920 sur les sociétés anonymes.*

The maritime provisions of the French Code de Commerce were also adopted in 1828 and after modifications in 1911 were kept in force until 1958 when a new Code of Private Maritime Law (N.3816/1958) was introduced. An English version of the code was prepared by Karatzas and Ready (1982) and a French version by Antapassis (1983). See also in English Deloukas (1993) *Admiralty and private maritime law* and Kiantou-Pampouki (1993) *Greek maritime law: recent developments.* The Code of Public Maritime Law was introduced by Law Decree 187 in 1973.

Code of Civil Procedure [*Kodikas Politikis Dikonomias*]

The first Code of Civil Procedure was introduced by the Bavarian jurist Ludwig von Maurer shortly after the establishment of the modern Greek state. The current code [*Kodikas Politikis Dikonomias* – KPolD], mainly influenced by German and Austrian Law, came into force on 16 September 1968.

The only available translation of the Code at all is in German by Baumgärtel and Rammos (1969) and does not include important subsequent amendments. The main treatises (in Greek) are by Rammos (1978–85), *Egchiridion politikis dikonomias* [Textbook of civil procedure], Kerameus (1986), *Astiko dikonomiko dikaio – geniko meros* [Civil procedure law – general part], and Beis (1984) *Mathimata politikis dikonomias* [Lectures on civil procedure]. In English see Kerameus (1993) *Judicial organization and civil procedure.* The article-by-article commentaries by Theodoropoulos (1992) and Beis (1973–1994) are the ones mostly used by practitioners. In English see Iatrou (1981), *Civil and criminal proceedings in Greece.*

Penal Code [*Poinikos Kodikas*] and Code of Criminal Procedure [*Kodikas Poinikis Dikonomias*]

The Penal Law of 1833 and the Code of Criminal Procedure Act of 1834 were replaced by the Penal Code [*Poinikos Kodikas*] and the Code of Criminal Procedure [*Kodikas Poinikis Dikonomias*] of 1950 which came into force on 1 January 1951. However, a great number of special statutes (e.g. the Code of Traffic Regulations, the Code of Market Regulations, the Military Penal Code, etc.) regulate most criminal offences. The Penal Code is translated into English by Lolis (1973) with an introduction by Mangakis.

The basic treatises are by Chorafas (1978) *Poinikon dikaion* [Penal law], Androulakis (1986 and 1991) *Poinikon dikaion I* and *II* [Penal law I and II], Mangakis (1984) *Poinikon dikaion – Genikon* [Penal law – General Part], and Dedes (1983) *Poiniki dikonomia* [Penal procedure]. In English see Spinellis (1993) *Criminal law and procedure*.

A commentary of the Penal Code, *Systimatiki Erminia tou Poinikou Kodika* [Systematic interpretation of the Penal Code] (1993–) has begun publication recently, while the commentary by Kontaxis (1993) *Erminia Kodika Poinikis Dikonomias* [Interpretation of the Code of Criminal Procedure], is widely used by practitioners.

Treaties

Although the President of the Republic may, among other duties, conclude treaties, these are not valid without a formal law which ratifies them (Constitution, art.36.2). Therefore international treaty-making powers are vested in the Parliament [*Vouli*]. The 1975 Constitution (art.28) states that the 'generally accepted rules of international law' and international treaties ratified by Greece constitute an integral part of Greek law and prevail over any contrary statutory provision. Therefore, in the hierarchy of the Greek legal system these rules and treaties rank between the Constitution and Acts of Parliament. Treaties are published in the *Efimeris tis Kyverniseos* [Official Gazette] but there is no official compilation of treaties. However, treaties concluded by Greece can be found at the Ministry of Foreign Affairs.

Law reports, judgments

There is no official collection of law reports in Greece, with the exception of the decisions of the Symboulio tis Epikrateias [Council of State] which are published in full in the *Evretirio kath'ylin ton apofaseon tou STE* [Subject Index of the Council of State Decisions] (1961–), recently in CD-ROM format also, together with extensive indexes. Court decisions are known by the name of the court, a serial number and the year, e.g. First Instance Court of Athens 12345/1996. A large number of decisions is published by legal periodicals and they normally state the names of the judges, the names of the attorneys and a brief summary. Some periodicals cover all cases while other specialise in certain branches of law. The best known legal periodicals are:

Nomiko Vima [Law Tribune] (1951–), edited by the Athens Bar Association, is one of the main sources of information for practitioners all over the country;

Poinika Chronika [Criminal Chronicles] (1951–), mainly for criminal cases and penal law;

Elliniki Dikeosyni [Greek Justice] (1960–), published by the Union of Judges and Public Prosecutors, covering all branches of law;

Archio Nomologias [Legislation File] (1950–) edited by G. Karageorgos in Athens;

Efimeris Ellinon Nomikon [Gazette of Greek Lawyers] (1934–) published by Zacheropoulos-Daidalos in Athens covering all branches of law;

Harmenopoulos (1946–), named after a Byzantine judge of the 14th century, edited by the Thessaloniki Bar Association;

Epitheorisis tou Emporikou Dikaiou [Review of Commercial Law] (1950–), covering commercial law cases;

Epitheorisis Ergatikou Dikaiou [Review of Labour Law] (1951–) covering labour law cases;

Epitheorisis Dimosiou Dikaiou kai Dioikitikou Dikaiou [Review of Public and Administrative Law] (1957–);

Revue Hellénique de Droit International (1948–) (see below under **Journals**).

Most of these periodicals are published by professional associations or special interest groups. For practical purposes it is better to order them through the main legal publishers who also act as booksellers and subscription agents and who also make available each year bound volumes (see 'Publishers and Booksellers' in the section of **Useful addresses** below).

A compilation of all decisions of the Areios Pagos [Supreme Court] in civil cases covering the period 1967 to 1982 has been published by the Athens Bar Association as *Vasiki nomologia* [Basic cases] with two supplements covering the periods 1983 to 1986 and 1986 to 1992 (Athens Bar Association, 1982). See also the volumes of *Nomologia, etisia evretiriasi* [Yearly index of case law] which is an index of both case law and articles (Beis, 1982–). A recent collection comes from Katralis (1993) *Nomologia tou areiou pagou 1951–1993* [Case law of Areios Pagos 1951–1993], which also includes a subject index. A collection of cases covering the Civil Code can be found in Vathrakokoilis (1989), *Analytiki erminia – nomologia Astikou Kodikos* [Analytical interpretation – case law of the Civil Code].

Computer-based systems

Two online systems offering legal information exist in Greece. The system operated by the Athens Bar Association does not have a particular name and is known simply as the 'system of the Athens Bar'. It started in 1995 and includes abstracts of reported and unreported cases of the past fifteen years. The system currently contains 30 000 decisions (in abstracts) and 45 000 bibliographic references indexing most legal periodicals. It has now expanded to include national and EU legislation. An online catalogue of the library of the Athens Bar provides reference for books. Furthermore the system supports a number of everyday activities of the Athens Bar practitioners such as finding whether a decision has been issued by the courts, keeping a track of personal records concerning contracts and court appearances made by lawyers, etc. The cost of subscription is around £2.70 per month including three hours of free use, subsequent time is charged at £3.50 per hour.

The NOMOS system is operated by the private company Databank. The NOMOS system covers all Greek legislation since the establishment of modern Greek state, all the repealed or amended legislation since 1944, a number of ministerial decisions and decisions of the Governor of the Bank of Greece, mainly of the past 15 years, and ratified international treaties. In case law the system includes most of the recently published decisions of the Supreme Court and of the Council of State; all the important decisions in abstract and full text since 1988 and most of the decisions of the period 1975 to 1988 in abstract. The average cost of using NOMOS is around £17 per month.

All the members of the Athens Bar Association, around 16 000, are registered and entitled to use the Athens Bar system while the NOMOS system claims 1000 connections. At the moment both systems are underused and everyday legal practice in Greece is still paper based. Furthermore the quality of telecommunications in Greece does not permit trouble-free connections for online systems. It is, however, expected that soon both systems will attain a higher volume of usage.

Directories

A list of lawyers in Athens is provided by the online service of the Athens Bar Association. A periodic edition of the Athens Bar, *O Odigos tou Dikigorou* [The directory of the lawyer] as well as the yearly calendars of the Athens Bar provide useful lists of government departments, courts and other legal institutions such as research institutes and law schools. These lists include addresses, telephones and fax numbers. Names of local lawyers, notaries and bailiffs are recorded with local bar associations.

Bibliographies

The lack of a general legal bibliography in Greece was remedied in 1992 by Katralis, *Vasiki nomiki pliroforisi* [Basic legal information]. This compilation provides subject and author indexes and, for case law, an index by decision number. The whole work covers monographs and articles in the period from 1951 to 1995 and is the only major legal bibliography in

Greece to include multi-search indexes. Supplements are published every year, while the publisher Sakkoulas issues a special update release every three to four months. The yearly catalogues of the two Sakkoulas legal publishers are considered useful but it is cumbersome to use them because they only list legal books by the author and not by subject. Recently the publishers P. Sakkoulas have released a catalogue partly arranged by subject. Further bibliographical reference can be found in the yearly indexes of the legal periodicals mentioned above, especially see Moustakas (1993) *Geniko evretirio Nomikou Vimatos* [General index of the Law Tribune].

Dictionaries

Two recent dictionaries of legal terms are more accurate than earlier attempts: by Zombolas, Tragakis and Karatzas (1991) and by Hiotakis (1992a). See also Hiotakis (1992b) *Shipping business and law dictionary*. The *Oxford English–Greek and Greek–English learner's dictionaries* (Stavropoulos, 1977 and 1988) are the standard reference for general translation.

Other reference books

The rules governing the legal profession and the Bar are compiled by Varibopiotis (1994) *Kodikas peri Dikigoron* [The Code of Lawyers].

Important reference books include: Maridakis (1967) *Idiotiko diethnes dikaion* [Private international law] and Vrellis (1988) *Idiotiko diethnes dikaio* [Private international law] are useful in the area of conflict of laws. For nationality law see Papasiopi-Pasia (1994) *Dikaio Ithagenias* [Nationality law]. *Syllogiko Ergatiko Dikaio* [Collective employment law] and *Atomiko Ergatiko Dikaio* [Personal employment law] (Karakantsanis, 1992 and 1995) and Kremalis (1985) *Dikaio Koinonikon Asfaliseon* [Social insurance law] are the standard references in the area of labour and social insurance law while Koniaris (1990) *Labour law and industrial relations in Greece* is the only source in English. The article-by-article commentary of Kerameus, Kremlis and Tagaras, (1989) *I symvasi ton Bryxellon gia ti diethni dikaiodosia kai tin ektelesi ton apofaseon* [The Brussels Convention on International Jurisdiction and the Enforcement of Judgments] is the standard work in the area of international jurisdiction and foreign judgments. For taxation law see Dryllerakis (1993) *Tax law and investment incentives*.

Current information sources

Journals, research reports

The periodicals already referred to in the section on **Law reports, judgments**, in particular mainly *Nomiko Vima* [the Law Tribune] of the Athens Bar Association and *Harmenopoulos* of the Thessaloniki Bar Association also act as journals for practising lawyers including updates and recent legal developments. *Revue Hellénique de Droit International* (1948–), is published by the Hellenic Institute of International and Foreign Law with contents in English, French and German.

News information

Apart from the Official Gazette there is no periodical edition of a legal newsletter by the government. However, each ministry issues press releases and circulars. Information on legislation in progress can be found in the *Praktika tis Voulis ton Ellinon* [Proceedings of the Parliament] and in the special parliamentary columns of the daily Athenian newspapers (*Kathimerini*, *Eleftheroptypia, Ta Nea* daily and *To Vima* on Sundays are considered to be the most serious Athenian newspapers).

The Hellenic Ministry of Press and Mass Media provides general information on the Internet about Greece including news about political life, foreign policy and economy and business at http://web.ariadne-t.gr/ which appears mainly in English. A mirror site which also includes other information about Greece is run by the Hellenic Resources Institute in the USA at http://www.hri.org.

Business and financial information

The *Doing business in Greece* guides can be used for information on business and finance, (e.g. Price Waterhouse, 1992). However, the revised and updated edition of the *Invest in Greece guide* of the Hellenic Industrial Development Bank (ETVA, 1996) is a must for those wishing to do business in Greece and includes a great deal of legal information. Reports also appear regularly from the Ministry of National Economy while the annual report of the Governor of the Bank of Greece (the Greek central bank) is quite significant for analysing the economy in Greece. The Organisation of Economic Cooperation and Development (1994) reviews on foreign direct investment include a section on Greece.

A central registry of companies does not exist. Different registries are kept by different authorities for each type of company. Therefore, searching the local registers of companies, patents and trade marks is rather cumbersome and bureaucratic and it would be recommended to consult a local lawyer.

Statistics

All statistics are issued by the National Statistical Service of Greece [Ethniki Statistiki Ypiresia Ellados – ESYE]. Limited information is available from the Ministry of Justice concerning the courts and the prisons system and from the local Bar Associations concerning the legal profession.

Useful addresses

Associations of lawyers

Dikogorikos Syllogos Athinon [Athens Bar Association], Akadimias 60, GR-10679 Athens, Greece. Tel: +30 1 3398200. Fax: +30 1 3610537

Dikigorikos Syllogos Peiraios [Piraeus Bar Association], Iroon Polytechniou 47, GR-18510 Peiraias, Greece. Tel: +30 1 4220625, 4176251

Dikigorikos Syllogos Thessalonikis [Thessaloniki Bar Association], Diakstiko Megaro, GR-54626 Thessaloniki, Greece. Tel: +30 31–528509/542987. Fax: +30 31–253444

Symvolaiografikos Syllogos Athinon [Athens Notaries Association], G. Genadiou 4, GR-10678 Athens, Greece. Tel: +30 1 3832501

Syllogos Dikastikon Epimenliton [Athens Bailiffs Association], Kapodistriou 24, GR-10682 Athens, Greece. Tel: +30 1 3837081

Government organizations

Ethniki Statistiki Ypiresia [National Statistical Service of Greece], Lykourgou 14–16, GR-10166 Athens, Greece. Tel: +30 1 3248511–9. Fax: +30 1 3222205

Ethniko Typografeio [National Printers], see under **Publishers and booksellers** below.

ETVA [Hellenic Industrial Development Bank], Leoforos Syngrou 87, GR-11745 Athens, Greece. Tel: +30 1 9242900, Fax: +30 1 9241513

Trapeza tis Ellados [Bank of Greece], El.Venizelou (Panepistimiou) 21, GR-10564 Athens, Greece. Tel: +30 1 3201111, Fax: +30 1 3232239

Vouli [Parliament], see Library of the Parliament under **Libraries** below.

Ypourgeio Anaptyxis – Tomeas Emporiou [Ministry of Trade and Commerce], Platia Kanigos, GR-10181 Athens, Greece. Tel: +30 1 3816241–9. This Ministry also keeps the trade marks registry.

Ypourgeio Dikaiosynis [Ministry of Justice], Mesogeion 96, GR-10179 Athens, Greece. Tel: +30 1 7711019, 7751303

Diefthinsi nomoparaskevastikis ergasias [Special Department for Legal Reform]. Tel: +30 1 7753230

Tmima Statistikon Dikaiosynis [Special Department for Legal Statistics]. Tel: +30 1 7705613

Ypourgeio Ethnikis Oikonomias [Ministry of National Economy], Platia Syntagmatos, GR-10180 Athens, Greece. Tel: +30 1 3332000. Fax: +30 1 3332130

Ypourgeio Exoterikon [Ministry of Foreign Affairs], Akadimias 1, GR-10671 Athens, Greece. Tel: +30 1 3610581–8. Fax: +30 1 6450028

Courts

Areios Pagos [Supreme Court], Leoforos Alexandras 121, GR-11522 Athens, Greece. Tel: +30 1 6411846–859. This is the highest court of civil and criminal appeal.

Elegktiko Synedrio [Auditors Court], Patision 34, GR-10682 Athens, Greece. Tel: +30 1 3819851. This is partly a court and partly an administrative authority deciding on pensions and auditing public accounts.

Symboulio tis Epikrateias [Council of the State], Panepistimiou 47 – Arsakio, GR-10564 Athens, Greece. Tel: +30 1 3234395. This is the highest administrative court; its legislative division has an advisory function for delegated legislation.

Education and training

There are three law schools in Greece:

Law School of the University of Athens, Solonos 57, GR-10672 Athens, Greece. Tel: +30 1 3601168/3610112/3620003

Law School of the University of Thessaloniki, University Campus, GR-54006 Thessaloniki, Greece. Tel: +30 31 210888. Fax: +30 31 206138

Law School of the University of Thrace, Dimokritou 17, GR-69100 Komotini, Greece. Tel: +30 531 26111-2. Fax: +30 531 26660/29398

Research institutions

The leading research institutions are connected to the departments of the law schools above.

Hellenic Institute of International and Foreign Law, Solonos 72, GR-10680 Athens, Greece. Tel: +30 1 3615646/3615856

Libraries

Dikogorikos Syllogos Athinon – Vivliothiki [Library of the Athens Bar Association], Akadimias 60, GR-10679 Athens, Greece. Tel: +30 1 3398125–9

Ethniki Vivliothiki [National Library], Panepistimiou 32, GR-10679 Athens, Greece. Tel: +30 1 3614413. Fax: +30 1 3608495

Nomiko Spoudastirio [Library of the Athens University Law School], Ippokratous 33, GR-10680 Athens, Greece.

Vivliothiki tis Voulis [Library of the Parliament], Megaro Voulis, GR-10021, Athens Tel: +30 1 3227958/3234290 (Secretariat). Fax: +30 1 3310013
Praktika tis Voulis ton Ellinon [Proceedings of Parliament]. Tel: +30 1 3233906
Diefthinsi nomothetikou ergou [Legislative Working Party]. Tel: +30 1 3232917
Archio evretiriasis nomothetikou ergou [Index of legislation]. Tel: +30 1 3235975
Epistimoniki Ypiresia [Scientific Service]. Tel: +30 1 3234064

Publishers and booksellers

The main legal publishers are also agents for most of the legal periodicals, or they can provide information on where to obtain them. Furthermore, they sell most legal books, even if they are published by other independent non-legal publishers. It is considered essential to look for information first from these legal publishers and ask for their catalogues.

Ethniko Typografeio [National Printers], Kapodistriou 34, GR-10432 Athens, Greece.

For copies of the Official Gazette only. For information on part A of the Official Gazette Tel: +30 1 5225713–5249547. For sales Tel: +30 1 5239762

Charis Karatzas, Mavromichali 51, GR-10680 Athens, Greece. Tel: +30 1 3600968. Fax: +30 1 3636422

Ant. N. Sakkoulas, Solonos 69, GR-10679 Athens, Greece. Tel: +30 1 3615440. Fax: +30 1 3610425

P. Sakkoulas Bros, Santarosa 1d, GR-10564 Athens, Greece. Tel: +30 1 3215842. Fax: +30 1 3214106. This publisher has opened another branch under the name Dikaio kai Oikonomia [Law & Economy] at Panemistimiou 49, GR-10564 Athens, Greece. Tel: +30 1 3310453–5. Fax: +30 1 3312710

Zacharopoulos-Daidalos, Arsaki 6, GR-10564 Athens, Greece. Tel: +30 1 3223218

Database suppliers

Databank S.A., Leoforos Kifissias 124, GR-11526 Athens, Greece. Tel: +30 1 6494830 Fax: +30 1 6490012. Distributor of the NOMOS system.

Dikogorikos Syllogos Athinon [Athens Bar Association], Akadimias 60, GR-10679 Athens, Greece. Tel: +30 1 3398142–9 (database system). Distributor of the database system of the Athens Bar Association.

List of works cited

Alivizatos, N. (1979) *Les institutions politiques de la Grèce travers les crises 1922–1974*. Paris: LDGJ.

Alivizatos, N. (1981) *Isagogi stin Elliniki Syntagmatiki Istoria 1821–1941* [Introduction to Greek constitutional history 1821–1941]. Athens: Sakkoulas.

Anastassopoulou, Ioanna G. (1993) *Corporations and partnerships in Hellas*. Deventer: Kluwer Law and Taxation; Athens: Sakkoulas.

Androulakis, N. (1986) *Poinikon dikaion I* [Penal law I]. (1991) *Poinikon dikaion II* [Penal law II]. Athens: Sakkoulas.

Antapassis, A. (1983) *Les Codes Maritimes Grecs*. Paris: n.p.

Archio Nomologias [Legislation File]. (1950–) Ed. by G. Karageorgos. Athens: G. Karageorgos, Panepistimiou 46, GR-10678, Athens, Greece. Tel: +30 1 381770.

Armenopoulos. See Harmenopoulos.

Athens Bar Association (1995) *O Odigos tou Dikigorou* [The directory of the lawyer]. Athens: Athens Bar Association. Annual.

Athens Bar Association (1982) *Vasiki nomologia* [Basic cases]. Athens: Athens Bar Association. 8 vols covering 1967–82. Two supplements: (1986) *Vasiki nomologia A*. 2 vols covering 1983–86 and (1993) *Vasiki nomologia B*. 2 vols covering 1986 to 1992.

Balis, G. (1961) *Genikes arches astikou dikeou* [General principles of civil law] 8th edn. Athens: n.p.

Baumgärtel, G. and Rammos, G. (1969) *Das griechische Zivilprozessgesetzbuch mit Enführungsgesetz*. Cologne: Carl Heymanns Verlag.

Beis, K. (1973–1994) *Politiki Dikonomia erminia kat'arthro* [Civil procedure, article-by-article interpretation]. Athens: n.p.

Beis, K. (1982–) *Nomologia, etisia evretiriasi* [Yearly index of case law]. Athens: n.p.

Beis, K. (1984) *Mathimata Politikis Dikonomias* [Lectures on civil procedure]. Athens: n.p.

Chorafas, N. (1978) *Poinikon dikaion* [Penal law] 9th edn. Athens: n.p.

Dedes, Ch. (1983) *Poiniki dikonomia* [Penal procedure] 6th edn. Athens: Sakkoulas.

Deloukas, N. (1993) Admiralty and private maritime law. In Kerameus and Kozyris (1993), pp. 231–246.

Deltion ergatikis nomothesias [Bulletin of labour legislation]. (1945–) Athens: administered by Meropi Petini-Pinioti, Emm.Benaki 18, GR-10678 Athens, Greece. Tel: +301 3820510/3226933.

Diarki evretiria nomologias kai nomothesias [Permanent indexes of cases and legislation]. (in progress) Athens: Zacharopoulos-Daidalos.

Dryllerakis, J. (1993) Tax law and investment incentives. In Kerameus K. and Kozyris P. (1993) (eds), pp. 321–338.

Efirmeris Ellinon Nomikon [Gazette of Greek Lawyers]. (1934–) Athens: Zacharopoulos-Daidalos.

Efimeris tis Kyverniseos tis Ellinikis Dimokratias [The official gazette of the Greek Republic]. (c.1833–) Athens: Ethniko Typografeio.

Eleftheroptypia. (n.d.) Athens: Ch. Tegopoulos. Daily newspaper.

Elliniki Dikeosyni [Greek Justice]. (1960–) Athens: Ekdosi enosis dikaston kai eisaggeleon.

Ephemeris tes kyverneseos. See *Efimeris tis kyverniseos*.

Epitheorisis Dimosiou Dikaiou kai Dioikitikou Dikaiou [Review of Public and Administrative Law]. (1957–) Athens: [the Review].

Epitheorisis Ergatikou Dikaiou [Review of Labour Law]. (1951–) Athens: P.Tsimpoukis. (Edited and administered by P.Tsimpoukis, Aristidou 9, GR-10559 Athens, Greece. Tel: +30 1 3218503. Fax: +30 1 3213428.

Epitheorisis tou Emporikou Dikaiou [Review of Commercial Law]. (1950–) Athens: K.N. Rokas. Administered by Galanis & Panayotis Mentzelopoulos, Solonos 140, GR-10677 Athens. Tel: +301 3647075/3821822.

ETVA (1996) *Invest in Greece guide*. Athens: Hellenic Industrial Development Bank (ETVA).

Evretirio kath'ylin ton apofaseon tou STE [Subject index of the Council of State decisions]. (1961–) Athens: Symboulio tis Epikrateias. Recently this index has also been published in CD-ROM format.

Flanz, Gisbert H. (1988) Greece. In *Constitutions of the Countries of the World*, ed. A.P. Blaustein and G.H. Flanz, vol.VII. Dobbs Ferry, NY: Oceana.

Forologiki epitheorisi [Tax Review]. (n.d.) Athens: administered by the Panellinia Omospondia Ergazomenon DOY [Greek Confederation of Internal Revenue Employees], Omirou 18, GR-10672, Athens, Greece.

Fragistas, C. (1978) Greece. In *International encyclopedia of comparative law*, ed. V. Knapp, vol.1, pp. G49–G62. Tübingen: J.C.B. Mohr.

Georgiadis, A. and Stathopoulos, M. (1978–93) *Astikos Kodix, erminia kat'arthro* [Civil Code, article-by-article commentary]. Athens: Sakkoulas. 8 vols.

Gofas, D. (1992) *Loi codifiée 2190/1920 sur les sociétés anonymes*. Athens: Sakkoulas.

Grammaticaki-Alexiou, A. (1993) Sources and materials. In Kerameus and Kozyris (1993), pp. 13–20.

Harmenopoulos. (1946–) Thessaloniki: Dikigorikos Syllogos Thessalonikis.

Hiotakis, M. (1992a) *English–Greek dictionary of legal and commercial terms*. Athens: Sakkoulas.

Hiotakis, M. (1992b) *Shipping business and law dictionary*. Athens: Sakkoulas.

Iatrou, A. (1981) *Civil and criminal proceedings in Greece*. Athens: n.p.

Iatrou, A. (1986) *An outline of the Greek Civil Code*. Athens: n.p.

International Business Lawyer: journal of the Section on Business Law of the International Bar Association. (1973–) London: International Bar Association.

Karakatsanis, A. (1992) *Syllogiko ergatiko dikaio* [Collective employment law] 3rd edn. Athens: Sakkoulas.

Karakatsanis, A. (1995) *Atomiko ergatiko dikaio* [Personal employment law] 4th edn. Athens: Sakkoulas.

Karatzas, T.B. and Ready, N.P. (1982) *Kodix Idiotikou Nautikou Dikaiou, The Greek Code of Private Maritime Law*. The Hague & London: Nijhoff.

Kathimerini. (n.d.) Athens: Th. Alafouzos. Daily newspaper.

Katralis, P. (1992) *Vasiki nomiki pliroforisi kai sympliroma* [Basic legal information and supplements]. Athens: Sakkoulas.

Katralis, P. (1993) *Nomologia tou Areiou Pagou 1951–1993* [Case law of Areios Pagos 1951–1993]. Athens: Sakkoulas.

Kerameus, K. (1986) *Astiko dikonomiko dikaio – geniko meros* [Civil procedure law – general part]. Thessaloniki: Sakkoulas.

Kerameus, K. and Kozyris, P. (1993) (eds) *Introduction to Greek law* 2nd edn. The Hague: Kluwer; Athens: Sakkoulas.

Kerameus, K. (1993) Judicial organization and civil procedure. In Kerameus and Kozyris (1993), pp. 265–299.

Kerameus, K., Kremlis, G. and Tagaras H. (1989) *I symvasi ton Bryxellon gia ti diethni dikaiodosia kai tin ektelesi ton apofaseon* [The Brussels Convention on International Jurisdiction and the Enforcement of Judgments]. Athens: Sakkoulas.

Kiantou-Pampouki, A. (1993) *Greek maritime law: recent developments*. Southampton: University of Southampton, Institute of Maritime Law.

Kodikas Nomikou Vimatos [Code of the Law Tribune]. (1951–) Athens: Athens Bar Association.

Koniaris, T. (1990) *Labour law and industrial relations in Greece*. Athens: Sakkoulas.

Kontaxis, A. (1993) *Erminia Kodika Poinikis Dikonomias* [Interpretation of the Code of Criminal Procedure]. Athens: Sakkoulas.

Kotsiris, L. (1993) *Greek company law*. Athens: Sakkoulas; The Hague: Kluwer.

Kozyris, P. (1993) Business associations. In Kerameus and Kozyris (1993), pp. 211–230.

Kremalis, K. (1985) *Dikaio koinonikon asfaliseon* [Social insurance law]. Athens: Sakkoulas.

Levantis, E. (1985–1991) *Dikaion emporikon etairion* [Law of commercial companies]. Athens: Sakkoulas. 6 vols.

Lolis, N.B. (1973) *The Greek Penal Code*. London: Sweet and Maxwell; South Hackensack, NJ: Rothman. Introduction by G.A. Mangakis.

Mamopoulos, P. (1982) *Code Civil Hellénique et Supplement*. Athens: Sakkoulas.

Mangakis, G.A. (1984) *Poinikon dikaion – geniko meros* [Penal law – general part] 3rd edn. Athens: Papazisis.

Maridakis, G. (1967) *Idiotiko diethnes dikaion* [Private international law] 2nd edn. Athens: Sakkoulas.

Mavrias, K. and Pantelis, A. (1990) *Syntagmatika keimena – Ellinika kai xena* [Constitutional texts – Greek and foreign] 2nd edn. Athens: Sakkoulas.

Moustakas, A. (1993) *Geniko evretirio Nomikou Vimatos* [General index of the Law Tribune]. Athens: Sakkoulas.

Ta Nea. (1946–) Athens: Lambrakis Press S.A. Daily newspaper.

Nomiko Vima [Law Tribune]. (1951–) Athens: Athens Bar Association.

NOMOS (available from Databank S.A.).

Organisation of Economic Cooperation and Development (1994) *Reviews on foreign direct investment – Greece*. Paris: OECD.

Pantelis A. (1979) *Les grands problèmes de la nouvelle Constitution hellénique*. Paris: LGDJ.

Papantoniou, N. (1983) *Genikes arches astikou dikaiou* [General principles of civil law] 3rd edn. Athens: Sakkoulas.

Papasiopi Pasia, Z. (1994) *Dikaio Ithagenias* [Nationality law]. Thessaloniki: Sakkoulas.

Phorologiki epitheoresi. See *Forologiki epitheorisi*.

Poinika Chronika [Criminal Chronicles]. (1951–) Athens: [the Chronicles].

Price Waterhouse (1992) *Doing business in Greece*. Price Waterhouse information guide. London: Price Waterhouse. And (1994) *Supplement to the 1992 edition*. London: Price Waterhouse.

Rammos, G. (1978–1985) *Egchiridion politikis dikonomias* [Textbook of civil procedure]. Athens: Sakkoulas. 4 vols.

Raptarchis: Diarkis kodikas tis ischyousas nomothesias [Permanent code of the legislation in force]. (1979–) Athens: Ypourgeio Esoterikon Apokentrosis kai Dimosias Dioikisis. Administered by A.Kontopodi, Ch.Trikoupi 5, GR-10678, Athens.

Revue Hellénique de Droit International. (1948–) Athens: Hellenic Institute of International and Foreign Law.

Rokas, I. (1992) *Greece: practical commercial law*. European Commercial Law Series. London: Longman.

Rokas, Ioannis (1993) *Hellenic insurance law*. Deventer: Kluwer Law and Taxation; Athens: Sakkoulas.

Simantiras, K. (1988) *Genikes arches astikou dikaiou* [General principles of civil law] 4th edn. Athens: Sakkoulas.

Spiliotopoulos, E. (1991) *Droit Administratif Hellénique*. Paris: LGDJ.

Spinellis, D. (1993) Criminal law and procedure. In Kerameus and Kozyris (1993), pp. 339–365.

Spyropoulos, P. (1995) *Constitutional law in Hellas*. The Hague & London: Kluwer Law International.

Stathopoulos, Michael P. (1995) *Contract law in Hellas*. The Hague: Kluwer Law International; Athens: Sakkoulas.

Stavropoulos, D. N. (1977) *Oxford English–Greek learner's dictionary*. Oxford: Oxford University Press.

Stavropoulos, D. N. (1988) *Oxford Greek–English learner's dictionary*. Oxford: Oxford University Press.

Systimatiki Erminia tou Poinikou Kodika [Systematic interpretation of the Penal Code]. (1993–) Athens: Sakkoulas.

Taliadoros, C. (1982) *Greek Civil Code*. Athens: n.p.

Taliadoros, C. (1983) *Greek commercial law*. Athens: n.p.

Taliadoros, C. (1985) *Business and trade laws of Greece*. Athens: n.p.

Theodoropoulos, P. (1992) *Erminia Kodika Politikis Dikonomias* [Interpretation of the Code of Civil Procedure]. Athens: n.p.

Varibopiotis, A. (1994) *Kodikas peri Dikigoron* [The Code of Lawyers]. Athens: n.p.

Vathrakokoilis, V. (1989) *Analytiki erminia – nomologia Astikou Kodikos* [Analytical interpretation – case law of the Civil Code]. Athens: Sakkoulas. 2 vols (A and B).

To Vima [Tribune]. (1922–) Athens: Lambrakis Press S.A. Sunday newspaper.

Vrellis, S. (1988) *Idiotiko diethnes dikaio* [Private international law]. Athens: Sakkoulas.

Yiannopoulos, A. N. (1993) Historical development. In Kerameus and Kozyris (1993), pp. 1–12.

Zombolas, T., Tragakis, G. and Karatzas, H. (1991) *English–Greek and Greek–English dictionary of legal terms*. Athens: n.p.

CHAPTER FOURTEEN

Iceland

HALVOR KONGSHAVN

Introduction to the legal system

Iceland is a small country with a long legal history. Iceland, an island between Norway and Greenland, now has approximately 267 000 inhabitants. The capital is Reykjavík; approximately half of the country's inhabitants live in the area of the capital. The country was settled, mostly by Norwegians, in the 9th and 10th centuries. The language, Icelandic, has evolved from Old Norse, the language of the Norwegian settlers.

The parliament, the Althing, is more than 1000 years old. The first Althing met in 930 AD 'on the famous site of Thingvellir . . . and a common law was adopted for the whole country with the institution of a firmly based legislative and judicial organisation. The code of law and the procedure derived from a body of Norwegian law adapted to meet Icelandic conditions' (Nordal and Kristinsson, 1987, p. 38). For a short overview on Thingvellir see Thorsteinsson (1987). As a civil law, or Romano-Germanic system, Iceland puts great emphasis on statutory law passed by the Althing. Delegated legislation usually takes the form of ministerial regulations and decrees and is also an important source of law.

The history of Icelandic private law from the year 1800, with emphasis on sources and literature, is described in German by Inger Dübeck in *Handbuch der Quellen und Literatur der neueren europäischen Privatrechtsgeschichte* (Dübeck, 1987).

The modern history of Iceland dates back to 1944 when the country became a constitutional republic after more than 650 years as a colony, first under Norway and from 1380 under Denmark. An English translation of the Icelandic Constitution with a bibliography can be found in *Constitutions of the countries of the world* (Flanz, 1988) which also contains a constitutional chronology (Flanz, 1988, pp. 1–10). Another translation, somewhat dated but with comments is in Peaslee (1956).

The Icelandic language does not share sufficient common elements with Norwegian, Danish and Swedish to make it commonly understood by other Scandinavians. Therefore, Icelandic law is not much used or referred to in the other Nordic countries. However, Iceland is one of the Nordic countries, it belongs to the same legal family and is a partner in the Nordic Council's uniform law cooperation. The member countries of the Nordic Council are Denmark, Finland, Iceland, Norway and Sweden. See Solem (1977) *The Nordic Council and Scandinavian integration*. The country is not a member of the European Union but participates through membership of the European Economic Area. The EES agreement has been translated into Icelandic, the English version is found in *Agreement on the European Economic Area* (Council of the European Communities, 1992).

Introductory works on the legal system and legal research

Jóhannesson's *Lög og réttur: thættir um íslenska réttarskipan* [Law and legal system: an introduction to the Icelandic system of law] now in its fourth edition (Jóhannesson, 1985) is the premier introductory book in Icelandic on Icelandic law.

For foreign readers the chapter on the legal system of Iceland by Sigurdsson and Simmons (1989) in *Modern legal systems cyclopedia* is more accessible. The chapter is divided into several sections: Introduction to Iceland; form of government; law-making process; the judicial system; legal education; admission to the Bar, nature and size of practice; and law reporting. In addition it gives some notes on the Nordic Co-operation and the so-called 'Cod Wars' against the UK in the early 1970s. The 'Cod Wars' are also described in Jónsson (1982). A 46-year old article by Orfield (1951) on Icelandic law is recommended by Sigurdsson and Simmons (1989, p. 4.50.41) as 'very interesting and informative . . . although somewhat dated'. The general introduction on Iceland by Snævarr (1961) in *Scandinavian legal bibliography* also still contains a great deal of interest.

Vilhjálmson's section on Iceland in the *International encyclopedia of comparative law* (Vilhjálmson, 1972) remains of great importance. His contribution gives a general view of the Icelandic governmental and legal system. Björgvinsson describes the Constitution and government in a chapter of the reference work *Iceland: the Republic* (Björgvinsson, 1996). His contribution is followed by Kristinsson (1996) writing about political developments and Palssón's contribution on foreign affairs (Palssón, 1996).

Of more specialised interest is Styrkársson and Skúlason (1983) on Iceland in *Digest of commercial laws of the world.*

Legislation

The official *Stjórnartídindi* (1874–) [Icelandic Statutory Law Gazette] is published in three sections: A. Statutes passed by the Althing; B. Delegated legislation, that is regulations and decrees; C. Treaties. The *Stjórnartídindi* is published approximately every second week. The normal way of citing an individual law is by number and year, for example: Lög nr.20/1986. Legislation comes into force on publication unless otherwise stated.

Lagasafn (1995) [consolidated Iceland law collection] published by the Ministry of Justice is the Icelandic lawyer's most important resource. It is organized systematically with both chronological and subject indexes. The oldest law still in force in the collection is Kristinréttur Árna biskups Thorlákssonar [Bishop Árna Thorláksson's Ecclesiastical Law] which dates back to the year 1275. *Lagasafn* has been published every five to ten years but the intention is now to publish the collection every three years.

Althingstídindi (1875–) [Parliamentary Gazette] is published by the Althing. It reports on all parliamentary proceedings, bills, laws passed and discussions and reports of parliamentary commissions. These discussions and reports are often the only legal history preceding the laws and are therefore often an important source in interpreting a particular law. *Althingstídindi* has, from 1972, two sections: A. Documents and B. Debates.

Treaties

Treaty-making power is vested in the Althing and treaties, once ratified, appear from 1962 in section C in the official gazette *Stjórnartídindi* (1874–) in both Icelandic and English with annual indexes. The Ministry of Foreign Affairs maintained a register of ratifications until 1986 and a register until 1995 is at http://www.adgengi.is/mrs/fjolintr.htm.

Law reports, judgments

Hæstaréttardómar (1920–) [Supreme Court Decisions] is a very important source of law and the interpretation of law. The judgments are published *in extenso*, together with decisions from the lower courts. All judgments are published. Indexes are only produced annually.

Nordisk domssamling (1958–) [Nordic Supreme Courts decisions collection] publishes supreme court decisions from the five Nordic countries including Iceland on subjects where the Nordic laws are fairly comparable. The Icelandic decisions are here translated into Danish. *Nordiske domme i sjøfartsanliggende* (1900–) [Nordic Court Decisions on Sea Law] publishes court decisions from the same countries on sea law.

Iceland has no district courts, the first level is the town or local court and appeal is to the Supreme Court. Some lower court decisions are also published, for example, extracts of the Reykjavík Town Court decisions have appeared in the recently established *Dómareifanir: borgardómaraembættid í Reykjavík 1987–* (1989–) of which only three annual volumes had been published by late 1995. Labour law decisions are found in *Dómar Félagsdóms* (1939–).

Computer-based systems

The *Lagasafn*, the Icelandic law collection, is available online and on disk in a full text database also entitled LAGASAFN which includes all Icelandic laws in force. LAGASAFN is produced by the Ministry of Justice and its host is Skyrsluvélar rikisins [the State Data Processing Centre] and Reykjavíkurborgar, SKYRR [Reykjavik Municipal Data Processing Centre]. Legislative material in Icelandic is available on the Internet at http://www.adgengi.is/ to registered paying subscribers. *Hæstarréttardómar* [the Supreme Court decisions] will be soon be published in full text on CD-ROM under the title ÍSLEX.

Encyclopedias

No encyclopedia of Icelandic law is published.

Directories

Lögfrædingatal (Haraldsson, 1993–) contains biographical information about every Icelandic lawyer, *Candidati juris* and *Examinati juris*, who has graduated in the period 1736–1992. Today approximately 1000 persons hold the Candidatus Juris degree [law degree].

A directory of parliament, government and government departments, courts, university, research and other institutions, with addresses and names of the persons working within the institutions can be found in *Ríkishandbók Íslands* (Thorlacius, 1988); this is somewhat outdated but a new edition is planned.

Bibliographies and indexes

The current national bibliography is *Íslenzk bókaskrá: the Icelandic National Bibliography* (1975–). It 'includes books and pamphlets, published or printed in Iceland, or published by Icelanders and printed abroad' according to Munch-Petersen (1984, p. 79). The bibliography is organized by the Dewey Decimal Classification system, so law is found under group 340 where the 'arrangement is alphabetical by author and title with ample cross references, arranged by first names of Icelandic authors and last names of foreign authors' (Munch-Petersen, 1984, p. 79). It should be noted that Icelanders use last names only when necessary for clarity. Last names are derived by adding '-son' for males or '-dóttir' for females to the father's or sometimes the mother's name. With few exceptions people are listed by first names in the telephone directory. A five-year cumulation for the years 1974–1978 was published in 1985 (*Íslensk bókaskrá*, 1985).

A 'selected list of books on Iceland in foreign languages' divided into eight groups, although law is not one of them, is found in a useful reference book for foreigners interested in the country *Iceland: the Republic* (Nordal and Kristinsson, 1996).

When it comes to legal bibliographies, two issues of the law review *Tímarit lögfrœdinga* cover Icelandic legal literature from the earliest times until the end of 1975, prepared by Skarphédinsson (1955) for the years until the end of 1955 and by Stefánsdóttir (1980) for the following years. See also Sigurdsson and Simmons (1989) who include an annotated bibliography at the end of their article on the legal system of Iceland. Volume 37 of the World Bibliographical Series, *Iceland*, has a section called Constitution, parliament and the law (Horton, 1983) with annotations to the bibliography; a new edition is in preparation. A general survey is presented in Danish by Gestsdóttir (1989) in the seminar report from the First Nordic Law Library Meeting in 1989. Furthermore, Icelandic legal literature is represented in the somewhat dated *Scandinavian legal bibliography* (Iuul *et al.*, 1961).

The collections of the University Library/National Library, and other academic libraries, are listed online in the catalogue GEGNIR using an automated library system called Libertas. The Internet address for a telnet call is saga.bok.hi.is and the home page address of the University Library/National Library on World Wide Web is http://www.bok.hi.is/. The transcription of Icelandic characters can cause some difficulties but one may enter the alphabetical indexes as close to the desired letter as possible and then browse as needed to overcome these difficulties, unless one has equipment which manages the ISO-8859/1 character set (see also *World wide web servers in Iceland* on http://www.isnet.is/WWW/servers.html).

Dictionaries

Lögbókin thin (Gudmundsson, 1989) is the major dictionary explaining Icelandic legal terms in Icelandic. There is no bilingual or multilingual dictionary of legal terms with the exception of the *Nordisk förvaltningsordbok* (1991) [Nordic dictionary of administrative terms] for the five Nordic languages.

The best general language dictionaries for translation between English and Icelandic, including legal terms, are *Ensk–íslensk ordabók* [English–Icelandic dictionary] (Sörensen *et al.*, 1991) and *Íslensk–ensk ordabók* [Icelandic–English dictionary] (Hólmarsson, 1989).

For business terms consult *Ensk–íslensk vidskiptaordabók* [English–Icelandic business dictionary] (Lacy and Einarsson, 1990) and *Ìslensk–ensk vidskiptaordabók* [Icelandic–English business dictionary) (Einarsson and Lacy, 1989).

Current information sources

Journals

The Icelandic law reviews publish articles on law solely in Icelandic. The two general law journals are *Tímarit lögfrædinga* (1951–) published by the Icelandic Lawyers Association and *Úlfljótur* (1947–) published by the Law Students Association, with a cumulative index covering 1947–1990 (*Úlfjótur: heildarregistur*, 1991).

In the following Nordic law reviews one will find contributions in English or Danish and sometimes Norwegian by Icelandic researchers: in English, *Nordic Journal of International Law* (1930–), *Scandinavian Studies in Criminology* (1965–) which has a cumulative alphabetical index (Hansen and Kongshavn, 1992), and *Scandinavian Studies in Law* (1957–) which has cumulative indexes in 1973 and 1989. Articles in Danish or Norwegian appear in *Nordisk Tidsskrift for Kriminalvidenskab* [Nordic Criminal Science Journal] (1949–), *Tidsskrift for rettsvitenskap* [Journal of Jurisprudence] (1888–) and *Nordisk administrativt tidsskrift* [Nordic Journal for Administrative Studies] (1920–).

Business and financial information

Some basic business and financial information about Iceland can be found in *Iceland: the Republic* (Nordal and Kristinsson, 1996), published by the Central Bank of Iceland. The Central Bank's annual report *Sedlabanki Íslands: Central Bank of Iceland* (1994), for the year 1993, is all in English, covering topics like money, credit and interest rates, the credit market and financial institutions, the exchange rate, the foreign exchange and the balance of payments, changes in legislation and other matters, external affairs, with a statistical appendix (see also the Icelandic Business Web on http://www1.mmedia.is/notes/fv/ibw.html).

Statistics

Landshagir: Statistical abstract of Iceland (1995), published by The Statistical Bureau of Iceland, gives an annual statistical overview of the country, including Supreme Court statistics. For justice statistics over some years consult the somewhat outdated *Dómsmálaskyrslur árin 1975–77 = Justice Statistics 1975–77* (1983). Statistics on the economy are published quarterly by the Central Bank in *Economic statistics* (1980–). The National Economic Institute has since 1979 published the annual *The Icelandic economy: developments [year] and outlook for [year]* (1979–). A new semi-annual publication is *The economy of Iceland* (1994–).

The Law Library

The Bókasafn Lagadeildar [Law Library] is a department of the Landsbókasafn Íslands – Háskólabókasafn [National Library – University of Iceland Library] and is situated at the law school. The study of law was established in 1908 and from 1911 it became a part of Háskóla Íslands [the University of Iceland]. The Faculty of Law is the single one in Iceland and has approximately 15 teachers, including 10 professors. About 600 students are presently enrolled at the Faculty of Law; study takes five to six years and around 30 to 35 persons graduate each year. Parts of the curriculum are in Danish, Norwegian and Swedish as the Nordic countries have a fairly uniform law. The Law Library employs one half-time librarian during term. In the summer the librarian works at the University Library and is called to the Law School when needed. The Law Library contains approximately 8000 volumes and subscribes to about 70 periodicals.

Useful addresses

Associations of lawyers

The Icelandic Bar Association, Lögmannafélag Íslands, Álftamyri 9, IS-108 Reykjavík, Iceland. Tel: +354 568 5620

Government organizations

Central Bank of Iceland, Sedalabanki Íslands, Kalkofnsvegi 1, IS-101 Reykjavík, Iceland. Tel: +354 569 9600

Ministry of Foreign Affairs, Utanríkisráduneytid, Raudarástig, IS-150 Reykjavík, Iceland. Tel: +354 560 9900

Ministry of Justice, Dóms-og kirkjumálarduneytid, Arnarhvoli, IS-101 Reykjavík, Iceland. Tel: +354 560 9010

World Wide Web address for governmental institutions of Iceland is http://www.stjr.is/en/stjren01.htm

Courts

The Supreme Court, Hæstiréttur, Lindargötu, IS-150 Reykjavík, Iceland. Tel: +354 551 3936

Education and training

The Law School, Háskóli Íslands, Lagadeild, IS-101 Reykjavík, Iceland. Tel: +354 569 4300

Research institutions

See The Law School above.

Libraries

Bókasafn Lagadeildar [The Law School Library], Landsbókasafn Íslands – Háskólabókasafn [National Library – University of Iceland Library], IS-101 Reykjavík, Iceland. Tel: +354 569 4372. The catalogue is available by telnet call to saga.bok.hi.is and the home page address of the University Library/National Library is http://www.bok.hi.is/ on the World Wide Web

Publishers and booksellers

Bókabud Larusar Blöndal (for documents from the Ministry of Justice), Skólavördustigur 2, IS-101 Reykjavík, Iceland. Tel: +354 551 5650

Bókaútgáfa Orators [The Law Students Association Publishers], P.O. Box 918, IS-121 Reykjavík, Iceland. Tel: +354 562 8202

Bóksala stúdenta [University Bookstore of Iceland], v/Hringbraut, IS-101 Reykjavík, Iceland. Tel: +354 561 5961

Háskólaútgáfan [The University Press], v/ Sudurgötu, IS-101 Reykjavík, Iceland. Tel: +354 525 4003

Skyrsluvélar rikisins [the State Data Processing Centre] and Reykjavíkurborgar, SKYRR [Reykjavik Municipal Data Processing Centre], Háaleitisbraut 9, IS-108 Reykjavík, Iceland

List of works cited

Althingstídindi. (1875–) Reykjavík: Althingi.

Björgvinsson, Davíd Thor (1996) Constitution and government. In Nordal and Kristinsson (1996), pp. 107–121.

Council of the European Communities (1992) *Agreement on the European Economic Area*. Luxembourg: Office for Official Publications of the European Communities.

Dómar Félagsdóms. (1939–) Reykjavík: Félagsdómur.

Dómareifanir: borgardómaraembættid í Reykjavík: 1987–. (1989–) Reykjavík: Borgardómur.

Dómsmálaskyrslur árin 1975–77 = Justice statistics 1975–77. (1983) Statistics of Iceland II, 77. Reykjavík: Hagstofa Íslands/The Statistical Bureau of Iceland.

Dübeck, Inger (1987) Island. In *Handbuch der Quellen und Literatur der neueren europäischen Privatrechtsgeschichte*, Bd.3: Das 19. Jahrhundert, Teilbd.4: Die nordischen Länder, pp. 629–654. Munich: C.H. Beck, 1973–.

Economic statistics: quarterly. (1980) Reykjavík: Central Bank of Iceland.

Economy of Iceland. (1994–) Reykjavík: Central Bank of Iceland, International Department.

Einarsson, Thorir and Lacy, Terry G. (1989) *Íslensk-ensk vidskipta ordabók*. Reykjavík: Örn og Örlygur.

Flanz, Gisbert H. (1988) Republic of Iceland: 1973–1987. In *Constitutions of the countries of the world*, ed. A.P. Blaustein and G.H. Flanz, vol.VIII. Dobbs Ferry, NY: Oceana.

GEGNIR (available from the National Library – University of Iceland Library [Landsbókasafn Íslands – Háskólabókasafn]).

Gestsdóttir, Audur (1989) Island. In *Seminarrapport: Det første nordiske juridiske bibliotekmøte: Oslo, 7–9 juni 1989*, pp. 51–57. Det juridiske fakultetsbibliotheks skriftserie, nr.6. Oslo: Det juridiske fakultetsbibliotek [The Law Faculty Library].

Gudmundsson, Björn Th. (1989) *Lögbókin thin*. Reykjavík: Örn og Örlygur.

Hansen, June and Kongshavn, Halvor (1992) *Scandinavian Studies in Criminology: vol.1–12 (1965–1991): alphabetical index*. Oslo: Scandinavian Research Council in Criminology.

Haraldsson, Gunnlaugur (1993–) *Lögfrædingatal: 1736–1992*. Reykjavík: Idunn (4 vols. when completed, three volumes are published at July 1995).

Hæstaréttardómar. (1920–) Reykjavík: Félagsprentsmidjan H/F.

Hólmarsson, Sverrir *et al.* (1989) *Íslensk-ensk ordabók*. Reykjavík: Idunn.

Horton, John J. (1983) (comp.) Constitution, parliament and the law. In *Iceland*, comp. John J. Horton, pp. 135–139. World Bibliographical Series, vol.37. Oxford: Clio Press.

Icelandic economy: developments [year] and outlook for [year]. (1979–) Reykjavík: National Economic Institute.

Íslenzk bókaskrá: The Icelandic National Bibliography (1975–) Reykjavík: Landsbókasafn Íslands (formerly *Ritaukaskrá Landsbókasafnsins*. [The National Library accession catalogue] (1887–1943) Reykjavík: Landsbókasafn Íslands and *Árbók Landsbókasafns Íslands: Yearbook of the Icelandic National Library*. (1944–1973) Reykjavík: Landsbókasafn Íslands).

Íslenzk bókaskrá: The Icelandic national bibliography 1974–1978. (1985) Reykjavík: Landsbókasafn Íslands.

Iuul, Stig *et al.* (1961) (comp.) *Scandinavian legal bibliography*. Stockholm: Almqvist & Wiksell.

Jóhannesson, Ólafur (1985) *Lög og réttur: thættir um íslenska réttarskipan* 4th edn., búid hefur til prentunar Sigurdur Líndal. Reykjavík: Hid Íslenska bókmenntafélag.

Jónsson, Hannes (1982) *Friends in conflict*. London: C. Hurst.

Kristinsson, Gunnar Helgi (1996) Political developments. In Nordal and Kristinsson (1996), pp. 122–133.

Lacy, Terry G. and Einarsson, Thorir (1990) *Ensk-íslensk vidskiptaordabók* 2nd edn. Reykjavík: Örn og Örlygur.

Lagasafn: Íslensk lög 1. október 1995. (1995) 2 vols. Reykjavík: Dóms-og kirkjumálaráduneytid.

LAGASAFN (available from Skyrsluvélar rikisins [the State Data Processing Centre] and Reykjavíkurborgar, SKYRR [Reykjavik Municipal Data Processing Centre]).

Landshagir: statistical abstract of Iceland 1994. (1995) Statistics of Iceland III, 21. Reykjavík: Hagstofa Íslands/Statistical Bureau of Iceland.

Munch-Petersen, Erland (1984) (ed.) *Guide to Nordic bibliography*. Copenhagen: Nordisk Ministerråd [Nordic Council].

Nordal, Jóhannes and Kristinsson, Valdimar (1987) (eds) *Iceland: the Republic. Handbook published by the Central Bank of Iceland*. Reykjavík: Central Bank of Iceland.

Nordal, Jóhannes and Kristinsson, Valdimar (1996) (eds) *Iceland: the Republic. Handbook published by the Central Bank of Iceland*. Reykjavík: Central Bank of Iceland.

Nordic Journal of International Law: Acta scandinavia juris gentium. (1986–) Copenhagen: The Journal. Continues *Nordisk Tidsskrift for International Ret: Acta scandinavia juris gentium*. (1930–1985).

Nordisk administrativt tidsskrift. (1920–) Copenhagen: Nordisk administrativt forbund [The Nordic Association for Administrative Studies].

Nordisk domssamling. (1958–) Oslo: Universitetsforlaget.

Nordisk förvaltningsordbok. (1991) Stockholm: Nordiska rådet/Almänna förlaget.

Nordisk Tidsskrift for Kriminalvidenskab. (1949–) Copenhagen: De nordiske kriminalistforeninger [The Nordic Criminalist Associations].

Nordiske domme i sjøfartsanliggende. (1900–) Oslo: Nordisk skibsrederforening [The Nordic Ship Owners Association].

Orfield, Lester (1951) Icelandic law. In *Dickinson Law Review*, vol.56, pp. 42–87.

Pálsson, Gunnar (1996) Foreign affairs. In Nordal and Kristinsson (1996), pp. 134–144.

Peaslee, Amos J. (1956) Iceland. In *Constitutions of nations*, Amos J. Peaslee, 2nd edn, vol.II, pp. 198–217. [n.p.]: Martinus Nijhoff.

Scandinavian Studies in Criminology. (1965–) Oslo: Universitetsforlaget.

Scandinavian Studies in Law. (1957–) Stockholm: Almqvist & Wiksell International. (cumulative indexes, 1973 and 1989, in vol.17, pp. 311–324 and vol.33, pp. 235–250).

Sedlabanki Íslands: Central Bank of Iceland: annual report 1993. (1994) Reykjavík: Sedlabanki.

Sigurdsson, Johannes and Simmons, Barry Keith (1989) The legal system of Iceland. In *Modern legal systems cyclopedia*, ed. K.R. Redden, vol.4, pp. 4.50. Buffalo, NY: Hein.

Skarphédinsson, Fridjón (1955) Skrár um lagabókmenntir eftir íslenska höfunda eda í íslenskum thydingum til ársloka 1955. In *Timarit lögfrædinga*, 1955, pp. 173–264.

Snævarr, Ármann (1961) Iceland. In Iuul, Stig *et al.* (1961), pp. 19–25.

Solem, Erik (1977) *The Nordic Council and Scandinavian integration*. Praeger Special Studies in International Politics and Government. New York: Praeger.

Sörensen, Sören *et al.* (1991) *Ensk-íslensk ordabók: med alfrædilegu ívafi*. Reykjavík: Örn og Örlygur.

Stefánsdóttir, Valborg (1980) Skrá um lagabókmenntir eftir íslenska höfunda eda í íslenskum thydingum 1956–75. In *Timarit lögfrædinga*, 1980, pp. 4–62.

Stjórnartídindi. (1874–) Reykjavík: Dómsmálaráduneytid.

Styrkársson, Gudjón and Skúlason, Pall (1983) The commercial laws of Iceland. In *Digest of commercial laws of the world*, ed. Lester Nelson, vol.3, 31pp booklet. Dobbs Ferry, NY: Oceana.

Thorlacius, Birigir (1988) (ed.) *Ríkishandbók Íslands 1988: skrá um stofnanir ríkisins, starfsmenn theirra o.fl.* 4th edn. Reykjavík: Ríkistjórn Íslands.

Thorsteinsson, Björn (1987) *Thingvellir: Iceland's national shrine: a visitors companion*. Reykjavík: Örn og Örlygur.

Tidsskrift for rettsvitenskap. (1888–) Oslo: Universitetsforlaget.

Timarit lögfrædinga. (1951–) Reykjavík: Lögfrædingafélag Íslands.

Úlfljótur. (1947–) Reykjavík: Orator.

Úlfjótur: heildarregistur Úlfljóts 1947–1990. (1991) Reykjavík: Orator.

Vilhjálmson, Thór (1972) Iceland. In *International encyclopedia of comparative law*, ed. V. Knapp, vol.1, pp. I1–I6. Tübingen: J.C.B. Mohr.

Note and Acknowledgements

This chapter is based on an article by the author published in *International Journal of Legal Information*, **21**, no.2, Summer 1993, pp. 167–173.

The author offers many thanks to the Librarian Audur Gestsdóttir at the Law School Library in Reykjavík for invaluable help and comments and greetings to the friendly and service-minded staff at the National Library/University Library in Reykjavík.

CHAPTER FIFTEEN

Ireland

JOHN FURLONG

Introduction to the legal system

The principal sources of modern Irish law were directly and significantly shaped by the events of over nine hundred years but mainly by the political and historical developments of the 19th and early 20th centuries.

The ancient Irish Brehon laws detailed in Kelly, F.K. (1988) had a slow demise as the influences of the Normans and the English spread throughout the island. Delany, V.T.H. (1975) outlines the attempts to impose the common law and extend the statutory powers of England to Ireland, most notably by Poynings Act of 1494 and coming to its conclusion with the Act of Union in 1800.

While Irish parliaments existed during the reigns of the Stuarts and Tudors, there is little legislative heritage of domestic origin from the period prior to 1800. Some English statutes of that time, as applied to Ireland, continue in force today although the courts may be inclined to view many as in a state of desuetude. The Act of Union of 1800, establishing the United Kingdom of Great Britain and Ireland, saw the commencement of the most fruitful period of legislative development prior to the foundation of the Irish State. Grimes and Horgan (1981) provides an historical overview of the development of the common law system through the last two centuries while McEldowney and O'Higgins (1990) and Boyle and Greer (1983) endeavour to analyse and identify the specifics of the common law system as it developed in Ireland.

The Government of Ireland Act 1920 and the Anglo Irish Treaty of 1921 established Saorstát Éireann (the Irish Free State) in respect of the larger part of the island of Ireland. Northern Ireland remained part of the United Kingdom. The Irish Free State adopted a written Constitution in 1922 with the consequent formal establishment of a parliament and legislature and the formation of an indigenous courts system.

In 1937, the people of the Irish Free State adopted a new Constitution [Bunreacht na hÉireann] which, with subsequent amendments, is the supreme legal authority. In 1948, Ireland declared itself a Republic. The Republic of Ireland Act 1948 provides that the description of the country is the Republic of Ireland or, in the Irish language, Poblacht na hÉireann. The constitutional name, which has precedence in law and is formally recognized as the correct form, is Ireland or, in the Irish language, Éire.

Ireland is thus a constitutional democracy with a common law jurisdiction. Through the Constitution, law making power is vested in the people by way of referendum, in the parliament, through its authority to enact statutory law and in the courts, through the power of judicial interpretation of the law.

Ireland became a member of the European Economic Community on 1 January 1973. The Constitution was amended by referendum to provide that nothing in it will invalidate any laws enacted or measures adopted as necessary to European Community membership and its laws.

Irish legal and political history has resulted in the continuing influence of law of the United Kingdom. Certain pre-1922 enactments of the United Kingdom parliament are still in full force and effect. Many areas of law have developed parallel to those in the UK. As a common law jurisdiction, decisions of the superior courts of the UK are a major reference source and have influential, though not binding, effect in the Irish courts. Over the past 25 years the influence of European Community law has led to further parallels between the legal systems of both jurisdictions.

Introductory works on legal system and legal research

The principal historical narrative on the development of the legal system is contained in Delany, V.T.H. (1975) which is now somewhat out of date. More recent introductions to the legal system are contained in Byrne and McCutcheon (1996) and in Grimes and Horgan (1981). Doolan (1991) and Faulkner, Kelly and Turley (1991) offer a more general introduction aimed at a student readership. Boyle and Greer (1983) provides an interesting comparative study of the legal systems in Ireland and Northern Ireland.

The most comprehensive work on legal research in Ireland is O'Malley (1993) which covers the primary and secondary sources of Irish law and other pertinent jurisdictions. It provides a more detailed and comprehensive approach to legal research than was previously available in other works. O'Malley has a very broad coverage of source materials and how to use them and is primarily aimed at law students. It includes a useful glossary of terms, listing of correct citations and common abbreviations.

Smith (1996) gives an overview of Irish law which is a valuable aid to research, containing illustrative examples of statutes and law reports.

Legislation

Constitution

From time to time, the revised text of the Constitution incorporating amendments passed by referendum of the people is published. *Bunreacht na hÉireann* [Constitution of Ireland] (1995) contains the amended text following the 10th amendment to the Constitution. Subsequent amendments (up to the 15th amendment) are provided on an insert sheet.

Kelly, J. (1994) provides a detailed and annotated text of the Constitution and is the definitive work. Also of considerable assistance is O'Reilly and Redmond (1980). Foley and Lalor (1995) incorporates a collated text up to and including the 14th Amendment.

The text of Constitutional amendments are also published as Acts of Parliament and are contained in the relevant yearly volume of the *Acts of the Oireachtas* (1922–).

Statutes

Primary legislation is enacted by the Oireachtas [Parliament] comprising Dáil Éireann [Chamber of Deputies], Seanad Éireann [Upper House or Senate] and the President.

BILLS

In general, a Bill, which is a draft version of legislative proposals, may be introduced or initiated in either House and bears the title and year of introduction. A Bill is published as initiated, usually with a useful Explanatory Memorandum which will explain the general objectives of the Bill and the purpose of each section. Further revised texts are published as the Bill progresses through both Houses usually after the Committee Stage and as passed by either Dáil Éireann or Seanad Éireann.

Committee Stage proceedings, which can often provide background detail on the purpose and intent of the Bill, are published in the *Dail Debates* and the *Seanad Debates* or (if the Bill is heard before a Special or Select Committee) in the Proceedings of the relevant Special or Select Committee.

The *Orders of the Day and Question Papers* are published separately for the Dáil and Seanad each day either House is in session. They are useful for tracking the initiation and progress of Bills through Parliament. They also list documents laid before either House.

Dooney and O'Toole (1992) and O'Donnell (1992) both detail the mechanics of parliamentary legislation. McGowan Smyth (1979) deals specifically with the structures and procedures of the parliament.

PUBLICATION AND CITATION

Public Acts: When a Bill has been signed, notice of its promulgation is published in *Iris Oifigiúil* (1922–) [Official Gazette] and it will receive a chronological number for its year of publication. An Act will commence on the date it is signed into law by the President unless it contains specific commencement provisions.

Acts are published singly and in bound yearly volumes as *Acts of the Oireachtas*. The bound yearly volumes from 1922 are available in two series: to 1980 in quarto size in bilingual format; from 1980 in A4 English language format. The correct citation for an Act is its title followed by its designation number and year. For example: Companies Act, 1990 (No.33 of 1990).

Private and Local Acts: Most legislation is of general application and will be known as a Public or General Bill or Act. A very small number of Private or Local Acts have been enacted. Private Acts are published in the back of the yearly volumes of the *Acts of the Oireachtas* and are cited thus: The Altamont (Amendment of Deed of Trust) Act, 1993 (No.1 (Private) of 1993).

OTHER GENERAL SERIES

Irish Current Law Statutes Annotated (1984–) comprises looseleaf volumes collecting the text of Acts issued in a series of releases each year, each release covering several Acts. The most important Acts have full annotations and most come with detailed general notes. There is a subject index which is updated with each release and the table of contents at the front of the volume lists the Acts both alphabetically and chronologically within each year from 1984.

PRE-1922 STATUTES

Some Irish Statutory law is still derived from the period prior to 1922. *The Statutes at Large . . . 1310 to 1786*, and continued until 1800 (edited by Grierson) contains in 20 volumes a comprehensive collection of laws enacted prior to the Act of Union in 1800. The *Irish Statutes Revised 1310–1800* (1885), reprinted 1995, while not entirely reliable, provides a single volume guide to Statutes of Pre-Union Parliaments. It purports to list all Pre-Union Statutes (including those repealed) accompanied by the texts of those Statutes which were still in force in 1885. It would be prudent when using this work to note the impact of the Statute Law Revision (Pre-Union Irish Statutes) Act 1962, which repealed many Statutes enacted for the period 1459–1800 and the Statute Law Revision Act 1983, which covered the period 1236 to 1796.

Vance (1862) contains commentaries on the text of Statutes published between 1215 and 1862 and Quinn (1992) is a modest selected collection of certain important Public Acts enacted prior to 1922 and which are still in force, presented in their amended form.

From the Act of Union in 1800 to 1921, both Public and Private Acts affecting Ireland form part of the annual volumes of the Acts of the Parliament of the United Kingdom. Oulton (1839) covers the period 1310 to 1838 listing Statutes then in force or affecting Ireland together with summaries of the relevant sections ordered by subject.

SPECIALIZED COLLECTIONS

Of particular note are the *Combined Companies Acts* (looseleaf) and *Butterworth Ireland Companies Acts 1963 to 1990* (1993) each of which consolidates the substantial body of law governing the incorporation and operation of companies. The latter also includes annotations to the legislation and reference to relevant case law.

Butterworths Taxes Acts (1991–), *Butterworths VAT Acts* (1992–) and *Butterworths Capital Tax Acts* (1993–) all consolidate complex areas of tax legislation and are published on a revised annual basis. Other notable consolidated and annotated texts are Clark (1995) and Delany, H. (1993). Kerr (1995) gathers full and annotated texts of all statutory material regarding termination of employment in one volume.

The detailed statutory code contained in statutes and regulations governing pensions law is available in a consolidated looseleaf format on subscription in The *Pensions Act and Regulations* (1992–).

INDEXES, TABLES AND CITATORS

The most recent cumulative *Index to the Statutes 1922–1982* (1986) has a separate supplement in the same volume and following the same format for the period 1983 to 1985. The Index, which is in seven sections, includes a subject index to the Statutes and to Statutory Instruments made under the provisions of the European Communities Act 1972. The Index also includes a number of separate chronological lists; one showing (where relevant) the Public General Acts from 1922 to 1982 which have been affected, repealed or amended and the others showing (where relevant) Pre-Union Irish Statutes, English Statutes, Pre-Union British Statutes and British Statutes up to 1922 which have been affected, repealed or amended for the period 1922 to 1982. Yearly non-cumulative Indexes, following the same format, are available for each subsequent year up to 1989. The 1989 year index contains a convenient list of the latest collective citations for groups of related Acts enacted between 1922 and 1989.

The *Chronological Table of the Statutes 1922–1995* (1996) provides new cumulative lists of Statutes enacted and Statutes affected, amended or repealed in the same format as the *Index to the Statutes 1922–1982* but without a subject index.

For each year since 1993, *Irish Current Law Statutes Annotated* (1984–) includes citators listing Acts and Statutory Instruments which have been amended either by Act or Statutory Instrument of the particular year or which have been judicially considered during that year. For each year since 1993, the work also sets out commencement dates of Statutes effected in the current year and a list of legislation not yet in force.

Volume II of the *Chronological Table and Index of the Statutes in Force* (1921) includes details of Statutes still in force and applying to Ireland in 1921. The Index covers the period 1235 to 1921 but does not include pre-Union Irish Acts or legislation applied by virtue of Poynings Act 1494.

Irish Current Law Monthly Digest (1995–) publishes on a monthly basis a cumulative list of Statutes enacted in the current year with details of their commencement.

Subordinate legislation

Subordinate or delegated legislation comprises Orders, Rules and Regulations made under authority of Statute by a specified Minister of the Government or by an authorized agency or body.

Until 1947 subordinate legislation was issued in the form of *Statutory Rules and Orders*. These are collected in three series (1922–1938), (1939–1945) and (1946–1947) each series with its own index volume. They are cited by title, number and year. For example: Milk and Dairies Regulations 1936 (SRO 310/36).

Subordinate legislation in the form of *Statutory Instruments* (1947–) is presently governed by the Statutory Instruments Act 1947. Several hundred Instruments are made each year. Statutory Instruments are cited by their name, instrument number and year of publication. For example: Local Government (Planning and Development) Regulations 1995 (SI 69/95).

Individual Statutory Instruments are published in stencil format, normally in the English language and subsequently in printed form in both Irish and English. The *Statutory Instruments* are issued in annual sets of bound volumes.

IMPLEMENTATION OF EC LEGISLATION

The European Communities Acts 1972–1994 enable the implementation of European Community measures, including Directives, by way of Statutory Instruments. A large number of measures have been given effect in this way. The Supreme Court has confirmed the capacity of such Statutory Instruments to repeal or amend existing Statute law.

INDEXES

An *Index to the Statutory Instruments* (1944–) which is non-cumulative is published on an occasional basis. Seven index volumes cover the period 1948–1995. Each index volume contains an alphabetical list of Statutes and the Statutory Instruments made thereunder together with an alphabetical list of Statutory Instruments made during the period. The indexes do not provide any information on the currency of the Statutory Instruments listed.

Irish Current Law Statutes Annotated includes both an alphabetical and chronological list of Statutory Instruments made for each year from 1984. Humphreys (1988) comprises a subject index and chronological index of Statutory Instruments, Orders and Regulations made from 1922 to 1984. It also indicates whether or not the indexed Instruments and Orders were revoked or were still in force at December 1988.

The *Chronological Table of the Statutes 1922–1995* (1996) includes a list of Statutory Instruments made under the provisions of the European Communities Acts.

Treaties

The executive power to make treaties is vested in the government. The Constitution requires that all international agreements must be laid before Dáil Éireann. The Department of Foreign Affairs occasionally publishes lists of recent international agreements in *Iris Oifigiúil*. The Stationery Office publishes each treaty as a separate document in a numbered *Treaty series* (1930–). The recommended citation for a treaty is by name and *Treaty series* number. For example: Treaty Series 10/1995 Air Transport Agreement between the Government of Ireland and the Government of the Russian Federation.

There have been seven general indexes to the *Treaty series* published covering the period 1930 to 1994, the last being the *General Index to the Treaty Series 1977–1994* (1994). Usually, the index lists the treaties for the period both alphabetically and chronologically.

Law reports, judgments, digests

The Irish Court system comprises the District Court, Circuit Court, Special Criminal Court, High Court, Court of Criminal Appeal and Supreme Court. While Delany, V.T.H. (1979) is still useful as an historical narrative on the development of the courts system, it is considerably out of step with more recent developments, notably the changes in the courts structures effected by the Court and Court Officers Act 1995.

The decisions of the Supreme Court are binding on all inferior courts although not on subsequent judgments of the Supreme Court itself. The decisions of the High Court are binding on the Circuit and District Courts and the decisions of the Court of Criminal Appeal are binding on inferior courts in criminal matters. The courts may adopt as persuasive but not as binding the decisions of courts in other jurisdictions notably those of the House of Lords and the US Supreme Court.

The *Legal Diary* (1854–) published daily during Court term lists all cases coming before the Superior Courts and Dublin Circuit Court together with advance warning notices of pending cases, certain court notices and practice directions.

General series

The principal source of law reporting is the *Irish Reports* (1894–), compiled under the authority of the Incorporated Council of Law Reporting for Ireland, published in six parts per annum and consolidated in three annual volumes. The seven series of the *Irish Reports* covering the years 1838–1894 were reprinted in 270 volumes in 1993. The *Irish Reports* are the principal preferred case reference in the Courts and are regularly cited in subsequent judgments. Each volume includes a subject index, details of Irish or English cases judicially cited and a list of Statutes which have been considered in the cases reported.

The *Irish Law Reports Monthly* (1976–) is usually published in fourteen issues per year with two indexes and is compiled since 1994 into two annual volumes. It includes a subject and citation index. A cumulative index has been published for the years 1976 to 1990 and 1991 to 1995. Each volume also lists cases under appeal at the time of publication.

Both these series enjoy full jurisprudential recognition. Both of these general law reports deal almost exclusively with the decisions of the Superior Courts (The High Court, Supreme Court and the Court of Criminal Appeal).

Specialized series

Judgments of the Courts of Criminal Appeal (1978 and 1984), in two volumes covering the years 1924–1978 and 1979–1983, collates the judgments of the Court of Criminal Appeal including previously unreported cases with headnotes of cases already reported. This work is continued as *Judgments of the Court of Criminal Appeal* (1991), for the period 1984–1989. It should be noted that the Court and Court Officers Act 1995 provides for the transfer of the functions of the Court of Criminal Appeal to the Supreme Court.

The *Employment Law Reports* (1991–) is published in four issues per year with an index and is also available in yearly volumes from 1991. It lists major decisions of the Employment Appeals Tribunal together with appeals and other significant cases relating to labour law and industrial relations in the High Court and Supreme Court. Generally, where not otherwise reported, copies of decisions of the Labour Court, Employment Appeals Tribunal and Labour Relations Commission may be obtained on a discretionary basis direct from the relevant body. The *Labour Court Annual Report* (1948–) lists recommendations, decisions and orders made under the provisions of industrial relations legislation.

Daly, B. (1995) has consolidated significant cases, including a number of previously unreported cases, on all areas of company law into one volume. *Irish Tax Reports 1922–1993* in five volumes, with a planned annual volume thereafter, collects together all major tax cases including a number of ones previously unreported.

Older reports

Breem, W. (1987: 177–178) contains a helpful overview of the history of Irish law reporting.

The *New Irish Jurist Reports* (1901–1905), the *Irish Jurist Reports* (1935–1965) and the *Irish Law Times Reports* (1867–1980), while no longer published, are of considerable assistance in providing reports of cases which are not contained in the *Irish Reports* series.

Unreported cases

A considerable body of Irish case law remains unreported. Since 1976 the Superior Courts have distributed copies of written judgments delivered by the High Court, the Court of Criminal Appeal and the Supreme Court to various bodies including the Law Society of Ireland and the Law Library. Since that date a subject index to these written judgments has also been published. This *Index to the Supreme and High Court Written Judgments* (1976–) (commonly called the 'Pink Pages') is issued on average three times a year with the third issue being a consolidation of Parts 1 and 2 together with some additional material. The index provides subject access only although recent copies have included a confirmatory alphabetical list of all cases included in the index.

Aston, J. *et al.* (1990) (ed.) *Index to Unreported Judgments of the Irish Superior Courts 1966–1975* provides a subject and case name index to written judgments issued prior to the introduction of the Pink Pages. It does not have keyword summaries but does include a citation index. Aston and Doyle (1984) (ed.) *Index to Irish Superior Court Written Judgments 1976–1982* and Aston, J. (1991) (ed.) *Index to Irish Superior Court Written Judgments 1983–1989* consolidate in two volumes, cases listed in the Pink Pages. Each of the two volumes contains an index by name of case together with a subject index and keyword summary of each case listed in the subject index.

Digests

O'Malley (1993) provides a list of the main digests of Irish law published since 1766. Since 1867 the Incorporated Council of Law Reporting in Ireland has published the *Irish Digest 1894–1993* (1995), which contains digests and indexes of those reports appearing in the *Irish Reports*, *The Irish Law Reports Monthly* (from 1976), the *Irish Law Times Reports* (1894–1980), the *New Irish Jurist Reports* (1901 to 1905) and since 1925 the *Northern Ireland Law Reports* (1925–). The volumes provide access to the various reports by names of parties, by subject matter or by citator (which lists case law and the legislation followed, overruled or considered by the reports digested). Of particular note are the summaries of cases contained in the Digest, which, in the absence of the law reports themselves provide basic research data.

Computer-based systems

There is no comprehensive computer-based system of access to legislation. The Finance Bill 1995 and the Finance Bill 1996 were both issued in disk format.

Itelis Limited compile a selection of reported cases most notably the *Irish Reports* (from 1950) and the *Irish Law Reports Monthly* (from 1980) together with selected unreported cases from 1985 which are available on the LEXIS-NEXIS system.

Online access is available to a small number of government agencies including the Companies Registration Office and the Land Registry. Internet access is available to a number of government departments and agencies.

Other important government documents

Parliamentary publications

Parliamentary papers including *Bills, Acts, Dáil and Seanad Debates, Orders of the Day* and Reports of Special Committees are published by the Stationery Office and may be purchased as separate items or by subscription.

Law Reform Commission

The Law Reform Commission publishes Reports and recommendations for statutory reform. The recommendations regularly provide the basis for new legislation and the Reports provide analytical and detailed reviews of particular aspects of Irish law. The *Law Reform Commission of Ireland Reports* (1994) collate the various reports of the Commission from 1977 to 1991 in ten volumes. O'Malley (1993) lists all of the published Law Reform Commission Papers as at 1993. Individual Reports are available from the Law Reform Commission.

Government departments

Many government departments issue reports of committees and working parties, as well as White Papers on proposed reforms, from time to time. The quarterly and cumulative *Annual Catalogue* (1922–) of the Stationery Office, Dublin, provides the best source of information as it contains a comprehensive list of annual reports, statistical analyses, tribunal findings and advisory papers published by various government departments and state agencies.

The Revenue Commissioners publish a wide range of detailed guidance notes on the tax code in the form of technical Statements of Practice, information brochures, memoranda and the *Tax Briefing* (1990–) which is published usually as four issues per year on a subscription basis.

A large number of other documents and briefing notes of legal interest are published by various departments and agencies on an occasional basis.

Encyclopedias, large collections and services

There is no true encyclopedia of Irish law. Ussher and O'Connor (1992) is a detailed exposition of Irish law, arranged under subject headings, and updated on a regular basis. Although styling itself as a dictionary, Murdoch (1993) provides concise information on most areas of Irish law including statutory and case law references and a guide to further reading.

The *Garda Síochána Guide* (1991), which is used extensively by the police force and practitioners in the District Court, contains references to, and extracts of, relevant case law and statute law in respect of various offences arranged in alphabetical order and is a practical source of general reference to the criminal law.

Directories

An indispensable reference book is the *Administration Yearbook and Diary* (1967–), published annually, and containing detailed lists of contact names and addresses as well as brief overviews of functions for all Government Departments, State Agencies, major corporations, trade associations, representative associations and groups, trade unions and the communications sector. It also includes statistical abstracts, lists of publications, journals, etc. and an overview of the Irish tax code.

Facts about Ireland (1995) is an official general overview of political, economic, social and cultural life. It includes historical and economic details as well as an outline of governmental structures. The annual *State Directory* (1966–) contains full details of all central government departments and agencies, with lists of key personnel in each individual unit.

The *Law Directory* (1886–) published annually, lists the names and business addresses of all solicitors and of barristers who subscribe to the Law Library together with details of judges and officers of all courts, dates and venues of court sittings, details of notaries, commissioners, summons servers, law searchers and expert witnesses. The *Directory* also contains a number of points of information in tabular form.

Bibliographies

Although there is no definitive or consolidated bibliography of Irish law, it is possible to trace publications from the 16th century to the present day using a number of different sources.

The most significant bibliography of early Irish law books and publications up to 1956 is Volume 4 of Sweet and Maxwell Ltd (1957), which is arranged by a combination of subject and author in the one index making it slightly unstructured in use. Another work regularly referred to is Twining and Uglow (1981) which attempted to extend the bibliography contained in Sweet and Maxwell from 1956 to 1980. The best and most comprehensive bibliography, covering the period from 1950 to 1993, is found in O'Malley (1993). Irish published law books are included in the annual *Irish Publishing Record* which was last published for the year 1993.

For journals and periodicals, the most comprehensive list is in O'Higgins (1966) with two supplements covering the period to 1983. It includes material from Irish and non-Irish journal sources with a subject and author index. There are no other comprehensive bibliographies of Irish journals, although *Irish Current Law Monthly Digest* lists articles from Irish journals and includes references to articles on Irish law contained in UK and other English language journals.

Indexing and abstracting services

Over twenty Irish journals are indexed and abstracted in the *Legal Journals Index* (1986–) and the *European Legal Journals Index* (1993–). This information is also used to compile the monthly subject digest in *Irish Current Law Monthly Digest*, which also summarizes all cases from the Superior Courts, legislation passed or in progress and recently published law books.

The *Irish Law Log Weekly* (1995–) seeks to provide focused coverage on a weekly basis of Circuit Court decisions and personal injury awards.

Dictionaries

Murdoch (1993) is an excellent source of defined terms and references to further research material, although it is not a dictionary in the true sense. It also contains a comprehensive list of abbreviations for Irish and other pertinent law reports.

Although Irish is the first official language, it is rare that any statutory materials, law reports or legal texts are published solely in that language. Usually such texts are published in English or in bilingual format. Where a translation is required from the Irish language the preferred dictionary is Ó Dónaill (1977).

Von Prondzynski and Richard (1994) provides explanations of specialist terms and legal terminology used in relation to Irish labour law.

Other reference works

The substantive guide to practice in the High Court and Supreme Court is contained in the *Rules of the Superior Courts* (1986), published initially as a one-volume Statutory Instrument, with subsequent amendments also published from time to time as individual Statutory Instruments. The Rules set out the requirements for practice in all areas of the High Court and Supreme Court and include copies of forms commonly used. Rules of practice for the lower Courts are contained in the series of *District Court Rules* (1997) and *Circuit Court Rules* (1950) which are similarly published as Statutory Instruments. O'Floinn (1996) provides comprehensive commentary on practice and procedure in the Superior Courts. Woods (1994) is the most recent in a well-used series of guides by the same author to practice in the District Court. Deale (1994) fulfils a similar role in respect of practice in the Circuit Court.

The *Guide to Professional Conduct of Solicitors in Ireland* (1988) sets out a code of conduct and practice for solicitors while the *Handbook of the Incorporated Law Society* (1976) includes the Charter, Statutes, Orders, Regulations and By-laws of the Law Society of Ireland together with opinions of its council. The various Committees of the Law Society publish regular practice notes for the solicitors profession in the monthly issues of the *Gazette of the Law Society of Ireland* (1907–).

The Irish Stock Exchange which is the competent authority and statutory regulator for listing of public companies publishes *Notes on the Listing Rules* (1995–) as a supplement to the Listing Rules of the London Stock Exchange. The Exchange has adopted the Listing Rules and the Notes set out the distinctions in their application to companies listed on the Irish Stock Exchange.

The *Annual Review of Irish Law* (1987–) traces statutory and judicial developments in annual volumes published for each year from 1987. The scale of the work is such that the 1993 volume was published as late as 1996. It includes a full review of legal developments for the given year under subject headings and includes analysis of important Superior Court and some Circuit Court decisions including unreported cases. It also includes an outline of each Statute and a listing of Statutory Instruments published in a given year. The volumes provide a comprehensive overview of Irish legal developments and are helpful both as annual digests and as continuing reference works.

Current information sources

Journals and research reports

The two leading legal journals are the *Irish Law Times and Solicitors Journal* (1983–), which contains detailed articles together with digests of case law and new legislation, and the *Gazette of the Law Society of Ireland*, which combines articles on legal topics with news of interest to the legal profession, including Practice Notes issued by the Law Society.

The *Dublin University Law Journal* (1976–), published annually, contains lengthy articles on legal matters, extended commentaries on selected cases and book reviews.

The *Irish Jurist* (5th Series) (1966–) comprises scholarly and academic writing on aspects of Irish jurisprudence.

Recently, a number of more specialized journals have begun publication, including the *Commercial Law Practitioner* (1994–), *Irish Planning and Environmental Law* (1994–) and the *Irish Journal of European Law* (1991–). Other journals of specialist interest include the *Irish Criminal Law Journal* (1991–) and the *Journal of the Irish Society of Labour Law* (1982–).

The Irish Centre for European Law regularly hosts seminars on issues in European Law and their implications for Ireland. Most papers are subsequently published in book format. The Irish Centre for Commercial Law Studies publishes its seminar papers dealing with a wide range of commercial law matters.

News information

Iris Oifigiúil [Official Gazette] is published on Tuesday and Friday of each week and is available, on subscription, from the Stationery Office. It lists Acts promulgated and Statutory Instruments published as well as other Stationery Office publications. It also contains legal notices, orders and other official and governmental information.

Reasonable coverage is afforded to legal developments in each of the two national broadsheet daily newspapers, although the *Irish Times* (1859–) provides the most extensive coverage of parliamentary affairs, court cases and business. It also publishes, each Monday, the Irish Times Law Report which summarizes recent cases in the Supreme Court, High Court or Circuit Court. The *Sunday Business Post* (1989–) provides extensive coverage of the week's financial, business and legal developments.

Most government departments have a press office and although some coordination is afforded through the Government Information Service, there is no mechanism to provide information on a systematic basis. The press officers will usually be able to source and provide copies of press releases and briefings on current legal developments. A list of departmental press officers is contained in the annual *Administration Yearbook and Diary*.

Business and financial information

The Central Bank of Ireland is the regulatory authority for banks, building societies, credit institutions and other designated financial service providers. Its *Quarterly Bulletin* (1943–) is a convenient source of detail on economic indicators and also lists all banks, credit institutions, etc., currently licensed by the Central Bank.

Business and Finance (1964–) magazine, published weekly, is a good source of contemporary information on all aspects of Irish business. The magazine also publishes an annual list of the top 500 Irish companies and has developed a database of corporate summaries, together with details of press coverage of Irish companies through its FACTFINDER CD-ROM and online service.

Other official sources of business information are Bord Tráchtála [Irish Trade Board] and the Department of Tourism and Trade. The Irish Business and Employers Confederation (IBEC) provides a comprehensive business information service to its members including a monthly business newsletter and the services of the Irish Business Bureau which monitors developments of relevance to Irish business at European level. The business reference section of the Dublin Central

Library operates a substantial reference service including access to newspaper files, trade directories, journals and business databases.

Statistics

The Central Statistics Office is a statutory body which compiles official statistical detail in respect of aspects of economic and social life. The Office produces an ongoing range of statistical information including data on crime, the court system and the prison service which are compiled into the annual *Statistical Abstract* (1931–). Useful summaries of economic indicators, labour force information, trade statistics and international comparative tables are included in the *Administration Yearbook and Diary*.

Useful addresses

Associations of lawyers

Law Society of Ireland, Blackhall Place, Dublin 7. Tel: +353 1 671 0711. Fax: +353 1 671 0704. Internet: http://www.iol.ie/resource/lawsociety

The Bar Council, P.O. Box 4460, 158–159 Church Street, Dublin 7. Tel: +353 1 804 5000. Fax: +353 1 804 5150. Internet: http://www./lawlibrary.ie/barcouncil

Government departments

An Bord Trachtála [Irish Trade Board] Merrion Hall, Strand Road, Sandymount, Dublin 4. Tel: +353 1 206 6000. Fax: +353 1 269 5820. Internet: http://www.irish-trade.ie

Central Bank of Ireland, PO Box 559, Dame Street, Dublin 2. Tel: +353 1 671 6666. Fax: +353 1 671 6561

Central Statistics Office, Skehard Road, Cork. Tel: +353 21 359000. Fax: +353 21 359090. Internet: http://www.hea.ie/cso

Department of Enterprise and Employment, Kildare Street, Dublin 2. Tel: +353 1 661 4444. Fax: +353 1 676 2654. Internet: http://www.irlgov.ie

Department of Equality and Law Reform, Dun Aimhirgin, 43–49 Mespil Road, Dublin 4. Tel: +353 1 667 0344. Fax: +353 1 667 0366

Department of Foreign Affairs (Information Section and Legal Division), 72–76 St Stephens Green, Dublin 2. Tel: +353 1 478 0822. Fax: +353 1 668 6518. Internet: http://www.irlgov.ie

Department of Justice, 72–76 St Stephens Green, Dublin 2. Tel: +353 1 678 9711. Fax: +353 1 661 5461

Department of Tourism and Trade, Kildare Street, Dublin 2. Tel: +353 1 662 1444. Fax: +353 1 676 6154. Internet: http://www.irlgov.ie

Government Information Services, Upper Merrion Street, Dublin 2. Tel: +353 1 662 4422. Fax: +353 1 676 3419. Internet: http://www.irlgov.ie

Houses of the Oireachtas (Dáil and Seanad), Leinster House, Kildare Street, Dublin 2. Tel: +353 1 678 9911. Fax: +353 1 678 5945

IDA Ireland (Industrial Development Agency) Wilton Park House, Wilton Place, Dublin 2. Tel: +353 1 603 4000. Fax: +353 1 603 4040. Internet: http://www.ida.ie

Irish Stock Exchange, 28 Anglesea Street, Dublin 2. Tel: 353 1 677 8808. Fax: +353 1 677 6045

Revenue Commissioners, Dublin Castle, Dublin 1. Tel: +353 1 679 2777. Fax: +353 1 671 1826. Internet: http://www.revenue.ie

Law reform bodies

Law Reform Commission, Ardilaun Centre, 111 St Stephens Green, Dublin 2. Tel: +353 1 671 5699. Fax: +353 1 671 5316

Courts

Employment Appeals Tribunal, 65a Adelaide Road, Dublin 2. Tel: +353 1 676 5861. Fax: +353 1 676 9047

Labour Court, Tom Johnson House, Haddington Road, Dublin 4. Tel: +353 1 660 8444. Fax: +353 1 660 8437

Labour Relations Commission, Tom Johnson House, Haddington Road, Dublin 4. Tel: +353 1 660 9662. Fax: +353 1 668 5069

Supreme Court and High Court, Four Courts, Dublin 7. Tel: +353 1 872 5555. Fax: +353 1 872 1620

Education and training

Faculty of Law, University College Cork. Tel: +353 21 276 871. Fax: +353 21 271 568. Internet: http://www.ucc.ie

Faculty of Law, University College Dublin, Belfield, Dublin 4. Tel: +353 1 706 7777. Fax: +353 1 269 4409. Internet: http://www.ucd.ie

Faculty of Law, University College Galway. Tel: +353 91 524 411. Fax: +353 91 525 700. Internet: http://www.ucg.ie

Faculty of Law, University of Dublin, Trinity College, Dublin 2. Tel: +353 1 677 2941. Fax: +353 1 677 2694. Internet: http://www.tcd.ie

Law School, Law Society of Ireland, Blackhall Place, Dublin 7. Tel: +353 1 671 0200. Fax: +353 1 671 0064

The Honorable Society of Kings Inns, Henrietta Street, Dublin 1. Tel: +353 1 874 4840. Fax: +353 1 872 6048

Research institutions

Institute of Public Administration, Landsdowne Road, Dublin 4. Tel: +353 1 668 6233. Fax: +353 1 668 9135

Irish Centre for Commercial Law Studies, University Industry Centre, University College Dublin, Belfield, Dublin 4. Tel: +353 1 706 8770. Fax: +353 1 269 3463

Irish Centre for European Law, Trinity College, Dublin 2. Tel: +353 1 702 1081. Fax: +353 1 679 4080

Libraries

Business Reference Section, Dublin Central Library, ILAC Centre, Henry Street, Dublin 1. Tel: +353 1 873 3996. Fax: +353 1 872 1451

Kings Inn Library, Henrietta Street, Dublin 1. Tel: +353 1 874 7134. Fax: +353 1 872 6048

The Law Society of Ireland, Blackhall Place, Dublin 7. Tel: +353 1 671 0711. Fax: +353 1 671 0704

The Law Library, P.O. Box 2424, Dublin 7. Tel: +353 1 872 0622. Fax: +353 1 872 0455

Publishers and booksellers

Business and Finance Business Information, 6 Merrion Row, Dublin 2. Tel: +353 1 661 8625. Fax: +353 1 676 2343. Internet: http://www.factfinder.ie

Butterworth Ireland Limited, 26 Upper Ormond Quay, Dublin 7. Tel: +353 1 873 1555. Fax: 353 1 873 1876

Fred Hanna Limited, Booksellers, 29 Nassau Street, Dublin 2. Tel: +353 1 677 1255. Fax: +353 1 671 4330

Gill & Macmillan, Goldenbridge Industrial Estate, Dublin 8. Tel: +353 1 453 1005. Fax: 353 1 454 1688

Government Publications Sales Office, Sun Alliance House, Molesworth Street, Dublin 2. Tel: +353 1 671 0309. No Fax

Itelis Limited, Legal Database, 9 D'Olier Street, Dublin 2. Tel: +353 1 671 7035. Fax: +353 1 671 7023

Round Hall Sweet & Maxwell, Brehon House, 4 Upper Ormond Quay, Dublin 7. Tel: +353 1 873 0101. Fax: +353 1 872 0078

Stationery Office, Government Supplies Agency, 4–5 Harcourt Road, Dublin 2. Tel: +353 1 661 3111. Fax: +353 1 478 0645. Internet: http://www.hea.ie/govpub

Other organizations

Irish Business and Employers Confederation (IBEC), Confederation House, 84/86 Lower Baggot Street, Dublin 2. Tel: +353 1 660 1011. Fax: +353 1 660 1717. Internet: http://ireland.iol.ie/ibec

List of works cited

Acts of the Oireachtas (1922–) annual volumes. Dublin: Stationery Office.

Administration yearbook and diary (1967–) annual. Dublin: Institute of Public Administration.

Annual catalogue (1922–). Dublin: Stationery Office.

Annual review of Irish Law (1987–). Dublin: Round Hall Sweet & Maxwell.

Aston, J. (1991) (ed.) *Index to Irish Superior Court Written Judgments 1983–1989*. Dublin: General Council of the Bar of Ireland.

Aston, J. *et al.* (1990) (ed.) *Index to Unreported Judgments of the Irish Superior Courts 1966–1975*. Dublin: Irish Association of Law Teachers.

Aston, J. and Doyle, M. (1984) (ed.) *Index to Irish Superior Court Written Judgments 1976–1982*. Dublin: Irish Association of Law Teachers.

Bills of the Oireachtas (1922–). Dublin: Stationery Office.

Boyle, C.K. and Greer, D.S. (1983) *The Legal Systems North and South*: A Study prepared for the New Ireland Forum. Dublin: Stationery Office.

Breem, W. (1987). *The Manual of Law Librarianship* 2nd edn. London: Gower.

Bunreacht na hÉireann [Constitution of Ireland] (1995 reprint). Dublin: Stationery Office.

Business and Finance (1964–) weekly. Dublin: Belenos Publications.

Butterworths Capital Tax Acts (1993–). Dublin: Butterworth Ireland.

Butterworth Ireland Companies Acts 1963–1990 (1993). Dublin: Butterworth Ireland.

Butterworths Taxes Acts (1991–). Dublin: Butterworth Ireland.

Butterworths VAT Acts (1992–). Dublin: Butterworth Ireland.

Byrne, R. and McCutcheon, P. (1996) *The Irish Legal System* 3rd edn. Dublin: Butterworth Ireland.

Central Bank of Ireland. *Quarterly Bulletin* (1943–). Dublin: Central Bank of Ireland.

Central Statistics Office. *Statistical Abstract* (1931–) annual. Dublin: Stationery Office.

Chronological Table of the Statutes 1922–1995 (1996). Dublin: Stationery Office.

Chronological Table and Index of the Statutes in Force (covering the period from 1235) (1921) 37th edn. London: HMSO.
Circuit Court Rules 1950 (SI 179/50) further revisions published as Statutory Instruments. Dublin: Stationery Office.
Clark, R. (1995) *Annotated Guide to Social Welfare Law*. Dublin: Round Hall Sweet & Maxwell.
Combined Companies Acts (looseleaf). Dublin: Gill & Macmillan.
Commercial Law Practitioner (1994–). Dublin: Round Hall Sweet & Maxwell.
Dail Debates (1922–). Dublin: Stationery Office.
Daly, B. (1995) (ed.) *Irish Company Law Reports 1963–1993*. Dublin: Round Hall Sweet & Maxwell.
Deale, J. (1994) *Circuit Court Practice and Procedure* 2nd edn. Dublin: Fitzbaggot Publications.
Delany, H. (1993) *The Courts Acts 1924–1991*. Dublin: Round Hall Sweet & Maxwell.
Delany, V.T.H. (1975) *Administration of Justice in Ireland* 4th edn. Dublin: Institute of Public Administration.
District Court Rules (1997) (SI 93/97) further revisions published as Statutory Instruments. Dublin: Stationery Office.
Doolan, B. (1991) *Principles of Irish Law* 3rd edn. Dublin: Gill & Macmillan.
Dooney, S. and O'Toole, J. (1992) *Irish Government Today*. Dublin: Gill & Macmillan.
Dublin University Law Journal (1976–). Dublin: Round Hall Sweet & Maxwell.
Employment Law Reports (1991–). Dublin: Round Hall Sweet & Maxwell.
European Legal Journals Index (1993–). Hebden Bridge: Legal Information Resources; Sweet & Maxwell.
FACTFINDER (available from Business and Finance Business Information).
Facts about Ireland (1995). Dublin: Stationery Office.
Faulkner, M. Kelly, G. and Turley, P. (1991) *Your Guide to Irish Law*. Dublin: Gill & Macmillan.
Foley, J.A. and Lalor, S.L. (1995) *Annotated Constitution of Ireland*. Dublin: Gill & Macmillan.
Garda Siochána Guide (1991) 6th edn. Dublin: Law Society of Ireland.
Gazette of the Law Society of Ireland (1907–). Dublin: Law Society of Ireland.
General Index to the Treaty Series 1977–1994 (1994). Dublin: Stationery Office.
Grimes, R.H. and Horgan, P.T. (1981) *Introduction to Law in the Republic of Ireland* with supplement (1988). Dublin: Wolfhound Press.
Guide to the Professional Conduct of Solicitors (1988). Dublin: Incorporated Law Society of Ireland.
Handbook of the Incorporated Law Society of Ireland (1976). Dublin: Incorporated Law Society of Ireland.
Humphreys, R. (1988) *Index to the Statutory Instruments*, 3 vols. Dublin: Butterworth Ireland.
Index to the Statutes 1922–1982 (1986) with Supplement to 1986. Dublin: Stationery Office.
Index to the Statutory Instruments (1944–). Dublin: Stationery Office.
Index to the Supreme Court and High Court Written Judgments (1976–). Dublin: Bar Council and Law Society of Ireland..
Iris Oifigiúil [Official Gazette] (1922–) published Tuesday and Friday of each week with occasional supplements. Dublin: Stationery Office.
Irish Criminal Law Journal (1991–). Dublin: Round Hall Sweet & Maxwell.
Irish Current Law Monthly Digest (1995–). Dublin: Round Hall Sweet & Maxwell.
Irish Current Law Statutes Annotated (1984–) Looseleaf to 1996 in 7 volumes with index volume. Dublin: Sweet & Maxwell.
Irish Digest 1894–1993. Reprint in 9 volumes (1995). Dublin: Butterworth Ireland.
Irish Journal of European Law (1991). Dublin: Round Hall Sweet & Maxwell.
Irish Jurist (5th Series) (1966–) published as 1 or 2 volumes annually. Dublin: Round

Hall Sweet & Maxwell in association with University College Dublin.

Irish Jurist Reports (1935–1965) Vols 1 to 31. Dublin: Jurist Publishing Co. Ltd.

Irish Law Log Weekly (1995–) published as 37 issues per year. Dublin: Round Hall Sweet & Maxwell.

Irish Law Reports Monthly (1976–). Dublin: Round Hall Sweet & Maxwell.

Irish Law Times Reports (1867–1980). Dublin: Iona Print.

Irish Law Times and Solicitors Journal (1983–). Dublin: Round Hall Sweet & Maxwell.

Irish Planning and Environmental Law Journal (1994–). Dublin: Round Hall Sweet & Maxwell.

Irish Publishing Record (1993). Dublin: National Library of Ireland (published up to 1989 by University College Dublin).

Irish Reports (1838–1894) Reprinted 1993 in 270 volumes. Dublin: Butterworth Ireland.

Irish Reports (1894–). Dublin: Incorporated Council of Law Reporting in Ireland.

Irish Statutes Revised 1310–1800 (1885). Reprinted 1995. Dublin: Round Hall Sweet & Maxwell.

Irish Tax Reports 1922–1993. 5 vols. Dublin: Butterworth Ireland.

The Irish Times (1859–) published Monday–Saturday with Business Supplement each Friday. (Internet ://www.irish-times.ie). Dublin: Irish Times Newspapers.

Journal of The Irish Society for Labour Law (1982–). Dublin: Round Hall Sweet & Maxwell.

Judgments of the Court of Criminal Appeal 1984–1989 (1991). Dublin: Round Hall Sweet & Maxwell.

Judgments of the Court of Criminal Appeal. 2 volumes: Vol.1 (1978); Vol.2 (1984). Dublin: Incorporated Council of Law Reporting for Ireland.

Kelly, F.K. (1988) *Guide to Early Irish Law*. Dublin: Dublin Institute of Advanced Studies.

Kelly, J. (1994) *The Irish Constitution* 3rd edn. Dublin: Butterworth Ireland.

Kerr, A. (1995) *Termination of Employment Statutes*. London: Sweet & Maxwell.

Labour Court Annual Report (1948–). Dublin: Stationery Office.

Law Directory (1886–). Dublin: Law Society of Ireland.

Law Reform Commission of Ireland Reports (1994 reprint in 10 volumes). Dublin: Butterworth Ireland.

Legal Diary (1854–) published daily during court term. Dublin: Mount Salus Press.

Legal Journals Index (1986–). Hebden Bridge: Legal Information Resources: Sweet & Maxwell.

LEXIS-NEXIS (available from Itelis).

McEldowney, J. and O'Higgins, P. (1990) (eds) *The Common Law Tradition*. Dublin: Irish Academic Press.

McGowan Smyth, J. (1979) *The Houses of the Oireachtas* 4th edn. Dublin: Institute of Public Administration.

Murdoch, H. (1993) *Dictionary of Irish Law* 2nd edn. Dublin: Topaz Publications.

New Irish Jurist Reports (1901–1905). Dublin: Dollard Printing House.

Northern Ireland Law Reports (1925–). Belfast: Incorporated Council of Law Reporting for Northern Ireland.

Notes on the Listing Rules (1995–) (Supplement to the Listing Particulars of the London Stock Exchange). Dublin: Irish Stock Exchange.

Ó Dónaill, N. (1977) *Foclóir Gaeilge Béarla*. Dublin: Stationery Office.

O'Donnell, J. (1992) *How Ireland is Governed* 6th edn. Dublin: Institute of Public Administration.

O'Floinn, B. (1996) *Practice and procedure in the Superior Courts*. Dublin: Butterworth Ireland.

O'Higgins, P. (1966) *Bibliography of Periodical Literature relating to Irish Law* (with 2 supplements to 1983). Belfast: NILQ and SLS.

O'Malley, T. (1993) *The Round Hall Guide to the Sources of Law*. Dublin: The Round Hall Press.

Orders of the Day and Question Papers (1922–). Dublin: Stationery Office.

O'Reilly, J. and Redmond, M. (1980) *Cases and Materials on the Irish Constitution.* Dublin: Incorporated Law Society of Ireland.

Oulton, A.N. (1839) *Index to the Statutes at Present in Force* 2nd edn. Dublin: Hodges and Smith.

Pensions Act and Regulations (1922–) (looseleaf). Dublin: An Bord Pinsean (The Pensions Board).

Quinn, S. (1992) *Statutes Revised on Commercial Law.* Bray: Irish Law Publishing.

Rules of the Superior Court 1986 (SI 15/86) with further revisions published as Statutory Instruments. Dublin: Stationery Office.

Seanad Debates (1922–). Dublin: Stationery Office.

Smith, G. (1996) Republic of Ireland law. In J. Dane and P.A. Thomas, *How to Use a Law Library* 3rd edn. London: Sweet & Maxwell.

State Directory (1966–). Dublin: Stationery Office.

The Statutes at Large Passed in the Parliaments held in Ireland from 1310–1786 edited by Grierson. (Continued to 1800 in 20 volumes). Dublin: Grierson.

Statutory Instruments (1947–). Dublin: Stationery Office.

Statutory Rules and Orders (1922–1947) 39 vols. Dublin: Stationery Office.

The Sunday Business Post (1989–). Dublin: Post Publications Limited.

Sweet & Maxwell Ltd (1957) *A Legal Bibliography of the British Commonwealth of Nations* 2nd edn. London: Sweet & Maxwell.

Tax Briefing (1990–). Dublin: Revenue Commissioners.

Treaty Series (1930–). Dublin: Stationery Office.

Twining, W. and Uglow, J. (1981) *Legal Publishing and Legal Information: Small Jurisdictions of the British Isles.* Commonwealth Legal Education Association. New York: Glanville Publishers.

Ussher, P. and O'Connor, B.J. (1992) (eds) *Doing Business in Ireland* (looseleaf). New York: Matthew Bender.

Vance, A (1862) *Green Book of Irish Statutes*. Dublin: White.

Von Prondzynski, F. and Richard. W. (1994) *European Employment and Industrial Relations Glossary: Ireland.* London: Sweet & Maxwell.

Woods, J.V. (1994) *District Court Practice and Procedure in Criminal Cases.* Limerick: published by the author.

Acknowledgements

Thanks are due to Jennefer Aston, Law Library, Dublin; Margaret Byrne, Librarian, Law Society of Ireland; and Jane Cantwell, William Fry, Solicitors, Dublin.

CHAPTER SIXTEEN

Italy

ETTORE SALVATORE D'ELIA AND MARIO RAGONA

Introduction to the legal system

Legal systems on the European Continent can be said to have had various origins but, in particular, to have descended from classical Roman law, which became with time *jus civile* and can be distinguished in many aspects from the common law.

The Italian legal order has two fundamental origins, *jus privatorum* and *jus publicum*; this traditional division of law, it is well known, does not exist in common law countries with an English tradition.

The former, concerning private law, draws its sources from ancient Roman law (the *Institutiones, Digesta, Codex* and *Novellae*) and substantially still mirrors those ancient principles today albeit filtered through the experience of the Medieval and Renaissance jurists (the glossators and commentators) and later summarized in the French Napoleonic codification of 1805, which in Italy was partially affected by the influx of German Pandectist doctrine.

The latter, concerning public law, finds its most direct and modern inspiration in the Declaration of the Rights of Man and of the Citizen of 1789 following the French Revolution. It was strongly influenced by the political experience of the Italian Risorgimento, partially incorporated in the Constitution of the State of Piedmont promulgated on 4 March 1848 by Carlo Alberto of Savoy (the so-called Statuto Albertino) and finally was fully expressed in the Republican Constitution in force today.

The description above provides a general outline of the system up to the promulgation of the new Constitution in 1947 which imposed a different and updated approach and interpretation of the old rule, influencing in a decisive manner the order of the powers of the individual and of the state and above all the relationship between the citizen and the state. Furthermore it also forced the latter to intervene strongly in the economic field.

It is usually said that the Italian Constitution is a compromise between the thrust for the simplified popular idea of justice deriving from 19th century socialist ideas and the innate natural law aspiration of religious Catholic origin. The Italian Constitution which came into force on 1 January 1948 clearly states that the rights of individuals exist and are protected but directs their exercise towards the benefit of the entire collectivity according to the principle, also dear to the early French constitution-makers, that the individual is everything in society but is nothing without it. It is the whole constitutional framework that, for the purpose of fully implementing the project for a new society, takes the doctrine formulated by Montesquieu as its own and clearly separates legislative, executive and judicial powers, giving each its own precise rules and autonomy.

The Constitution was published in a special issue of the *Gazzetta Ufficiale* [Official Gazette] on 27 December 1947. The text can almost always be found together with publications of the Codes. English translations of it can be found in the following works: *The Constitution of the Italian Republic. Rules of the Chamber of Deputies,* edited by the Camera dei Deputati (1990); *The Italian legal system: an introduction* (Cappelletti, Merryman and Perillo, 1967); *Constitutions of countries of the world* (Flanz, 1987 supplemented 1994); on the Internet site http://www.uni-wuerzburg.de/law/index.html; and on the site http://www.mi.cnr.it/WOI/deagosti/constitu/welcome.html, there is, in English, an illustration of the Constitution and the general principles of the legal order within an historical and political framework. The *Commentario della Costituzione,* edited by Branca and Pizzorusso (1975–96) in 30 volumes, can be considered the most important treatise on constitutional law.

Legislative power is exercised by the *Parlamento* [Parliament]: that is the *Camera dei Deputati* [Chamber of Deputies] and the *Senato della Repubblica* [Senate of the Republic]. Legislative initiative belongs also to the Consiglio Nazionale dell'Economia e del Lavoro (CNEL) [National Council of Economy and Labour] and the People. The *Corte Costituzionale* [Constitutional Court] exercises control over the constitutional legitimacy of laws. Executive power is attributed to the *Governo* [Government], while the *Consiglio di Stato* [Council of State] and the *Corte dei Conti* [State Audit Court] have a measure of control and advisory role over the executive. Judicial power is exercised by magistrates distinguished in functions and competencies as shown in Figure 1.

Figure 1. Italian jurisdiction

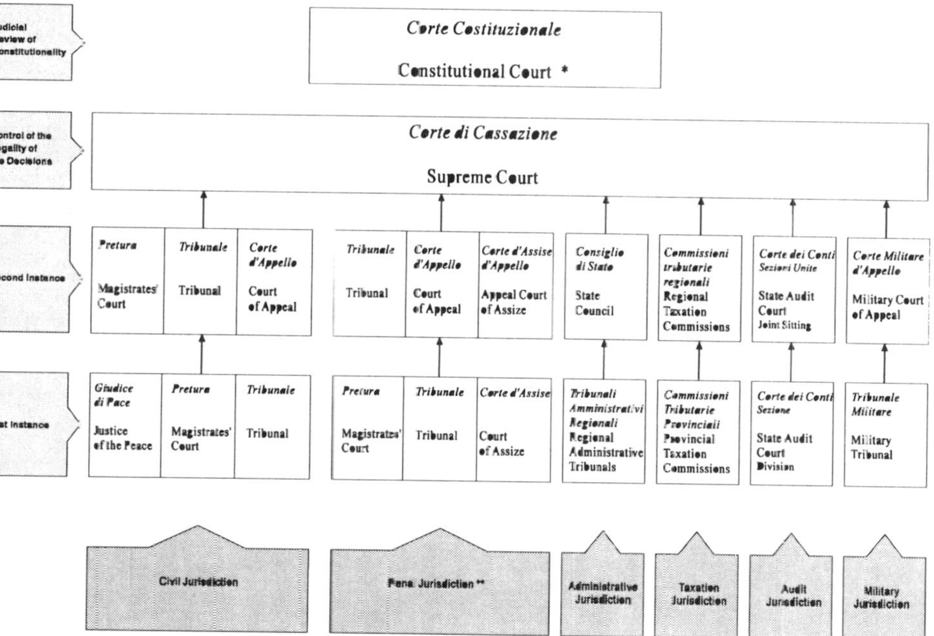

* Any judge can refer a case to the Constitutional Court

** Here is considered only the adjudicating judges

Introductory works on the legal system and legal research

An excellent historical introduction to the birth and development of Italian law can be found in the entry 'Diritto italiano, storia' [Italian Law, History] by Crifò (1972) in the *Enciclopedia Feltrinelli-Fischer.* An introduction of a general philosophical nature can be found in entry 'Diritto' [Law] by Cordero (1978) in *Enciclopedia* and also in the entry 'Ordinamento giuridico' [Legal Order] by Frosini (1980) in the *Enciclopedia del diritto.*

In English, reference should be made to the works by Cappelletti, Merryman and Perillo (1967) *The Italian legal system: an introduction,* and by Certoma (1985) *The Italian legal system.* The former shows signs of the time in which it was written, the latter more recent work ends with a detailed bibliography. For a historical framework of Italian law up until the end of World War II reference should be made to *1859–1945. A history of Italian law* (Calisse, 1969).

The reader can find excellent aids to methods of legal research in Meloncelli (1990), *Come si cerca il diritto* and in Sciullo (1989) *Introduzione alla ricerca dei dati giuridici.*

Research on the speculative or academic aspects of Italian law should be assisted by the bibliographical tools referred to below. The reader may find a bibliography in English in Certoma's book cited above and in the article by Lamaro (1994). Finally, mention should be made of Grisoli (1965) *Guide to foreign legal materials: Italian,* and the series by the Associazione Italiana di Diritto Comparato [Italian Association of Comparative Law] published by Giuffrè in which, periodically, national reports on various aspects of Italian law presented at international conferences on comparative law are published in English and French.

Legislation

Official publications

The *Gazzetta Ufficiale* [Official Gazette] (1860–) comes out every day with the exception of holidays and is edited by the Ufficio pubblicazione delle leggi e dei decreti [Office for the Publication of Laws and Decrees] at the Ministry of Justice, printed at the Istituto Poligrafico e Zecca dello Stato which also distributes it throughout the country at the Librerie dello Stato [state bookshops] and related foreign bookshops. It is available online on the GURITEL system (see below).

The Gazette is made up of a general series and four special series (entitled Corte Costituzionale [Constitutional Court], Comunità Europee [European Communities], Regioni [regions], Concorsi pubblici ed esami

[Public competitive tests and exams]), where the following kinds of legislative acts are published: 1. legislative measures enacted by the central organs of the state; 2. regulations by the regions and autonomous provinces; 3. legislative acts by the European Communities; 4. decisions and ordinances of the Corte Costituzionale, as well as referrals to the Court by the other courts; 5. government and ministerial circulars and regulations. Together with the legislative text, a series of coordinating notes to facilitate understanding of the legislation is published and often the full text of the legislation in force is printed when a legislative text has been frequently amended. The Constitution lays down that a law comes into force on the fifteenth day after its publication in the *Gazzetta Ufficiale*, unless it does not specifically make other provisions.

There are other legislative instruments ènacted by the government and by ministers. It is quite often useful in legal practice to know about the executive acts of government adopted on the basis of state and regional laws. These documents which are on each occasion defined as either *decreti* [decrees] or *ordinanze* [ordinances] or *regolamenti* [regulations], in the most important cases or whenever they are of significance outside the administration, are published in the *Gazzetta Ufficiale*.

The Gazette has monthly indices and an annual index: the monthly indices are by subject and number, while the annual index is only numeric.

The *Raccolta ufficiale degli atti normativi della Repubblica Italiana* (1987–) is an official collection of laws which is also important and considerably more convenient to use than the Gazette. It contains the texts of legislative instruments in the numerical order in which they appear and it has two annual indexes: an alphabetical analytical index by subject and a chronological index.

Finally, there are offices of the Senate of the Republic and the Chamber of Deputies that, on a daily basis, publish shorthand summaries or brief extracts of the work done in parliament while sitting or in the parliamentary commissions as well as draft bills; see the addresses of their information services below. This material is also available through the information retrieval systems of the two houses of parliament, see below.

Commercial publications

Beside the official collections, specialized publications on the law are available on the market which only contain legislative texts in a convenient format, such as *Lex* (1861–), *Legislazione italiana* (1943–), *Leggi d'Italia nel testo vigente* (1963–) a looseleaf compilation of the laws in force, *Le Leggi* (1951–) and others, or those which contain an commentary written by the most eminent Italian jurists such as *Le nuove leggi civili commentate* (1978–) or those which contain references to the publication of legislative texts coordinated with the texts previously dealing with the same matter such as *La legislazione vigente* (1951–).

Codes and commentaries

The Italian system of civil rights is based on the *Codice civile* [Civil Code] and on the laws of updating and integration issued by ordinary legislation. Also in the area of penal law reference is made to the *Codice penale* [Penal Code] and other laws. Judicial procedures are guided by the *codici di procedura civile e di procedura penale* [codes of civil procedure and criminal procedure]. Procedures for administrative and taxation judgments are ruled by laws specifically issued.

The Civil Code which is now in force was promulgated in 1942 and has never been comprehensively amended except in 1975 for the part concerning family law. Apart from family law, the most important amendments have occurred following action by the Corte Costituzionale and, in company law, as a consequence of the implementation of European Union directives. Otherwise it can be said that the general framework of the Civil Code has remained the same as that of 1942. The Code of Civil Procedure was promulgated in 1940; it was amended in 1950 and then with the most recent reform in 1990. There have also been many partial amendments brought about by the action of the Corte Costituzionale.

The Penal Code was enacted in 1930 and has been amended at different times solely in the part concerning the way individual crimes are treated. It is worthwhile mentioning, for example, the innovations introduced on several occasions between 1975 and 1987 to combat terrorism and subversive activities and amendments to fight the Mafia. Specific and individual modifications were introduced by the Corte Costituzionale. The Code of Criminal Procedure was completely redrafted and promulgated in 1988.

The law on bankruptcy was enacted together with the Civil Code in 1942 and the special laws on credit instruments (cheques and promissory notes) were passed in 1933. Until 1942 the legal order specifically regulated commercial activities in the *Codice di commercio* [Commercial Code]. As a result of wide debate that involved Italian jurists for over twenty years, the 1942 reform unified civil and commercial law, arguing that the law did not have to distinguish between the rights and duties of the citizen and the entrepreneur.

Apart from the official collections of legislation and those sold commercially which are described above, the codes, with or without annotations, are available in printed form for everyday use and extensively in electronic form both commercially and on the Internet (see **Computer-based systems** below). Among these the following types of edition can be mentioned: codes annotated with references of a numerical type to the various provisions of the same code or of another code; codes that have the case law that is applicable to the various provisions in note form; and, finally, those codes that provide annotations on both legal literature and case law.

Among the most famous of the first kind are *I quattro codici,* edited by Franchi, Feroci and Ferrari (1994) and *I codici per l'udienza,* edited by Carnelutti, Bigiavi and Crespi (1953). An English translation of the Civil Code can be found in Beltramo (1991) *The Italian Civil Code*, and the Penal Code is found in Wise (1978) *The Italian Penal Code*. Some parts of the Civil Code have been translated into English: Book V on Labour in *The Italian Civil Code. Labour articles 2060–2642* (1993) and the articles that deal with business corporations but not partnerships in Frignani and Elia (1992) *Italian company law*. Furthermore, the Code of Navigation has an English edition, somewhat out of date: *The Italian Code of Navigation* (Manca, 1958).

Among the numerous codes of the second kind, provided with case law, there are *Codice civile annotato con giurisprudenza* (Cendon, 1995) annotated with case law updated to 1995, and *Codice penale annotato con la giurisprudenza e le norme complementari* by Lattanzi (1995).

As to individual codes annotated with legal authority and case law, the most important annotation of the Civil Code is the one edited first by Scialoja and Branca (1946–) entitled *Commentario del codice civile* which is currently made up of 79 volumes. The most recent section, edited by Galgano, is the *Commentario alla legge fallimentare* composed so far of 13 volumes. The six volumes of the *Codice civile annotato con la dottrina e la giurisprudenza* (Perlingieri, 1991), in which the state of the debate in legal authority and the most important decisions on the matter are given for every provision, should also be mentioned.

More recent works include the *Commentario al Codice civile* (Cendon, 1994–95) which is supplied with a basic bibliography and a succinct statement of the legal authority and case law on every single article. Among the works more penetrating and significant for their content about both legal authority and case law, the reader's attention should be referred to Satta (1966–71) *Commentario al Codice di procedura civile*. Another useful commentary in monographic form is the *Commentario breve al Codice di procedura civile* (Carpi, Colesanti and Taruffo, 1984).

With regard to commentaries on the Penal Code, the *Commentario breve al Codice Penale,* edited by Crespi, Stella and Zuccalà (1992), together with a volume of *Complemento giurisprudenziale* which is regularly updated and well organized, and *Codice penale commentato* (Dall'Ora, 1982) are worth attention. The former is only annotated on the basis of case law, the latter contains many references to theories and the evolution of legal authority.

Among the works relating to the new Code of Criminal Procedure, the following is recommended: *Commentario del nuovo codice di procedura penale* (Amodio and Dominioni, 1989–90) in 4 volumes.

Treaties

The State body with competence to sign international treaties is the Government of the Republic and, in accordance with Art.80 of the Constitution, Parliament ratifies them. Treaties are published together with the law ratifying them in the *Gazzetta Ufficiale* and come into force in accordance with the provisions of the law that ratifies them.

Law reports, judgments

Officially published reports

Even though in the Italian legal order cases do not take on the same binding force as in the common law, they are not without great importance in the study and interpretation of legal rules. For this reason the higher courts and some of the lower courts (Corte Costituzionale, Corte di Cassazione, Consiglio di Stato, Corte dei Conti, Commissioni Tributarie) must by law publish a summary or extract (so called massima [maxim]) of the legal principle upheld in the decision that has been made. For this purpose at these courts there is an Ufficio del Massimario [Maxim Office] which periodically publishes a journal entitled *Rivista ufficiale del Massimario*, circulated almost exclusively to judicial offices and not generally available for sale. Furthermore, the Corte Costituzionale publishes the *Raccolta ufficiale delle sentenze e ordinanze della Corte Costituzionale* [Official Collection of the Case Law of the Constitutional Court] (1956–) as well as individual decisions in the *Gazzetta Ufficiale*.

The ITALGIURE is a very extensive online system which contains court decisions (see below).

Commercially published reports

Apart from these official publications, private publishing companies produce dozens of reports both of a general nature and of a specialized nature in relation to the case law of a specific court or a particular legal discipline.

The main series are: *Repertorio del Foro Italiano* (1947–), *Repertorio della Giurisprudenza Italiana* (1848–) and *Repertorio generale annuale di legislazione, bibliografia, giurisprudenza* (1955–). The most important specialized series are: *Cassazione Penale* (1961–), *Consiglio di Stato* (1950–), *Il Foro Italiano* (1876–), *Giurisprudenza costituzionale* (1956–) which also contains significant comments on legal authority, *Giurisprudenza di merito* (1969–), *Giurisprudenza Italiana* (1849–), *Giustizia civile* (1951–), *Settimana giuridica* (1960–) and *Tribunali Amministrativi Regionali* (1975–).

The works that systematically collect case law in digested and annotated form in one or more volumes and usually examine the evolution of case law from the origin of the rule to its most recent applications are extremely important and worth noting. The most important works in this area are the 46 volumes of *Giurisprudenza sistematica di diritto civile e commerciale* (1977–93) with full citations of the legal authority in the field, *Raccolta sistematica di giurisprudenza commentata* (1987–) which is a series of volumes by subject containing the most relevant decisions printed in full and, finally, *Nuova rassegna di giurisprudenza sul codice civile* (Ruperto and Sgroi, 1994–95).

Computer-based systems

There are two major online information systems: the ITALGIURE system of the Centro Elettronico di Documentazione [Centre of Electronic Documentation] of the Corte di Cassazione [Supreme Court] and the GURITEL system of the Istituto Poligrafico e Zecca dello Stato that places the *Gazzetta Ufficiale della Repubblica Italiana* online. Both systems can be accessed after a subscription contract has been made according to differentiated fees without however offering any guarantees about the officiality of the data stored therein.

The ITALGIURE system is the most important online information retrieval system in Italy. It is very extensive, well established and sophisticated. With its 50 databases, it provides the user with a service that globally covers Italian legal information, including legislation, case law including all the maxims of the decisions handed down by the Supreme Courts. A detailed description of the ITALGIURE system is available in English with useful hints for training in researching data; it can be found in Giannantonio (1984), *Italian legal information retrieval*.

The Constitution and the four Codes (the Civil Code and the Code of Civil Procedure, the Penal Code and the Code of Criminal Procedure) can be searched on the Internet site: http://infosistemi.com/jura/codici/index.htm in Italian.

With regard to CD-ROM, the most important products for legislation are CODICI E LEGGI D'ITALIA published by De Agostini and JURIS DATA LEGISLAZIONE published by Giuffrè; the former provides the text of the legislative measures in force (accompanied by the case law) and stores not only the Civil Code, the Penal Code, the Code of Civil Procedure and the Code of Criminal Procedure but also the Code of Navigation, the Military Penal Code in Peacetime and the Military Penal Code in Wartime, annotated with the last ten years of case law of the Corte di Cassazione.

Among the CD-ROM on general case law, reference should be made to: REPERTORIO DELLA GIURISPRUDENZA ITALIANA published by Utet, REPERTORIO

DEL FORO ITALIANO published by Zanichelli, JURIS DATA GIURISPRUDENZA and JURIS DATA – LE SENTENZE DELLA CASSAZIONE CIVILE – TESTO INTEGRALE published by Giuffrè.

Other electronic materials are mentioned below, particularly in relation to bibliographies.

Encyclopedias

Among Italian legal encyclopedias the following are considered as the most significant.

The *Novissimo Digesto Italiano*, published between 1957 and 1975 in twenty volumes (between 1980 and 1987 seven volumes of updating appeared), is addressed to practitioners of law in such a way that it represents, within a sufficient but limited number of pages, not only a general overview of the theory of the subject, but also the examination and solution of the various specific and practical aspects.

The *Enciclopedia del diritto*, published between 1958 and 1993, with an overall total of 46 volumes, plus a subject index and an index of legal sources from Roman sources to those of the present day, represents the greatest effort on the part of jurists to condense the century-long elaboration of Italian legal thought into a single work.

The *Enciclopedia giuridica* started in 1988 and, still in progress, issued volume 32 in 1994. It is currently the most up-to-date encyclopedia and is widely appreciated for its capacity to provide, in a limited space, accurate references to the materials covered.

Published since 1987, the *Digesto – Quarta Edizione* is planned in 60 volumes and divided into four parts: 'Private Law Disciplines: Civil Section'; 'Private Law Disciplines: Commercial Section'; 'Public Law Disciplines'; and 'Penal Law Disciplines'. Treatment of the subject matter is generally detailed, without being dull, and case law and bibliographical references are sufficient for facing the examination of a problem with confidence.

Treatises, studies

The most highly regarded work in the field of public law is the *Trattato di diritto amministrativo* (Santaniello, 1988–); 24 volumes of this work have been published so far.

In the field of civil law works of great importance because many of them have become university textbooks over time are: *Trattato di diritto civile e commerciale* (Cicu and Messineo, 1957–95), *Trattato di diritto civile italiano* (Vassalli, 1961–94), *Trattato di diritto commerciale e di diritto pubblico dell'economia* (Galgano, 1977–95), which is outstanding for the actuality and breadth with which it deals with the chosen topics so that it constitutes a series of up-to-date monographs, *Trattato di diritto privato* edited by Rescigno (1989–95) in 22 volumes, *Diritto civile e commerciale* (Galgano, 1990) in 7 volumes and, finally, the now classic and basic work by Messineo (1952–72) *Manuale di diritto civile e commerciale* in 7 volumes.

In English, limited to specific branches of civil law, it is possible to refer to the following works: *Italian law of contract* (Criscuoli, 1991); *The Italian law of agency and distributorship agreements* (La Villa, 1977); *Italy: practical commercial law* (Barbalich, 1991); *Italian patent law* (Jacobacci, 1985) and, finally, *Italian company law* (Verrucoli, 1985). *The Italian Unified Banking and Credit Act* offers an English translation of that 1993 Act together with selected implementing regulations (Bernascone and Donald, 1994).

In the branch of civil procedure, the most important works are *Trattato di diritto processuale civile* (Rocco, 1957–64) in eight volumes, *Diritto processuale civile* (Andrioli, 1979) in two volumes, *Diritto processuale civile* (Redenti, 1949–51) in three volumes with a new edition in progress (1995–) and, finally, the *Commentario al Codice di procedura civile* by Satta (1966–71). The work of Cappelletti and Perillo (1965) *Civil procedure in Italy*, and also the two volumes of the *Italian Yearbook of Civil Procedure* edited by Fazzalari (1991–93) can be consulted in English.

In the domain of criminal law and procedure, the *Trattato di diritto penale italiano* by Manzini (1985–87) in eleven volumes and the *Manuale di diritto penale* by Antolisei (1994–95) in five volumes, as well as the *Commentario al Codice di procedura penale* by Chiavario (1995) in ten volumes, should be considered.

Bibliographies and indexing services

The most important bibliographical collection in Italy is *Dizionario bibliografico delle riviste giuridiche italiane*. Edited by Napoletano since 1958, it annually publishes the bibliographical data referring to both articles and other legal works published in Italy. Another bibliography of a general nature is *Diritto* edited by Armani (1989), in the series *Strumenti di studio. Guide bibliografiche*. Sources of Italian legal bibliography in English have already been mentioned above. As we have noted for legislation and case law, the ITALGIURE system of the Corte di Cassazione also offers various bibliographical databases online. The databases include BNI (*Bibliografia nazionale italiana* [Italian national bibliography]); BIGIUR (*Biblioteca del Ministero di Grazia e Giustizia* [Library of the Ministry of Justice]); DOTTR (abstracts of articles published in Italian law journals and in Italian daily newspapers); RIV (references to the publication of notes commenting on jurisdictional provisions published in law journals); BID (*Bibliografia internazionale di informatica e diritto* [International bibliography on computers and law]); FIURIS (sources of Roman law).

Internet users can consult the DOGI database of the Istituto per la Documentazione Giuridica at http://www.idg.fi.cnr.it/eng/information/information.htm which contains abstracts in Italian of articles published in Italian legal journals since 1970.

Many libraries and, above all, university libraries provide users with their electronic catalogues. A list of Italian libraries of legal interest with online information and catalogues can be found at http://www.idg.fi.cnr.it/ita/informazione/biblioteche/bibliote.htm through the Internet. Almost all these catalogues offer a search interface in English.

With regard to CD-ROMS, we refer our readers to what has been said about case law products in the section on **Computer-based systems** above. In fact, these products reproduce the bibliographical references to relevant works of legal authority together with the court decisions. A CD-ROM of the catalogues of the works of the most important Italian legal publisher, the Giuffrè publishing house of Milan, is also available. The CD-ROM, in Italian, may be requested directly from the publisher.

The Zanichelli publishing house, which produces a large number of books of legal interest, has put its catalogue at the following site: http://www.doit.it/Zanichelli/ on the Internet.

Dictionaries

No dictionary of Italian legal language exists. Some dictionaries within the ambit of special legal domains were published between 1910 and 1950 but they have proved not only to be impossible to find and out of date but very insignificant from both the linguistic and legal points of view. Instead, in the wide field of Italian language dictionaries, recommended works are: *Grande lessico italiano* and *Grande dizionario enciclopedico* (1991). Within the sphere of typically legal terms they give exhaustive and scientifically accurate explanations and examples.

With regard to non-specialized bilingual dictionaries, limited only to English, the reader should consult *Dizionario inglese–italiano italiano–inglese* by Ragazzini (1995). Among bilingual legal dictionaries, the following exist: Mastellone (1980) *Legal and commercial dictionary* (only English–Italian), and one that is a little older, Parisi (1950–55) *Dizionario giuridico italiano–inglese inglese–italiano*.

The reader should also be aware of the two-volume work by de Franchis, *Dizionario giuridico/Law dictionary*, which specializes in the field of comparative law between English and American law and Italian law. More than this, it is a legal vocabulary. The work is really directed towards illustrating both the English and American legal orders to the

Italian reader through a brief but comprehensive representation of the conceptual content underlying the listed terms. A translation of this work in English would be desirable as it is certainly a cornerstone of modern comparative law literature.

Finally, a relevant multilingual law dictionary is *West's law & commercial dictionary* (1988), where the translation of terms from English can be found in German, Spanish, French and Italian. The work is also published by Zanichelli which enriches the American edition with a part of the dictionary completely dedicated to the translation of terms from Italian into English.

Legal profession

Law schools and institutes for legal research

In Italy there are 35 law faculties with about 300 000 students in the 1994–1995 academic year. Such a large number of students results from the fact that, in the majority of faculties in Italian universities, no preselection requirements exist for entry except that students have obtained their high school diploma. The law degree course usually lasts four years but a large percentage of students exceed this period and continue their studies *fuori corso* [outside the established length of their course]. So in 1994–1995 one-third of the students were *fuori corso* and only a little more than 16 000 took their degree. The most famous law faculties are those of the universities of Rome, Milan, Bologna, Naples, Bari and Florence. There are approximately one hundred courses for research doctorates at these faculties which range from historical–theoretical materials to positive law, including legal informatics.

Research institutes are generally within the faculties and have their own *scuole di specializzazione* [schools for specialization], for example, the Advanced School in Civil Law at the University of Camerino, the Advanced School in Labour Law at the University of Bari and the post-graduate course for corporate lawyers at the University of Bologna. Apart from the university, the state has instituted a second public research network which is most significantly represented by the Consiglio Nazionale delle Ricerche [National Research Council], which has six research institutes in various legal domains.

Branches of the legal professions

The intellectual professions in which the law operates in Italy are essentially divided into the judiciary, the bar, the notary public profession and teaching and research in the legal field.

Once students have obtained a degree in law, they can join the judiciary after having passed a single national competitive examination (open only to a fixed number of students) which includes three written tests and one test in ten or so subjects. The highest level of the judiciary is constituted by the Chief Justice of the Italian Supreme Court.

A law graduate becomes a member of the Bar once he has passed a professional qualification examination made up of two written tests and one oral test in ten or so subjects. Once he has passed the exam he is called a procuratore legale and after 6 years he becomes an avvocato. Notaries public have the nature and character of public officials and their declarations and certifications have full validity. They are selected through a single national competitive examination consisting of three written tests and an oral one. Apart from state laws, the last two types of professionals are also regulated by rules of professional conduct, passed, within the sphere of their autonomy, by their respective professional associations: the Consiglio Nazionale Forense [National Bar Council] and the Consiglio Nazionale del Notariato [National Council of Notaries Public].

In order to become a law professor or researcher, it is generally necessary to carry out a long period of post-graduate qualification either at university (also abroad or at research institutions). The Ministero dell'Università e della Ricerca Scientifica e Tecnologica [Ministry for Universities and Scientific and Technological Research], independently or together with public research bodies, manages the competitive examinations that give access to these professions.

Current information sources

Journals

Today Italian legal periodicals include about 300 national journals and there is no single journal which covers all the disciplines of law. Clearly, one can only cite here the most important journals within the main disciplinary fields out of this excessive number.

For constitutional law, public law in general and administrative law, the reader will find the most important contributions in the following journals: *Giurisprudenza costituzionale* (1956–), *Rivista trimestrale di diritto pubblico* (1951–), *Il foro amministrativo* (1925–), *Diritto processuale amministrativo* (1983–) and *Rivista giuridica dell'edilizia* (1958–), as well as *Le Regioni* (1973–).

In the civil law sector, we find the following journals: *Rivista di diritto civile* (1955–), *Rivista trimestrale di diritto e procedura civile* (1947–), *Rivista di diritto processuale* (1946–), *Rivista del notariato* (1947–), *Il diritto della famiglia e delle persone* (1972–), *Diritto e giurisprudenza* (1886–), and *Le nuove leggi civili commentate* (1978–), which is recommended to the reader for the rapidity with which legal authority relating to legislative changes is updated.

The following journals are important in the area of commercial law: *Bancaria* (1945–), *Banca borsa e titoli di credito* (1934–), *Rivista di diritto commerciale e del diritto generale delle obbligazioni* (1903–), *Rivista delle società* (1956–), *Giurisprudenza commerciale – Società e fallimento* (1974–), *Il diritto fallimentare e delle società commerciali* (1924–) and *Rivista di diritto industriale* (1952–).

In the field of criminal law, there are: *Rivista italiana di diritto e procedura penale* (1958–), *La legislazione penale* (1956–), *Archivio penale* (1949–), *L'indice penale* (1967–), *Rivista trimestrale di diritto penale dell'economia* (1988–).

Among international and community law journals, the following should be considered: *Rivista di diritto internazionale* (1918–), *Rivista di diritto internazionale privato e processuale* (1965–), *Rivista di diritto europeo* (1961–), *Il diritto marittimo* (1899–), *Rivista italiana di diritto pubblico comunitario* (1991–) and *Il diritto comunitario e degli scambi internazionali* (1962–).

The following law journals are mentioned because of their international interest: *Iura – Rivista internazionale di diritto romano e antico* (1950–), *Labeo – Rassegna di diritto romano* (1955–) and *Studia et Documenta Historiae et Iuris* (1935–) which publish contributions in various languages.

The following law journals are mainly directed towards practising lawyers: *Il Foro Italiano* (1876–), *Giurisprudenza Italiana* (1849–), *Giustizia civile* (1951–), *Rivista penale* (1875–), *Diritto e pratica tributaria* (1930–).

News information

Apart from the Official Gazette and Official Bulletins, no other publication for updating news of legal interest which has an official legal character exists in Italy. Nevertheless, there are several authoritative daily newspapers which, on a daily basis, publish news regarding laws, politico-legislative initiatives in course, bills that have passed one of the houses of parliament or, finally, current and emergency ministerial decrees within the sphere of economic and legal activities (for example, duties and taxes, amendments to administrative or fiscal regulations, information regarding the courts and procedures to be followed before those courts, etc.). The most important amongst these are *Il Sole 24 Ore* (1865–) and *Italia Oggi* (1986–): the former also has a site http://www. sole24ore.iol.it on the Internet.

The Giuffrè publishing house in collaboration with the daily newspaper *Italia Oggi* publishes the *Gazzetta giuridica* [Legal Gazette] (1993–) once a week. It contains news about parliamentary activities, information and abstracts about domestic and community legislative measures, as well as references to the most interesting cases; whenever one of these documents is considered to be of particular importance, it is published in full.

Business, financial and statistical information

For readers working in the business world, it may be useful to consult the publications of ISTAT (Istituto nazionale di statistica) [National Institute of Statistics]. This Institute publishes every year the *Annuario statistico italiano* in which macroeconomic information and data of a political and social nature are presented, in both analytical and synthetic form through graphs and tables. There is also an abridged edition of the *Annuario* in English available on the market, entitled *Italian Statistical Abstract*, and the same data can be retrieved in English at the site http://www.istat.it/Inglese.html via the Internet.

For financial and monetary information the reader may find it useful to consult the annual report to shareholders of the Governor of the Banca d'Italia [Bank of Italy], of which there is also an English edition entitled *Ordinary general meeting of the shareholders*. Furthermore, the Banca d'Italia always publishes an economic bulletin in English once every six months.

Additional and more specific information or statistics of an economic kind or of interest to the businessman can be found in the periodical publications of Consob (Commissione nazionale per le società e la borsa) [National Commission for Companies and the Stock Exchange], of the Ufficio Italiano dei Cambi [Italian Exchange Office], of the Istituto Nazionale per il Commercio Estero [National Institute for Foreign Trade], of Cerved, the operational arm of the Unione italiana delle Camere di Commercio Industria Artigianato Agricoltura (Unioncamere) [Italian Union of Chambers of Commerce, Industry, Artisanship and Agriculture]), addresses for which are below.

Useful addresses

Associations of lawyers and other professional bodies

ABI (Associazione Bancaria Italiana) [Association of Italian Bankers], piazza del Gesù 49, 00186 Rome, Italy. Tel: +39 6 67671. Fax: +39 6 6767457

Consiglio Nazionale del Notariato [National Council of Notaries Public], via Flaminia 160, 00196 Rome, Italy. Tel: +39 6 3215866. Fax: +39 6 3221594. Internet: http://www.notariato.it

Consiglio Nazionale Forense [National Bar Council], via Arenula 71, 00186 Rome, Italy. Tel: +39 6 68802689. Fax: +39 6 6876871

Government organizations

Banca d'Italia – Divisione Biblioteca e pubblicazioni [Bank of Italy, Library and Publications Division], via Nazionale 91, 00184 Rome, Italy. Tel: +39 6 47922333. Fax: +39 6 47922059

Camera dei Deputati [Chamber of Deputies], piazza di Montecitorio, 00186 Rome, Italy. Tel: +39 6 67601. (Servizio Informatica Tel: +39 6 67609395/6)

Consiglio di Stato [Council of State], piazza Capo di Ferro 13, 00186 Rome, Italy. Tel: +39 6 68271

Consiglio Nazionale dell'Economia e del Lavoro (CNEL) [National Council of Economy and Labour], viale David Lubin 2, 00196 Rome, Italy. Tel: +39 6 36921. Fax: +39 6 3202867

Consiglio Superiore della Magistratura [Superior Council of Judges], piazza Indipendenza 6, 00185 Rome, Italy. Tel: +39 6 44491. Fax: +39 6 4457175

Consob (Commissione nazionale per le società e la borsa) [National Commission of Companies and the Stock Exchange], via Isonzo 19/d/e, 00198 Rome, Italy. Tel: +39 6 84771. Fax: +39 6 8417707

Istat (Istituto nazionale di statistica) [National Statistical Institute], via Cesare Balbo 16, 00184 Rome, Italy. Tel: +39 6 46735115–6. Fax: +39 6 46735198. Internet: http://www.istat.it/Inglese.html

Ministero degli Affari Esteri [Ministry of Foreign Affairs], piazzale della Farnesina 1, 00194 Rome, Italy. Tel: +39 6 36911

Ministero del Commercio con l'Estero [Ministry of Foreign Trade], viale America 341, 00144 Rome, Italy. Tel: +39 6 59931

Ministero delle Finanze [Ministry of Finance], viale Europa, 00144 Rome, Italy. Tel: +39 6 59971. Internet: http://www.finanze.interbusiness.it

Ministero dell'Industria, del Commercio e dell'Artigianato [Ministry of Industry, Commerce and Artisanship], via Molise 2, 00187 Rome, Italy. Tel: +39 6 47051

Ministero dell'Università e della Ricerca Scientifica e Tecnologica [Ministry of Universities and Scientific and Technological Research], piazzale J.F. Kennedy 20, 00144 Rome, Italy. Tel: +39 6 5991. Internet: http://www.murst.it

Ministero di Grazia e Giustizia [Ministry of Justice], via Arenula 70, 00186 Rome, Italy. Tel: +39 6 65101

Presidenza del Consiglio dei Ministri [Office of the President of the Council of Ministers], piazza Colonna 370 Palazzo Chigi, 00187 Rome, Italy. Tel: +39 6 67791

Senato della Repubblica [Senate of the Republic], piazza Madama, 00186 Rome, Italy. Tel: +39 6 67061 (Servizio Informatica Tel: +39 6 67062051)

Ufficio Italiano dei Cambi [Italian Exchange Office], via Quattro Fontane 123, 00184 Rome, Italy. Tel: +39 6 46631. Fax: +39 6 4825591

Courts

Corte Costituzionale [Constitutional Court], piazza del Quirinale 41, 00187 Rome, Italy. Tel: +39 6 46981. Fax: +39 6 4825706

Corte dei Conti [Audit Court], via Baiamonti 25, 00195 Rome, Italy. Tel: +39 6 38761

Corte di Cassazione [Supreme Court], piazza Cavour, 00193 Rome, Italy. Tel: +39 6 686001

Education, training and research

The law faculties of universities cannot all be listed and the reader is referred to *Guide to legal studies in Europe* (1996) or *World of learning* (1947–).

Consiglio Nazionale delle Ricerche (CNR) [National Council for Research], piazzale A. Moro 7, 00185 Rome, Italy. Tel: +39 6 49931. Fax: +39 6 4461954. Internet: http://www.cnr.it

Istituto per la Documentazione Giuridica del Consiglio Nazionale delle Ricerche [Institute for Legal Documentation of the Italian National Research Council], via Panciatichi 56/16, 50127 Florence, Italy. Tel: +39 55 43995. Fax: +39 55 4221637. E-mail: idg@idg.fi.cnr.it Internet: http://www.idg.fi.cnr.it

Email of authors of this chapter: delia@idg.fi.cnr.it and ragona@idg.fi.cnr.it

Libraries

Biblioteca Nazionale Centrale, piazza Cavalleggeri 4, 50122 Florence, Italy. Tel: +39 55 244441. Fax: +39 55 2342482

Biblioteca Nazionale Centrale 'Vittorio Emanuele II', viale Castro Pretorio 105, 00185 Rome, Italy. Tel: +39 6 4989. Fax: +39 6 4959292

Other

Cerved s.p.a. (operational arm of the Unione italiana delle Camere di Commercio Industria Artigianato Agricoltura), via Staderini 93, 00155 Rome, Italy. Tel: +39 6 2280708. Fax: +39 6 2280928. Internet: http://cerved.pitagora.it/internet/cervmenu.htm

Istituto Nazionale per il Commercio Estero [National Institute for Foreign Trade], via Liszt 21, 00144 Rome, Italy. Tel: +39 6 59921. Fax: +39 6 59926900

Unione italiana delle Camere di Commercio Industria Artigianato e Agricoltura – Unioncamere [Italian Union of Chambers of Commerce, Industry, Artisanship and Agriculture], piazza Sallustio 21, 00187 Rome, Italy. Tel: +39 6 47041. Fax: +39 6 4744741

Publishers and booksellers

Cedam, via Jappelli 5/6, 35121 Padua, Italy. Tel: +39 49 656677. Fax: +39 49 8752900

Corte di Cassazione – Centro Elettronico di Documentazione (sistema ITALGIURE), via Damiano Chiesa 24, 00136 Rome, Italy. Tel: +39 6 35081. Fax: +39 6 35057005

De Agostini, via G. da Verrazzano 15, 28100 Novara, Italy. Tel: +39 321 4241. Fax: +39 2 471286. E-mail: info@deagostini.it

Ebsco Italia (subscription agents), corso Brescia 75, 10152 Turin, Italy. Tel: +39 11 2480870. Fax: +39 11 2482916

Edizioni Scientifiche Italiane, via Chiatamone 7, 80121 Naples, Italy. Tel: +39 81 7645443. Fax: +39 81 7646477. E-mail: esi@dial.it Internet: http://www.dial.it/esi

Giuffrè, via Busto Arsizio 40, 20151 Milan, Italy. Tel: +39 2 380891. Fax: +39 2 38009582. Internet: http://www.giuffre.it

Hoepli, via Ulrico Hoepli 5, 20121 Milan, Italy. Tel: +39 2 864871. Fax: +39 2 8052886

Ipsoa, Strada 1 Palazzo F6 Milanofiori, 20090 Assago (Milan), Italy. Tel: +39 2 824761. Fax: +39 2 82476689. Internet: http://www.vol.it/ipsoa

Istituto della Enciclopedia Italiana, piazza della Enciclopedia Italiana, 00186 Rome, Italy. Tel: +39 6 68961. Fax: +39 6 68982175. E-mail: romano.gorga@treccani.inet.it

Istituto Poligrafico e Zecca dello Stato [official publisher], piazza Giuseppe Verdi 10, 00198 Rome, Italy. Tel: +39 6 85081. Fax: +39 6 85082517

Italedi, piazza Cavour 19, 00193 Rome, Italy. Tel/Fax: +39 6 3210803. E-mail: italedi@flashnet.it

Jovene, via Mezzocannone 109, 80134 Naples, Italy. Tel: +39 81 5521019. Fax: +39 81 5520687

Laterza, piazza Umberto I 54, 70121 Bari, Italy. Tel: +39 80 5216713. Fax: +39 80 5243461. E-mail: laterza@iqsnet.it Internet: http://www.iqsnet.it/laterza/html/home.html

La Tribuna, via Don Minzoni 51, 29100 Piacenza, Italy. Tel: +39 523 759015. Fax: +39 523 757219

Piccin Nuova Libraria, via Altinate 107, 35100 Padua, Italy. Tel: +39 49 655566. Fax: +39 49 8750693

Il Sole 24 Ore Pirola, via Parabiago 19, 20151 Milan, Italy. Tel: +39 2 30221. Fax: +39 2 38011205

Utet, corso Raffaello 28, 10125 Turin, Italy. Tel: +39 11 65291. Fax: +39 11 6529240

Zanichelli, via Irnerio 34, 40126 Bologna, Italy. Tel: +39 51 293111. Fax: +39 51 249782. E-mail: zanichelli@zanichelli.it Internet: http://www.doit.it/Zanichelli/

List of works cited

Amodio, E. and Dominioni, O. (1989–90) (eds) *Commentario del nuovo codice di procedura penale*. Milan: Giuffrè. 4 vols.

Andrioli, V. (1979) *Diritto processuale civile*. Naples: Jovene. 2 vols.

Annuario statistico italiano. (1995) Rome: Istat (Istituto nazionale di statistica). Also issued in English as: *Italian Statistical Abstract*.

Antolisei, F. (1994–95) *Manuale di diritto penale*. Milan: Giuffrè. 5 vols.

Archivio penale. (1949–) Naples: Edizioni Scientifiche Italiane.

Armani, G. (1989) (ed.) *Diritto*. Strumenti di studio. Guide bibliografiche. Milan: Garzanti.

Banca borsa e titoli di credito. (1934–) Milan: Giuffrè.

Banca d'Italia (1995) *Ordinary general meeting of the shareholders. Report*. Rome: Banca d'Italia. English edition of the annual report.

Bancaria. (1945–) Rome: ABI.

Barbalich, R. (1991) *Italy: practical commercial law*. London: Longman.

Beltramo, M. (1991) *The Italian Civil Code and complementary legislation*. New revised edn. Dobbs Ferry, NY: Oceana. 2 vols, looseleaf.

Bernascone, G. and Donald, D.C. (1994) *The Italian Unified Banking and Credit Act*. The Hague: Kluwer Law International.

Branca, G. and Pizzorusso, A. (1975–96) (eds) *Commentario della Costituzione*. Bologna: Zanichelli. 30 vols.

Calisse, C. (1969) *1859–1945. A history of Italian law*. South Hackensack, NJ: Rothman.

Camera dei Deputati (1990) *The Constitution of the Italian Republic. Rules of the Chamber of Deputies*. Rome: Camera dei Deputati, Segreteria Generale.

Cappelletti, M., Merryman, J.H. and Perillo, J.M. (1967) *The Italian legal system: an introduction*. Stanford, Cal.: Stanford University Press.

Cappelletti, M. and Perillo, J.M. (1965) *Civil procedure in Italy*. L'Aja.

Carnelutti, F., Bigiavi, W. and Crespi, A. (1953) (eds) *I codici per l'udienza*. Padua: Milani Ed.

Carpi, F., Colesanti, V. and Taruffo, M. (1984) (eds) *Commentario breve al Codice di procedura civile*. Padua: Cedam.

Cassazione Penale. (1961–) Milan: Giuffrè.

Cendon, P. (1994–95) (ed.) *Commentario al Codice civile*. Turin: Utet. 7 vols.

Cendon, P. (1995) (ed.) *Codice civile annotato con la giurisprudenza*. Turin: Utet. 4 vols.

Certoma, G.L. (1985) *The Italian legal system*. London: Butterworths.

Chiavario, M. (1995) *Commentario al Codice di procedura penale*. Turin: Utet. 10 vols.

Cicu, A. and Messineo, F. (1957–95) (eds) *Trattato di diritto civile e commerciale*. Milan: Giuffrè.

CODICI E LEGGI D'ITALIA (available from De Agostini).

Consiglio di Stato. (1950–) Rome: Italedi.

Cordero, F. (1978) Diritto. In *Enciclopedia*, vol.4, pp. 895–1003. Turin: Einaudi.

Crespi, A., Stella, F. and Zuccalà, G. (1992) (eds) *Commentario breve al Codice Penale*. Series Breviaria juris, no.5 Padua: Cedam.

Crespi, A., Stella, F. and Zuccalà, G. (1992–) (eds) *Commentario breve al Codice Penale. Complemento giurisprudenziale*. Series Breviaria juris, no.5 Padua: Cedam.

Critò, G. (1972) Diritto italiano, storia. In *Enciclopedia Feltrinelli-Fischer*, vol.30: Diritto 1, pp. 219–244. Milan: Feltrinelli.

Criscuoli, G. (1991) *Italian law of contract*. Naples: Jovene.

Dall'Ora, A. (1982) *Codice penale commentato*. Turin: Utet. Reprinted 1984. 2 vols.

de Franchis, F., *Dizionario giuridico/Law Dictionary*, vol.I: *Inglese–Italiano/English–Italian*, Milan, Giuffrè, 1984, pp. xi-1545; vol.II: *Italiano–Inglese/Italian–English*, Milan, Giuffrè, 1996, pp. 1467.

Digesto – Quarta Edizione. (1987–) Turin: Utet.
Il diritto comunitario e degli scambi internazionali. (1962–) Naples: Editoriale Scientifica.
Il diritto della famiglia e delle persone. (1972–) Milan: Giuffrè.
Diritto e giurisprudenza. (1886–) Naples: Jovene.
Diritto e pratica tributaria. (1930–) Padua: Cedam.
Il diritto fallimentare e delle società commerciali. (1924–) Padua: Cedam.
Il diritto marittimo. (1899–) Genoa: Dirmar.
Diritto processuale amministrativo. (1983–) Milan: Giuffrè.
Enciclopedia del diritto. (1958–93) Milan: Giuffrè. 46 vols.
Enciclopedia giuridica. (1988–) Rome: Istituto della Enciclopedia Italiana. 32 vols.
Fazzalari, E. (1991–93) (ed.) *Italian yearbook of civil procedure*. Milan: Giuffrè. 2 vols.
Flanz, Gisbert H. (1987) Italy. In *Constitutions of the countries of the world*, eds A.P. Blauistein and G.H. Flanz, vol.IX. Dobbs Ferry, NY: Oceana. Supplement issued November 1994.
Il foro amministrativo. (1925–) Milan: Giuffrè.
Il foro Italiano. (1876–) Bologna: Zanichelli.
Franchi, L., Feroci, V. and Ferrari, S. (1994) (eds) *I quattro codici*. Milan: Hoepli.
Frignani, A. and Elia, G. (1992) *Italian company law: with the Italian text of the Civil Law. Book 5, arts. 2325–2548*. Deventer: Kluwer; Milan: Ipsoa.
Frosini, Vittorio (1980) Ordinamento giuridico. In *Enciclopedia del diritto*, vol.XXX, pp. 639–654.
Galgano, F. (1977–95) (ed.) *Trattato di diritto commerciale e di diritto pubblico dell'economia*. Padua: Cedam. 20 vols.
Galgano, F. (1990) *Diritto civile e commerciale*. Padua: Cedam. 7 vols.
Gazzetta giuridica. (1993–) Milan: Giuffrè.
Gazzetta Ufficiale della Repubblica Italiana. (1860–) Rome: Istituto Poligrafico e Zecca dello Stato.
Giannantonio, E. (1984) *Italian legal information retrieval*. Milan: Giuffrè.
Giurisprudenza commerciale – Società e fallimento. (1974–) Milan: Giuffrè.
Giurisprudenza costituzionale. (1956–) Milan: Giuffrè.
Giurisprudenza di merito. (1969–) Milan: Giuffrè.
Giurisprudenza Italiana. (1849–) Turin: Utet.
Giurisprudenza sistematica di diritto civile e commerciale. (1977–93) Turin: Utet. 46 vols.
Giustizia civile. (1951–) Milan: Giuffrè.
Grande dizionario enciclopedico. (1991) 3rd edn. Turin: Utet. 22 vols.
Grande lessico italiano. Turin: Utet.
Grisoli, A. (1965) *Guide to foreign legal materials: Italian*. Dobbs Ferry, NY: Oceana.
Guide to legal studies in Europe 1996–1997. (1996) Brussels: Law Books in Europe.
GURITEL (available from Istituto Poligrafico e Zecca dello Stato).
L'indice penale. (1967–) Padua: Cedam.
Italia Oggi: quotidiano economico finanziario e politico. (1986–) Milan: Finedit 2000. Daily newspaper.
The Italian Civil Code. Labour articles 2060–2642. (1993) Milan: Giuffrè.
ITALGIURE (available from the Centro Elettronico di Documentazione, Corte di Cassazione).
Iura – Rivista internazionale di diritto romano e antico. (1950–) Naples: Jovene.
Jacobacci, G. (1985) *Italian patent law*. Milan: Giuffrè.
JURIS DATA: LE SENTENZE DELLA CASSAZIONE CIVILE: TESTO INTEGRALE (available from Giuffrè).
JURIS DATA GIURISPRUDENZA (available from Giuffrè).
JURIS DATA LEGISLAZIONE (available from Giuffrè).
La Villa, G. (1977) *The Italian law of agency and distributorship agreements*. London: Oyez.
Labeo – Rassegna di diritto romano. (1955–) Naples: Jovene.

Lamaro, E. (1994) References in the Italian law literature. In *Rapports nationaux italiens au XIV Congrès International de Droit Comparé*, ed. A. Pizzorusso, pp. 521–530. Milan: Giuffrè.

Lattanzi, G. (1995) *Codice penale annotato con la giurisprudenza e le norme complementari*. Milan: Giuffrè.

Le Leggi. (1951–) Bologna: Zanichelli.

Leggi d'Italia nel testo vigente. (1963–) Rome: PEM. Looseleaf.

Legislazione italiana. (1943–) Milan: Giuffrè.

La legislazione penale. (1956–) Turin: Utet.

La legislazione vigente. (1951–) Turin: Utet.

Lex. (1861–) Turin: Utet.

Manca, P. (1958) (ed.) *The Italian Code of Navigation*. Milan: Giuffrè. Reprinted 1969.

Manzini, V. (1985–87) *Trattato di diritto penale italiano*. New edn. by P. Nuvolone and G. Pisapia. Turin: Utet. 11 vols. Original edn. 1933–39 in 11 vols.

Mastellone, L. (1980) *Legal and commercial dictionary. English/Italian*. Sydney: Butterworths.

Meloncelli, A. (1990) *Come si cerca il diritto (La ricerca di leggi, giurisprudenza e letteratura attraverso biblioteche, bibliografie e banche dati. Strumenti e metodi)*. Rimini: Maggioli.

Messineo, F. (1952–72) *Manuale di diritto civile e commerciale*. Milan: Giuffrè. 7 vols.

Napoletano, V. (1958–) *Dizionario bibliografico delle riviste giuridiche italiane*. Milan: Giuffrè.

Novissimo Digesto Italiano. (1957–87) Turin: Utet. 27 vols.

Le nuove leggi civili commentate. (1978–) Padua: Cedam.

Parisi, G.A. (1950–55) *Dizionario giuridico italiano–inglese inglese–italiano*. Milan: Giuffrè. 2 vols.

Perlingieri, P. (1991) (ed.) *Codice civile annotato con la dottrina e la giurisprudenza*. Naples: Edizioni Scientifiche Italiane; Bologna: Zanichelli. 6 vols.

Raccolta sistematica di giurisprudenza commentata. (1987–) New series. Padua: Cedam. 28 vols, in progress.

Raccolta ufficiale degli atti normativi della Repubblica Italiana. (1987–) Rome: Istituto Poligrafico e Zecca dello Stato. Earlier series 1861–1946 and 1947–1986 under slightly variant titles.

Raccolta ufficiale delle sentenze e ordinanze della Corte Costituzionale [Official Collection of the Case Law of the Constitutional Court]. (1956–) Rome: Palazzo della Consulta.

Ragazzini, G. (1995) *Il Ragazzini terza edizione. Dizionario inglese–italiano italiano–inglese* 3rd edn. Bologna: Zanichelli. There is also a CD-ROM version.

Redenti, E. (1949–51) *Diritto processuale civile*. Milan: Giuffrè. 3 vols. 4th edn. by M. Vellani in progress 1995– .

Le Regioni. (1973–) Bologna: Il Mulino.

Repertorio del Foro Italiano. (1947–) Bologna: Zanichelli. Also CD-ROM version available from Zanichelli.

Repertorio della Giurisprudenza Italiana. (1848–) Turin: Utet. Also CD-ROM version available from Utet.

Repertorio generale annuale di legislazione, bibliografia, giurisprudenza. (1955–) Milan: Giuffrè.

Rescigno, P. (1989–95) (ed.) *Trattato di diritto privato*. Turin: Utet. 22 vols.

Rivista del notariato. (1947–) Milan: Giuffrè.

Rivista delle società. (1956–) Milan: Giuffrè.

Rivista di diritto civile. (1955–) Padua: Cedam.

Rivista di diritto commerciale e del diritto generale delle obbligazioni. (1903–) Padua: Piccin Nuova Libraria-Vallardi.

Rivista di diritto europeo. (1961–) Roma: Istituto Poligrafico e Zecca dello Stato.

Rivista di diritto industriale. (1952–) Milan: Giuffrè.

Rivista di diritto internazionale. (1918–) Milan: Giuffrè.
Rivista di diritto internazionale privato e processuale. (1965–) Padua: Cedam.
Rivista di diritto processuale. (1946–) Padua: Cedam.
Rivista giuridica dell'edilizia. (1958–) Milan: Giuffrè.
Rivista italiana di diritto e procedura penale. (1958–) Milan: Giuffrè.
Rivista italiana di diritto pubblico comunitario. (1991–) Milan: Giuffrè.
Rivista penale. (1875–) Piacenza: La Tribuna.
Rivista trimestrale di diritto e procedura civile. (1947–) Milan: Giuffrè.
Rivista trimestrale di diritto penale dell'economia. (1988–) Padua: Cedam.
Rivista trimestrale di diritto pubblico. (1951–) Milan: Giuffrè.
Rocco, U. (1957–64) *Trattato di diritto processuale civile*. Turin: Utet. 8 vols.
Ruperto, C. and Sgroi, V. (1994–95) (eds) *Nuova rassegna di giurisprudenza sul codice civile*. Milan: Giuffrè.
Santaniello, G. (1988–) (ed.) *Trattato di diritto amministrativo*. Padua: Cedam. 24 vols.
Satta, S. (1966–71) *Commentario al Codice di procedura civile* 2nd edn. Milan: Vallardi. 6 vols.
Scialoja, A. and Branca, G. (1946–) (eds) *Commentario del codice civile*. Bologna: Zanichelli. In progress, 76 volumes at time of writing. Currently edited by F. Galgano but known by the original editors.
Sciullo, G. (1989) (ed.) *Introduzione alla ricerca dei dati giuridici*. Turin: Giappichelli. Contributions by M. Leonelli, F. Martoni, M. Masotti and M.A. Stefanelli.
Settimana giuridica. (1960–) Rome: Italedi.
Il Sole 24 Ore. (1865–) Milan: Editrice Il Sole. Daily newspaper.
Studia et Documenta Historiae et Iuris. (1935–) Rome: Pontificia Universitas Lateranensis.
Tribunali Amministrativi Regionali. (1975–) Rome: Italedi.
Vassalli, F. (1961–94) (ed.) *Trattato di diritto civile italiano*. Turin: Utet. 15 vols.
Verrucoli, P. (1985) *Italian company law*. London: Oyez.
West's law & commercial dictionary in five languages. (1985) St. Paul, Minn: West. 2 vols. Italian edition with Italian–English dictionary, (1988) Bologna: Zanichelli.
Wise, E.M. (1978) (ed.) *The Italian Penal Code*. Littleton, Colo.: Rothman; London: Sweet & Maxwell.
World of learning. (1947–) London: Europa Publications.

Acknowledgements

Written in May 1996 at the Istituto per la Documentazione Giuridica del Consiglio Nazionale delle Ricerche (see the section of **Useful addresses**). Translation by *Deirdre Exell Pirro*. Linguistic revision by *Domenico Torretta.*

CHAPTER SEVENTEEN

Luxembourg

CHRISTIAN F. VERBEKE

Introduction to the legal system

The development of the Grand Duchy's legal history can be traced from its feudal origins and customary law period covering the 10th to 15th centuries, the successive Burgundian reigns, Charles V and the archducal period of Albert and Izabel, which produced the *Édit perpétuel* of 1611 regulating criminal law, administration of justice and the civil law in the Netherlands of which Luxembourg was a part (*Ordonnance et Édit . . .*, 1611). This was followed by the publication in 1623 of the *Coutumes du pays de Luxembourg* [customary laws of Luxembourg], hailed to this day as a juridical monument (*Coutumes générales . . .*, 1623).

There follows the Habsburg period (described by most historians as the *ancien régime*, but not to be confused with the French Old Regime) which ends with the French Revolution. The entire historical process has been described in considerable detail in *Histoire du droit dans le G.D. de Luxembourg* (Majerus, 1949).

The Congress of Vienna (articles 67 and 85) signed on 9 June 1815 made the Duchy of Luxembourg an independent state (some legal historians choose to define it as 'une cession définitive aux Pays-Bas', Ruppert, *Le Grand Duché dans ses relations internationales*, 1892), the appanage of the King of the Netherlands, subject to that country's constitution of 1815, yet part of the German Confederation. Luxembourg was subject to the same laws as those of the seventeen provinces of the Netherlands, whose King was also the first Grand Duke. After Belgium's secession from the Netherlands in 1830, Luxembourg, with the exception of the fortress-city Luxembourg, remained attached to Belgium until 1839. The Grand Duchy of Luxembourg, as a constitutional monarchy with a parliamentary form of government, came into being in 1839 when Luxembourg gained autonomy (Treaty of London 19 April 1839), not without having lost five of its eight districts to Belgium to become the Belgian province of Luxembourg.

The Constitution of 1841 effectively brought an end to the Dutch period. The dissolution of the German Confederation in 1867 brought guarantees of neutrality under the provisions of the Treaty of London of 11 May 1867. Upon the death of William III of the Netherlands, succeeded by his daughter Wilhelmina under the Salic law of succession, the Grand Duchy passed to the House of Nassau-Weilburg, still the present-day rulers.

A first constitution was adopted in 1841, followed by a broader based 'democratic' constitution in 1848, inspired by, if not a copy of the Belgian Constitution, followed by the authoritarian constitution of 1856. A substantively changed constitution saw the light in 1868. Further major changes of the constitution were made in 1919, with further revisions in 1948 and 1987. A reliable study on the Constitution of the Grand Duchy of Luxembourg is Majerus (1990) *L'État luxembourgeois. Manuel de droit constitutionnel.* Excellent contributions on the Constitution by divers hands appear in a 'livre jubilaire' (*Conseil d'État du Grand Duché de Luxembourg: livre jubilaire . . .*, 1957) in which is also outlined the crucial role played by the Conseil d'État, created on 28 June 1857, in the political and constitutional evolution of the Grand Duchy. A concise sketch of public and constitutional law in English is found in *The institutions of the Grand Duchy of Luxembourg* (Majerus, 1977). The supreme source of law in Luxembourg is the Constitution of 17 October 1868. A trilingual (French, German, English) text of the Constitution is *Constitution du 17 octobre 1868, revisée* (1968) and an English translation incorporating amendments to November 1983 appears with a detailed chronology in Weirich (1985).

The Constitution is pre-eminent. The legislative function, as directed by the Constitution, is shared or exercised jointly by the Grand Duke, the government, the Chamber of Deputies, and the Council of State. Substantive law consists essentially of the adoption the laws of countries with which Luxembourg was connected. The country's framework of legislation is statute law, hence enacted law is the principal source of law.

Luxembourg legislation is in French, the sole language for authentic texts; records submitted to parliament must be drafted in French. The spoken, and official, language is Letzeburgesch; the languages of the administration are French and to some extent German, translations into the latter are now infrequent and are made *ex post facto*.

Introductory works on the legal system and legal research

An introductory work of lasting importance and the only one in English is Graulich, *Introduction to the law of Luxembourg* (1968). Although it is dated, its lacunae can be filled by the use of Krieger's *Bibliographie* (Krieger, Spielmann and Graas-Lorang, 1989) and the more balanced earlier *Bibliographie* (Maul *et al.*, 1967). Graulich's manual remains essential, however, as nothing better even in French has taken its place. Although not a work on legal research, a useful general introductory work is Pescatore, *Introduction à la Science du Droit* [Introduction to the science of law], which contains an exceptionally complete list of Luxembourg law sources (Pescatore, [1978], pp. 443–505). A concise but informative introduction in English is supplied by Pescatore (1973).

The absence of a law faculty in the Grand Duchy of Luxembourg compels law students to turn to Belgian or French institutions for their law studies; the proportion appears to be half and half. The inevitable consequence is that their first exposure to legal research methods will be *Précis de méthodologie juridique* (de Theux and Kovalovsky, 1995), likely to become the standard work for some years to come. In French law faculties the standard works on legal research would be *Documentation juridique* (Dunes, 1977) and the later *Recherche documentaire en droit* (Tanguy, 1991).

A detailed examination of the Luxembourg law bibliographies of Maul *et al.* (1967) and Krieger, Spielmann and Graas-Lorang (1989) reveals the paucity of full scale manuals, commentaries and law treatises, to which Graulich had already drawn attention in 1968. While both bibliographies reveal the existence of an abundance of essays and articles, the lack of major studies is apparent. There is thus a great dependence on foreign legal literature, principally Belgian, for constitutional and penal law, and in a large measure French for civil law. It is noteworthy that in Pescatore's preliminary general bibliography (Pescatore, 1978), out of twenty-seven authors cited, seventeen are French jurists, two are Belgian, and seven are German, the latter chiefly legal philosophy specialists, with H. Coing heading the list.

Legislation

The publication of Luxembourg laws is governed by the Royal Decree of 22 October 1842, completed by the Decree of 20 April 1854 (of which some articles have been repealed) and these decrees remain basic today.

The Grand Duchy of Luxembourg's official record of laws and statutes is the *Mémorial. Journal officiel du Grand Duché de Luxembourg*, published since 1 January 1832 after having undergone several title changes. This publication is divided into three distinct sections: A. Recueil de législation; B. Recueil administratif et économique; C. Recueil spécial des sociétés et associations. For an extensive survey of previously published law collections see Graulich on Luxembourg (Graulich *et al.*, 1968, pp. 89–119).

Parliamentary debates in the Chambre des Députés [Chamber of Deputies] are published in the *Compte rendu de séances*, published since 1842. This publication has appeared in two parts since 1872: Part 1. Introductions, Discussions, which contains the debates and an alphabetical index; Part 2. Annexes, Sommaires, which comprises the text of the bills with the opinions of the Conseil d'État, also governmental decisions.

A major unofficial and widely used publication is the *Pasinomie luxembourgeoise* (1830–). Chronologically arranged, this collection records the statutes, decrees, ministerial orders and special regulations extracted from the *Mémorial.*

The laws in civil, commercial and penal matters, aside from the major codes, are collected in the unofficial *Recueil des lois spéciales* (1972–), an ambitious undertaking in looseleaf form which is regularly updated. Legislation affecting companies and associations has also been treated separately in *Recueil de la législation sur sociétés et associations* (Ministère d'État, 1991). Luxembourg banking laws are found in *Droit bancaire et financier au Grand Duché de Luxembourg* (Elvinger, 1994). Essential knowledge of the provisions of art.24 of the Constitution on the means of mass communication, media law, is found in *Recueil de législation sur les médias* (Ministère d'État, 1994).

Codes and commentaries

The principal collection of privately published codes is Gontier-Grigy, *Les Vingt-cinq codes de la législation luxembourgeoise* (1884), a work to be used with some circumspection. Later editions of the Civil Code are Gillissen (1959), *Code civil et code de procédure civile*, to be used in conjunction with Gillissen (1952), *Complément au Code civil*, as it records all the special laws relating to the civil law in force up to 1952. The Civil Code is also published in an official version with annotations by the Ministère de la Justice (1995a).

The Luxembourg Penal Code of 1879 follows the Belgian Penal Code of 1867 and is found in Hammes (1953) *Code de la législation pénale*, which includes the Code of Criminal Procedure, and is now updated by *Code pénal et Code d'instruction criminelle* (Ministère de la Justice, 1990). The standard edition of the commercial code is Ruppert (1915) which includes the special laws pertaining to commerce. A new edition is available, *Code de procedure civile et code de commerce* (Ministère de la Justice, 1995b). In administrative law Ruppert (1907) *Code politique et administrative* is of lasting importance.

The laws affecting the Conseil d'État with a chronological record of its orders and decisions can be found in *Le Conseil d'État: recueil de législation* (Biever and Ensch, 1946). A new official collection of the *Code administratif* (1994) has now been published, which renders Biever and Ensch virtually obsolete. *Le contentieux administratif* (Schockweiler, 1987) provides information on current procedures in non-disputed administrative claims.

In addition to the large Belgian collections of commentaries on the Belgian Codes and case law (see the chapter on Belgium for, e.g. De Page, 1949–90, *Répertoire pratique du droit belge,* 1930–61, and *Les Novelles,* 1931–91), Luxembourg practitioners would also turn to French classics such as Aubry and Rau (1950–90), Baudry-Lacantinerie (1905–30) and Planiol and Ripert (1952–54).

Treaties

Treaty-making power is exercised by the Grand Duke under the control of parliament (Constitution, art.37). Treaties become effective after approval, ratification, and publication. Treaties are published in the *Mémorial.* An important retrospective study and record of treaty literature is found in Ruppert (1892) *Le Grand-Duché de Luxembourg dans ses relations internationales: recueil des traités.* The conflict of laws in the international private law of Luxembourg is analysed by Schockweiler (1985) *Les conflits des lois et de jurisdiction.* An essential introduction to the subject is Pescatore (1964) *Conclusion et effets des traités internationaux.*

Law reports, judgments

The Cour supérieure de Justice comprises: the Cour de Cassation, the cassation court or highest court of appeal in civil, criminal and military justice cases which deals with judicial form not substance or facts and comprises a single chamber; the Cour d'Appel, or court of appeals, comprising seven chambers; and the Cour Supérieure de Justice proper, which deals solely with cases involving members of the government, the disciplining of magistrates and appeals against decisions of the disciplinary council of the Bar.

The principal collection of Luxembourg case law is *Pasicrisie luxembourgeoise* (1881–). The first volume covers the years 1867–1880; subsequent volumes each cover several years of decisions on civil, commercial, criminal and public law.

Earlier series of reports of cases in the Cour supérieure de Justice, Cour de Cassation, and other tribunals are described in detail in Graulich *et al.* (1968, pp. 118–119).

Earlier collections include decisions of the Council of State, Luxembourg's highest administrative jurisdiction, covering 1867–74 (Schon, 1874), which is now supplemented and continued by Glodt (1983) *Répertoire analytique de la jurisprudence administrative du Conseil d'État à partir de 1859.*

Computer-based systems

The legal documentation service of the Chambre des Députés is conducting a development project for a legislative database; the decision on the selection of a server or the form of access remain to be made and it is assumed that in its preliminary stages access will be restricted. Online services are available through the Belgium-based CREDOC which contains LJUS, a database of Luxembourg case law.

Encyclopedias

The French looseleaf collections *Encyclopédie juridique Dalloz* and *Juris-classeurs* are widely used, with the latter placing more emphasis on European and international law. Sets of volumes on single subjects from within these major multi-volume sets can be purchased separately.

Directories

Judicial and administrative Luxembourg is treated in the comprehensive *Annuaire Officiel d'Administration et de Législation* (1995), in two looseleaf volumes. It is based on information supplied by administrative and judicial bodies, e.g. the Conseil d'État maintains a special file and bibliography of all legislation and jurisprudence affecting this institution.

Bibliographies

Although dated, the fundamental legal bibliography of the Grand Duchy in English is in *Guide to foreign legal materials: Belgium, Luxembourg, Netherlands* (Graulich *et al.*, 1968, pp. 89–119). Concise and condensed in format, it is the only bibliographic guide to the intricacies of early depositories of law. The author describes some 60 collections (frequently of an ephemeral nature), law series or seminal pieces of legislation covering 1788 to 1968. See also in this respect 'Chronologie des sources du droit depuis la Révolution française' (Pescatore, [1978], Annexe XXVI, pp. 497–505).

The *Bibliographie du droit luxembourgeois* (Maul *et al.*, 1967), is a detailed survey of the literature which was followed by *Bibliographie juridique luxembourgeoise* (Krieger, Spielmann and Graas-Lorang, 1989), an awkwardly arranged work which has tended to limit itself to the periodical literature. I have found no entry in the subject index for 'Codes', while 'Jurisprudence' yields at best some articles on European law. The *Catalogue* of the Staatsbibliothek Preussischer Kulturbesitz has a useful section of Luxembourg legal materials. The arrangement is alphabetic (author or title entries), with a comprehensive country and subject index in vol.III (Staatsbibliothek . . ., 1987).

The *Catalogue* of the library of the Luxembourg Chambre des Députés records a nearly complete collection of Luxembourg legal literature (Chambre des Députés, 1994). However, admission to the collections is restricted. A printed catalogue of the comprehensive law reference collections of the Conseil d'État is in existence but not published; access to the collections is restricted. Requests for consultation or information, on a need-to-know basis, should be addressed to Mr Marc Besch, Clerk to the Justices, to whom I am indebted for the reading of the preliminary draft of this chapter.

Indexing and abstracting services

No privately published indexing and abstracting service exists, but the respective jurisdictions and administrative bodies maintain their own resources. An internal online legislative index and abstract service is planned to come on-stream in the Chambre des Députés.

Dictionaries

For the most frequently used dictionaries in all categories see the chapter on Belgium.

Other reference books

Administrative law and its conflicts have been analysed by Bonn (1966) *Le Contentieux administratif.* A panoramic survey of modern Luxembourg law has been realized with the massive *Diagonales à travers le droit* (Conférence Saint-Yves, 1986) in 60 essays by various authors.

Miscellaneous studies on constitutional law and the historical evolution of commercial and company law is found in Metzler (1949) *Mélanges de droit Luxembourgeois.* Fiscal law practice is found in Olinger (1994) and his *Procédure contentieuse* (Olinger, 1989) deals with disputed fiscal claims.

In English, *Belgium and Luxembourg: practical commercial law* (Van Crombrugghe and Arendt, 1992) is useful. The laws of holding companies, a broad-based Luxembourg activity, is found in Bernard (1979) *Les sociétés holding au Grand Duché de Luxembourg.* A useful study in English of banking secrecy is Kauffman (1991) *Professional secrecy of bankers.* Several up-to-date studies are published by the publications departments of the Banque Internationale de Luxembourg and Kredietbank (Luxembourg).

Current information sources

Journals, research reports

Although a recent addition to the legal literature, the yearly *Annales du droit luxembourgeois* (1991–) have tackled wide subject areas such as maritime law (Luxembourg flag registrations), the Constitution and builders' liability in addition to a host of other legal themes and the articles are substantial scholarly contributions. Recent developments in Luxembourg law are discussed in *Bulletin du Cercle François Laurent.* A similar periodical slanted perhaps more narrowly towards the civil law is *Feuille de liaison de la Conférence Saint-Yves.*

News information

The government's information service is the Service Information et Presse, a part of the Ministry of State. The government presence on the Internet is at http://www.restena.lu/luxembourg/lux_welcome.html which gives a wide range of general information. Authoritative official news and notices are found in the privately published daily *Luxemburger Wort* (1848–).

Business and financial information

Luxembourg economic and financial news is found in the Belgium-based *L'Écho: le quotidien de l'économie et de la finance.* There is a journal with contents in English and French entitled *Luxembourg Business.* The Luxembourg Stock Exchange produces a booklet every six months with general statistical and organizational information (Luxembourg Stock Exchange, 1983–).

Statistics

The irregularly published *Annuaire* is a reliable and comprehensive work on the statistics of the Grand Duchy (Ministère de l'Économie, 1909–). An exhaustive statistical study of the Grand Duchy is *Statistiques historiques 1839–1989* (Ministère de l'Économie, 1990).

Useful addresses

Associations of lawyers

Association of Banking Jurists, Association luxembourgeoise des juristes de banque, BP 245, L-2012 Luxembourg. An important component group of the Luxembourg legal profession.

Bar Association of Diekirch, Ordre des Avocats de Diekirch, Palais de Justice, L-9265 Diekirch, Luxembourg. Tel: +352 808397. The Bar Association for the Grand Duchy's north-eastern jurisdictions.

Bar Association of Luxembourg, Ordre des Avocats de Luxembourg, rue du Palais de Justice, L-1841 Luxembourg. Tel: +352 224850

Government organizations

The 'central number' noted in entries below is for a central government switchboard which connects to all participating ministries and is recommended for those unfamiliar with the structure of Luxembourg government.

Institut Monétaire Luxembourgeois, 63 avenue de la Liberté, L-2983 Luxembourg. Tel: +352 402929/402203. Fax: +352 492180. Formerly known as the Banking Commission.

Ministère d'État, Service Information et Presse, 43 boulevard F.D. Roosevelt, L-2450 Luxembourg. Tel: +352 478 2183. Fax: +352 470285/467492

Ministère de l'Économie, 19–21 boulevard Royal, L-2914 Luxembourg. Tel: +352 478 4268. Fax: +352 460448

Ministère de l'Économie, Service central de la Statistique et des Études économiques (STATEC), BP 304, L-2013 Luxembourg. Tel: +352 478–1. Fax: +352 464289

Ministère de l'Intérieur, 19 rue Beaumont, L-2933 Luxembourg. Tel: +352 478-1 (central number). Fax: +352 41846

Ministère de la Justice. 16 Boulevard Royal, L-2934 Luxembourg. Tel: +352 478-1 (central number). Fax: +352 227661. Ministry of Justice's information service: Service d'accueil et d'information juridique, 12 Côte d'Eich, L-1450 Luxembourg. Tel: +352 221846

Ministère des Affaires étrangères, du Commerce extérieur et de la Coopération, 5 rue Notre Dame, BP 1602, L-1016 Luxembourg. Tel: +352 478-1 (central number). Fax: +352 223144 (juridical service only)

Ministère des Finances, 3 rue de la Congrégation, L-2931 Luxembourg. Tel: +352 478-1 (central number). Fax: +352 475241

Trésorerie d'État, 3 rue de la Congrégation, L-2931 Luxembourg. Tel: +352 478-1 (central number). Fax: +352 466212

Courts

Cour supérieure de Justice, 12 Côte d'Eich, Luxembourg. Tel: +352 4759811. Fax: +352 475 981396

Conseil d'État, 5 rue Sigefroi, L-2536 Luxembourg. Tel: +352 473071 1. Fax: +352 464322

Education and training

As described earlier in the chapter, there is no law faculty in the Grand Duchy. There is a Département de Formation juridique and a Département de Droit et des Sciences Économiques attached to the Centre Universitaire de Luxembourg (below).

Research institutions

Centre Universitaire de Luxembourg, 162A avenue de la Faiencerie, L-1511, Luxembourg. Tel: +352 4666441. Fax: +352 466644203

Libraries

Bibliothèque du Conseil d'État, Conseil d'État, 5 rue Sigefroi, L-2536 Luxembourg. Tel: +352 473071 1. Fax: +352 464322. A major law library, access highly restricted.
Bibliothèque du Parlement, Chambre des Députés, 19 rue du Marché-aux-Herbes, L-1728 Luxembourg. Tel: +352 466966 1. A major law library, access highly restricted.
Bibliothèque nationale, 37 boulevard Roosevelt, L-2450, Luxembourg. Tel: +352 226255. The principal research library.

Law publishers and booksellers

Credoc asbl-vzw: documentation juridique, rechtsdocumentatie, rue de la Montagne 34, Box 11, B-1000 Brussels, Belgium. Tel: +32 2 511 6941. Fax: +32 2 513 3195
Editpress Luxembourg, 15 route d'Esch, L-1470, Luxembourg. Tel: +352 251880
Imprimerie Saint-Paul, 2 rue Christophe-Plantin, Gasperich, L-2339 Luxembourg. Tel: +352 4993 1
Imprimerie Victor Bück, Printers to the Grand-Ducal Court, 6 rue F. Hogenberg, L-1735, Luxembourg. Tel: +352 499866 1

List of works cited

Annales de droit luxembourgeois. (1991–) Brussels: Bruylant.
Annuaire Officiel d'Administration et de Législation. (1995) Luxembourg: Ministère d'État. 2 looseleaf vols.
Aubry, C. and Rau, C.F. (1950–90) *Cours de droit civil*. . . ed. by Esmein. Paris: Librarie Marchal et Billard. 12 vols. with supplements, multiple concurrent editions.
Baudry-Lacantinerie, G. (1905–30) *Traité théorique et pratique de droit civil* . . . 3rd edn. *Compléments* by J. Bonnecase. Paris: Recueil Sirey. 29 vols and 6 vols of supplements.
Bernard, G. (1979) *Les sociétés holding au Grand Duché de Luxembourg*. Luxembourg: Institut Universitaire International.
Biever, Tony and Ensch, Paul (1946) *Le Conseil d'État: recueil de législation et de jurisprudence*. Luxembourg: Bourg-Bourger.
Bonn, Alex (1966) *Le contentieux administratif en droit luxembourgeois*. Luxembourg: Éditions Armand Peiffer.
Bulletin du Cercle François Laurent. (1957/58–) Luxembourg: Cercle François Laurent.
Chambre des Députés (1994) *Catalogue de la Bibliothèque*. Luxembourg: Chamber of Deputies. 2 vols.
Code administratif: vol.I Institutions; II Procedures; III Fonctions publiques. (1994)

Luxembourg: Service Central de Législation. 3 vols.

Compte Rendu des séances de la Chambre des Députés du Grand Duché de Luxembourg édité par le Greffe. . . . (1842–) Luxembourg: Bück.

Conférence Saint-Yves (1986) *Diagonales à travers le droit luxembourgeois.* Luxembourg: Impr. Saint-Paul. Contains 60 essays.

Le Conseil d'État du Grand Duché de Luxembourg: livre jubilaire du centième anniversaire. (1957) Luxembourg: Bourg-Bourger.

Constitution du 17 octobre 1868 revisée. (1968) Luxembourg: Ministère de l'État. Service central de Législation. Trilingual edition in French, German and English.

Coutumes générales des Pays Duché de Luxembourg et Comté de Chiny. (1623) Luxembourg: Pierre Reulandt.

CREDOC (available from Credoc asbl-vzw).

De Theux, Axel and Kovalovsky, I. (1995) *Précis de méthodologie juridique: les sources documentaires du droit.* Brussels: Publications des Facultés Universitaires Saint-Louis.

Dunes, A. (1977) *Documentation juridique.* Collection Méthodes du Droit. Paris: Dalloz.

L'Écho: le quotidien de l'économie et de la finance. (1881–) Brussels: L'Écho. Published at 131 Rue de Birmingham, 1070 Brussels, Belgium. Tel. +32 2 526 5511. Fax: +32 2 526 5526

Elvinger, A. (1994) (ed.) *Droit bancaire et financier au Grand Duché de Luxembourg.* Brussels: Larcier, for the Association Luxembourgeoise de Juristes de Banque. 2 vols.

Encyclopédie juridique Dalloz. (original publications dates vary, currently updated by looseleaf pages) 2nd edn. Paris: Éditions Dalloz. 38 vols, looseleaf.

Études Fiscales. Revue consacrée à la Fiscalité Luxembourgeoise. (1963–) Luxembourg: Impr. Saint-Paul.

Feuille de liaison de la Conférence Saint-Yves. (1952–) Luxembourg: Conférence Saint Yves. New series started 1956– ; the Conférence is a group of law historians.

Gillissen, Frédéric (1952) *Complément au Code civil comprenant les lois spéciales en matière civile en vigueur dans le Grand Duché de Luxembourg, mises à jour jusqu'en 1952.* Luxembourg: Bück.

Gillissen, Frédéric (1959) *Code civil et Code de procédure civile en vigueur dans le Grand Duché de Luxembourg, annotés d'après la jurisprudence luxembourgeoise, française et belge. Mis à jour jusqu'en 1958, publiés par le Gouvernement.* Diekirch: Impr. de Diekirch.

Glodt, G. (1983) *Répertoire analytique de la jurisprudence administrative du Conseil d'État à partir de 1859.* Luxembourg: Ministère de la Justice.

Gontier-Grigy, Denis-Antoine (1884) *Les vingt-cinq codes de la législation luxembourgeoise* [The twenty five codes of Luxembourg legislation] 4th edn. Luxembourg: J. Beffort.

Graulich, Paul (1968) Introduction to the law of Luxembourg. In Graulich *et al.*, 1968, pp. 91–101.

Graulich, Paul *et al.* (1968) *Guide to foreign legal materials: Belgium, Luxembourg, Netherlands.* Dobbs Ferry, NY: Oceana.

Hammes, Charles-Leon (1953) (ed.) *Code de la législation pénale en vigueur dans le Grand-Duché de Luxembourg.* Luxembourg: Bourg-Bourger. 2 vols, looseleaf.

Juris-classeur. (original publications dates vary, currently updated by looseleaf pages) Paris: Éditions Techniques. The complete collection including European law comprises 167 vols, looseleaf.

Kauffman, Jacques (1991) *Professional secrecy of bankers in Luxembourg law.* Luxembourg: Banque Internationale à Luxembourg.

Krieger, G., Spielmann, D. and Graas-Lorang, Cl. (1989) *Bibliographie juridique luxembourgeoise.* Brussels: Nemesis.

Luxembourg Business. (1987–) Luxembourg: International City Magazines.

Luxembourg Stock Exchange (1983–) *Facts and figures.* Luxembourg: Luxembourg Stock Exchange, PO Box 165, 11 Avenue de la Porte Neuve, L-2011 Luxembourg. Tel: +352 4779361. Fax: +352 473298

Luxemburger Wort. (1848–) Luxembourg: Impr. Saint-Paul. Daily.

Majerus, Nicolas (1949) *Histoire du droit dans le Grand-Duché de Luxembourg*. Luxembourg: Impr. Saint-Paul. 2 vols.

Majerus, Pierre (1977) *The Institutions of the Grand Duchy of Luxembourg*. Luxembourg: Ministère d'État.

Majerus, Pierre (1990) *L'État luxembourgeois. Manuel de droit constitutionnel et de droit administratif* 6th edn. Luxembourg: Editpress.

Maul, Roger *et al.* for the Association Internationale des Sciences Juridiques. Comité national Luxembourgeois (1967) *Bibliographie du droit luxembourgeois*. Brussels: F. Larcier.

Mémorial. Journal officiel du Grand Duché de Luxembourg. (1832–) Luxembourg: Bück.

Metzler, Léon (1949) *Mélanges de droit Luxembourgeois, 1949*. Luxembourg: Impr. de la Cour, J. Beffort.

Ministère d'État (1991) *Recueil de la législation sur sociétés et associations. Textes coordonnés et jurisprudence*. Luxembourg: Service Central de Législation.

Ministère d'État. (1994) *Recueil de législation sur les médias*. Luxembourg: Ministère d'État. Looseleaf.

Ministère de l'Économie, Service Central de la Statistique et des Études économiques (STATEC) (1909–) *Annuaire*. Luxembourg: Service Central de la Statistique et des Études économiques.

Ministère de l'Économie, Service Central de la Statistique et des Études économiques (STATEC) (1990) *Statistiques historiques 1839–1989*. Luxembourg: Service Central de la Statistique et des Études économiques. Published every ten years.

Ministère de la Justice (1990) *Code pénal et Code d'instruction criminelle en vigueur dans le G.-D. de Luxembourg, annotés d'après la Jurisprudence Luxembourgeoise*. Esch-sur-Alzette: Impr. Cooperative Luxembourgeoise.

Ministère de la Justice (1995a) *Code civil en vigueur dans le G.D. de Luxembourg. Annoté d'après la Jurisprudence luxembourgeoise*. Luxembourg: Editpress.

Ministère de la Justice (1995b) *Code de procedure civile et code de commere en vigueur dans le Grand-Duché de Luxembourg*. Luxembourg: Bück.

Olinger, Jean (1989) La procédure contentieuse en matière d'impôts directs. In *Études fiscales*, November 1989.

Olinger, Jean (1994) Le droit fiscal. Introduction à l'Étude du droit fiscal Luxembourgeois. In *Études Fiscales*, September 1994.

Ordonnance et Édit Perpétuel des Archiducqz . . . pour meilleure direction des affaires de la Justice, en leur pays de par deça. (1611) Brussels: R. Velpius & H. Antoon.

Pasicrisie luxembourgeoise. Recueil de la jurisprudence luxembourgeoise en matière civile, commerciale, criminelle, de droit public, fiscal, administratif et notarial. (1881–) Luxembourg: J. Beffort.

Pasinomie luxembourgeoise. Recueil des lois, décrets, arrêtés, règlements . . . qui peuvent être invoqués dans le Grand Duché de Luxembourg. (1830–) Luxembourg: Bück.

Pescatore, Pierre (1964) *Conclusion et effets des traités internationaux selon le droit constitutionnel, les usages et la jurisprudence du Grand Duché de Luxembourg*. Luxembourg: Office des Imprimés de l'État.

Pescatore, Pierre (1973) Luxembourg. In *International encyclopedia of comparative law*, ed. V. Knapp, vol.1, L47–L52. Tübingen: J.C.B. Mohr.

Pescatore, Pierre (1978) *Introduction à la science du droit* 2nd edn. Luxembourg: Offices des Imprimés de l'État.

Planiol, M. and Ripert, G. (1952–54) *Traité pratique de droit civil français*. Paris: Librairie Générale de Droit et de Jurisprudence. 14 vols.

Recueil des lois spéciales en matière civile, commerciale et pénale. (1972–) Luxembourg: Impr. Saint-Paul. 7 vols, looseleaf.

Ruppert, Pierre (1892) *Le Grand-Duché de Luxembourg dans ses relations internationales: recueil des traités, conventions, et arrangements internationaux et dispositions législatives diverses concernant les étrangers*. Luxembourg: Bück.

Ruppert, Pierre (1907) *Code politique et administratif du Grand Duché de Luxembourg, lois règlements, arrêtés sur l'organisation politique, judiciaire, et administrative* 3rd edn. Luxembourg: Impr. Bück.

Ruppert, Pierre (1915) *Code du commerce, de l'industrie et du travail en vigueur dans le Grand Duché de Luxembourg. Nouv. éd. compl., amplifiée et commentée par la jurisprudence de 1915.* Luxembourg: Bück.

Schockweiler, Fernand (1985) *Les conflits des lois et les conflits de jurisdictions en droit international privé luxembourgeois.* Luxembourg: Ministère de la Justice.

Schockweiler, Fernand (1987) *Le contentieux administratif et la procedure administrative non contentieuse en droit Luxembourgeois.* Luxembourg: Impr. Hermann.

Schon, Michel (1874) (ed.) *Journal des Décisions du Conseil d'État et autres decisions d'un intérêt administratif du Grand-Duché de Luxembourg.* Vol.1, Nos. 1–118. Luxembourg: Bück.

Staatsbibliothek Preussischer Kulturbesitz (1987) *Catalogue of the holdings pertaining to the law of the Romanic Law Countries. Europe-Africa. Acquisitions since 1946.* Berlin: Staatsbibliothek Preussischer Kulturbesitz. 3 vols.

Tanguy, Y. (1991) *La recherche documentaire en droit.* Paris: P.U.F.

Van Crombrugghe, Nicole and Arendt, Guy (1992) *Belgium and Luxembourg: practical commercial law.* European Commercial Law Series. London: Longman.

Weirich, Malou (1985) The Grand Duchy of Luxembourg. In *Constitutions of the countries of the world*, ed. A.P. Blaustein and G.H. Flanz, vol.X. Dobbs Ferry, NY: Oceana.

CHAPTER EIGHTEEN

Malta

JOANNA DRAKE, P.G. XUEREB AND EUGENE BUTTIGIEG

Introduction to the legal system

In general, it can be stated that Maltese private law follows the European continental system, while Maltese public law, including conflict of laws, follows the British system. There are several exceptions to this dual classification. For example, Maltese maritime law, company law, the law of evidence and the law on adoption follow English Law.

The first known organized system of law that applied in Malta was Roman Law, as in 216 BC Malta became a Roman colony. It was previously a Carthaginian outpost and the local population derived from an early Phoenician settlement. The influence of Roman Law continued almost uninterruptedly. During the Middle Ages, Malta's vicissitudes were similar to those of Sicily, as Malta was subject to the same forces and main historical events, particularly the Moorish invasion and the Aragonese influence.

In relatively modern times, before the commencement of the British period, the most influential developments took place during the domination of the Knights of St John (normally referred to as the Knights of Malta) to whom Malta was granted in 1530 in feudal tenure by the King of Spain. Several Grandmasters of the Order of St John enacted important laws. Particular attention was given to maritime and mercantile legislation and traditionally the Consolato del Mare of Messina was followed. At the time of Grandmaster Perellos (1697–1720) a special Consolato del Mare was enacted for Malta but it was provided that, in the absence of an express provision of the local law, the Consolato del Mare of Messina was to be followed. A digest of the laws obtaining in Malta was enacted by Grandmaster De Vilhena (1722–1736) and although the previous legislation was followed, it was provided that on matters not specifically dealt with by local legislation, any controversy was to be decided in accordance with the rules of the Consolato del Mare of Barcelona and the one of Messina.

A voluminous Municipal Code was enacted by Grandmaster De Rohan in 1784 and continued to be in force up to the middle of the 19th century when it was substituted by the new Codes. As there was no express general revocation, the Courts held that various provisions continued to apply and this code, also referred to as the Code De Rohan, must be regarded still as an immediate source of Maltese law.

The Constitution now in force is the Malta Independence Constitution as amended particularly in 1974. Malta is a republic within the British Commonwealth of Nations. The members of the House of Representatives are elected by proportional representation with a system of one transferable vote based on universal suffrage. The Executive is headed by the Prime Minister, who is the leader of the party in power. The President of the Republic has the function of calling on the member of the House of Representatives whom he/she believes has the support of the House. That system and the Cabinet that controls the Executive is built on the British pattern. On the constitutional development of Malta in general, reference may be made to Cremona (1963, 1994).

Malta is divided into 13 electoral districts for the election of the Members of Parliament. As the numbers of voters in the electoral districts are not precisely the same and may vary up to the limit of 5 per cent, it may happen that a party having a majority of votes on a national basis obtains a minority of seats. This has happened on two occasions in recent years. The law was therefore amended to provide that should the party obtaining a clear majority of number one votes in the election itself with a minority of parliamentary seats, that party would automatically be allocated more seats to enable it to have a majority of seats in Parliament.

According to Act XV of 1993, Malta and the sister island of Gozo were divided into 67 districts for the purpose of the election of local councils, each one of which is presided over by a mayor.

Introductory works on legal system and legal research

On the general outlines of Maltese law and its origins, reference may be made to the following publications: de Bono (1897); J.M. Ganado (1947, 1950, 1961); *Sweet & Maxwell's legal bibliography of the British Commonwealth of Nations* (1964); Busuttil (1973); H.W. Harding (1980); A. Ganado (1991).

Other works in English, which are of historical interest, include Cremona (1959) and Lee (1973). Another treatise that gives a substantial insight into Maltese public law at the end of the 18th century but which is not available in translation is De Giovanni (1983).

Legislation

All laws in Malta are promulgated in the two official languages of the archipelago, namely Maltese and English. As a rule, the Maltese version prevails in case of conflict. The most up-to-date and official source of Maltese legislation is the *Government Gazette* which is published twice weekly by the Department of Information, from where it may be purchased by subscription or as individual copies. Supplements A, B, C and recently D are also issued on a regular basis together with the *Gazette* but all are on sale separately (Maltese and English versions). Supplement A consists of legislation as it is carried through Parliament. Supplement B contains subsidiary legislation (by-laws, regulations, legal notices, etc.) and Supplement C contains Bills and/or White Papers. An annual cumulation of Supplements A and B is also published. Since the introduction of Local Councils by virtue of the Local Councils Act (Act XV of 1993), local by-laws are published in a new Supplement D of the *Government Gazette*. An index to the *Gazette* and Supplements is published annually, although publication is usually two years overdue.

Although in practice the coming into force of a law usually coincides with its publication date, specific provision is usually made in each particular law for the date of the entry into effect of that law.

The complete set of the *Laws of Malta* (official version) 1984 edn., eight volumes and an index, was first published by the Law Revision Commission which was set up in 1980 (Act IX) and was entrusted with the task of preparing, from time to time, at intervals of not less than ten years, a revised edition of the Statute Laws of Malta which include both principal and subsidiary legislation. The first six volumes were originally published in book form and contain the principal legislation in force on 31 December 1983. Volumes VII and VIII were published in looseleaf form and contain the principal legislation after 1983. The whole edition is now being published in looseleaf format and two volumes, that is II and III have been so published updated to 31 December 1993. The remaining volumes are being updated to 31 December 1994 and are due to be published shortly.

A widely used commercial version of Maltese laws is that published by Legal (Publishing) Enterprises which are the principal publishers in Malta specializing in legal publications. This enterprise provides its subscribers, which include most lawyers, the law courts, judges and magistrates and most government departments, with several services, namely:

- the conversion into looseleaf format of the original set of the *Laws of Malta* as published by the Law Revision Commission;
- an amendment service to the *Laws of Malta* on a quarterly basis;
- the reprinting of the original *Laws of Malta*, which is now out of print;

- the publishing of a collection of all subsidiary legislation in Malta (legal notices and local council by-laws), indexed and regularly updated;
- the publication of special sectional collections such as *Building, construction and land laws*; *Company law, accountancy and other fiscal legislation; Medical and kindred professions laws and legislation; Criminal laws and other laws relating to the police;* and *Laws and legislation relating to tourism (1996).*

Codes and commentaries

The Code of Organization and Civil Procedure [*Il-Kodici ta' l'Organizzazzjoni u Procedura civili*] was enacted in 1855 and subsequently amended on many occasions.

The Criminal Code [*Il-Kodici Kriminali*], including criminal procedure, as well as the Code of Police Laws, were enacted in 1854 and subsequently amended on many occasions.

The Commercial Code [*Il-Kodici Kummercjali*] was enacted in 1857 and the Ordinances dealing with Maritime Law were enacted in 1858. In 1931, certain parts of the Commercial Code were revised. The sections relating to commercial partnerships, including companies, were replaced by a new law enacted in 1962.

The Civil Code [*Il-Kodici Civili*] was enacted piecemeal and later consolidated in 1868 insofar as the Law of Property ('Things' in the Code) was concerned and in 1873 insofar as it related to the Law of Persons. Various amendments were naturally made along the years. Mention may be made of the new sections on the law of adoption enacted in 1962, and of the new sections on family law enacted in 1973, 1975 and 1993. There is at present a programme of revision of various parts of the Civil Code.

All the main Codes including the Code of Police Laws (English and Maltese versions) are available from Legal (Publishing) Enterprises for sale separately. For details see the List of Works Cited at the end of the chapter.

Commentaries on the various Codes take the form of lecture notes written by university professors for circulation to students. Further information may be obtained from the Faculty of Laws, University of Malta.

Treaties

Treaty-making power is vested in Parliament if the provisions of a particular treaty include matters which necessitate amendments to national laws. Once ratified, treaties appear in the *Government Gazette*.

The best source to ascertain whether Malta is a signatory to a treaty is through the Ministry of Foreign Affairs which maintains a register of ratification, accessions or signature. The United Nations *Treaty series*, an annual publication of multilateral treaties deposited with the Secretary-General also includes entries for treaties adopted by Malta.

Law reports, judgments, digests

The Maltese court system branches into two main divisions: the Superior Courts (presided over by Judges) and the Inferior Courts (presided over by Magistrates). In the civil jurisdiction, magistrates can hear cases where the amount involved is liquidated and can be specified and does not exceed LM (Maltese lira) 1000. The competence of the Inferior Courts was extended from the previous maximum limit of LM250 to LM1000 with effect from 1 July 1996. The Criminal Court hears criminal cases where the maximum term of imprisonment does not exceed three years. If the maximum term exceeds three years but not ten, then the accused may opt to have his case heard before a magistrate, failing which the case is heard before the Superior Courts.

The Superior Courts comprise the Criminal Court (where the accused can choose to have a trial by jury or else have his/her case decided by a Judge), the Civil Court (First Hall of contentious jurisdiction and Second Hall of voluntary jurisdiction), the Commercial Court, the Constitutional Court and the Courts of Appeal. Only one appeal subsists from the judgment of the Court of First Instance. However, in constitutional cases where human rights are involved, recourse may be made to the European Court of Human Rights.

The official version of the decisions of the Superior Courts of Malta 1789–1969, *Decizjonijiet tal-Qrati Superjuri ta' Malta* have long been out of print but are still available for reference at the major libraries in Malta and in some major UK research libraries. The volumes from 1789 up to 1933 are mainly in the Italian language and are of particular interest not only to the legal profession but to researchers and melitensia scholars. From 1934 to 1969 (apart from a few in the English language, due to English-speaking parties in particular cases) the judgments are in the Maltese language as they are delivered up to this day. Legal (Publishing) Enterprises have published reprints of these judgments in 185 volumes: *Kollezzjoni ta' decizjonijiet tal-Qrati Superjuri ta' Malta [1781–1969]* and are also publishing on an ongoing basis an official government authorized version of the Superior Courts' judgments from 1970 onwards in order to close the lacuna that had existed since that date when government had ceased the publication of these judgments. So far 18 volumes have been published containing decisions from 1986 to 1995. All the volumes, including the past and the recent judgments, are indexed by subject and by contending parties. There are also cross-references to the relevant legislation and articles.

The decisions of the Inferior Courts of Malta, *Kollezzjoni ta' Decizjonijiet tal-Qrati Inferjuri* (1939–) which contain the main decisons of the Magistrates' Courts (criminal and civil judicature) have also been published by Legal (Publishing) Enterprises. A selection of the more important decisions of the main Maltese Adminstrative Tribunals (including the Rent Regulation Board, the Agricultural Leases Board, the old Arbitration Board and the more recent judgments of the Malta Industrial Tribunals) have been collected in volumes and published by Legal (Publishing) Enterprises as *Gabra tas-Sentenzi tat-Tribunali ta' Dawn il-Gzejjer*. The official reporting and publishing of the cases decided by administrative tribunals is however not yet fully operational. The Department of Information, however, has published some of the more important awards given by the Malta Arbitration Tribunal (dealing with industrial disputes) in a work entitled *Decizjonijiet tat-Tribunal ta' l'Arbitragg ghal Malta = Awards by the Malta Arbitration Tribunal 1949–1973*. Of particular interest is the publication by Legal (Publishing) Enterprises of the *Planning appeals decisions* which comprises the decisions of the Planning Appeals Board of Malta (set up in 1993), appeals from such decisions to the Court of Appeal and cabinet decisions from Planning Appeals Board recommendations. These are an invaluable source for the interpretation of the Maltese Structure Plan, the Planning Authority and the overall regulation of building in Malta. A selection of decisions of the Malta Constitutional Court covering the years 1964–1968 have been compiled and published in two volumes by Law Students Society [Ghaqda Studenti tal-Ligi] and the work is entitled *Decizjonijiet Kostituzzjonali 1964–1978*. A summary and index of the decisions of the Court of Appeal 1964–1980 has also been published as *Decizjonijiet Qorti ta' l'Appell: Sommarji u Indicijiet 1964–1980*.

A comprehensive index of all the decisions of the Maltese Courts and administrative tribunals covering the period from 1939 to 1970 has been published by Legal (Publishing) Enterprises: *Indici: Qrati, Tribunali u Ligijiet*. It is divided into three particular indexes relating to subject matter, names of the parties to the suit and the relevant section of the legislation mentioned in the respective decisions. The Law Students Society [Ghaqda Studenti tal-Ligi] had also published, through the services of the University of Malta, an index: *Indici Decizjonijiet tal-Qrati ta' Malta*, complete with cross-references to the relevant law section, of the decisions of Maltese courts (commercial, civil and criminal jurisdiction) covering the period from 1890 to 1960.

An invaluable source of court decisions' summaries on the law relating to banking may be found in a thirteen volume work (including index) entitled *The word of the Court* edited by Ph. Farrugia Randon (1992).

Computer-based systems of basic legal texts

Since June 1995 both statutes and case law are available electronically at the Ministry of Justice central Client Server (Mini host). These are cross-referenced for maximum utility and practicability. All information held will be updated regularly through the contracted services of the University of Malta. Due to technical and linguistic limitations, access to computer-held information (statutes, case law, case management and diary) has been restricted to Maltese advocates and legal procurators from their homes and offices through telephone link via modem. Statistical data will also be generated by the system on MIS basis.

In collaboration with various Maltese computer firms, Legal (Publishing) Enterprises is also setting up a modem accessible database to include all present legislation of Malta and to cater for immediate updating of legislation in general. This database will also include all decisions of the Maltese Superior and Inferior Courts as well as the Administrative Tribunals. It will also include a third section relating to a sample system of forms, contracts, etc. within the Maltese jurisdiction.

Other important government documents

Parliamentary proceedings are published by the House of Representatives.

The Permanent Law Reform Commission occasionally produces White Papers/Reports advocating the reform of certain aspects of Maltese Law. Two such reports which are still available from the offices of the Law Reform Commission are *The Law relating to legal aid* (1992b) and *Law relating to foundations* (1992a). The Department of Information, also produces other relevant reports such as the *Economic Survey* which is published quarterly.

Encyclopedias, large collections and services

There is no current publication.

Directories

A list of law firms and practising lawyers/notaries public, together with a list of judges and magistrates and other legal personnel is published by the Camera degli Avvocati [Chamber of Advocates] in *The legal and court directory 1994/1995*. This publication also contains a list of government ministries and departments with addresses, telephone numbers and faxes. A more detailed and frequently updated list of *Government departments* incorporating names and numbers of important contact persons is published by the Department of Information and is available on request.

The *University of Malta calendar 1994/1995* lists all the major legal institutions/research institutes and their respective contact addresses and telephone/fax numbers.

Bibliographies

Since 1983 the National Library of Malta has published annually a *Malta national bibliography* which lists new works published in the Maltese islands during a particular year and describes each work in detail. The material catalogued is based upon the items received at the National Library of Malta by way of legal deposit. There is a law section and included are all books or other works with eight pages or more of text which could either deal with aspects of Maltese law or are written by Maltese nationals abroad. In another part of this publication, subtitled 'The Classified Bibliography', entries are arranged by subject according to the Dewey Decimal Classification. The bibliography is followed by two indexes. In the 'Index of Authors, Titles and Series' are entries in a single alphabetical sequence for all authors, editors, compilers, illustrators and contibutors, as well as for titles of works and for series. The 'Index of Subjects' should guide the user to where a work or works on a particular subject can be found in the 'Classified Bibliography'.

Indexing and abstracting services

An analytical index of the Laws of Malta is published periodically (latest edition covers the laws in force at the end of 1994) in *Laws of Malta – Analytical Index of Titles* (in English), compiled by Judge Riccardo Farrugia.

The Special Collections Department of the University of Malta Library has published a classified list of *Dissertations presented for the degree of Doctor of Laws: a classified list 1958–1988*. This publication, which has recently been updated as *Dissertations of Doctor of Law up to 1993*, contains a subject and author index. The Library also maintains a card index by author of these dissertations which are all written in English.

Dictionaries

No legal dictionary exists. Researchers may however refer to Joseph Aquilina's *Maltese–English Dictionary* (1987), for a general language dictionary which also translates the major legal terms.

Current information sources

Journals, research reports

The main source of current information on Maltese legal developments is the large number of dissertations submitted at the Faculty of Laws, University of Malta, in part fulfilment of the requirements for the degree of Doctor of Laws.

Other regular publications (books, research and information papers) include those of the European Documentation and Research Centre at the University of Malta and other university institutes.

Legal articles appear regularly in the *Bank of Valletta Review*, the *Commercial Courier*, *Industry Today*, the *Management Journal* and other professional journals.

The Camera degli Avvocati [Chamber of Advocates] publishes the proceedings of conferences/seminars organized by it from time to time.

Forum, published twice yearly, is a scholarly review of annulment and separation decisions of the Maltese Ecclesiastical Tribunal which, according to Canon Law, enjoys jurisdiction over marriages celebrated within the Roman Catholic Church.

News information

English-language newspapers (which include *The Times*, published daily, *Sunday Times, Malta Independent* and *Malta Business Weekly*) carry law reports as well as articles of legal interest and general news, including parliamentary reports.

Government departments issue press releases and information circulars through the Department of Information.

Business and financial information

One of the best sources of business and financial information is the *Trade Directory* published annually by the Malta Chamber of Commerce. Other information is obtainable directly from government departments or constituted bodies such as the Malta Chamber of Commerce, the Federation of Industry, the Malta Financial Services Centre, the Malta Stock Exchange, the General Retailers and Traders Union, and the Malta Institute of Management and the Malta Export Trade Corporation (METC).

Of particular interest is an annual publication by the Department of Partnerships (within the Department of Trade), which lists the companies in existence in a particular year, e.g. *Commercial partnerships appearing on the Register on 31/03/96 (indicating companies in liquidation).*

An updated list of companies is maintained on a database. The Department also maintains a list of companies which have been wound up. The memoranda of association and articles together with the file of each company are available for inspection on demand.

Statistics

The *Reports on the working of government departments* published annually by the Department of Information comprises a collection of reports of the performance of the respective departments, including the Ministry of Justice. The report of this Ministry, together with its various departments, usually includes statistics regarding the number of cases disposed of in the courts, prison service statistics and other related figures.

The main source of business statistics giving basic economic and trade indicators is the *Economic Survey* published quarterly by the Department of Information and the *Economic Review of the Maltese Islands* published biannually by the Ministry of Economic Services. The Central Office of Statistics also publishes a compendium of the statistics of the main economic sectors in Malta in an annual publication, *Abstract of Statistics,* as well as other specialized publications containing statistics of specific sectors of the economy (trade, tourism, education, demography, import/export, GNP/GDP, etc.) and which are published regularly every two or three months.

Useful addresses

Associations of lawyers

Camera degli Avvocati (Chamber of Advocates), The Law Courts, Valletta. Tel: +356 248601/223281, ext. 316. Fax: +356 248601

Government organizations

Ministry of Justice and the Arts, Floriana, CMR 02. Tel: +356 244041. Fax: +356 243025

Ministry of Foreign Affairs, Palazzo Parisio, Merchants Street, Valletta CMR 02. Tel: +356 242191. Fax: +356 220494/247229

Ministry for Economic Services, Auberge d'Aragon, Independence Square, Valletta CMR 02. Tel: +356 245391/245380. Fax: +356 233081

Department of Trade (Partnerships section), Malta Financial Services Centre, Attard. Tel: +356 441155. Fax: +356 441188

Department of Information, 3 Castille Place, Valletta CMR 02. Tel: +356 224901 or 250550/60. Fax: +356 237170

The Malta Export Trade Corporation, Trade Centre, San Gwann, SGN 09. Tel: +356 446186

The Malta Stock Exchange, Valletta. Tel: +356 244051. Fax: +356 244071

Law reform bodies

The Law Reform Commission, The Palace, Valletta, CMR 02. Tel: +356 245320/242623. Fax: +356 241874

Courts

The Courts of Justice, Valletta, Malta. Tel: +356 223281. Fax: +356 240458

Education and training

Faculty of Laws, University of Malta, Tal-Qroqq MSD 06. Tel: +356 333998 or +356 3290 2836 or +356 3290 2780

RESEARCH INSTITUTES AT THE UNIVERSITY OF MALTA

European Documentation and Research Centre. Tel: +356 3290 2001 or +356 3290 2998. Fax: +356 337624. E-mail: edrc@cs.uni.edu.mt

International Maritime Law Institute. Tel: +356 310816/319343. Fax: +356 343092

International Ocean Institute. Tel: +356 346528. Fax: +356 346502

Centre for Communications Technology, Law and Information Technology Research Unit. Tel: +356 3290 2781 or +356 3290 2782

Mediterranean Academy of Diplomatic Studies. Tel: +356 483090. Fax: +356 483091

Institute of Forensic Studies. Tel: +356 3290 2268

Institute of Criminology. Tel: +356 3290 2771

Foundation for International Studies, St Pauls Street, Valletta. Tel: +356 234121. Fax: +356 230551

Libraries

The University of Malta Library, University of Malta, Tal-Qroqq MSD 06. Tel: +356 333903. Fax: +356 314306

The National Library of Malta, 36, Old Treasury Street, Valletta, CMR 02. Tel: +356 224338. Fax: +356 235992

The Central Bank Library, Central Bank Annexe, Valletta. Tel: +356 247480. Fax: +356 623051

The EU Directorate Library, EU Directorate, The Palace, Valletta CMR 02. Tel: +356 242580. Fax: +356 240210

The EDRC Library, University of Malta, Tal-Qroqq. Tel: +356 3290 2001 or +356 3290 2998. Fax: +356 337624

Publishers and booksellers

Government Publisher, The Department of Information, 3, Castille Place, Valletta CMR 02. Tel: +356 224901 or 250550/60. Fax: +356 237170

Legal (Publishing) Enterprises, Il-Gnejna, Triq F Castagna, Gudja ZTN 12. Tel: +356 696272

List of works cited

Abstract of Statistics. (1959–) Valletta: Central Office of Statistics

Aquilina, J. (1987) *Maltese–English Dictionary*, Volumes 1 and 2. Valletta, Midsea Books Ltd.

Bank of Valletta Review. (1990–) Valletta: Bank of Valletta Ltd.

Building construction and land laws. (1993–1994) 4 vols. Gudja: Legal (Publishing) Enterprises.

Busuttil, E (1973) Malta. In *The international encyclopedia of comparative law*, Volume 1, pp. M46–51. Tubingen: J.C.B. Mohr (Paul Siebeck).

Code of Police Laws. (1992) Gudja: Legal (Publishing) Enterprises.

Commercial Courier. (1947–) Valletta: Malta Chamber of Commerce.

Commercial partnerships appearing on the Register on 31/03/[96] (indicating companies in liquidation). (Annual) Malta: Ministry of Finance.

Company law, accountancy and other fiscal legislation. Main laws, 1993, 3 vols. Subsidiary legislation, 1994, 3 vols. Gudja: Legal (Publishing) Enterprises in collaboration with the Malta Institute of Accountants.

Cremona, J.J. (1959) *The Malta Constitution of 1835 and its historical background.* Malta: Giov. Muscat.

Cremona, J.J. (1963) *An outline of the constitutional development of Malta under British rule.* Malta: Malta University Press.

Cremona, J.J. (1994) *The Maltese Constitution and constitutional history since 1813.* San Gwann: PEG.

Criminal laws and other laws relating to the Police. (1996) (2 vols). Gudja: Legal (Publishing) Enterprises.

De Bono, P. (1897) *Storia della Legislazione in Malta.* Malta: (no publisher named).

De Giovanni, G. (1983) *Il diritto pubblico del Principato di Malta alla fine del settecento: Lineamenti.* Roma: Unione Nazionale Insegnanti

Decizjonijiet Kostituzzjonali 1964–1978. (1979) Msida: Ghaqda Studenti tal-Ligi.

Decizjonijiet Qorti ta' l'Appell: Sommarji u Indicijiet 1964–1980. (1964–1980) Valletta: l'Awturi.

Decizjonijiet tal-Qrati Superjuri ta' Malta 1789–. (1858–) Valletta: Department of Information. Reprinted (1981–) as *Kollezzjoni ta' Decizjonijiet tal-Qrati Superjuri ta' Malta 1781–.* Gudja: Legal (Publishing) Enterprises.

Decizjonijiet tat-Tribunal ta' l'Arbitragg ghal Malta = Awards by the Malta Arbitration Tribunal 1947–1973. (1949–1983) Valletta: Department of Information.

Dissertations of Doctor of Law up to 1993. (1995) Msida: University of Malta Library.

Dissertations presented for the degree of Doctor of Laws: a classified list 1958–1988 (1988). Msida: Malta University Library.

Economic Review of the Maltese Islands. (1995–) Valletta: Ministry of Economic Services.

Economic Survey. Valletta: Department of Information (quarterly publication).

Farrugia, Riccardo (comp.) (1994–95) *Laws of Malta – Analytical Index of Titles* [in English] Malta: (no publisher named).

Farrugia Randon, Ph. (1993) (ed.) *The word of the court.* Valletta: Mid-Med Bank Ltd.

Forum. Mons, Bajada J. (1990–) (ed.) Valletta: Malta Ecclesiastical Tribunal.

Gabra tas-Sentenzi tat'-Tribunali ta' dawn il-Gzejjer (1995–) Malta: T. De Gaetano.

Ganado, A.(1991) Storja tal-Legislazzjoni ta' Malta. In *Oqsma tal-Kultura Maltija.* Beltissebh: Ministeru ta' l'Edukazzjoni u ta' l'Intern.

Ganado, J.M. (1947) Maltese Law. *Journal of Comparative Legislation and International Law*, 32–*et seq.*

Ganado, J.M. (1950) British Public Law and the Civil Law in Malta. *Current Legal Problems*, 195–213.

Ganado, J.M. (1961) The overseas influence of English Law – Malta. *Solicitor's Journal*, 105, nos.48–49, 1 and 8 December, pp. 999–1001, 1025–1027.

Government departments. (irregular) Valletta: Department of Information.

Government Gazette. (1813–) Valletta: Department of Information.

Harding, H.W. (1980) *Maltese legal history under British rule (1801–1836).* Malta: Royal University of Malta.

Harding, H.W. (1994) History of Maltese Legislation. In *Malta – Culture and Identity*, eds H. Frendo and O. Friggieri, pp. 205–219. Floriana: Ministry for Youths and the Arts.

Indici Decizjonijiet tal-Qrati ta' Malta. (197?–) (3 vols). Msida: Ghaqda Studenti tal-Ligi.

Indici: Qrati, Tribunali u Ligijiet. (1980–) Malta: T. De Gaetano.

Industry today. (1972–) Floriana: Federation of Malta Industries.

Il-Kodici Civili. (1992) Gudja: Legal (Publishing) Enterprises.

Il-Kodici Kriminali. (1992) Gudja: Legal (Publishing) Enterprises.

Il-Kodici Kummercjali. (1992) Gudja: Legal (Publishing) Enterprises.

Il-Kodici ta' l'Organizzazzjoni u Procedura Civili. (1992) Gudja: Legal (Publishing) Enterprises.

Kollezzjoni ta' Decizjonijiet tal-Qrati Inferjuri [1939–]. (1982–) Malta: T. De Gaetano.

Law Reform Commission (1992a) *Law relating to foundations* (Permanent Law Reform Commission Report no.2) Valletta: Malta University Services.

Law Reform Commission (1992b) *Law relating to legal aid* (Permanent Law Reform Commission Report no.1) Msida: Malta University Services.

Laws and legislation relating to tourism (1996) Gudja: Legal (Publishing) Enterprises.

Laws of Malta. (1986 and 1992) Gudja: Legal (Publishing) Enterprises.

Lee, H.I (1973) *Malta 1813–1914: a study in constitutional and strategic development*. Malta: Progress Press.

The legal and court directory 1994/1995. Valleta, Camera degli Avvocati.

Malta Business Weekly. (1994–) Sliema: Standard Publications Ltd.

Malta independent. (1992–) Sliema: Standard Publications Ltd.

Malta national bibliography. (Annual) Valletta, National Library of Malta.

Management Journal (1989–) Valletta: Institute of Management.

Medical and kindred profession (laws and legislation). (1996) (2 vols). Gudja: Legal (Publishing) Enterprises.

Planning appeals decisions. (1995) Gudja: Legal (Publishing) Enterprises.

Reports on the working of government departments. (190?–) Valletta: Department of Information.

Revised edition of the laws of Malta in force on 1st January 1984. (1985) 8 vols and index. Valletta: Law Revision Commission.

Subsidiary legislation for the year . . . (1965–)(Annual cumulation) Valletta: Department of Information.

Subsidiary legislation of Malta [amended up till 31/12/93]. Gudja: Legal (Publishing) Enterprises.

Sunday Times. (1978–) Valletta: Progress Press.

Sunday Times of Malta. (1929–) Valletta, Allied Malta Newspapers.

Sweet & Maxwell's legal bibliography of the British Commonwealth of Nations (1964). pp. 384–394. London: Sweet & Maxwell.

The Times. (1978–) Valletta: Progress Press.

The Times of Malta. (1935–) Valletta: Allied Malta Newspapers.

Trade Directory. (Annual) Valletta: Malta Chamber of Commerce.

United Nations (1947–) *Treaty series*. New York: United Nations.

University of Malta calendar 1994/1995. Tal-Qroqq: University of Malta.

CHAPTER NINETEEN

Netherlands

CHRISTIAN F. VERBEKE

Introduction to the legal system

The history of Dutch law is closely connected with the legal history of its immediate neighbours, Belgium, France and Germany. The division of a historical process into distinct periods is by necessity arbitrary. Most legal authors have however adopted the following phases of the evolution of Dutch law: first, the early Germanic period; second, the Frankish period which spans the 5th to 9th century; third, the Middle Ages, the 9th to the 16th century, or seignorial period, called the 'feodale' or 'landsheerlijke tijdperk'; see Fockema Andreae (1906) *Oud-Nederlandsch Burgerlijk Recht* [early Dutch civil law]. This period is characterized by the emergence of regional and local customary laws.

Fourth, there is the advent of the Republic of the United Netherlands (1581–1795) with William of Orange at its head. The period begins with the key date of 24 July 1581 and the Act of Abjuration which declared forfeit Philip II of Spain's sovereignty over the provinces of Brabant, Flanders, Holland, Zeeland, Gelderland and Utrecht. However, Professor René Dekkers, bibliographer of Dutch–Belgian law, in *Bibliotheca Belgica Juridica* (Dekkers, 1951) rejects the rigour of what he called 'the fatal date of 1581' in distinguishing main currents of early Dutch legal science. An important contribution to the legal history of this phase is de Blécourt (1959) *Kort begrip van het burgerlijk recht* [a concise survey of early Dutch civil law]. A useful modern survey is *Voortgangh des rechtes* [the progress of law] (Gerbenzon and Algra, 1972).

Full independence of the Netherlands from Spain and the German Empire was not confirmed until 1648 with the Treaty of Westphalia. The 15th and 16th centuries saw the reception of Roman law, and its outcome Roman–Dutch law, a term coined by Simon van Leeuwen in the subtitle of his *Paratitula* (or *paratitla) juris novissimi*: 'appendices to single Justinian codification titles edited by a Byzantine jurist' (Van Leeuwen, 1652). 'Rooms Hollands Regt' was expatriated to South Africa with Jan van Riebeeck in 1651 and remains the basis of that country's legal system to this date.

The advent of the Batavian Republic (1795–1806) marks the abolition of feudal privilege and regional power; its first written Constitution was adopted in 1798. Under Napoleonic pressure the Republic was transformed into the Kingdom of Holland (1806–1810) followed by incorporation into the French Empire (1810–1813). Roman–Dutch law was rescinded in 1809 and replaced by the 'Wetboek Napoleon ingerigt voor het Koningrijk Holland', itself replaced outright by the French Code civil on 1 March 1811. Napoleon Bonaparte's demise in 1815 led to the establishment of the Kingdom of the Netherlands under King William I of Orange Nassau. Now a parliamentary democracy under a constitutional monarchy, the Netherlands' legislature, the Staten Generaal, comprises two chambers, the Eerste Kamer [First Chamber], and the directly elected larger Tweede Kamer [Second Chamber], which has the dominant legislative power shared with the former.

The first Dutch Constitution was adopted in 1814 and modified in 1815 resulting from the annexation of Belgium by the Netherlands, with a major revision in 1840 resulting from Belgium's independence in 1830. Further significant constitutional revisions took place in 1848, 1884, 1887, 1917 (universal suffrage), 1922, 1938, 1953, 1956, 1963, and the most recent one of 1987, although further amendments were published in 1995. These revisions with their texts up to 1987 are recorded in Van Hasselt (1987) *Verzameling van Nederlandse Staatsregelingen en Grondwetten*, a collection of all the relevant historical constitutional documents and notes. For the specific study of organic changes in the constitutional text *De grondwet, met aantekeningen* . . ., (*Grondwet* . . ., 1964) called the 'rode grondwet' [the red constitution] is of considerable interest as it prints in red type the latest state of the constitution while earlier versions of articles appear in black type. A modern and comprehensive commentary is by Akkermans and Koekkoek (1992) and also the noteworthy Waaldijk (1991). The Constitution is cited as G or Grw, e.g. *art.57, Grw.1992.*

An English translation of the Constitution with amendments up to 10 July 1995 appears in Flanz (1996). The Direction Communication of the Ministry of Home Affairs also publishes French and German translations.

The treatise in English by Kortmann and Bovend'Eert (1993) *Dutch constitutional law* provides an excellent introduction for law students and also includes the text of the Constitution of 1987 in English. A broader treatment in Dutch by Kortmann (1994) is *Constitutioneel recht.*

Introductory works on the legal system and legal research

The new edition of *Introduction to Dutch law for foreign lawyers* by Chorus, Gerver and Hondius (1993), formerly edited by Fokkema, is a sure guide which takes into consideration major changes in Dutch law since 1978, the year of the first edition. Dated but still useful is Graulich *et al.* (1968) which is not only a guide in English to legal materials but also to the legal system itself. Also in English is the concise chapter by Koopmans (1971).

Gokkel (1981) *Juridische literatuurgids* is a competent guide to the use of legal literature and juridical methodology when used in conjunction with *Data Juridica (1975–)*, a looseleaf current awareness legal bibliography. The intricacies of legal methodology, research and construction for law students are successfully covered by Wessels (1992) *Juridische vaardigheden* [juridical proficiency and skills], a work destined for academic use, which regrettably is not available for other countries or law systems; databases and OPACs are widely covered. A more advanced and complex, albeit indispensable work is Franken (1993–94) *Practicum methoden en technieken*.

Legislation

The primary official source of legislation is the *Staatsblad van het Koninkrijk der Nederlanden*, where statutes and decrees are published in pamphlet form which can total 700 numbers per year; it is commonly referred to as *Staatsblad* (cited as S. or Stb.), published since 1813 with a yearly analytical index of subjects. A microfiche edition of the *Staatsblad* is available. *Nederlandse Staatscourant*, the official gazette of the Netherlands, is a separate publication which has a range of contents including lesser decrees and orders but not the main legislation. A useful retrospective index to the *Staatsblad*, covering the years 1813–1955 is *Van Stockum's Naam en zaakregister* (Audier, 1956) followed by *Klapper op de wetgeving te vinden in het Staatsblad, de Staatscourant, het Tractatenblad* (1955–74). A current index is provided by Editie Schuurman an Jordens described below.

The proceedings of the Eerste en Tweede Kamer [First and Second Chambers] which compose the Staten Generaal [Parliament] are found in the *Handelingen van de Staten Generaal* (1840–). Numbered original draft statutes, verbatim reports, parliamentary commission proposals and government replies are transcribed and yearly and ten-year cumulative indexes are available to access this unwieldy publication.

The most ambitious project in private publishing of the codes and statutes is the Schuurman and Jordens collection *Nederlandse staatswetten editie Schuurman & Jordens* commonly called 'Editie Schuurman en Jordens' and cited as S&J. This massive undertaking which commenced over a century ago and is still in progress has now grown to 215 titles, supplemented and reprinted in new editions as required by changes in the law. Each volume contains all the relevant critical apparatus including digests of cases and extracts from parliamentary proceedings. Quarterly index volumes, registers, are published and are also available in CD-ROM format.

Of major interest is *De Nederlandse Wetboeken* (Fruin, 1940–), commonly referred to as 'Fruin', a compact widely used annual reference work which contains the codes and also selected statutes and international treaties. Equally popular with practitioners is the *Editie Cremers* of the codes published in multi-volume looseleaf format (Cremers, 1951–), whereas the handiest and most economical solution is *Verzameling Nederlandse Wetgeving 1995/96,* cited as VNW, (Alkema, *et al.,* 1996).

Codes and commentaries

Civil Code

The French *Code civil* of 1804 made applicable in the Netherlands in 1811 remained in force until 1 October 1838 when it was replaced by the *Burgerlijk Wetboek*, cited as BW, modelled on the *Code civil* but with a specific national character. *Le droit civil en Belgique et en Hollande de 1800 à 1940* (Van Dievoet, 1948) remains a useful comparative introduction to the history of the Netherlands civil law codification. The Civil Code has been amended numerous times (54 statute modifications between the period of 1838–1948) specially in family law. The concise survey by Cohen Jehoram (1970) *Over codificatie* [on codification] brings its history up to the period of E.M. Meijers, the spiritual father and first draftsman of the New Civil Code, see *Bibliographie der geschriften van Prof. Mr. E.M. Meijers* (Feenstra *et al.*, 1957).

The drafting of the Nieuw Burgerlijk Wetboek or NBW [New Civil Code] began in 1947 and is still proceeding with new sections or 'books' being promulgated when complete while sections of the 1838 code remain in force. A sketch of the 'transitional' civil code is found in Wessels (1990) *Overgangsrecht Nieuw B[urgerlijk] W[etboek] in kort bestek.* Book 1, persons and family, law became effective in 1970, followed in 1976 by Book 2, juridical personality of corporations. It should be noted that Books 3, 5, 6 and 7, property rights, of the New Civil Code only became effective on 1 January 1992. The introduction of Book 4, laws of inheritance and succession, has been postponed for a few years. Book 8, transport and haulage, is also incorporated in the NBW. Book 9 on intellectual property law envisaged by Professor Meijers will likely not be forthcoming soon, if at all. A draft proposal for Book 10 on international private law was published in 1992 by the Ministry of Justice.

A useful current desk edition of the Civil Code, with commentaries of the Nieuw BW, is *Tekst & commentaar Burgerlijk Wetboek* (Nieuwenhuis *et al.*, 1993) while a handy pocket text is van Zeeben (1994) *Burgerlijk Wetboek 1994/1995*.

The Nieuw Burgerlijk Wetboek and its transitional stages and levels (a subject of which the complete history remains to be written) might at first sight appear complicated but fortunately a number of useful aids to the problem have been published. A lucid and concise text explaining the implications of the NBW is *Nieuw Burgerlijk Wetboek: Inleiding*, an introductory supplement by Wessels (1995) which accompanies another edition of the Civil Code, *Burgerlijk Wetboek boek 1 t/m 8, uitgave 1995/1996* (Wessels and Splinter-van Kan, 1995–96).

Wessels explains in his introduction the risks of contradictions and conflicts between the former Burgerlijk Wetboek and the NBW, which must be viewed against the background of the some one hundred rules of the 'overgangsrecht', the transitional laws. The author states unambiguously that even experienced Dutch practitioners do not escape perplexities and confusion. Leading Dutch magistrates have used words such as 'jungle' and 'labyrinthine'. It cannot be stressed sufficiently that foreign jurists, even those thoroughly experienced in the old civil law (BW), must familiarize themselves thoroughly with the full implications of the NBW. For further study an excellent outline is Van Dam and Hondius (1990) *Het Nieuw BW in 400 trefwoorden* [the new civil code in 400 keywords], and in the same vein Zwitser, *NBW in 100 uur* [the NBW in one hundred hours], its arch and time-oriented title notwithstanding, is a most competent introduction.

Wessels also recommends that practitioners plunging straight into the NBW must resist the temptation to bypass the earlier BW. These texts remain available from the standard legal publishers, e.g. Kluwer, Gouda Quint, Tjeenk Willink, and Koninklijke Vermande's *Oud Burgerlijk Wetboek* (Vermandes Wettenreeks, 1993), to name but a few.

Translations of parts of the Civil Code and other codes appear in some of the works described below in **Other reference books**.

Commercial Code

The *Wetboek van Koophandel* [Commercial Code] of 1838, cited as WvK, replaced the French *Code de Commerce* of 1807. Commercial law was considered an extension of the civil law in the Netherlands and numerous subjects related to both the civil and commercial law are not treated in codes but in specific statutes. In 1947 Professor Meijers was appointed to draft a new Civil Code which would incorporate the Commercial Code. This is now largely an accomplished fact as detailed above.

The general conclusion is that commercial law as well as civil law are an integral part of Dutch private law. The difference between the two has grown historically but not in reality and in the NBW the differences have been levelled and the two are merged. This also explains the absence of specific rules for commercial procedure.

A separate edition of the WvK, the commercial code, is found in Cremers (1994) *Wetboek van Koophandel en Faillissementswet.* Additional information on the 'shrinking' of the WvK by the absorption of many of its titles including maritime law into Book 8 and others of the NBW is intelligently set out in de Vries (1994) *Wetboek van Koophandel* [Commercial Code].

Code of Civil Procedure

The French Code de procédure civile of 1806 was replaced in 1838 by the *Wetboek van burgerlijke Rechtsvordering* [Code of Civil Procedure], cited as WBRv. The standard work on the WBRv, as its provisions stand on 1 January 1992, is *Burgerlijke rechtsvordering* (Asser *et al.*, 1995). A compact text is *Compendium van het burgerlijk procesrecht* (Stein, 1994) which encompasses changes since 1992 in particular in divorce proceedings. Civil injunction and provisional order procedure is covered in *Het kort geding* [summary procedure] (Schenk and Blaauw, 1992).

Code of Criminal Procedure

Likewise the French Code d'instruction criminelle [Code of Criminal Procedure] of 1808 was replaced in 1838 by the *Wetboek van Strafvordering*, cited as WvSv, of which the latest edition is *Wetboek van Strafvordering* (Koopstra *et al.*, 1995). Text and commentary on WvSv is provided by *Tekst & Commentaar Wetboek van Strafvordering* (Cleiren and Nijboer, 1994).

Penal Code

The French Penal Code of 1810 remained in force in the Netherlands from 1811 to 1886 when it was replaced with the *Wetboek van Strafrecht*, cited as WvS. The reasons for this long hiatus are set forth in Bosch (1965) *Het ontstaan van het WvS.* [The origin of the Dutch penal code]. The standard text is Koopstra (1995) *Wetboek van strafrecht.* A current work of practice in the criminal courts is Cleiren and Nijboer (1994) *Tekst & Commentaar Strafrecht* [criminal law].

Treaties

From 1951 treaties have been published in *Tractatenblad van het Koninkrijk der Nederlanden* [bulletin of Netherlands treaties], commonly called *Tractatenblad* and cited as Trb., with text translations and consecutive numbering, to which easy access is gained by comprehensive annual indexes covering analytical/chronological tables and country registers. Treaties published before the end of 1950 may be found in *Staatsblad.*

The following specialized publications may be of particular use: Bosmans and Visser (1921) *Répertoire des engagements internationaux* covers the first quarter of the 20th century. Of particular importance is Stuyt (1953) *Repertorium van door Nederland tussen 1813 en 1950 gesloten verdragen* [summary of concluded treaties . . .]. A shorter time frame is covered by the International Intermediary Institute (1926) *Répertoire général des traités et autres actes diplomatiques conclus 1895–1920.* Of considerable historical interest is *Recueil des traités et conventions conclus par le royaume des Pays-Bas avec les puissances étrangères depuis 1813 à nos jours* (Lagemans and Breukelman, 1858–1915). For advanced legal research in international law of the Netherlands, two works, vastly broader in scope, appear unavoidable: Myers (1922) *Manual of collections of treaties* and Molhuysen and Oppenheim, *Catalogue. Bibliothèque du Palais de la Paix* (1916–61), both of which give worldwide coverage but the latter is particularly rich in Dutch materials.

Law reports, judgments

Case law [*rechtspraak* or *jurisprudentie*] (and jurisprudence in French) in the Netherlands legal system, its manifest importance notwithstanding, is not a binding or compulsory source of the law. This was laid down formally in the *Wet houdende algemene bepalingen betreffende de wetgeving van het Koninkrijk* [Law concerning the general provisions of legislation of the Kingdom] of 1829. Decisions of the Hoge Raad [High Court of Justice] although not binding are generally followed by the lower jurisdictions. Law reports, of which no official collections are published, are thus important sources in legal research.

Current unofficial collections are headed by *Nederlandse Jurisprudentie* (1913–) which consists of weekly reports on High Court decisions and lower court civil and criminal cases, the latter two categories are also published separately. Access to this series is provided by quarterly indexes, the NJ-Kaartsystem [jurisprudential card index] for interfiling by subscribers and JURIDISCHE DATABANK [judicial database] on CD-ROM. Selected decisions, especially on widely covered articles of the codes, are available in the so-called 'Kaartenboekjes' [card booklets] divided into series. A wide range of periodicals on particular areas of law publish reports of decisions.

Hoge Raad [High Court] weekly reports of the most important decisions are found in *Rechtspraak van de Week*, annotated, with a biyearly index. *Rechtspraak van de Week*, published since 1939, originally in conjunction with *Nederlands Juristenblad* which is now published as a general law journal. Specific retrospective High Court decisions 1843–1903 are found in *Verzameling van arresten van den Hoogen Raad* (Van den Honert, 1904).

Important general retrospective collections include *Luttenberg's Chronologische verzameling*, a composite compilation generally covering 1830 to 1950 consisting in part I of the statutes and decrees, in part II of High Court, administrative and lower court decisions since 1813, cited as 'Luttenberg'. Decisions for the period 1839–1935 are found in the *Weekblad van het Recht* (1839–1941), a weekly covering cases in the civil, criminal and administrative courts. Access is by an annual alphabetical subject index which must be supplemented by the use of *Léon's Rechtspraak*, a digest of case law which includes bibliographical material (described under **Bibliographies** below).

Computer-based systems

INFORMATIERIJK. The Executive of the Netherlands (all departments and ministries), the Tweede Kamer der Staten Generaal and the Foreign Office's databanks are available on one CD-Rom from Koninklijke Vermande.

NLEX. The data bank Nederlandse Wetgeving [Dutch legislative database], an initiative of the law publishers Koninklijke Vermande, records integral legislative texts, administrative directives, ministerial decisions, and all laws effective in the Netherlands.

JURIDISCHE DATABANK [judicial database] on CD-ROM comprises both case law and bibliographical data, published by Tjeenk Willink.

NESTOR (Netherlands Educational Scientific Titles for Online Retrieval). A national database containing all scientific publications in print, a project in which all law publishers collaborate.

PARAC (Parlementair Automatiserings Centrum) provides parliamentary documents and law texts; this database is only accessible to official bodies but this includes Dutch universities.

PICA (Project Geïntegreerde Catalogus-automatisering) is a central databank providing an online national union catalogue produced by a collective of libraries part of the Wetenschappelijke en Speciale Bibliotheken [scientific and special collections libraries] group. Although a general catalogue of printed books, the holdings in legal literature are considerable. The system is run via the Koninklijke Bibliotheek (KB) in The Hague.

WET-DISK Burgerlijk Wetboek. The NBW (new civil code), the transitional laws, and code of civil procedure on diskette published by Koninklijke Vermande in cooperation with Van Rensch Advocaten.

A useful Internet site is at http://www.evr.nl/frg/English/fol.html provided by the Faculty of Law at the Erasmus University, Rotterdam.

Encyclopedias, large collections

There is no equivalent of the *Pandectes belges* or the *Novelles*, the massive Belgian encyclopedic works, in Dutch legal literature. A major exposition of the civil law is Asser (1967–83) *Handleiding tot de beoefening van het Nederlands Burgerlijk recht* [manual of civil law practice]. This comprehensive encyclopedic undertaking, known as the *Asser Serie*, began its first edition in 1878. Although cited as Asser, it has been continued by a collective of specialists in multiple editions of its various volumes. It deals with the civil code texts, case law, doctrine and legal history. Its indispensable continuation *Asser Actueel* [Asser update] is published three times per year in five editions, each one belonging to the original Asser series subject manuals.

Directories

The leading administrative and judicial directory is *Gids voor de rechterlijke macht* (Berger-Wiegerinck, 1995), a massive looseleaf manual with names, addresses, telephone and fax numbers (when known). Names of magistrates, lawyers, notaries and bailiffs are recorded in the greatest detail for each jurisdiction, as well as the different courts and tribunals with local Bar Associations. Also covered are regional and municipal structures, tax exempt institutions, foundations, trusts, higher education institutions, and museums.

The Groep Juridische Bibliothecarissen, Documentalisten en Literatuuronderzoekers [law librarians, documentalists and bibliographers], cited as GJB, publishes a very useful directory of law collections in the Netherlands, *Gids van Juridische Collecties in Nederland* (Groep Juridische . . ., 1990).

Bibliographies

Legal bibliography of the Netherlands presents at first sight a confusing array of interwoven retrospective legal bibliographies, law collection catalogues and current bibliographies. It is this very abundance which makes the prior consultation of the standard bibliographies of law bibliographies and law bibliographies proper an imperative before engaging in any legal history research project. To mind come: Stollreither (1955) *Internationale Bibliographie der juristischen Nachslagewerke*, an ambitious albeit dated reference work whose only drawback to the uninitiated might be the dispersal of materials by category rather than by law system throughout the work, a bibliographic configuration for which the author, perhaps justifiably, has been severely criticized, see Goedan (1992) *International legal bibliographies*, pp. 253–4. Besterman (1971) *Law and international law, a bibliography of bibliographies*, with all its faults, remains indispensable. Lansky (1987) *Bibliographical handbook on law* has a chapter on 'Netherlands', pp. 299–306, which contains much useful information; the text is in German with some French and English abstracts.

A useful starting point remains *Bibliotheca Belgica Juridica* (Dekkers, 1951), which should be used for the period after 1800 with *Bibliografische inleiding . . . negentiende eeuw* [bibliographic introduction to Dutch law history of the 19th century] (Brüggemann and Coppens, 1985). The transition to modern law is accomplished by the use of Nijhoff (1874) *Bibliotheca juridica, 1837 [to] 1873* and *Législation et codification dans les Pays-Bas* (Nijhoff, 1902–04). Another valuable transitional law bibliography is Van Oppen and Sasse (1884–85) *Nederlandsche rechtsliteratuur*. Although essentially a digest of case law, *Léon's Rechtspraak* (1848–1938) contains exhaustive law bibliographies and literature reviews.

An essential but overlapping current bibliography is *Repertorium van de nederlandsche jurisprudentie en rechtsliteratuur* (1878–1944), continued by the much lamented *Klapper op de rechtspraak en de rechtsliteratuur* (1952–87) and the earlier publication *Overzicht van de rechtspraak, rechtsliteratuur, administratieve beslissingen* [overview of jurisprudence, legal literature and administrative decisions] (1926–52). These now defunct series are continued by the current *Data juridica* (1975–) which indexes over 120 journals; it is also available in electronic form as the DATA JURIDICA databank or DJ. Literature surveys can also be found in *Nederlands juristenblad* (1925–).

Important information about the publications of the leading legal history and research institutions in the Netherlands (and in other countries), is found in *Repertorium Bibliographicum Institutorum* (Feenstra, 1980).

Indexing and abstracting services

The periodical indexing service *Data juridica* is described above. Particularly useful is *Overzicht recent verschenen tijdschriftenartikelen*, an index with abstracts of some 150 Dutch and foreign law reviews available from the Ministry of Justice, law serials division.

Dictionaries

Boele-Woelki and Van der Velden's *Nederlandse Rechtsbegrippen vertaald: Frans–Engels–Duits* [Dutch legal concepts translated into French, English, German] (1992) is placed intentionally at the head of this section in view of its manifest usefulness. This is in fact the one indispensable reference work which should be present in any Dutch law collection for foreign use.

Dictionnaire des termes juridiques en quatre langues (Le Docte, 1988) is a widely used translating legal dictionary in four languages, French, Dutch, English, German. A more recent Dutch (Nederlands) work is Moors (1991) *Dictionnaire juridique Français–Néerlandais, Néerlandais–Français*, which should be used with some caution as Dutch legal terminology can be vastly different from Belgian/Flemish legal phraseology. This applies also to other similar dictionaries reviewed in the chapter on Belgium. The problems of definition and interpretation of contracts drafted in English, subject to Dutch law, are illustrated in Drion (1994) *Subject to the laws of the Netherlands*, a work based on Hoge raad [High Court] guidelines.

Leliard (1991) *Gerechtelijke terminologie* [legal terminology], although essentially a Belgian reference work, can be used with the *caveat actor* cited in the preceding paragraph. This useful and specialized word list of Dutch–French civil procedure and administration of justice terms is frequently encountered in Dutch law collections.

A Dutch language dictionary and essential starting point for historical legal research is Fockema Andreae (1981) *Rechtsgeleerd handwoordenboek* [juridical dictionary] and his *Juridisch woordenboek* (Fockema Andreae, 1993).

Latin remains inextricably linked with continental legal science and the Netherlands is no exception. A recent lexicon fills this need: De Koninck (1993) *Glossarium*. Equally important is Ankum and Hartkamp (1985) *Romeinsrechterlijk handwoordenboek* [Latin for lawyers], of which a new edition is in preparation.

Other reference books

For the Anglo-American legal practitioner intending to practise law in the Netherlands, an excellent concise introduction in English is *Dutch legal culture* (Blankenburg and Bruinsma, 1994); the work surveys aspects of Dutch legal culture, the legal profession, the civil law, penal and public law practice.

There is a wide range of books in English on aspects of law in the Netherlands. The rules of Dutch civil evidence in English are displayed in Hebly (1992) *The Netherlands Civil Evidence Act 1988*. In English, the provisions of the Dutch law of estates can be found in Haanappel and Mackaay (1990) *New Netherlands civil code: patrimonial law (property, obligations, and special contracts)* and Book 8 of the new Civil Code on transport is translated into English and French by the same authors in 1995. An authorized translation into German of several books of the new Civil Code has appeared edited by Nieper and Westerdijk, Book 2 (1995a), Books 6, 7 and 7a (1995b) and Books 3, 4 and 5 (1996). Administration of justice in the Netherlands is covered by *Wet op de rechterlijke organisatie* (Ende, 1995). A concise survey of Dutch criminal justice is found in Tak (1993) *Criminal justice systems in Europe: the Netherlands.*

Also in English *Dutch business law* (Schuit, Zeevenboom and Romijn, 1989), updated by looseleaf pages, unravels the intricacies of Dutch commercial law; another work is Hoyng, Roelvink and Schlingmann (1991). In this context *Netherlands arbitration law* may be useful (Van den Berg, Van Delden and Snijders, 1993). An English translation of the new Dutch Patent Act officially approved by the Dutch Patent Office has been produced by the consultants Nederlandisch Octrooibureau (1995). Information needs on Dutch labour laws in English are covered by *Labour law in the Netherlands* (Jansen, 1994), a concise guide. Dutch computer law in English is covered by Schmidt (1994) and international telecommunications by Hins and Hugenholtz (1988). *Private international law in the Netherlands* (Van Rooij and Valentijn, 1987) is also worthy of mention.

Current information sources

Journals, research reports

Reports in English on Dutch judicial decisions involving private international law are provided in *Netherlands International Law Review* (1953–). Dutch private law and notarial decisions are covered in the weekly *Weekblad voor privaatrecht, notariaat en registratie* (1975–), cited as WPNR. The *Advocatenblad* (1918–) is an influential journal published by the national bar association. *THEMIS Rechtsgeleerd Magazijn* (1840–), *Rechtskundig Weekblad* (1931–) and *Nederlands Juristenblad* (1925–) all carry current material. As described above, *Data Juridica* (1975–) indexes over 120 journals, mainly Dutch with some English language titles on European law, and all are listed with the publisher's name and address.

News information

Nederlandse Staatscourant, the official journal of the Netherlands, broad in its objective news coverage, judicial news, publishes everything not published in the *Staatsblad.*

Business and financial information

A wide range of information on economic and financial affairs is available from the 'Economische Voorlichtingsdienst' [economic intelligence unit] van het Ministerie van Economische Zaken. Economic planning and forecasts information can be obtained from Centraal Planbureau. Also useful is the *Financieel Memo* (1996), a financial yearbook.

Statistics

The Centraal Bureau voor de Statistiek publishes the annual *Statistisch Jaarboek* of which an edition in English is available and the quarterly *Netherlands Official Statistics*.

Useful addresses

Associations of lawyers

Nederlandse Orde van Advocaten [Netherlands Bar Association], Houtweg 60, Postbus 30851, 2500 GW The Hague, Netherlands. Tel: +31 70 342 9191. Fax: +31 70 365 1909

Practizijns Sociëteit [Law Society], Parnassusweg 222, Postbus 84500, 1080 BN Amsterdam, Netherlands. Tel: +31 20 541 2112. The society functions essentially as a study group on new legislation and has a library

Government organizations

Centraal Bureau voor de Statistiek [Central Statistical Office], CBS Voorburg, Prinses Beatrixlaan 428, postbus 959, 2270 AZ Voorburg, Netherlands. Tel: +31 70 337 3800. Fax: +31 70 387 7429. One of two offices, see below.

Centraal Bureau voor de Statistiek [Central Statistical Office], CBS Heerlen, Kloosterweg 1, postbus 4481, 6401 CZ Heerlen, Netherlands. Tel: +31 45 706000. Fax: +31 45 727440. General information telephone number for both institutions +31 45 707070 and for access to the comprehensive reference library.

Centraal Planbureau [Central planning office], Van Stolkweg 14, 2585 JR The Hague, Netherlands. Tel: +31 70 351 14151

Economische Voorlichtingsdienst [Economic Intelligence Unit] van het Ministerie van Economische Zaken, Bezuidenhoutseweg 151, 2594 AG The Hague, Netherlands. Tel: +31 70 381 4111

Ministerie van Binnenlandse Zaken [Ministry of Internal Affairs], Documentatie en Bibliotheek, Schedeldoekshaven 100, 2500 EA The Hague, Netherlands. Tel: +31 70 371 6637

Ministerie van Buitenlandse Zaken [Foreign Office], Research and Documentation Centre, Bezijdenhoutseweg 67, Postbus 20061, 2500 EB The Hague, Netherlands. Tel: +31 70 348 4028. Fax: +31 70 348 4848. Of central importance for its online research services: RCC data bases, Kluwer Datalex, Celex, SCAD, Dialog, Profile, Echo, Agralin, FAO, IDRIS, UNBIS, UNSIS, UNPRESS and its free, open access.

Ministerie van Financiën [Ministry of Finance], Library and Documentation Centre. Korte Voorhout 7, Postbus 2021, 2500 EE The Hague, Netherlands. Tel: +31 70 342 6226

Ministerie van Justitie [Ministry of Justice], Central Library and Documentation Centre, Schedelhoekshaven 100, 2500 EA The Hague, Netherlands. Tel: +31 70 370 6934/35. Has three major legal research libraries.

Tweede Kamer der Staten-Generaal [Parliament], Bibliotheek en Documentatie, Binnenhof 1A, 2513 AA The Hague, Netherlands. Tel: +31 70 336 14911

Law reform

See Practizijns Sociëteit above under Associations of Lawyers.

Courts

Hoge Raad der Nederlanden [the Supreme Court], Kazernestraat 52, Postbus 20303, 2500 EH The Hague, Netherlands. Tel: +31 70 361 1180. The Library is at this address.

Raad van State [Council of State], Kneuterdijk 22, Postbus 20019, 2500 EA The Hague, Netherlands. Tel: +31 70 624 871. The library of the highest administrative jurisdiction of the land established in 1533 comprises one of the largest administrative and public law collections.

Education and training

Rijksuniversiteit Leiden, Faculteit der Rechtsgeleerdheid, Juridisch Studiecentrum Gravensteen, Pieterskerkhof 6, Postbus 9501, 2300 RA Leiden, Netherlands. Tel: +31 71 277 448.

Rijksuniversiteit Utrecht, Faculteit der Rechtsgeleerdheid, Janskerkhof 3, 3512 BK Utrecht, Netherlands. Tel: +31 30 393 089. Fax: +31 30 393 073. The Juridische Bibliotheek is at this address.

Research institutions

Stichting tot bevordering der Notariële Wetenschap [foundation for the study of notarial science], Herengracht 278, 1016 BX Amsterdam, Netherlands. Tel: +31 20 262 574

T.M.C. Asser Instituut, Alexanderstraat 20–22, Postbus 30461, 2500 GL The Hague, Netherlands. Tel: +31 70 342 0300. Fax: +31 70 342 0359. The Institute library is at this address.

Libraries

Libraries are noted with institutions listed above.

Koninklijke Bibliotheek, Prins Willem Alexanderhof 5, Postbus 90407, 2509 LK The Hague, Netherlands. Tel: +31 70 314 0911. Fax: +31 70 3140 0450

Nederlandse Orde van Advocaten (see address listed under Associations of Lawyers above). The Library of the Bar specializes in ethics of the legal profession and advocacy.

Wetenschappelijk Onderzoek- en Documentatie Centrum (WODC), Ministerie van Justitie, Schedeldoekhaven 100, 2500 EH The Hague, Netherlands. Tel: +31 70 370 6553

Publishers and booksellers

Koninklijke Vermande b.v., Platinastraat 33, 8211 AR Lelystad/Postbus 20, 8200 AA Lelystad, Netherlands. Tel: +31 320 237777. Fax: +31 320 226334. The only law publishers to apply an integral publishing on demand system. All publications are available in the format and number selected by the client, i.e. CD-Rom, looseleaf, printed paperback, hardback or online access, as Vermande's entire published list of titles is coded in SGML, the Standardized Generalized Markup Language.

M.I.C.R.O., Microfiche Informatie Centrum Rijks Overheid, Fluwelen Burgwal 18, 2511 CH The Hague, Netherlands. Tel: +31 70 335 0015. Publishers of microfiche editions of *Handelingen*, *Staatsblad*, *Staatscourant*, and other parliamentary publications.

NESTOR-Secretariaat, Plein 26, 2511 CS The Hague, Netherlands. Information from Marga ter Borgt, Information Officer, Tel: +31 70 361 7183

Staatsdrukkerij [Government Printers], sdu/uitgeverij, Christoffel Plantijnstraat 2, 2515 TZ The Hague, Netherlands. Tel: +31 70 378 9911. Fax: +31 70 378 9783 (specific number for law publications).

Uitgeverij Kluwer b.v., Postbus 23, 7400 GA Deventer, Netherlands. Tel: +31 5700 47111. Fax: +31 5700 31419

Wolters Kluwer Rechtswetenschappen b.v., (same address as above) which via the consolidated catalogues in the *Algemeen Register* gives access to the following well-known legal imprints: Uitgeverij FED, Gouda Quint b.v., W.E.J. Tjeenk Willink. Tel: +31 5700 47066. Fax: +31 5700 27771

List of works cited

Advocatenblad. (1918–) The Hague: Nederlandse Orde van Advocaten. 24 issues per year. Subscriptions: Tjeenk Willink.

Akkermans, P.W.C. and Koekkoek, A.K. (1992) (eds) *De Grondwet, een artikelgewijs commentaar* 2nd edn. Zwolle: Tjeenk Willink.

Algemeen Register 1995/1996. (1995) Deventer: Wolters Kluwer Rechtswetenschappen bv.

Alkema, E.A. *et al.* (1996) (eds) *Verzameling Nederlandse Wetgeving 95/96.* Lelystad: Koninklijke Vermande.

Ankum, J.A. and Hartkamp, A.S. (1985) *Romeinsrechterlijk handwoordenboek* 2nd edn. Zwolle: Tjeenk Willink. New edn in preparation.

Asser, C. (1967–83) *Handleiding tot de beoefening van het Nederlands Burgerlijk recht.* Zwolle: Tjeenk Willink. 11 vols; multiple editions and editors in the current set; updated by *Asser Actueel.*

Asser, W.D.H. *et al.* (1995) *Burgerlijke rechtsvordering.* Deventer: Kluwer. 6 vols. Looseleaf. 12 contributors.

Audier, J.A. (1956) (ed.) *Van Stockum's Naam en zaakregister op de Nederlandse wetgeving 1813–1955.* The Hague: Nijhoff.

Berger-Wiegerinck, M.F.M. (1995) (ed.) *Gids voor de rechtelijke macht en het rechtswezen in het Koninkrijk der Nederlanden.* Deventer: Gouda Quint bv. 2 vols.

Besterman, Theodore (1971) *Law and international law, a bibliography of bibliographies.* Totowa, NJ: Rowman & Littlefield.

Blankenburg, E. and Bruinsma, F. (1994) *Dutch legal culture* 2nd edn. Deventer: Kluwer.

Boele-Woelki, K. and Van der Velden, F.J.A. (1992) *Nederlandse Rechtsbegrippen vertaald: Frans–Engels–Duits* [Dutch legal concepts translated into French, English, German]. The Hague: Asser Institute.

Bosch, A.G. (1965) *Het ontstaan van het Wetboek van Strafrecht.* Zwolle: Tjeenk Willink.

Bosmans, C.J.E. and Visser, M. (1921) *Répertoire des engagements internationaux au XXe siècle concernant les Pays-Bas.* The Hague: Nijhoff.

Brüggemann, G.W.F. and Coppens, E.C. (1985) *Bibliografische inleiding in de Nederlandsche rechtsgeschiedenis van de negentiende eeuw.* Zutphen: De Walburg Pers.

Chorus, J.M.J., Gerver, P.H.M. and Hondius, E.H. (1993) *Introduction to Dutch law for foreign lawyers* 2nd edn. Deventer: Kluwer.

Cleiren, C.P.M. and Nijboer, J.F. (1994) *Tekst & Commentaar Strafrecht, Wetboek van Strafrecht en enkele aanverwante wetten en regelingen.* Deventer: Kluwer.

Cleiren, C.P.M. and Nijboer, J.F. (1994) *Tekst & Commentaar Wetboek van Strafvordering, en enkele aanverwante wetten en regelingen, voorzien van commentaar.* Deventer: Kluwer.

Cohen Jehoram, H. (1970) *Over codificatie; van Portalis to na [E.M.] Meijers* 2nd edn. Deventer: Kluwer.

Cremers, W.A.M. *et al.* (1951–) (eds) *Editie Cremers* [of the Codes and Statutes]. Gouda: Quint. Multi-volume, looseleaf, kept up to date by supplements; different codes began publication in looseleaf form at different dates; originally published from various dates beginning with Wetboek van Strafordering in 1951.

Cremers, W.A.M. (1994) *Wetboek van Koophandel en Faillissementswet*. In Cremers, W.A.M. *et al.* (1951–).

DATA JURIDICA (available from Kluwer).

Data juridica: documentatie van juridische literatuur. (1975–) Ed. by J.N.Troost-Boland *et al.* Deventer: Kluwer. Quarterly.

de Blécourt, A.S. (1959) *Kort begrip van het Oudvaderlands burgerlijk recht* 7th edn. by H.F.W.D. Fisher. Groningen: Wolters. [Reprint] with a bibliographic suppl. by J.A. Ankum, 1967.

De Koninck, Constant (1993) *Glossarium van latijnse en romeinse rechtstermen*. Brussels: Bruylant.

De Vries, L. (1994) *Wetboek van Koophandel* [Commercial Code]. Zwolle: Tjeenk Willink.

Dekkers, René (1951) *Bibliotheca Belgica Juridica, een bio-bibliographisch overzicht der Rechtsgeleerdheid in de Nederlanden tot 1800*. Brussels: Royal Flemish Academy of Letters.

Drion, C.A. (1994) *Subject to the laws of the Netherlands*. Deventer: Kluwer.

Ende, P. (1995) *Wet op de rechterlijke organisatie*. Lelystad: Koninklijke Vermande.

Feenstra, Robert *et al.* (1957) *Bibliographie der geschriften van Prof. Mr. E.M. Meijers*. Leiden: Universitaire Pers.

Feenstra, Robert (1980) *Repertorium bibliographicum institutorum et sodalitatum iuris historiæ*. Leiden: E.J. Brill. For the Association internationale d'Histoire du Droit et des Institutions.

Financieel Memo (1996). Deventer: Kluwer. Annual.

Flanz, Gisbert H. (1996) Kingdom of the Netherlands. In *Constitutions of the countries of the world*, ed. A.P.Blaustein and G.H.Flanz, vol.XIII. Dobbs Ferry, NY: Oceana.

Fockema Andreae, S.J. (1906) *Het Oud-Nederlandsch burgerlijk recht* [the early Dutch civil law]. Haarlem: Tjeenk Willink. 2 vols.

Fockema Andreae, S.J. (1981) *Rechtsgeleerd Handwoordenboek*. Alphen aan den Rijn: Tjeenk Willink.

Fockema Andreae, S.J. (1993) *Juridisch woordenboek*. Alphen aan den Rijn: Samson.

Franken, H. (1993–94) *Practicum methoden en technieken: werkmateriaal, 4e druk. Practicum II, 3e druk.* Deventer: Gouda Quint bv. Vol.1 currently in 4th edn, 1994, vol.2 currently in 3rd edn, 1993.

Fruin, J.A. (1940–) *De Nederlandse Wetboeken*. Zwolle: Tjeenk Willink. Annual.

Gerbenzon, P. and Algra, N.E. (1972) *Voortgangh des rechtes, de ontwikkeling van het Nederlands recht* 3rd edn. Groningen: Tjeenk Willink.

Goedan, J.C. (1992) *International legal bibliographies, a worldwide guide and critique*. Ardsley-on-Hudson, NY: Transnational Publishers.

Gokkel, H.R.W. (1981) *Juridische literatuurgids* 3rd edn. Zwolle: Tjeenk Willink.

Graulich, Paul *et al.* (1968) *Guide to foreign legal materials: Belgium, Luxembourg, Netherlands*. Dobbs Ferry, NY: Oceana.

Groep Juridische Bibliothecarissen, Documentalisten en Literatuuronderzoekers (1990) *Gids van Juridische Collecties in Nederland*. Duivendrecht: Stichting De Prom.

De Grondwet met aantekeningen van de gelijksoortige bepalingen van vroeger tijd bij elk artikel. (1964) Zwolle: Tjeenk Willink.

Haanappel, Peter P.C. and Mackaay, E. (1990) *The Netherlands civil code: patrimonial law (property, obligations, and special contracts)*. Deventer: Kluwer Law and Taxation.

Haanappel, Peter P.C. and Mackaay, E. (1995) *New Netherlands Civil Code/Nouveau Code civil néerlandais. Book 8 means of transport/Livre 8 des moyens de transport et du transport*. Deventer: Kluwer Law International.

Handelingen van de Staten Generaal. (1840–) The Hague: Staten Generaal. Appears in two series: *Het verslag der Handelingen van de Tweede Kamer* and *Het verslag der*

Handelingen van de Eerste Kamer generally known as the *Handelingen*; much material appears as 'bijlagen' [supplements] to the main publication.

Hebly, Jan M. (1992) *The Netherlands Civil Evidence Act 1988 and related provisions of the Netherlands law of evidence*. Deventer: Kluwer Law and Taxation.

Hins, Wouter and Hugenholtz, Bernt (1988) *The law of international telecommunications in the Netherlands*. Baden-Baden: Nomos.

Hoyng, Willem, Roelvink, Julie and Schlingmann, Francine (1991) *The Netherlands: practical commercial law*. European Commercial Law Series. London: Longman.

INFORMATIERIJK (available from Koninklijke Vermande).

International Intermediary Institute (1926) *Répertoire général des traités et autres actes diplomatiques conclus 1895–1920*. Haarlem, The Hague: I.I.I.

Jansen, Ernst P. (1994) *Labor law in the Netherlands*. The Hague: Kluwer International.

JURIDISCHE DATABANK (available from Tjeenk Willink).

Klapper op de rechtspraak en de rechtsliteratuur. (1952–87) Zwolle: Tjeenk Willink.

Klapper op de wetgeving te vinden in het Staatsblad, de Staatscourant, het Tractatenblad (1955–74) Zwolle: Tjeenk Willink.

Koopmans, Thijmen (1971) The Netherlands. In *International encyclopedia of comparative law*, ed. V. Knapp, vol.1, N11–N28. Tübingen: J.C.B. Mohr.

Koopstra, W. *et al.* (1995) *Wetboek van strafrecht*. Lelystad: Koniklijke Vermande.

Koopstra, W. *et al.* (1995) *Wetboek van Strafvordering*. Lelystad: Koninklijke Vermande.

Kortmann, C. (1994) *Constitutioneel recht*. Deventer: Kluwer.

Kortmann, C. and Bovend'Eert, P. (1993) *The kingdom of The Netherlands. An introduction to Dutch constitutional law*. Deventer: Kluwer.

Lagemans, E.G. and Breukelman, J.B. (1858–1915) *Recueil des traités et conventions conclus par le royaume des Pays-Bas avec les puissances étrangères depuis 1813 à nos jours*. The Hague: Belinfante. 18 vols.

Lansky, Ralph (1987) *Bibliographisches Handbuch der Rechts- und Verwaltungswissenschaften*. Band I. Allgemeines und Europa. Frankfurt am Main: Vittorio Klostermann.

Le Docte, Edgard (1988) *Dictionnaire de termes juridiques en quatre langues* [French, Dutch, English, German]. Antwerp-Apeldoorn: Maklu.

Leliard, J.D.M. (1991) *Gerechtelijke terminologie Nederlands – Franse lijst van termen en uitdrukkingen uit het burgerlijk procesrecht en de rechtelijke organisatie*. Antwerp-Apeldoorn: Maarten Kluwer. Also French edition: (1991) *Terminologie judiciaire*, id.

Léon's Rechtspraak. (1848–1938) The Hague: Belinfante, later Leiden: Sijthoff, etc. 80 vols.

Luttenberg, G. (1899–1950) *Chronologische verzameling der wetten, besluiten, betreffende het openbaar bestuur in de Nederlanden sedert . . . 1813*. Zwolle: Tjeenk Willink. 27 plus index vols.

Meijers, H. (1959) *Repertorium van de Sociale Wetenschappen, Rechtswetenschap*. Amsterdam: Elsevier.

Molhuysen, Philip Christiaan and Oppenheim, E.R. (1916–61) *Catalogue de la Bibliothèque du Palais de la Paix*. Leiden: A.W. Sijthoff. Original catalogue in 1916 by Molhuysen and Oppenheim, supplements with others.

Moors, J. (1991) *Dictionnaire juridique Français–Néerlandais, Néerlandais–Français*. Brussels: Bruylant.

Myers, Denys P. (1922) *Manual of collections of treaties*. Cambridge, Mass.: Harvard University Press.

Nederlandisch Octrooibureau (1995) *The new Dutch Patent Act*. The Hague: Kluwer Law International.

Nederlands Juristenblad. (1925–) Zwolle: Tjeenk Willink.

Nederlandse Jurisprudentie. (1913–) Zwolle: Tjeenk Willink. Available in a variety of formats, i.e. on index cards for interfiling, in looseleaf and bound volumes.

Nederlandse Staatscourant. (1814–) The Hague: Ministry of the Interior. Daily; microfiche edition also available.

Nederlandse staatswetten editie Schuurman & Jordens. Ed. by M.D. van Wolferen *et al.* Zwolle: Tjeenk Willink. Publication dates vary; about 250 vols each supplemented and issued in a new edition as its subject requires. Also: *Registers editie Schuurman & Jordens. Alfabetisch trefwoordenregister; Chronologisch register per deel; Overzicht van wetten*. (1995) Zwolle: Tjeenk Willink. An annual suite of indexes also available as: *Register Schuurman & Jordens CD-ROM*: (1995) Deventer: Schuurman & Jordens.

NESTOR (available from NESTOR-Secretariaat).

Netherlands International Law Review. (1953–) The Hague: Kluwer International Law. 3 issues per year.

Netherlands Official Statistics. (1985–) The Hague: Sdu/uitgeverij for the Centraal Bureau voor de Statistiek (CBS). Quarterly.

Nieper, F. and Westerdijk, A.S. (1995a) (eds) *Niederländisches Bürgerliches Gesetzbuch. Buch 2: Juristische Personen*. The Hague: Kluwer Law International.

Nieper, F. and Westerdijk, A.S. (1995b) (eds) *Niederländisches Bürgerliches Gesetzbuch. Buch 6: Allgemeiner Teil des Schuldrechts; Bücher 7 und 7A Besondere Verträge*. The Hague: Kluwer Law International.

Nieper, F. and Westerdijk, A.S. (1996) (eds) *Niederländisches Bürgerliches Gesetzbuch. Buch 3: Allgemeiner Teil des Vermögensrechts; Buch 4: Erbrecht; Buch 5: Sachenrecht*. The Hague: Kluwer Law International.

Nieuwenhuis, J.H. *et al.* (1993) (eds) *Tekst & commentaar Burgerlijk Wetboek*. Deventer: Kluwer. 3 vols.

Nijhoff, Martinus (1874) *Bibliotheca juridica. Catalogus van alle boeken sedert 1837 in het Koninkrijk der Nederlanden verschenen over staatswetenschappen, wetgeving en rechtsgeleerdheid*. The Hague: M. Nijhoff.

Nijhoff, Martinus (1902–04) *Législation et codification dans les Pays-Bas*. The Hague: M. Nijhoff. Vol.1: avant 1795; vol.2: 1795–1904.

NLEX (available from Koninklijke Vermande).

Overzicht van de rechtspraak, rechtsliteratuur, administratieve beslissingen [overview of jurisprudence, legal literature and administrative decisions]. (1926–52) Zwolle: Tjeenk Willink.

Overzicht recent verschenen tijdschriftenartikelen. (current) The Hague: Ministry of Justice, Law Serials Division.

PARAC (available from Koninklijke Vermande bv).

PICA (available from the Koninklijke Bibliotheek).

Rechtskundig Weekblad. (1931–) Antwerp: Maklu.

Rechtspraak van de Week. (1939–) Zwolle: Tjeenk Willink. Originally appeared as a supplement to *Nederlands Juristenblad*.

Repertorium van de nederlandsche jurisprudentie en rechtsliteratuur. (1878–1944) s'Hertogenbosch: van Heuseden. Continued by: *Klapper op de rechtspraak en de rechtsliteratuur* (1952–).

Schenk, W. and Blaauw, J.H. (1992) *Het kort geding* 5th edn. Deventer: Kluwer.

Schmidt, A.H.J. (1994) (ed.) *Information technology and the law in the Netherlands*. Lelystad: Koninklijke Vermande.

Schuit, Steven R., Zeevenboom, G.H. and Romijn, M. (1989) *Dutch business law* 3rd edn. The Hague: Kluwer International Law. Looseleaf with twice yearly updates.

Schuurman & Jordens. See: *Nederlandse staatswetten editie Schuurman & Jordens*.

Staatsblad van het Koninkrijk der Nederlanden. (1813–) The Hague: Ministry of Justice. Entitled *Staatsblad de Nederlanden* from 1813–15. Irregular.

Statistisch Jaarboek. (1996) The Hague: Sdu/uitgeverij for the Centraal Bureau voor de Statistiek (CBS). Also an edition in English, (1996) *Statistical yearbook of the Netherlands*.

Stein, P.A. (1994) *Compendium van het burgerlijk procesrecht* 10th edn. Deventer: Kluwer.

Stollreither, Konrad (1995) *Internationale Bibliographie der juristischen Nachschlagewerken*. Frankfurt am Main: Vittorio Klostermann.

Stuyt, A.B. (1953) *Repertorium van door Nederland tussen 1813 en 1950 gesloten verdragen*. The Hague: Nijhoff.

Tak, Peter J.P. (1993) *Criminal justice systems in Europe: the Netherlands*. The Hague: Kluwer.

THEMIS Rechtsgeleerd Magazijn. (1840–) Zwolle: Tjeenk Willink. 10 issues yearly.

Tractatenblad van het Koninkrijk der Nederlanden. (1951–) The Hague: Staatsdrukkerij.

Van Dam, C.C. and Hondius, E.H. (1990) (eds) *Het Nieuw BW in 400 trefwoorden: gids bij het hanteren van de Boeken 3 t/m 7 NBW* [the new civil code in 400 keywords . . .] 2nd edn. Deventer: Kluwer.

Van den Berg, A.J., Van Delden, R. and Snijders, H.J. (1993) *Netherlands arbitration law*. Deventer: Kluwer Law and Taxation.

Van den Honert, J. (1904) (ed.) *Verzameling van arresten van den Hoogen Raad der Nederlanden*. Amsterdam: Veen. Covers 1843–1903.

Van Dievoet, Émile (1984) *Le droit civil en Belgique et en Hollande de 1800 à 1940, les sources du droit*. Brussels: Bruylant.

Van Hasselt, W.J.C. (1987) *Verzameling van Nederlandse Staatsregelingen en Grondwetten* 17th edn. Alphen: Samson.

Van Leeuwen, Simon (1652) *Paratitula juris novissimi. Dat is: een kort begrip van het Rooms Hollands regt. . . .* Leiden: Pieter Leffen.

Van Oppen, L.J. and Sasse, J.C. (1884–86) *Nederlandsche rechtsliteratuur*. The Hague: Belinfante. 5 parts.

Van Rooij, René and Valentijn, Maurice (1987) *Private international law in the Netherlands*. Deventer: Kluwer.

Van Zeeben, C.J. (1994) (ed.) *Burgerlijk Wetboek 1994/1995, Boek 1 t/m 8 incl. Overgangswet*. Deventer: Kluwer.

Vermandes Wettenreeks (1993) *Oud Burgerlijk Wetboek*. Lelystad: Koninklijke Vermande.

Waaldijk, C. (1991) *Grondwet*. Lelystad: Koninklijke Vermande.

Weekblad van het Recht. (1839–1941) The Hague: Nijhoff.

Weekblad voor privaatrecht, notariaat en registratie. (1975–) The Hague: Koninklijke Notariële Broederschap. Weekly; distributed by Koninklijke Vermande. Originally entitled: *Weekblad voor privaatrecht, notaris-ambt en registratie* (1870–1974).

Wessels, B. (1990) *Overgangsrecht Nieuw B[urgerlijk] W[etboek] in kort bestek*. Lelystad: Koninklijke Vermande.

Wessels, B. (1992) *Juridische vaardigheden* 5th edn. Deventer: Kluwer.

Wessels, B. (1995) *Nieuw Burgerlijk Wetboek: Inleiding*. In Wessels and Splinter-van Kan (1995–96).

Wessels, B. and Splinter-van Kan, H.A.G. (1995–96) *Burgerlijk Wetboek boek 1 t/m 8 uitgave 1995/1996*. Lelystad: Koninklijke Vermande.

WET-DISK Burgerlijk Wetboek (available from Koninklijke Vermande).

Zwitser, R. (n.d.) *NBW in 100 uur*. Deventer: Gouda Quint.

CHAPTER TWENTY

Norway

PÅL A. BERTNES

Introduction to the legal system

Historical points

Norway became one kingdom at the end of the 9th century. Earlier the country consisted of several regional kingdoms, each with its own legal system. A proper administration of justice based on law took place at the *Althing*, which was a public meeting, representative of the rural community or the larger community units.

From the middle of the 10th century the *Lagting* was established. It consisted of representatives from all regions, chosen among men of proven wisdom. The *Lagting* had legislative, executive and judiciary power within its section of the realm. Gradually the *Lagrett* was developed. It was constituted of selected members of the *Lagting* and functioned as a court.

In the 12th century written laws appeared. The oldest codifications of law known to us date from the 12th and 13th centuries, the so-called *landsskapslovene* or regional laws. In 1274 King Magnus Lagabøte (Magnus the Law Mender) compiled and revised the regional law codifications, called *Landslov*, which became the national codification of law. The *Landslov* bears the name of the king. The corpus of the law created by King Magnus Lagabøte remained the governing law for more than 400 years.

The King had legislative power even before this was officially established in the *Landslov*. This continued during Norway's union with Denmark from 1380. In 1604 a revised version of the National Codification of Law was translated from Old Norse to Danish and renamed (King) Christian IV's Norwegian Law. This law incorporated most of the provisions issued by previous kings.

In 1687 Norway was given a new comprehensive codification of law in Christian V's Norwegian Law, which introduced Danish rules of law to a considerable extent. It was, however, only slightly influenced by the legal concepts of Roman law, which was to such a marked degree reflected in the legislation of many other countries. Some of the provisions of Christian V's Norwegian law still remain in force.

The Norwegian legal system has primarily developed from national roots, as in the other Nordic countries. However, there has been some influence from other countries. The governing ideas behind the Norwegian constitution were largely the result of influence by English and French political philosophers (Locke, Montesquieu and Rousseau). As to British and American law their influence is mainly limited to criminal procedure and to criminal remedies.

Constitution

Norway adopted its own Constitution at Eidsvoll in 1814 and established its own parliament, the Storting, in 1815. The underlying reason was the renunciation by the King of Denmark/Norway of all his rights to the Norwegian kingdom in favour of the King of Sweden. Norway opposed the union with Sweden and section 1 of the Norwegian Constitution provides that 'The Kingdom of Norway is a free, independent and indivisible realm'. Norway had, however, to submit to a union with Sweden, but as a sovereign nation. In 1905 the union with Sweden was dissolved by the Storting and a new independent Norwegian kingdom was declared in 1907. The European Economic Area (EEA) Agreement was incorporated into Norwegian law in November 1992 and EC directives are implemented by Acts passed by the Norwegian parliament or by government regulations.

The Constitution of 17 May 1814, as amended, appears at the front of *Norges Lover* (1994); a Norwegian text and a translation into English as amended to 29 May 1990 can be found in Flanz (1993) together with a chronology of recent constitutional developments and a bibliography; a translation as amended to June 1988 is in Risa (1993). The Constitution, with amendments and a commentary in English is in Andenæs and Wilberg (1987).

The courts of justice

The historical development of the court system is too diverse to be addressed here. It is important to notice, though, that one year after Norway became an independent constitutional monarchy in 1814, the Supreme Court [Høyesterett] was established as the Constitution provided (the Supreme Court was previously situated in Denmark).

Simply expressed there are three judicial authorities within the Norwegian court system: first, the County Court as court of the first instance; second, the High Court or Crown Court; third, the Supreme Court as court of the last instance. In special cases a case may be referred directly to the High Court due to its grave nature.

The courts' role as law makers began at the end of the 18th century. Later a law was passed which required the Supreme Court to publish written decisions setting forth the reasoning underlying its decisions and also its voting. In 1926 another law was passed which allowed a case to be dealt with in plenary session if two or more judges felt that a case might be decided in a way that would conflict with previous decisions. Even though grounds for judgment are thus published, they are considerably briefer than what is common in Germany and especially in the USA. Even so the Norwegian Supreme Court's decisions have a relatively substantial legislative effect. It is unlikely that a court that has rendered a judgment in one case will reach an inconsistent result in a later case.

The Norwegian hierarchy of legal norms

Norway is a unitary state. In spite of The EEA Agreement, the Norwegian legal system can still be regarded as a hierarchy of norms. The highest level is represented by the Constitution of 17 May 1814. Statute law is adopted pursuant to the Constitution and is consequently subordinate to the Constitution according to the 'Lex Superior' principle. Regulations adopted pursuant to a statute are subordinate to such law.

Introductory works on the legal system and legal research

The major introductory work on the legal system is *Knophs oversikt over Norges rett* [Knoph on Norwegian Law] (Knoph, 1993), a comprehensive book with many authors each dealing with the main points in an area of law. *Innføring i juss* contains advice on methods of studying, legal theory and a summary of certain areas of law (Boe, 1993). *Innføring i rettstudiet* (Andenæs, 1994), *Rettskildelære* (Eckhoff, 1993) and *Rettskilder* (Fleischer, 1995) are all theoretical works in Norwegian with primary emphasis on the relative importance of the various sources of law.

In English there are some minor publications and also some articles. One of the most recent articles is *The Norwegian legal system: an introductory guide* (Hagelien and Vonen, 1993), also published separately in 1994. The Ministry of Justice has published *Administration of justice in Norway* (1980). There is a chapter in the *Modern legal systems cyclopedia* with the title 'The legal system of Norway' (Risa, 1993) and a more dated but valuable chapter on Norway in the *International encyclopedia of comparative law* (Lødrup, 1972). Several projects are in progress to meet the demand for English-language legal literature from foreign students under the ERASMUS program and students at summer schools held by the Faculty of Law, University of Oslo.

Praktisk rettskildelære. Juridisk kildesøking i Norge, øvrige nordiske land og EF [Practical textbook on sources of legal information. Legal information retrieval in Norway, the other Nordic Countries and the EEC] (Bertnes and Kongshavn, 1992) describes and evaluates legal literature and sources of law and also provides guidance on how to perform legal research by the use of both printed and electronic sources. Birger Stuevold Lassen has written *Presentasjon av rettsvitenskapelige arbeider på norsk* (Lassen, 1993). In English there are articles by Bertnes (1993), 'Sources to legal information in Norway' and by Aarbakke and Helgesen (1982) 'Sources of law in Norway'.

Legislation

Acts or statutes

There are two official periodic publications of statute law. According to special statute *Norsk Lovtidende* (1877–) must include new statutory law and resolutions about when laws come into force, their abolition and their scope. *Norsk Lovtidende* is published twice a month and is the publication necessary to keep updated regarding statutory law, regulations, tax resolutions, and so forth. *Norsk Lovtidende* is divided into two parts: Avd.I [Part 1] contains statutory law and central regulations, while Avd.II [part 2] contains regional and local regulations. In addition to annual indexes, cumulative quarterly indexes are published. The *Norsk Lovtidende* also contains an index of regulations authorized under each statutory provision. Members of the civil service in Norway may receive *Norsk Lovtidende* without payment, others subscribe with Grøndahl and Dreyer's Forlag (publishers).

The public authorities also publish *Lover: vedtatt på det . . . ordentlige storting* at the end of each annual session of parliament with the formal text of new statute laws and amendments to old laws. The publishers Grøndal/Dreyer produce the most used statutes separately as offprints.

The most frequently used and most comprehensive Norwegian collection of laws is *Norges Lover*, privately published by the Faculty of Law in Oslo. It is produced every two years in one heavy volume and contains both a subject and an alphabetic index. The Constitution of 1814 forms the first part, then follows what still applies of King Christian V's Norwegian law from 1687; the rest of the statutes in force are arranged chronologically according to the date they were adopted. Amendments are incorporated into the existing statute with a reference to the amending statute in a footnote. Since 1992 a supplementary volume has been published containing laws passed during the intervening year between main editions. *Norges Lover* has official status and is used by lawyers and judges; with an edition of more than 40 000 copies, this is one of the 'best sellers' in Norway.

In 1994 a new collection of laws in force with commentary, *Karnov. Norsk kommentert lovsamling*, appeared in three volumes and a comprehensive index volume. The index volume contains a chronological index of all statutes in Karnov, an alphabetical index based on the abbreviated titles of the statutes with reference to the standardized abbreviations of the separate statutes. There is an index of the reported court decisions and criminal judgments mentioned in the commentaries. Pamphlet supplements will be published when required and a new edition of the code will be published every two years. The 196 authors include scientists, solicitors, judges and other prominent Norwegian lawyers who have all contributed to this achievement. The model is the Danish Karnov's code of laws which has been published since the 1930s. Karnov's code of laws is much more expensive than *Norges lover* and the first edition was issued in about 3000 copies.

The supplier of the text to both of the above mentioned codes of laws is LOVDATA, the semi-official legal information database in Norway. By agreement with the authorities LOVDATA receives the text of the statutes as soon as they are passed and consequently always has the best updated electronic code of laws in Norway. Institutions and individuals may obtain access to LOVDATA for a fee (see below).

Very few statutes are translated into other languages. Some may be found in the somewhat antiquated *Norwegian laws etc. selected for the foreign service* (Ministry of Foreign Affairs, 1980). Over the years some statutes have been translated into English, some by the Foreign Office department of translations, some by other offices and a few by private organizations. None of them, however, has the status of public translations and they are seldom published. The library at the Foreign Office and the Faculty of Law Library in Oslo have endeavoured to collect all the translations they can find. Attempts are being made to make them available in a database. The Faculty of Law Library in Oslo is conducting an experimental project by making certain translated statutes available at http://www.ub.uio.no:80/ujur/text/uten/lov.html on the Internet.

Norwegian laws are referred to by their titles and date. If more than one law is passed on a certain date, which often occurs, each law gets a number in addition e.g. *Lov om arv m.m. av 3. mars 1972 nr.5* (Law of inheritance of 3 March 1972 no.5). Sometimes the law's abbreviated title is used, with or without the date and number, e.g. *Arveloven av 3. mars 1972 nr.5,* (The inheritance law of 3 March 1972 no.5), or just *Arveloven*. Authors often use abbreviations and the above-mentioned law would then be referred to just as *al.* Such abbreviations are usually listed. To trace an abbreviation one may use the index to Karnov (1994) or to Lassen (1993). *Norske lovtitler. Fortegnelse over lover trykt i Norges Lover 1685–1993* (Strømø, 1994) is primarily addressed to the Norwegian library world. It gives a chronological survey of laws with full titles and Dewey library classification numbers, systematically arranged and with an index of abbreviated law titles. This information is also available within the database system of the University of Oslo Library, TRIP, under the name LOV.

Regulations

Regulations issued by the central administration as authorized by statute are called *forskrifter* [provisions] and are published in *Norsk Lovtidende*. A regulation [forskrift] is referred to by its title and the date it was passed. *Norges forskrifter* (1989–) is a collection of regulations in nine volumes where all valid regulations from the 17 ministries should be found; a new edition is being planned. In addition there are special collections which contain laws, regulations and circulars within limited legal fields. LOVDATA receives regulations from all the ministries which issue regulations and is responsible for editing *Norsk Lovtidende*. LOVDATA contains all regulations in force, always updated and available to subscribers.

In addition selections are published in specialist periodicals, e.g. *K-kontakt* published by Konkurransetilsynet [Competition Inspectorate] (1994–). Konkurransetilsynet (1994) has also published a compilation of current regulations in the area of competition, *Konkurranseregler for foretak i EØS. Regelsamling*, with extracts from the Agreement on the European Economic Area and its protocols.

Legislative history

The legislative history of statutes contained in various preparatory documents may give useful guidance in the process of interpretation. When a statute is published in *Norsk Lovtidende* references are made to the documents that constitute the preparatory work for the statute.

The reports of committees or commissions appointed to look into the need for a new law and give recommendations about its contents are usually published as 'NOU' in a special publication series *Norges offentlige utredninger* (1972–), previously entitled *Innstillinger og betenkninger* (1935–72), with regular cumulative indexes. Indexes to all NOUs and reports since 1814 are found in a special microfilm edition called *Norske utredninger 1814–1986* (1987).

After consultation on the committee's report, the responsible ministry prepares a proposition with its underlying motives, which the government presents to the Storting as a bill called an *Odelstingsproposisjon* (proposition to the *Odelsting*, abbreviated: Ot.prp.) and is the basis for further discussions in the Storting. The *Odelstingsproposisjon* and the documents from the discussions are published in the publication series *Stortingsforhandlinger* (1814–), which is a comprehensive parliamentary series in nine volumes containing bills, white papers and documents from most areas of government. It also contains the minutes of the debates in the Storting.

The preparatory documents of Norwegian statutory law are assembled in *Forarbeid til lovene* (Ministry of Justice, 1897–). This collects the Storting documents regarding laws: *Odelstingsproposisjoner* (Ot.prp.), recommendations to the *Odelsting*, the debates in the *Odelsting* and in the *Lagting*, in addition to the preparatory work for the law, today mainly the NOUs.

Codes and commentaries

The codes of laws in Norway give the date of a statute according to the year it was originally passed, so the most important statutes often have dates from long ago. This does not mean that Norwegian law making is less updated. Amendments are usually integrated into the text of existing statutes; only when comprehensive changes are made does the legislature choose to pass a complete new statute simultaneously abolishing the old.

In certain areas of law separate committees are continually working on law revision efforts. In other areas special committees are appointed to prepare propositions for concrete amendments. The Law Section at The Ministry of Justice is the authority which is responsible for the administration of the law revision work.

The most important statutes within civil procedure are: Tvistemålsloven av 13. august 1915 nr.6 [the Code of Civil Procedure]; Tvangsfullbyrdelsesloven av 26. juni 1992 nr.86 [the Enforcement Code]; and Domstolloven av 13. august 1915 nr.5 [the Courts Code]. In the field of criminal law: Straffeloven av 22. mai 1902 nr.10 [the Penal Code] and Straffeprosessloven av 22. mai 1981 nr.25 [the Code of Criminal Procedure]. Among other important statute laws are: Kjøpsloven av 13. mai 1988 nr.27 [the Sale of Goods Code]; Avtaleloven av 31. mai 1918 nr.4 [the Code on Contracts]; Forvaltningsloven av 10. februar 1967 [the Code of Administrative Procedure]; and Skatteloven av 18. august 1911 nr.8 [the Tax Code].

It has long been common practice to publish special editions with detailed commentaries to specific statutes. This practice may continue despite the appearance of *Karnov. Norsk kommentert lovsamling* with commentaries on all statutes in force. Since Norway is a small country, it is a substantial undertaking to produce a thorough commentated edition to the most important statutes. The most competent among the judges and legal scholars are chosen and the editions may get grants from various funds. They seldom have competitors and each edition is a great authority on its area. For less important statutes and those concerning trades and industries there will be competing editions, often tailormade for certain occupational groups or industries. The publishers Ad Notam/Gyldendal have started to publish many commentaries to statutes called *Norsk lovnøkkel. Lovkommentarer i lommeformat* [Key to Norwegian laws. Commentaries to laws in a nutshell]. There are no updated commentary editions translated into English.

Treaties

In order to find which treaties Norway has entered into, the chief reference work is *Norges traktater 1661–* [Norwegian treaties 1661–] (Ministry of Foreign Affairs, 1967–88), a collection of treaties in five volumes, the fifth being an important index. The texts appear chronologically in Norwegian and in the original language. *Overenskomster med fremmede stater* [Treaties with foreign governments] (Ministry of Foreign Affairs, 1879–) publishes international treaties on an ongoing basis. From time to time the most important treaties are collected and issued, e.g. *Folkerettslige tekster: samling med opplysninger til studiebruk* [Texts pertaining to international law: a collection of information for students] (Møse, 1991). *Nordisk statuttsamling* [Scandinavian body of statutes] (1970–) is published by the Nordic Council every third year and contains texts concerning cooperation between the Nordic countries. *Norske skatteavtaler* (Sanfelt, 1987) contains all tax agreements that Norway has entered into with foreign countries.

Law reports, judgments

As previously mentioned, court decisions play an important role among the legal sources in Norway, especially decisions of the Supreme Court. Most of the decisions of the Supreme Court are published twice per month in *Norsk Retstidende* (1836–), nearly all in extenso, with the dissenting opinions where appropriate. Extracts of decisions made by the Supreme Court's Committee on Appeals are also published here. The editor, Hans Stenberg Nilsen, provides headnotes and Pål A. Bertnes is responsible for comprehensive annual and five-year indexes. The Norwegian Bar Association edits *Norsk Retstidende*, abbreviated Rt, in cooperation with the Supreme Court of Norway and it is considered to be the official record of the Supreme Court decisions.

Supreme Court decisions are referred to by publishing year and first page of the decision e.g.: Rt 1994 s.1063 (s is the abbreviation for the

Norwegian 'page'). The decisions also have reference numbers, e.g. no.113 B/1994 for the above decision, and a publisher's reference number in brackets, e.g. for the same decision: [338–94]; neither reference is much used.

As to decisions by subordinate courts; the county courts, high courts and crown courts, only a selection is reported in *Rettens Gang* (1933–), abbreviated RG, also published by the Norwegian Bar Association twice per month. Citation is in the form: *RG 1994 s. 334*; in scholarly publications the name of the court or its abbreviation is often added.

When referring to unpublished legal decisions, one should state the name of the court, the date of the judgment and the case number. With this information, a copy of the decision can usually be obtained from the court for a fee.

There are ways to search for decisions other than the indexes of Rt and RG. In *Juridisk oppslagsbok* [Legal reference book] (Bertnes, Kongshavn and Eckhoff, 1993) an index of legal key words gives references to various sources, including judgments published in Rt and RG. *Lov og Dom* (Høgh, 1990a, 1990b and 1992) is a cumulative index to decisions in *Norsk retstidende* 1836–1968 and 1969–1988 and in *Rettens Gang* 1933–1989 by statute and specific section of statute.

LOVDATA has Supreme Court decisions in full text from 1945 onwards and headnotes of decisions of the courts of first instance published in RG from 1945 onwards. Since the beginning of the 1990s LOVDATA has received the decisions from the courts of first instance electronically and made them available in full text as well.

In addition to the main series above there are special collections of decisions such as *Dommer og kjennelser av arbeidsretten* (1916/17–) and *Dommer, uttalelser m.v. i skattesaker og skattespørsmål* (1922–). *Nordisk Domssamling* (1958–) contains selected decisions from the Nordic countries and *Nordiske domme i sjøfartsanliggender* (1900–) contains Nordic decisions based on maritime law.

Administrative practice

The practice of the public administrative agencies and their decisions are often referred to and relied on by the courts. This applies especially with tax legislation, so *Dommer, uttalelser m.v. i skattesaker og skattespørsmål* (1922–) is much used. The annual report from the Ombudsman is another publication of the practice of the public administration (it appears as Document no 4 in volume 5 of *Stortingsforhandlingene*). The Ministry of Justice, Law Section, annually publishes a collection of legal interpretations: *Lovavdelingens Uttalelser* (Matheson and Woxholth, 1990–).

Private practice

Today the practice of private people does not play the same dominant part as in former times. Private practice is still a source of law and in certain areas it carries a lot of weight, e.g. commercial law other than contract law and in relation to usufruct. Some private conflict solving bodies publish their decisions such as Avkortningsnemnda [Committee of reduction concerning reductions in insurance cases] (1990), Forsikringsskadenemnda [Committee of Insurance Damages] (1992–) and Bankklagenemnda [Complaints Board for consumers in banking and finance matters] (1988/89–). Decisions from the last two committees are also available in LOVDATA.

Computer-based systems

LOVDATA [Law data]

LOVDATA is an independent foundation which cooperates with the public authorities to make a legal information system available which is well updated and contains several of the most important printed sources of law in Norway as noted above under **Legislation** and **Law reports**. The system carries material from public authorities and other publishers.

LOVDATA contains several online databases: NORLEX contains Norwegian sources of law, among others court decisions, statutes and regulations and legal literature; NORIM contains NORLEX, CELEX and EEA-documents; PETROLEX contains NORLEX plus information on petroleum.

Price examples at the time of writing: NORLEX costs NKr500 for regular monthly subscription and a searching fee of NKr3 per minute. The price for storing of texts is NKr1 per 1000 characters. The subscription price for NORIM is NKr700. LOVDATA also publishes a CD-ROM, NORLEX CD, which contains the same legal information as the online database NORLEX, price NKr8000. For further information about LOVDATA see their home page at: http://www.lovdata.no on the Internet.

Through Statens Datasentral one may obtain access to several public databases containing public indexes, documents from the Storting, the government and ministries.

Encyclopedias

In Norway there are no common collective works of legal sources as we know from other countries. The most comprehensive is *Karnov. Norsk kommentert lovsamling*, described above under **legislation**, which contains statute laws with commentaries to each section with mention of the most important court decisions and the index gives a whole range of possibilities for finding current sources.

Samfunnsboka (Statens informasjonstjeneste, 1982–) is a concise but encyclopedic work published every two years which states the law affecting various areas of society and gives practical instructions on how to proceed, including current addresses and telephone numbers.

Directories

The Norwegian Bar Association has published *Aktive medlemmer av Den Norske Advokatforening 1993* (Norske Advokatforening, 1993) listing practising members of the Association. The *Norges Statskalender* is the annual official yearbook and contains a survey of institutions and individuals with a separate name index. The universities and other educational institutions in Norway also appear. The *Telefonkatalogen. Departementene og Forvaltningstjenesten* [Telephone directory for the Ministries] is published annually and includes information on the separate government ministries, their departments and individuals in charge, with telephone numbers and the addresses of the separate offices.

Hvem svarer på hva i Staten (Statens informasjonstjeneste, 1956–) leads the reader to the department responsible for a particular matter. *Samfunnsboka* (Statens informasjonstjeneste, 1982–), described above, also acts as a directory.

Bibliographies

General bibliographies

The *Guide to Nordic bibliography* (Munch-Petersen, 1988) is a descriptive guide in English which covers all the Nordic countries.

Norsk bokfortegnelse [the Norwegian National Bibliography] is the most comprehensive bibliographic tool (Universitetsbiblioteket i Oslo, 1870–). National bibliographic registration covers the period from 1814 to the present day. The database of the University of Oslo Library UBO:BOK contains among other things references to Norwegian books from 1971 onwards. The database is available online and also as a CD-ROM with the title NASJONALBIBLIOGRAFISKE DATA.

Norsk Samkatalog (Norwegian union catalogue) is an important aid in the world of Norwegian research libraries. It registers foreign books in about 350 cooperating Norwegian libraries from 1939; from 1988 on Norwegian professional books and periodicals are included. It is to be found online in UBO:BOK (http://www2.nbo.uio.no/ubobok/uboboknor.html) with the title SAMBOK and as a CD-ROM. Among more than 40 databases of the University of Oslo Library, some are of special interest to lawyers, e.g. JURHOPP with a survey of students' theses at the Faculty of Law in Oslo and LOVTITLER, a survey of Norwegian law titles.

BIBSYS is the name of the common electronic library system used by universities and higher education institutions in Norway. Besides being an automated library management system, the online catalogue, with approximately 1.8 million records is an excellent help with reference work, particularly since it has been connected to the Internet for searching on World Wide Web (http://www.bibsys.no/search/pubn.html).

Law bibliographies

Among the many international bibliographies of law which cover Nordic law, two need to be mentioned. For older literature the *Scandinavian legal bibliography* (Iuul, Malmstrøm and Søndergaard, 1961) is useful. A more recent international bibliography is volume 1 of *Bibliographisches Handbuch der Rechts- und Verwaltungswissenschaften* (Lansky, 1987).

In Norway there is no general Norwegian law bibliography, only one covering the years 1962–1966 (Haukaas, 1967a). The Faculty of Law Library in Oslo is, however, working on a legal bibliography covering the period after 1945. Nordic legal literature is frequently used and Sweden, Finland and especially Denmark have enviable publications in this field. There exists, however a small special bibliography, *Norwegian legal publications in English, French and German up to 1965* (Haukaas, 1967b) supplemented for 1966–1977 (Haukaas, 1977). The *International Journal of Legal Information* has published a bibliography of Nordic legal literature written in English, German, French and Italian 1982–1992 (Haider, 1993). *Juridisk oppslagsbok* (Bertnes, Kongshavn and Eckhoff, 1993) is a tool with strong elements of a bibliographic nature, where the main part consists of references to books and articles.

Publikasjonsliste fra Storting og Regjering is a current list of publications from the Norwegian Parliament and the Ministries which is published monthly.

Praktisk rettskildelære [Practical textbook on sources of legal information] (Bertnes and Kongshavn, 1992), described above, not only surveys and evaluates sources of legal information and methods of legal research but also contains a full list of suggested reading. The list is arranged alphabetically and systematically and is the bibliography in its field.

Bibliographies on the works of individuals which may be found in Festschriften, give easy access to relevant literature. Halvor Kongshavn has prepared a bibliography on the contents of Norwegian Festschriften (Kongshavn, 1991, 1994). He has also published *A bibliography of articles in non-Scandinavian languages 1963–1993 in Norwegian festschriften* (Kongshavn, 1994).

An extensive bibliography on tax law covers the period after 1945 (Selberg, 1990).

In connection with the twenty-fifth anniversary of the Faculty of Law at The University of Bergen, a bibliography was prepared of the legal writings of faculty members (Jacobsen, 1994).

LOVDATA has a separate legal literature data base with bibliographic information received from the National Library and the Faculty of Law Library in Oslo. BIBJURE is an electronic library system with a database of legal literature developed especially for Norwegian lawyers. The database has 10 000 bibliographic records, mainly Norwegian and Nordic books, and about 3000 Norwegian legal articles, the professional legal part of which was prepared by Pål A. Bertnes. Because of the system's powerful retrieval capabilities BIBJURE is an interesting tool when searching for legal literature. The most important courts of law and firms of lawyers in Norway have adopted the system.

Indexing and abstracting services

Until 1995 the Norwegian National Library was part of the University of Oslo Library. Here a selection of Norwegian periodicals, including the most important legal periodicals, is indexed. The index to articles is made available both as a publication *Norske tidsskriftartikler* (*NOTA*) (Universitetsbiblioteket i Oslo, 1981–) and online on the file NOTA of UBO:BOK and as part of the national bibliographic CD-ROM mentioned above. The literature file of LOVDATA includes the index entries for law articles from *NOTA*. BIBJURE analyses legal periodicals and seeks to cover all legal articles in periodicals, festschriften and anthologies in Norway. For the period 1966–1979 we lack easy access to the literature in Norwegian periodicals. Prior to 1966 *Norsk tidsskriftindex* (1919–1966) covers the field fairly well.

Juridisk oppslagsbok is published in one volume: part I – Civil law and part II – Administrative law (Bertnes, Kongshavn, and Eckhoff, 1993). This reference book is arranged alphabetically by keywords and provides references to literature, books and papers, and also laws and legal practice, i.e. reported decisions. *Juridisk oppslagsbok* deals with civil law and administrative law, not criminal law, tax law, constitutional law or procedural law.

Dictionaries

The only recent legal dictionary in Norway is *Juridisk leksikon* (Gulbransen, 1994) which gives short explanations of some Norwegian legal terms. In English there is the *Anglo-Scandinavian law dictionary of legal terms used in professional and commercial practice* (Anderson, 1977). A specialist dictionary for international contract terminology in Norwegian, English and French is *Leksikon om internasjonale kontrakter: med norsk, engelsk og fransk terminologi* (Rigault, 1992).

There are a few other dictionaries which may help foreign lawyers: *Fransk–norsk juridisk oppslagsbok = Lexique juridique Franco-Norvégien* (Fife, 1991), *Franske fagtermer: fransk–norsk/norsk–fransk ordbok* (Schlyter, Nordli and Hustad, 1987), *Deutsch–Norwegisches Juristisches Wörterbuch* (Simonnæs, 1985) and *Forsikringsordbok: Norsk–engelsk/Engelsk-norsk* [Insurance dictionary: Norwegian–English/English–Norwegian] (Lind, 1989).

Lately some new dictionaries have been published to assist Norwegian lawyers in making interpretations into other languages. These dictionaries with English–Norwegian indexes may also be of interest to foreigners: in contract law *Norsk–engelsk juridisk ordbok: kontraktsrett* (Craig, 1992), in criminal law and procedure *Norsk–Engelsk Juridisk ordbok. Strafferett, straffeprosess og andre termer* (Chaffey and Walford, 1992), in civil and criminal law *Norsk–engelsk juridisk ordbok. Sivilrett og strafferett* (Lind, 1992), *Norsk–Engelsk økonomisk ordbok* [Norwegian–English economic dictionary] (Aagenæs, 1993), *Norsk–engelsk administrativ ordbok* [Norwegian–English administrative glossary] (Chaffey, 1988) and *Norsk–tysk juridisk ordbok* [Norwegian–German legal dictionary] (Simonnæs, 1994).

Current information sources

Journals, research reports

The Norwegian Bar Association publishes *Advokatbladet* (1985–), with information on activities of lawyers and their associations and short articles about recent legislation and significant court decisions. The publication also contains a separate section of news concerning sources of law. The other important association Norges Juristforbund [Norwegian Association of Lawyers], publishes *Juristkontakt* (1967–). Besides information about the association it contains some relatively short scholarly articles. Both publications are issued monthly and are important sources for keeping up to date. *Lov og Rett* (1962–), abbreviated to LoR, is a general law publication whose authors are mostly academic lawyers, practising lawyers or judges. *Tidsskrift for rettsvidenskap* (1888–), abbreviated to TfR, is a Nordic publication issued in Norway which is considered more theoretical and contains long scholarly articles and a large number of book reviews of Nordic legal literature.

The separate departments of the different faculties of law at the universities in Oslo, Bergen and Tromsø all issue separate monograph series. The series *Marius* (1975–) from the Scandinavian Institute of Maritime Law and *Complex* (1981–) from the Centre for Computers and Law, both under the Faculty of Law in Oslo, have many contributions written in English.

Business and financial information

In Norway there are several types of business indexes. *Norges Handelskalender* is published annually and contains a survey of business firms, arranged according to trade with addresses and some statistics. *Kompass* in its printed, CD-ROM and online versions and Kierulf's annual *Håndbok* are other sources to find information about firms, agencies, and their products and services. Otherwise, the Export Council of Norway is the office to approach to contact Norwegian firms. The Council has an EU information office which answers inquiries concerning Norway's harmonization with the EU, following the EEA agreement, and adjustment to the internal market. The Ministry of Industry has within its remit to answer questions about the legal aspects of trades and industries, e.g. oil, gas and petroleum activities. The Confederation of Norwegian Business and Industry also renders information services.

Statistics

The main supplier of statistics in Norway is the Statistisk sentralbyrå [Central Bureau of Statistics]. It issues weekly, monthly and annual statistics including law and legal institutions, trade and business. The statistics are written with both Norwegian and English text. In 1994 the 119th statistical yearbook appeared containing 550 tables and both contents and detailed index in English and Norwegian. The Bureau has issued a separate *Guide to Norwegian statistics* (Statistisk sentralbyrå, 1980–).

Useful addresses

Associations of lawyers and judges

Den Norske Advokatforening [Norwegian Bar Association], Kristian Augusts Gate 9, N-0164 Oslo, Norway. Tel: +47 22 03 50 50. Fax: +47 22 11 53 25

Den Norske Dommerforening [Norwegian Association of Judges], Kristian Augusts Gate 9, N-0164 Oslo, Norway. Tel: +47 22 03 50 50. Fax: +47 22 11 51 18

Norges Juristforbund [Norwegian Association of Lawyers], Kristian Augusts Gate 9, N-0164 Oslo, Norway. Tel: +47 22 03 50 50. Fax: +47 22 11 51 18

Government organizations

Justis- og politidepartementet [Ministry of Justice and Police], Akersgaten 42, Pb 8005 Dep, N-0030 Oslo, Norway. Tel: +47 22 34 90 90. Fax: +47 22 34 27 20

Justis- og politidepartementet, Lovavdelingen [Ministry of Justice and Police, Law

Section], Akersgaten 42, Pb 8114 Dep, N-0032 Oslo, Norway. Tel: +47 22 34 53 99. Fax: +47 22 34 27 25

Nærings- og energidepartementet [Ministry of Industry], Pløens gate 8, Pb 8014 Dep, N-0030 Oslo, Norway. Tel: +47 22 34 90 90

Utenriksdepartementet [Ministry of Foreign Affairs], 7. juni-plass 1, Pb 8114 Dep, N-0032 Oslo, Norway. Tel: +47 22 34 90 90/22 34 36 00. Fax: +47 22 34 95 80/81

Courts

Høyesterett [Supreme Court], Grubbegaten 1, Pb 8016 Dep, N-0030 Oslo, Norway. Tel: +47 22 03 59 00. Fax: +47 22 33 23 55

Education and training and research institutions

Universitetet i Bergen, Det juridiske fakultet [University of Bergen, Faculty of Law], Magnus Lagabøtes plass 1, N-5020 Bergen, Norway. Tel: +47 55 58 95 95. Fax: +47 55 58 95 22

Universitetet i Oslo, Det juridiske fakultet [University of Oslo, Faculty of Law], Urbygningen, Karl Johans gate 47, N-0162 Oslo, Norway. Tel: +47 22 85 93 00. Fax: +47 22 85 98 40. E-mail: fak.sekr@jus.uio.no

Universitetet i Tromsø, Institutt for rettsvitenskap [University of Tromsø, Department of Jurisprudence], Breivika, N-9037 Tromso, Norway. Tel: +47 77 64 45 65/77 64 41 97. Fax: +47 77 64 47 75

Libraries

Det juridiske fakultetsbibliotek [Faculty of Law Library], Karl Johans gate 47, N-0162 Oslo, Norway. Tel: +47 22 85 98 85. Fax: +47 22 85 98 80

Nobelinstituttets bibliotek [The Nobel Institute Library], Drammensveien 19, N-0255 Oslo, Norway. Tel: +47 22 44 20 63. Fax: +47 22 43 01 68

Stortingsbiblioteket [The Storting Library, i.e. Library of the Norwegian Parliament], Stortinget, N-0026 Oslo, Norway. Tel: +47 22 31 36 90. Fax: +47 22 31 38 59

Universitetsbiblioteket i Oslo [University of Oslo Library], N-0242 Oslo, Norway. Tel: +47 22 85 50 50. Fax: +47 22 85 90 50

Law librarians

Fakultetsbibliotekar [Faculty Librarian] Pål A. Bertnes, Universitetsbiblioteket i Oslo, Det juridiske fakultetsbibliotek [University of Oslo Library, Faculty of Law Library], Karl Johans gate 47, N-0162 Oslo, Norway. Tel: +47 22 85 98 84. Fax: +47 22 85 94 99. E-mail: p.a.bertnes@ub.uio.no

Fakuletetsbibliotekar [Faculty Librarian] Halvor Kongshavn, Universitetet i Bergen, Det juridiske fakultetsbibliotek [University of Bergen, Faculty of Law Library], Magnus Lagabøtes plass 1, N-5020 Bergen, Norway. Tel: +47 55 58 95 25. Fax: +47 55 58 95 22. E-mail: halvor.kongshavn@ub.uib.no

Universitetsbibliotekar [Academic Librarian] Hanne E. Strømø, Universitetsbiblioteket i Oslo, Det juridiske fakultetsbibliotek [University of Oslo Library, Faculty of Law Library], Karl Johans gate 47, N-0162 Oslo, Norway. Tel: +47 22 85 98 79. Fax: +47 22 85 98 80. E-mail: hanne.stromo@jus.uio.no

Publishers and booksellers

Ad Notam Gyldendal AS (Publishers), Universitetsgaten 14, Pb 6730 St Olavs Plass, N-0130 Oslo, Norway. Tel: +47 22 03 43 00. Fax: +47 22 03 05

Akademika Universitetsbokhandel, Juridisk avdeling [Akademika University Bookshop, Law Department], Karl Johans gate 47, N-0162 Oslo, Norway. Tel: +47 22 42 54 50. Fax: +47 22 41 17 08

Akademika. Avdeling for Offentlige Publikasjoner [Department of Official Publications], Møllergaten 17, N-0179 Oslo, Norway. Tel: +47 22 11 67 70. Fax: +47 22 42 05 51

Diagnostica [Law Library System — BIBJURE], Sondreveien 1, N-0378 Oslo, Norway. Tel: +47 22 92 40 40. Fax: +47 22 92 40 09

Karnovs Forlag AS (Publishers), Rådhusgaten 7B, N-0155 Oslo, Norway. Tel: +47 22 41 87 08. Fax: +47 22 42 22 66

LOVDATA (Law Information Systems), Rådhusgaten 7B, N-0151 Oslo, Norway. Tel: +47 22 41 82 00. Fax: +47 22 41 81 80

Norlis Bokhandel [Norli's Bookshop], Universitetsgaten 20–24, N-0162 Oslo, Norway. Tel: +47 22 42 91 35. Fax: +47 22 42 26 51

Tano A/S (Publishers), Stortorvet 10, N-0155 Oslo, Norway. Tel: +47 22 42 55 00. Fax: +47 22 42 01 64

Statens Datasentral [Norwegian Government Computing Centre], Ulvenv. 89B, Pb 6664 Rodeløkka, N-0502 Oslo, Norway. Tel: +47 22 88 60 00. Internet: http://daneel.sds.no/htdocs/sds/SDS-hoved-n.html

Universitetsforlaget A/S (Publishers), Kolstadgaten 1, Pb 2959 Tøyen, N-0608 Oslo, Norway. Tel: +47 22 57 53 00. Fax: +47 22 57 53 53

Business information organizations

Norges Eksportråd [Export Council of Norway], Drammensveien 40, N-0243 Oslo, Norway. Tel: +47 22 92 63 00. Fax: +47 22 92 64 00

Næringslivets Hovedorganisasjon [Confederation of Norwegian Business and Industry], Middelthuns gate 27, Pb. 5250 Majorstua, N-0303 Oslo, Norway. Tel: +47 22 96 50 00. Fax: +47 69 55 93

List of works cited

Aagenæs, Janet (1993) *Norsk–engelsk økonomisk ordbok* [Norwegian–English economic dictionary]. Oslo: Kunnskapsforlaget.

Aarbakke, Magnus and Helgesen, Jan (1982) Sources of law in Norway. In *The sources of law. A comparative study. National systems of sources of law*, ed. Chantal Kourilsky, Attila Rácz and Heinz Schäffer, pp. 189–225. Budapest: Akadémiai Kiadó.

Advokatbladet. Medlemsblad for Den Norske Advokatforening. (1985–) Oslo: Den Norske Advokatforening.

Andenæs, Johs (1994) *Innføring i rettsstudiet* [Introduction to the study of law] 4th edn. Oslo: Grøndahl Dreyer.

Andenæs, Mads T. and Wilberg, Ingeborg (1987) *The Constitution of Norway: a commentary.* Oslo: Universitetsforlaget.

Anderson, Ralph J.B. (1977) *Anglo-Scandinavian law dictionary of legal terms used in professional and commercial practice.* Oslo: Universitetsforlaget.

Avkortningsnemnda (1990) *Avkortningsnemndas uttalelser* [Committee of Reduction concerning reduction in insurance cases]. Oslo: Avkortningsnemnda.

Bankklagenemnda (1988/89–) *Bankklagenemndas uttalelser* [The Complaint Board for Consumers in Banking and Finance Matters]. Oslo: Bankklagenemnda.

Bertnes, Pål A. and Kongshavn, Halvor (1989) *Juridisk kildesøking* [Legal information retrieval]. Det juridiske fakultetsbiblioteks skriftserie, no.4. Oslo: Det juridiske fakultetsbibliotek.

Bertnes, Pål A. and Kongshavn, Halvor (1992) *Praktisk rettskildelære. Juridisk kildesøking i Norge, øvrige nordiske land og EF* [Textbook on sources to legal information. Legal information retrieval in Norway, the other Nordic countries and EEC]. Oslo: Det juridiske bibliotekfond, Ad Notam Gyldendal.

Bertnes, Pål A. (1993) Sources to legal information in Norway. *International Journal of*

Legal Information, **21**, 154–166.
Bertnes, Pål A., Kongshavn, Halvor and Eckhoff, Torstein (1993) *Juridisk oppslagsbok* 18th edn. Oslo: Ad Notam Gyldendal.
BIBJURE (available from Diagnostica).
BIBSYS (available from University of Oslo Library at http://www.bibsys.no/search/pubn.html).
Boe, Erik (1993) *Innføring i juss* [Introduction to law]. Oslo: Tano.
Chaffey, Patrick N. (1988) (ed.) *Norsk–engelsk administrativ ordbok. Navn og termer fra offentlig virksomhet. Norwegian–English administrative glossary*. Rev. edn. Oslo: Universitetsforlaget.
Chaffey, Patrick N. and Walford, Ronald (1992) *Norsk–engelsk juridisk ordbok. Strafferett, straffeprosess og andre termer. Norwegian–English law dictionary. Criminal law and procedure and miscellaneous terms*. Oslo: Universitetsforlaget.
Complex. (1981–) Oslo: Universitetsforlaget.
Craig, Ronald L. (1992) *Norsk–engelsk juridisk ordbok. Kontraktsrett. Norwegian–English law dictionary. Contract law*. Oslo: Universitetsforlaget.
Dommer og kjennelser av arbeidsretten [Decisions of the Labour Disputes Court]. (1916/17–) Oslo: Grøndahl.
Dommer, uttalelser m.v. i skattesaker og skattespørsmål [Decisions and opinions in tax cases]. (1922–) Bergen: Ligningsnevndenes landsforbund.
Eckhoff, Torstein (1993) *Rettskildelære* [Sources of law theory] 3rd edn. Oslo: Tano.
Fife, Rolf Einar (1991) *Fransk–norsk juridisk oppslagsbok. Lexique juridique franco-norvegien*. Rev.edn. Oslo: Tano.
Flanz, Gisbert H. (1993) Norway. In *Constitutions of the countries of the world*, eds A.P. Blaustein and G.H. Flanz, vol.XIV. Dobbs Ferry, NY: Oceana.
Fleischer, Carl August (1995) *Rettskilder* [Sources of law]. Oslo: Ad Notam Gyldendal.
Forsikringsskadenemda, Avkortningsnemda for forbrukersaker, Avkortningsnemda for næringssaker (1992–) *Nemdsuttalelser*. Oslo: Norges forsikringsforbund.
Gulbransen, Egil (1994) *Juridisk leksikon* [Law dictionary] 8th edn. Oslo: Kunnskapsforlaget.
Hagelien, Per and Vonen, Marie (1993) The Norwegian legal system. In *EFTA legal systems. An introductory guide*, eds Maurice Sheridan, James Cameron and John Toulmin pp. i-51. London: Butterworths.
Hagelien, Per and Vonen, Marie (1994) *The Norwegian legal system: an introductory guide*. Bergen: Advokatfirmaet Schødt.
Haider, Inger Erikson (1993) Recent legal developments in the Nordic countries. A selected bibliography of works written in English, German, French and Italian, 1982–1992. *International Journal of Legal Information*, **21**, 33–64.
Haukaas, Kaare (1967a) *Norsk juridisk litteratur 1962–1966*. Oslo: Universitetsforlaget.
Haukaas, Kaare (1967b) *Norwegian legal publications in English, French and German. A list*. Norsk bibliografisk bibliotek, no.33. Oslo: Universitetsforlaget.
Haukaas, Kaare (1977) Norwegian legal publications in English, French and German 1966–76. A list. *Scandinavian Studies in Law*, **21**, 261–293.
Høgh, Tom Arbo (1990a) *Lov og dom. Lovregister til Norsk retstidende 1836–1968* [Statutory index to Norsk retstidende 1836–1968]. Oslo: Det juridiske bibliotekfond, Ad Notam Gyldendal.
Høgh, Tom Arbo (1990b) *Lov og dom. Lovregister til Norsk retstidende 1969–1988* [Statutory index to Norsk retstidende 1969–1988]. Oslo: Det juridiske bibliotekfond, Ad Notam Gyldendal.
Høgh, Tom Arbo (1992) *Lov og dom. Lovregister til Rettens Gang 1933–1989* [Statutory index to Rettens Gang 1933–1989]. Oslo: Det juridiske bibliotekfond, Ad Notam Gyldendal.
Iuul, Stig, Malmstrøm, Åke and Søndergaard, Jens (1961) (eds) *Scandinavian legal bibliography*. Acta Instituti Upsaliensis iurisprudentiae comparativae, no.4. Stockholm: Almqvist & Wiksell.

Jacobsen, Kirsti Lothe (1994) *Juridisk fakultetsbibliografi. Systematisk og alfabetisk bibliografi over publikasjoner utgitt ved Det juridiske fakultet. Biografi over ansatte ved fakultetet 1969–1994*. Det juridiske fakultets skriftserie, no.47. Bergen: Universitetet i Bergen.

Juristkontakt. Medlemsblad for Norges juristforbund. (1967–) Oslo: Norges juristforbund.

Karnov. Norsk kommentert lovsamling [Karnov. Norwegian code of laws with commentaries]. (1994) Oslo: Karnovs forlag.

Kierulf, Carl (annual) *Håndbok over norske obligasjoner og aksjer* [List of Norwegian bonds and shares]. Oslo: Carl Kierulf.

Knophs oversikt over Norges rett [Knoph on Norwegian law]. (1993) 10th edn. Oslo: Universitetsforlaget.

Kompass. (1992) Oslo: Kompass-Norge. 2 vols. Also available as an international database online and on CD-ROM as EUROPEAN KOMPASS.

Kongshavn, Halvor (1991) *Norske juridiske festskrift 1870–1990. En bibliografi over innholdet* [Norwegian legal festschriften 1870–1990. A bibliography of the contents]. Oslo: Det juridiske bibliotekfond, Ad Notam Gyldendal.

Kongshavn, Halvor (1994) *A bibliography of articles in non-Scandinavian languages 1963–1993 in Norwegian legal festschriften.* Det juridiske fakultetsbiblioteks skriftserie, no.10. Oslo: Det juridiske bibliotekfond.

Kongshavn, Halvor (1994) *Tilleggshefte 1991–1993 til Norske juridiske festskrift 1870–1990 En bibliografi over innholdet* [Appendix 1991–1993 to Norwegian legal festschriften 1870–1990. A bibliography of the contents]. Bergen: Institutt for privatrett.

Konkurransetilsynet [Competition Inspectorate]. (1994–) *K-kontakt.* Oslo: Konkurransetilsynet. Formerly *Pristidende.* (1940–) Oslo: Prisdirektoratet [Price Directorate].

Konkurransetilsynet [Competition Inspectorate]. (1994) *Konkurranseregler for foretak i EØS. Regelsamling* [Competition rules for enterprises within the EEA]. Rev. edn. Oslo: Konkurransetilsynet.

Lansky, Ralph (1987) *Bibliographisches Handbuch der Rechts- und Verwaltungswissenschaften: Band 1: Allgemeines und Europa.* Frankfurt am Main: Klostermann.

Lassen, Birger Stuevold (1993) *Presentasjon av rettsvitenskapelige arbeider på norsk. Med forslag til en norsk rettsvitenskapelig forkortelsesstandard* [A presentation of works of jurisprudence in Norwegian]. Oslo: Stiftelsen Tidsskrift for rettsvitenskap.

Lind, Åge (1989) *Forsikringsordbok. Norsk–engelsk, engelsk–norsk* [Insurance dictionary: Norwegian–English/English–Norwegian]. Oslo: Kunnskapsforlaget.

Lind, Åge (1992) *Norsk–engelsk juridisk ordbok. Sivilrett og strafferett* [Norwegian–English legal dictionary. Civil law and criminal law]. Oslo: Bedriftsøkonomens forlag.

Lødrup, Peter (1972) Norway. In *International encyclopedia of comparative law*, ed. V. Knapp, vol.1, pp. N73–N86. Tübingen: J.C.B. Mohr.

Lov og rett. (1962–) Oslo: Universitetsforlaget.

LOVDATA (available from LOVDATA Law Information Systems).

Lover: vedtatt på det . . . ordentlige Storting [Statutory law: passed at the . . . assembly of the Storting]. (Annual) Oslo: Stortingets kontor.

Marius. (1975–) Oslo: Nordisk institutt for sjørett.

Matheson, Wilhelm and Woxholth, Geir (1990–) *Lovavdelingens uttalelser* [Reports from the Law Section, Ministry of Justice]. Oslo: Juridisk forlag.

Ministry of Foreign Affairs (1879–) *Overenskomster med fremmede stater* [Treaties with foreign governments]. Oslo: Fabritius.

Ministry of Foreign Affairs (1980) *Norwegian laws etc. selected for the Foreign Service.* Oslo: Ministry of Foreign Affairs.

Ministry of Foreign Affairs (1988) *Norges traktater 1661–* [The treaties of Norway 1661–]. Oslo: Grøndahl.

Ministry of Justice (1897–) *Forarbeid til lovene* [Preparatory work on statutes]. Oslo: Justisdepartementet.

Ministry of Justice (1980) *Administration of justice in Norway. A brief summary* 2nd edn. Oslo: Universitetsforlaget.
Møse, Erik (1991) (ed.) *Folkerettslige tekster* [Texts pertaining to international law] 3rd edn. Oslo: Universitetsforlaget.
Munch-Petersen, Erland (1988) (ed.) *Guide to Nordic bibliography*. Copenhagen: Nordisk Ministerråd.
Nordisk domssamling [Selected decisions from the Nordic countries]. (1959–) Oslo: Universitets-forlaget.
Nordisk statuttsamling [Scandinavian body of statutes]. (1970–) Oslo: Nordic Council. Every three years.
Nordiske domme i sjøfartsanliggender [Nordic decisions based on maritime law]. (1990–) Oslo: Nordisk skibsrederforening.
Norges forskrifter. (1989) 2nd edn. Oslo: Grøndahl. 9 vols.
Norges handelskalender. Adressebok for handel, håndverk, industri og skipsfart [A survey of business firms, arranged according to trade]. (1994) Oslo: Bryde. Annual.
Norges lover. 1685–1995 (1996) Oslo: Ad Notam Gyldendal. Biennial publication with supplementary volume in intervening years.
Norges offentlige utredninger. (1972–) Oslo: Universitetsforlaget. Entitled: *Innstillinger og betenkninger* (1935–72).
Norges statskalender. Fortegnelse over konstitusjonelle organer og statsforvaltning m.v. [The Norwegian official yearbook]. (Annual) Oslo: Universitetsforlaget.
NORLEX CD (available from LOVDATA Law Information Systems).
Norsk lovtidende Avd.I (1877–) *Avd.II.* (1885–) Oslo: Grøndahl.
Norsk retstidende. (1836–) Oslo: Den Norske Advokatforening.
Norsk tidsskriftindex [Norwegian periodical index]. (1919–1966) Oslo: Universitetsforlaget.
Norske Advokatforening (1993) *Aktive medlemmer av Den Norske Advokatforening 1993* [Current members of the Norwegian Bar Association]. Oslo: Dokumentarforlaget.
Norske utredninger 1814–1986. (1987) Oslo: Universitetsforlaget.
Publikasjonsliste fra Storting og Regjering [Current list of publications from the Norwegian Parliament and the Ministries]. (Monthly) Oslo: Forvaltningstjenestene.
Rettens Gang. (1933–) Oslo: Den Norske Advokatforening.
Rigault, Didier (1992) *Leksikon om internasjonale kontrakter. Med norsk, engelsk og fransk terminologi* [Dictionary of international contracts. With Norwegian, English and French terminology]. Oslo: Norges eksportråd.
Risa, Staale T. (1993) The legal system of Norway. In *Modern legal systems cyclopedia*, ed. K.R. Redden, vol.4B, pp. 4.100.1–61. Buffalo, NY: Hein.
Sanfelt, Trond (1987) (ed.) *Norsk skatteavtalesamling* [Norwegian survey of tax agreements]. Oslo: Universitetsforlaget.
Schlyter, Børje, Nordli, Knut E. and Hustad, Tom (1987) *Franske fagtermer. Fransk–norsk, norsk–fransk ordbok over vanlig brukte ord og uttrykk i samfunnslivet* [French technical terms. French–Norwegian/Norwegian–French]. Oslo: Universitetsforlaget.
Selberg, Kjersti (1990) *Norsk skatterett 1945–1988. En bibliografi* [Norwegian tax law 1945–1988. A bibliography]. Oslo: Universitetsforlaget.
Simonnæs, Ingrid (1985) *Deutsch–Norwegisches juristisches Wørterbuch* [German–Norwegian legal dictionary] 2nd edn. Bergen: Norges handelshøgskole.
Simonnæs, Ingrid (1994) *Norsk–tysk juridisk ordbok* [Norwegian–German legal dictionary]. Bergen: Fagbokforlaget.
Statens informasjonstjeneste (1956–) *Hvem svarer på hva i staten* [Subject guide to the Ministries]. Oslo: Tano.
Statens informasjonstjeneste (1982–) *Samfunnsboka.* Oslo: Universitetsforlaget. Published every two years.
Statistisk sentralbyrå [Central Bureau of Statistics] (1980–) *Veiviser i norsk statistikk. Guide to Norwegian statistics.* Oslo: Statistisk sentralbyrå.
Stortingsforhandlinger [Proceedings and debates of the Parliament]. (1814–) Oslo: Forvaltningstjenestene.

Strømø, Hanne (1994) (ed.) *Norske lovtitler. Fortegnelse over lover trykt i 'Norges lover 1685–1993'* [Norwegian law titles. Inventory in 'Norwegian Laws 1685–1993']. Oslo: Ad Notam Gyldendal.

Telefonkatalogen. Departementene og Forvaltningstjenesten [Telephone directory for the Ministries]. (Annual) Oslo: Forvaltningstjenestene.

Tidsskrift for rettsvitenskap [Periodical of jurisprudence]. (1888–) Oslo: Aschehoug.

UBO:BOK (available from the University of Oslo Library at http://www2.nbo.uio.no/ubobok/ uboboknor.html)).

Universitetsbiblioteket i Oslo (1870–) *Norsk bokfortegnelse. Årskatalog. The Norwegian National Bibliography*. Oslo: Den norske bokhandlerforening.

Universitetsbiblioteket i Oslo (1981–) *Norske tidsskriftartikler* [Norwegian periodical articles]. Oslo: Universitetsbiblioteket.

CHAPTER TWENTY-ONE

Poland

MARIA SMOLKA-DAY

Introduction to the legal system

Polish statehood was established over one thousand years ago, an event of great importance for Polish culture and national traditions. However, old Polish law has had little impact on the contemporary legal system. Legal continuity was broken by partitions in the late 18th century which divided Poland among Russia, Prussia and Austria, resulting in a loss of independence for over one hundred years. When the Polish state was reborn in 1918, a mosaic of various legal systems was in force in different parts of the country. All of them developed in the civil law tradition. During twenty years of the inter-war period most law was unified and some important parts were codified, following examples from continental Western Europe. Legal education and practice thoroughly incorporated the spirit of the civil law tradition.

The post-World War II period of communist domination brought Polish law under Soviet influence but no sharp rejection of earlier legislation took place. Some inter-war laws remain in force although usually in amended form. These laws primarily regulated economic activity in the private sector which, under communism, was very limited. After the economic reforms and political changes of 1989, they gained new prominence and helped to speed transformation to a market economy. The whole system, however, underwent legal reform with frequent and substantial legislative changes. Although reforms are still in progress, major legal changes have taken place and present efforts are directed mainly at perfecting the existing legal structure and harmonizing it with European law. Poland concluded the Association Agreement with the European Union and hopes eventually to become a full member.

Because of rapid changes in all aspects of Polish life, information sources are changing constantly. New legislative enactments affect the contents of legal sources and a spirit of free enterprise results in the proliferation of new publishers and products while some old sources are disappearing. Therefore the researcher should keep in mind that some of the sources discussed below are not well established.

The transitional character of Polish law is exemplified by its Constitution. The old Constitution of 22 July 1952, although frequently and substantially amended, is still in force as regards those parts dealing with civil rights and judicial powers. However, the main branches of government are regulated by the so-called 'Little Constitution' adopted in 1992 (Dz.U. nr.84, poz. 426). Work on a new constitution is in progress. Drafts already prepared are available on the electronic web page of the Polish Council of Ministers [Urząd Rady Ministrów] at http://www.urm.gov.pl/ along with texts currently in force. The English translation of the Constitution is also on the University of Würzburg web site (see International Constitutional Law in the **Useful addresses** below). A printed updated text of the Constitution is published in *Konstytucja* (1994) and an English translation appears in Flanz (1991 supplemented in 1993). Constitutional developments can be monitored in *Przegląd sejmowy* (1993–) and in English in the *Journal of Constitutional Law in Eastern and Central Europe* (1994–) and the *East European Constitutional Review* (1992–).

Under current law the Republic of Poland is a democracy based on the doctrine of the separation of powers. The *Sejm* [House of Representatives] and the *Senat* [Senate] are the two houses of the legislative branch making laws signed by the President and reviewed by the Constitutional Tribunal. The government, chaired by the prime minister, nominated by the president but approved by the *Sejm* to which it is responsible, is in charge of implementing the laws by issuing secondary legislation. Independent courts apply the law to individual cases. Although nuances of relations between these powers are a subject of national debate, there is no indication that this basic structure will change in the new constitution.

Introductory works on the legal system and legal research

Because the Polish legal system has been changing fundamentally during the last few years, introductory works summarizing the law of the country are not easily written. Therefore one must turn to older works which may still be used for understanding the historic background, basic structure, and research techniques in Polish law.

The most up-to-date summary is the chapter on Poland in the latest annual edition of the *Martindale-Hubbell international law digest*

(1993–), available also online on LEXIS (Library: MARHUB, File: INTDIG). Concentrating primarily on private law, it gives a quite detailed summary of various topics of law arranged alphabetically. The *Business law guide to Poland* (Seibel 1996) provides detailed information on business-related law for foreign investors and is up to date to about November 1995. An excellent research guide by Reynolds and Flores (1989–) is published in looseleaf format; at the time of writing its part on Poland in vol.2A was last updated in 1995. In addition to detailed information on English sources of Polish law, it also provides a short but informative general introduction. Among older books the collections of essays edited by Wagner (1970), Sokolewicz (1978), and Kurowski (1984) are still of use to a limited degree.

Legislation

The nomenclature of legislative acts in Poland may vary for different historical periods, but the primary form of legislative enactment is an *ustawa* [a law or statute] which must be passed by the parliament and signed by the president. At different times Polish constitutions have also provided for some exceptional simplified procedures for issuing, in extraordinary circumstances, legislative acts by bodies other than the parliament: for example in the form of a *dekret* [decree] or *rozporządzenie Prezydenta* [Presidential regulation]. They equal statutes in the hierarchy of legal acts. The most important subordinate legislation is a *rozporządzenie* [regulation] issued by the Council of Ministers or an individual minister only after explicit statutory authorization. The only official source for the above enactments is *Dziennik Ustaw* (1918–) (Dz.U.) published by the official government publisher, Urząd Rady Ministrów, Wydział Wydawnictw.

Other less important kinds of subordinate legislation, such as a *zarządzenie* [order] or an *uchwała* [decision], are published in *Monitor Polski* (1918–) (M.P.) or in official gazettes of individual ministries and administrative agencies. Unless explicitly stated otherwise in the act itself, Polish legislation comes into force upon publication in an appropriate official journal. Both *Dziennik Ustaw* (1918–) and *Monitor Polski* (1918–) follow a similar pattern of publication. At the beginning of each calendar year two independent sequences of numbers are started, namely by issue number and item number. Both have to be used when citing individual laws. The citation also has to include the type of enactment, date and title of an act, as well as the abbreviated title of an official journal in which it appears. No reference to the page number is needed. For example: Ustawa z dnia 23 kwietnia 1964 r. Kodeks cywilny. (Dz.U. nr.16, poz. 93) which translates as: Law of 23 April 1964. Civil Code. (Journal of Laws. no.16, item 93).

Individual pieces of legislation are not, as a rule, published as single laws and may not be purchased separately. However, individual issues of both gazettes may be purchased from the publisher (see **Useful addresses** below). A somewhat dated but still correct description in English of the official publishing of legislation in Poland is in Siekanowicz (1964, pp. 51–58). A complete list of currently published official gazettes appears in part 02 of the annual volumes of *Polska bibliografia prawnicza* (1962–).

Both *Dziennik Ustaw* (1918–) and *Monitor Polski* (1918–) have annual indexes with the title *Skorowidz alfabetyczny*. Cumulative subject indexes are available separately. *Skorowidz przepisów prawnych* (1992), the official index to legislation covering 1918–1939 and 1944–1992, is prepared by Wydział Prawny Urzędu Rady Ministrów [Legal Office of the Office of the Council of Ministers]. It is published irregularly but has appeared more frequently in recent years. Its commercial competitor, *Skorowidz obowiązujących przepisów prawnych* (1993–), is an annual publication. The latter index, derived from the publisher's computerized database, is also advertised in two computerized versions: on many computer disks as INFO-LEX. SKOROWIDZ OBOWIĄZUJĄCYCH PRZEPISÓW PRAWNYCH; and on a CD-ROM as KARTOTEKA (see below). The biggest advantage of the commercial title seems to be its frequent updating. However, the new publication introduces new subject headings and a different system of citation making it more difficult to use in conjunction with official annual indexes and other sources. The effort of learning a new system would be worthwhile if updates are truly current.

There is no official publication that rearranges legislation by subject and incorporates amendments. In the case of some significant acts with frequent and complex changes, the only official 'help' comes with the occasional issue of a consolidated text [*jednolity tekst*] (j.t.) of individual acts. Such a text incorporating all up-to-date changes is published in *Dziennik Ustaw* (1918–) and has become the official text of a law for all but historic research. For example, the Law of 26 March 1982 on the Tribunal of State, whose official consolidated text was published in May 1993, is found at Dz.U. 1993, nr.38, poz. 172. However, since the publication does not introduce any substantive changes, it is placed in *Dziennik Ustaw* (1918–) under the heading *Obwieszczenia* [announcements], rather than under *Ustawy* [statutes].

Another way of finding the text of legislation by subject is by using unofficial publications. The most comprehensive collections are looseleaf services published in Polish by the German publisher C.H. Beck, in cooperation with the reputable Polish publisher PWN. The set consists of:

- *Polskie ustawy* (1993–) covering civil, criminal, and procedural laws as well as economic laws such as commerce, intellectual property, etc.;

- *Prawo administracyjne* (1995–) covering constitutional and administrative law, including administrative procedure;
- *Prawo podatkowe* (1994–) covering tax laws and regulations;
- *Prawo pracy* (1995–) covering labour and social law.

The laws, regulations, and other acts included in these publications are updated by incorporating amendments and are arranged in broad subject categories. They also include alphabetical lists of all acts and quick guides to major legislation. Although complementing one another, each title is purchased and updated separately.

For those interested only in legislation on a specific subject, specialized collections of laws are published from time to time, such as *Prawo ubezpieczeniowe* (1993). They are usually edited by specialists in the field and frequently include a substantial introduction or commentary. The most important among this genre are one volume publications of major codes related by subject, for example, the Civil Code, Code of Civil Procedure, and Family Code (*Kodeks cywilny*, 1993).

Translations of legislation

It is difficult to find English translations of Polish laws. After World War II an attempt was made to publish systematically important Polish laws in English in the series *Legislation of Poland* (1949–1959). No current equivalent of this publication exists. Only selected statutes and very few pieces of subsidiary legislation are translated at all and there is no single source which would include all acts available in translation. Among publications worth consulting is Pechota (1990–), a looseleaf service which includes some Polish legislative acts primarily but not exclusively relevant to business law. The Polish Society of Economic, Legal and Court Translators (TEPIS) specializes in publishing legal texts in translation. They have published several books in English: *Polish business law, 1992*, *Polish Labour Code* (1992) and a few others. The National Technical Information Service (NTIS) distributes selected texts of legislation provided by the US Department of Commerce.

Various pieces of legislation can occasionally be found in periodicals such as *Droit polonais contemporain* (1963–) and *Review of Central and East European Law* (1992–). Polish law is also frequently included in topical collections of legislative texts from many countries: for example, in the International Labour Office's *Labour law documents* (1990–), Blanpain (1977–), and Sanders (1984–). A chapter on Poland in Reynolds and Flores (1989–) is very helpful in locating sources of translated legislation on a specific subject. Computerized sources are discussed below. If no translation is available, a good detailed summary of selected legislation is provided in *European current law* (1992–).

Codes and commentaries

Most of Poland's major codes were enacted in the 1960s and 1970s and they are still in force, although significantly amended in some parts. Therefore, the latest possible editions should be consulted. On the other hand, many parts were not changed at all and even older translations can still be used with caution. All codes in Polish are published frequently, although irregularly, in separate updated and annotated editions. The traditional legal publisher, Wydawnictwo Prawnicze, now faces increasing competition both from new local publishing houses and from abroad, for example C.H. Beck.

Kodeks cywilny [Civil Code] of 23 April 1964 (Dz.U. no.16, item 93). A recent Polish edition: *Kodeks cywilny* (1994); a recent English translation: *Polish Civil Code* (1994). Commentaries: Winiarz (1989) in Polish; Lasok (1973–75) in English.

Kodeks postępowania cywilnego [Code of Civil Procedure] of 17 November 1964 (Dz.U. no.43, item 296). A recent Polish edition: *Kodeks postępowania cywilnego* (1993). No English translation exists, but an Italian one does: *Il processo civile polacco* (1981) and also a German one: *Zivilverfahrensgesetzbuch der Volksrepublik Polen* 1967). A commentary: Ereciński (1989).

Kodeks handlowy [Commercial code] of 27 June 1934 (Dz.U. no.57, item 502). Practically, only parts regulating company law are in force. It has been amended extensively since the late 1980s and only recent editions should be used. A recent Polish edition: *Kodeks handlowy* (1993); a recent English translation: *The Polish Commercial Code* (1991). New commentary: Sołtysiński *et al.* (1994–1996).

Kodeks karny [Criminal Code] of 19 April 1969 (Dz.U. no.13, item 94). A recent Polish edition: *Kodeks karny* (1994); an English translation: *Penal Code* (1973). Commentaries: Bafia, Mioduski and Siewierski (1987) and Buchała (1994).

Kodeks postępowania karnego [Code of Criminal Procedure] of 19 April 1969 (Dz.U. no.13, item 96). A recent Polish edition: *Kodeks karny* (1994); an English translation: *Code of Criminal Procedure* (1979); a commentary: Grajewski and Skrętowicz (1995).

In addition to the five major codes, other codifications exist: *Kodeks postępowania administracyjnego* [Code of Administrative Procedure] of 1960; *Kodeks morski* [Maritime Code] of 1961; *Kodeks rodzinny i opiekuńczy* [Family and Guardianship code] of 1964; *Kodeks pracy* [Labour Code] of 1974, and others. References to the official text and an English translation (when available) may be located under the appropriate subject in the chapter on Poland in Reynolds and Flores (1989–).

Treaties

International treaties [*umowy międzynarodowe*] concluded by Poland are published in *Dziennik Ustaw* (1918–). Multilateral conventions sometimes appear in special supplements. One may also consult the periodical *Zbiór Umów Międzynarodowych* (1952–) published by the Polski Instytut Spraw Międzynarodowych [Polish Institute of International Affairs]. The same Institute also publishes the *Polish yearbook of international law* (1968–), which includes useful information on Polish treaty actions. Both indexes of legislation, *Skorowidz przepisów prawnych* (1992) and *Skorowidz obowiązujących przepisów prawnych* (1993–), provide subject access to the international treaties to which Poland is a party.

Law reports, judgments

As a matter of legal principle, court decisions do not have precedential value in Polish law. However, in legal practice and scholarship, decisions of the highest courts are watched and followed. They are published selectively.

The Trybunał Konstytucyjny [Constitutional Tribunal] was created in 1985 and since then has issued numerous decisions on a variety of subjects. Although its opinions must win the approval of the Sejm, it has established itself as an important factor in Polish life. The conclusions of its decisions are published in *Dziennik Ustaw* (1918–) and full decisions appear in *Orzecznictwo Trybunału Konstytucyjnego* (1986–). The Tribunal's powers are likely to be strengthened in a new constitution.

The Sąd Najwyższy [Supreme Court] consists of chambers whose decisions are published in two separate series: *Orzecznictwo Sądu Najwyższego. Izba Cywilna* (1962–); and *Orzecznictwo Sądu Najwyższego. Izba Karna* (1962–). The former includes cases from civil, administrative, labour and social insurance law, the latter from criminal and military law. The highest administrative court, Naczelny Sąd Administracyjny, created in 1980, has its decisions published in *Orzecznictwo Naczelnego Sądu Administracyjnego* (1981–).

Some law reports include selected decisions from, but not necessarily exclusively, various of the highest courts. The most important are: *Orzecznictwo sądów polskich* (1957–) and *Wokanda* (1992–). Traditionally, decisions can also be found in legal periodicals such as *Państwo i prawo* (1946–), *Przegląd ustawodawstwa gospodarczego* (1948–), *Monitor prawniczy* (1993–), *Przegląd sejmowy* (1993–), etc. If selected for such publication, decisions are frequently accompanied by a commentary, called a 'glosa' and written by scholars or practitioners.

Polish cases are published without the names of the parties to the litigation. They are referred to by the name of a court deciding the case, followed by the date and docket number. When indexed or digested they are organized by subject or by the list of the statutes, analysed section by section, interpreted by decisions. Most reports are accompanied by annual subject indexes. From time to time they also include multi-year cumulations for the given reporter. However, better access to case law is through the annotated commentaries to major legislative acts. There are also collections of court decisions dealing with specific subjects; for example, see Piszczek (1994). Polish court decisions are not generally translated into English. However, the most significant Polish cases have recently been digested in *European current law* (1992–).

Computer-based systems

A computerized version of Polish law has been available for some time but, having been developed for computer disks, its use and storage were cumbersome and inconvenient. A new CD-ROM version is much more promising. It consists of three major parts: KARTOTEKA [Index], TEKSTY [legislative texts] and TEMIDA [court decisions]. The first two parts are planned to be updated (at least in Poland) monthly, the third quarterly. All major parts of the Polish government maintain an internet homepage and from time to time add texts of official documents. The most useful homepage is that of Urząd Rady Ministrów [Office of the Council of Ministers] at http://www.urm.gov.pl/ which includes texts of the current Constitution, all official drafts of constitutional proposals and the tables of contents of *Dziennik Ustaw* (1918–) and *Monitor Polski* (1918–). Some information is also in English.

In English there are some very selective legislative materials (statutes in force, drafts, other documents) on both LEXIS (library: EUROPE, file: EELEG) and WESTLAW (database: INT-EUROPE). Both include primarily laws of commercial interest and use texts supplied by NTIS. Additionally NEXIS has among its journals the *Polish News Bulletin* (file: PNBUL) and the *Warsaw Voice* (1988–) (file: WARSAWV) which occasionally publish the full texts of the most important legislation. Searching these and other NEXIS files can also help one to follow legislative developments in Poland.

Ombudsman

The Ombudsman [Rzecznik Praw Obywatelskich] was introduced in Poland in 1987. From the beginning she established herself as an important factor in Polish political and legal life due to her vigorous and visible activity in pursuing the proper implementation of law on behalf of the people. Her *Annual report* and other publications may be consulted in legal research, especially in human rights issues (Rzecznik Praw Obywatelskich, 1989–).

Encyclopedias and large collections

Poland is waiting for a major encyclopedic publication covering the entire legal system. Instead, for the systematic explanation of law, researchers should consult subject-oriented textbooks or treatises. The latter can be recognized by the word 'system' in the title: for example, Czachórski (1985–).

Directories

Law firms involved in international practice are listed in major international directories. The most complete information is in *Martindale-Hubbell international law directory* (1992–) but *Kime's international law directory* (1892–) also gives addresses of national and local offices of the Polish Bar Association [Rada Adwokacka] where further information may be obtained. For addresses of government offices, including courts, see *Worldwide government directory* (1987–) or *Europa world year book* (1990–). Information about law schools is available in *Informator nauki polskiej* (1958–), the *World of learning* (1947–), and in the *World law school directory* (1993).

Bibliographies and indexes to periodicals

The most comprehensive bibliography of Polish legal publications, including the contents of legal periodicals, is *Polska bibliografia prawnicza* (1962–) prepared by the Instytut Nauk Prawnych PAN. It may be updated by consulting the monthly bibliography published in *Państwo i prawo* (1946–) and is now also available in computer readable form. The publisher's address is below in the **Useful addresses** section. Among many selected bibliographies the 'Polish bibliography of international law' is published regularly in English in the *Polish yearbook of international law* (1968–). For older materials consult Suligowski (1911) and Siekanowicz (1964).

Dictionaries

In the mid-1980s the Instytut Nauk Prawnych PAN sponsored an effort to prepare dictionaries translating Polish legal terminology into major

European languages: English, French, German, and Russian. The English version is *Slownik prawniczy polsko–angielski* (1986); it also has an English–Polish index. The English–Polish dictionary by Jaślan and Jaślan (1991) covers both law and economics. An extensive list of commonly used legal abbreviations is included in the annual volumes of *Polska bibliografia prawnicza* (1962–).

Current information sources

Journals

Among many legal journals published in Poland, the most important for legal practice are: *Palestra* (1957–), *Przegląd ustawodawstwa gospodarczego* (1948–), and *Przegląd sądowy* (1991–). *Palestra* (1957–), sponsored by the Główna Rada Adwokacka [Polish Bar Association], covers a broad range of topics of interest for the general practitioner, while *Przegląd ustawodawstwa gospodarczego* (1948–) addresses the needs of business lawyers by publishing not only articles, but also selected legislation and relevant court decisions. *Przegląd sądowy* (1991–), which continues *Nowe prawo* (1950–1991), addresses primarily the needs of litigation lawyers. Among scholarly journals *Państwo i prawo* (1946–) plays a leading role because it is the most general and easily available. It publishes not only scholarly articles but also reports on conferences, book reviews, and case notes. It includes an ongoing bibliography of Polish legal publications, both books and periodical articles. All these periodicals are published monthly.

In addition scholars should not neglect journals and monographic series published by Polish law schools and specialized legal periodicals dealing with specific areas of law. The leading Polish legal periodical published in foreign languages, *Droit polonaise contemporain* (1963–), is far behind in schedule which limits its usefulness as a source of current information.

More and more frequently developments in Polish law are covered by journals published abroad. Journals and updated services devoted to Central and East Europe, such as the *Parker School Journal of East European Law* (1994–), *SEEL, Survey of East European Law* (1991–), the *Review of Central and East European Law* (1992–), *BNA's Eastern Europe reporter* (1991–), and *Doing business in Eastern Europe* (1992–), are particularly useful.

News information

The most current source of legal information is the daily *Rzeczpospolita* (1982–) which not only covers current events thoroughly, but also provides the full text of important legislation. Selected materials from this paper are available in English, together with other translations from the Polish press in the *Polish News Bulletin*. Weeklies, the *Warsaw Voice* (1988–) and *Gazeta international* (1990–), can also serve as valuable sources of information. All three English titles are available on NEXIS.

Business information

Basic business information on Poland can be found in the annual *General trade index & business guide: Poland* (1991–) prepared by the Business Foundation in Warsaw (see address in **Useful addresses** below). For the largest businesses the *Eastern European business directory* (1992–) may also be used. The US government through the Central and Eastern Europe Business Information Center (see address below) publishes a monthly, the *Eastern Europe Business Bulletin* (1992–), which publicizes business opportunities and gives the names and addresses of contact people.

Statistics

Official statistical information is published annually in *Rocznik statystyczny*.

Useful addresses

Government organizations

Ministerstwo Spraw Zagranicznych [Ministry of Foreign Affairs], Al. Szucha 23, 00-580 Warszawa, Poland. Tel: +48 2 623-90-00. Fax: +48 2 625-76-52

Ministerstwo Sprawiedliwósci [Ministry of Justice], Al. Ujazdowskie 11, 00-950 Warszawa, Poland. Tel: +49 2 628-44-31. Fax +48 22 28-16-92. Telex: 813891

Urząd Rady Ministrów [Office of Council of Ministers], Wydział Wydawnictw [sales office for government publications], ul. Powsińska 69/71, 00–979 Warszawa, Poland. Tel: +48 22 42-14-78 or +48 22 694-67-50. Fax: +48 22 694-62-06. Telex: 825944WW. Internet: http://www.urm.gov.pl/

Research institutes

Instytut Nauk Prawnych PAN [Institute of Law, Polish Academy of Science] (publisher of bibliography), ul. Nowy Swiat 72, 00 330 Warszawa, Poland. Tel: +48 22 26-52-31 ex. 68 (for computerized bibliography) or +48 22 26-75-71 (other publications). Fax: +48 22 26-78-53

Publishers and booksellers

Business Foundation Co. (publisher of business directory), ul. Krucza 38/42, 00–512 Warszawa, Poland. Tel: +48 22 21-99-93. Fax: +48 22 21-97-61

Central and Eastern Europe Business Information Center, International Trade Administration, US Department of Commerce, Room 7414, Washington, D.C. 20230, USA. Tel: +1 202 482-2645. Fax: +1 202 482-4473. Flashfax: +1 202 482-5745. Internet: http://www.itaiep.doc.gov E-mail: eebicl@usita.gov

International Constitutional Law, University of Würzburg. Internet: http://www.uni-wuerzburg.de/law/index.html

Kubon & Sagner (bookseller), Buchexport-Import GmbH, D-80328 München, Germany. Tel: +49 89 54 218130. Fax: +49 89 54 218218. Telex: 5 216 711 kusa d

LEXIS-NEXIS, see the addresses given on page 19 in the **General sources** chapter.

Orbis Books (London) Ltd (bookseller), 66 Kenway Road, London SW5 ORD, UK. Tel: +44 171 370 2210. Fax: +44 171 602 5541

TEPIS Publishing House, ul. Brodzińskiego 4, 01–557 Warsaw, Poland

WESTLAW. West Information Publishing Group, 620 Opperman Drive, Eagan, MN 55123, USA. Tel: +1 612 687 4064. E-mail: westmedia@westpub.com Internet: http://www.westpub.com London Office: West Publishing UK Ltd, 2 London Wall Buildings, London Wall, London EC2M 5PP, UK. Tel: +44 171 638 9997. Fax: +44 171 638 9908

Wydawnictwo Prawnicze (leading legal publisher), ul. Wiśniowa 50, 02–520 Warszawa, Poland. Tel: +48 22 49-47-05. Fax: +48 22 49-94-10

Wydawnictwo Prawnicze LEX (publisher of legal databases/legislation index), ul. Śląska 12, 80–389 Gdańsk, Poland. Tel/Fax: +48 58 52-00-21 to 24

List of works cited

Bafia, J., Mioduski, K. and Siewierski, M. (1987) *Kodeks karny: komentarz* [Criminal Code with commentary] 3rd edn. Warsaw: Wydawnictwo Prawnicze. 2 vols.

Blanpain, R. (1977–) (ed.) *International encyclopaedia for labour law and industrial relations*. Deventer: Kluwer. Looseleaf.

BNA's Eastern Europe reporter. (1991–) Washington, DC: Bureau of National Affairs.

Buchała, K. (1994) (ed.) *Komentarz do kodeksu karnego: cześć ogólna* [Criminal Code with commentary] 2nd edn. Warsaw: Wydawnictwo Prawnicze.

Code of Criminal Procedure of the Polish People's Republic. (1979) Warsaw: Wydawnictwo Prawnicze.

Czachórski, W. (1985–) (ed.) *System prawa cywilnego* [Treatise on civil law] 2nd edn. Wrocław: Ossolineum.

Doing business in Eastern Europe. (1992–) Wiesbaden: CCH Europe; Bicester: CCH Editions Ltd.

Droit polonais contemporain. (1963–) Wrocław: Ossolineum.

Dziennik ustaw Rzeczypospolitej Polskiej [Journal of laws of the Republic of Poland]. (1918–) Warsaw: Urząd Rady Ministrów.

East European Constitutional Review. (1992–) Chicago, Ill: Center for the Study of Constitutionalism in Eastern Europe at the University of Chicago Law School in partnership with the Central European University.

Eastern Europe Business Bulletin. (1992–) Washington, DC: Eastern Europe Business Information Center.

Eastern European business directory. (1992–) Detroit, Mich: Gale Research.

Ereciński, T. *et al.* (1989) *Kodeks postępowania cywilnego z komentarzem* [Code of Civil Procedure with commentary]. Warsaw: Wydawnictwo Prawnicze. 3 vols.

Europa world year book. (1989–) London: Europa Publications.

European current law. (1992–) London: European Law Centre, Sweet & Maxwell.

Flanz, Gisbert H. (1991) Poland. In *Constitutions of the countries of the world*, ed. A.P. Blaustein and G.H. Flanz, vol.XV. Dobbs Ferry, NY: Oceana Pub. Also Poland supplement dated October 1993. Looseleaf.

Gazeta international. (1990–) Warsaw: Agora. English translations of selected articles from the daily *Gazeta wyborcza*. Also available on NEXIS.

General trade index & business guide: Poland. (1991–) Warsaw: Business Foundation. Annual.

Grajewski, J. and Skrętowicz, E. (1995) *Kodeks postępowania karnego z komentarzem* [Code of Criminal Procedure with a commentary] 2nd edn. Gdańsk: IUS.

INFO-LEX. SKOROWIDZ OBOWIĄZUJĄCYCH PRZEPISÓW PRAWNYCH (available from Wydawnictwo Prawnicze LEX). Computer disk.

Informator nauki polskiej. (1958–) Warsaw: Państwowe Wydawnictwo Naukowe. Directory of institutions of higher learning.

Jaślan, J. and Jaślan, H. (1991) *Słownik terminologii prawniczej i economicznej angielsko–polski* [Dictionary of legal and economic terms: English–Polish]. Warsaw: Wiedza Powszechna.

Journal of Constitutional Law in Eastern and Central Europe. (1994–) Den Bosch: BookWorld Pub.

KARTOTEKA (available from Wydawnictwo Prawnicze LEX). CD-ROM.

Kime's international law directory. (1892–) London: Bowden.

Kodeks cywilny ze skorowidzem; Kodeks postępowania cywilnego ze skorowidzem; Kodeks rodzinny i opiekuńczy [Civil Code; Code of Civil Procedure; Family and Guardianship Code]. (1993) Gdańsk: Info-Trade.

Kodeks cywilny ze skorowidzem rzeczowym [Civil Code]. (1994) Warsaw: Wydawnictwo Prawnicze.

Kodeks handlowy i inne teksty prawne [Commercial Code]. (1993) Warsaw: C.H. Beck/PWN.

Kodeks karny; Kodeks postępowania karnego; Kodeks karny wykonawczy [Criminal Code, Code of Criminal Procedure and related statutes]. (1994) 4th edn. Gdańsk: LEX, Wydawnictwo Prawnicze.

Kodeks postępowania cywilnego i inne teksty prawne [Code of Civil Procedure]. (1993) Warsaw: C.H. Beck/PWN.

Konstytucja Rzeczypospolitej Polskiej [Constitution of the Republic of Poland]. (1994) 3rd edn. Lublin: Lubelskie Wydawnictwa Prawnicze.

Kurowski, L. (1984) (ed.) *General principles of law of the Polish People's Republic*. Warsaw: Polish Scientific Publishers.

Labour law documents. (1990–) Geneva: International Labour Office.

Lasok, D. (1973–1975) (ed.) *Polish civil law*. Leiden: Sijthoff. 4 vols.

Legislation of Poland. (1949–1959) Warsaw: Polish Institute of International Affairs.

LEXIS (available from LEXIS-NEXIS).

Martindale-Hubbell international law digest. (1993–) New Providence, NJ: Martindale Hubbell. Also available on LEXIS.

Martindale-Hubbell international law directory. (1992–) New Providence, NJ: Martindale Hubbell. Also available on LEXIS.

Monitor Polski: dziennik urzędowy Rzeczypospolitej Polskiej [Official gazette of the Republic of Poland]. (1918–) Warsaw: Urząd Rady Ministrów.

Monitor prawniczy. (1993–) Warsaw: C.H. Beck/PWN. Monthly legal journal.

NEXIS (available from LEXIS-NEXIS).

Orzecznictwo Naczelnego Sądu Administracyjnego [Reports of the Administrative Tribunal]. (1981–) Warsaw: Wydawnictwo Prawnicze.

Orzecznictwo sądow polskich [General law reports]. (1957–) Warsaw: Państwowe Wydawnictwo Naukowe.

Orzecznictwo Sądu Najwyższego. Izba Cywilna oraz Izba Administracyjna, Pracy i Ubezpieczeń Społecznych [Supreme Court reports. Civil, Administrative, and Labour & Social Insurance chambers]. (1962–) Warsaw: Wydawnictwo Prawnicze.

Orzecznictwo Sądu Najwyższego. Izba Karna i Izba Wojskowa [Supreme Court reports. Criminal and Military chambers]. (1962–) Warsaw. Wydawnictwo Prawnicze.

Orzecznictwo Trybunału Konstytucyjnego [Reports of the Constitutional Tribunal]. (1986–) Warsaw: Zakład Wydawniczy Letter Quality.

Palestra. (1957–) Warsaw: Wydawnictwo Prawnicze. Monthly legal journal.

Państwo i prawo. (1946–) Warsaw: Instytut Nauk Prawnych PAN. Monthly legal journal.

Parker School Journal of East European Law. (1994–) New York: Parker School of Foreign and Comparative Law, Columbia University.

Pechota, V. (1990–) (ed.) *Central and east European legal materials.* Ardsley-on-Hudson, NY: Transnational Juris; London: Graham & Trotman. Looseleaf.

Penal code of the Polish People's Republic. (1973) South Hackensack, NJ: F.B. Rothman.

Piszczek, P. (1994) *Orzecznictwo Sądu Najwyższego: prawo cywilne* [Selected Supreme Court civil law cases] 2nd edn. Bia ystok: Oficyna Prawnicza IUSTITIA.

Polish business law, 1992. (1992) Warsaw: Information Centre, Ministry of Privatization (TEPIS series).

Polish Civil Code. (1994) Warsaw: Polish Society of Economic, Legal and Court Translators TEPIS.

Polish Commercial Code. (1991) Warsaw: Polish Society of Economic, Legal and Court Translators (TEPIS).

Polish Labour Code. (1992) Warsaw: Polish Society of Economic, Legal and Court Translators.

Polish News Bulletin of the American and British Embassies. Warsaw: [s.n.]. Also available on NEXIS.

Polish yearbook of international law. (1968–) Wrocław: Ossolineum.

Polska bibliografia prawnicza [Polish legal bibliography]. (1962–) Warsaw: Instytut Nauk Prawnych PAN.

Polskie ustawy: zbiór przepisów. (1993–) Warsaw: C.H. Beck, PWN. Looseleaf. Polish statutes.

Prawo administracyjne: zbiór przepisów. (1995–) Warsaw: C.H. Beck. Looseleaf. Administrative and constitutional legislation.

Prawo podatkowe: zbiór przepisów. (1994–) Warsaw: C.H. Beck. Looseleaf. Tax legislation.

Prawo pracy i ubezpieczeń spolecznych: zbiór przepisów. (1995–) Warsaw: C.H. Beck. Looseleaf. Labour and social legislation.

Prawo ubezpieczeniowe: zbiór przepisów. (1993) 2nd edn. Gdańsk: LEX. Insurance legislation.

Il processo civile polacco. (1981) Rimini: Maggioli.

Przegląd sądowy. (1991–) Warsaw: Wydawnictwo Prawnicze. Formerly *Nowe prawo* (1950–1991). Monthly legal journal.

Przegląd sejmowy. (1993–) Warsaw: Wydawnictwo Sejmowe. Quarterly legal journal.

Przegląd ustawodawstwa gospodarczego. (1948–) Warsaw: Państwowe Wydawnictwo Ekonomiczne. Business law journal.

Review of Central and East European Law. (1992–) Dordrecht: M. Nijhoff. Formerly *Review of Socialist Law* (1975–1991).

Reynolds, T.H. and Flores, A.A. (1989–) *Foreign law: current sources of codes and legislation in jurisdictions of the world.* Littleton, Colo: F.B. Rothman. Looseleaf.

Rocznik statystyczny [statistical yearbook]. Warsaw: GUS.

Rzecznik Praw Obywatelskich (1989–) *Annual report.* Warsaw: Biuro Rzecznika Praw Obywatelskich.

Rzeczpospolita. (1982–) Warsaw: Nakł. PPW 'Rzeczpospolita'. Daily newspaper.

Sanders, P. (1984–) (ed.) *International handbook on commercial arbitration.* Deventer: Kluwer. Looseleaf.

SEEL, Survey of East European Law. (1991–) Ardsley-on-Hudson, NY: Transnational Juris.

Seibel, Claudia (1996) (ed.) *Business law guide to Poland.* Bicester: CCH Europe.

Siekanowicz, P. (1964) *Legal sources and bibliography of Poland.* New York: Praeger.

Skorowidz obowiązujących przepisów prawnych. (1993–) Gdańsk: LEX. Index to legislation.

Skorowidz przepisów prawnych ogłoszonych w Dzienniku Ustaw i Monitorze Polskim w latach 1918–1939 oraz 1944–1992 według stanu prawnego na dzień 1 lipca 1992. (1992) 2nd edn. Warsaw: Urząd Rady Ministrów, Biuro Prawne. Official index to legislation.

Słownik prawniczy polsko–angielski [Polish–English legal dictionary]. (1986) Wrocław: Ossolineum, PWN.

Sokolewicz, W. (1978) (ed.) *The law in Poland: the chosen problems.* Warsaw: Wydawnictwo Prawnicze.

Sołtysiński, S., Szajkowski, A. and Szwaja, J. (1994–1996) *Kodeks handlowy: komentarz.* Warsaw: C.H. Beck, PWN. 2 vols.

Suligowski, A. (1911) *Bibliografja prawnicza polska XIX i XX wieku, poprzedzona słowem wstępnym i rzutem oka na twórczość piśmienniczą prawników polskich w ciagu XIX i pierwszego dziesięciolecia XX wieku.* Warsaw: Nakł. M. Arcta. Legal bibliography.

Wagner, W.J. (1970) (ed.) *Polish law throughout the ages.* Stanford, Cal.: Hoover Institution Press.

Warsaw Voice. (1988–) Warsaw: Polish Interpress Agency. Weekly. Also available on NEXIS.

WESTLAW (available from West Information Publishing Group).

Winiarz, J. (1989) (ed.) *Kodeks cywilny z komentarzem* [Civil Code with commentary]. Warsaw: Wydawnictwo Prawnicze. 2 vols.

Wokanda: orzecznictwo Sądu Najwyższego, Naczelnego Sądu Administracyjnego, Sądów apelacyjnych, Sądu Antymonopolowego. (1992–) Warsaw: Wydawnictwo 'Librata' Monthly.

World law school directory. (1993) Buffalo, NY: Hein. Included also in the volume 'Indices and World Law School Directory' of the looseleaf *Modern legal systems cyclopedia* (1984–) ed. K.R. Redden by the same publisher.

World of learning. (1947–) London: Europa Publications.

Worldwide government directory with international organizations. (1987–) Bethesda, Md: Worldwide Government Directories Inc.

Zbiór umów międzynarodowych Rzeczypospolitej Polskiej [Collection of international treaties]. Warsaw: Polski Instytut Spraw Międzynarodowych.

Zivilverfahrensgesetzbuch der Volksrepublik Polen. (1967) Berlin: Osteuropa-Institut.

CHAPTER TWENTY-TWO

Portugal

MÁRIO BIGOTTE CHORÃO AND
MARIA MANUELA FARRAJOTA

Introduction to the legal system

Historical background

The Portuguese legal system dates back to the foundation of Portugal as a state in 1140. It has as its conceptual predecessors, which influenced it to a greater or lesser extent, Roman law, Teutonic law (mainly visigothic), Christian canon law and Muslim law. The several consecutive periods are distinguished by their dominant features:

- the development of customs and *forais* as sources of law, the latter being enactments by means of which the competent authority (the king or lord) conferred certain privileges on his local community and established the basis of their legal status (1140–1248);
- reception of the *direito comum* [common law, i.e. Roman and canon laws], and compilation of the sources of law [*ordenações*] on the initiative of the king (1248–1750);
- influence of illuminist rationalism (1750–1820);
- predominance of liberal and individualistic ideas, reflected by the movement towards codification initiated in 1833 with the Commercial Code (1820–c.1918);
- emphasis on social concerns in the legal order (c.1918 onwards).

The Portuguese legal system belongs to the civil law family (the romano-germanic, romano-canonic or romanistic legal tradition). The following features stand out: a romanistic base; significant influence of Teutonic and canon law with deep Christian motivations; a normative structure (based in general and abstract norms), and primacy of the (statute) laws as the source of law to which the *jurisprudência* [judgments of the courts] is subordinated; a high degree of technical and scientific elaboration of the law, being the object of university teaching since the foundation of the university system in 1288–1290. Due to the process of discovery and colonization Portuguese law has been projected throughout the world; it is to be found in Angola, Brazil, Cape Verde, East Timor, Guinea-Bissau, Macao, Mozambique, Portuguese India, and São Tomé and Príncipe.

For study of the history of the legal system, one can profitably be referred to, among others: Albuquerque and Albuquerque (1993), Caetano (1992), Almeida Costa (1996), Hespanha (1982), and Gomes da Silva (1992).

Constitution

The Portuguese political and legal system has suffered profound alteration as a consequence of the revolution of 25 April 1974, which led to a new constitution in 1976. This constitution was subject to revisions in 1982, 1989 and 1992. It asserts the unitary character of the Portuguese state, but recognizes the archipelagos of the Azores and Madeira as autonomous regions with self-government and their own politico-administrative rules. Copies of the Constitution of the Portuguese Republic [Constituição da República Portuguesa (CRP)] may be obtained directly from the government printer: Imprensa Nacional – Casa da Moeda (INCM) or from most bookshops. An English translation of the text of the CRP with a constitutional chronology can be found in the encyclopedia *Constitutions of the countries of the world* (Flanz, 1991).

Portugal is a member of the European Union. Its treaty of accession was signed in Lisbon on 12 June 1985. By way of the extraordinary revision of 1992, the indispensable modifications required for the approval and ratification of the European Union treaty (7 February 1992) were introduced into the Constitution.

Sources of law

In addition to sources of international and community origin, the principal formal sources (that is, ways of formation of legal norms) of the Portuguese legal system are:

- the constitutional laws [*leis constitucionais*], including those produced by constitutional revision [*leis de revisão*], the observance of which is specifically reserved to the constitutional court to oversee;
- the ordinary laws [*leis ordinárias*], emanating from the exercise of legislative functions of (i) the *Assembleia da República* [Parliament] (*leis*, statutes); (ii) the government (*decretos-leis*, decree-laws); (iii) the regional legislative assemblies of the Azores and

Madeira (*decretos legislativos regionais*, regional legislative decrees);

- regulations [*regulamentos*] (*decretos regulamentares, portarias, despachos* and *resoluções do Conselho de Ministros* – statutory decrees, orders, dispatches and resolutions of the Council of Ministers), within the administrative competence of the government;
- regulations [*regulamentos*] (*decretos regulamentares regionais* – regional regulatory decrees) within the competence of the regional legislative assemblies and of the regional governments of the Azores and Madeira;
- regulations [*regulamentos*], at the initiative of local authorities (*freguesias, municípios* and *regiões administrativas*);
- collective labour bargaining agreements [*convenções colectivas de trabalho*], made by unions and employers; and
- certain decisions of the courts (including the Constitutional Court) also have the nature of a source of law, and they produce rules with 'general obligatory force'.

Custom occupies a modest position in the system of sources. The latter is given definition mainly by the Constitution, and is further defined by the Civil Code.

The *Diário da República* (DR) [Official Journal] (1976–), 1st Series or Part 1, is the authoritative source publication for: the constitutional laws, international conventions, laws, decree-laws, and regional legislative decrees, decisions of the constitutional court and those of other courts on the decisions of which are conferred generally obligatory force, regulations of the government, and regional regulatory decrees. Labour bargaining agreements [Instrumentos de Regulamentação Colectiva de Trabalho (IRCT)] are gazetted in the *Boletim do Trabalho e do Emprego* [Bulletin of Labour and Employment] (1975–) by the Scientific and Technical Information Service of the Ministry of Labour [Ministério para a Qualificação e o Emprego]. This Bulletin is also available on CD-ROM (see below in **Computer-based systems**).

Introductory works on the legal system and legal research

The more helpful general introductory works on Portuguese law are often cited as those by Oliveira Ascensão (1995) *O Direito. Introdução e Teoria Geral. Uma Perspectiva Luso-Brasileira* [The law. Introduction and general theory. A Luso-Brazilian perspective] and Baptista Machado (1985) *Introdução ao Direito e ao Discurso Legitimador* [Introduction to law and to judicial reasoning]. As to questions of methodology, of special interest are the contemporary studies of

Castanheira Neves (1993 and 1995). An important work of reference with a wide base of information on the Portuguese legal and political systems is the encyclopedia *POLIS. Enciclopédia VERBO da Sociedade e do Estado* (1983–1987).

In English, reference may be made to the chapter 'The legal system of Portugal' by Hostetler (1989) in *Modern legal systems cyclopedia*, as a good general and concise work.

Legislation

The *Diário da República* [Official Journal] (1976–) which is published daily, has been mentioned above. This is the instrumental source *par excellence* for legislation because in it is required to be published the principal normative texts of laws. The legislation generally enters into force on the date specified in the enactment, or otherwise on the date established in special legislation. Presently, Law 6/83 of 29 July establishes entry into force on the fifth day from publication for the continent, on the fifteenth day for the Azores and Madeira, and on the thirtieth day for Macao and abroad. The DR is presented in three parts or 'series'. The first one is, in turn, subdivided into two parts (A and B): in Part A are included the more categorized sources (see above), and for Part B are left, among others, government regulatory decisions and regional regulatory decrees.

Enactments are identified by their given serial number, the year and the date of publication in the DR, e.g. Lei n.° 6/83, de 29 de Julho (unofficially abbreviated as: L 6/83, 29–7) refers to Law no.6 of 1983 passed on 29 July; Decreto-Lei n.° 1/91, de 2 de Janeiro (unofficially abbreviated as: DL 1/91, 2–1) refers to Decree-Law no.1 of 1991 signed on 2 January. The enactments of the autonomous regions have their own enumeration series and are also identified by the letters 'A' (Azores) and 'M' (Madeira).

The DR may be acquired directly from the Government Printer – National Mint, either by annual subscription or by individual daily editions. There is no published index to the DR, either by the INCM, or by a private publisher. However, one may have recourse to a few legal databases for search/reference to the more recent enactments, generally since 1982 (see below under **Computer-based systems**).

The Ministry of Justice edits a bimonthly compilation of the most important legislation with references and a brief summary of other legislation in *Legislação* (1968–), which is a supplement to the *Boletim do Ministério da Justiça* [Bulletin of the Ministry of Justice] (1940–). Other law journals also summarize legislation, for example, *Revista de Legislação e Jurisprudência* [Legislation and Cases Review] (1868–) and *Revista da Ordem dos Advogados* [Bar Association

Review] (1941–). Parliamentary works relating to the making of laws are documented by the *Diário da Assembleia da República* [Diary of the Assembly of the Republic/Parliament] (1976–) also available through the INCM.

Codes and commentaries

Codes

Excluding the constitutional legislation, the codification movement has had the following evolution in Portugal: *Código Comercial* [Commercial Code] with codes promulgated in 1833, 1888; *Código Administrativo* [Administrative Code] 1836, 1842, 1878, 1886, 1895–96, 1936; *Código Penal* [Penal Code] 1852, 1886, 1982; Código Civil [Civil Code] 1867, 1966; *Código de Processo Civil* [Civil Procedure Code] 1876, 1939, 1961; *Código de Processo Comercial* [Commercial Procedure Code] 1895, 1896, 1905; *Código de Processo Penal* [Penal Procedure Code] 1929, 1987.

The principal codified sources now in force are: *Constituição da República Portuguesa* (CRP) [Constitution of the Portuguese Republic] 1976, with revisions; *Código Administrativo* [Administrative Code] 1936, with substantial amendments; *Código Civil* [Civil Code] 1966, with modifications; *Código Comercial* [Commercial Code] 1888, substantially altered, and complemented by prolific legislation, for example, the *Código das Sociedades Comerciais* [Commercial Companies Code] 1986; *Código de Processo Civil* [Civil Procedure Code] 1961 as amended; *Código de Processo Penal* [Penal Procedure Code] 1987; *Código Penal* [Penal Code] 1982, revised in 1995. Mention is also made of the *Código dos Direitos de Autor e Direitos Conexos* [Copyright and Related Rights Code] 1985, *Código do Mercado de Valores Mobiliários* [Securities Market Code] 1991, *Código do Procedimento Administrativo* [Administrative Procedure Code] 1991, and the *Código da Propriedade Industrial* [Industrial Property Code] 1995.

There are compilations of the main laws and complementary/ancillary legislation in different areas of law: for administrative law one should make recourse to the recent publication of Sousa (1995); on economic legislation to Sousa Franco and Paz Ferreira (1996); on tax law to Soares Martínez (1994); on commercial law to Caeiro and Nogueira Serens (1996); on banking and finance law to Neto (1994); and labour law to Monteiro Fernandes and Lourenço (1992). There are several other publications, used widely by practitioners, on some of the codes and related legislation with cases and materials, among which reference may generally be made to the publications of Abílio Neto.

Commentaries and treatises

Each of the following is regarded as the classic book or authority in its own field of law.

Administrative law: Caetano (1980–1991) and Freitas do Amaral (1996);
Civil law: Pires de Lima and Antunes Varela (1987–1995), Mota Pinto (1994), Antunes Varela (1994–1995 and 1996), Oliveira Ascensão (1993), and Galvão Telles (1991);
Civil procedure law: Ferral de Brito, Luso Soares and Mesquita (1994), and Antunes Varela, Bezerra and Sampaio e Nora (1985);
Commercial law and Company law: Ventura (1988, 1989–1993, 1990, 1992, 1993, 1994), Pinto Furtado (1993), and Ferrer Correia (1991);
Constitutional law: Gomes Canotilho and Vital Moreira (1993) and J. Miranda (1991–1996);
Finance law and Tax law: Teixeira Ribeiro (1995), Sousa Franco (1996), and Soares Martínez (1995);
Labour law: Lobo Xavier (1993), and Monteiro Fernandes (1994–1996);
Penal/Criminal law: Cavaleiro de Ferreira (1992), Figueiredo Dias (1993), and Leal Henriques and Sima Santos (1995–1996);
Penal procedure law: Maia Gonçalves (1996) and Marques da Silva (1993–1996);
Private international law: Baptista Machado (1995).

On tax and finance law, there are some useful texts in English. *The Portuguese tax system* is published by the Centro de Estudos Fiscais [Centre for Tax Studies] (1993), and in French there is *Portugal juridique – fiscal, social, comptable* in Dossiers Internationaux Francis Lefebvre (1992). On labour law, there is the recently published *European employment and industrial relations glossary: Portugal* by Pinto, Furtado Martins and Nunes de Carvalho (1996a) who also published a commentary in Portuguese in 1994 on the labour laws of Portugal. Reference should also be made to the section prepared by Pinto (1990) entitled 'Portugal' in the *International encyclopaedia for labour law and industrial relations*, and to the article 'Portugal: industrial relations under democracy' in *Industrial relations in the new Europe* by Barreto (1992).

From an outsider's point of view, the work by Wolf (1993), *Corporate acquisitions and mergers in Portugal: a practical guide to the legal, financial, and administrative implications*, offers the reader a general overview on the Portuguese legal system with a strong emphasis on commercial, company and finance law.

Treaties

The power to negotiate and conclude international conventions (treaties and agreements) is vested in the government (Article 20(1)(b) of the CRP). The approving or ratifying bodies are, as the case may be, the Assembly of the Republic (Article 164(j)) or the Government (Article 200(1)(c)). The President of the Republic ratifies treaties (Article 138(b)), and signs resolutions for the approval of international agreements (Article 137(b)). Article 8(2) of the CRP states as follows: 'The provisions of international conventions properly ratified or approved enter into force as part of Portuguese internal law after their official publication and remain so for as long as they are binding internationally on the Portuguese State'. That publication is in Part A of the 1st Series of the *Diário da República* (1976–). Some treaties are published by the Ministry of Justice in the journal *Documentação e Direito Comparado* [Documentation and Comparative Law] (1980–).

Law reports, judgments

In the Portuguese legal system the judgments of the courts [*jurisprudência*] are not, in principle, a formal source of law, nor are they binding precedents for future cases. Yet some decisions [*acórdãos*] of certain courts are a binding source of law, with a normative nature and of general obligatory force. This is so in the case of decisions of the Constitutional Court [*Tribunal Constitucional* (TC)] which state the unconstitutionality or illegality of rules (Articles 281 and 282 of the CRP); of some decisions [*assentos*] of the Supreme Court of Justice [*Supremo Tribunal de Justiça* (STJ)] by which conflicts between the decisions of superior courts (of the STJ itself or of the Appeal Courts [*Tribunais da Relação*]) are resolved on the same fundamental issue of law, although the general obligatory force of the *assentos* has recently been declared unconstitutional by the Constitutional Court; and of the decisions of the Supreme Administrative Court [*Supremo Tribunal Administrativo* (STA)] stating the illegality of regulations. All these judicial decisions are published in Part A, 1st Series of the *Diário da República* (1976–).

However, even when lacking general normative effectiveness, the *jurisprudência*, especially that of the higher levels of courts exercise a significant influence on formulating and clarifying the legal order. In addition, judges, in making decisions, should take into consideration judgments on similar cases, so as to obtain, as much as possible, a uniform interpretation and application of the law (Article 8(3) of the Civil Code).

Besides the DR, many other publications disclose, to a greater or lesser extent, the decisions of the courts, for example: *Boletim do*

Ministério da Justiça (BMJ) [Ministry of Justice Bulletin] (1940–) which comprises the decisions of several courts; *Acórdãos do Tribunal Constitucional* [Constitutional Court Reports] (1983–); *Acórdãos Doutrinais do Supremo Tribunal Administrativo* [Supreme Administrative Court Doctrine Reports] (1962–); *Dicionário de Legislação e Jurisprudência* [Dictionary of Legislation and Cases] (1930–) which, besides a selection of relevant cases, also includes notes on the most relevant recent legislation; *Colectânea de Jurisprudência* [Collection of Reports] (1976–); *Corpus Juris: Revista de Jurisprudência da Primeira Instância* [Corpus juris: First Instance Reports Review] (1992–). Some of these compilations of reports are indexed every five to ten years in a separate index volume. Cases are usually indexed by court and then by subject or by the articles of the relevant code.

The main legal journals, such as *Revista de Legislação e Jurisprudência* [Legislation and Cases Review] (1868–), *O Direito* [The Law] (1868–), and *Revista da Ordem dos Advogados* [Bar Association Review] (1941–), usually include sections with comments on the case law.

Among the most recent topical reports of judgments are Miranda (1996) on constitutional law, Sima Santos and Leal Henriques (1995) on criminal law, and Mendes Baptista (1996) on labour law.

Selected parts of judgments may also be found on databases (see **Computer-based systems** below).

Computer-based systems

The Ministry of Justice has online databases of documentation and legal information. The electronic access system used is not very user friendly. However, this is expected to change in the near future. The current databases include: (1) JSTJ – JURISPRUDÊNCIA DO STJ [Reports of the STJ] which is not yet complete; (2) JTRP – JURISPRUDÊNCIA DO TRIBUNAL DA RELAÇÃO DO PORTO; (3) JTRL – JURISPRUDÊNCIA DO TRIBUNAL DA RELAÇÃO DE LISBOA [Reports from the Appeal Courts of Lisbon and Oporto] with earlier years still to be loaded; (4) JSTA – JURISPRUDÊNCIA DO STA which is up to date; (5) ATCO – JURISPRUDÊNCIA DO TRIBUNAL CONSTITUCIONAL [Reports from the STA and TC] which is presently inoperative; (6) BPGR – BIBLIOTECA DA PGR; (7) PGRP – PARECERES DO CONSELHO CONSULTIVO DA PGR [Library and Opinions of the Consultative Council of the Attorney General's Office] which is up to date; (8) TJCE – JURISPRUDÊNCIA DO TRIBUNAL DAS COMUNIDADES EUROPEIAS [European Court of Justice Reports]; (9) CELE – TRATADOS E DIREITO DERIVADO COMUNITÁRIO [Treaties and EC Law]; and (10) CELJ – JURISPRUDÊNCIA DO TRIBUNAL DE JUSTIÇA DA UNIÃO EUROPEIA [Reports of the European Court of Justice].

This list includes a number of European Commission databases which are accessible from Portugal (the STAIRS system). Access to the national databases (1 to 8) is still free but access to the EC databases (9 and 10) is already on a fee-paying basis after a trial period of two months. To obtain access to these databases, contact should be established with the Directorate-General of Computing Service or the Head Department for Judicial Informatics, at the Ministry of Justice (addresses below).

The Cabinet Office manages the DIGESTO – SISTEMA INTEGRADO PARA O TRATAMENTO DA INFORMAÇÃO JURÍDICA project, which provides access online to PCMLEX, the central database of legislative information, which covers Parts (Series) 1 and 2 of the DR (the latter only partially); to MFLEX, a sectoral database of the Ministry of Finance, and SOCIOLEX, by the Ministry of Labour; DGCP/DOUT, a specialized database of the Directorate-General of Public Accounting; and REGTRAB, another specialized database of labour regulations. All databases are updated regularly (either daily or weekly). So far, this system provides the most reliable databases in terms of completeness of the current law, although it does not yet provide the full text of the law. The system used by DIGESTO is not user friendly, although this is expected to change within one or two years. Access was free until 1995. A monthly fee is now being asked from private users. Access is obtained through the Secretariat-General at the Cabinet Office (address below).

There is also a commercial database, LEXDATA from the company JURINFOR, with the full text of the law from 1984 to the present. From 1970 until 1984 there are available only the summaries of the 1st Series of the DR, with the risk that they do not reflect the full content of the law. This database is available on disk and on CD-ROM. JURINFOR also has available on disk the most relevant codes.

For citations to the current laws published in the 1st and 2nd Series of the DR with an abstract of each one (but not full text), reference should be made to a few commercial databases: DATAJURIS is an online database of legislation and reports of judgments; as well as LEJURIS, which is mainly on administrative law; ECOLEGIS-ECOJURIS as a database of statutory, regulatory and jurisprudential references provided on disk and with a monthly updating disk sent by post. These databases should be used with caution as most of the summaries provided are those of the DR, which often do not reflect the full content of the law.

On tax law, reference may be made to INFORFISCO, an online database including administrative decisions, tax department statements, and opinions on the law and other government department administrative documents.

As referred to under **Sources of law**, the *Boletim do Trabalho e do Emprego* [Bulletin of Labour and Employment] (1975–) is also available on CD-ROM. The full text of the IRCT from 1979 to 1995 is reproduced in chronological sequence and searching by subject may easily be carried out by means of a thesaurus. A quarterly update accompanies the bulletin itself.

Also managed by the Cabinet Office, but through its Secretariat for the Modernization of the Administration, there is available to the general public through multimedia public kiosks, the Internet at http://www.infocid.pt/ or two disks, a database called INFOCID. This database results from the collaboration between several ministries and includes the 'Guide-book to Government Administration', which has all relevant addresses and telephone numbers, and which is also available in hardcopy on request directly from the Secretariat. INFOCID comprises information from different sources and is organized by subject matter such as legal aid, the law and court services, employment and education, social security, housing, health, etc. The information provided is addressed mainly to the common citizen.

Other important government documents

The governmental initiative for producing legal documentation has belonged mainly to the Ministry of Justice. The Ministry edits the *Boletim do Ministério da Justiça* (BMJ) (1940–) and its supplement, *Legislação* (1968–) and the publication *Documentação e Direito Comparado* (1980–) which includes inter alia treaties and decisions of the European Court of Justice. The BMJ includes a section on legal opinions [*Pareceres*] of the Attorney-General's Office [*Procuradoria-Geral da República*], the directing body of the State Prosecution Service [*Ministério Público*]. This body has the power to 'represent the state, to commence and participate in criminal proceedings, to defend the democratic legality and the interests that the law may determine' (Article 221(1) of the CRP). These legal opinions are also published privately as a collection by Dias (1988–1993).

Presently, the Cabinet Office (*Presidência do Conselho de Ministros*) has an important role in the production and coordination of legal information through the DIGESTO project (see **Computer-based systems**). Within the Cabinet Office, the Legal Centre (CEJUR), further to participating in DIGESTO, performs the functions of a consultancy specialized in the drafting and analysis of the normative acts which fall within the powers of the government, as well as its bills. In this connection see the study by Beleza (1989) on the form of those normative acts.

Encyclopedias

The best Portuguese work of an encyclopedic nature on legal and political matters is the *POLIS. Enciclopédia VERBO da Sociedade e do Estado* (1983–1987), cited above. The second edition is in the course of publication.

In the general work *Verbo. Enciclopédia Luso-Brasileira de Cultura* (1963–1995) may be found a very broad and valuable source of legal and political information. A new edition is now in preparation.

Directories

The only Portuguese directory of lawyers and law firms in Portugal, *Relação dos Advogados e das Sociedades de Advogados* is published with some regularity by the Ordem dos Advogados Portugueses [Portuguese Bar Association] (1996); this directory is organised by judicial district (*comarcas*).

The INFOCID database described above includes a 'Guide-book to Government Administration' which has all relevant addresses and telephone numbers. The *Index* (Ministério da Justiça, Direcção-Geral dos Serviços Judiciários, 1991) contains practical information covering government departments, central government administration, the police department, prison services and the courts. This directory has not been updated. One may ask for a photocopy of updates from the department.

Reference should also be made to a special issue of the *Boletim do Ministério da Justiça* in 1994, which is current to 1992, listing the current and former Ministers of Justice, judges, notaries, registrars, and judicial staff.

Bibliographies

There is no general and exhaustive Portuguese legal bibliography. Apart from several specialized bibliographic lists, complete to a greater or lesser extent, contained in authoritative works on Portuguese law such as those noted in the **Commentatives and treatises** section above, one may consult: Hespanha (1973–1979) 'Introdução bibliográfica à História do Direito Português' [Bibliographic introduction to the history of Portuguese law] in *Boletim da Faculdade de Direito de Coimbra*, and Associação Portuguesa de Editores e Livreiros (1995), a general listing of books in print which shows the law books available through publishers and booksellers.

The *Instituto da Biblioteca Nacional e do Livro* (1995–96) of the Portuguese National Library have now available for purchase on two CD-ROMs a new part of the national bibliography comprising records of all books published from 1985 up until 1995, including law books.

The journal *Scientia iuridica* (1951–) publishes in its first issue each year a bibliographic list by subject matter of legal works published in Portugal in the previous year.

Indexing and abstracting services

There is an exhaustive index to articles in law journals and reviews from 1868 until 1990 by Casanova (1992). The *Boletim do Ministério da Justiça* has a section with a selected bibliography of law journal articles published both in Portugal and abroad.

Dictionaries

Among the Portuguese legal dictionaries, reference should be made to the work of a general character by Ferreira da Cunha (1995), to the collective work *Dicionário Jurídico da Administração Pública* (Fernandes, 1965–1993), to Prata (1995) for civil law, civil procedure law and judicial system, and to Pinto, Furtado Martins and Nunes de Carvalho (1996b) for a glossary on labour law and industrial relations.

For translation one may use the legal dictionaries of Andrade and Saraiva (1991) (English–Portuguese), and Noronha Goyos Jr. (1994) (English–Portuguese and Portuguese–English). As to the German language, there is now a German–Portuguese legal dictionary by Silveira Ramos (1995).

For the banking and finance area, there is the Portuguese–English dictionary by Correia Cunha (1984). For general commercial and international contract drafting, there is a guide to English, French and Portuguese terminology by Boyé (1993) translated and adapted to the Portuguese language.

Reference is also made to the dictionary of Latin adages and legal principles by Simões Correia (1958–1959).

Other reference books

Sousa Santos *et al.* (1996) *Os Tribunais nas Sociedades Contemporâneas: o Caso Português* [The courts in contemporary societies: the Portuguese case] consists of an exhaustive sociological study of the Portuguese legal system, including the delays in court proceedings and access to justice, with an indication of the necessary reforms.

Current information sources

Journals

The main scholarly law journals include *Revista de Legislação e Jurisprudência* (1868–), which also contains jurisprudential commentary on selected laws, *O Direito* (1868–), the *Revista da Ordem dos Advogados* (1941–) from the Bar Association, the *Boletim da Faculdade de Direito da Universidade de Coimbra* (1914–), the *Revista da Faculdade de Direito da Universidade de Lisboa* (1917–), *Direito e Justiça* (1980–) from the Catholic University of Portugal, the *Revista de Direito Luso-Brasileiro* (1982–), from the Luso-Brazilian Institute for Comparative Law, and *Scientia iuridica* (1951–), a biannual journal also on Portuguese and Brazilian comparative law.

Law journals devoted to particular subjects have emerged only relatively recently. On banking and finance law one may refer to *Revista da Banca* (1987–) published by the Portuguese Association of Banks; on competition law, *Boletim da Direcção-Geral de Concorrência e Preços* (1982–); on tax law, *Ciência e Técnica Fiscal* (1964–) by the Centre for Fiscal Studies of the Directorate-General of Inland Revenue, and *Fisco: doutrina: jurisprudência: legislação* (1988–); on criminal law, *Revista Portuguesa de Ciência Criminal* (1991–); on law and economics, *Revista de Direito e Economia* (1975–) by the Interdisciplinary Centre for Legal and Economic Studies of the University of Coimbra; and on public law, *Revista de Direito Público* (1985–).

News information

Covering the major legal developments and recent events related to the legal profession is the *Boletim da Ordem dos Advogados* [Bar Association Bulletin] which is published bimonthly and is distributed on a gratis basis to all members of the Association. It may be obtained directly from the Association.

Business and financial information

For business and financial information about Portugal, one should refer to the government agency operating under the aegis of the Ministry of the Economy, ICEP – *Investimentos, Comércio e Turismo de Portugal* [Investment, Trade and Tourism of Portugal]. Its activities concentrate on the export of Portuguese goods and services, foreign investment in Portugal, Portuguese direct investment abroad, tourism promotion by means of supplying specialized information, advising on investment projects, and managing incentive programmes. This agency supplies information in English about the Portuguese economy, its sectors of activities, laws and regulations, e.g. a guide for investors and a brochure on investment news updates. As to specific information on financial transactions, one should refer to the Securities Market Commission, the regulatory body of the Lisbon Stock Exchange and Oporto Derivatives Exchange, or to the exchanges themselves, which regularly publish brochures and booklets with updated information on recent transactions, turnover and statistics, a quarterly analysis of the functioning of the markets in both Portuguese and English, all available directly from the exchanges (addresses below).

The major business-orientated daily newspaper is the *Diário Económico.*

An interesting work in English on the Portuguese economy, its evolution and current analysis, published inhouse by the Catholic University of Portugal is *The Portuguese economy: a picture in figures. XIX and XX centuries* by César das Neves (1994).

Statistics

The Instituto Nacional de Estatística [National Institute of Statistics] (INE) publishes the bilingual *Anuário Estatístico de Portugal–Statistical Yearbook of Portugal* (1875–), the *Boletim Mensal de Estatística* [Statistical Monthly Bulletin] (1929–), and several other publications on sectoral statistics.

The Ministry of Justice, through the Studies and Planning Department, published a complete book on the statistics of the Portuguese legal system (Ministério da Justiça, Gabinete de Estudos e Planeamento, 1994). It comprises general data on the courts, police departments, organizations for the execution of sentences and social rehabilitation measures, registries and notaries, civil and criminal identification centres, the ombudsman's office services, traffic services, coroners, department for the planning and coordination of combating drug trafficking, etc. It also includes statistics on different categories such as personnel, costs, volume of court proceedings and movements of prisoners, prison establishments, movement of minors and social rehabilitation, notarial and registration activities.

Useful addresses

Professional associations

Associação de Oficiais de Justiça [Court Service Staff Association], Rua Nova do Almada, 45, 1200 Lisboa, Portugal. Tel: +351 1 347 20 66

Associação dos Magistrados Judiciais [Association of Judges], Palácio da Justiça, Rua Marquês da Fronteira, 1070 Lisboa, Portugal. Tel: +351 1 387 0618

Associação Portuguesa de Notários [Portuguese Notaries Association], Rua dos Sapateiros, 115, 3° D, 1100 Lisboa, Portugal. Tel: +351 1 346 3876

Ordem dos Advogados Portugueses (OA) [Portuguese Bar Association], Largo de S. Domingos, n° 14–1°, 1150 Lisboa, Portugal. Tel: +351 1 886 7152. Fax: +351 1 886 2403. E-mail: boa@telepac.pt Internet: http://www.oa.pt

Sindicato dos Magistrados do Ministério Público [Union of State Prosecutors], Palácio da Justiça, Piso 4, Rua Marquês da Fronteira, 1070 Lisboa, Portugal. Tel: +351 1 388 0130/387 0603

Government organizations

Comissão do Mercado de Valores Mobiliários (CMVM) [Securities Market Commission], Avenida Fontes Pereira de Melo, 21, 1050 Lisboa, Portugal. Tel: +351 1 350 3000. Fax: +351 1 353 7077/78

ICEP – Investimentos, Comércio e Turismo de Portugal [Investment, Trade and Tourism of Portugal], Av. 5 de Outubro, 101, 1050 Lisboa, Portugal. Tel: +351 1 793 0103. Fax: +351 1 793 5028. Headquarters in Lisbon but has six regional offices and 42 offices abroad offering business information.

Instituto Nacional de Estatística (INE) [National Institute of Statistics], Av. António José de Almeida, 2, 1000 Lisboa, Portugal. Tel: +351 1 847 0050. Fax: +351 1 795 1507

Ministério da Justiça [Ministry of Justice], Praça do Comércio, 1194 Lisboa Codex, Portugal. Tel: +351 1 347 4780. Fax: +351 1 346 0028

Gabinete de Gestão Financeira (Distribuição de publicações) [Department of Financial Management (Publications distribution)], Rua do Comércio, 56, r/c, 1100 Lisboa, Portugal. Tel: +351 1 888 4402–4. Fax: +351 1 342 7858

Direcção-Geral dos Serviços Judiciários [Directorate-General of Judicial Services], Av. Casal Ribeiro, 48, 1000 Lisboa, Portugal. Tel: +351 1 315 5282/315 3264. Fax: +351 1 353 8702

Gabinete de Direito Europeu [Department of European Law], Av. Óscar Monteiro Torres, 39, 2°, 1000 Lisboa, Portugal. Tel: +351 1 793 5535

See also Databases of the Ministry of Justice under **Legal databases** below.

Ministério dos Negócios Estrangeiros [Ministry of Foreign Affairs], Palácio das Necessidades, Largo do Rilvas, 1350 Lisboa, Portugal. Tel: +351 1 397 0201

Direcção-Geral dos Assuntos Comunitários [Directorate-General of Community Affairs], Cova da Moura, 1, 1350 Lisboa, Portugal. Tel: +351 1 395 4600.

Biblioteca [Library], Cova da Moura, 1, 1350 Lisboa, Portugal. Tel: +351 1 396 5041

Ministério para a Qualificação e o Emprego [Ministry of Labour], Praça de Londres, 2, 1000 Lisboa, Portugal. Tel: +351 1 847 0430. Fax: +351 1 840 6171 (also for the Biblioteca and BTE [Library and Bulletin] and for the Serviço de Informação Científica e Técnica [Scientific and Technical Information Service]).

Presidência do Conselho de Ministros [Cabinet Office], Rua Prof. Gomes Teixeira, 1350 Lisboa, Portugal. Secretaria-Geral. Tel: +351 1 397 7001. Fax: +351 1 397 5349. Centro Jurídico (CEJUR). Tel: +351 1 397 7001. See also INFOCID under **Legal databases** below.

Other organizations

Assembleia da República [Parliament], Palácio de S. Bento, 1249 Lisboa Codex, Portugal. Tel: +351 1 395 3620. Fax: +351 1 397 4865/397 5327

Divisão de Informação Legislativa e Parlamentar [Division of Legislative and Parliamentary Information]. Tel: +351 1 391 2031

Divisão de Edições [Publishing Division]. Tel: +351 1 391 2053. Fax: +351 1 604039

Biblioteca [Library]. Tel: +351 1 397 6289

Banco de Portugal (BP) [Bank of Portugal], Rua do Comércio, 148, 1100 Lisboa, Portugal. Tel: +351 1 346 2931. Fax: +351 1 346 4843. Also: Rua Francisco Ribeiro, 2, 1150 Lisboa, Portugal. Tel: +351 1 313 0000. Fax: +351 1 314 3938

Bolsa de Derivados do Porto (BDP), Departamento de Relações Externas [Oporto Derivative Exchange, External Relations Department], Av. da Boavista, 3433, 4150 Porto, Portugal. Tel: +351 2 618 5858. Fax: +351 2 618 5566

Bolsa de Valores de Lisboa (BVL), Gabinete de Estudos [Lisbon Stock Exchange, Studies Department], Rua Soeiro Pereira Gomes, 1600 Lisboa, Portugal. Tel: +351 1 790 9904. Fax: +351 1 795 2021

Provedoria de Justiça [Ombudsman], R. Pau da Bandeira, 9, 1200 Lisboa, Portugal. Tel: +351 1 60 8161/397 9101. Fax: +351 1 396 1243

Courts

Procuradoria-Geral da República [Attorney General's Office] see under **Libraries** below.

Supremo Tribunal Administrativo [Supreme Administrative Court], Rua de S. Pedro de Alcântara, 75, 1250 Lisboa, Portugal. Tel: +351 1 346 7797. Fax: +351 1 346 6129

Supremo Tribunal de Justiça [Supreme Court of Justice], Praça do Comércio, 1100 Lisboa, Portugal. Tel: +351 1 347 5536/347 2501. Fax: +351 1 347 4919

Tribunal Constitucional [Constitutional Court], Palácio Ratton, Rua de O Século, 111, 1200 Lisboa, Portugal. Tel: +351 1 346 0024. Fax: +351 1 342 1564

Education and training

Centro de Estudos Judiciários [Centre for Judicial Studies] under **Libraries** below.

Among others, one may refer the following law faculties:

Universidade Católica Portuguesa, Faculdade de Direito [Catholic University of Portugal, Faculty of Law], Caminho da Palma de Cima, 1600 Lisboa, Portugal. Tel: +351 1 721 4000. Fax: +351 1 727 0256

Universidade de Coimbra, Faculdade de Direito [University of Coimbra, Faculty of Law] see **Libraries** below.

Universidade de Lisboa, Faculdade de Direito [University of Lisbon, Faculty of Law] see **Libraries** below.

Libraries

Assembleia da República, Biblioteca [Library of Parliament] see **Other organizations** above.

Biblioteca Nacional [National Library], Rua Ocidental, 83, Campo Grande, 1751 Lisboa, Portugal. Tel: +351 1 795 0130. Fax: +351 1 793 3607

Centro de Documentação, Centro Jean Monnet (Comissão das Comunidades Europeias) [Documentation Centre, Commission of the European Communities], Largo Jean Monnet, 1, 3°, 1250 Lisboa, Portugal. Tel: +351 1 350 9870/350 9890

Centro de Estudos Judiciários, Biblioteca [Library of the Centre for Judicial Studies], Largo do Limoeiro, 1100 Lisboa, Portugal. Tel: +351 1 887 4713

Gabinete de Documentação e Direito Comparado [Department of Documentation and Comparative Law], Ministério da Justiça, Rua do Vale de Pereiro, nº 2– 4°, 1250 Lisboa, Portugal. Tel: +351 1 388 1141–4/388 8065. Fax: +351 1 387 1360

Imprensa Nacional – Casa da Moeda, Biblioteca [Library of the Government Printer] see **Publishers and booksellers** below.

Ordem dos Advogados Portugueses, Biblioteca [Library of the Portuguese Bar Association] see **Professional associations** above.

Procuradoria-Geral da República, Biblioteca [Library of the Attorney General's Office], Rua da Escola Politécnica, 140, 1250 Lisboa, Portugal. Tel: +351 1 395 5296/395 1038. Fax: +351 1 397 5255

Universidade Católica Portuguesa, Biblioteca João Paulo II [John Paul II Library, Catholic University of Portugal], Caminho da Palma de Cima, 1600 Lisboa, Portugal. Tel: +351 1 721 4016. Fax: +351 1 726 6160

Universidade de Coimbra, Biblioteca da Faculdade de Direito [Library of the Coimbra Faculty of Law], 3049 Coimbra Codex, Portugal. Tel: +351 39 410 9801. Fax: +351 39 23 353

Universidade de Lisboa, Biblioteca da Faculdade de Direito [Library of the University of Lisbon Faculty of Law], Alameda da Universidade, Cidade Universitária, 1600 Lisboa, Portugal. Tel: +351 1 797 7051. Fax: +351 1 795 0303

Publishers and booksellers

Universidade Católica Editora, Caminho da Palma de Cima, 1600 Lisboa, Portugal. Tel: +351 1 721 4000. Fax: +351 1 727 0256

Coimbra Editora Lda., Rua do Arnado, Apartado 101, 3002 Coimbra Codex, Portugal. Tel: +351 39 25 459. Fax: +351 39 37 531

Edições Cosmos – Livraria Arco-Íris (Publisher and Bookseller), Centro Comercial Arco-Íris, Av. Júlio Dinis, 6–A, loja 23 e 30, 1050 Lisboa, Portugal. Tel: +351 1 795 5140–6. Fax: +351 1 796 9713

Imprensa Nacional – Casa da Moeda (INCM) [Government Printer – National Mint], Rua da Escola Politécnica, 135, 1250 Lisboa, Portugal. Tel: +351 1 397 4768. Fax: +351 1 397 8239. For photocopies of old issues of the Official Journal (DR), Library, Biblioteca, Tel: +351 1 396 2125

Lex, Avenida de Berna, nº 31, r/c Esq., 1050 Lisboa, Portugal. Tel: +351 1 793 1585. Fax: +351 1 796 0747

Livraria Almedina (Publisher and Bookseller), Arco de Almedina, 15, 3000 Coimbra, Portugal. Tel: +351 39 26 980. Fax: +351 39 22 507

Legal databases

DATAJURIS. Direito e Informática, Lda., Rua João Machado, 100, 2º, sala 201, 202, 204, 3000 Coimbra, Portugal. Tel: +351 1 39 32511/32 532. Fax: +351 1 39 32 555

Databases of the Ministry of Justice:

Direcção-Geral dos Serviços de Informática [Directorate General of Computing Service], Av. Casal Ribeiro, 16, 1096 Lisboa codex, Portugal. Tel: +351 356 1061. Fax: +351 1 355 7208

Gabinete Director da Informatização Judiciária [Head Department for Judicial Informatics], Av. Infante Santo, 42–8º, 1350 Lisboa, Portugal. Tel: +351 1 395 3192/395 0787. Fax: +351 1 397 5349

DIGESTO. Secretaria-Geral da Presidência do Conselho de Ministros, Rua Prof. Gomes Teixeira, 1350 Lisboa, Portugal. Tel: +351 1 397 7001. Fax: +351 1 396 8448

ECOLEGIS-ECOJURIS. ATAC, Rua Dr. Teófilo Braga, 3–A, cave, 1200 Lisboa, Portugal. Tel: +351 1 395 2231/395 2274

INFOCID. Secretariado para a Modernização Administrativa, Presidência do Conselho de Ministros, Rua Almeida Brandão, 7, 2º e 3º, 1200 Lisboa, Portugal. Tel: +351 1 392 1500. Fax: +351 1 392 1599. Internet: http://www.infocid.pt/

INFORFISCO. Fiscobase – Gestão de Bases de Dados, Lda. (Internet), Av. Conde Valbom, 30–8º, 1000 Lisboa, Portugal. Tel: +351 1 315 7590. Fax: +351 1 315 7589

LEJURIS. Simões Correia, Editores, Rua Dr. António Loureiro Borges, 1, Arquiparque, Miraflores, 1495 Lisboa, Portugal. Tel: +351 1 790 7075. Fax: +351 1 790 7043

LEXDATA. JURINFOR, Rua Luciano Cordeiro, 123, 3º Esq., 1050 Lisboa, Portugal. Tel: +351 1 352 3316. Fax: +351 1 352 3602

List of works cited

Acórdãos do Tribunal Constitucional [Constitutional Court Reports]. (1983–) Lisbon: Coimbra Editora.

Acórdãos Doutrinais do Supremo Tribunal Administrativo [Supreme Administrative Court Doctrine Reports]. (1962–) Lisbon: Simões Correia, Editores.

Albuquerque, Ruy de and Albuquerque, Martim de (1993) *História do Direito Português. I.* [History of Portuguese law]. 8th edn. Lisbon: Pedro Ferreira.

Almeida Costa, M.J. (1996) *História do Direito Português* [History of Portuguese law] 3rd edn. Coimbra: Almedina.

Andrade, Maria Paula Gouveia and Saraiva, A. Dias (1991) *Dicionário Jurídico Inglês–*

Português [Legal dictionary English–Portuguese]. Porto: ELCLA.

Antunes Varela, J.M. (1994–1995) *Das Obrigações em Geral* [Obligations in general] Coimbra: Almedina. 2 vols.: vol.I, 8th edn; vol.II, 6th edn.

Antunes Varela, J.M. (1996) *Direito da Família. I.Introdução. II.Direito Matrimonial* [Family law. I.Introduction. II.Matrimonial law] 4th edn. Lisbon: Petrony.

Antunes Varela, J.M., Bezerra, J.M. and Sampaio e Nora (1985) *Manual de Processo Civil* [Manual of civil procedure] 2nd edn. Coimbra: Coimbra Editora.

Anuário Estatístico de Portugal – Statistical Yearbook of Portugal. (1875–) Lisbon: INE.

Associação Portuguesa de Editores e Livreiros (1995) *Livros Disponíveis. 1995* [Available books. 1995]. Lisbon: Associação Portuguesa de Editores e Livreiros.

Baptista Machado, J. (1985) *Introdução ao Direito e ao Discurso Legitimador* [Introduction to law and to judicial reasoning]. Coimbra: Almedina.

Baptista Machado, J. (1995) *Lições de Direito Internacional Privado* [Lessons of private international law] 3rd edn. (repr.) Coimbra: Almedina.

Barreto, José (1992) Portugal: industrial relations under democracy. In *Industrial relations in the new Europe*, ed. A. Ferner and R. Hyman, pp. 445–481. London: B. Blackwell.

Beleza, Maria dos Prazeres Pizarro (1989) *Forma Externa dos Actos Normativos do Governo* [External form of the normative acts of the government]. Lisbon: Presidência do Conselho de Ministros – CETAL.

Boletim da Direcção-Geral de Concorrência e Preços [Bulletin of the Directorate-General of Competition and Prices]. (1982–) Lisbon: Direcção-Geral de Concorrência e Preços.

Boletim da Faculdade de Direito da Universidade de Coimbra [Coimbra University Law Faculty Bulletin]. (1914–) Coimbra: Faculdade de Direito da Universidade de Coimbra.

Boletim da Ordem dos Advogados [Bar Association Bulletin]. (1986–) 3rd series. Lisbon: Ordem dos Advogados.

Boletim do Ministério da Justiça [Ministry of Justice Bulletin]. (1940–) Lisbon: Gabinete de Documentação e Direito Comparado da Procuradoria-Geral da República, Ministério da Justiça. A *Número Especial* [Special issue] in 1994 carried a directory of officials.

Boletim do Trabalho e do Emprego [Bulletin of Labour and Employment]. (1975–) Lisbon: Serviço de Informação Científica e Técnica, Ministério para a Qualificação e o Emprego. Also available in CD-ROM format.

Boletim Mensal de Estatística [Statistical Monthly Bulletin]. (1929–) Lisbon: INE.

Boyé, Eric (1993) *Guia da linguagem de contratos internacionais Inglês–Francês–Português* [Guide to the language of international contracts English–French–Portuguese]. Trans. Pedro Marcelino. Lisbon: Publicações Dom Quixote.

Caeiro, António and Nogueira Serens, M. (1996) *Código Comercial. Código das Sociedades Comerciais. Legislação Complementar* [Commercial Code. Commercial Companies Code. Complementary legislation] 8th edn. Coimbra: Almedina.

Caetano, Marcello (1980–1991) *Manual de Direito Administrativo* [Manual of administrative law]. Coimbra: Almedina. 2 vols: vol.I, 10th edn. (repr.), 1991; vol.II, 9th edn. (repr.), 1980.

Caetano, Marcello (1992) *História do Direito Português I. Fontes – Direito Público (1140–1495)* [History of Portuguese law I. Sources – public law] 3rd edn. Lisbon: Verbo.

Casanova, J. F. de Salazar (1992) *O Direito nas Revistas Portuguesas* [The law in Portuguese journals]. Coimbra: Almedina.

Castanheira Neves, A. (1993) *Metodologia Jurídica. Problemas Fundamentais* [Legal methodology. Fundamental problems]. Coimbra: Coimbra Editora.

Castanheira Neves, A. (1995) *Digesta. Escritos acerca do Direito, do Pensamento Jurídico, da sua Metodologia e Outros* [Digesta. Written works on the law, on legal thought, on its methodology and others] Coimbra: Coimbra Editora. 2 vols.

Cavaleiro de Ferreira, M. (1992) *Lições de Direito Penal. Parte Geral. I. A Lei Penal e a Teoria do Crime no Código Penal de 1982* [Lessons of criminal law. General part. I. The criminal law and the theory of crime in the Criminal Code of 1982] 4th edn. Lisbon: Verbo.

Centro de Estudos Fiscais, Direcção-Geral das Contribuições e Impostos (1993) *The Portuguese tax system*. Lisbon: Ministério das Finanças.

César das Neves, João (1994) *The Portuguese economy: a picture in figures. XIX and XX centuries*. Lisbon: Universidade Católica Editora.

Ciência e Técnica Fiscal [Fiscal science and techniques]. (1964–) Lisbon: DGCI-Centro de Estudos Fiscais, Ministério das Finanças.

Colectânea de Jurisprudência [Collection of Reports]. (1976–) Coimbra: Associação Sindical dos Magistrados Judiciais Portugueses.

Corpus Juris: Revista de Jurisprudência da Primeira Instância [Corpus juris: First Instance Reports Review]. (1992–) Porto: Ad Omnes Edições.

Correia Cunha, A. (1984) *Dicionário Bancário Português–Inglês* [Banking dictionary Portuguese–English]. Lisbon: Publicações Europa-América.

DATAJURIS (available from Direito e Informática, Lda.).

Diário da Assembleia da República [Diary of the Assembly of the Republic/Parliament]. (1976–) Lisbon: INCM.

Diário da República [Official Journal]. (1976–) Lisbon: INCM. Published since the 18th century under various titles such as: *Gazeta de Lisboa, Diário do Governo, Diário de Lisboa.*

Diário Económico. Lisbon: Diário Económico. Daily newspaper.

Dias, Francisco M. (1988–1993) *Colectânea de Pareceres da Procuradoria-Geral da República* [Collection of opinions of the Attorney-General's Office]. Coimbra: Coimbra Editora. 5 vols.

Dicionário de Legislação e Jurisprudência [Dictionary of legislation and cases]. (1930–) Lisbon: Simões Correia, Editores.

DIGESTO – SISTEMA INTEGRADO PARA O TRATAMENTO DA INFORMAÇÃO JURÍDICA (available from Secretariat-General of the Cabinet Office).

O Direito. (1868–) Lisbon: E.I.– Editora Internacional.

Direito e Justiça. (1980–) Lisbon: Universidade Católica Editora.

Documentação e Direito Comparado [Documentation and Comparative Law]. (1980–) Lisbon: Gabinete de Documentação e Direito Comparado da Procuradoria-Geral da República, Ministério da Justiça.

Dossiers Internationaux Francis Lefebvre (1992) *Portugal juridique – fiscal, social, comptable*. Paris: Éditions Francis Lefebvre.

ECOLEGIS-ECOJURIS (available from ATAC)

Fernandes, J.P. (1965–1993) (ed.) *Dicionário Jurídico da Administração Pública* [Public administration legal dictionary]. Lisbon: José Pedro Fernandes. 5 vols. Vol.1 (1990) in 2nd edn.

Ferral de Brito, W., Luso Soares, F. and Mesquita, D.R. (1994) *Código de Processo Civil* [Civil Procedure Code] 9th edn. Coimbra: Almedina.

Ferreira da Cunha, P. (1995) *Tópicos Jurídicos* [Legal topics]. Porto: Asa.

Ferrer Correia, A. (1991) *Lições de Direito Comercial* [Lessons of commercial law]. Lisbon: Lex.

Figueiredo Dias, J. (1993) *Direito Penal Português. Parte Geral. II. As Consequências Jurídicas do Crime* [Portuguese criminal law. General part. II. The legal consequences of crime]. Lisbon: Aequitas-Editorial Notícias.

Fisco: doutrina: jurisprudência: legislação [Tax: doctrine: reports: legislation]. (1988–) Lisbon: Lex.

Flanz, Gisbert H. (1991) Portugal. In *Constitutions of the countries of the world*, eds A.P. Blaustein and G.H. Flanz, vol.XV. Dobbs Ferry, NY: Oceana.

Freitas do Amaral, Diogo (1996) *Curso de Direito Administrativo I*. [A course of administrative law I.] 2nd edn. Coimbra: Almedina.

Gabinete de Estudos e Planeamento (1994) *Estatísticas de Justiça, 1994* [Statistics on justice]. Lisbon: Ministério da Justiça.

Galvão Telles, Inocêncio (1991) *Direito das Sucessões. Noções Fundamentais* [Succession law. Fundamental notions] 6th edn. Coimbra: Coimbra Editora.

Gomes Canotilho, J.J. and Moreira, Vital (1993) *Constituição da República Portuguesa Anotada* [Constitution of the Portuguese Republic annotated] 3rd edn. Coimbra: Coimbra Editora.

Gomes da Silva, N. J. Espinosa (1992) *História do Direito Português. Fontes do Direito* [History of Portuguese law. Sources of law] 2nd edn. Lisbon: Fundação Calouste Gulbenkian.

Hespanha, A.M. (1973–1979) Introdução bibliográfica à História do Direito Português [Bibliographic introduction to the history of Portuguese law], *Boletim da Faculdade de Direito de Coimbra*, **49** (1973), pp. 47–133; **50** (1974), pp. 1–106; **55** (1979), pp. 39–89.

Hespanha, A.M. (1982) *História das Instituições. Épocas medieval e moderna* [History of institutions. Medieval and modern epochs]. Coimbra: Almedina.

Hostetler, C.L. (1989) (ed.) The legal system of Portugal. In *Modern legal systems cyclopedia*, ed. K.R. Redden, vol 4, pp. 4.110.1–35. Buffalo, NY: Hein. Looseleaf. Date from title page of volume, partly revised 1993.

INFOCID (available from Secretariat for the Modernization of the Administration, Cabinet Office).

INFORFISCO (available from Fiscobase – Gestão de Bases de Dados, Lda.).

Instituto da Biblioteca Nacional e do Livro (1995–96) *Bibliografia Nacional Portuguesa* [Portuguese National Bibliography]. Lisbon: Instituto da Biblioteca Nacional e do Livro. Covers 1985–1995. 2 CD-ROM.

Leal Henriques, M. and Sima Santos, M. (1995–1996) *Código Penal* [Criminal Code]. Lisbon: Rei dos Livros. 2 vols.

Legislação [Legislation]. (1968–) Lisbon: Gabinete de Documentação e Direito Comparado da Procuradoria-Geral da República, Ministério da Justiça.

Leite de Campos, D. (1990) (ed.) *Direito das Empresas* [Law of Enterprises]. Oeiras: Instituto Nacional de Administração.

LEJURIS (available from Simões Correia, Editores).

LEXDATA (available from JURINFOR).

Lobo Xavier, B. da Gama. (1993) *Curso de Direito do Trabalho* [Labour law course] 3rd edn. Lisbon: Verbo.

Maia Gonçalves, M. Lopes (1996) *Código de Processo Penal Anotado* [Criminal Procedure Code annotated] 7th edn. Coimbra: Almedina.

Marques da Silva, Germano (1993–1996) *Processo Penal* [Criminal procedure]. Lisbon: Verbo. 3 vols: vol.I. (1996), 3rd edn; vol.II. (1993); vol.III. (1994).

Mendes Baptista, A. (1996) *Jurisprudência do Trabalho Anotada. Relação Individual de Trabalho.* [Labour cases annotated. Conditions of employment] 2nd edn. Lisbon: SPB.

Ministério da Justiça, Direcção-Geral dos Serviços Judiciários (1991) *Index*. Lisbon: Ministério da Justiça.

Miranda, Jorge (1991–1996) *Manual de Direito Constitucional* [Manual of constitutional law] 2nd edn. Coimbra: Coimbra Editora. 4 vols: Tomo I (1996), 5th edn; Tomo II (1991), 3rd edn; Tomo III (1994), 3rd edn; Tomo IV (1993).

Miranda, Jorge (1996) *Jurisprudência Constitucional Escolhida* [Selected constitutional reports] vol.1 Lisbon: Universidade Católica Editora.

Monteiro Fernandes, A. (1994–1996) *Direito do Trabalho* [Labour Law] Vol.I. *Introdução. Relações Individuais de Trabalho* [Introduction. Conditions of employment] 9th edn. Vol.II. *Relações Colectivas de Trabalho* [Collective bargaining agreement] 4th edn. Coimbra: Almedina.

Monteiro Fernandes, A. and Lourenço, J.A. (1992) *Leis do Trabalho* [Labour laws] 6th edn. Coimbra: Almedina.

Mota Pinto, C.A. (1994) *Teoria Geral do Direito Civil* [General theory of civil law] 3rd edn. Coimbra: Coimbra Editora.

Neto, Abílio (1994) *Legislação Bancária e Financeira* [Banking and financial legislation] 2nd edn. Lisbon: Ediforum.

Noronha Goyos Jr, D. (1994) *Dicionário Jurídico Inglês-Português, Português–Inglês*

[English–Portuguese, Portuguese–English legal dictionary]. São Paulo: Noronha.
Oliveira Ascensão, J. (1993) *Direito Civil. Reais* [Civil law. Property] 5th edn. Coimbra: Coimbra Editora.
Oliveira Ascensão, J. (1995) *O Direito. Introdução e Teoria Geral. Uma Perspectiva Luso-Brasileira* [The law. Introduction and general theory. A Luso-Brazilian perspective] 9th edn. Coimbra: Almedina.
Ordem dos Advogados Portugueses (1996) *Relação dos Advogados e das Sociedades de Advogados* [Directory of lawyers and law firms]. Lisbon: Ordem dos Advogados.
Pinto, Mário (1990) Portugal. In *International encyclopaedia for labour law and industrial relations*, ed. R. Blanpain. Dordrecht: Kluwer. Looseleaf.
Pinto, M., Furtado Martins, P. and Nunes de Carvalho, A. (1994) *Comentário às Leis do Trabalho I. Regime Jurídico do Contrato Individual de Trabalho (Dec.-Lei nº. 49 408, de 24–XI-69)* [Commentary to the labour laws I. Legal regime of the employment contract (Decree-Law no.49 408, of 24 November 1969)]. Lisbon: Lex.
Pinto, M., Furtado Martins, P. and Nunes de Carvalho, A. (1996a) *European employment and industrial relations glossary: Portugal*. London: Sweet & Maxwell.
Pinto, M., Furtado Martins, P. and Nunes de Carvalho, A. (1996b) *Glossário de Direito do Trabalho e Relações Industriais* [Glossary of labour law and industrial relations]. Lisbon: Serviço de Publicações Oficiais das Comunidades Europeias – Universidade Católica Editora.
Pinto Furtado, J. (1993) *Deliberações dos Sócios (Artigos 53º a 63º) – Comentário ao Código das Sociedades Comerciais* [Resolutions of the partners (articles 53 to 63) – commentary to the Commercial Companies Code]. Coimbra: Almedina.
Pires de Lima, F.A. and Antunes Varela, J.M. (1987–1995) *Código Civil Anotado* [Civil Code annotated]. Coimbra: Coimbra Editora. 4 vols: vol.I *(Artigos 1º–761º)*, 4th edn; vol.II *(Artigos 762º–1250º)*, 3rd edn; vol.III *(Artigos 1251º–1575º)*, 2nd edn; vol.IV *(Artigos 1576º–1795º)*, 2nd edn; vol.V *(Artigos 1796º–2023º)*.
POLIS. Enciclopédia VERBO da Sociedade e do Estado (1983–1987) Lisbon: Verbo. 5 vols.
Prata, Ana (1995) *Dicionário Jurídico. Direito Civil. Direito Processual Civil. Organização Judiciária* [Legal dictionary. Civil law. Civil procedure law. Judicial system] 3rd edn. Coimbra: Almedina.
Revista da Banca [Bank Review]. (1987–) Lisbon: Associação Portuguesa de Bancos.
Revista da Faculdade de Direito da Universidade de Lisboa [University of Lisbon Law Faculty Review]. (1917–) Lisbon: Faculdade de Direito da Universidade de Lisboa.
Revista da Ordem dos Advogados [Bar Association Review]. (1941–) Lisbon: Ordem dos Advogados.
Revista de Direito e Economia [Law and Economics Review]. (1975–) Coimbra: Centro Interdisciplinar de Estudos Juridico–Económicos da Universidade de Coimbra.
Revista de Direito Luso–Brasileiro [Portuguese–Brazilian Law Review]. (1982–) Rio de Janeiro: Instituto de Direito Comparado Luso-Brasileiro.
Revista de Direito Público [Public Law Review]. (1985–) Lisbon: Copi.
Revista de Legislação e Jurisprudência [Legislation and Cases Review]. (1868–) Coimbra: Coimbra Editora.
Revista Portuguesa de Ciência Criminal [Portuguese Criminal Science Review]. (1991–) Lisbon: Aequitas.
Scientia iuridica – Revista de Direito Comparado Português e Brasileiro [Journal of Portuguese and Brazilian Comparative Law]. (1951–) Braga: Associação Jurídica de Braga, Universidade do Minho.
Silveira Ramos, F. (1995) *Dicionário Jurídico Alemão–Português* [Legal dictionary German–Portuguese]. Coimbra: Almedina.
Sima Santos, M. and Leal Henriques, M. (1995) *Jurisprudência Penal* [Penal cases]. Lisbon: Rei dos Livros.
Simões Correia, A. (1958–1959) *Dicionário de Adágios e Princípios Jurídicos* [Dictionary of adages and legal principles]. Lisbon: Livraria Ferin.

Soares Martínez, P. (1994) *Impostos Portugueses* [Portuguese taxes]. Coimbra: Almedina.
Soares Martínez, P. (1995) *Direito Fiscal* [Tax law] 7th edn. Coimbra: Almedina.
Sousa, A. Francisco de (1995) *Legislação Administrativa* [Administrative legislation]. Lisbon: *i* Editores.
Sousa Franco, A.L. (1996) *Finanças Públicas e Direito Financeiro* [Public finance and finance law] 4th edn. Coimbra: Almedina. 2 vols.
Sousa Franco, A. L. and Paz Ferreira, E. (1996) *Colectânea de Legislação de Direito Económico* [Collection of legislation of economic law]. Coimbra: Almedina.
Sousa Santos, B. *et al.* (1996) *Os Tribunais nas Sociedades Contemporâneas: o Caso Português* [The courts in contemporary societies: the Portuguese case]. Porto: Edições Afrontamento.
Teixeira Ribeiro, J.J. (1995) *Lições de Finanças Públicas* [Lessons on public finance]. 5th edn. Coimbra: Coimbra Editora.
Ventura, Raúl (1988) *Alterações do Contrato de Sociedade – Comentário ao Código das Sociedades Comerciais* [Alterations to the memorandum and articles of association – commentary to the Commercial Companies Code] 2nd edn. Coimbra: Almedina.
Ventura, Raúl (1989–1993) *Sociedade por Quotas – Comentário ao Código das Sociedades Comerciais* [Limited partnership – commentary to the Commercial Companies Code]. Coimbra: Almedina. 3 vols: vol.I (Artigos 197° a 239°), 2nd edn, 1993; vol.II (Artigos 240° a 251°), 1989; vol.III (Artigos 252° a 264°), 1991.
Ventura, Raúl (1990) *Fusão, Cisão, Transformação de Sociedades (Parte Geral – Artigos 97° a 140°) – Comentário ao Código das Sociedades Comerciais* [Merger, cision, alteration of companies' status (general part – articles 97 to 140) – commentary to the Commercial Companies Code]. Coimbra: Almedina.
Ventura, Raúl (1992) *Estudos Vários sobre Sociedades Anónimas – Comentário ao Código das Sociedades Comerciais* [Various studies on public limited companies – commentary to the Commercial Companies Code]. Coimbra: Almedina.
Ventura, Raúl (1993) *Dissolução e Liquidação de Sociedades – Comentário ao Código das Sociedades Comerciais* [Dissolution and liquidation of companies – commentary to the Commercial Companies Code] 2nd edn. Coimbra: Almedina.
Ventura, Raúl (1994) *Novos Estudos sobre Sociedades Anónimas e Sociedades em Nome Colectivo – Comentário ao Código das Sociedades Comerciais* [New studies on public limited companies and unlimited partnership- commentary to the Commercial Companies Code]. Coimbra: Almedina.
Verbo. Enciclopédia Luso-Brasileira de Cultura. (1963–1995) Lisbon: Verbo. 23 vols.
Wolf, Ronald C. (1993) *Corporate acquisitions and mergers in Portugal: a practical guide to the legal, financial, and administrative implications.* London: Graham & Trotman.

CHAPTER TWENTY-THREE

Romania

ANNE PRIES

Introduction to the legal system

The foundations of Romania as an independent state were laid after the Crimean war. The Paris Agreement of 1858 recognized the unification of the two Romanian principalities of Moldavia and Wallachia. The first Constitution, enacted in 1866, was a liberal one based on the Belgian Constitution of 1831, which at that time was considered to be the most advanced in Europe. All the major codes were modelled on the French legislation.

After World War I the 'old Kingdom', as it is called, was extended to 'Greater Romania' with the Romanian provinces of Transylvania and Bukovina from the Austro-Hungarian empire and Bessarabia from Russia. A new constitution was enacted in 1923. This constitution, which was in force until 1938, was based on the same principles as its predecessor. A third constitution was adopted on 20 February 1938 but was suspended in September 1940. After World War II King Michael I re-enacted the Constitution of 1923 but on 30 December 1947 he was forced to abdicate and Romania was proclaimed a 'People's Republic' [*Republica Populară Romănă*]. The Romanian provinces Bessarabia and Bukovina were incorporated into the Soviet Union. A history up to this point is contained in Hitkins (1994) *Rumania 1866–1947*.

The Constitution of 1948 which followed was completely different in ideology. More than four decades of communist dictatorship followed. A second communist constitution was proclaimed in September 1952 and in July 1965 the third communist constitution dubbed Romania a 'Socialist Republic' [*Republica Socialistă România*].

In December 1989 the communist regime of Nicolae Ceauşescu collapsed. A new constitution was adopted in the Constituent Assembly

Session of 21 November 1991. It entered into force after its approval by a national referendum of 8 December 1991. The text was published in the *Monitorul Oficial* [Official Gazette], part I, no.233. The traditional French influence can be found in the new constitution. The new parliament, the supreme representative body of the Romanian people and the sole legislative body of the state, consists of the Chamber of Deputies [*Camera Deputaţilor*], the second chamber with 341 members and the Senate [*Senat*], the first chamber with 143 members. The government consists of the prime minister, ministers and other members as established by organic law. The President of Romania, elected by popular vote, represents the state; he designates the prime minister.

The introduction of the Ombudsman [*Avocatul Poporului*] is something quite new in the Romanian Constitution (art.55–57). He is appointed by the Senate for a term of four years and reports to the two Chambers annually or on request. The reports may contain recommendations on legislation or measures of any other nature for the defence of the citizens' rights and freedoms.

A printed bilingual (Romanian and English) version of the Romanian Constitution (*Constituţia României*, 1991) was edited and published by the 'Monitorul Oficial – Self-managed Public Company'. An English translation of the new Constitution of Romania can also be found in *The rebirth of democracy: 12 constitutions of central and eastern Europe* (1995, pp. 429–493) as well as in *The constitutions of new democracies in Europe* (Raina, 1995) and in *Constitutions of central and eastern Europe* (Flanz, 1995).

An English translation of the communist constitution was published in *The constitutions of the communist world* (Simons, 1980). German translations of the Constitution and other documents are to be found in a looseleaf edition of Brunner, Schmidt and Westen (1992–) *Wirtschaftsrecht der osteuropäischen Staaten*. Recent commentary appears in a chapter by Mihai (1995), Constitutional law of Romania.

Introductory works on the legal system and legal research

The chapter in the looseleaf *Modern legal systems cyclopedia* is a comprehensive introduction to the legal system which was re-issued in December 1995 although the date of writing is not apparent (Top, 1995). The article by Reynolds (1992) on socialist legal systems in the *International Journal of Legal Information* gives useful background information as does the book by Michta (1994). The chapter on Romania in the work of Gsovski and Grzybovski (1959) deals with an earlier period.

Good guides to earlier material are the chapter on Romania by Hunter (1982) in *Official publications of the Soviet Union and eastern Europe 1945–1980* and the basic work of Stoicoiu (1964).

Legislation

The official gazette *Monitorul Oficial al României* [Official Monitor of Romania] has been published since 1879. The title has varied, as has the subdivision into separate parts, but this title was adopted again when publication recommenced on 22 December 1989 after the fall of the Ceauşescu regime.

Laws and decrees, decisions of the Council of Ministers and other normative acts as well as international treaties are published in Part I; the proceedings of the Grand National Assembly are published in Part II and official communiques, publications and announcements of central organizations in Part III. In Supplement A the list of prices issued by the Ministry of Home Trade is published and a special economic section can be found in Part IV. An index to the *Monitorul Oficial* Part I has been published annually in the *Repertoriul anual al actelor normative* (1971–1991) covering the years from 1970 until it was succeeded by the *Anuarul Legislativ al actelor publicate in Monitorul Oficial al României: in anul* . . . (1992–) covering the years from 1991 onwards.

Decisions of the National Assembly, decrees of the Council of State and of the Communist Party, Presidential Decrees and Resolutions of mass organizations were published in the *Colecţia de legi şi decrete* [Collection of laws and decrees] from 1949 until 1988. In 1991 it was succeeded by *Legislaţia României* [Legislation of Romania], a quarterly with texts of laws issued by the Romanian parliament. Starting with 1994 the *Parliamentary Bulletin* has been issued by the Chamber of Deputies. Besides news of standing committees and other parliamentary issues, it contains legislative summaries of draft laws, legislative proposals and texts of laws in English.

Collections of Decisions of the Council of Ministers, and other normative acts which form secondary legislation, have been published in 1951–1962 and 1969–1988: *Colecţia de hotărîri de Consiliului de Miniştri şi alte acte normative*; they include alphabetical and chronological indexes. Starting with 1992, Decisions of the Government and other normative acts are published in the *Hotărâri ale Guvernului României şi alte acte normative*.

A retrospective compilation of legislation *Repertoriul legislaţiei României* has been published in 1938–1947, 1957 and 1966 by the Legislative Council and thereafter by the Ministry of Justice. The *Repertoriul Legislaţiei*, issued in 1976 again by the Legislative Council, was supplemented in 1978, 1979, 1985, and 1989 and most recently by the Parliament in 1992. In 1995 the *Repertoriul actelor publicate în Monitorul Oficial al României, Partea I, în perioada 22 decembrie 1989–31 ianuarie 1995* [Repertoire of acts, published in the official gazette in the period 22 December 1989–31 January 1995] was published covering the important period of rapid change in the legal system.

A selection of Romanian legislation in Romanian and in translation can be found in *Législation Roumaine = Romanian Legislation*, a trilingual publication of the Parliament of Romania, issued irregularly since 1991. It is also entitled *Digest of general laws of Rumania*. Up to now 15 volumes have been published. A survey of the most important laws and international agreements published in the official gazettes of Romania and the other countries of Central and East Europe is given in *WGO: Monatshefte für Osteuropäisches Recht*. It contains German translations of the full text of some laws.

Codes and commentaries

Official publications are published by the press of the *Monitorul Oficial*. During the post-war period all publishing was state controlled but now several private publishers (associations of jurists) are active in this field.

Before 1944 Romania had a Civil Code which came into force on 1 December 1865, inspired by the Code civil français. That old civil code is in force again (*Monitorul Oficial* 21 November 1991), albeit with changes and amendments especially in the fields of business activities such as companies, banking, joint ventures, bankruptcy and or antitrust. Romania lacked many laws of this kind. A printed version of the current civil code was published in 1993 entitled *Codul Civil*. A recent introduction to Romanian civil law is *Drept civil Român* (Beleiu, 1994). The textbook of Vlachide (1994) on the principles of civil law should also be mentioned.

The Code of Civil Procedure, originally of 11 September 1865, was amended 27 February 1973 and recently on 23 July 1993 (*Monitorul Oficial*, 26 July 1993). A textbook of current Romanian civil procedure has been written by Ungureanu (1994).

The first Commercial Code was promulgated in the *Monitorul Oficial* of 10 May 1887, amended in 1895, 1900, 1902, 1906, 1929, 1930, 1931, 1932, 1933, 1934 and 1943. In 1946–1947 the state-guided economy was introduced and the Code was not applied during the period up to 1989. After the collapse of the communist regime, the Commercial Code in force in 1940 was reintroduced. A printed edition of the current Commercial Code is the *Codul commercial Român* (1991). New in Romanian legislation is financial law and a recent publication in this field is *Drept financiar* (Condor, 1994). Thanks to the resuscitation of the Civil Code and Commercial Code, both dating from the 19th century, Romania now has at its disposal a civil law infrastructure.

Since the start of 1990 the Criminal Code and the Code of Criminal Procedure have been changed in several aspects. For example, the death penalty has been abolished (*Monitorul Oficial*, 4/1990). The Criminal Code in force was promulgated 21 June 1968, amended on 27 February 1973,

29 March 1973, 6 July 1992 and 22 September 1992. A printed edition of the current criminal code *Codul Penal* was published in 1995 (up to date to 31 December 1994). A handbook for criminal law covering the special part, i.e. the separate delicts, is *Drept penal Român: partea specială* (Loghin and Toader, 1994). Works on the general part were written by Zolyneak (1993), Bulai and Mitrache (1994) and by Mitrache (1995).

The Code of Criminal Procedure was promulgated 12 November 1968, amended 27 February 1973, 29 March 1973 and 1 July 1993. The *Codul de procedură penală* (1994) has been published by Lumina Lex. In the same year the treatise *Procedură penală (partea generală)* by Mateuţ was published. A combined edition of the Criminal Code and the Code of Criminal Procedure was edited by Răvescu (1992).

Laws on the organization and function of several ministries, including the Ministry of Justice, were promulgated on 28 December 1992 and again on 29 July 1994.

Treaties

Texts of international treaties are published in the *Monitorul Oficial* Part I.

Law reports, judgments

The Law on Judicial Organization was published in the *Monitorul Oficial* I, no.197, 13 August 1992; an English translation has been published in the series *Romanian Legislation*. The courts are divided into: courts of first instance; tribunals; courts of appeal; the Supreme Court of Justice. There is a Superior Council of Magistracy which performs the role of a disciplinary council for judges.

Decisions of the Supreme Court were promulgated annually in the *Culegere de decizii ale Tribunal suprem pe anul . . .* covering 1952 until 1987 (1955–1989). For the first few years decisions in civil cases and in criminal cases were published together in one volume, from 1958 in separate volumes. A few selected decisions appear in Romanian law journals (see below).

A new institution in Romanian constitutional law is the Constitutional Court consisting of nine judges, appointed for a term of nine years. Three judges have to be appointed by the Chamber of Deputies, three by the Senate and three by the President. Decisions of the Constitutional Court are published in the *Monitorul Oficial*. Legislation on the Constitutional Court is given in art.140–145 of the Constitution of Romania of 8 December 1991, *Monitorul Oficial* I, 1991, no.233; in Law no.47 of 1992, 16 May 1992, on the Organization and Functioning of the Constitutional Court, *Monitorul Oficial* I, 1992 no.101 and in Regulations on the Organization and Functioning of the Constitutional Court of 18 June 1992, *Monitorul Oficial* I, 1992 no.190. A description of the development of a constitutional judiciary in Eastern Europe has been given by Brunner (1992). Decisions of the Constitutional Court taken in 1994, are collected in *Curtea Constituţională: Culegere de decizii şi hotărâri 1994* (1995) and appear regularly in *Legislaţia României* (1991–). Selected decisions may appear in *East European Case Reporter of Constitutional Law* (1994–).

The *OMRI Daily Digest* published by the Open Media Research Institute contains English summaries of selected court decisions.

Directories

The *Romania directory: public institutions and organizations*, published in 1990 by Editura Cronos, is still of use for the names and contact details of government and public bodies.

Bibliographies

The Biblioteca Naţională [National Library] in Bucharest is the centre of current national bibliographies. It publishes the *Bibliografia natională a Româniaei* in four series which is the only current bibliographical source for law books published in Romania. Since 1992 official publications can be found in *Publicaţii oficiale*, arranged by subject with an alphabetical index. The Juridical Institute of the Romanian Academy of Sciences has published a bilingual, Romanian and French, retrospective legal bibliography for the periods 1944–1968 and 1968–1973, both edited by Ionascu (1969 and 1974).

Dictionaries

No Romanian legal dictionaries of any value have been published after 1990. The most recent one discovered is *Dicţionar juridic, selectiv* (Ghimpu *et al.*, 1985). General dictionaries are: *Dictionary English–Romanian, Romanian–English*, compiled by a board of scholars in New Delhi in 1991, and the new New York edition of the dictionary compiled by Schönkron (1992).

Other reference books

Useful background information on the country can be found in Grothusen (1977) and in the annual survey of Economist Publications

Country profile: annual survey of political and economic background. Since 1992 several series have been published including one on Romania. The dissertation of Verheijen (1995) and the work of Brown (1994) may also be helpful.

Current information sources

Journals, research reports

The juridical departments of the Romanian universities have their own journals: *Analele Ştiinţifice ale Universităţii 'Al.I. Cuza' din Iaşi. Secţiunea III (Ştiinţe juridice)* [Scientific annals of the University 'Al.I. Cuza' in Iaşi. Section III, Juridical sciences] (1954–) and *Analele Universităţii Bucureşti. Drept* [Annals of the University of Bucharest. Law]. Both are general legal periodicals covering a wide range of topics and containing several articles in French.

The Association of Jurists in Bucharest publishes *Revista Justiţia nouă* (1991?–), formerly *Dreptul* (1990–1991?), formerly *Revista româna de drept* (1967–1989), formerly *Justiţia nouă* (1944–1966), a general legal periodical covering subjects relevant to legal practice. The Academia Româna, Institutul de Cercetări Juridice [Juridical Institute of the Academy of Sciences] issues *Studii de drept Românesc: serie nouă* [Studies in Romanian Law: new series] (1989–), formerly *Studii şi cercetări juridice* (1956–1989) [Juridical studies and research], focused on legal sciences and civil law, and the *Revue Roumaine des Sciences Juridiques* (1964–) in French.

A new periodical issued by the publisher Lumina is *Revista de drept commercial* [Review of commercial law] (1991–) which appeared quarterly 1991–1993 and in six issues per year from 1993. Members of the editorial board include the Minister of Justice, the Governor of the Central Bank, judges of the Supreme Court, the Court of Bucharest and the court of commercial arbitration, and other well-known lawyers. It consists of two parts: studies and commentaries in the field of commercial law and reports of court decisions.

Developments in Romanian law are covered more and more frequently by journals published abroad devoted to Central and Eastern Europe such as the *Review of Central and East European Law* (1992–), published in cooperation with the Institute of East European Law and Russian Studies of Leiden University, and the *Parker School Journal of East European Law* (1994–). Other information on legal issues in Romania can be found in *BNA's Eastern Europe Reporter* (1991–), *East European Constitutional Review* (1992–) published by the Center for the Study of Constitutionalism in Eastern Europe at the University of Chicago Law School, in the *Journal of Constitutional Law in Eastern and Central Europe* (1994–), published in the Netherlands, and in the *Eastern European Forum Newsletter* (1993–), a publication of the London International Bar Association. Newsletters from law firms operating in the area often provide valuable information, for example, *Central Europe Newsletter* (1992–) and *Central European and CIS Legal Update* (1993–) among others.

Recht in Ost und West (1957–), published in Berlin, gives legal information in German, as does *Osteuropa-Recht* (1955–). An overview of the legal changes in Romania and the other Central and East European states can be found in the *Jahrbuch für Ostrecht* (1960–).

News information

The Open Media Research Institute in Prague publishes *Transition: Events and Issues in the Former Soviet Union and East Central and Southeastern Europe* (1995–), a weekly journal of analyses and news focusing on the political, social, economic, legal and other affairs.

Business and financial information

The *Monitorul Oficial* publishes the List of Prices issued by the Ministry of Home Trade in Supplement A and a special economic section in Part IV. The International Center for Entrepreneurial Studies (ICES), an affiliate of the Institute for Contemporary Studies in San Francisco, issues the *ICES: Quarterly Newsletter* (1992–) focused on the economic restructuring in Romania.

Many foreign periodicals are also focused on Romanian economic activities and business such as *Image on Central + Eastern Europe* (1991–), KPMG's International newsletter, *Law in Transition, a Newsletter on Legal Cooperation and Training* (1994–) from the European Bank for Reconstruction and Development, and *Doing business in eastern Europe* (1992–). A German periodical devoted to legal aspects of commercial activities in Eastern Europe is *WiRO: Wirtschaft und Recht in Osteuropa* (1992–).

The electronic periodical *OMRI Daily Digest* (1994–) gives political, economic and legal information; Part II covers Central, Eastern and Southeastern Europe. Political and economic information on the country can also be found in the *SWB: Summary of World Broadcasts*, (1993–).

Statistics

The *Anuarul statistic al Republicii Socialiste România* [Statistical yearbook of the Socialist Republic of Romania] was published by the Central Statistical Board in the period 1904–1940 and 1957–1989. Since 1990 it has been succeeded by a new series *Anuarul statistic al României* [Statistical yearbook of Romania]. English and French editions are also published.

Useful addresses

Associations of lawyers

Asociaţia de drept internaţional şi relaţii internaţionale din România [Association of international law and international relations of Romania], Şos. Kiseleff 47, 71268 Bucharest, Romania. Tel: +40 1 185462

Uniunea Advocatilor din Romania [Union of Romanian Advocates], Palatul Justitiei, Calea Rahovei no.2–4, sector 4, 70502 Bucharest, Romania. Tel: +40 1 314 9229. Fax: +40 1 312 1085

Uniunea Juriştilor democraţi din România [Democratic Lawyers Union of Romania], Bd. Magheru 22, 70158 Bucharest, Romania. Tel: +40 1 593440

Government organizations

Office of the Prime Minister, Piaţa Victoriei 1, 71201 Bucharest, Romania. Tel: +40 0 143400. Fax: +40 0592018

Ministerul Justiţiei [Ministry of Justice], Bd. Mihail Kogălniceanu 33, 70602 Bucharest, Romania. Tel: +40 1 144400/0 148623. Fax: +40 0 131219

National Statistical Office, Str. Stavropoeos 6, 70075 Bucharest, Romania. Tel: +40 1 6155528/6140262. Fax: +40 1 6145910/6415055

Education and training

Universitatea Buchareşti, Blvd. M. Kogălniceanu 64, 70609 Bucharest, Romania. Tel: +40 1 3120419. Fax: +40 1 6131760

Research institutes

Academia Româna. Institutul de Cercetări Juridice [Romanian Academy. Institute of Juridical Studies], Calea 13 Septembrie 13, Sector 5, 76117 Bucharest, Romania. Tel: +40 1 312 4496

International Center for Entrepreneurial Studies (ICES), University of Bucharest, Blvd. Mihail Kognălniceanu 64, Bucharest, Romania. Tel/Fax: +40 1 6133340

Libraries

Biblioteca Academiei Române [Library of the Romanian Academy], Calea Victoriei 125, 71102 Bucharest, Romania. Tel: +40 1 6503043

Biblioteca Centrală Universitară, Str. Transilvaniei 6, 70778 Bucharest, Romania. Tel: +40 1 6154240. Fax: +40 1 6132842

Biblioteca Naţională, Str. Ion Ghica 4, Bucharest, Romania. Tel: +40 1 6157063. Fax: +40 1 3123381

Camera Deputatilor, Biblioteca [Library of the Chamber of Deputies], Alleea Mitropolici no.5, Bucharest, Romania. Tel: +40 1 6385090, ext 43. Fax: +40 1 3120826

Senat, Oficiul de Informare-Documentare, Biblioteca [Library and Information Service of the Senate], Piata Revoluţiei no.1, sect.1, Bucharest, Romania. Tel: +40 1 617061 ext.186 and 172. Fax: +40 1 3121184

Publishers and booksellers

Centrala Editoriala, Piata Scinteii no.1, R-71341 Bucharest, Romania. Coordinates book publishing and distribution in Rumania. Publishes a quarterly: *Romanian Books* (in English, French, German and Russian).
Editura Lumina Lex SRL, Str. Prof. Ion Filibiliu 5, sector 3, 74238 Bucharest, Romania. Tel: +40 1 6217650
Monitorul Oficial al României, Publicitate [Official Gazette of Romania. Publishing House], Str. Blanduziei 1, 70132 Bucharest, Romania. Tel: +40 1 117702
Open Media Research Institute (OMRI), 140 62 Prague 4. Motokov Building. Na Strzi 63., Prague, Czech Republic. Tel: +42 2 6114 2114. Fax +42 2 6114 3323. Internet: http://www.omri.cz/Publications/Digests/DigestIndex.html
ROMPRESFILATELIA, PO Box 12–201, Galea Grivitei no.60–64, Bucharest, Romania. Handles orders for Romanian periodicals.

General

Romania home page. Internet: http://www.info.polymtl.ca/Romania/
Romanian Chamber of Commerce, Blvd. Nicolae Balcescu 22, 79502 Bucharest, Romania. Tel: +40 1 3121312. Fax: +40 1 3122091

List of works cited

Analele Ştiinţifice ale Universităţii 'Al.I. Cuza' din Iaşi, Secţiunea III (Ştiinţe juridice) [Scientific annals of the University 'Al.I. Cuza' in Iaşi. Section III (Juridical sciences)]. (1954–) Iaşi: Universitãea 'Al.I. Cuza' din Iaşi.
Analele Universităţii Bucureşti. Drept [Annals of the University of Bucharest. Law]. (1951–) Bucharest: Universitatea Buchareşti.
Anuarul Legislativ al actelor publicate in Monitorul Oficial al României: in anul. . . . (1992–) Bucharest: Monitorul Oficial. Covers 1991–.
Anuarul statistic al Republicii Socialiste România [Statistical yearbook of the Socialist Republic of Romania]. (1904–1940; 1957–1989) Bucharest: Direcţia Centrală de Statistică.
Anuarul statistic al României [Statistical yearbook of Romania]. (1990–) Bucharest: Direcţia Centrală de Statistică.
Beleiu, G. (1994) *Drept civil Român.* Bucharest: Sansa SRL.
Bibliografia naţională a Româniaei. (1990–) Bucharest: Biblioteca naţională. Earlier series: 1951–1989).
BNA's Eastern Europe Reporter. (1991–) Washington, DC: Bureau of National Affairs.
Brown, J.F. (1994) *Hopes and shadows: eastern Europe after communism.* Durham, NC: Duke University Press.
Brunner, G. (1992) Development of a constitutional judiciary in eastern Europe. *Review of Central and East European Law* 1992, no.6, pp. 535–553.
Brunner, G., Schmidt, K. and Westen, K. (1992–) *Wirtschaftsrecht der osteuropäischen Staaten.* Baden-Baden: Nomos.
Bulai, C. and Mitrache, C. (1994) *Drept Penal Român: partea generală. Culegere de probleme din practica juriciară* [Romanian civil law: general part. Collection of problems in the juridical practice]. Bucharest: Sansa SRL.
Central Europe Newsletter. (1992–) London: Clifford Chance.

Central European and CIS Legal Update. (1993–) London: Baker & McKenzie.
Codul Civil. (1993) Bucharest: Editura ALL.
Codul commercial Român. (1991) Iaşi: Editura Coda.
Codul de procedură penală. (1994) Bucharest: Lumina Lex.
Codul Penal. (1995) Bucharest: Lumina Lex.
Colecţia de hotărîri de Consiliului de Miniştri şi alte acte normative [Collection of Decisions of the Council of Ministers and other normative acts]. (1951–1962; 1969–1988) Bucharest: Monitorul Oficial.
Colecţia de legi şi decrete [Collection of laws and decrees]. (1949–1988) Bucharest : Monitorul Oficial. Title varies.
Condor, I. (1994) *Drept financiar*. Bucharest: Monitorul Oficial.
Constituţia României = The Constitution of Romania. (1991) Bucharest: 'Monitorul Oficial – Self-managed Public Company'.
Country profile: annual survey of political and economic background [Romania]. (1992–) London: Economist Publications.
Culegere de decizii ale Tribunal suprem pe anul . . . (1955–1989) Bucharest: Editura de Stat. Covering 1952–1987.
Curtea Constituţională: Culegere de decizii şi hotărâri 1994. (1995) Bucharest: Regia Autonomă 'Monitorul Oficial'.
Dictionary English–Romanian, Romanian–English (1991) New Delhi: J.L.N. University of International Studies.
Digest of general laws of Romania. (1991–) Bucharest: Parlamentul Romaniei. Also entitled *Législation roumaine = Romanian legislation*. English, French and Romanian text.
Doing business in eastern Europe. (1992–) Bicester: CCH Editions Ltd.
Dreptul. (1990–1991?) Bucharest: Association of Jurists.
East European Case Reporter of Constitutional Law. (1994–) Den Bosch: Bookworld.
East European Constitutional Review. (1992–) Chicago, Ill.: Center for the Study of Constitutionalism in Eastern Europe at the University of Chicago Law School in partnership with the Central European University.
Eastern European Forum Newsletter. (1993–) London: International Bar Association.
Flanz, G.H. (1995) *Constitutions of central and eastern Europe*. Dobbs Ferry, NY: Oceana.
Ghimpu Sanda *et al.* (1985) *Dicţionar juridic, selectiv*. Bucharest: Albatros.
Grothusen, K. (1977) (ed.) *Rumänien = Romania*. Südosteuropa-Handbuch Bd.2 = Handbook on South Eastern Europe; vol.2. Göttingen: Vandenhoeck & Ruprecht.
Gsovski, V. and Grzybovski, K. (1959) (eds) *Government, law and courts in the Soviet Union and eastern Europe*. London: Stevens & Sons; The Hague: Mouton & Co. 2 vols.
Hitkins, K. (1994) *Rumania 1866–1947*. Oxford: Clarendon Press.
Hotărâri ale Guvernului României şi alte acte normative. (1992–) Bucharest: Guvernul Romaniei.
Hunter, B. (1982) Romania. In *Official publications of the Soviet Union and eastern Europe 1945–1980: a select annotated bibliography*, ed. G. Walker, pp. 221–262. London: Mansell.
ICES: Quarterly Newsletter. (1992–) Bucharest: International Center for Entrepreneurial Studies, Bucharest University.
Image on Central + Eastern Europe: the International KPMG Newsletter. (1991–) Brussels: KPMG.
Ionascu, T.R. (1969) *Bibiliographie juridique roumaine: Bibliografie juridica romana (1944–1968)*. Bucharest: Academia Româna, Institutul de Cercetări Juridice.
Ionascu, T.R. (1974) *Bibiliographie juridique roumaine: Bibliografie juridica romana (1968–1973)*. Bucharest: Academia Româna, Institutul de Cercetări Juridice.
Jahrbuch für Ostrecht. (1960–) Munich: Beck.
Journal of Constitutional Law in Eastern and Central Europe. (1994–) Den Bosch: Bookworld.
Justiţia nouă. (1944–1966) Bucharest: Association of Jurists.

Law in Transition: a Newsletter on Legal Cooperation & Training from the European Bank for Reconstruction and Development. (1994–) London: European Bank for Reconstruction and Development.

Legislaţia României [Legislation of Romania]. (1991–) Bucharest: Parlamentul Romaniei.

Législation Roumaine = Romanian Legislation. (1991–) Bucharest: Parlamentul Romaniei. English, French and Romanian text. Also entitled *Digest of general laws of Romania.*

Loghin, O. and Toader, T. (1994) *Drept penal Român: partea specială.* Bucharest: Sansa SRL.

Mateuţ, G. (1994) *Procedură penală (partea generală).* Iaşi: Chemarea.

Michta, A. (1994) *The government and politics of postcommunist Europe.* Westport, Conn.: Praeger.

Mihai, L. (1995) Constitutional law of Romania. In *Legal reform in post-communist Europe*, eds S. Frankowski and P.B. Stephan III, pp. 51–59. Dordrecht: Martinus Nijhoff Publishers.

Mitrache, C. (1995) *Drept Penal Român: partea generală.* [Revised and enlarged edition]. Bucharest: Sansa SRL.

Monitorul oficial al României. (1879–) Bucharest: Monitorul oficial. Under this title with new numbering, Annul 1 onwards, from 22 December 1989. Formerly *Buletinul oficial* 1949–1989 and *Monitorul oficial* until 1949.

OMRI Daily Digest. (1994–) Prague: Open Media Research Institute. Electronic periodical (available at Listserv@ubvm.cc.Buffalo.edu).

Osteuropa-Recht. (1955–) Stuttgart: Gesellschaft für Osteuropakunde.

Parker School Journal of East European Law. (1994–) New York: Parker School of Foreign and Comparative Law, Columbia University School of Law.

Parliamentary Bulletin. (1994–) Bucharest: Monitorul Oficial. Compiled by the Chamber of Deputies of the Parliament of Romania. English language.

Publicaţii oficiale. (1992–) Bucharest: Monitorul Oficial.

Raina, P. (1995) (ed.) *The constitutions of new democracies in Europe.* Cambridge: Merlin Books.

Răvescu, V. (1992) (ed.) *Codul penal şi codul de procedură penală.* Bucharest: Editura 'Cutuma'.

The rebirth of democracy: 12 constitutions of central and eastern Europe. (1995) Edited by The International Institute for Democracy. Strasbourg: Council of Europe Press.

Recht in Ost und West. (1957–) Berlin: Arno Spitz.

Repertoriul actelor publicate în Monitorul Oficial al României, Partea I, în perioada 22 decembrie 1989–31 ianuarie 1995 [Repertoire of acts, published in the official gazette in the period 22 December 1989–31 January 1995]. (1995) Bucharest: Monitorul oficial.

Repertoriul anual al actelor normative. (1971–1991) Bucharest: Monitorul oficial. Covering 1970–1990.

Repertoriul legislaţiei României. (1992–) ed. by the Romanian Parliament. Bucharest. See the **Legislation** section of the chapter for the publishing history prior to 1992.

Review of Central and East European Law. (1992–) Dordrecht: Kluwer. Published in cooperation with the Institute of East European Law and Russian Studies of Leiden University. Formerly *Review of Socialist Law.*

Review of Socialist Law. (1975–1991) Dordrecht: Nijhoff. Published in cooperation with the Institute of East European Law and Russian Studies of Leiden University. Superseded by *Review of Central and East European Law* (1992–).

Revista de drept commercial. (1991–) Bucharest: Lumina.

Revista Justiţia nouă. (1991?–) Bucharest: Association of Jurists.

Revista româna de drept. (1944–1989) Bucharest: Association of Jurists.

Revue Roumaine des Sciences Juridiques. (1964–) Bucharest: Academia Româna,

Institutul de Cercetări Juridice.

Reynolds, T.H. (1992) Socialist legal systems: reflections on their emergence and demise. *International Journal of Legal Information*, **20**, pp. 215–237.

Romania directory: public institutions and organizations. (1990) Bucharest: Editura Cronos.

Romanian Législation = Législation Roumaine (1991–) Bucharest: Parlamentul Romaniei. English, French and Romanian text. Also entitled *Digest of general laws of Romania.*

Schönkron, Marcel (1992) *Romania–English, English Romanian dictionary*. New York: Hippocrene Books.

Simons, William B. (1980) *The constitutions of the communist world.* Alphen aan den Rijn: Sijthoff & Noordhoff.

Stoicoiu, V. (1964) *Legal sources and bibliography of Romania.* Praeger Publications in Russian History and World Communism, no.24. Westport, Conn.: Praeger.

Studii de drept Românesc: serie nouă [Studies in Romanian law: new series]. (1989–) Bucharest: Academia Româna, Institutul de Certecari Juridice.

Studii şi cercetări juridice [Juridical studies and research] (1956–1989) Bucharest: Academia Româna, Institutul de Cercetări Juridice.

SWB: Summary of World Broadcasts: part 2, Central Europe, the Balkans. (1993–) Reading: BBC Monitoring.

Top, T. (1995) The legal system of the Socialist Republic of Romania (SRR.). In *Modern legal systems cyclopedia*, ed. K.R. Redden, vol.8, pp. 8.130.1–8.130.121. Buffalo, NY: Hein. Looseleaf.

Transition: Events and Issues in the Former Soviet Union and East Central and Southeastern Europe. (1995–) Prague: OMRI.

Ungureanu, O. (1994) *Actele de procedură în procesul civil: (La instanţa de fond)*. Bucharest: Sansa SRL.

Verheijen, A.T.G. (1995) *Constitutional pillars for new democracies: the cases of Bulgaria and Romania.* Leiden: DSWO Press.

Vlachide, P.C. (1994) *Repetiţia principilor de drept civil*. Bucharest: Europea Nova. 2 vols.

WGO: Monatshefte für Osteuropäisches Recht. (1959–) Heidelberg: Müller.

WiRO: Wirtschaft und Recht in Osteuropa. (1992–) Munich: Beck.

Zolyneak, M. (1993) *Drept Penal: (Partea Generala)*. Iaşi: Chemarea.

CHAPTER TWENTY-FOUR

Russia

W.E. BUTLER

Introduction to the legal system

This chapter contains a bibliography of the principal official publications of the Russian Federation (RF) and subjects of the RF, together with references to secondary sources that develop observations or provide documentation relating to the main text. The references to secondary sources are confined chiefly to those in the English language and to those relating to the RF since independence in 1991. For the Soviet period see chapter 21 of *Soviet law* (Butler, 1988: pp. 403–14).

Introduction to the legal system

While Russian law dates back to at least the 10th century, in its most recent autonomous incarnation Russian law dates from the dissolution of the Union of Soviet Socialist Republics (USSR) on 8 December 1991. The USSR was formed by the Treaty of the Union, concluded on 30 December 1922, by the Russian Soviet Federated Socialist Republic (RSFSR), Ukrainian SSR, Belorussian SSR, and Transcaucasian SFSR. The last soon broke up into Armenia, Azerbaidzhan, and Georgia. When the RSFSR, Belorussian SSR, and Ukrainian SSR on 8 December 1991 denounced the Treaty of the Union in their capacities as original signatories, joined on 21 December 1991 by most of the remaining union republics who expressed their assent in the Declaration of Alma Ata (the three Baltic republics already having seceded from the USSR), the USSR disappeared as a state and juridical person.

The members of the Commonwealth of Independent States (CIS), formed in late December 1991 at Almaty, are presently twelve, consisting of Armenia, Azerbaidzhan, Estonia, Georgia, Kazakhstan, Kyrgyzia, Moldova, Russian Federation, Tadzhikistan, Turkmenistan, Ukraine, and Uzbekistan. The three Baltic republics are not members. The CIS is an international organization with its own charter, secretariat (Minsk, Belarus), organs, and jurisdiction; it operates on the basis of international treaties concluded among the members. The principal constitutive documents are translated in *Basic legal documents of the Russian Federation* (Butler, 1992).

The demise of the USSR did not, however, mean that Soviet law simultaneously disappeared in Russia. In the Russian Federation, Soviet law continues in force insofar as: it has not been expressly repealed; or it has not been superseded by RF legislation; or it is not inconsistent with RF legislation. Soviet law in this sense means normative acts adopted or issued by agencies or officials of the USSR itself. In another sense Soviet law also continues to operate in the RF: in the form of rules enacted by agencies or officials of the RSFSR but identical or similar to those adopted by the USSR. Here the legacy of Soviet law is most substantial, for a massive body of RSFSR legislation in force prior to December 1991 substantially replicated that of the USSR.

The verbatim transcripts, materials, and documents of the Constitutional Assembly convoked to draft the 1993 Constitution of the Russian Federation have been published in twenty-one volumes, *Konstitutsionnoe soveshchanie. Stenogrammy, Materialy, Dokumenty. 29 aprelia–10 noiabria 1993 g.* (1995–96). The Constitution in English is available in Blaustein (1994) and also at the International Constitutional Law Internet site (http://www.uni-wuerzburg.de/law/index.html).

Introductory works on the legal system and legal research

On the late Soviet period, see *Soviet law* (Butler, 1988) and *Demise of the Soviet Union: a bibliographic survey of English writings on the Soviet legal system, 1900–1991* (Kavass, 1992), which has been updated for 1992 in the *International Journal of Legal Information* (Kavass, 1993). Similar bibliographical works on earlier periods are also by Kavass (1988 and 1991). Books published on the subject are recorded annually in *Russian Law Books* (1997–) edited by Butler and Murjas.

Legislation

Official gazettes

The RF always has regarded itself as the legal successor to the Russian Empire and as the legal continuer of the former Soviet Union.

Accordingly, when the USSR was dissolved in December 1991, the Parliament of the RF continued to publish its weekly official gazette without interruption, the *Vedomosti s"ezda narodnykh deputatov Rossiiskoi federatsii i verkhovnogo soveta Rossiiskoi federatsii*. When the Congress of People's Deputies was suspended in September 1993 after the abortive attempt to capture the White House, publication ceased after issue No.34 and was resumed in spring 1994, back-dated to January 1994, as *Vedomosti federal'nogo sobraniia Rossiiskoi federatsii*.

Parliamentary, presidential, and governmental enactments have been published in the *Sobranie zakonodatel'stva Rossiiskoi federatsii* weekly from May 1994, replacing the *Sobranie aktov Prezidenta i Pravitel'stva Rossiiskoi federatsii*, issued weekly from 1 July 1992.

The newspaper *Rossiiskaia gazeta* (1990–), published five days per week, enjoys the status of an official gazette.

The State Duma issues eighteen times annually the *Sbornik federal'nykh konstitutsionnykh zakonov i federal'nykh zakonov* (1994–) and a monthly collection of its decrees and other documents: *Gosudarstvennaia Duma. Postanovleniia i drugie dokumenty* (1994–) and verbatim transcripts of its sessions in *Gosudarstvennaia Duma. Stenogrammy zasedanii (biulleten')* (1994–) published in sixty parts each year, to which the *Dnevnik zasedanii Gosudarstvennoi Dumy* (1994–) is issued bimonthly as a supplement.

Departmental gazettes

The general gazette specializing in departmental legislation is that published by the Ministry of Justice of the RF, succeeding the bulletin commenced in 1972 by the Ministry of Justice of the USSR. Issued monthly, it is presently titled: *Biulleten normativnykh aktov ministerstv i vedomostv Rossiiskoi federatsii*. The same Ministry also issues the *Biulleten' Ministerstva iustitsii RF* (1995–) appearing six times yearly. With effect from 1 July 1996 and appearing twice monthly, the *Biulleten' normativnykh aktov federal'nykh organov ispolnitel'noi vlasti* (1996–) is an official publication containing the full texts of normative acts adopted by federal agencies of executive power which have been registered at the Ministry of Justice of the Russian Federation.

The newspaper *Rossiiskaia gazeta* contains a weekly Departmental Supplement [*Vedomstvennoe prilozhenie*] which as a rule is subscribed to separately and contains departmental enactments registered by the Ministry of Justice. The draft Russian Civil Code was published therein in instalments.

The Federal Commission for Securities and the Stock Market publishes *Vestnik federal'noi komissii po tsennym bumagam i fondovomu rynku pri pravitel'stve Rossiiskoi federatsii* (1996–), the experimental issue being dated 30 January 1996. The State Customs Committee of the

RF publishes a monthly bulletin of official materials issued by it, *Tamozhennye vedomosti* (1994–) and the monthly *Tamozhennyi vestnik* (1993–). *Nalogovyi vestnik* (1995–), founded by the State Tax Service of the RF, is issued monthly. The Ministry of Labour of the RF publishes the monthly *Biulleten' Ministerstva truda Rossiiskoi federatsii* which includes all material relating to labour, pension, social security, veterans and relevant Constitutional Court decisions. *Patenty i litsenzii* (1966–) from the Committee of the RF for Patents and Trademarks contains informational materials, normative acts, and occasional international treaties in its subject area. *Panorama privatizatsii* (November 1992–), issued twice monthly by the State Committee of the Russian Federation for the Administration of State Property, contains key GKI enactments.

Unofficial collections of legislation

Among journals publishing current legislation are the weekly *Kadastr* (1991–); normative acts of other CIS states are sometimes published. Also see *Normativnye akty po finansam, nalogam i strakhovaniiu* (1991–), issued monthly as an annex to *Zakonodatel'stvo i ekonomika* (1992–) which contains economic legislation and commentary, issued twice monthly. KODEKS is published at St Petersburg weekly and contains legislation and commentary, see **Computer-based systems** below. Also see *Pravovoe obozrenie*, a monthly journal issued the Ministry of Justice of the RF, Iniurkollegiia, and others.

Current legislative acts are also published by various newspapers such as *Iuridicheskaia gazeta*, issued weekly by the Union of Jurists and the weekly *Iuridicheskii vestnik* (1991–), issued by the Ministry of Justice of the RF. *Ekonomika i zhizn'* (1918–), *Finansovaia gazeta* (July 1991–), *Biznes i banky* (1990–) is an important weekly for departmental tax, financial, economic, and banking materials. Published twice monthly, *Nalogi* (1993–) contains tax legislation and instructions.

Legislation in translation

Translations of the major codes are noted in the next section. Much legislation including many of the earlier codes are in *Collected legislation of the USSR and Constituent Union Republics* (Butler, 1979–91). For more recent materials see *Russia and the Republics: legal materials* (Hazard and Pechota, 1993–), a looseleaf service which uses texts supplied by many sources. *Soviet Statutes and Decisions* (1964–1991) which was renamed *Statutes and Decisions* (1991/92–) is a journal of translations of selected laws of the USSR's successor states; there tends to be considerable delay between promulgation and the appearance of the translation. *Sudebnik* (1996–), described under **Journals** below, also contains translated documents, for example vol.1, no.1, March 1996 contains among others a translation of the Federal Law on Joint-Stock Societies adopted on 24 November 1995. Both Simmonds and Hill and Interlist (addresses below) publish translations and commentaries on codes and laws of the RF and other CIS states and only a selection are mentioned specifically below.

Codes

Civil Code. The Civil Code of the Russian Federation is being adopted in three separate parts, Part One having been enacted on 21 October 1994 (in force from 1 January 1995) and Part Two, on 22 December 1995 (in force from 1 March 1996). Both parts have since been amended. Countless texts of each or both parts have been issued in the Russian Federation and both parts are translated in *Civil Code of the Russian Federation* (Butler and Gashi-Butler, 1997). Until Part Three is enacted, in 1997, the RSFSR Civil Code of 1964 and the 1991 Fundamental Principles of Civil Legislation of the USSR and Republics remain in force in relevant part. The modern generation of intellectual property legislation in Russia is collected in *Intellectual property in the Russian Federation: collected legislation* (Butler and Gashi-Butler, 1994).

Family Code. The Russian Family Code was adopted on 8 December 1995.

Labour Code. The 1971 Labour Code of the RSFSR as amended to 1 December 1993 is available in a translation by Butler (1993) *The Labour Code of the Russian Federation.*

Criminal Code. The Russian Criminal Code was adopted 24 May 1996 and entered into force as from 1 January 1997, replacing the 1960 Criminal Code of the RSFSR as amended.

Code of Civil Procedure. The Code of Civil Procedure in force remains that of the RSFSR adopted in 1964 as amended. The most recent translation in English appears in *Soviet codes of law* (Simons, 1980).

Code of Criminal Procedure. The Code of Criminal Procedure in force is that of the RSFSR adopted in 1960, as amended. The most recent translation in English appears also in Simons (1980).

Other Codes. Among the principal codes adopted during the Soviet era and still in force in the Russian Federation are the Air Code of the USSR, the Merchant Shipping Code, and the Code on Administrative Violations; see Butler (1995) *The Merchant Shipping Code of the USSR.*

Treaties

The publication of international treaties of the RF commenced in the monthly *Biulleten' mezhdunarodnykh dogovorov* (March 1993–), which is issued by the Administration of the President of the RF.

The Ministry of Foreign Affairs of the RF continues to publish the annual collection of treaties in force, renamed in 1994 (vol.47) *Sbornik mezhdunarodnykh dogovorov SSSR i Rossiiskoi federatsii*, containing treaties which entered into force during the calendar year 1991 and which are treaties of the Russian Federation as the state-continuer of the USSR. The monthly journal *Diplomaticheskii Vestnik* (1992–), issued by the Ministry of Foreign Affairs, contains the texts of diplomatic documents.

International treaties are also published in the *Ezhegodnik mezhdunarodnogo prava Rossiiskoi federatsii 1992–*, published since 1994 at St Petersburg by the Russian Association of International Law (continuing the *Sovetskii ezhegodnik mezhdunarodnogo prava (1958–91)*, and in the journals *Moskovskii zhurnal mezhdunarodnogo prava* (quarterly, 1991–) and *Zhurnal mezhdunarodnogo chastnogo prava* (twice yearly, St Petersburg, 1993–).

Vneshniaia torgovlia (1931) continues to be issued monthly in separate Russian and English (*Foreign Trade*), French, German and Spanish language versions by the Ministry of Foreign Economic Relations and contains the texts of commercial treaties.

Law reports, judgments

The Supreme Court of the RF continues to publish the monthly *Biulleten' verkhovnogo suda Rossiiskoi federatsii* (1992–).

From December 1992 the Supreme Arbitrazh Court of the RF commenced publication of the monthly *Vestnik vysshego arbitrazhnogo suda Rossiiskoi federatsii*, devoted principally to commentary, legislation, and decrees of the Plenum of the court.

The *Vestnik konstitutsionnogo suda Rossiiskoi federatsii*, issued bimonthly, commenced publication in January 1993 with an experimental number '0'.

Computer-based systems

The information below has been gathered from a variety of sources, including advertising material of the firms themselves. Direct inquiries should be made in each case regarding upgrading policies, software details, CD-ROM and online availability, compatibility, networking, and delivery. Addresses of suppliers are given below in the **Useful addresses** section. Most sources are adding daily to their databases and changing their technologies to meet recent developments. In addition, both LEXIS/NEXIS and WESTLAW contain a selection of translated laws and treaties affecting foreign economic activity and extensive coverage of law and business-related periodicals.

ARGUMENT: Issued by Agentstvo 'Biznes-Press' in Moscow, the databases include material on central and local governmental structures and officials, as well as the press centres of State agencies of the RF. Thematic offerings include the Regions of Russia, the Structures of Power of Russia, the CIS, and Baltic Countries.

DELO I PRAVO: Moscow-based, this complex of databases claims to have all legislation 'from the commencement of the formation of market relations in Russia.' Three basic services are offered: Russia, Moscow and Moscow Region, and Taxes.

ETALON: Created by the Scientific Centre for Legal Information of the Ministry of Justice of the Russian Federation for courts and justice agencies, but widely installed in central government offices and available commercially from the Ministry of Justice.

GARANT: One of the earliest legislative database systems to appear on the market, GARANT is widely used in Russian government offices despite its limitations. It is available online or in diskette or CD-ROM form. A separate English-language version is to be avoided.

INEK (INEC): Situated in Moscow, this firm offers more than 15 000 documents in subject categories: Economic Law and the Market (tax, land, labour, housing, investment, and other legislation), Insurance, Banking Law (includes basic legislation, instructions, letters, telegrams), foreign economic activity, legislative acts of the city of Moscow. Commentaries on individual enactments and branches of law are a speciality. Fully cross-referenced, including later upgrades.

IUSIS (JUSIS): Issued by the Legal Information Agency Interlex, legislative databases exist for Russian legislation (State Duma, President, Government, Central Bank, Ministry of Finances, Ministry of Labour), Moscow, Moscow Region, St Petersburg, Leningrad Region, court decisions, notarial practice, arbitrazh practice, commentaries, and model documents.

KODEKS: St Petersburg-based, this is one of the best legal databases available, with a variety of subject categories: economic legislation, bookkeeping and finances for enterprises, banking and finance, customs law, international law, securities and privatization, arbitrazh law and practice, construction and architecture, insurance, legal commentaries and advice, samples of legal and business documents, customs legislation of the CIS and the Baltic, banking legislation of the CIS and Baltic. It is updated weekly and available online, on CD-ROM or on disk from Tsentr Komp'iuternykh razrabotok.

KONSUL'TANT PLIUS: The Regional'nyi informatsionnyi tsentr GRANT [Regional Information Centre GRANT] offers systems including Russian legislation divided into 525 thematic topics, both current and repealed versions, documents of the Supreme Court and Supreme

Arbitrazh Court, Moscow legislation, Central Bank, Ministry of Finances, State Tax Service, and other departmental acts, sample notarial, legal, and financial documents.

PRAVO: Information regarding Russian legislation in force, full texts with issuance data, renewable weekly or monthly. The publisher, Iuridicheskii dom Iustitsinform, also offers electronic versions of journals which it publishes.

Internet

Several relevant Internet sites are fee based or contain some fee-based services. Sites with materials in Russian require support for the Cyrillic character set.

Jurweb Bayreuth has a Russian Federation page (at http://www.uni-bayreuth.de/students/elsa/jura/geo/jurweb-russland.html) which includes selected laws and regulations, governmental decrees and other official documents, mostly in English. It also includes links to other useful pages including: ICL, the International Constitutional Law server mentioned above in the introductory section; the Internet Law Library – Russia maintained by the US House of Representatives (at http://law.house.gov/80.htm) which contains selected current and proposed legislation and articles and assessments on RF law; the Russian Legal Server privately maintained (at http://www.friends-partners.org/partners/fplegal/main.html) which includes Russian legal news and a listservice, selected Russian laws mainly in Russian only, and articles on Russian legal research.

The Inforis web server (at http://www.inforis.ru) is one of the oldest web sites in Russia and claims to be the only free of charge, full-text legislative database available on the Internet; it is in Russian, with advice on installing the Cyrillic character set and has keyword searching.

The Russia-On-Line site (at http://online.ru/emain/enews/) has a variety of useful news and economics sources; some sources such as *Izvestiia*, *Kommersant*, *Finansovye Izvestiia* are for subscribers only.

Directories

RIA-Novosti produce regularly updated directories. The *Russian Federation directory* contains basic data on all 89 Russian federation republics and regions, with a guide to regional executive power structures and names and telephone numbers to the offices of the leadership of each region/republic. The *Russian Federation government* directory gives the names and titles of ministers and includes state committee chairmen and other senior officials.

Bibliographies

A bibliography of recent books on Russian law appears in each issue of the quarterly journal *Sudebnik* (1996–). A general bibliography is RUSSIAN NATIONAL BIBLIOGRAPHY PLUS (1996) on CD ROM which has bibliographic information on 800 000 books published in Russia and former Soviet Union between 1980 and 1995. See also *Russian Law Books* (1997–).

The works by Kavass mentioned above are excellent annotated bibliographies of works in the English language on Russian law and can be supplemented by reference to the English language journals described below.

Dictionaries

For Russian legal terminology, the best dictionary is *Russian–English legal dictionary* (Butler, 1995); also see Kuznetsov, *Russian–English legal dictionary* (1995). Russian equivalents of English legal terminology are to be found in *Anglo-russkii iuridicheskii slovar'* (1994).

Current information sources

Journals

The pre-eminent law review in the RF is the venerable monthly journal of the Institute of State and Law of the Russian Academy of Sciences, *Gosudarstvo i pravo* (1930–). The Law Faculty of Moscow State University publishes *Vestnik Moskovskogo universiteta, seriia 11: pravo*, bimonthly. St Petersburg University continues to combine law with philosophy, politology, sociology, and psychology in *Vestnik Sankt-Peterburgskogo universiteta, seriia 6: pravo*, issued quarterly. In Ekaterinburg the *Rossiiskii iuridicheskii zhurnal*, founded by the Ural State Legal Academy and the Ministry of Justice of the RF, is published quarterly, and in Saratov the *Vestnik Saratovskoi gosudarstvennoi akademii prava* appears.

A number of law societies issue journals and newspapers. The Moscow City Advokatura together with the International Union of Advocates publishes a monthly newspaper, *Advokat* (1993–). *Rossiiskii advokat* was founded by the Guild of Russian Advocates. *Iurist* (1994–) is issued with the participation of the Youth Union of Jurists which publishes *Molodoi iurist*, a monthly newspaper, and also *Moskovskii iurist* (1996–). The Youth Union of Jurists also issues two annual reference volumes: *Vsia iuridicheskaia Rossiia* (1994–) and *Vsia iuridicheskaia Moskva* (1994–).

Rossiiskaia iustitsiia (1923–) contains articles for the practitioner and the notary. The procuracy reads the *Zakonnost'* (1922–) and notaries have a special publication in Moscow, *Notarius* (1996–). *Militsiia* (1992–) is published for policemen and the professional investigator consults *Sledovatel'* (1996–). For those interested in military law, *Zakon i Armiia* (1996–) appears independently, as an annex to the journal *Iurist* (1994–).

An excellent monthly journal, each issue devoted to a particular theme, combining commentary with selected legislation is *Zakon* (1992–), published by Izvestiia. Commentary on issues of economic law, including court decisions, is to be found in *Khoziaistvo i pravo* (1977–), presently the organ of the Supreme Arbitrazh Court and the Ministry of Justice of the RF. A wide range of subject orientated journals includes: *Bukhgal'terskii uchet* (1937–) in which legislation on bookkeeping and accounting is discussed and sometimes reproduced; intellectual property is treated in the monthly journals such as *Izobretatel' i ratsionalizator*; *Den'gi i kredit* (1932–) contains much of legal interest; securities are treated in *Rynok tsennykh bumag* (1995–); international legal matters are treated with frequency in *Morskoi sbornik*, issued monthly since the 19th century by the Russian navy; on merchant shipping, see *Morskoi flot* (1886–).

The president and the government each have popular informational journals intended for the layman but containing much of legal interest: *Rossiiskaia federatsiia* (1994–) is twice monthly by the government of the RF and *Presidentskii kontrol'* (1994–) bimonthly from the administration of the president of the RF. The layman continues to be catered for by the monthly *Chelovek i zakon* (1968–) issued by the Ministry of Justice of the RF.

Foreign language journals

Among Western journals, the *Review of Socialist Law* (1975–1991), published at the University of Leiden, renamed the *Review of Central and East European Law* as from 1992 and the *Parker School Journal of East European Law* (1994–) are of particular importance. Several other journals covering Central and East European countries in general are described in the chapters in this book on the Czech Republic and Poland. *Sudebnik* (1996–), the law review of the Moscow Higher School of Social and Economic Sciences and the Vinogradoff Institute at University College London, contains articles in English, a current bibliography and translated documents.

Several serials are being published in the RF in foreign languages, for example *Law* is a Russian legal journal in the English language issued by the International Publishing Group 'Pravo' at Moscow.

Business and news information

The Chamber of Commerce and Industry of the RF (address below) produces a range of publications on economic activity and maintains various databases including member companies, banking and finance facilities, legislation affecting commercial enterprises, joint venture proposals, searchable by the staff of the Chamber on payment of a fee.

The commercial press contains much of legal interest. *Kommersant* (1989–), a weekly business newspaper with a less frequent English-language version, is a leading example, but its texts of legislation often contain misprints or omissions. *Delo i pravo* (1992–) is linked to the computer database service (see above). *Pravo i ekonomika* appears twice monthly under the auspices of the Russian Union of Industrialists and Entrepreneurs in Moscow. *Norma* is issued by the Conference of Unions of Entrepreneurs of Russia.

Russian Business Monitor (1993–) is targeted at foreign business people entering the Russian market; *Russian Economic Trends* (1992–), co-sponsored by the Centre for Economic Performance at the London School of Economics and Political Science and the Centre for Economic Performance in Russia, contains commentary and statistics on various sections of the economy. RIA Novosti, with offices in London as well as Moscow, produce a range of news and business publications and alerting services including *Daily Review*, a summary of significant items from the Russian press available in print and also online. The newspaper *Izvestiia* (1917–) has a weekly supplement on financial and business matters, *Finansovye Izvestiia* from October 1992 and *Financial Izvestiia* (1992–) is an English language version produced in conjunction with the Financial Times. Both the general newspaper and the supplement along with other news materials such as *Kommersant* are available on the Russia-On-Line web site (see Internet above).

Useful addresses

Associations of lawyers

Moskovskaya Gorodskaya Kollegiya Advokatov [Moscow City College of Advocates], Bldg no.6, 9 Pushkin Street, 103009 Moscow, Russia. Tel: +7 95 229 9007. Fax: +7 95 229 6960

Moskovskaya Oblastnaya Kollegiya Advokatov [Moscow Regional College of Advocates], Izmailovskii Prospekt 49, 105037 Moscow, Russia. Tel: +7 95 292 3260

Rossiiskaia assotsiatsiia mezhdunarodnogo prava [Russian Association of International Law], ul. Znamenka 10, 119841 Moscow, Russia

Government organizations

Ministry of Justice, ul. Mikhalkovskaia 65, korpus 1, 125438 Moscow, Russia. Tel: +7 95 459 0515. Fax: +7 95 450 3260

Russian Central Bank, ul. Zhitnaya 12, 117049 Moscow, Russia. Tel: +7 95 237 5965. Fax: +7 95 237 6625

State Committee for the Administration of State Property, Prospekt Vladimirova 9, Moscow, Russia. Tel: +7 95 206 1525

Statistical Office of the RF, Maly Cherkassy per 2/6, 103616 Moscow, Russia. Tel: +7 95 9243762

Commercial organizations

Chamber of Commerce and Industry of the RF, 6 Ilyinka, 103684 Moscow, Russia. Tel: +7 95 921 7205/923 0215. Fax: +7 95 921 7405

Moscow International Stock Exchange, 4 Prosvirin per, 103045 Moscow, Russia. Tel: +7 95 923 3339

Education and training

Faculty of Law, Moscow Higher School of Social and Economic Sciences, Prospekt Vernadskii 82, 117571 Moscow, Russia. Tel: +7 95 436 5314. Fax: +7 95 434 7547

Faculty of Law, Moscow State University, Leninskie Gory, 117234 Moscow, Russia. Tel: +7 95 939 5340 (general university number)

Research institutions

Institute for Legislation and Comparative Law, Vozdvizhenka 4/22, 103728, Russia. Tel: +7 95 291 0207. Fax: +7 95 290 5856

Institute of State and Law, Russian Academy of Sciences, 10 ul. Znamenka, 119841 Moscow, Russia. Tel: +7 95 291 3381

Libraries

Institute for Scientific Information on the Social Sciences of the Russian Academy of Sciences, ul.Krasikova 28/21, 117418 Moscow, Russia. Tel: +7 95 128 8881. Fax: +7 95 420 2261

Rossiiskaia Gosudarstvennaia Biblioteka [Russian State Library], Prospekt Kalinina 3, 101000 Moscow, Russia. Tel: +7 95 202 4956

Rossiiskaia Natsionalnaia Biblioteka [National Library of Russia], Sadovaia 18, 191069 St Petersburg, Russia. +7 812 310 2856. Fax: +7 812 310 6148

Publishers

Agenstvo 'Biznes-Press', Volgogradskii pr-t 26, Office 608, Moscow, Russia. Tel: +7 95 277 0660/215–5610. Fax: +7 95 270 9090

Bowker-Saur, Maypole House, Maypole Road, East Grinstead, West Sussex RH19 1HH, UK. Tel: +44 342 330100. Fax: +44 342 330192

Delo i pravo, ul. Iablochkova dom 5, 127254 Moscow, Russia. Tel/Fax: +7 95 210 2221

Garant, Leninskie Gory MGU NPP 'Garant-Servis', 119899 Moscow, Russia. Tel: +7 95 939 1888/939 1605/939 0804. Fax: +7 95 938 2873/939 0071

INEK (INEC). Tel: +7 95 150 8608/150 9213/150 8604

Interlist, 11–13 Charterhouse Buildings, London EC1M 4DT, UK. Tel: +44 171 490 3036. Fax: +44 171 490 2296

Iuridicheskii dom Iustitsinform, Kotel'nicheskaia nab. 17, 109240 Moscow, Russia. Tel/Fax: +7 95 298 3841

IUSIS, Giliarovskii ul. 44, 129110 Moscow, Russia. Tel: +7 95 288 7923/281 3767. E-mail: postmaster@intralex.msk.su

LEXIS/NEXIS. See the addresses given on page 19 in the **General sources** chapter.

Mezhdunarodnaya Kniga (distributors), B. Yakimanka 39, 116049 Moscow, Russia
Ministry of Justice see above under **Government organizations**
Regional'nyi informatsionnyi tsentr GRANT, Neglinnaia ul. 17, 103051 Moscow, Russia. Tel/Fax: +7 95 200 4306/207 9288/207 9439
RIA-Novosti, 3 Rosary Gardens, London SW7 4NW, UK. Tel +44 171 370 3002. Fax: +44 171 244 7875
Simmonds and Hill Publishing, 58 Carey Street, London WC2A 2JD, UK. Tel: +44 171 405 5145. Fax: +44 181 523 5926. E-mail: bhill@shpub.win-uk.net
Tsentr Komp'iuternykh razrabotok, Isaakievskaia pl. 6, 190107 St Petersburg, Russia. Tel: +7 812 119 8611. Fax: +7 812 314 1143
WESTLAW. West Information Publishing Group, 620 Opperman Drive, Eagan, MN 55123, USA. Tel: +1 612 687 4064. E-mail: westmedia@westpub.com Internet: http://www.westpub.com London office: West Publishing UK Ltd., 2 London Wall Buildings, London Wall, London EC2M 5PP, UK. Tel: +44 171 638 9997. Fax: +44 171 638 9908

List of works cited

Advokat. (1993–) Moscow: Moscow City Advokatura, International Union of Advocates.
Anglo-russkii iuridicheskii slovar'. (1994) Moscow: izd-vo Russkii iazyk.
ARGUMENT (available from Agenstvo 'Biznes-Press').
Biulleten' mezhdunarodnykh dogovorov. (1993–) Moscow: Administration of the President of the RF.
Biulleten' Ministerstva iustitsii RF. (1995–) Moscow: Ministry of Justice. 6 pa.
Biulleten' Ministerstva truda Rossiiskoi federatsii. (199?–) Moscow: Ministry of Labour of the RF.
Biulleten' normativnykh aktov federal'nykh organov ispolnitel'noi vlasti. (1996–) Moscow: Ministry of Justice. 12 pa.
Biulleten normativnykh aktov ministerstv i vedomostv Rossiiskoi federatsii. (1972?–) Moscow: Ministry of Justice. Monthly. Title varies
Biulleten' verkhovnogo suda Rossiiskoi federatsii. (1992–) Moscow: Supreme Court of the RF.
Biznes i banky. (1990–) Moscow.
Blaustein, A.P. (1994) The Russian Federation. In *Constitutions of the countries of the world*, ed. A.P. Blaustein and G.H. Flanz, vol.XVI. Dobbs Ferry, NY: Oceana. Looseleaf.
Bukhgal'terskii uchet. (1937–) Moscow: Ministerstvo Finansov, distr. by Mezhdunarodnaya Kniga. Monthly.
Butler, William E. (1979–91) (transl.) *Collected legislation of the USSR and Constituent Union Republics.* Dobbs Ferry, NY: Oceana. 7 looseleaf vols.
Butler, William E. (1988) *Soviet law* 2nd edn. London: Butterworths.
Butler, William E. (1992) *Basic legal documents of the Russian Federation.* Dobbs Ferry, NY: Oceana.
Butler, William E. (1993) *The Labour Code of the Russian Federation.* London & Moscow: Interlist.
Butler, William E. (1995) *Russian–English legal dictionary.* Moscow: Zertsalo; London: Simmonds & Hill.
Butler, William E. (1995) (transl.) *The Merchant Shipping Code of the USSR.* London & Moscow: Interlist.
Butler, William E. and Gashi-Butler, Maryann E. (1994) (transl.) *Intellectual property in the Russian Federation: collected legislation.* Moscow & London: Interlist.
Butler, William E. and Gashi-Butler, Maryann E. (1997) *Civil Code of the Russian Federation.* London: Simmonds & Hill.

Chelovek i zakon. (1968–) Moscow: Ministry of Justice of the RF.
Daily Review. London: RIA Novosti. Also available online.
DELO I PRAVO (available from Delo i Pravo).
Delo i pravo. (1992–) Moscow: Delo i Pravo. Monthly.
Den'gi i kredit. (1932–) Moscow: Den'gi i kredit, distr. Mezhdunarodnaya Kniga.
Diplomaticheskii Vestnik. (1992–) Moscow: Ministry of Foreign Affairs of the RF.
Dnevnik zasedanii Gosudarstvennoi Dumy. (1994–) Moscow: Gosudarstvennaia Duma. Bimonthly. Supplement to *Gosudarstvennaia Duma. Stenogrammy zasedanii (biulleten')*.
Ekonomika i zhizn'. (1918–) Moscow: Ekonomika i zhizn'. Until 1990 entitled *Ekonomicheskaya gazeta*.
ETALON (available from the Ministry of Justice of the Russian Federation).
Ezhegodnik mezhdunarodnogo prava Rossiiskoi federatsii 1992– [Russian yearbook of international law]. (1994–) St Petersburg: Rossiiskaia assotsiatsiia mezhdunarodnogo prava [Russian Association of International Law]. Continues *Sovetskii ezhegodnik mezhdunarodnogo prava* [Soviet yearbook of international law] (1958–91).
Financial Izvestiia. See *Izvestiia*.
Finansovaia gazeta. (July 1991–) Moscow: Finansovaia gazeta.
GARANT (available from Garant).
Gosudarstvennaia Duma. Postanovleniia i drugie dokumenty. (1994–) Moscow: Gosudarstvennaia Duma. Monthly.
Gosudarstvennaia Duma. Stenogrammy zasedanii (biulleten'). (1994–) Moscow: Gosudarstvennaia Duma. 60 issues pa.
Gosudarstvo i pravo. (1930–) Moscow: Institute of State and Law.
Hazard, J.N. and Pechota, V. (1993–) (eds) *Russia and the Republics: legal materials*. New York: Transnational Juris Publications. Looseleaf.
Iuridicheskaia gazeta. (no start date known) Moscow: Union of Jurists.
Iuridicheskii vestnik. (1991–) Moscow: Ministry of Justice of the RF.
Iurist. (1994–) Moscow: Youth Union of Jurists.
Izobretatel' i ratsionalizator. (1929–) Moscow: Society of Russian Inventors and Innovators.
Izvestiia. (1917–) Moscow: Sovety Deputatov Trudiaskchikhsia SSSR. Weekly supplement: *Finansovye Izvestiia* (1992–). *Financial Izvestiia* (1992–), English language, in conjunction with the Financial Times.
Izvestiia soveta deputatov goroda Moskvy. (1940–1992?) Moscow: Moscow Chamber of Deputies. Continued by *Vestnik merii Moskvy*.
Kadastr. (1991–) Moscow: Informbank Agency.
Kavass, Igor I. (1988) *Soviet law in English: research guide and bibliography, 1970–1987*. Buffalo, NY: Hein.
Kavass, Igor I. (1991) *Gorbachev's law: a bibliographic survey of English writings on Soviet legal developments, 1987–1990*. Buffalo, NY: Hein.
Kavass, Igor I. (1992) *Demise of the Soviet Union: a bibliographic survey of English writings on the Soviet legal system, 1900–1991*. Buffalo, NY: Hein.
Kavass, Igor I. (1993) Sources for post-Soviet law in Russia and the other republics: an annotated bibliography of books and articles in English, 1992. *International Journal of Legal Information*, **21**, 211–319.
Khoziaistvo i pravo. (1977–) Moscow: Supreme Arbitrazh Court and the Ministry of Justice of the RF.
KODEKS (available from Tsentr Komp'iuternykh razrabotok).
Kommersant. (1989–) Moscow: Kommersant.
Konstitutsionnoe soveshchanie. Stenogrammy, Materialy, Dokumenty. 29 aprelia-10 noiabria 1993 g. (1995–96) Moscow: Izd Administratsii Prezidenta Rossiiskoi Federatsii.
KONSUL'TANT PLIUS (available from Regional'nyi informatsionnyi tsentr GRANT [Regional Information Centre GRANT]).

Kuznetsov, A. (1995) *Russian–English legal dictionary*. Moscow: no publisher information.
Law. (no start date known) Moscow: International Publishing Group 'Pravo'.
LEXIS/NEXIS (available from LEXIS).
Militsiia. (1992–) Moscow: Ministerstvo Vnutrennikh. Monthly.
Molodoi iurist. (no start date known) Moscow: Youth Union of Jurists.
Morskoi flot. (1886–) Moscow: Ministerstvo Kommercheskog Flota. Bimonthly.
Morskoi sbornik. (1848–) Moscow: Izdatel'stvo Krasnaya Zvezda/Russian Navy.
Moskovskii iurist. (1996–) Moscow: Youth Union of Jurists.
Moskovskii zhurnal mezhdunarodnogo prava. (1991–) Moscow: no publisher information.
Nalogi. (1993–) Moscow: no publisher information.
Nalogovyi vestnik. (1995–) Moscow: State Tax Service of the RF.
Norma. (no start date known) Moscow: Conference of Unions of Entrepreneurs of Russia.
Normativnye akty po finansam, nalogam i strakhovaniiu. (1991–) Moscow: no publisher information.
Notarius. (1996–) Moscow: Youth Union of Jurists.
Panorama privatizatsii. (November 1992–) Moscow: State Committee of the Russian Federation for the Administration of State Property.
Parker School Journal of East European Law. (1994–) New York: Parker School of Foreign and Comparative Law, Columbia University School of Law.
Patenty i litsenzii. (1966–) Moscow: Committee of the RF for Patents and Trademarks.
PRAVO (available from Iuridicheskii dom Iustitsinform).
Pravo i ekonomika. (no start date known) Moscow: Russian Union of Industrialists and Entrepreneurs. 24 pa.
Pravovoe obozrenie. (no start date known) Moscow: Ministry of Justice of the RF, Iniurkollegiia, *et al.*
Presidentskii kontrol'. (1994–) Moscow: Administration of the President of the RF.
Review of Central and East European Law. (1992–) Dordrecht: Kluwer. Published in cooperation with the Institute of East European Law and Russian Studies of Leiden University. Formerly *Review of Socialist Law*.
Review of Socialist Law. (1975–1991) Dordrecht: Nijhoff. Published in cooperation with the Institute of East European Law and Russian Studies of Leiden University. Superseded by *Review of Central and East European Law* (1992–).
Rossiiskaia federatsiia. (1994–) Moscow: Government of the RF.
Rossiiskaia gazeta. (1990–) Moscow: Izd-vo. Verkhovnogo Soveta RSFSR. With weekly Departmental Supplement [*Vedomstvennoe prilozhenie*].
Rossiiskaia iustitsiia. (1923–) Moscow: Ministry of Justice of the RF. Monthly.
Rossiiskii advokat. (no start date known) Moscow: Guild of Russian Advocates.
Rossiiskii iuridicheskii zhurnal. (no date known) Ekaterinburg: Ural State Legal Academy and the Ministry of Justice of the RF.
Russian Business Monitor. (1993–) Moscow: RBM Eurokosmos. 6 pa.
Russian Economic Trends. (1992–) London: Whurr Publishers. Quarterly.
Russian Federation directory. (1996) London: RIA-Novosti.
Russian Federation government. (1996) London: RIA-Novosti.
Russian Law Books. (1997–) ed. W.E. Butler & Murjas. London: Simmonds & Hill. Annual.
RUSSIAN NATIONAL BIBLIOGRAPHY PLUS (1996) Munich: K.G. Saur. CD-ROM. Annual.
Rynok tsennykh bumag. (1995–) Moscow: no publisher information.
Sbornik federal'nykh konstitutsionnykh zakonov i federal'nykh zakonov. (1994–) Moscow: Gosudarstvennaia Duma.
Sbornik mezhdunarodnykh dogovorov SSSR i Rossiiskoi federatsii. (1994–) Moscow: Ministry of Foreign Affairs of the RF.
Simons, William B. (1980) (ed.) *Soviet codes of law*. Leiden: Sijthoff.
Sledovatel'. (1996–) Moscow: Youth Union of Jurists.
Sobranie zakonodatel'stva Rossiiskoi federatsii. (May 1994–) Moscow: Iuridicheskaia literatura. Previously entitled *Sobranie aktov Prezidenta i Pravitel'stva Rossiiskoi*

federatsii. (July 1992–April 1994) Moscow: Izd Administratsii Prezidenta Rossiiskoi Federatsii.

Soviet Statutes and Decisions: a journal of translations. (1964–1991) White Plains, NY: International Arts and Sciences Press. Continued by *Statutes and Decisions.*

Statutes and Decisions: the laws of the USSR and its successor states: a journal of translations. (1991/92–) Armonk, NY: M.E. Sharpe. Continues *Soviet Statutes and Decisions.*

Sudebnik. (1996–) London: Simmonds & Hill.

Tamozhennye vedomosti. (1994–) Moscow: State Customs Committee of the RF.

Tamozhennyi vestnik. (1993–) Moscow: State Customs Committee of the RF.

Vedomosti federal'nogo sobraniia Rossiiskoi federatsii. (1994–) Moscow: Izd. Verkhovnogo Soveta Rossiiskoi Federatsii.

Vedomosti moskovskoi Dumy. (1992?–) Moscow: Moscow Duma. Previously entitled *Vedomosti Mossoveta.*

Vedomosti s"ezda narodnykh deputatov Rossiiskoi federatsii i verkhovnogo soveta Rossiiskoi federatsii. (1992–93) Moscow: Izd. Verkhovnogo Soveta Rassiiskoi Federatsii. Previously entitled: *Vedomosti Verkhovnogo Soveta Soiuza Sotsialistichskikh Republik* (1938–1957) and *Vedomosti Verkhovnogo Soveta RSFSR* (1957–1992). Continued by: *Vedomosti federal'nogo sobraniia Rossiiskoi federatsii*. (1994–).

Vedomosti Sverdkovskoi oblastnoi dumy. (1994–) Sverdlovsk: Sverdlovsk Regional Duma.

Vedomosti Verkhovnogo Soveta Respubliki Tatarstan. (1992–) Kazan: Supreme Soviet of the Republic of Tatarstan.

Vestnik federal'noi komissii po tsennym bumagam i fondovomu rynku pri pravitel'stve Rossiiskoi federatsii. (1996–) Moscow: Federal Commission for Securities and the Stock Market.

Vestnik konstitutsionnogo suda Rossiiskoi federatsii. (January 1993–) Moscow: Constitutional Court.

Vestnik merii Moskvy. (1992?–) Moscow: Mayorate. Continues *Izvestiia soveta deputatov goroda Moskvy.*

Vestnik merii Sankt-Peterburga. (1993–) St Petersburg: Mayorate.

Vestnik Moskovskogo universitata, seriia 11: pravo. (no start date known) Moscow: Law Faculty of Moscow State University.

Vestnik Moskovskoi oblastnoi Dumy. (1994–) Moscow: Moscow Regional Duma.

Vestnik Sankt-Peterburgskogo gorodskogo sobraniia. (1995–) St Petersburg: City Assembly.

Vestnik Sankt-Peterburgskogo universiteta, seriia 6: pravo. (no start date known) St Petersburg: St Petersburg University.

Vestnik Saratovskoi gosudarstvennoi akademii prava. Pravo i zhizn'. (no start date known) Saratov: State Academy.

Vestnik vysshego arbitrazhnogo suda Rossiiskoi federatsii. (December 1992–) Moscow: Supreme Arbitrazh Court of the RF.

Vneshniaia torgovlia [Foreign trade]. (1931–) Moscow: Ministerstvo Vneshnei Torgovli [Ministry of Foreign Economic Relations]. English language edition: *Foreign Trade*; French, German and Spanish editions also published.

Vsia iuridicheskaia Moskva. (1994–) Moscow: Youth Union of Jurists.

Vsia iuridicheskaia Rossiia. (1994–) Moscow: Youth Union of Jurists.

WESTLAW (available from Westlaw).

Zakon. (1992–) Moscow: Izvestia.

Zakon i Armiia. (1996–) Moscow: Youth Union of Jurists. Monthly as an annex to *Iurist.*

Zakonodatel'stvo i ekonomika. (1992–) Moscow: no publisher information.

Zakonnost'. (1922–) Moscow: General'naya Prokuratura Rossiiskoi Federacii. Monthly. Until 1992 entitled: *Sotsialisticheskaya Zakonnost'*.

Zhurnal mezhdunarodnogo chastnogo prava. (1993–) St Petersburg: no publisher information.

CHAPTER TWENTY-FIVE

Slovak Republic

ANNE PRIES

Introduction to the legal system

The historical background: Czechoslovakia

A brief introduction to some of the historical background to the Slovak legal system including the various forms of Czechoslovakia up to its dissolution on 1 January 1993 is included in the chapter on the Czech Republic; that chapter also contains references to relevant legal materials published during the period which also applied to the Slovak Republic. Much of the comparative material mentioned in the chapter on the Czech Republic is of equal relevance to the Slovak Republic.

The legal system of the Slovak Republic

The Slovak Republic was under the influence of, part of, and even at the centre of the Hungarian Empire for centuries. Its legal system was derived from Hungarian rather than Germanic sources in the period up to independence from the Austro-Hungarian Empire, 14 November 1918. During the period from 1918, as part of a unified Czechoslovakia, and even after the measures of 1968 to introduce some local autonomy within a federal structure, the legal system of the Slovak Republic was strongly influenced by its dominant partner. Slovakia adopted a new constitution as an independent state on 3 September 1992, in advance of the Czech Republic's new constitution, precipitating the dissolution of the federal republic.

The Slovak Republic [Slovenská Republika] has a unicameral National Council [Národná rada Slovenskej Republiky], a parliament consisting of 150 deputies, the sole constitutional and legislative body, and an independent judiciary. Executive power is exercised by the president and the government. The president is elected by the National Council for a five-year term; he appoints the prime minister and his cabinet. The tasks and duties of the president are to be found in art.102 of the Slovak Constitution.

The Constitutional Court is an independent judicial body composed of ten judges appointed by the president for a seven year term. Art.124–140 deal with the Constitutional Court. All court judges are elected by the National Council for a five year term. The judicial system of the Slovak Republic is described in art.141–151 of the Constitution.

The original text of the Constitution of the Slovak Republic, with a summary in English and German, was published in 1992: *Ústava Slovenskej republiky*. An English translation of the new Constitution can be found in *The rebirth of democracy: 12 constitutions of central and eastern Europe* (1995, pp. 495–552), as well as in *The constitutions of new democracies in Europe* (Raina, 1995) and in *Constitutions of central and eastern Europe* (Flanz, 1995). It is also available in English at http://www.sanet.sk/court/c-index.html on the Internet. German translations of the Constitution and other documents are to be found in the looseleaf *Wirtschaftsrecht der osteuropäischen Staaten* (Brunner, Schmidt and Westen, 1992–).

An English translation of the communist constitution was published in *The constitutions of the communist world* (Simons, 1980).

Introductory works on legal system and legal research

No introductory works on the current Slovak legal system could be found. The materials mentioned in the chapter on the Czech Republic refer to the federal period but contain useful material relevant to the Slovak Republic: the chapter by Glos (1992) in *Modern legal systems cyclopedia*, the article by Reynolds (1992) on socialist legal systems and the chapter on Czechoslovakia in Michta (1994).

Knapp (1979) in the *International encyclopedia of comparative law* predates the period of reform from 1990 onwards. For study of the earlier period, see the chapter on Czechoslovakia in Gsovski and Grzybovski (1959), the chapter on Czechoslovakia (Chrástek, 1982) in *Official publications of the Soviet Union and eastern Europe 1945–1980* and the basic work of Bohmer (1959).

Legislation

For the purposes of this chapter it must be assumed that there is some continuity between the existing federal Czechoslovak legislation and the legislation of the new Slovak Republic, although it is not clear how far federal legislation has been adopted.

The Slovak official legislation appears in the *Zbierka Zákonov Slovenskej republiky* [Collection of laws of the Slovak Republic], issued by the Ministry of Justice [Ministerstvo spravodlivosti Slovenskej republiky], since 1993 in Bratislava. It is partly a continuation of *Sbírka zákonů republiky Československé* [Collection of laws of the Czechoslovak Republic] (1918–1992). An electronic collection of laws in Slovak, called ASPI, is available on http://www.sanet.sk/court/aspi.html.

The most significant new reforming legislation of the federal period from 1990 to 1992 was translated into English in the *Bulletin of Czechoslovak Law* (1960–). A survey of the most important laws and international agreements published by the Slovak Republic is given in *WGO: Monatshefte für Osteuropäisches Recht* which also contains German translations of the full text of some laws.

Parliamentary papers

Slovak parliamentary papers are entitled: *X. volebné obdobie/Slovenská národná rada.* The stenographic reports of debates are published under the title *Stenografické správy* (1993–). An illustrated periodical, published monthly by the Slovakian National Council since 1993, is the *Parlamentny Kuriér: Časopis Národnej Rady Slovenskej republiky*, which contains general information on legal issues and has a special section on legislation.

Codes and commentaries

The current Slovak codes are based upon the federal codes of the former Czechoslovakia and much of the description in the chapter on the Czech Republic and the translations cited are relevant here.

The Slovak Civil Code [Občiansky zákonník] is based on the Czechoslovakian Civil Code of 1964, which has been amended several times and most recently reformed with a consolidated text published in *Sbírka zákonů* no.47 of 1992 amended in no.264 of 1992. The current Civil Code has been published by Hušek and Kopáčová (1992). The Slovak Code of Civil Procedure is based upon the Czechoslovak one of 1963, which has been amended several times since then, with a consolidated text appearing in *Sbírka zákonů* no.501 of 1992. An edition of the Code of Civil Procedure has also been edited by Hušek (1992).

The Commercial Code of Slovakia is based upon the federal commercial code of 5 November 1991, promulgated as Act 513/1991 in *Sbírka zákonů* no.98 of 1991. A translation appears in the *Bulletin of Czechoslovak Law* by Pelikánová (1992). The *Obchodný zákonník* has been edited by Kopáč and Bartošiková (1992).

A recent edition of criminal law and procedure and related regulations has been published in *Trestný zákon – Trestný poriadok a súvisiace predpisy* (1994).

There is no Slovak equivalent for the Beck looseleaf editions of current Czech legislation.

Treaties

International treaties concluded by Slovakia are published in the *Zbierka Zákonov*. It is, as yet, unclear how far treaties made by the federal republic have been adopted by the new Slovak Republic but much work has been done to bring legal arrangements into line with recent events and a large number of revised agreements have been printed.

Law reports, judgments

Starting with 1994, decisions of the courts of the Slovak Republic are published in the *Zbierka rozhodnutí a stanovísk súdov Slovenskej Republiky* [Collection of the decisions and opinions of the courts of the Slovak Republic], published by the Supreme Court of the Slovak Republic [Najvyšší Súd SR]. This is partly a continuation of *Sbírka soudních rozhodnutí a stanovisek* (1948–1993) published by the Supreme Court of Czechoslovakia. The decisions of the Supreme Court are published in *Nálezy a rozhodnutia Najvyššieho súdu SR* [Judgments and decisions of the Supreme Court of the Slovak Republic]. Selected decisions are also reported in the Slovak legal journals such as *Právnické štúdie* and *Právny obzor* (see below).

Slovakia had already passed the legislation to establish a constitutional court before the breakup of the federation. The Constitutional Act on the Constitutional Court of the Slovak Republic of 2 December 1991 has been published in the *Sbírka zákonů* 1992, no.7; the Act on the Organization of the Constitutional Court of the Slovak Republic of 3 December 1991 can be found in the *Sbírka zákonů* 1992, no.8. Proceedings of the Constitutional Court have been published in Čič (1993), *Konanie pred Ústavný súdom Slovenskej Republiky* [Proceedings of the Constitutional Court of the Slovak Republic]. The Constitutional Court has an informative Internet site at http://www.sanet.sk/court which contains selected passages in Slovak from the decisions of the Court and the full text in English of the legislation noted above.

The *OMRI Daily Digest* (1994–) published by the Open Media Research Institute contains English summaries of selected court decisions.

Bibliographies

The *Slovenská národná bibliografia* [Slovak national bibliography] is published in several series; series 1 lists official documents.

Dictionaries

A specialized dictionary for commercial law is *Slovník obchodného práva* (1994). A Slovak–English dictionary on economic issues has been compiled by Caforio (1994).

Current information sources

Journals, research reports

The Ministry of Justice has published *Justičná Revue. Časopis pre právnu prax* [Review of law practice] since 1990 with an annual index; it is a continuation of *Socialistické súdnictvo*. *Právnické štúdie* [Studies in legal science] was a periodical of the Slovak Academy of Sciences (1953–1989). Starting with 1990 it has appeared as a series of monographs on several legal issues.

The Law Faculty of the University of Bratislava has its own periodical: *Acta Facultatis Iuridicae Universitatis Comenianae* (1966?–). The Faculty of Law of the Šafárika University in Košice publishes the *Acta Iuridica Cassoviensia* (1974?–); the latest issue received at the time of writing was volume 20, 1994. The Institute of State and Law of the Academy of Sciences in Bratislava has published *Právny obzor: Teoretický časopis pre otázky štátu a práva* [Legal review of problems of state and law] since 1918.

A description of comparative law journals published outside the Slovak Republic, in English and in German, which may contain relevant material can be found under this heading in the chapter on the Czech Republic.

News information

The electronic periodical *OMRI Daily Digest* (1994–) gives political, economic and legal information; part II covers Central, Eastern and Southeastern Europe. OMRI also publishes *Transition: Events and Issues in the Former Soviet Union and East Central and Southeastern Europe* (1995–), a weekly journal of analysis and news focusing on political, social, economic, legal and other affairs. Political and economic information on the country can also be found in the *SWB: Summary of world broadcasts* (1993–), part 2: Central Europe, the Balkans.

General Internet addresses are given below including the Slovak Republic home page.

Business and financial information

The weekly electronic periodical: *OMRI Economic Digest* (1995–97) carried reports on recent economic and business developments in all the countries of Eastern Europe and the former Soviet Union; it is continued in part by *Transition* mentioned above. Business and financial information is available from the Slovak Chamber of Commerce and Industry (address below) and from regional sources published outside the Slovak Republic which are listed under this heading in the chapter on the Czech Republic.

Statistics

The Slovak Statistical Office in Bratislava (address below) publishes the bilingual *Štatistická ročenka Slovenskej republiky – Statistical yearbook of the Republic of Slovakia* (1993–) and the *Ekonomiká štatistika* [Economic statistics] (1993?–). During the federal period the *Štatistická ročenka regiónov SR* [Statistical yearbook of the regions of the Slovak Republic] was published in Slovakia. The *Československá statistica* [Czechoslovak statistics] (1922–1992) and *Statistická ročenka československe Republiky* [Statistical yearbook of the Czechoslovak Republic] (1934–1992) were published in Prague by the Federal Statistical Office and included material on Slovakia, the former superseded by *Slovenská statistica e demografia* (1991–).

Useful addresses

Associations of lawyers

Slovenská Advokatska Komoro [Slovak Bar Association], Octobrove nám. 13, 81 342 Bratislava, Slovak Republic. Tel: +42 7 315813. Fax: +42 7 315807

Government organizations

Ministerstvo spravodlivosti [Ministry of Justice], Zupné námestie 13, 81311 Bratislava, Slovak Republic. Tel: +42 7 353454. Fax: +42 7 316035/330732

Slovak Statistical Office, Mileticova 3, 82 467 Bratislava, Slovak Republic. Tel: +42 7 2018201. Fax: +42 7 214601

Education and training

Univerzita Komenského v Bratislave, právnická fakulta UK [Law Faculty of the Comenius University of Bratislava], Šafarikovo nám. 6, 818 05 Bratislava, Slovak Republic. Tel: +42 7 304111

Univerzita Pavla Josefa Šafárika, právnická fakulta UPJS [Law Faculty of the Šafárik University], Kováčska 26, 041 01 Košice, Slovak Republic. Tel: +42 95 27104/20481

Research institutes

Institute of State and Law, Klemensova 19, 842 34 Bratislava, Slovak Republic. Tel +42 7 361833. Fax: +42 7 373567

Libraries

Matica Slovenská [Slovak National Library] L. Novomeského 32, 036 52 Martin, Slovak Republic. Tel: +42 04842/34035/32454. Fax: +42 04842/33012/33188. E-mail: matica@uvt.utc.cs

Slovak Parliamentary Library, Mudro ova ul. 1, 842 44 Bratislava, Slovak Republic. Tel: +42 7 313443/311500 ext.277. Fax: +42 7 313281/313200. E-mail: gadugeor@ncsr.sk/malaceva@ncsr.sk

Knižnica právnickej fakulty UK [Library of the Law Faculty of the Comenius University], Šafarikovo nám. 6, 818 05 Bratislava, Slovak Republic. Tel: +42 7 304111 ext.518. Fax: +42 7 366126. E-mail: kniznica@flaw.uniba.sk

General

Slovak Republic home page. Internet: http://nic.uakom.sk/hypertext/mew/homepage.html and also Internet: http://www.eunet.sk/slovakia/slovakia.html

Slovak Chamber of Commerce and Industry, Grokého 9, 816 03 Bratislava, Slovak Republic. Tel +42 7 316402. Fax: +42 7 330754

List of works cited

Acta Facultatis Iuridicae Universitatis Comenianae. (1966?–) Bratislava: Univerzita Komenského v Bratislave, právnická fakulta UK.

Acta Iuridica Cassoviensia. (1974–) Košice: Univerzita Pavla Josefa Šafárika, právnická fakulta UPJS.

Bohmer, A. *et al.* (1959) *Legal sources and bibliography of Czechoslovakia*. Praeger Publications in Russian History and World Communism, No.19. New York: Praeger.

Brunner, G., Schmidt, K. and Westen, K. (1992–) *Wirtschaftsrecht der osteuropäischen Staaten*. Baden-Baden: Nomos. Looseleaf.

Bulletin of Czechoslovak Law. (1960–) Prague: Association of Lawyers of the Czech and Slovak Federal Republic.

Caforio, A. (1994) *Slovensko–anglický ekonomický slovník* [Slovak–English economic dictionary]. Bratislava: Tronet.

Československá statistica [Czechoslovak statistics]. (1922–1992) Prague: Federal Statistical Office.

Chrástek, D. (1982) Czechoslovakia. In *Official publications of the Soviet Union and eastern Europe 1945–1980: a select annotated bibliography*, ed. Gregory Walker, pp. 43–64. London: Mansell.

Čič, M. (1993) *Konanie pred Ústavným súdom SR* [Proceedings of the Constitutional Court of the SR]. Košice: Cassoviapress.

Ekonomiká štatistika. (1993?–) Bratislava: Slovak Statistical Office.

Flanz, Gisbert H. (1995) *Constitutions of central and eastern Europe*. Dobbs Ferry, NY: Oceana. Looseleaf.

Glos, G. (1992) The legal system of Czechoslovakia. In *Modern legal systems cyclopedia*, ed. K.R. Redden, vol.8, pp. 8.40.1–8.40.40. Buffalo, NY: Hein.

Gsovski, V. and Grzybovski, K. (1959) (eds) *Government, law and courts in the Soviet Union and eastern Europe*. London: Stevens & Sons; The Hague: Mouton & Co. 2 vols.

Hušek, J. (1992) (ed.) *Občiansky súdny poriadok a notársky poriadok* [Code of Civil Procedure and Notarial Procedure]. Bratislava: Omega.

Hušek, J. and Kopáčová, V. (1992) (eds) *Občiansky zákonik* [Civil Code]. Bratislava: Omega.

Justičná Revue. Časopis pre právnu prax [Review of law practice]. (1990–) Bratislava: Ministerstvo spravodlivosti.

Knapp, Viktor (1979) Czechoslovakia. In *International encyclopedia of comparative law*, ed. V. Knapp, vol.1, pp. C111–C126. Tübingen: J.C.B. Mohr.

Kopáč, L. and Bartošiková, M. (1992) (eds) *Obchodný zákonník a živnostenský zákon* [Commercial law and trade law]. Bratislava: Omega.

Michta, A. (1994) *The government and politics of postcommunist Europe*. Westport, Conn.: Praeger.

Nálezy a rozhodnutia Najvyššieho súdu SR. [Judgments and decisions of the Supreme Court of the Slovak Republic]. (1993?–) Bratislava: Najvyšší súd SR.

OMRI Daily Digest. (1994–) Prague: Open Media Research Institute. Electronic periodical (available at Listserv@ubvm.cc.Buffalo.edu).

OMRI Economic Digest. (1995–97) Prague: Open Media Research Institute. Electronic periodical (available at Listserv@ubvm.cc.Buffalo.edu).

Parlamentny Kuriér. (1993–) Bratislava: Slovak National Council.

Pelikánová, I. (1992) The Czechoslovak Commercial Code. *Bulletin of Czechoslovak Law*, **31**, pp. 3–152 and 4 unnumbered index pages. The brief commentary and translation of the extensive text forms the whole of volume 31.

Právnické štúdie [Studies in legal science]. (1953–1989) Bratislava: Vydavatel'stvo Slovenskej académie vied [Slovak Academy of Sciences]. From 1990 it has appeared as a series of monographs.

Právny obzor: Teoretický časopis pre otázky štátu a práva [Legal review of problems of state and law]. (1918–) Bratislava: Institute of State and Law.

Raina, P. (1995) (ed.) *The constitutions of new democracies in Europe*. Cambridge: Merlin Books.

The rebirth of democracy: 12 constitutions of central and eastern Europe. (1995) Edited by The International Institute for Democracy. Strasbourg: Council of Europe Press.

Reynolds, T.H. (1992) Socialist legal systems: reflections on their emergence and demise. *International Journal of Legal Information*, **20**, pp. 215–237.

Sbírka soudních rozhodnutí a stanovisek [Collection of court decisions and determinations]. (1948–1993) Prague: Supreme Court [Nejvyšš soud]. Czech and Slovak Federal Republic.

Sbírka zákonů Republiky Československé [Collection of laws of the Czechoslovak Republic]. (1918–1992) Prague.

Simons, William B. (1980) *The constitutions of the communist world.* Alphen aan den Rijn: Sijthoff & Noordhoff.

Slovenská národná bibliografia [Slovak national bibliography]. (1922–) Bratislava: Matica Slovenská.

Slovenská statistica e demografia [Slovak statistics and demography] (1991–) Bratislava: Slovak Statistical Office.

Slovník obchodného práva [Dictionary of commercial law]. (1994) Bratislava: Iura Edition.

Statistická ročenka Československe Republiky [Statistical yearbook of the Czechoslovak Republic]. (1934–1992) Prague: Federal Statistical Office. Title varies.

Štatistická ročenka regiónov SR [Statistical yearbook of the regions of the Slovak Republic]. (1969?–1992) Bratislava: Slovak Statistical Office.

Štatistická ročenka Slovenskej republiky – Statistical Yearbook of the Republic of Slovakia. (1993–) Bratislava: Slovak Statistical Office.

Stenografické správy [Minutes of debates]. (1993–) Bratislava: Slovak National Council.

SWB: Summary of World Broadcasts: part 2, Central Europe, the Balkans. (1993–) Reading: BBC Monitoring.

Transition: Events and Issues in the Former Soviet Union and East Central and Southeastern Europe. (1995–) Prague: OMRI.

Trestný zákon – Trestný poriadok a súvisiace predpisy [Criminal law – Criminal procedure and related regulations]. (1994) Bratislava: Ister Science Press. 2 vols.

Ústava Slovenskej republiky [Constitution of the Slovak Republic]. (1992) Bratislava: Remendium.

WGO: Monatshefte für Osteuropäisches Recht. (1959–) Heidelberg: Müller.

X. volebné obdobie/Slovenská národná rada [X. election period/the Slovak National Council] (1993–) Bratislava.

Zbierka rozhodnutí a stanovísk súdov Slovenskej Republiky [Collection of the decisions and opinions of the courts of the Slovak Republic]. (1994–) Bratislava: Najvyšší Súd SR.

Zbierka Zakonov Slovenskej Republiky [Collection of laws of the Slovak Republic]. (1993–) Bratislava: Ministerstvo spravodlivosti Slovenskej republiky.

CHAPTER TWENTY-SIX

Spain

POMPEU FABRA UNIVERSITY LIBRARY

Introduction to the legal system

Constitution

The current Spanish Constitution [*Constitución española*] (cited *CE*), establishes Spain as a social and democratic state, subject to the rule of law. The political form is parliamentary monarchy. The *CE* was approved by the Cortes Generales [Spanish legislative chamber] on 31 October, 1978, ratified by popular referendum on 7 December, 1978, and sanctioned by his Majesty the King before the Cortes Generales on 27 December, 1978. Spain became a member of the European Communities, now the European Union, in 1986.

The Constitution was published in the *Boletín oficial del Estado* [Spanish state official gazette] (BOE, 311, 29 December 1978) and came into force on 29 December, 1978. Several publishers, either public such as the Boletín Oficial del Estado (BOE), or private such as Tecnos or Civitas, have issued editions of the *CE*. Many of them include annotations of related acts, statutes and judgments.

There are also compilations of the organic laws required by the Constitution known as political laws of the state, for example Aja and Alberti (1994). An edition with commentary which should be mentioned is Garrido Falla (1985). English versions of the *CE* have been issued both by Spanish publishers, *Spanish Constitution* (1982) by the BOE, and by foreign publishers (Flanz and Hernandez, 1991); French and German versions of the *CE* have been also published by BOE. The text of the *CE* in Spanish and English is accessible through the Internet (at http://www.redestb.es/personal/vmaroto/Constitucion.htm).

There have been constitutions adopted by Spain prior to 1978: in 1812, in 1834, in 1837, in 1845, in 1869, in 1876 and in 1931. All these constitutions can be found in *Constituciones españolas* (1991), which also reproduces facsimiles of the original documents. Historical material can be found in Tierno Galván (1984) and Clavero (1990).

Autonomous communities

Article 2 of the Constitution defines Spain as a unitary and indissoluble state but recognizes the principle of autonomy for the nationalities and regions. The political organization of Spain lies somewhere between a unitary and a federal state. Between 1979 and 1983 statutes have been enacted for seventeen *comunidades autónomas* [autonomous communities] which have reached autonomy through the processes established by the 1978 Constitution: Basque Country and Catalonia in 1979, Andalusia, Asturias, Cantabria and Galicia in 1981, Aragon, Canary Islands, Castile-La Mancha, Murcia, Navarre, La Rioja and Valencia in 1982, Balearic Islands, Castile-León, Extremadura and Madrid in 1983 and finally Ceuta and Melilla in 1995.

The autonomy of these communities established by the 1978 Constitution is not only a question of administrative decentralization but also provides a real element of self-government. The Constitution grants each autonomous community legislative and executive powers in matters over which it has jurisdiction. Article 149.3 of the *CE* ordains that the matters not expressly assigned to the state by the Constitution may fall under the jurisdiction of the autonomous communities by virtue of their respective statutes. So, the level of self-government is not the same for all the communities. Matters for which jurisdiction has not been assumed by the statutes of autonomy shall fall within the jurisdiction of the state, whose laws shall prevail in case of conflict. State law is, in all cases, supplementary to that of the autonomous communities.

Autonomous statutes of all the communities have been issued by the official publisher in a series called *Estatutos de autonomía*. Each autonomous community, through its official publisher, issues separate editions of the statute in the official language. Castilian is the official language of the state, but some communities are bilingual: Basque is also official in the Basque Country and in a part of Navarre; Galician is also official in Galicia; Catalan is also official in Catalonia and Balearic Islands; Valencian is also official in Valencia (Catalan and Valencian are two different designations of the same language). Editions have also been issued in foreign languages including English. Compilations of all the statutes can be found in publications such as Ripollés Serrano and Jiménez Díaz (1994) or Aja and Carrillo (1989) which includes the institutional laws of each community.

Legislative and executive power

The state's legislative power is exercised by the *Cortes Generales*. It is a bicameral institution consisting of the *Congreso de los Diputados* [Congress of Deputies] and the *Senado* [Senate]. The Senate is the chamber of territorial representation. Each autonomous community has its own legislative Assembly or Parliament [*Asamblea legislativa* or *Parlamento*] which exercises legislative power within their territory.

At state level, executive power is exercised by the Spanish government [*Gobierno español*] which possesses the statutory authority. Each region has an autonomous government [*Gobierno autónomo*] which exercises executive power and statutory authority within its own territory.

Constitutional court

The Constitutional Court is regulated by Title IX of the *CE* and by the *Ley Orgánica 2/1979, de 3 de Octubre* (*BOE*, 239, 5 October 1979), partially modified in 1988. This court has jurisdiction over the whole of Spain and is competent to hear appeals against the alleged unconstitutionality of laws and regulations having the force of law, individual appeals for protection [*recursos de amparo*] against violation of the rights and liberties referred in article 53.2 of the *CE*, conflicts of competence between the state and the autonomous communities or between the autonomous communities themselves, and other matters.

Decisions given by the Constitutional Court are published by statutory requirement in the State's official gazette (*BOE*) in fortnightly supplementary issues. The most notable compilations are *Jurisprudencia constitucional* (1982–), which is published by BOE and the Constitutional Court itself, and the monthly *Boletín de jurisprudencia constitucional: BJC* (1981–), which is published by the Cortes Generales. The latter includes relevant judgments of the Supreme Court, selected judgments of the European Court of Human Rights, European Commission of Human Rights, and selected judgments of other European constitutional courts.

Privately published sources include publications entirely dedicated to constitutional judgments, e.g. *Repertorio Aranzadi del Tribunal Constitucional 1981–* (1982–), and publications reporting judgments of the highest regular courts as well as doctrinal opinions, see **Law reports, judgments** below.

Introductory works on the legal system and legal research

There are some handbooks considered essential to understand Spanish legal literature. They are not only useful for students, but also for any jurist or individual interested in the Spanish legal order. Their contents contribute to the correct application of Spanish law because they include references to related legislation and judgments, and also explanation of concepts, features, principles, and sources of the Spanish law.

Introductory works to the legal system, from the point of view of constitutional law, are: Viver Pi-Sunyer (1987), Aja *et al.* (1989), Aparicio Pérez (1991), and López Guerra *et al.* (1991–1992). For further reading about the background, composition and functioning of the Spanish legislative body, the Cortes Generales, it can be useful to consult Capo Giol *et al.* (1990). A concise explanation of the judicial system in English, German and French can be found in the chapter on Spain in Simons (1994–).

A synopsis of the Spanish legal system in English can be found in Spain (1992) and at the Embassy of Spain in Canada website at http://www.DocuWeb.ca/SiSpain/english/politics/form/index.html for form of government and http://www.DocuWeb.ca/SiSpain/english/politics/autonomo/index.html for autonomous communities.

Two general introductions in English to the legal system are the chapter by Martin (1989) in the *Modern legal systems cyclopedia* and the chapter on Spain in the *International encyclopedia of comparative law* (Cánovas and Domínguez, 1986). Two useful books in English giving recent and practical descriptions of business law are by Cremades (1992) and by the law firm Bufete Cuatrecasas (1994).

On particular areas of law, the following authors should be mentioned:

Administrative law: García de Enterría and Fernández (1980–1991).
Civil law: Albaladejo (1982), Lacruz Berdejo (1988), and Puig Brutau (1975–1989).
Civil procedure: Ramos Méndez (1992).
Commercial law: Vicent Chuliá (1995) and Uría (1995).
Criminal law: Mir Puig (1990) and Muñoz Conde (1995).
Criminal procedure: Oliva *et al.* (1993).
Ecclesiastical law of Spain: Navarro-Valls (1993).
Legal history: Tomás y Valiente (1990).
Labour law: Alonso Olea and Casas Baamonde (1995).
Mortgage law: Roca i Sastre and Roca-Sastre Muncunill (1979).
Planning law: Fernández (1993).
Social Security law: Alarcón Caracuel (1990).
Tax law: Ferreiro Lapatza (1995).

Legislation

Sources of law

Article 1 of the *Código Civil* [Spanish Civil Code] (cited CC,) establishes, as sources of the Spanish law: *ley* [law], *costumbre* [custom] and *principios generales del derecho* [general principles of law]. As in all members of the Civil law system, the written law is the preeminent source; custom and general legal principles are subsidiary sources. *Tratados internacionales* [international treaties] are also sources of the law once published completely in the official state gazette. The jurisprudence of the *Tribunal Supremo* [Supreme Court], the highest judicial organ except in constitutional matters, is a complementary source.

Approval of the *CE* in 1978 and incorporation of Spain into the European Communities in 1986 introduced important changes in the Spanish system of sources of the law: the Constitution itself became the main source of the law. Laws are not only enacted by the Cortes Generales but also by the legislative assemblies of the different autonomous communities and jurisprudencia is not only produced by the Supreme Court but also by the Constitutional Court in constitutional matters and by the *tribunales superiores de las comunidades autónomas* [high courts of the autonomous communities] in some matters (see below). Finally, European Union law itself must not be forgotten. An outline in English of the sources of law in Spain by Díez-Picazo (1994) makes particular reference to the relationship with European Union law.

National legislation

Acts of the Cortes Generales are either organic or ordinary. Organic acts [*leyes orgánicas*], as established by *CE* art.81.1, are those relative to the exercise of fundamental rights and public liberties, those which approve the Statutes of Autonomy and the general electoral system and others provided for in the *CE*. Ordinary laws [*leyes ordinarias*] are all the other laws produced by the Cortes Generales. These appear cited simply in the form 'ley'.

The Executive also produces other acts with the status of law. They are either legislative decrees [*decretos legislativos*] or decree-laws [*decretos-ley*]. A legislative decree, as established by *CE* arts. 82–85, is a disposition of the government containing delegated legislation. This legislative delegation must be granted by means of a basic law when its objective is the formation of articled texts, or by an ordinary law when it is a matter of arranging several legal texts into a single one. A decree-law, as it is established by *CE* art.85, is a provisional legislative decision issued by the government in the case of extraordinary and urgent necessity.

The legislative process prior to the enactment of laws can be monitored through the official publications of the Cortes Generales. Proposals [*proposiciones de ley*] and parliamentary bills [*proyectos de ley*], and related legislative papers are published in the *Boletín oficial de las Cortes Generales* [the official gazette of the Cortes Generales], which is divided into three sections since 1961, each subdivided into several series: *Sección Cortes Generales; Sección Congreso de los Diputados; Sección Senado.* Proceedings of plenary sessions and parliamentary commissions have been published since 1977 in three different official journals: *Diario de sesiones de las Cortes Generales. Comisiones Mixtas* [official journal of the Cortes Generales' joint commissions and sessions proceedings]; *Diario de sesiones del Congreso de los Diputados* [official journal of the Congress of Deputies' proceedings]; *Diario de sesiones del Senado* [the official journal of the Senate proceedings]. All these publications appear irregularly and their frequency depends on the chambers' activity.

According to the *CE* art.97 and related laws, the Spanish government exercises regulatory power at the central level. Regulations can adopt one of the following forms: decrees [*decretos*] issued by the Spanish government; orders [*órdenes*] issued either by the delegated committees of government [*órdenes de las comisiones delegadas*] or by the ministers [*órdenes ministeriales*].

Laws and regulations are published in the *Boletín oficial del Estado*, the *BOE*, according to the principle of publication of the norms guaranteed by the *CE* art.9.3. The *BOE* is published by the Boletín Oficial del Estado, an autonomous office within the Ministerio de la Presidencia [Ministry of the Presidency].

The predecessor of the *BOE* was the *Gaceta de Madrid* published since 1697 to 1936. Although initially a private publication, it become the Spanish government's official gazette in 1762. During the Spanish Civil War, the *Gaceta de Madrid* was substituted by two different official publications: *Boletín oficial de la Junta de Defensa Nacional de España* published by the Nationalist Government from 25 July 1936 to 2 October 1936, and the *Gaceta de la República* (1936–1938) published by the Republican government. The *Boletín oficial del Estado* (1936–) succeeded the *Boletín de la Junta de Defensa Nacional de España* as official gazette.

Currently, the *BOE* is published daily except Sundays and includes the following five sections: *I. Disposiciones generales*, which provides the full text of statutes (produced either by the Legislative or by the Executive), Executive decrees and orders, treaties and international agreements, and statutes produced by the Legislative and Executive of autonomous communities; *II. Autoridades y personal* [Government and civil service staff]; *III.* Otras disposiciones; *IV. Administración de Justicia* [Administration of Justice] which includes judicial edicts, notifications, and advertisements; *V. Anuncios* [Government advertisements]. The *BOE* provides monthly indexes by subject, by date of enactment, by law and decree numbers, and chronologically by institutions and government departments. It is also available in microfiche and microfilm.

The state official publisher BOE provides also series of individual laws or legislative compilations relating to particular subjects: *Códigos*, *Compilaciones*, *Separatas*, *Textos legales*, etc. Most series include annotations of legislation and judgments and indexes. Information about all publications edited by BOE are provided by its annual catalogue, called *Catálogo general* or direct (address below).

The most widely used and comprehensive full text sources of state legislation issued by private publishers are the following monthly publications: the *Repertorio cronológico de legislación* (1930–) known as 'Aranzadi' from its publisher's name, the *Legislación española 'Ledico'* (1987–), and *La Ley legislación* (1989–).

The *Nuevo diccionario de legislación* . . . (1975–1978) includes the full text of all Spanish legislation in force at 1 January 1975, 52 000 legislative dispositions classified under 5395 subject headings alphabetically ordered; the dispositions are in chronological order under subject heading. The *Nuevo Diccionario* . . . is updated by the *Apéndice 1975–1985 al Nuevo diccionario de legislación* (1986–1990), which also mentions if the dispositions included in the earlier work are in force or if they have been repealed or modified. The *Apéndice* is in turn annually updated by the *Tabla de puesta al día*. . . .

Legislation of the autonomous communities

At the autonomous communities level, there are two kinds of acts: statutes produced by their legislative assemblies or parliaments [*leyes*], and legislative decrees produced by the autonomous governments [*decretos legislativos*]. They are published in the official gazette of each autonomous government as a primary source, and also in the *BOE*. Proposals, parliamentary bills and related legislative papers are also published in the official gazette of the autonomous assembly. Regulations enacted by autonomous communities' government can adopt one of the following forms, ordered by normative hierarchy: decrees [*decretos*] enacted by the councils of government and orders [*órdenes*] enacted by the councillors.

Autonomous communities' laws and regulations must be published in the official gazette of its government to come into force. These official gazettes are entitled, e.g. *Boletín oficial de Aragón*, or for the Balearic Islands: *Butlletí oficial de la Comunitat Autònoma de les Illes Balears* (includes Catalan and Castilian versions) or for the Basque Country: *Boletín oficial del País Vasco = Euskal Herriko agintaritzaren aldizkaria* (includes Castilian and Basque versions). Some of the official publishers of these gazettes also provide series of individual laws or legislative compilations relating to particular subjects. In most series, text includes annotations of legislation and judgments, and indexes.

Aranzadi (address below) has published a monthly series of legislation since 1991 for each autonomous community in a more convenient form than the official gazette; the monthly issues are compiled in annual volumes including comprehensive indexes. These 17 series succeed the *Legislación de las comunidades autónomas* which included the legislation produced by all the autonomous communities.

Codes and commentaries

All the codes and laws cited below are published by major legal publishers such as BOE, Tecnos, Civitas (addresses below), and contain annotations of amendments and relevant judgments; there are also editions which include complementary legislation.

Civil Code

The current Civil Code [*Código Civil*] was enacted on 24 July, 1889 (*Gaceta de Madrid*, 211, 30 July 1889) and came into force on 27 July. Its precedents are the 1851 legislative bill (*Proyecto de Código Civil*) and the 1888 basic law (*Ley de Bases de 11 de Mayo de 1888*).

Since 1904, it has been modified by several laws e.g. Law on horizontal property (Ley 49/1960), Royal decree on majority (Real Decreto-ley 33/1978), Law modifying articles relative to filiation, patria potestas and matrimonial property (Ley 11/1981), Law modifying the matrimonial regulation and procedure in nullity, separation and divorce actions (Ley 30/1981), Law on nationality (Ley 18/1990), etc. The most recent change, at the time of writing in 1996, was the law authorizing mayors to perform civil marriage (Ley 35/1994).

Some of the autonomous communities have their own traditional civil law that was compiled and approved during Franco's regime. Once the 1978 Constitution was approved, each of these communities adapted by law their compilation to the new legal order and assumed the competence to modify and develop its particular civil law. Currently these compilations coexist with the state's Civil Code:

- Biscay and Álava (Basque Country): Ley 42/1959, de 30 de Julio de 1959, and Ley 3/1992 de 1 Julio;
- Catalonia: Ley 40/1960, de 21 Julio and Ley 13/1984 de 20 de Marzo;
- Balearic Islands: Ley 5/1961, de 19 Abril, and Ley 8/1990 de 28 de Junio;

- Galicia: Ley 147/1963, de 2 Diciembre, and Ley 7/1987 de 10 de Noviembre;
- Aragon: Ley 15/1967, de 8 Abril, and Ley 3/1985 de 21 de Mayo;
- Navarre: Ley 1/1973, de 1 Marzo, and Ley Foral 5/1987 de 1 de Abril.

A noteworthy commentary of the Cc and the compilations is Albaladejo (1978–).

Commercial Code

The first Spanish Commercial Code (*Código de Comercio*, cited Ccom) was approved in 1829; the current one was enacted by Real Decreto de 22 de Agosto de 1885 (*Gaceta de Madrid*, 298–328, 16 October–24 November 1885) and came into force on 1 January 1886. The most widely used editions of the Ccom include complementary laws and regulations, e.g. Arroyo Martínez (1993). A notable edition with commentary is Castro Mieje *et al.* (1992).

Some of the laws which complement the Ccom are: Law on exchange and checks (Ley 19/1985), Law on intellectual property (Ley 22/1987), Law on patents (Ley 11/1986), Law on trademarks (Ley 32/1988), Law on unfair competition (Ley 3/1991), Royal Decree on stock corporations (Real Decreto Legislativo 1564/1989), Law on private companies (Ley 2/1995), etc. An English translation of the laws on the stock company and the limited liability company are in a volume by Legal Language Services and Ernst & Young (1996) and a more general work is *Spain practical commercial law* (Miranda, 1993).

Code of Civil Procedure

Spanish Civil Procedure is regulated by the Ley de Enjuiciamiento Civil (LEC), which was enacted by the Real Decreto de 3 de Febrero de 1881 (*Gaceta de Madrid*, 36–53, 5–22 February 1881; text corrections on 5 March, 1881) and came into force on 1 April. Its precedent is the 1880 basic law (Ley de bases de 21 de Junio de 1880).

Since 1888, parts of the Code have been revised many times. The most recent partial reform, at the time of writing, was by the Law on rents (Ley 29/1994). In addition, there are some special procedures regulated by other laws, e.g. Law on protection of liberties and fundamental rights before ordinary jurisdiction (Ley 62/1978), Law on civil protection of the right of honour, personal and family privacy and identity (Ley 1/1982).

Penal Code

Several texts of the Penal Code (*Código Penal*, cited CP) have been approved in Spain: in 1822, in 1848, in 1850, in 1870, in 1928, in

1932, in 1944 and in 1973. The current Penal Code was enacted by Ley Orgánica 10/1995 de 23 de Noviembre (*BOE*, 281, 24 November 1995). An edition with commentary such as Quintero Olivares (1996) can be recommended.

Code of Criminal Procedure

Spanish Criminal Procedure is regulated by the Ley de Enjuiciamiento Criminal (LECr) that was approved by Real Decreto de 14 de Septiembre de 1882 (*Gaceta de Madrid*, 260–283, 17 September–10 October 1882). It has been amended by many laws; the most recent reform was of the jury by Ley Orgánica 5/1995, de 22 de Mayo, del Tribunal del Jurado (*BOE*, 122, 23 May 1995) later reformed by Ley Orgánica 8/1995, de 6 de Noviembre.

Treaties

The Spanish government, which directs foreign policy (*CE* art.97), has the main role in the treaty-making process: to initiate treaty negotiations, to negotiate, and, even in some sorts of treaties, to ratify. Nevertheless, prior authorization by the Cortes Generales to consent is required in cases enumerated by the *CE* art.94.

Legislative papers relevant to international treaties are published in *Boletín oficial de las Cortes Generales. Sección Congreso de los Diputados. Serie C: Tratados y convenios internacionales* and in *Sección Senado. Serie IV: Tratados y convenios internacionales*. Once ratified, international treaties appear in the *BOE*.

The Ministry of Foreign Affairs [Ministerio de Asuntos Exteriores] provides general collections of international treaties. The *Censo de tratados internacionales suscritos por España* (1976) includes citations to all international treaties signed since 16 September 1125 to 21 October 1975, in three volumes: bilateral treaties, multilateral treaties and a comprehensive key word index. The *Colección de tratados internacionales suscritos por España: bilaterales* (1977–) includes the full text of treaties signed since 1911 to 1943. It succeeds the compilation of Marques de Olivart (1890). Most treaties are in Spanish or French.

The Ministry of Foreign Affairs and some other ministries issue collections of treaties by subject, e.g. *Tratados bilaterales sobre materias civiles* (1992) published by the Ministry of Justice and Interior. Private publishers also provide thematic compilations, e.g. Civitas, Tecnos, CISS, Actualidad.

Law reports, judgments

The Spanish judicial system

CE proclaims the exclusivity of the judiciary in exercising judicial authority, the independence of the Judiciary, the establishment of the General Council of the Judiciary [Consejo General del Poder Judicial] as a self-governing body, and the principle of jurisdictional unity as the basis of the organization and operation of the courts. The laws which regulate the Spanish judicial system are Ley Orgánica 6/1985, de 1 de Julio, del Poder Judicial (*BOE*, 157, 2 July 1985) and Ley 38/1988, de 28 de Diciembre, de Demarcación y Planta Judicial (*BOE*, 313, 30 December 1988), modified by Ley 3/1992, de 20 de Marzo (*BOE*, 70, 21 March 1992). The system is based on two main criteria: a hierarchical basis which determines the court's rank and the territorial structure of the Spanish State which determines the court's jurisdiction. The highest courts at state and autonomous communities levels, with the corresponding chambers are shown in Table 1.

The Supreme Court is the highest judicial body for the courts excepting cases concerning constitutional rights and constitutional interpretations in which the Constitutional Court is the only body entitled to decide.

Table 1. Spain, the courts

State jurisdiction		Autonomous communities' jurisdiction
Tribunal Supremo (Supreme Court)	Audiencia Nacional (High Court)	Tribunal Superiores de Justicia (Autonomous Communities High Courts)
• Sala de lo Civil (Civil Chamber)	• Sala de lo Penal (Criminal Chamber)	• Sala de lo Civil y de lo Penal (Civil and Criminal Chamber)
• Sala de lo Penal (Criminal Chamber)	• Sala de lo Contencioso-Administrativo (Administrative Chamber)	• Sala de lo Contencioso-Administrativo (Administrative Chamber)
• Sala de lo Contencioso-(Administrative Chamber)	• Sala de lo Social (Social Chamber)	• Sala de lo social (Social Chamber)
• Sala de lo Social (Social Chamber)		
• Sala de lo Militar (Military Chamber)		

In addition, judgments pronounced by the autonomous communities' high courts in some matters are not appealable at the Supreme Court (e.g. matters of particular civil law, acts ordered by the autonomous Government and by the autonomous administration in matters where legislation is the sole responsibility of the self-governing community).

Publications of decisions of the Constitutional Court are described in **Introduction to the legal system** above.

Compilations

The BOE publishes *Jurisprudencia del Tribunal Supremo*, an official reporter of sentencias [judgments] and *autos* [interlocutory orders] of the Supreme Court from 1986. Currently, it appears in the following series: *Sala Primera de lo Civil* [Civil Chamber] (1987–), *Sala Segunda de lo Penal* [Criminal Chamber] (1987–), *Sala Tercera de lo Contencioso-Administrativo* [Administrative Chamber] (1987–), *Sala Cuarta de lo Social* [Social Chamber] (1993–), *Sala Quinta de lo Militar* [Military Chamber] (1989–) and *Tribunal de Conflictos de Jurisdicción y salas especiales* [litigation and special chambers] (1990–). Most series are quarterly with indexes by date and subject and a comprehensive annual index. This official publication includes the full text of all judicial resolutions, while most privately published compilations include only the legal bases, i.e. the part of the judgment containing the interpretation of the court which can become jurisprudence, one of the sources of the law.

The most well-known and widely used privately published reporter of Supreme Court judgments is the *Repertorio de jurisprudencia* (1931–), published weekly by Aranzadi, with three-monthly cumulative volumes. Privately published series are published by PPU and by Colex.

Selected judgments of the Supreme Court, the National High Court and the high courts of the autonomous communities are selectively reported in various publications, the most important and comprehensive being: *Actualidad y derecho: revista semanal de actualidad jurídica* (1988–), *La ley: revista jurídica española de doctrina, jurisprudencia y bibliografía* (1980–) and *Revista general del derecho* (1944–).

Some autonomous communities have publications of judgments of their high court, with or without judgments of the provincial courts. This kind of publication is very common in communities with their own particular civil law: Aragon, Balearic Islands, Basque Country, Catalonia, Galicia and Navarre. Most are published by provincial, even regional, bar associations and by academic institutions. Private publishers such as Actualidad and Aranzadi also provide selections of judgments pronounced by all or some of the highest courts at central, autonomous and provincial level.

Computer-based systems

The official publisher, BOE, provides different computer-based versions of the dispositions included in the *BOE*. IBERLEX provides all the dispositions included in Section I since 1968, a selection of dispositions from Section III, selected judgments of the Constitutional Court and Supreme Court, etc. It is accessible online, via videotext, and available on CD-ROM. PERSONAL provides the full text of Section II, INDILEX offers full text of Section III and PUBLIBOE contains the full text of official advertisements included in sub-section V.A. These last three databases are accessible online and via videotext. *BOE*'s daily summary is accessible online and via videotext through INDIBOE which includes summaries from 1992 onwards, through the BOE's web homepage at http://www.boe.es and via audiotex, an answerphone service with a recorded reading of the day's summary (see Boletín Oficial del Estado in **Useful addresses** below).

Other information services relevant to legislation provided by the BOE (addresses also below) are the Centro de información legislativa [Legislative Information Centre], a legislation searching and retrieval service, document supply service and legislative information by telephone service, and Centro de Información de *BOE* y *BORME* [Information centre about *BOE* and *BORME*] which supplies copies of documents from the *Boletín oficial del Estado* and the *Boletín del Registro Mercantil* (1990–), or BORME, the official publication of the Spanish mercantile register.

Legislative papers produced by the Cortes Generales are accessible online through ARGO (Congress of Deputies) and GELABERT (Senate).

Some autonomous communities have made accessible online (either dial-up or videotext or Internet) their government's official gazette and even their assembly's official publications, e.g. Andalusia, Aragon, Basque Country, Catalonia, Navarre and Valencia: *Butlletí oficial de les Corts Valencianes (BOCV)* at gopher://gopher.gva.es:70/1/.bocv, *Diari oficial de la Generalitat Valenciana (DOGV)* at gopher://gopher.gva.es:70/1/.dogv, *Sumarios del Boletín oficial de Aragón* at http://wzar.unizar.es/boa/boa.html and the government's online databases of Catalonia, BASE DE DADES DEL DIARI OFICIAL DE LA GENERALITAT DE CATALUNYA, and Valencia G.V. LEXDATA:BASE DE DADES LEGISLATIVA DE LA GENERALITAT VALENCIANA.

The MAP-LEXTER CD-ROM database from BOE includes the full text of the national legislation relating to the autonomous communities since 1978 and the full text of autonomous communities' laws and legislative decrees.

The most widely used privately published databases of legislation and judgments of the state and the autonomous communities are the B.D.A.: BASE DE DATOS ARANZADI, the COMPULEY (databases: *Administrativo*,

Civil, Fiscal, Laboral, Jurisprudencia) both available on CD-ROM, and the COLEX DATA available online and on CD-ROM. Their publishers also issue thematic databases in different areas of law which include both legislation and judgments. A fax service of judgments is provided by Colex Data for Supreme Court judgments cited in its database and by Aranzadi for judgments cited in its weekly journal *Actualidad jurídica Aranzadi* (1991–).

The Spanish government Internet site is at http://www.la-moncloa.es/ with searchable links to other Spanish websites. Another useful Internet resource is the LOCIS database of foreign law LAWL-INTERNATIONAL LEGAL DATABASE (telnet://locis.loc.gov) which includes abstracts of Spanish legislation since the 1970s.

Directories

A comprehensive list of Spanish law firms is Westweber and Vives (1994) which includes names of practising lawyers, addresses, etc.

Los Cargos en el poder (1987–) and the *Fichero de altos cargos* (1940–), a card index also available on floppy disk, include updated information on official institutions including names, addresses, individuals, etc., at the central, autonomous and local levels. Organizational charts of the state's administration can be found in the *Guía de la Administración general del estado: organigramas* (1994–), a looseleaf service updated monthly, which also includes addresses, telephone and fax numbers, etc. The website *Directorio de la Administración Pública*, created by the Ministry of Public Administration (at http://www.map.es) offers links to the websites of public bodies which include contact information in addition to other information about the public administration services.

Indexing and abstracting services

The CSIC and COMPULEY databases, available on CD-ROM, and COLEX DATA, available on CD-ROM and online, are the main indexing services of Spanish law journals. COLEX DATA provides indexing for the complete sets of approximately thirty Spanish law journals.

Dictionaries

The best Spanish legal dictionary is Ribó Durán (1995), which is also available on CD-ROM. Further information is provided by Montoya Melgar (1995), which also includes a list of the most common legal abbreviations.

As a bilingual Spanish and English legal dictionary Muñiz Castro (1992) should be mentioned and as a multilingual dictionary the *West's law and commercial dictionary in five languages: English to German, Spanish, French, Italian* (1985).

Other reference resources

The *GUIDE: guia de informacion sobre derecho español* will soon be accessible through the Pompeu Fabra University Library website (http://www.upf.es/bib). This electronic resource will contain references to and abstracts of publications which include Spanish primary legal texts and a directory of official bodies, bar associations, law schools and law libraries and private publishers.

Current information sources

In this section, a selection of most cited and representative journals in each area of Spanish law is given. Some of these law journals are privately published but there are also important publications by public bodies such as the Ministry of Justice and the Interior. These law journals contain scholarly opinion, a selection of judgments and legislation with commentary and specialized bibliography. The services indexing the journals are shown in brackets after the title.

As comprehensive law journals *Revista general de derecho* (1944–) (COLEX, COMPULEY, CSIC and *Index to Legal Periodicals*) and *Revista jurídica de Catalunya* (1895–) (COLEX DATA), published by the Col·legi d'Advocats de Barcelona with articles either in Spanish or the Catalan language, are two of the most consulted journals by jurists.

Constitutional law: the *Revista española de derecho constitucional* (COMPULEY, CSIC, *International Political Science Abstracts*) published by the Centro de Estudios Constitucionales.

Civil law: *Anuario de derecho civil* (1948–) (COLEX, COMPULEY, CSIC, *Index to Legal Periodicals*) published by the Ministry of Justice and Interior and the Centro Superior de Investigaciones Científicas or CSIC, *Cuadernos Civitas de jurisprudencia civil* (1983–) (COLEX, COMPULEY), and *Revista crítica de derecho inmobiliario* (1925–) (COLEX, COMPULEY, CSIC).

Civil procedure: *Revista de derecho procesal* (CSIC, *Index to Foreign Legal Periodicals*).

Commercial law: *Revista de derecho mercantil* (1946–) (COLEX, COMPULEY, CSIC, *Index to Legal Periodicals*), *Revista de derecho bancario y bursátil* (1981–) (CSIC) are two of the most used journals.

Administrative law: *Revista española de derecho administrativo* (1974–) (COMPULEY, CSIC) and *Revista de administración pública* (1950–) (COMPULEY, CSIC, PAIS, *Index to Legal Periodicals, International Political Science Abstracts*).

Labour law: *Relaciones laborales* (1984–) (COMPULEY, CSIC), *Revista española de derecho del trabajo* (1980–) (COMPULEY, CSIC) and *Revista de trabajo y seguridad social* (1990–) edited by the Ministerio de Trabajo y Seguridad Social.

Tax law: *Impuestos: revista de doctrina, legislación y jurisprudencia* (1984–) (COMPULEY, CSIC), and *Revista española de derecho financiero* (1974–) (COMPULEY, CSIC).

Criminal law: *Anuario de derecho penal y ciencias penales* (1948–) (CSIC) published by the Ministry of Justice and Interior and CSIC and *Cuadernos de política criminal* (1977–) (CSIC), published by the Universidad Complutense de Madrid.

Finally, it could be useful to emphasize the *Anuario de historia del derecho español* (1924–) (CSIC) on **history of law**, and the *Anuario de derecho eclesiástico del estado* (1985–) (CSIC) on **ecclesiastical law** of the state.

Useful addresses

Associations of lawyers

Col·legi d'Advocats de Barcelona [Barcelona Bar Association], c/ Mallorca 283, 08037 Barcelona, Spain. Tel: +34 3 4872814. Library. Tel: +34 3 4872814. Fax: +34 3 4871128

Colegio de Abogados de Madrid [Madrid Bar Association], c/ Serrano 9, 28001 Madrid, Spain. Tel: +34 1 4357810/4358133. Library. Tel: +34 1 3086151. Fax: +34 1 3086078

Consejo General de la Abogacía Española [General Council of Bar Associations], c/ Serrano 9, 28001 Madrid, Spain. Tel: +34 1 4357810. Fax: +34 1 4319365

Government organizations

Congreso de los Diputados, c/ Floridablanca, 28014 Madrid, Spain. Tel: +34 1 3906000. Library. Tel: +34 1 3906220. Fax: +34 1 4296765

Dirección de Informática, c/ Floridablanca, 28071 Madrid, Spain. Tel: +34 1 3906359. Fax: +34 1 4200309

Servicio de Publicaciones, Carretera de San Jerónimo, 28071 Madrid, Spain. Tel: +34 1 4295193

Ministerio de Asuntos Exteriores, Plaza de la Provincia 1, 28012 Madrid, Spain. Tel: +34 1 3665000

Centro de Publicaciones y Documentación, c/ Imperial 9, 4°, 28012 Madrid, Spain. Tel: +34 1 3665000. Fax: +34 1 3665500

Ministerio de Justicia e Interior, c/ San Bernardo 47, 28071 Madrid, Spain. Tel: +34 1 3902000. Library of the Interior Dept: Tel: +34 1 5371362. Fax: +34 1 5371160. Library of the Justice Dept: Tel: +34 1 3902142. Fax: +34 1 3902141

Centro de Publicaciones, Gran Vía 76, 8°, 28013 Madrid, Spain. Tel: +34 1 5475422

Ministerio de Trabajo y Seguridad Social, Nuevos Ministerios, 28003 Madrid, Spain. Tel: +34 1 5536000

Ministerio para las Administraciones Públicas, Paseo de la Castellana 3, 28046 Madrid, Spain. Tel: +34 1 5861000

Senado, Plaza de la Marina Española 8, 28013 Madrid, Spain. Tel: +34 1 5381000. Library. Tel: +34 1 5381339/5381460. Fax: +34 1 5381020
Departamento de Informática: Tel: +34 1 5381379. Fax: +34 1 5381018
Servicio de Publicaciones, c/ Bailén 3, 28071 Madrid, Spain. Tel: +34 1 5381364

Courts and judicial system

Audiencia Nacional, c/ García Gutiérrez 1, 28004 Madrid, Spain. Tel: +34 1 3101097

Consejo General del Poder Judicial [General Council of the Judiciary], c/ Marqués de la Ensenada 8, 28004 Madrid, Spain. Tel: +34 1 3199700

Tribunal Constitucional, c/ Domenico Scarlatti 6, 28003 Madrid, Spain. Tel: +34 1 5490400. Fax: +34 1 5449268. Library. Tel: +34 1 5490400. Fax: +34 1 5449268

Tribunal Supremo de Justicia, Plaza de la Villa de París, 28004 Madrid, Spain. Tel: +34 1 3971000. Library. Tel: +34 1 3971000. Fax: +34 1 3194720

Research institutions

Centro de Estudios Constitucionales, Plaza de la Marina Española 9, 28071 Madrid, Spain. Tel: +34 1 5415000. Library. Tel: +34 1 5415000

Real Academia de Jurisprudencia y Legislación, c/ Marqués de Cubas 13, 28071 Madrid, Spain. Tel: +34 1 5222069. Library. Tel: +34 1 5326789. Fax: +34 1 5234021

Education and training

Euskal Herriko Unibertsitatea/Universidad del País Vasco. Zuzenbide Fakultatea/Facultad de Derecho, c/ Manuel De Lardizabal 4, 20009 San Sebastian-Donostia, Spain. Tel: +34 43 210300 ext. 243. Library. Tel: +34 43 210300 ext. 243. Fax: +34 43 215488. E-mail: sdzaztac@sd.chu.es

Universidad Autónoma de Madrid. Facultad de Derecho, Carretera de Colmenar Viejo, km. 15,500, Ciudad Universitaria de Cantoblanco, 28049 Madrid, Spain. Tel: +34 1 3978133. Fax: +34 1 3978216. Library. Tel: +34 1 3978714. Fax: +34 1 3975058

Universidad Carlos III. Facultad de Ciencias Sociales y Jurídicas, c/ Madrid 126–128, 28903 Getafe (Madrid), Spain. Tel: +34 1 6249500. Fax: +34 1 6249757. María Moliner Library. Tel: +34 1 6249722. Fax: +34 1 6249783. E-mail: zamarra@pa.uc3m.es

Universidad Complutense de Madrid. Facultad de Derecho, Ciudad Universitaria, 28040 Madrid, Spain. Tel: +34 1 3945438. Library. Tel: +34 1 3945608

Universidad de Salamanca. Facultad de Derecho, c/ Francisco Vitoria 6–16, 37008 Salamanca, Spain. Tel: +34 23 294441. Fax: +34 23 294516. Library. Tel: +34 23 294441. Fax: +34 23 294516

Universidade de Santiago de Compostela. Facultade de Dereito, Campus Universitario, 15706 Santiago de Compostela (a Coruña), Spain. Tel: +34 81 563100. Fax: +34 81 591554. Library. Tel: +34 81 563100. Fax: +34 81 591554

Universidad de Sevilla. Facultad de Derecho, Plaza del Cid, 41004 Sevilla, Spain. Tel: +34 5 4220835. Library. Tel: +34 5 4551218. Fax: +34 5 4551216

Universidad de Zaragoza. Facultad de Derecho, Ciudad Universitaria, 50009 Zaragoza, Spain. Tel: +34 76 550406. Fax: +34 76 550080. Library. Tel: +34 76 564512. Fax: +34 76 550080

Universitat Autònoma de Barcelona. Facultat de Dret, Campus Universitari de Bellaterra, 08193 Bellaterra (Vallès Occidental), Spain. Tel: +34 3 5811062. Fax: +34 3 5812732. Social Sciences Library. Tel: +34 3 5811818. Fax: +34 3 5812009. E-mail: iybs5@cc.uab.es

Universitat de Barcelona. Facultat de Dret, Avinguda Diagonal 684, 08034 Barcelona, Spain. Tel: +34 3 4024346. Fax: +34 3 4024354. Library (law section). Tel: +34 3

4024455. Fax: +34 3 4024459. E-mail: edoagen.bib.ub.es

Universitat de València. Facultat de Dret, Avinguda Blasco Ibáñez, 46010 València, Spain. Tel: +34 6 3864440. Fax: +34 6 3864443. Library. Tel: +34 6 3864446. Fax: +34 6 3864732

Universitat Pompeu Fabra. Facultat de Dret, Edifici de Franca, Passeig de Circumval·lació 8, 08003 Barcelona, Spain. Tel: +34 3 5422500. Fax: +34 3 5421719. Library. Tel: +34 3 5422457. Fax: +34 3 5422455. E-mail: biblioteca-franca@grup.upf.es

Publishers and booksellers

See also **Government organizations** above for publishing sections of ministries and parliament.

Actualidad Editorial, c/ Aragoneses 71, Polígono Industrial Alcobendas, 28100 Alcobendas (Madrid), Spain. Tel: +34 1 6616284. Fax: +34 1 6615937

Aranzadi, Carretera de Aoiz, km 3'5, 31486 Elcano (Navarra), Spain. Tel: +34 48 330226. Fax: +34 48 330845

Boletín Oficial del Estado (official publisher), c/ Trafalgar 27–29, 28071 Madrid, Spain. Tel: +34 1 5382290. Internet: http://www.boe.es
Databases: Tel: +34 1 5382292. Fax: +34 1 5382345
Audiotex: Tel: +34 1 5382245
Legislative information service: Tel: +34 1 5382253. E-mail: cil@docu.boe.es
Information centre about BOE and BORME: Tel: +34 1 5382331. Fax: +34 1 5382349

Bosch, c/ Comte d'Urgell 51 bis, 08011 Barcelona, Spain. Tel: +34 3 4544629. Fax: +34 3 3236736

Ciss, c/ Colom 1, 5è., 46004 València, Spain. Tel: +34 6 3523461. Fax: +34 6 3522538

Civitas, c/ Ignacio Ellacuría 3, 28017 Madrid, Spain. Tel: +34 1 7255137. Fax: +34 1 7252673

Colex, c/ Rafael Calvo 42, bajos izquierda, 28010 Madrid, Spain. Tel: +34 1 3196506. Fax: +34 1 3194397

Colex Data, Avinguda Diagonal 579, 2n., 08014 Barcelona, Spain. Tel: +34 3 4012757. Fax: +34 3 4012826. Available from Mapfre Lex below.

Consejo Superior de Investigaciones Científicas (CSIC), Centro de Informacion y Documentacion (CINDOC), Joaquin Costa 22, 28002 Madrid, Spain. Tel: +34 1 5635482. Fax: +34 1 5642644. E-mail: DSDI@cti.csic.es

Distribuciones de Derecho y Economía, c/ Ardemans 60, 28028 Madrid, Spain. Tel: +34 1 3560579

Edersa, c/ Valverde 32, 1°, 28004 Madrid, Spain. Tel: +34 1 5210246. Fax: +34 1 5210539

Gaceta del Foro, c/ Narváez 7, 28009 Madrid, Spain. Tel: +34 1 5778668

Generalitat de Catalunya. Entitat Autònoma del Diari Oficial I de Publicacions, c/ Bisbe 6, Casa dels Canonges, 08002 Barcelona. Tel: +34 3 3026483. Fax: +34 3 4121014

Generalitat Valenciana. Gabinet de Coordinació Interdepartamental, c/ Miquelet 5, 46001 Valencia, Spain. Tel: +34 6 3866300. Fax: +34 6 3866398

Lex Nova, Avenida Reyes Católicos 11, 47006 Valladolid, Spain. Tel: +34 83 222551. Fax: +34 83 472884

La Ley, Carretera de la Coruña, km 17 200, Edificio La Ley, Monterrey 1, 28230 Las Rozas (Madrid), Spain. Tel: +34 1 6342200. Fax: +34 1 6346561

Mapfre Lex, Manuel Cortina 2, 28010 Madrid, Spain. Tel: +34 1 5815120. Fax: +34 1 5815381

Marcial Pons, c/ Bárbara de Braganza 8, 28004 Madrid, Spain. Tel: +34 1 3194250. Fax: +34 1 319 43 73

PPU, c/ Marquès de Campo Sagrado 16, 08015 Barcelona, Spain. Tel: +34 3 4420391. Fax: +34 3 4421401

Tecnos, c/ Juan Ignacio Luca de Tena 15, 28027 Madrid, Spain. Tel: +34 1 3200119. Fax: +34 1 7426631

Tirant lo Blanch, c/ Arts Gràfiques 14, València, Spain. Tel: +34 6 3610048. Fax: +34 6 3615480

List of works cited

Actualidad jurídica Aranzadi. (1991–) Madrid: Aranzadi.

Actualidad y derecho: revista semanal de actualidad jurídica. (1988–) Alcobendas: Actualidad.

Aja, E. and Carrillo, M. (1989) (eds) *Leyes políticas autonómicas* 2nd edn. Madrid: Civitas.

Aja, E. *et al.* (1989) *El sistema jurídico de las comunidades autónomas*. Madrid: Tecnos.

Aja, E. and Alberti, E. (1994) (eds) *Leyes políticas del Estado*. Madrid: Civitas.

Alarcón Caracuel, M. R. (1990) *Compendio de seguridad social* 3rd edn. Madrid: Tecnos.

Albaladejo, M. (1978–) *Comentarios al Código Civil y a las compilaciones forales*. Madrid: EDERSA. In progress.

Albaladejo, M. (1982) *Curso de derecho civil español común y foral*. Barcelona: Librería Bosch. 5 vols. Different editions of each volume have been published.

Alonso Olea, M. and Casas Baamonde, M. E. (1995) *Derecho del trabajo* 14th edn. Madrid: Universidad de Madrid, Facultad de Derecho.

Anuario de derecho civil. (1948–) Madrid: Ministerio de Justicia, Consejo Superior de Investigaciones Científicas.

Anuario de derecho eclesiástico del estado. (1985–) Madrid: EDERSA, Editorial de la Universidad Complutense de Madrid.

Anuario de derecho penal y ciencias penales. (1948–) Madrid: Ministerio de Justicia, Consejo Superior de Investigaciones Científicas.

Anuario de historia del derecho español. (1924–) Madrid: Ministerio de Justicia, Consejo Superior de Investigaciones Científicas.

Aparicio Pérez, Miguel A. (1991) *Introducción al sistema político y constitucional español* 5th edn. Barcelona: Ariel.

ARGO (available from Congreso de los Diputados. Dirección de Informática).

Arroyo Martínez, I. (1993) (ed.) *Código de Comercio y legislación mercantil* 9th edn. Madrid: Tecnos.

B.D.A.: BASE DE DATOS ARAZADI: JURISPRUDENCIA: TEXTO COMPLETO E ÍNDICES and . . .: LEGISLACIÓN: TEXTO COMPLETO E ÍNDICES (available from Aranzadi).

BASE DE DADES DEL DIARI OFICIAL DE LA GENERALITAT DE CATALUNYA (available from Generalitat de Catalunya. Entitat Autònoma del Diari Oficial i de Publicacions).

Boletín de jurisprudencia constitucional: BJC. (1981–) Madrid. Congreso de los Diputados.

Boletín del Registro Mercantil. (1990–) Madrid: Ministerio de Justicia, BOE.

Boletín oficial de las Cortes Generales. (1979–) Madrid: Cortes Generales. Formerly *Boletin oficial de las Cortes Españolas.*

Boletín oficial del Estado. (1936–) Madrid: BOE. Supersedes *Gaceta de la República* (1936–1936), *Boletín oficial de la Junta de Defensa Nacional de España* (1936).

Boletín Oficial del Estado. (1996) *Catálogo general* . . . Madrid: BOE. Annual.

Bufete Cuatrecasas (1994) *Business law guide to Spain* 2nd edn. Bicester: CCH Europe.

Cánovas, Diego Espín and Domínguez, Justino Duque (1986) Spain. In *International encyclopedia of comparative law*, ed. V. Knapp, vol.1, pp. S91–123. Tübingen: J.C.B. Mohr.

Capo Giol, J. *et al.* (1990) By consociationalism to a majoritarian parliamentary system: the rise and decline of the Spanish Cortes. In *Parliament and democratic consolidation in Southern Europe: Greece, Italy, Portugal, Spain and Turkey*, eds Ulrike Liebert and Maurizio Cotta, pp. 92–130. London: Frances Pinter.

Los Cargos en el poder. (1987–) Madrid: Los Cargos en el poder.

Castro Mieje, F. J. *et al.* (1992) *Código de Comercio y legislación mercantil complementaria: legislación básica sobre el Código de Comercio y leyes complementarias* 3rd edn. Madrid: Colex.

Censo de tratados internacionales suscritos por España. (1976) Madrid: Ministerio de Asuntos Exteriores. 3 vols.

Clavero, B. (1990) *Manual de historia constitucional de España*. Madrid: Alianza.

Colección de tratados internacionales suscritos por España: bilaterales. (1977–) Madrid: Ministerio de Asuntos Exteriores. 7 vols., in progress.

COLEX DATA (available from Mapfre Lex).

COMPULEY. JURISLEY. BASE DE DATOS (available from La Ley División Informática).

Constituciones españolas. (1991) Madrid: Congreso de los Diputados. Secretaría General. Gabinete de Publicaciones, Boletín Oficial del Estado.

Cremades, Bernardo M. (1992) *Business law in Spain*. London: Butterworths.

CSIC (available from Consejo Superior de Investigaciones Científicas).

Cuadernos Civitas de jurisprudencia civil. (1983–) Madrid: Civitas.

Cuadernos de política criminal. (1977–) Madrid: Instituto Universitario de Criminología. Universidad Complutense de Madrid.

Diario de sesiones de las Cortes Generales. Comisiones Mixtas. (1977–) Madrid: Cortes Generales.

Diario de sesiones del Congreso de los Diputados. (1977–) Madrid: Cortes Generales.

Diario de sesiones del Senado. (1977–) Madrid: Cortes Generales.

Díez-Picazo, Luis María (1994) *Sources of law in Spain: an outline*. EUI Working Paper, LAW no.94/10. Florence: European University Institute.

Fernández, T.-R. (1993) *Manual de derecho urbanístico* 10th edn. Madrid: El Consultor de los Ayuntamientos y Juzgados.

Ferreiro Lapatza, J. J. (1995) *Curso de derecho financiero español* 17th edn. Madrid: Marcial Pons.

Fichero de altos cargos. (1940–) Madrid: FICESA.

Flanz, Gisbert H. and Hernandez, Eugenio A. (1991) Spain. In *Constitutions of the countries of the world*, eds A.P. Blaustein and G.H. Flanz, vol.XVIII. Dobbs Ferry, NY: Oceana.

García de Enterría, E. and Fernández, T.-R. (1980–1991) *Curso de derecho administrativo* 3rd edn. Madrid: Civitas.

Garrido Falla, F. (1985) (ed.) *Comentarios a la Constititución*. Madrid: Civitas.

GELABERT (available from Senado. Departamento de Informática).

Guía de la Administración general del estado: organigramas. (1994–) Madrid: Ministerio para las Administraciones Públicas.

G.V. LEXDATA: BASE DE DADES LEGISLATIVA DE LA GENERALITAT VALENCIANA (available from Generalitat Valenciana. Gabinet de Coordinació Interdepartamental).

IBERLEX (available from BOE).

Impuestos: revista de doctrina, legislación y jurisprudencia. (1984–) Madrid: La Ley.

Index to Foreign Legal Periodicals. (1960–) Berkeley, Cal.: University of California Press for the American Association of Law Libraries. Also available on CD-ROM and online.

Index to Legal Periodicals. (1908–) New York: H.W. Wilson. Also available on CD-ROM and online via (for example LEXIS, WESTLAW AND WISONLINE).

INDIBOE (available from BOE).

INDILEX (available from BOE).

International Political Science Abstracts. (1951–) Oxford: Basil Blackwell. Also available in electronic formats.

Jurisprudencia constitucional. (1982–) Madrid: Tribunal Constitucional/Boletín Oficial del Estado.

Jurisprudencia del Tribunal Supremo. Madrid: BOE. Appears in the following series: *Sala Cuarta de lo Social* (1993–); *Sala Primera de lo Civil* (1987–); *Sala Quinta de lo Militar* (1989–); *Sala Segunda de lo Penal* (1987–); *Sala Tercera de lo Contencioso-Administrativo* (1987–); *Tribunal de Conflictos de Jurisdicción y salas especiales* (1990–).

Jurisprudencia española: 'Ledico'. (1989–) Madrid: Gaceta del Foro.

Lacruz Berdejo, J. L. (1988) *Elementos de derecho civil*. Barcelona: Librería Bosch. Different editions of each volume have been published.

Legal Language Services and Ernst & Young (1996). *Spanish corporation law and limited liability company law*. The Hague: Kluwer Law International.

Legislación española 'Ledico'. (1987–) Madrid: Distribuciones de Derecho y Economía.

La Ley legislación. (1989–) Madrid: La Ley.

La Ley: revista jurídica española de doctrina, jurisprudencia y bibliografía. (1980–) Madrid: La Ley.

López Guerra, Luis *et al.* (1991–1992) *Derecho constitucional*. Valencia: Tirant lo Blanch.

MAP-LEXTER (available from BOE).

Marqués de Olivart (1890) *Colección de los tratados, convenios y documentos internacionales*. Madrid: El Progreso Editorial.

Martin, George R. (1989) The legal system of Spain. In *Modern legal systems cyclopedia*, ed. K.R. Redden, vol.4, pp. 4.160.1–36. Buffalo, NY: Hein. Partly revised in 1993.

Mir Puig, S. (1990) *Derecho penal: parte general: fundamentos y teoría del delito* 3rd edn. Barcelona: PPU.

Miranda, Susana (1993) *Spain practical commercial law*. European Commercial Law Series. London: Longman.

Montoya Melgar, A. (1995) (ed.) *Enciclopedia jurídica básica*. Madrid: Civitas. 4 vols.

Muñiz Castro, E.-G. (1992) *Diccionario terminológico de derecho: inglés/español–español/inglés = Dictionary of legal terminology: English/Spanish–Spanish/English*. Las Rozas: La Ley.

Muñoz Conde, F. (1995) *Derecho penal: parte especial* 10th edn. Valencia: Tirant lo Blanch.

Navarro-Valls, R. (1993) (ed.) *Derecho eclesiástico del Estado Español* 3rd edn. Pamplona: Ediciones Universidad de Navarra.

Nuevo diccionario de legislación: toda la legislación española en vigencia al 31 Diciembre 1974. (1975–1978) Pamplona: Aranzadi. 25 vols. Updated by: *Apéndice 1975–1985 al Nuevo diccionario de legislación* (1986–1990) and annually by: *Tabla de puesta al día. . . .* Supersedes: *Diccionario de legislación* (legislation in force to 1950) and *Apéndice 1951–1966*.

Oliva, Andrés de la *et al.* (1993) *Derecho procesal penal*. Madrid: Centro de Estudios Ramón Areces.

PERSONAL (available from BOE).

PUBLIBOE (available from BOE).

Puig Brutau, José (1975–1989) *Fundamentos de derecho civil*. Barcelona: Bosch.

Quintero Olivares, G. (1996) (ed.) *Comentarios al nuevo Código penal*. Pamplona: Aranzadi.

Ramos Méndez, F. (1992) *Derecho procesal civil* 5th edn. Barcelona: Bosch. 2 vols.

Relaciones laborales. (1984–) Madrid: La Ley.

Repertorio Aranzadi del Tribunal Constitucional 1981– . (1982–) Pamplona: Aranzadi.

Repertorio cronológico de legislación. (1930–) Pamplona: Aranzadi.

Repertorio de jurisprudencia. (1931–) Pamplona: Aranzadi.

Revista Crítica de derecho immobiliario. (1925–) Madrid: [s.n.].

Revista de administración pública. (1950–) Madrid: Centro de Estudios Constitucionales.

Revista de derecho bancario y bursátil. (1981–) Madrid: Centro de Estudios y Comunicación Económica.

Revista de derecho mercantil. (1946–) Madrid: [s.n.].

Revista de derecho procesal. (1985–) Madrid: EDERSA.

Revista de trabajo y seguridad social. (1990–) Madrid: Ministerio de Trabajo y Seguridad Social.

Revista española de derecho administrativo. (1974–) Madrid: Civitas.

Revista española de derecho constitucional. (1981–) Madrid: Centro de Estudios Constitucionales.

Revista española de derecho del trabajo. (1980–) Madrid: Civitas.

Revista española de derecho financiero. (1974–) Madrid: Civitas.
Revista general de derecho. (1944–) Valencia: [s.n.].
Revista jurídica de Catalunya. (1895–) Barcelona: Il·lustre Col·legi d'Advocats de Barcelona.
Ribó Durán, L. (1995) *Diccionario de derecho* 2nd edn. Barcelona: Bosch.
Ripollés Serrano, M. R. and Jiménez Díaz, A. (1994) (eds) *Estatutos de autonomía*. Madrid: Senado. Secretaría General. Dirección de Estudios y Documentación.
Roca i Sastre, R. M. and Roca-Sastre Muncunill, Ll. (1979) *Derecho hipotecario* 7th edn. Barcelona: Bosch. 5 vols.
Simons, Th. (1994–) (ed.) *Directory of European lawyers = Europäisches Anwaltsverzeichnis = Répertoire éuropéen d'avocats*. Munich: IPR. Annual. Also available on floppy disk.
Spain. (1992) In *Public management: OECD countries profiles*. Paris: OECD.
Spanish Constitution. (1982) Madrid: Servicio Central de Publicaciones. Presidencia del Gobierno.
Tierno Galván, E. (1984) (comp.) *Leyes políticas españolas fundamentales: 1808–1978*. Madrid: Tecnos.
Tomás y Valiente, F. (1990) *Manual de historia del derecho español* 4th edn. Madrid: Tecnos.
Tratados bilaterales sobre materias civiles. (1992) Madrid: Ministerio de Justicia.
Uría, R. (1995) *Derecho mercantil* 22nd edn. Madrid: Marcial Pons.
Vicent Chuliá, F. (1995) *Introducción al derecho mercantil* 8th edn. Valencia: Tirant lo Blanch.
Viver Pi-Sunyer, C. (1987) *Constitución: conocimiento del ordenamiento constitucional* 7th edn. Barcelona: Vicens-Vives.
West's law and commercial dictionary in five languages: English to German, Spanish, French, Italian. (1985) St. Paul, Minn.: West. 2 vols.
Westweber, U. and Vives, M. (1994) Spain = Spanien = Espagne. In Simons (1994–), pp. 779–862.

CHAPTER TWENTY-SEVEN

Sweden

GUNNEL JARBRANT

Introduction to the legal system

Earlier than in other European countries the law of Sweden was unified, around 1350, by the legislation of King Magnus Eriksson. There were two general codes, one for the countryside and the other for the towns. In 1734 one single code was promulgated, which consisted of nine *Balkar* [Books]. The present *Sveriges Rikes lag* [the Book of Statutes] is still divided into these Balkar, although almost nothing remains of the original text. Sweden belongs to the continental law tradition with its dependence on statutory law.

The first written Constitution was drawn up in the middle of the 14th century in the *Magnus Erikssons allmänna landslag*; this is translated by Holmbäck and Wessén (1962) as part of the Rättshistoriskt bibliotek series. The first Instrument of Government, dating from 1634, consisted primarily of rules for the administration. The following one from 1809 tried to achieve a balance of power between the king and the parliament. This instrument was influenced by the constitutional theorists of that time especially Montesquieu. The king held executive power. Legislative power was vested jointly between the king and the parliament. The constitution of 1809 remained in force until 1975, when the present Instrument of Government of 1974 was adopted. It is based on the principles of the sovereignty of the people, representative democracy and parliamentarism. Important political and constitutional changes were incorporated in amendments to the Instrument in 1994 which came into effect on 1 January 1995, including, among other measures, provisions for Sweden's membership of the European Union. Apart from the Instrument of Government there are three other constitutional laws: the Act of Succession of 1810, the Freedom of the Press Act of 1949 and the

Freedom of Expression Act of 1991.

The texts of the constitutional laws in Swedish can be found in *Sveriges Rikes Lag* (1861–) and *Sveriges grundlagar och Riksdagsordningen* (1995). The texts in English can be found in *Constitutions of the countries of the world* (Nergelius, 1996), reproducing official translations and the Swedish texts and including an extremely useful introduction, and in *Constitutional documents of Sweden* (1990) which is now somewhat dated.

Introductory works on the legal system and legal research

A usable introductory work on the Swedish legal system and the sources of legal information is *Finna rätt* by Bernitz *et al.* (1996). This book is intended for students but is widely read by practitioners. *Norstedts juridiska handbok* (1994), first published in 1946 by Norstedts, is a valuable source of information on the Swedish legal system, written for practitioners as well as the legally untrained. There are several introductory works available in English. *Swedish law*, edited by Tiberg, Sterzel and Cronhult (1994) gives a concise presentation of the Swedish law in English. Each chapter, written by an expert, is an independent survey of an area of law, for example private, criminal and procedural law. Some chapters have bibliographical notes. Another source of information about the Swedish legal system in English is *An introduction to Swedish law* edited by Strömholm (1988), which provides a broad survey. The chapters of the book are also written by experts and have useful bibliographical notes. A third work in English describing the Swedish legal system is a chapter by Åke Malmström (1983) in the *International encyclopedia of comparative law*; there is a detailed reference list at the end of the article both for material on Sweden and on Nordic countries generally. There is also a chapter by Bramstang (1993) in *Modern legal systems cyclopedia* which concentrates on constitutional law.

Legislation

The most important acts and ordinances are published in the series *Svensk författningssamling: SFS* [Official Statutes Publication] founded in 1825. It contains all acts promulgated by the cabinet and the parliament together, while ordinances by the cabinet are included selectively. Other ordinances by the cabinet are published in statute collections published by public authorities and county administrations.

The acts in the SFS are cited by year and number in the collection for example SFS 1995:18. Information about legislative preparatory materials is given in an annotation. There are quarterly indexes published with chronological and alphabetical lists which are cumulated in a yearly index. Amendment acts are also mentioned.

An important register, *Register över gällande SFS-författningar* (1996), is published at irregular intervals. This includes all acts and ordinances in force. Besides chronological and alphabetical indexes there is a table of cancelled acts.

Från riksdag & departement [News from parliament and ministries] (1976–) gives information continuously about new acts (see below).

Sveriges Rikes lag (1861–) is the most frequently used Swedish collection of legislation. It is privately published by Norstedts annually in a large volume containing a selection of the most important acts in force. *Sveriges Rikes lag* is divided into two sections, the 'Main law' and the Appendix [Bihanget]. The 'Main law' is based on the Code of 1734 with its division into Balkar (Books). In the Appendix other acts not related to the subject matter of the original Codes are arranged chronologically according to their enactment year and number in the publication SFS. *Sveriges Rikes lag* contains a chronological index and a subject index. There are references to case law in connection with the paragraphs in the law.

Some acts are translated into other languages and are annotated in *Svenska författningar i översättning till främmande språk* (1994).

Parliamentary publications and legislative preparatory materials

In Sweden the legislative preparatory materials are of great importance for the interpretation of new acts. These legislative materials are assembled in the collections of the parliamentary publications and the government inquiry commissions. Of considerable importance as legislative materials are the government bills and committee reports. Legislation often needs a comprehensive preparatory process before the final government proposal is laid before the parliament.

Riksdagstrycket [Parliamentary publications], first published in 1809, contains the printed records of the parliament and all the other documents concerning the activity of the parliament. The publications are delivered in issues which are bound together after the session. For every sessional year there are subject and personal indexes. The parliamentary publications are expensive and voluminous. Those who are interested can address themselves to the Parliamentary Library or the university libraries which have complete collections of the publications. They can be purchased from the Information Centre for the Swedish Parliament or Fritzes, the publishers.

The reports and drafts of important government inquiry commissions are published in the series *Statens offentliga utredningar* [Official Reports of the Government Commissions] (1922–), abbreviated as SOU. They are cited by indicating the year and the number in the series e.g. SOU 1995:15. Less important reports and drafts are published in the series *Ds: departementsserien* [Official Report series published by the Ministries] (1961–). They are also cited by indicating the year and number in the series e.g. Ds 1995:26. In every SOU and Ds there is a chronological index and a systematic subject index, divided according to the ministries. There are irregular bibliographies of the SOU and Ds. The latest published is *SOU och Ds 1981–1987: bibliografi* (1988).

A convenient method to trace the relevant parts of the legislative material concerning new acts is to consult the privately published review *Nytt juridiskt arkiv, Avd II* (1976–), abbreviated as NJA II. Its index is arranged according to the Balkar in *Sveriges Rikes Lag* (see above).

Från riksdag & departement (1976–) follows continually the work of the Parliament, government and commissions (see below). The annually published *Riksdagens årsbok* (1974–) gives a survey of the decisions of the parliament.

Codes and commentaries

There are four main series providing code commentaries: *Norstedts blå bibliotek* (1965–), *Norstedts gula bibliotek* (1963–), *Norstedts laghandböcker* (1983–) and *Publica* 1970–). The first three are published by Fritzes/Norstedts Juridik and the last mentioned by Fritzes/Publica. *Norstedts blå bibliotek* contains code commentaries to the Balkar in *Sveriges Rikes lag*, e.g. *Kommentar till Brottsbalken* [Commentary on the Penal Code] whose latest edition was published in three volumes in 1994. There is an English translation of this code, *The Swedish Penal Code*, published by the Ministry of Justice (1990). *Norstedts gula bibliotek* contains commentaries to independent acts. *Norstedts laghandböcker* which all are published in looseleaf format contain commentaries to both the Balkar and the independent acts e.g. *Rättegångsbalken* [The Code of Judicial Procedure] by Gullnäs *et al.* (1984–). This Code, which encompasses both civil and criminal procedure, is also translated into English in a volume entitled *The Swedish Code of Judicial Procedure* by National Council for Crime Prevention (1985).

Sweden has no special civil and commercial codes. Some acts can be found within the structure of the old Code of 1734 (see above under **Introduction to the legal system**) and in a great number of independent acts.

Treaties

The main publication concerning international treaties is *Sveriges internationella överenskommelser* (1991–), abbreviated as SÖ, which is the official publication published by the Ministry for Foreign Affairs. The treaty series was called *Sveriges överenskommelser med främmande makter* between 1912 and 1990. SÖ contains all international treaties binding on Sweden which have been agreed by the government, including amendments. The treaties are arranged chronologically with French or English translations where available.

An index to the SÖ entitled *Register över Sveriges internationella överenskommelser* is published every second year. The last one (1995) covers the period up to the 31 December 1994. This index covers both bilateral and multilateral treaties to which Sweden is a party and lists the treaties in order of the date on which they were signed. There is also a subject index.

Information about later treaties is available from the Utrikesdepartementet [Ministry for Foreign Affairs].

Law reports, judgments

The primary responsibility for the enforcement of law devolves upon the courts and the administrative authorities. The system of general courts consists of three instances: *tingsrätter* [courts of the first instance, district courts]; *hovrätter* [courts of appeal]; *Högsta Domstolen* [the Supreme Court] as court of the highest instance.

Since 1874 the cases of the Supreme Court are reported in a privately published collection, *Nytt juridiskt arkiv, Avd. I*, abbreviated to NJA. The publisher is Norstedts. The cases are cited by indicating year and page in the reports, e.g. NJA 1995, p. 157. Cases of judicial concern are reported in their entirety while other cases of less legal interest are reported as notices. NJA appears in instalments seven times a year. These are later published in one annual volume with statute and subject indexes. There are also cumulative indexes covering a period of ten years.

Cases since 1980 from the six Courts of Appeal are reported in *Rättsfall från hovrätterna* (1981–), published by Domstolsverket with indexes arranged in the same way as in NJA. Earlier cases are published in *Svensk juristtidning* (1916–). These cases are not to be considered as precedents. There are also indexes covering terms of five years. Cases in the District Courts are not reported.

Commentaries and periodical articles on a case can be traced by using *Rättspraxis i litteraturen* by Regner, Berggren and Lindh (1993) (see below).

Questions in the field of administrative law are in general not brought before the ordinary courts. The Regeringsrätten [Supreme Administrative Court] is the last instance for such cases which are published in *Regeringsrättens årsbok*, abbreviated to RÅ. The cases are cited by year and reference number, e.g. RÅ 1995 ref.5. RÅ contains statute and subject indexes. Current publishing of cases during the year appears in the looseleaf *Rättsfallsreferat från Regeringsrätten* (1988–), abbreviated to RR.

Besides the ordinary courts there are also some special courts. Their decisions are issued in the following publications: the decisions of the Labour Court are reported in *Arbetsdomstolens domar* (1930–); the decisions of the House Court in *Rättsfall från bostadsdomstolen*, RBD, (1975/76–); the decisions of the Market Court in *Marknadsdomstolens avgöranden* (1974–); and the decisions of the Insurance Court in *Rättsfall från försäkringsöverdomstolen*, RF, (1993–). All are published by Domstolsverket [the National Swedish Courts Association].

Computer-based systems

Within the last few years many of the legal texts have become available in computer databases and CD-ROM versions. The first Swedish legal database, RÄTTSBANKEN, became accessible for the public in 1981. RÄTTSBANKEN consists of two groups of databases. The first and older one contains cases from different courts such as the Supreme Court and the Courts of Appeal in full text. It also contains legislation; it updates continuously the SFS (see above) with information about amendments also in full text. The other group of databases includes for example collections of materials from ministries, the SOU and Ds (see above). Anyone who wants to have access to RÄTTSBANKEN must contact the SEMA Group Sweden to agree a contract.

The CD-LAG X on CD-ROM started in 1995. It contains in full text acts and ordinances of the SFS in force, information about amendments, cases of the Supreme Court and the Supreme Administrative Court from 1985 to the date of publication, reports and notices of *Nytt juridiskt arkiv, Avd.I* and *Regeringsrättens årsbok* and also a number of government bills. CD-LAG X is published by Norstedts and will be updated twice a year.

The Swedish Parliament's database RIXLEX became accessible in 1995. For the present it contains among other things the parliamentary publications in full text from the 1987/88 session and all acts and ordinances of the SFS in force. Anyone who wants to have access to RIXLEX must contact the Swedish Parliament, Dokument- och registerenheten.

The government Internet site at http://www.sb.gov.se provides information in Swedish with English translations due in the near future on the government and its ministries with recent press releases.

Directories

The Swedish Bar Association every year publishes *Sveriges Advokatsamfund: förteckning över advokater och advokatbyråer* (1996) which gives an alphabetical list of lawyers as well as lawyers' firms in different geographical areas. The annual *Sveriges statskalender* (1876–) gives addresses of public authorities, ministries, courts and prosecution authorities and also members of parliament are listed. There are institutional and personal indexes.

Bibliographies and indexing services

The main source of information for Swedish books is *Svensk bokförteckning* [the Swedish national bibliography] (1953–) published by Tidskriftsaktiebolaget Svensk bokhandel appearing weekly as an appendix to the journal *Svensk bokhandel* (1952–). At the end of the year an annual volume is produced. Entries for law books will be found under Oe in the classified subject arrangement. National bibliographical registration covers the period from 1830 up to the present. The Swedish national bibliography is also available in LIBRIS, the online bibliographic database of the Swedish research libraries and on the corresponding CD-ROM version. LIBRIS is produced by the Royal Library, LIBRIS Department.

The information source for Swedish articles in journals is *Svenska tidskriftsartiklar* (1961–) and for articles in newspapers *Svenska tidningsartiklar* (1961–). Both are published by Bibliotekstjänst. The references to the articles are also available on CD-ROM and online under the name ARTIKELSÖK.

Svensk juridisk litteratur by Regner (1957–1993) published by Norstedts is the easiest way to find out what has been written on a particular subject. The bibliography covers monographs, articles in journals and special collections from 1865 to 1991 so far. It is arranged according to the Balkar in the *Sveriges Rikes Lag* (see above) There is a subject index and from volume three the bibliography also includes an author index. Parts of the bibliography (the years 1976–1991) are available on a CD-ROM entitled CD-LITT, as at the second release for 1995, published by Norstedts.

Rättspraxis i litteraturen by Regner, Berggren and Lindh (1993), also published by Norstedts, is a way to find out where in the legal literature commentary on cases of the Supreme Court and the Courts of Appeal appears. This bibliography covers cases from *Nytt juridiskt arkiv, Avd. I* and *Rättsfall från hovrätterna* during the period 1930–1992. The cases are presented chronologically with literature references. There is also an author and an index to the works in which the commentaries appear.

Statliga publikationer (1985–) published by the Parliamentary Library is an annual bibliography of printed Swedish official publications. Public authorities and institutions in *Sveriges statskalender* (see above) are included in alphabetical order and titles are listed alphabetically within each publishing authority. This bibliography has subject and personal indexes as well as an index of public authorities.

Dictionaries

Juridikens termer by Bergström *et al.* (1993) and *Norstedts juridiska ordbok* by Martinger (1991b) are sources of information on legal terms in Swedish. These books are intended for practitioners and students but are also useful for lay people. *Förkortningsordbok* by Collinder and Svenblad (1987) is a Swedish abbreviation dictionary containing the most exhaustive general selection of abbreviations in all fields.

Three valuable multilingual dictionaries of legal terms are *Brottsbalkens termer på 6 språk* by Backe (1969) covering six languages, *Fyrspråkig juridisk ordbok* by Lindberg (1995) and *Ordlista för exekutionsväsendet på engelska, franska och tyska.*

Swedish–English and English–Swedish law dictionaries are respectively *Kortfattad svensk–engelsk juridisk ordlista* by Backe, Bruzelius and Wångstedt (1973), *Kortfattad engelsk–svensk juridisk ordbok* by Bruzelius, Wångstedt and Norking (1980). Others are *English law dictionary: engelsk–svensk–engelsk* by Collin (1989), *Juridikordbok: svensk–engelsk fackordbok* by Martinger (1991a) and *Ordlista för domstolsväsendet* (1994) published by the Courts Administration.

Swedish–French and French–Swedish dictionaries are *Juridisk ordbok* by Bouvier (1988) and *Juridikordbok* by Hellberg (1983).

Dictionaries in other languages are *Fachwörterbuch für Recht und Wirtschaft* (Swedish–German–Swedish) by Parsenow (1985) and *Juridisk ordbok* (Swedish–Polish–Swedish) by Drews (1987) and *Svensk–finsk och finsk–svensk juridisk ordlista* (Swedish–Finnish–Swedish) by Grönholm (1988).

Current information sources

Journals

The principal journals in legal science are *Svensk juristtidning* (1916–) and *Juridisk tidskrift vid Stockholms Universitet* (1989/90–). *Svensk juristtidning*, published since 1916, is intended for the practising lawyer, which can be noted from the selection of the articles. This journal also contains case law surveys and book reviews. *Juridisk tidskrift vid Stockholms universitet* is an academic journal containing longer articles and book reviews. It has a special part for comments on recent cases from the Supreme Court.

Advokaten (1983–) is the members' journal of the Sveriges advokatsamfund [Swedish Bar Association] containing articles and debates.

Another category of journals are the specialist ones, which contain articles on a special field of law. Examples of such journals are *Förvaltningsrättslig tidskrift* (1938–), which is a theoretical journal with articles on public administration. *Skattenytt* (1951–) and *Svensk skattetidning* (1934–) are specialist journals dealing with tax law. *Tidskrift för rättssociologi* (1983–) contains articles on the sociology of law. *Lag & avtal* (1978–) contains articles on labour law.

Från riksdag & departement (1976–) appearing in 40 issues per year follows the work of the parliament, the government and the commissions, and gives information continuously about committees, government bills and new acts.

Scandinavian studies in criminology (1965–) and *Scandinavian studies in law* (1957–) are published annually and contain articles in English on all the Nordic countries.

Business and financial information

An easy way to find information about Swedish enterprises is *Kompass-Sverige* (1957–), which provides facts on a great number of companies. Many products and services are listed, as well as the companies that manufacture or sell them. The daily newspaper for business people is *Dagens industri* (1976–).

Statistics

The official statistics are produced by Statistiska centralbyrån. The annual *Statistisk årsbok för Sverige* [Statistical yearbook of Sweden] (1914–) is a statistical abstract which provides summary statistics on a broad range of conditions and activities in Sweden inter alia the legal system. *Rättsstatistisk årsbok* [Yearbook of judicial statistics] (1975–), published annually, contains more comprehensive statistics on legal matters.

Useful addresses

Associations of lawyers and other professional organizations

Sveriges advokatsamfund [Swedish Bar Association], Box 27321, S-102 54 Stockholm, Sweden. Tel: +46 8 459 03 00. Fax: +46 8 660 07 79

Sveriges industriförbund [Federation of Swedish Industries], Box 5501, S-114 85 Stockholm, Sweden. Tel: +46 8 783 80 00. Fax: +46 8 662 35 95

Government organizations

Brottsförebyggande rådet [National Council for Crime Prevention], Box 6494, S-113 82 Stockholm, Sweden. Tel: +46 8 769 84 00. Fax: +46 8 32 83 64

Justitiedepartementet [Ministry of Justice], S-103 33 Stockholm, Sweden. Tel: +46 8 405 10 00. Fax: +46 8 20 27 34

Riksdagen [Parliament], S-100 12 Stockholm, Sweden. Tel: +46 8 786 40 00

Riksdagens InfoCentrum [Information Centre for the Swedish Parliament], S-100 12 Stockholm, Sweden. Tel: +46 8 786 54 62. Fax: +46 8 786 54 18

Riksskatteverket [National Swedish Tax Board], Tritonvägen 21, S-171 94 Solna, Sweden. Tel: +46 8 764 80 00. Fax: +46 8 28 03 32

Statistiska centralbyrån [Statistics Sweden], S-115 81 Stockholm, Sweden. Tel: +46 8 783 40 00. Fax: +46 8 661 52 61

Statsrådsberedningen [Cabinet Office], S-103 33 Stockholm, Sweden. Tel: +46 8 405 10 00. Fax: +46 8 723 11 71

Utrikesdepartementet [Ministry for Foreign Affairs], Box 16121, S-103 23 Stockholm, Sweden. Tel: +46 8 22 28 60. Fax: +46 8 723 11 76

Courts

Domstolsverket [National Swedish Courts Administration], S-551 81 Jönköping, Sweden. Tel: +46 36 15 53 00. Fax: +46 36 16 57 21

Högsta domstolen [Supreme Court], Box 2066, S-103 12 Stockholm, Sweden. Tel: +46 8 617 64 00. Fax: +46 8 617 65 2

Regeringsrätten [Administrative Supreme Court], Box 2293, S-103 17 Stockholm, Sweden. Tel: +46 8 617 62 00. Fax. 08 617 62 58

Education, training and research institutions

Juridiska fakulteten vid Lunds universitet [University of Lund. Faculty of Law], P.O. Box 207, S-221 00 Lund, Sweden. Tel: +46 46 222 00 00. Fax: +46 46 10 47 20

Stockholms universitet. Juridiska institutionen [Stockholm University. Faculty of Law], S-106 91 Stockholm, Sweden. Tel: +46 8 16 20 00. Fax: +46 8 612 60 87

Uppsala universitet. Juridiska fakulteten [Uppsala University. Faculty of Law], Box 512, S-751 20 Uppsala, Sweden. Tel: +46 18 18 25 00. Fax: +46 18 18 20 00

Libraries

Juridiska fakulteten vid Lunds universitet. Biblioteket [University of Lund. Faculty of Law. Library], PO Box 207, S-221 00 Lund, Sweden. Tel: +46 46 222 31 45. Fax: +46 46 222 44 33

Regeringskansliets förvaltningskontor, Rosenbadsbiblioteket, S-103 33 Stockholm, Sweden. Tel: +46 8 405 48 26. Fax: +46 8 21 06 35

Riksdagsbiblioteket [Parliamentary Library], S-100 12 Stockholm, Sweden. Tel: +46 8 786 40 00. Fax: +46 8 796 82 74

Stockholms universitetsbibliotek. Juridiska avdelningen [Stockholm University Library. Department of Law], S-106 91 Stockholm, Sweden. Tel: +46 8 16 20 00. Fax: +46 8 15 28 00

Uppsala universitet. Juridiska biblioteket [Uppsala University. Law Library], Box 6508, S-751 08 Uppsala, Sweden. Tel: +46 18 18 78 50. Fax: +46 18 69 56 65

Publishers and booksellers

Bibliotekstjänst AB, Box 200, S-221 00 Lund, Sweden. Tel: +46 46 18 00 00. Fax: +46 46 18 01 25

Fritzes AB, S-106 47 Stockholm, Sweden. Tel: +46 8 690 90 90. Fax: +46 8 690 91 66

Kungliga biblioteket. LIBRIS-avdelningen [Royal Library. LIBRIS Department], Box 5039, S-102 41 Stockholm, Sweden. Tel: +46 8 783 39 00. Fax: +46 8 783 39 30

Norstedts Juridik, Fritzes AB, S-106 47 Stockholm, Sweden. Tel: +46 8 690 90 90. Fax: +46 8 21 99 03

SEMA Group Sweden, Box 34101, S-100 26 Stockholm, Sweden. Tel: +46 8 738 50 00. Fax: +46 8 13 72 03

List of works cited

Advokaten: tidskrift för Sveriges advokatsamfund. (1983–) Stockholm: Samfundet. 1935–1982 with the title: *Tidskrift för Sveriges advokatsamfund.*

Arbetsdomstolens domar. (1930–) Stockholm: Allmänna förlaget (distr.) for Domstolsverket.

ARTIKELSÖK (available from Bibliotekstjänst).

Backe, T. (1969) *Brottsbalkens termer på 6 språk: med rättegångsformulär: svenska, tyska, engelska, franska, italienska, spanska.* Lund: Gleerups.

Backe, T., Bruzelius, A. and Wångstedt, E. (1973) *Kortfattad svensk–engelsk juridisk ordlista = Concise Swedish–English glossary of legal terms.* Lund: Gleerups.

Bergström, S. *et al.* (1993) (eds) *Juridikens termer* 8th edn. Stockholm: Almqvist & Wiksell.

Bernitz, U. *et al.* (1996) *Finna rätt: juristens källmaterial och arbetsmetoder* 4th edn. Stockholm: Juristförlaget.

Bouvier, M. (1988) *Juridisk ordbok: svensk–fransk och fransk-svensk = Dictionnaire juridique = suedois français et français–suedois.* Stockholm: Exportrådet.

Bramstang, Nils (1993) The legal system of Sweden. In *Modern legal systems cyclopedia,* ed. K. Redden, vol.4, pp. 4.200.1–4.200.41. Buffalo, NY: Hein.

Bruzelius, A., Wångstedt, E. and Norking, M.-L. (1980) *Kortfattad engelsk–svensk juridisk ordbok = A concise English–Swedish glossary of legal terms.* Lund: Liber Läromedel.

CD-LAG X (available from Norstedts Juridik).

CD-LITT (available from Norstedts Juridik).

Collin, P.H. (1989) *English law dictionary.* Stockholm: Esselte ordbok.

Collinder, B. and Svenblad, R. (1987) *Förkortningsordbok: åttatusen svenska och internationella förkortningar med förklaringar* 2nd edn. Stockholm: Liber.

Constitutional documents of Sweden. (1990) Stockholm: Riksdagen.

Dagens industri. (1976–) Stockholm: Affärsförlaget.

Drews, J. (1987) *Juridisk ordbok: svensk–polsk och polsk–svensk = Slownik prawniczy: szwedzko–polski i polsko–szwedzki.* Trångsund: XYZ.

Ds: departementsserien. (1961–) Stockholm: Allmänna förlaget.

Förvaltningsrättslig tidskrift. (1938–) Stockholm: Norstedt (distr.).

Från riksdag & departement. (1976–) Stockholm: Från riksdag & departement.

Grönholm, B. (1988) *Svensk–finsk och finsk–svensk juridisk ordlista = Ruotsalais-suomalainen ja suomalais-ruotsalainen alkikielen sanasto* 2nd edn. Turku: Grönholm.

Gullnäs, I. *et al.* (1984–) *Rättegångsbalken.* Stockholm: Norstedt. Looseleaf.

Hellberg, O. (1983) *Juridikordbok: fransk–svensk och svensk–fransk med begreppsförklaringar = Lexique juridique: français–suedois et suedois–français avec des explications de conception* 2nd edn. Stockholm: Norstedt.

Holmbäck, Å. and Wessén, E. (1962) *Magnus Eriksson Landslag.* Rättshistoriskt bibliotek. Skrifter utgivna av Institutet för rättshistorisk forskning, Ser. I, Band 6. Stockholm: Nordiska bokhandeln (distr.).

Juridisk tidskrift vid Stockholms universitet. (1989/90–) Stockholm: Juridisk tidskrift.

Kommentar till brottsbalken. (1994–) Stockholm: Fritze. 3 vols.

Kompass-Sverige: handbok över Sveriges industri och näringsliv. (1957–) Stockholm: Kompass-Sverige.

Lag & avtal: specialtidningen för arbetsrätt. (1978–) Stockholm: Stiftelsen Arbetsrättslig tidskrift.

LIBRIS (available from Royal Library, LIBRIS Department).

Lindberg, E. (1995) *Fyrspråkig juridisk ordbok = International law dictionary = Dictionnaire international de droit = Internationales Rechtswörterbuch*. Stockholm: Juridik & Samhälle.

Malmström, Å. (1983) Sweden. In *International encyclopedia of comparative law*, ed. V. Knapp, Vol.1, pp. S157–S176. Tübingen: Mohr.

Marknadsdomstolens avgöranden. (1974–) Stockholm: Norstedt.

Martinger, S. (1991a) *Juridikordbok: svensk–engelsk fackordbok* 2nd edn. Stockholm: Norstedt.

Martinger, S. (1991b) *Norstedts juridiska ordbok: juridik från A till Ö* 3rd edn. Stockholm: Norstedt.

Ministry of Justice (1990) *Swedish Penal Code*. Stockholm: Allmänna förlaget (distr.).

National Council for Crime Prevention (1985) *Swedish Code of Judicial Procedure: the translation is that of the wording of the Code of Judicial Procedure as at January 1, 1985*. Stockholm: Allmänna förlaget (distr.).

Nergelius, Joakim (1996) Sweden. In *Constitutions of the countries of the world*, ed. by A.P. Blaustein and G.H. Flanz, vol.XVIII. Dobbs Ferry, NY: Oceana. In 3 booklets.

Norstedts blå bibliotek. (1965–) Stockholm: Norstedt.

Norstedts gula bibliotek. (1963–) Stockholm: Norstedt.

Norstedts juridiska handbok. (1994) 15th edn. Stockholm: Fritze.

Norstedts laghandböcker. (1983–) Stockholm: Norstedt.

Nytt juridiskt arkiv: Avd. I: Rättsfall från Högsta Domstolen. (1874–) Stockholm: Norstedt.

Nytt juridiskt arkiv: Avd. II: Tidskrift för lagstiftning m. m. (1976–) Stockholm: Norstedt.

Ordlista för domstolsväsendet: svensk–engelsk, engelsk–svensk. (1994) Jönköping: Domstolsverket.

Ordlista för exekutionsväsendet på engelska, franska och tyska: svensk–engelsk, engelsk–svensk: svensk–fransk, fransk–svensk: svensk–tysk, tysk–svensk. (1994) Stockholm: Riksskatteverket.

Parsenow, G. (1985) *Fachwörterbuch für Recht und Wirtschaft: Schwedisch/Deutsch – Deutsch/Schwedisch = Fackordbok för juridik och ekonomi: svensk/tysk – tysk/svensk* 2nd edn. Cologne: Heymann.

Publica. (1970–) Stockholm: Fritze.

RÄTTSBANKEN (available from SEMA Group Sweden).

Rättsfall från Bostadsdomstolen. (1975/76–) Stockholm: Allmänna förlaget (distr.) for Domstolsverket. 1969/1970–1974/1975 with the title: *Praxis i hyresmål*.

Rättsfall från Försäkringsöverdomstolen. (1993–) Stockholm: Allmänna förlaget (distr.) for Domstolsverket. 1986–1992 with the title: *Rättsfall från Försäkringsöverdomstolen och försäkringsrätterna*.

Rättsfall från Hovrätterna. (1981–) Stockholm: Allmänna förlaget (distr.) for Domstolsverket.

Rättsfallsreferat från Regeringsrätten. (1988–) Stockholm: Allmänna förlaget (distr.) for Domstolsverket. Looseleaf. 1973–1987 with the title: *Rättsfallsreferat från Regeringsrätten och kammarrätterna*.

Rättsstatistisk årsbok. (1975–) Stockholm: Statistiska centralbyrån.

Regeringsrättens årsbok. (1909–) Stockholm: LiberFörlag/Allmänna förlaget for Domstolsverket.

Register över gällande SFS-författningar 1 januari 1996. (1996) Stockholm: Justitiedepartementet.

Register över Sveriges internationella överenskommelser den 31 dec. 1994. (1995) Stockholm: Utrikesdepartementet.

Regner, N. (1957–1993) *Svensk juridisk litteratur*. Stockholm: Norstedt. Coverage: Band 1: 1865–1956; Band 2: 1957–1970; Band 3: 1971–1978; Band 4: 1971–1982; Band 5: 1971–1986; Band 6: 1976–1991.

Regner, N., Berggren, N.-O. and Lindh, O. (1993) *Rättspraxis i litteraturen: Nytt juridiskt arkiv 1930–1992: Rättsfall från hovrätterna 1930–1992*. Stockholm: Norstedts juridik.

Riksdagens årsbok. (1974–) Stockholm: Allmänna förlaget. (1906–1948 with the title: *Lagtima riksdagen*; 1949–1973 with the title: *Riksdag*).

Riksdagstrycket. (1809–) Stockholm: Riksdagen.

RIXLEX (available from Riksdagen, Dokument- och registerenheten).

Scandinavian studies in criminology. (1965–) Oslo: Universitetsforlaget.

Scandinavian studies in law. (1957–) Stockholm: Almqvist & Wiksell International.

Skattenytt. (1951–) Stockholm: Skattenytt.

SOU och Ds 1981–1987: bibliografi. (1988) Stockholm: Allmänna förlaget.

Statens offentliga utredningar. (1922–) Stockholm: Allmänna förlaget.

Statistisk årsbok för Sverige. (1914–) Stockholm: Statistiska centralbyrån.

Statliga publikationer: Årsbibliografi. (1985–) Stockholm: Riksdagsbiblioteket. 1976/1978–1984 with the title: *Sveriges statliga publikationer: Bibliografi*; 1931/1933–1974/1975 with the title: *Årsbibliografi över Sveriges offentliga publikationer*.

Strömholm, S. (1988) (ed.) *An introduction to Swedish law*. Stockholm: Norstedt.

Svensk bokförteckning. (1953–) Stockholm: Tidningsaktiebolaget Svensk Bokhandel. Weekly issues appear as an appendix to *Svensk bokhandel*. Edited by the Bibliographical Department at the Royal Library in Stockholm.

Svensk bokhandel. (1952–) Stockholm: Svensk bokhandel.

Svensk författningssamling: SFS. (1825–) Stockholm: Liber/Allmänna förlaget.

Svensk juristtidning. (1916–) Stockholm: Norstedt.

Svensk skattetidning. (1934–) Stockholm: Norstedt.

Svenska författningar i översättning till främmande språk. Ds 1994:107. Stockholm: Fritze.

Svenska tidningsartiklar. (1961–) Lund: Bibliotekstjänst. 1953–1960 with the title: Svensk tidningsindex.

Svenska tidskriftsartiklar. (1961–) Lund: Bibliotekstjänst. 1953–1960 with the title: *Svensk tidskriftsindex*.

Sveriges advokatsamfund: förteckning över advokater och advokatbyråer. (1996) Stockholm: Samfundet.

Sveriges grundlagar och Riksdagsordningen. (1995) Stockholm: Riksdagen.

Sveriges internationella överenskommelser. (1991–) Stockholm: Utrikesdepartementet. 1912–1990 with the title: *Sveriges överenskommelser med främmande makter*.

Sveriges Rikes Lag. (1861–) Stockholm: Norstedt. Now annual.

Sveriges statskalender. (1876–) Stockholm: Fritzes.

Tiberg, H., Sterzel, F. and Cronhult, P. (1994) (eds) *Swedish law: a survey*. Stockholm: Juristförlaget.

Tidskrift för rättssociologi. (1983–) Lund: Tidskrift för rättssociologi.

CHAPTER TWENTY-EIGHT

Switzerland

JARMILA LOOKS

Introduction

Switzerland is a relatively small country (41 300 sq. km, 6.9 million inhabitants) situated in the central part of Europe. The beginning of its history is traditionally seen in the event of *Rütlischwur*, a solemn oath which took place on 1 August 1291, when the countrymen of three Alpine valleys met to form a league principally to defend themselves against the Habsburgs. This league of three is considered to be the foundation of the Swiss Confederation of today. During the centuries new members, called cantons, came to join the original *Eidgenossenschaft* and today's Switzerland counts 26 of them. To understand Swiss federalism it is important to know that the cantons, although bound together, always retained their autonomy and the people feel they belong more strongly to their commune and their canton than they do to the federal state.

This is certainly the reason for the diversity that characterizes Switzerland. Four languages are spoken: French in the west, Swiss German in the east, Italian and Romanche in the south. Two religions, Catholic and Protestant, co-exist equally. Four political parties form the collegiate government of seven members.

Introduction to the legal system

The first Swiss federal Constitution was promulgated in 1848. It replaced the inter-cantonal treaties and made Switzerland a federal state with its own legislative and executive authorities. This Constitution was totally revised in 1874. The federal state was given more power to legislate and the political rights of the people were extended. A Federal

Court was created to guarantee the compatibility of cantonal and federal laws and a uniform application of the latter.

The federal state received the competence to legislate in all important fields of private and public law and the most significant texts unifying the old cantonal laws were adopted during the years that followed: Civil Code, Code of Obligations, Criminal Code, Federal Statute on Debt Collection and Bankruptcy. Both civil and criminal procedure remained within the sphere of cantonal competence, which means that Switzerland has 26 cantonal Codes of Civil Procedure and the same number of cantonal Codes of Criminal Procedure. While some consider this eminently interesting and desirable, others wonder how a uniform application of federal law can be ensured under these circumstances. The most important procedural principles, however, are fixed in federal law, either in the Federal Constitution, or in the federal codes and statutes.

The Swiss federal Constitution in its present form has over 120 articles. The official text can be found in the *Systematische Sammlung des Bundesrechts* (1974–), see below. It can also be obtained in a separate booklet from the Federal Printing Office. An unofficial English translation can be found in *Constitutions of the countries of the world* which also contains a chronology of the constitutional history, although there may be some certain delay in the updates of the text (Flanz and Klein, 1982 and supplement 1994).

The Constitution contains the classic constitutional provisions such as articles on the structure of the state, on its authorities, on division of powers and competences, on fundamental rights of individuals, etc. The Swiss Constitution also contains a number of provisions which may seem curious to a foreigner because they determine, sometimes in quite a detailed way, the contents of federal legislation. For example, article 24novies deals with the protection of the environment and human beings from abuses that might be caused by the techniques of medically assisted procreation and genetic engineering. This phenomenon can be explained by the active role Swiss citizens play in the law-making process. They can exercise their right of initiative (see below) to ask for a modification of the Constitution. As they do not have the same right in regard to statutes, they have to request changes in the Constitution whenever they aim at changes in federal law. Moreover, any changes in the federal Constitution are submitted to a compulsory referendum, so that, in order to encourage the voters' agreement, the constituent tries to give more insight into the effect on future legislation (this is, for instance, apparent in the case of article 34quater dealing with old age and invalidity pensions). On the other hand, some of the fundamental rights of individuals are unwritten, even though guaranteed, such as personal freedom, freedom of expression.

The most important commentary on the Swiss Constitution is the looseleaf *Commentaire de la Constitution Fédérale de la Confédération*

Suisse du 29 mai 1874 (Aubert *et al.*, 1987–), also in German under the title *Kommentar zur Bundesverfassung der Schweizerischen Eidgenossenschaft vom 29 Mai 1874*. Aubert is also the author of the treatise entitled *Traité de droit constitutionnel suisse* (1967, supplemented in 1982), translated into German in 1991 as *Bundesstaatsrecht der Schweiz*.

Several attempts to undertake a total revision of the Swiss Constitution have been made in order to allow for more structure and coherence. Three drafts have been presented since 1978, the last one has been published in 1995 (*Reform der Bundesverfassung, Réforme de la Constitution fédérale, Riforma della Costituzione federale*, all three linguistic versions published by the Federal Printing Office). The electronic version, in German, French and Italian, can be found at the following URL (http://www.admin.ch/bj/bve96/).

The three main Swiss federal authorities are the Federal Council (executive), the Federal Assembly (legislative) and the Federal Court (judiciary).

The Federal Council [*Bundesrat, Conseil fédéral*] is a collegiate body of seven members elected every four years by the Federal Assembly who have to observe a rule, called 'magic formula', on the distribution of the seats according to representation of the political parties and to geographic area and linguistic group. Members who wish to be re-elected usually succeed and, although elected by the Federal Assembly, the Federal Council cannot be revoked by them. For these reasons the Swiss government remains very stable. Each of the seven members is head of one of the seven departments of federal administration. There is no real President *stricto sensu* even though each year one of the federal councillors is elected 'president'. This only means that he or she presides over the sessions of the Federal Council and represents the Swiss Confederation. The Federal Council decides as a unity.

The Federal Assembly [*Bundesversammlung, Assemblée fédérale*] is composed of two chambers. The National Council [*Nationalrat, Conseil national*] comprises 200 representatives of the Swiss people directly elected according to the principle of proportionality. The election is governed by federal law. The Council of the States [*Ständerat, Conseil des Etats*] has 46 deputies of the cantons. Their election is governed by cantonal law and varies therefore from one canton to another. The two chambers deliberate separately and only exceptionally sit together, for example, for the election of members of the Federal Council and the Federal Tribunal. There are four sessions of parliament in a year. Draft laws from the Federal Council are sent from one chamber to the other until all differences in opinion are settled.

The Federal Court [*Bundesgericht, Tribunal fédéral*] is the supreme court of Switzerland. It is situated in Lausanne and not in Bern, the Swiss capital. The section dealing with social security has its seat in

Luzern. The judges are elected by the Federal Assembly for six years and they usually are re-elected if they wish. The Federal Court has constitutional, administrative, civil, criminal, debt collection and bankruptcy jurisdiction. It is bound by federal statutes and cannot invalidate them in case they are contrary to the federal constitution. The deliberations of the judges are public. As a court of last instance, the Federal Court guarantees uniform application of federal statutes. Quite detailed information on federal institutions can be found at http://www.admin.ch on the Internet.

The cantonal authorities are different from one canton to another but correspond largely to the federal ones. The legislative body usually is unicameral. There are still a few cantons where the legislative power is exercised by the assembly of all, until recently exclusively male, citizens [*Landsgemeinde*]. The cantons may only exercise powers which are not within the competence of the Confederation. The distribution of competences is defined in the federal Constitution.

Two typical institutions of the Swiss democracy should be mentioned here: the 'initiative' and the referendum. On federal level the initiative is a right to propose a total or, more usually, partial modification of the Constitution, provided that 100 000 signatures of Swiss citizens can be collected within 18 months. A popular vote then decides if the constitutional change should be accepted. A double majority of the people and of the cantons is necessary to pass the change. The referendum is the right to provoke, within 90 days after publication, a popular vote on a law, provided that 50 000 Swiss citizens or 8 cantons request it. This means that a law cannot enter into force in any case during this 90-day period after its publication and, in case of a referendum, before the voters have decided. The majority of people is sufficient (that of the cantons not being necessary). Both institutions also exist on cantonal level where an initiative is possible to propose directly a modification of the legislation and not only of the constitution, as it is the case on federal level.

Switzerland is not a member of the European Union. In a relatively recent popular vote (6 December, 1992) the people and the cantons rejected participation in the European Economic Area. However, the membership of the European Union remains one of the political goals of Swiss foreign affairs.

Introductory works on the legal system and legal research

A very good introduction to the legal system of Switzerland (Legal system of Switzerland in general, 1989) is contained in the *Modern legal systems cyclopedia*. The *International encyclopedia of comparative law* has an excellent chapter on Switzerland (Stoffel, 1987) although this is also slightly outdated on some points because there have been changes in Swiss law, for example company law, since 1987. Another good chapter on Switzerland can be found in *EFTA legal systems: an introductory guide* (Sheridan, Cameron and Toulmin, 1993). Price Waterhouse published a guide in 1989 *Doing business in Switzerland* which still contains useful information for a business-oriented reader. More recent and complete are the *Business law guide to Switzerland* (Pestalozzi, Gmuer and Heinz, 1991) which also has a glossary of English, French and German terms at the end, and *Introduction to Swiss law* (Dessemontet and Ansay, 1995). The *Guide juridique suisse* (Baudraz, Colombini and Vogel, 1993) is another introductory work which can be recommended.

There is no major work in English on legal research in Switzerland. The looseleaf *Transnational law research* (Germain, 1992–) has a chapter on Switzerland but it is more a bibliography than a research guide. The same may be said about the chapter on Switzerland in volume II of the looseleaf *Foreign law* (Reynolds and Flores, 1989–), although the information is more detailed. Dumoulin and Frossard (1992) have published quite a complete work on legal research entitled *Les sources du droit, la documentation juridique et l'informatique documentaire*. Even though the text has been written mainly for a French-speaking Swiss readership, a list of federal laws which have been translated into English is published in an annex. *La recherche et la rédaction en droit suisse* (Tercier, 1995) makes little reference to English sources.

Legislation

There are three degrees of federal legislation. The first one in the hierarchy is the federal Constitution (see above). The second is legislative acts, federal laws [*Bundesgesetz, loi fédérale*], which have an unlimited validity in time and federal decrees [*Bundesbeschluss, arrêté fédéral*] which are limited in time. Finally, on the third level, there are regulations [*Verordnung, ordonnance*] which are merely executory norms for laws upon which they are based. International treaties are part of the federal law and have priority over earlier federal legislation.

Federal legislation is published weekly in three official languages, German, French and Italian, in the official collection of federal laws *Amtliche Sammlung des Bundesrechts*, AS = *Recueil officiel des lois fédérales*, RO = *Raccolta ufficiale delle leggi federali*, RU (1988–). The laws enter in force only when the 90-day period for referendum has expired or, when there is a vote, if the law has been accepted by the people (see above). Citation is made to the annual volume and page, for example, AS 1995 90, RO 1995 1022, RU 1995 471. All linguistic versions have exactly the same value; none is preferred if there are divergences. Recently an Internet site giving information on entry into force of legislation was created (http://www.admin.ch/ch/f/gg/ikt/index.html).

Individual laws, as well as the explanatory reports produced during the preparatory stage, can be obtained from the Eidgenossische Drucksachen- und Materialzentrale, Office central des imprimés et du matériel [Federal Printing Office] commonly known under the abbreviation EDMZ.

A consolidated version of the federal legislation in force is published in a very large multi-volume looseleaf compilation in systematic subject order, *Systematische Sammlung des Bundesrechts*, SR, *Recueil systématique du droit fédéral*, RS, *Raccolta systematica del diritto federale*, RS (1974–), updated in principle every three months. Citation is made to the subject classification number which appears in the upper right corner on each page, e.g. SR 220, RS 822.11. Treaties are included in this collection with classification numbers starting with 0., for example, SR 0.191.01 (see below).

In general, the publication of the Swiss legislation is very well organized and it is usually relatively easy to find legislative texts. A chronological index to federal legislation is published every five years and a systematic subject index appears annually, although with a two-year delay. The indexes give citations to both the official collection and to the systematic compilation. A bimonthly publication *Gesetzgebungs-Bulletin = Bulletin de législation* (1987–) provides information on the newest legislation, both federal and cantonal, and on the legislation in preparation. In addition, the systematic collection of federal legislation can be consulted on the Internet (http://www.admin.ch/f/rs/rs.html).

Draft laws submitted to the Federal Assembly and the explanatory reports (*Botschaft*, *message*, *messagio*) are published in the federal gazette, *Schweizerisches Bundesblatt*, BBl., *Feuille fédérale suisse*, FF, *Foglio federale svizzero*, FF (1848–). It is published weekly and citation is to the annual volume, its part in Roman numerals, and page number, for example, FF 1978 I 1493.

Schweizerisches Handelsamtsblatt = Feuille officielle suisse du commerce = Foglio ufficiale svizzero di commercio (1883–) is published five times per week by the Federal Department of Public Economy and gives, among other business related information, a selection of federal legislation in the field of commerce and industry.

There is also a commercial edition of civil, commercial and criminal laws in German entitled *Schweizerische Gesetze*, edited by Rehbinder and Zäch (1993–). It comprises one looseleaf volume which is much more compact and affordable than the multi-volume official publication and contains the most important legislation selected from the areas of law covered, regularly updated.

Each canton publishes a collection of its cantonal legislation. The systematic compilations of the cantonal legislation correspond more or less to the federal one. A complete survey of cantonal publications can be found in Dumoulin and Frossard, *Les sources du droit*, pp. 104–108.

Codes and commentaries

The Swiss Civil Code (*Zivilgesetzbuch, Code civil, Codice civile*) of 10 December 1907, came into force in 1912. It is a fruit of the unification of ancient cantonal private law which varied considerably from one canton to another under the respective influence of Germanic, Austrian, French, and the old customary law, depending on the region. The Code has a preliminary part containing fundamental principles and four main parts dealing with the law of persons, family law, law of inheritance, and law of property. The text has been partially revised several times, for example, adoption in 1972 (in force 1973), child–parent relationship in 1976 (in force 1978) and marriage law in 1984 (in force 1988).

The Code of Obligations (*Obligationenrecht, Code des obligations, Codice delle obbligazioni*) of 30 March 1911 constitutes the fifth part of the Civil Code but is often published separately. It was in fact enacted before the Civil Code (1881) and made part of it subsequently, keeping a separate numbering of sections. Divided into five parts, the Code of obligations deals with general provisions, different kinds of contracts (such as sale and exchange, rent and hire, employment, etc.), commercial law and companies, commercial register, firm names and commercial accountancy, and securities. The major modifications concerned for instance the employment contract in 1971 and the joint stock company in 1991. There is no Commercial Code as such.

The official versions of the Codes are included in the collections of federal laws described above. They can also be obtained separately from the Federal Printing Office. The most used commercial annotated editions are those by Schönenberger and Gauch (1994), *Schweizerisches Zivilgesetzbuch mit Obligationenrecht*, abbreviated to ZGB and OR, and by Scyboz and Gilliéron (1993), *Code civil suisse et Code des obligations annotés*, abbreviated to CC&CO. English translations exist for both codes: *The Swiss Civil Code* (Williams, 1987), originally translated by Ivy Williams and completely revised and updated by Sigfried and Barbara Wyler, *Swiss Code of Obligations – Volume 1: Contract law* (Reber *et al.*, 1990) and *The Swiss Federal Code of Obligations (as of January 1, 1984)* by Simon L. Goren, published in 1987 with a 1988 supplement. It does not include the new Swiss company law but separate translations have been published: *Swiss corporation law* (Bösch and Würsch, 1992) and *Swiss company law in the European context* (Wyler, Watter and Wyler, 1994). The latter also has a vocabulary of terms in German, French, Italian and English.

The two principal commentaries are the *Berner Kommentar* (1909–)

and the *Kommentar zum schweizerischen Zivilgesetzbuch* (1908–) known as the *Zürcher Kommentar*, both published in German. They each represent a series of volumes following the divisions and subdivisions of the Codes. Neither has been completed in their first edition, however the second and third editions have been simultaneously started for both of them. The state of both publications is rather difficult to survey and the use is often complicated. A helpful synopsis of the existing volumes and respective editions has been published in Dumoulin and Frossard (1992, pp. 323–).

As mentioned above, there is a variety of Codes of civil procedure as procedure is mostly within the competence of the cantons. However, mention should be made of international arbitration which is regulated on federal level as part of the Private International Law statute of 18 December 1987 (in force 1989). There is a commercial edition by Patocchi and Geisinger (1995), *Code de droit international privé suisse annoté*, which also contains a selection of relevant conventions. A major commentary in German was published under the title *IPRG Kommentar* (Heini *et al.*, 1993). An English translation with an introduction and annotations entitled *Switzerland's Private International Law Statute of December 18, 1987* by Karrer and Arnold (1989) is also available.

Treaties

International treaties are principally within the competence of the Confederation. Exceptionally the cantons have treaty-making power which is limited to the fields of public economy, police and neighbourhood conventions (art.8 and 9 of the Federal Constitution). The power to negotiate, sign and ratify international treaties is vested in the Federal Council. However, treaties which incur new obligations or modify the rights of the Confederation have to be approved by the Federal Assembly. The vote of the Chambers takes place after the signature and before the ratification of the treaty. It is very rare, though, that the approval of the Federal Assembly is refused. Some treaties are also subject to popular vote. Once a treaty has been ratified, it becomes part of the internal legislation and in principle has the priority over the internal rules.

Treaties are published in the official collection of federal laws, appearing in chronological order together with the internal legislation. As already mentioned, they are also published in the systematic compilation of laws, where they receive classification numbers starting with 0, e.g. RS 0.111. However, there is some delay in the publication of the treaties in the systematic collection. The Federal Department of Foreign Affairs has a documentation centre (address below) where information on treaties ratified by Switzerland can be obtained. A systematic plan of treaties can be found on the Internet (http://www.admin.ch/ch/f/rs/index.html).

Law reports, judgments

Judicial decisions play an important role, even though the status of precedents cannot be compared to that of common law countries. Mention should be made especially of private law, where, according to art.1 of the Civil Code, in the absence of a rule or a custom the judge has the power to decide according to the rules he would create if he had to act himself as legislator.

Only about 15 to 20 per cent of the decisions of the Federal Court are published, the choice being made by the Presidents of each chamber of the Court according to the criteria of general interest. The decisions appear in the official collection called *Entscheidungen des schweizerischen Bundesgerichtes : Amtliche Sammlung = Arrêts du Tribunal fédéral suisse : recueil officiel* (1875–), abbreviated to BGE or ATF. Each decision appears in the language in which the judgment was given. The collection is divided in five parts (six volumes as one part is further subdivided) and the current issues for each part are supplied four or five times a year. The subdivisions are as follows: Ia Constitutional Law; Ib Administrative Law; II Civil Law; III Debt Collection and Bankruptcy; IV Criminal Law; V Social Security.

Citation is to the number of the volume (and not the year), the number of the part and the page number, for example, BGE 112 Ia 36, or ATF 112 Ia 36. Each volume has a summary of decisions at the beginning and, until 1984 (ATF 110), a list of the names of the parties at the end. A decennial index called 'Répertoire général' is published, the last one covering 1975–1984. It is composed of a systematic list of legal dispositions applied by the Court (using the subject classification numbering of the systematic compilation of laws) and an alphabetical list by subject. Annual, three-year and five-year indexes following the same structure are published.

Most of the decisions are released in German. Translations of some of them, sometimes incomplete, are published in *Journal des tribunaux* (1846–), JT or JdT, *La Semaine judiciaire* (1879–), SJ, and *Repertorio di giurisprudenza Patria* (1935–), RGP, (French and Italian respectively). *Die Praxis* (1912–) brings German translations of decisions published originally in French or, more rarely, in Italian.

Unpublished decisions are sometimes reported in specialized periodicals, for example *Blätter für zürcherische Rechtsprechung* (1902–), *La Semaine judiciaire* (1879–), *Revue de droit administratif et de droit fiscal* (1945–), etc. Otherwise, they can be obtained from the Court itself. The request should be addressed to the Chancery or to the Managing Director. However, the decision as to whether the request will be satisfied is that of the President of the chamber which heard the case.

Specialized periodicals such as *Schweizerische Zeitschrift für internationales und europäisches Recht = Revue suisse de droit international et de droit européen = Rivista svizzera di diritto internationale e di diritto europeo = Swiss review of international and European law* (1991–), *Schweizerische Zeitschrift für Wirtschaftsrecht = Revue suisse de droit des affaires = Swiss review of business law* (1990–) and others often publish surveys of decisions with commentary. Mention should also be made of numerous publications compiling the case law in various fields, for example, *Schweizerische Verwaltungsrechtsprechung* (Rhinow and Krähenmann, 1990) and *Schweizerisches Obligationenrecht: Rechtsprechung des Bundesgerights* (Gauch, Aepli and Casanova, 1993).

Although of limited scientific value, the reports of Federal Court judgments published regularly in the daily *Neue Zürcher Zeitung* (1780–) are generally well documented and sufficiently neutral to be recommended as a source of up-to-date information.

Computer-based systems

The legal database SWISSLEX enables access to statutes and judicial decisions in full text. In addition to the decisions of the Federal Court as published in the official collection from 1954, it also contains jurisprudence (federal and cantonal) taken from about thirty periodicals, with special emphasis on tax law. SWISSLEX also contains electronic versions of the systematic compilation of federal legislation (described above) and the Bibliography of Swiss law (see below).

Full-text research is now possible using German and French terminology. In the future a trilingual thesaurus [*thesaurus de droit suisse*] should replace the existing vocabulary and enable searches in German, French, or Italian with retrieval of texts irrespective of the language they have been written in.

SWISSLEX is available online and subscription fees depend on individual contracts which are concluded either on an effective consultation time basis or for a given amount of hours of consultation per month. The former option at the time of writing costs a monthly fee of SFr100.- plus SFr10.- per minute of consultation, the latter option costs SFr650.- for two hours per month, SFr1045.- for four hours, etc., whether the monthly hours are used or not, additional minutes SFr10.- each.

Decisions of the Federal Court have been made accessible at http://antares.ethz.ch/BUGE on the Internet.

Encyclopedias, large collections

The only large legal encyclopedic publication covering Swiss law is the *Schweizerische juristische Kartothek, Fiches juridiques suisses*. It is a collection of more than 1000 booklets or leaflets, in all about 10 000 pages, containing comments on various subjects of law. The publication started in 1941 and is updated. A general subject index is published regularly in a consolidated version.

Directories

The Federal Chancery publishes each year a federal directory, *Eidgenössischer Staatskalender = Annuaire fédéral = Annuario federale* (1984–) with organizational schemes, names, addresses and telephone numbers of the federal administration. It further contains a list of the members of the government, of the Federal Assembly, and of the Federal Court, and it indicates the office hours and public holidays. The Swiss administration also has a home page on the World Wide Web (http://www.admin.ch/).

The *Staatskunde Lexikon* by Huber (1994) contains general information on law, economy, and society, organized by subject in alphabetical order. It is available in German and knowledge of the language is necessary for consulting it. *Publicus* (1958–) is a yearbook of Swiss public life. It partly gives the same information as the federal directory, but includes in addition cantons, communes, and further information on political parties, commercial organizations, social security institutions, science and culture, etc. *Jahrbuch der eidgenössischen Behörden... = Annuaire des autorités . . . = Annuario delle autorità . . .* (1958–) is another directory of public authorities, the administration and private enterprises; it lists members of the organizations with photograph and a short curriculum vitae. *Der Bund kurz erklärt, Conféderation en bref, Confederazione in breve* (1979–) is a concise yearly booklet containing basic information on how Swiss political life is organized. A list of Swiss embassies and consulates, *Verzeichnis der schweizerischen Botschaften . . . = Liste des ambassades et consulats . . . = Elenco delle ambasciate . . .* with their addresses and representatives is published separately by the Department of Foreign Affairs.

The Schweizer Anwaltsverband [Swiss Federation of Lawyers] publishes each year a list of members, *Mitgliederverzeichnis = Tableau des membres* (1994); some 5000 names and addresses according to canton are listed in the 1994 edition. The Association suisse d'arbitrage [Swiss Arbitration Association] has published a directory under the title *Profiles of ASA Members 1994–1996* (Blessing, 1994), including photographs and curricula. Finally, the *Schweizer Rechtspraxis = La pratique juridique suisse* (1985–) is a yearly directory of useful addresses for law, fiduciary and notarial practice and the administration. *Guide to legal studies in Europe 1996–1997* gives among other things information and addresses of law schools in Switzerland.

Bibliographies

One of the classics is the Szladits' *Guide to foreign legal materials: French, German, Swiss* published in 1959. It is still a very good bibliographic introduction to Swiss law. The *Schweizer Rechtsbibliographie = Bibliographie juridique suisse = Bibliografia giuridica svizzera* by Christen (1965–80) is a compilation of law books, periodicals and articles published in Switzerland on Swiss law or by Swiss authors from 1901 to 1978. It is continued from December 1980 as a monthly publication under the title *Summa jus*. The entries are classified by subject in around 20 main groups but there is no cumulation or index. *Rechtsbibliographie* (Cerutti, 1978–82) was published yearly in two volumes of which volume one concerns Switzerland. The entries are in alphabetical order, by author or title, with an author-title index at the end. The *Bibliographie des schweizerischen Rechts = Bibliographie du droit suisse = Bibliografia del diritto svizzero* (Frossard and Pop, 1987–) is published yearly as supplement to the *Zeitschrift für Schweizerisches Recht*. It contains publications, including books and periodical or other articles, from Swiss authors or about Swiss law, published in Switzerland or abroad. A systematic classification scheme is used to present the entries and an index of authors and titles appears at the end of each volume.

Dictionaries

There is no Swiss dictionary of legal terms, the French and German dictionaries being used in the country. One should note, though, that the terminology sometimes varies. As already mentioned, a trilingual (German, French, Italian) thesaurus of Swiss law is in preparation for SWISSLEX and a possible English translation is in discussion for the future.

Let us mention here the *Schweizerische Abkürzungen und Akronyme = Swiss abbreviations and acronyms* by Sokoll (1992), even if the publication does not concentrate specifically on law. Lists of abbreviations can be found in numerous monographic (e.g. Tercier) or periodical publications. An unofficial list is published at the beginning of each volume of the *Entscheidungen des schweizerischen Bundesgerichtes : Amtliche Sammlung*, the official collection of the decisions of the Federal Court.

Current information sources

Journals, research reports

There are some 90 Swiss law periodicals. The most important and currently used are the following ones. The *Aktuelle juristische Praxis* (AJP) = *Pratique juridique actuelle* (PJA), is a monthly published in German and French since 1992. It regularly contains articles, choice of court decisions, comments on cases, bibliography and book reviews. The *Schweizerische Juristen-Zeitung* (SJZ) = *Revue suisse de jurisprudence* (RSJ) (1904–) is published twice a week and contains articles, decisions of cantonal tribunals, book reviews and other information. It is more oriented to the practising lawyer than, for instance, the *Zeitschrift für Schweizerisches Recht* (ZSR) = *Revue de droit suisse* (RDS) which is a classic academic journal published since 1852 in German, French and Italian. Since 1882 when a new series began, it consists of two parts; the first part is more general and is published five times a year, the second is reserved for the publication of the reports of the Swiss Society of Lawyers [Schweizerischer Juristenverein, Société suisse des juristes, Società svizzera dei giuristi]. The periodicals mentioned above in the section on law reports, for example, *Journal des tribunaux*, *La Semaine judiciaire*, also sometimes publish articles.

News information

The most authoritative daily newspaper probably is the *Neue Zürcher Zeitung*, which is very well documented and publishes for instance a detailed programme and summary of debates in the Parliament during the sessions. It also regularly publishes more or less extensive articles on current legal problems, often written by legal academics or professionals. As already mentioned, the reports of cases before the Federal Court which the paper publishes regularly are also of interest to a legal practitioner.

Useful addresses

Associations of lawyers

Schweizer Anwaltsverband, Sekretariat, Bollwerk 21, Postfach 8321, 3001 Bern, Switzerland. Tel: +41 31 312 2505. Fax: +41 31 312 31 03

Association suisse d'arbitrage (ASA) [Swiss Arbitration Association], St. Alban-Graben 8, PO Box 1548, 4001 Basel, Switzerland. Tel: +41 61 272 18 88. Fax: +41 272 80 60

Government organizations

Eidg. Justiz- und Polizeidepartement = Office fédéral de justice et police [Ministry of Justice and Police], 3003 Bern, Switzerland. Tel: +41 31 322 41 11. Fax: +41 31 322 78 32

Eidg. Department für auswärtige Angelegenheiten = Office fédéral des affaires étrangères [Foreign Ministry], 3003 Bern, Switzerland. Tel: +41 31 322 21 11. Fax: +41 31 322 32 37. Also: Direktion für Völkerrecht = Direction du droit international public [documentation centre/treaties], Tel: +41 31 322 30 79. Fax: +41 31 322 30 73

Office suisse d'expansion commercial (OSEC) [Swiss Office of Trade Development], Stampfenbachstrasse 85, 8006 Zürich, Switzerland. Tel: +41 1 365 51 51. Fax: +41 1 365 52 21

Courts

Bundesgericht = Tribunal fédéral, 1000 Lausanne 14, Switzerland. Tel: +41 21 318 91 11. Fax: +41 21 323 37 00

Eidg. Versicherungsgericht = Tribunal fédéral des assurances, Adligenswilerstr. 24, 6006 Luzern, Switzerland. Tel: +41 41 59 25 56. Fax: +41 41 59 26 69

Education and training

Universität Basel, Petersplatz 1, 4003 Basel, Switzerland. Tel: +41 61 293111

Universität Bern, Hochschulstrasse 4, 3012 Bern, Switzerland. Tel: +41 31 658111

Université de Fribourg, Miséricorde, 1700 Fribourg, Switzerland. Tel: +41 37 219248

Université de Genève, Place de l'Université, 1200 Genève, Switzerland. Tel: +41 22 705 71 11

Research institutes

Institut suisse de droit comparé [Swiss Institute of Comparative Law], 1015 Lausanne, Switzerland. Tel: +41 21 692 49 11. Fax: +41 21 692 49 49. E-mail: Secretariat@isdc-dfjp.unil.ch. Internet: http://www.unil.ch/isdc/Welcome.html

Publishers and booksellers

Eidg. Drucksachen- und Materialzentrale = Office fédéral des imprimés et du matériel [Federal Printing Office], EDMZ, 3000 Bern, Switzerland. Tel: +41 31 322 39 51 (for legislative materials, incl. treaties), +41 31 322 39 52 (general). Fax: +41 31 322 39 75

Schulthess, Zwingliplatz 2, Postfach, 8022 Zürich, Switzerland. Tel: +41 1 251 93 36. Fax: +41 1 261 63 94

SWISSLEX, Banque suisse de données juridiques SA, Hirschengraben 8/case postale, 3001 Bern, Switzerland. Tel: +41 31 382 83 84. Fax: +41 31 382 35 04

Stämpfli, Hallerstr.7, 3012 Bern, Switzerland. Tel: +41 31 300 6666. Fax: +41 31 300 66 88

Chambers of commerce

British–Swiss Chamber of Commerce, Freiestrasse 155, 8032 Zürich, Switzerland. Tel: +41 1 422 31 31. Fax: +41 1 422 32 44

Swiss–American Chamber of Commerce, Talacker 41, 8001 Zürich, Switzerland. Tel: +41 1 211 24 54. Fax: +41 1 211 95 92

List of works cited

Aktuelle juristische Praxis = Pratique juridique actuelle. (1992–) Lachen: Dike.

Amtliche Sammlung des Bundesrechts. (1988–) Bern: Bundeskanzlei. Issued under various similar titles from 1848. In looseleaf format from 1973.

Aubert, J.F. (1967) *Traité de droit constitutionnel suisse*. Neuchâtel: Ides et Calendes. Supplement 1982.

Aubert, J.F. (1991) *Bundesstaatsrecht der Schweiz*. Fassung von 1967. Neubearbeiteter Nachtrag bis 1990. Basel: Helbing & Lichtenhahn.

Aubert, J.F. *et al.* (1987–) (eds) *Commentaire de la Constitution Fédérale de la Confédération Suisse du 29 mai 1874*. Basel: Helbing & Lichtenhahn; Zürich: Schulthess. Looseleaf.

Aubert, J.F. *et al.* (1987–) (eds) *Kommentar zur Bundesverfassung der Schweizerischen Eidgenossenschaft vom 29 Mai 1874*. Basel: Helbing & Lichtenhahn; Zürich: Schulthess. Looseleaf.

Baudraz, H. *et al.* (1993) *Guide juridique suisse* 6th edn. Lausanne: Marguerat.

Berner Kommentar. (1909–) Bern: Stämpfli. Multi-volume work in multiple editions.

Blätter für zürcherische Rechtsprechung. (1902–) Zürich: Orell Füssli.

Blessing, M. (1994) (ed.) *Profiles of ASA members 1994–1996*. Basel: Association suisse d'arbitrage.

Bösch, René and Würsch, Daniel (1992) *Swiss corporation law*. Zürich: Schulthess.

Der Bund Kurz erklärt. (1979–) Bern: EDMZ.

Cerutti, N.M. (1978–82) *Rechtsbibliographie = Law bibliography = Bibliographie juridique*. Zürich: Studio.

Christen, H. (1965–80) *Schweizer Rechtsbibliographie = Bibliographie juridique suisse = Bibliografia giuridica svizzera*. Zürich: Juris. Continued by *Summa jus*.

Conféderation en bref. (1979–) Bern: EDMZ.

Confederazione in breve. (1979–) Bern: EDMZ.

Dessemontet, F. and Ansay, T. (1995) (eds) *Introduction to Swiss law* 2nd edn. Deventer & Antwerp: Kluwer.

Dumoulin, J-F. and Frossard, G. (1992) *Les sources du droit, la documentation juridique et l'informatique documentaire*. Basel/Frankfurt a M : Helbing & Lichtenhahn.

Eidgenössischer Staatskalender = Annuaire fédéral = Annuario federale. (1984–) Bern: EDMZ.

Entscheidungen des schweizerischen Bundesgerichts = Arrêts du Tribunal fédéral suisse. (1875–) Lausanne: Imprimeries réunies.

Feuille fédérale. (1848–) Bern: Stämpfli. Title varies.

Fiches juridiques suisses. (1941–) Genève.

Flanz, Gisbert H. and Klein G.E. (1982) Switzerland. In *Constitutions of the countries of the world*, eds A.P. Blaustein and G.H. Flanz, vol.XIX. Dobbs Ferry, NY: Oceana. Updated 1973–81 by J.K. Siegenthaler. Supplement by Gisbert H. Flanz issued August 1994.

Foglio federale. (1848–) Bellinzona: Grassi. Title varies.

Frossard, G. and Pop, T. (1987–) (eds) *Bibliographie des Schweizerischen Rechts = Bibliographie du droit suisse = Bibliografia del diritto svizzero*. Basel: Helbing & Lichtenhahn. Supplement to *Zeitschrift für schweizerisches Recht*.

Gauch, P., Aepli, V. and Casanova, H. (1993) (eds) *Schweizerisches Obligationenrecht: Rechtsprechung des Bundesgerichts* 3rd edn. Zürich: Schulthess.

Germain, C.M. (1992–) *Transnational law research*. Ardsley-on-Hudson, NY: Transnational Juris Publications. Looseleaf.

Gesetzgebungs-Bulletin = Bulletin de législation. (1987–) Zürich: Orell Füssli.

Goren, Simon L. (1987) *The Swiss Federal Code of Obligations (as of January 1, 1984)*. Littleton, Colo.: Rothman. Supplement published 1988.

Guide to legal studies in Europe 1996–1997. (1996) Brussels: Law Books in Europe.

Heini, A. *et al.* (1993) (eds) *IPRG Kommentar*. Zürich: Schulthess.

Huber, A. (1994) *Staatskunde Lexikon*. Luzern: Verlag Schweizer Lexikon.

Jahrbuch der eidgenössischen Behörden = Annuaire des autorités fédérales = Annuario delle autorità federali. (1958–) Bern: Benteli.

Journal des tribunaux. (1846–) Lausanne: Impr. Ruckstahl.

Karrer, P.A. and Arnold, K.W. (1989) *Switzerland's Private International Law Statute of December 18, 1987*. Deventer & Boston: Kluwer.

Kommentar zum schweizerischen Zivilgesetzbuch (Zürcher Kommentar). (1908–) Zürich:

Schulthess. Multi-volume work in multiple editions.
Legal system of Switzerland. (1989) In *Modern legal systems cyclopedia*, ed. K.R. Redden, vol.4, pp. 4.210.1–4.210.73. Buffalo, NY: Hein. No author given. Publication date of volume is 1989, minor updating of chapter in 1993.
Mitgliederverzeichnis = Tableau des membres. (1994) Zürich: Schweizerischer Anwaltsverband, Fédération Suisse des Avocats. Annual.
Neue Zürcher Zeitung. (1780–) Zürich: Neue Zürcher Zeitung.
Patocchi, P.M. and Geisinger, E. (1995) *Code de droit international privé suisse annoté*. Lausanne: Payot.
Pestalozzi, Gmuer and Heinz (1991) *Business law guide to Switzerland*. Wiesbaden & Bicester: CCH Europe.
Die Praxis: wichtige Entscheidungen des Schweizerischen Bundesgerichts.... (1912–) Basel: Helbing und Lichtenhahn.
Price Waterhouse (1989) *Doing business in Switzerland*. Zürich & Lausanne: Price Waterhouse.
Publicus. (1958–) Basel: Schwabe.
Raccolta sistematica del diritto federale. (1974–) Bern: EDMZ. Looseleaf.
Raccolta ufficiale delle leggi federali. (1988–) Bern: Cancelleria federale. Issued under various similar titles from 1848. In looseleaf format from 1973.
Reber, A. *et al.* (1990) *Swiss Code of Obligations – Volume 1: Contract law*. Zürich: Swiss–American Chamber of Commerce.
Recueil officiel des lois fédérales. (1988–) Berne: Chancellerie fédérale. Issued under various similar titles from 1848. In looseleaf format from 1973.
Recueil systématique du droit fédéral. (1974–) Berne: Chancellerie fédérale. Looseleaf.
Reform der Bundesverfassung. (1995) Bern: EDMZ. 2 vols.
Réforme de la Constitution fédérale. (1995) Bern: EDMZ. 2 vols.
Rehbinder, M. and Zäch, R. (1993–) *Schweizerische Gesetze: Sammlung des Zivil-, Wirtschafts- und Strafrechts*. Bern: Stämpfli, etc. Looseleaf.
Repertorio di giurisprudenza Patria. (1935–) Belinzona: Salvioni.
Revue de droit administratif et de droit fiscal. (1945–) Lausanne & Geneva: the Revue.
Reynolds, T.H. and Flores, A.A. (1989–) *Foreign law: current sources of codes and basic legislation in jurisdictions of the world*. Littleton, Colo.: Rothman. Looseleaf.
Rhinow, R.A. and Krähenmann, B. (1990) *Schweizerische Verwaltungsrechtsprechung* 6th edn. Basel & Frankfurt a.M.: Helbing & Lichtenhahn.
Riforma della Costituzione federale. (1995) Bern: EDMZ. 2 vols.
Schönenberger, W. and Gauch, P. (1994) *Schweizerisches Zivilgesetzbuch mit Obligationenrecht*. Zürich: Schulthess.
Schweizer Rechtspraxis = La Pratique juridique suisse. (1985–) Zürich: Orell Füssli.
Schweizerische Juristen-Zeitung = Revue suisse de jurisprudence. (1904–) Zürich: Schulthess.
Schweizerische juristische Karthotek. (1941–) Geneva: Schweizerische Juristische Karthotek.
Schweizerische Zeitschrift für internationales und europäisches Recht = Revue suisse de droit international et de droit européen = Rivista svizzera di diritto internationale e di diritto europeo = Swiss review of international and European law. (1991–) Zürich: Schulthess. Formerly *Schweizerisches Jahrbuch für internationales Recht*.
Schweizerische Zeitschrift für Wirtschaftsrecht = Revue suisse de droit des affaires = Swiss review of business law. (1990–) Zürich: Schulthess.
Schweizerisches Bundesblatt. (1848–) Bern: Stämpfli. Title varies.
Schweizerisches Handelsamtsblatt = Feuille officielle suisse du commerce = Foglio ufficiale svizzero di commercio. (1883–) Bern: Bundesamt für Aussenwirtschaft des Eidgenössischen Volkswirtschaftsdepartments.
Scyboz, G. and Gilliéron, P-R. (1993) *Code civil suisse et Code des obligations annotés*. Lausanne: Payot.

La Semaine judiciaire. (1879–) Geneva: Imprimerie Fornara for the Greffe de la Cour de Justice.

Sheridan, M., Cameron, J. and Toulmin, J. (1993) (eds) *EFTA legal systems: an introductory guide*. London: Butterworths.

Sokoll, A.H. (1992) *Schweizerische Abkürzungen und Akronyme = Swiss abbreviations and acronyms*. Munich: Alkos.

Stoffel, W.A. (1987) Switzerland. In *International encyclopedia of comparative law*, ed. V. Knapp, vol.1, pp. S177–S204. Tübingen: J.C.B. Mohr.

Summa Jus. (1980–) Zürich: Juris.

Systematische Sammlung des Bundesrechts. (1974–) Bern: EDMZ. Looseleaf.

Szladits, C. (1959) *Guide to foreign legal materials: French, German, Swiss*. New York: Oceana.

Tercier, P. (1995) *La recherche et la rédaction en droit suisse*. 2nd edn. Fribourg: Editions universitaires.

Verzeichnis der Schweizerischen Botschaften und Konsulate = Liste des ambassades et consulats de Suisse = Elenco delle ambasciate e dei consolati di Svizzera. (no date) Bern: EDMZ.

Williams, Ivy (1987) *The Swiss Civil Code*. Zürich: ReMak.

Wyler, Sigfried, Watter, Rolf and Wyler, Juerg (1994) *Swiss company law in the European context*. St. Gallen: ReMak.

Zeitschrift für schweizerisches Recht = Revue de droit suisse = Rivista di diritto svizzero. (1852–) Basel: Helbing & Lichtenhahn. Annual supplement: *Bibliographie des schweizerischen Rechts = Bibliographie du droit suisse = Bibliografia del diritto svizzero*.

CHAPTER TWENTY-NINE

Turkey

OSMAN DOĞRU

Introduction to the legal system

The Republic of Turkey was established in 1923 and its secular legal system has evolved with the reception of important laws, both civil and penal, from continental European countries.

The first Constitution [Anayasa] of the Republic of Turkey was in force between 1924 and 1960. Although the 1924 Constitution established the basic institutions of democratic government, a one-party regime ruled the country until the end of World War II. A multi-party system commenced in 1946 and the opposition Democratic Party gained power in the elections of 1950; it was in government until 27 May 1960 when it was removed from power by a *coup d'état*. A military regime was established and an extraordinary tribunal tried the deputies of the Democratic Party; the former Prime Minister and two other Ministers were executed in September 1961.

A new constitution was prepared during the military regime and power was transferred to civilian authorities after the elections in October 1961. The Constitution of 1961 secured the rights and freedoms of individuals by establishing a Constitutional Court and also recognized the social and economic rights of citizens. After a warning from the commanding officers of the armed forces on 12 March 1971, the cabinet resigned and their successors, with the support of the armed forces, declared martial law. Parliament amended some of the articles of the 1961 Constitution at the proposition of the new government.

The last military intervention in civilian politics took place on 12 September 1980. A military junta composed of five members ruled the country for three years. A new constitution was prepared by a consultative assembly during the period of military rule and it was approved at a referendum in 1982 by a majority of 92 per cent. Elections were held in November 1983 for a return to civilian rule. An English translation, *Constitution of the Republic of Turkey* (Prime Ministry, 1990) has been published by the Prime Ministry Directorate General of Press and Information. Flanz (1994) provides both the Turkish text and an official translation of the text as at May 1987 into English with a bibliography and translations of further amendments of July 1995 in a supplement.

The Constitution of 1982 defines the Republic of Turkey as a democratic, secular and social state governed by the rule of law. Some provisions of the 1982 Constitution and some other laws enacted by the junta but still in force are the subject of criticism for not fulfilling the basic requirements of a Western democracy and the rule of law. However, Turkey is now a member of the Council of Europe and a contracting state of the European Convention for the Protection of Human Rights and Fundamental Freedoms and has accepted the competence of the European Commission on Human Rights and the European Court of Human Rights. It could be expected that the decisions of these bodies will help to reinforce democracy and the rule of law.

Turkey is not a full member of the European Union but the government has applied for membership and a customs union between the European Union and Turkey is now in force.

Among textbooks on Turkish constitutional law, the following can be consulted: *Anayasa bilimi* [Science of constitution] by Çağlar (1988), *Türk anayasa hukuku* [Turkish constitutional law] by Özbudun (1992), *Siyasi kurumlar ve anayasa hukuku* [Political institutions and constitutional law] by Tunaya, 1982 and *Türkiye'nin insan haklari sorunu* [Human rights issues in Turkey] by Tanör (1994).

Introductory works on the legal system and legal research

The outstanding work among introductory works on the legal system in Turkish is *Hukuk Başlangici* [Introduction to law] by Bilge (1986). There are also useful general works in English such as *The legal system of Turkey* (Özman and Sírman, 1990), *Introduction to Turkish law* by Ansay and Wallace (1987), which has a selected bibliography of books and articles in English on Turkish law and the chapter on Turkey in the *International encyclopedia of comparative law* (Davran and Kubali, 1973). Two more specialized books worthy of mention are *The Turkish legal system on foreign investments* by Altuğ (1987) and *Fundamentals of Turkish private law* by Adal (1991).

Legislation

The legislation of the country is published in the *Resmî Gazete* [Official Gazette]. All the laws enacted by Parliament, decrees having the force of law issued by the Council of Ministers, regulations issued by the Council of Ministers for the implementation of laws, by-laws issued by ministries and public corporate bodies in order to ensure the application of laws, and regulations or decrees issued by ministries, appear in the Official Gazette which is a daily publication. Legislation comes into force on publication in the gazette. The form of the citation to an individual law is, e.g. The Constitution of the Republic of Turkey, RG: 9.11.1982–17863; the first figures are the date and the second is the number of the part of the Official Gazette in which the law is published. There is an index to the Gazette published quarterly.

There is a looseleaf compilation of the laws, *Yürürlükteki Kanunlar Külliyati* [The Laws in Force], in force at a certain date, published by the Prime Ministry. It is arranged by the number of the enactment with an index by name. It is kept up to date by releases of new pages every three months which incorporate amendments into the text of each act. There is also a similar and reliable compilation under the same title published by a private company, Kazanci Yayinlari, which tends to be more up to date. There is also an officially published annual collection of legislation, with index, called *Düstur* but the looseleaf compilations are generally preferred because they contain more up-to-date consolidated texts.

Certain laws, such as the Civil Code and the Penal Code, are reproduced in their amended forms by private publishers and are widely purchased. Proceedings in Parliament, including debates on new laws and draft legislation, are contained in *Meclis Tutanaklari* [Parliament Records].

Codes and commentaries

The *Medeni Kanun* [Civil Code] and the *Borçlar Kanunu* [Code of Obligations] originate in 1926. They are adaptations of the equivalent codes of Switzerland to the Turkish legal system. The Civil Code includes articles on personal status, family, inheritance and property. There are several commercial annotated editions of which the most used by lawyers are Şener (1991) and Yavuz (1996). Commentaries used by lawyers on the Code of Obligations include editions by Dalamanli and Kazanci (1990), Karahasan (1992) and Uygur (1990–1994).

The *Türk Ticaret Kanunu* [Turkish Commercial Code], which came into force in 1957, comprises articles on all aspects of commercial law including maritime law. The commentaries are by Domaniç and Çamoğlu (1992) and Doğanay (1990).

The *Hukuk Muhakemeleri Usulü Kanunu* [Code of Civil Procedure] came into force in 1927. The commentaries are by Üstündağ (1989) and Kuru (1995).

The *Türk Ceza Kanunu* [Turkish Criminal Code] originates in 1926. In addition there are several other provisions relating to criminal acts such as the Law on Combating Terrorism which is often applied by the courts. The leading commentaries are by Erem (1993), by Içel and Yenisey (1994) and Gözübüyük (1989). The *Ceza Muhakemeleri Usulü Kanunu* [Code of Criminal Procedure] came into force in 1929. The Code of Military Criminal Procedure and the Code of Criminal Procedure of State Security Courts are also applied in criminal procedure matters.

There are many laws relating to administrative matters. All acts and decisions of the administration are subject to judicial review and provisions appear in the *Idari Yargilama Usulü Kanunu* [Code of Administrative Procedure], which came into force in 1982.

Treaties

Treaty-making power is vested in Parliament according to article 90 of the Turkish Constitution. Treaties, once ratified, are published in the *Resmî Gazete*; they are indexed under 'Milletlerarasi Andlaşmalar ve Sözleşmeler' (*Andlaşma* [treaty] and *Sözleşme* [convention]). The best source to discover if Turkey is a signatory to a treaty is to look in *Türk Antlaşmalor Rehberi* [The treaties to which Turkey is a contracting party] by Ökçün (1974), a guide to treaties covering 1920 to 1972. An earlier work, *A guide to Turkish treaties*, in English covers 1920–1964 and is arranged by general subject with a detailed subject index (Ökçün, 1966). There is also a compilation of treaties relating to public international law by Gündüz (1994).

Law reports, judgments

The Turkish legal system has three main branches: juridical, administrative and military. The *Yargitay* [High Court of Appeals] is the supreme court in the juridical field and some of its judgments are published in the monthly *Yargitay Kararlar Dergisi* [Journal of the High Court of Appeals] with a subject index. Some of the most important judgments of the Court can also be found in compilations published by private companies. The *Danıştay* [Council of State] is the supreme court in the administrative field and most of its decisions have been published annually with a subject index in the *Danıştay Dergisi* [Journal of the Council of State] since 1970; from 1939 to 1969 the publication was entitled *Danıştay Kararlar Dergisi* [Journal of Decisions of the Council of State].

Cases are normally known by the number allocated by the court in the form Y.2.C.D.; E.1992/232; K.1994/126; K.T.:12.07.1994. The first section refers to the court, Second Chamber of the High Court of Appeals; the second section is the year of registration of the case and the running number for that year; the third section is the year and the number of judgment in that year; the fourth section is the date of judgment. The registry of each court keeps a file of transcripts of every judgment.

There is also the Constitutional Court established in 1961 and its decisions are published individually in the *Resmî Gazete*. The decisions of the Constitutional Court also appear annually with an index in the *Anayasa Mahkemesi Kararlar Dergisi* [Journal of Decisions of the Constitutional Court]. Extracts from the decisions have been published in the three-volume compilation *Anayasa Yargisi* [Constitutional Review] (Aykonu and Özkul, 1981).

Computer-based systems

The YARGITAY KARARLARI VERI TABANI [Information Bank of the Istanbul Bar Association] is a computer-based system containing texts of the fifteen main laws (a recognized corpus of the most important laws) and thousands of decisions of the High Court of Appeals on fifty high-density disks. The database is supplemented every two months by the issue of new disks. The system is commercially produced by Hukuk Programlari Ltd. They also produce a database of the decisions of the Council of State.

Directories

The *Ístanbul Barosu Avukatlar Listesi* [List of the Advocates of the Istanbul Bar] (1992) includes all the names and addresses of the advocates practising in Istanbul. There is no publication which lists the names of judges. *Devlet Teşkilati Rehberi* [Guidebook of State Organization] includes addresses and brief notes on the structure and function of all the departments of government and was published by the Institute of Middle Eastern Public Administration in 1992.

Bibliographies

Bibliographies of Turkish law have been compiled by Erciyeş in 1956 and its supplement in 1959; by Tanilli and Aybay in 1959 and its supplement in 1967; by Akünal and Bayraktar in 1970; by Yurtcan in 1971; and by Yilmaz and Çağlayan in 1981 in two volumes covering 1970–74 and 1975–79. *Yüksek Öğretim Kurumlari Bilimsel Yayinlar Katalogu*

[Academic publications of higher education institutions] has been published in 1982, 1988 and 1990 and includes bibliographies on Turkish law; further volumes are planned. Bibliographies on human rights are published in the *Insan Haklari Yilliği* [Annual of human rights].

Dictionaries

There are law dictionaries by Ejder Yilmaz, *Hukuk Sözlüğü* [Law dictionary] (Yilmaz, 1992) and by Hüseyin Özcan, *Ansiklopedik Hukuk Sözlüğü* (Özcan, 1980).

Current information sources

The essential journals for practising lawyers are published by the Bar Associations in Ankara, Istanbul and Izmir: *Ankara Barosu Dergisi* (1953–), *İstanbul Barosu Dergisi* (1927–), *İzmir Barosu Dergisi* (1935–). There is also the *Çağdaş Hukuk* [Journal of contemporary law] (1992–) published by the Association of Contemporary Lawyers. These journals comprise articles on specific subjects and extracts from the judgments of the courts. The major journals published by faculties of the universities of Ankara, Istanbul, and Marmara should also be mentioned: *A.Ü. Hukuk Fakültesi Dergisi* [Journal of the Faculty of Law of Ankara University]; *A.Ü. Siyasal Bilgiler Fakültesi Dergisi* [Journal of the Faculty of Political Science of Ankara University]; *İ.Ü. Hukuk Fakültesi Mecmuasi* [Journal of the Faculty of Law of Istanbul University]; *M.Ü. Fakültesi Hukuk Araştirmalari Dergisi* [Journal of Legal Research of the Faculty of Law of Marmara University]. General business news is carried by the daily newspaper *Dünya* [The world].

Adalet Istatistikleri [Judicial statistics] have been published by the State Institute of Statistics every year since 1937. The data given in the annual publications cover the Constitutional Court, Supreme Courts, Council of State, Ministry of Justice, Ministry of National Defence, Chief Public Prosecutors, notaries and prisons.

Useful addresses

Associations of lawyers

Ankara Barosu [Ankara Bar Association], Ankara, Turkey. Tel: +90 312 3124729

Çağdaş Hukukçular Derneği [Association of Contemporary Lawyers], Inkilap sokak No:5/6, Kizilay – Ankara, Turkey. Tel/Fax: +90 312 4335540

Insan Haklari Derneği [Association of Human Rights], Yüksek cd. No:29/13, Yenişehir – Ankara, Turkey. Tel: +90 312 4320957/58. Fax: +90 312 4259547

Istanbul Barosu [Istanbul Bar Association], Tünel, Istiklal Cad., Av. Orhan Adli Apaydin sk. No:1, Baro Han, Beyoğlu – Istanbul, Turkey. Tel: +90 212 2454816, 212 2457693. Fax: +90 212 2448960

Türkiye Baralor Birliği [Union of Turkish Bar Associations], Karanfil sok. No:5 D.33, Kizilay – Ankara, Turkey. Tel: +90 312 4177700. Fax: +90 312 4181002

Türkiye Insan Haklari Vakfi [Human Rights Foundation of Turkey], Menekşe 2 sokak No:16/6–7–8, Kizilay 06440 – Ankara, Turkey. Tel: +90 312 4177180. Fax: +90 312 4254552

Government organizations

Diş Ticaret Müsteşarliği [Permanent Under-Secretary for Foreign Trade], Inönü Bulvari, Eskişehir Yolu, Balgat – Ankara, Turkey. Tel: +90 312 2128800. Fax: +90 312 2128778

T.C.Adalet Bakanliği [Ministry of Justice], Bakanliklar – Ankara, Turkey. Tel: +90 312 4177770

T.C.Dişişleri Bakanliği [Ministry of Foreign Affairs], Balgat – Ankara, Turkey. Tel: +90 312 2872555. Fax: +90 312 2871886

T.C.Sanayi ve Ticaret Bakanliği [Ministry of Industry and Trade], Gazi Mustafa Kemal Bulvari No.28, Ankara, Turkey. Tel: +90 312 2317280

Courts

Anayasa Mahkemesi [Constitutional Court], Simon Bolivar Bulvari No:23, Çankaya – Ankara, Turkey. Tel: +90 312 4407878/79/80/81/82

Yargitay [High Court of Appeals], Bakanliklar – Ankara, Turkey. Tel: +90 312 4179036, 4171516

Education and training

Avrupa Topluluğu Enstitüsü [Institute of the European Community], Kuyubaşi, Kadiköy – Istanbul, Turkey. +90 212 2441636

Istanbul Üniversitesi, Hukuk Fakültesi [Istanbul University Law School], Beyazit – Istanbul, Turkey. Tel: +90 212 5140301

Marmara Üniversitesi, Hukuk Fakültesi [Marmara University Law School], Haydarpaşa – Istanbul, Turkey. Tel: +90 216 3498400. Fax: +90 216 3387710

Libraries

Central Library of Istanbul University, Istanbul Üniversitesi Merkez Kütüphanesi, Beyazit – Istanbul, Turkey. Tel: +90 212 5111219

Documentation Centre of the Institution of Higher Education, YÖK Dökümantasyon Merkezi, Bilkent – Ankara, Turkey. Tel: +90 312 2664700

Library of the Grand National Assembly, T.B.M.M. Kütüphanesi, Ankara, Turkey. Tel: +90 312 2251352

Publishers and booksellers

Beta Basim Yayim Dağitim A.Ş., Ilimayc-i Etfal sk., Talas Han No:13–15, Cağaloğu – Istanbul, Turkey. Tel: +90 212 5281320. Fax: +90 212 5138705

Hukuk Programlari Ltd, Büyükdere cad. No: 19/5, Şişli 80220 – Istanbul, Turkey. Tel: +90 212 2321504/05. Fax: +90 212 2489340

Kazanci Kitap Ticaret A.Ş., Isakpaşa Mah. Çayiroğlu Sok. No:14, 34400 Sultahmet – Istanbul, Turkey. Tel: +90 212 5168407. Fax: +90 212 5170218

Yetkin Yayinlari, Kazimkarabekir cad. No: 95/7–8, Ankara, Turkey. Tel: +90 312 3410006

List of works cited

A.Ü. Hukuk Fakültesi Dergisi [Journal of the Faculty of Law of Ankara University]. (1943–) Ankara: Ankara Üniversitesi, Hukuk Fakültesi.

A.Ü. Siyasal Bilgiler Fakültesi Dergisi [Journal of the Faculty of Political Science of Ankara University]. (1943–) Ankara: Ankara Üniversitesi, Siyasal Bilgiler Fakültesi.

Adal, Erhan (1991) *Fundamentals of Turkish private law.* 3rd edn. Istanbul: Beta Basim Yayim Dağitim AŞ.

Adalet Istatistikleri [Judicial statistics]. (1937–) Ankara: Başbakanlik Devlet İstatistik Genel Müdürlüğü [State Institute of Statistics, Prime Ministry].

Akünal, Teoman and Bayraktar, Köksal (1970) *Türk Hukuk Bibliyografyasi* [Bibliography of Turkish law]. (Istanbul Universitesi Yayinlari, no.1518) Istanbul: Istanbul Üniversitesi Yayinlari.

Altuğ, Yilmaz (1987) *The Turkish legal system on foreign investments*. Istanbul: Fakülteler Matbaasi.

Anayasa Mahkemesi Kararlar Dergisi [Journal of Decisions of the Constitutional Court]. (1964–) Ankara: Anayasa Mahkemesi Yayinlari.

Ankara Barosu Dergisi [Journal of the Bar Association of Ankara]. (1953–) Ankara: Ankara Barosu.

Ansay, Tuğrul and Wallace, Don (1987) *Introduction to Turkish law*. 3rd edn. Deventer: Kluwer Law and Taxation.

Aykonu, M.S. and Özkul, E.A. (1981) *Anayasa Yargisi* [Constitutional review]. 3 vols. Ankara: Anayasa Mahkemesi Yayinlari.

Bilge, Necip (1986) *Hukuk Başlangici* [Introduction to law]. Ankara: Turhan Kitabevi.

Çağdaş Hukuk [Journal of Contemporary Law]. (1992–) Ankara: Çağdaş Hukukçular Derneği [Association of Contemporary Lawyers].

Çağlar, Bakir (1988) *Anayasa bilimi* [Science of constitution]. Istanbul: BFS Yayinlari.

Dalamanli, Lütfü and Kazanci, Faruk (1990) *Borçlar Kanunu* [On the Code of Obligations]. 4 vols. Istanbul: Kazanci Yayinlari.

Daniştay Dergisi [Journal of the Council of State]. (1970–) Ankara: Daniştay Yayinlari.

Daniştay Kararlar Dergisi [Journal of Decisions of the Council of State]. (1939–1969) Ankara: Daniştay Yayinlari.

Davran, Bülent and Kubali, Hüseyin Nail (1973) Turkey. In *International encyclopedia of comparative law*, ed. V. Knapp, vol.1, T45–T55. Tübingen: J.C.B. Mohr.

Devlet Teşkilati Rehberi [Guidebook of state organization]. (1992) Ankara: Institute of Middle Eastern Public Administration.

Doğanay, Ismail (1990) *Türk Ticaret Kanunu* [Turkish Commercial Code]. 3 vols. Istanbul: n.p.

Domaniç, Hayri and Çamoğlu, Ersin (1992) *Ticaret Kanunu* [Commercial Code]. Istanbul: n.p.

Düstur [Official collection of laws]. (Vth series, 1962–) Ankara: Prime Ministry.

Erciyeş, Bülent (1956) *Türk Hukuk Bibliyografyasi* [Bibliography of Turkish law]. (1956) Ankara: Fakülteler Matbaasi and (1959) *Türk Hukuk Bibliyografyasina Ek* [Supplement]. Ankara: Güzel Istanbul Matbaasi.

Erem, Faruk (1993) *Türk Ceza Kanunu* [Turkish Criminal Code]. 3 vols. Ankara: Seçkin Yayinevi.

Flanz, Gisbert H. (1994) Turkey. In *Constitutions of the countries of the world*, eds A.P. Blaustein and G.H. Flanz, vol.XIX. Dobbs Ferry, NY: Oceana. Supplement November 1995.

Gözübüyük, A. Pulat (1989) *Türk Ceza Kanunu* [Turkish Criminal Code]. 4 vols. Ankara: Kazanci Kitap ve Ticaret AŞ.

Gündüz, Aslan (1994) *Milletlerarasi Andlaşmalar* [A compilation of treaties relating to public international law]. Istanbul: Beta Basim Yayim Dağitim AŞ.

Içel, Kiyihan and Yenisey, Feridun (1994) *Ceza Kanunlari* [Criminal Codes]. Istanbul: Beta Basim Yayim Dağitim AŞ.

İ.Ü. Hukuk Fakültesi Mecmuasi [Journal of the Faculty of Law of Istanbul University]. (1922–) Istanbul: Istanbul Üniversitesi, Hukuk Fakültesi. Note: vol.1–5, 1922–27, in Arabic script; vol.6– , 1928– , in the Turkish alphabet.

Insan Haklari Yilliği [Annual of human rights]. (1979–) Ankara: TODAIE.

İstanbul Barosu Avukatlar Listesi [List of the Advocates of the Istanbul Bar]. (1992) Istanbul: Istanbul Barosu Yayini.

İstanbul Barosu Dergisi [Journal of the Bar Association of Istanbul]. (1927–) Istanbul: İstanbul Barosu.

İzmir Barosu Dergisi [Journal of the Bar Association of Izmir]. (1935–) Izmir: İzmir Barosu.

Karahasan, M. Reşit. (1992) *Borçlar Kanunu* [On the Code of Obligations]. 6 vols. Istanbul: Beta Basim Yayim Dağitim AŞ.

Kuru, Baki (1995) *Hukuk Muhakemeleri Usulü* [Civil procedure law]. Istanbul: Alfa Basim, Yayim, Dağitim.

Meclis Tutanaklari [Parliament records]. (n.d.) Ankara: n.p.

M.Ü. Fakültesi Hukuk Araştirmalari Dergisi [Journal of Legal Research of the Faculty of Law of Marmara University]. (1986–) Marmara: Marmara Üniversitesi, Hukuk Fakültesi.

Ökçün, A. Gündüz (1966) *A guide to Turkish treaties (1920–1964)*. Ankara: Faculty of Political Science, University of Ankara.

Ökçün, A. Gündüz (1974) *Türk Antlaşmalor Rehberi* [The Treaties to which Turkey is a contracting party]. Ankara: A.Ü. Siyasal Bilgiler Fakültesi Yayinlari.

Özbudun, Ergun (1992) *Türk anayasa hukuku* [Turkish constitutional law]. Ankara: Yetkin Yayinlari.

Özcan, Hüseyin (1980) *Ansiklopedik Hukuk Sözlüğü* [Encyclopedic law dictionary]. Ankara: Olgaç Matbaasi.

Özman, M. Aydoğan and Sírman, Lâle (1990) The legal system of Turkey. In *Modern legal systems cyclopedia*, ed. K.R. Redden, pp. 5A.20.1–38. Buffalo, NY: Hein.

Prime Ministry (1990) *Constitution of the Republic of Turkey*. Ankara: Prime Ministry, Directorate General of Press and Information, Turkey.

Resmî Gazete [Official gazette]. (1920–) Ankara: Başbakanlik Mevzuati Geliştirme ve Yayin Genel Müdürlüğü

Şener, Esat (1991) *Türk Medeni Kanunu* [Turkish Civil Code]. Ankara: Seçkin Yayinlari.

Tanilli, Server and Aybay, Rona (1959) *Türk Hukuk Bibliyografyasi* [Bibliography of Turkish law]. Istanbul: Fakülteler Matbaasi and (1967) *Türk Hukuk Bibliyografyasina Ek* [Supplement]. Istanbul: Fakülteler Matbaasi.

Tanör, Bülent (1994) *Türkiye'nin insan haklari sorunu* [Human rights issues in Turkey]. Istanbul: BDS Yayinlari.

Tunaya, Tarik Zafer (1982) *Siyasi kurumlar ve anayasa hukuku* [Political institutions and constitutional law]. Istanbul: Aroştirma, eğitim, ekin yayinlari.

Üstündağ, Saim (1989) *Medeni Yargilama Hukuku* [The law of civil procedure]. Istanbul: Beta Basim Yayim Dağitim AŞ.

Uygur, Turgut (1990–1994) *Borçlar Kanunu* [On the Code of Obligations]. 7 vols. Ankara: n.p.

Yargitay Kararlar Dergisi [Journal of the High Court of Appeals]. (1975–) Ankara: Yargitay Yayinlari.

YARGITAY KARARLARI VERI TABANI [Information Bank of the Istanbul Bar Association] (available from Hukuk Programlari Ltd).

Yavuz, Cevdet (1996) *Türk Medeni Kanunu* [Turkish Civil Code]. Istanbul: Beta Basim Yayim Dağitim AŞ.

Yilmaz, Ejder and Çağlayan, Tacar (1981) *Türk Hukuk Bibliyografyasi* [Bibliography of Turkish law]. 2 vols. Ankara: Fakülteler Matbaasi.

Yilmaz, Ejder (1992) *Hukuk Sözlüğü* [Law dictionary]. Ankara: Yetkin Yayinlari.

Yüksek Öğretim Kurumlari Bilimsel Yayinlar Katalogu [Scientific publications of higher education institutions]. (1982, 1988 and 1990) Ankara: Yök.

Yurtcan, Erdener (1971) *Türk Hukuk Bibliyografyasi* [Bibliography of Turkish law]. Istanbul: Fakülteler Matbaasi.
Yürürlükteki Kanunlar Külliyati [The laws in force]. (n.d.) Ankara: Kazanci Yayinlari.
Yürürlükteki Kanunlar Külliyati [The laws in force]. (1987–) Ankara: Prime Ministry.

CHAPTER THIRTY

United Kingdom and dependencies

GUY HOLBORN

General introduction

The UK, in full the United Kingdom of Great Britain and Northern Ireland, contains within it three distinct legal systems: (1) England and Wales, (2) Scotland and (3) Northern Ireland. Each has a separate court structure, legal profession, and in many areas of the law its own legislative provisions and binding court decisions. The sources of legal information for each, together with introductions on their constitutional history in relation to their union, are given in the separate sections that follow. At this stage, the point to be emphasised is that expression 'English law' (which is the usual shorthand for the law pertaining in both England and Wales) should not be treated loosely as referring to the law throughout the UK.

Not part of the UK, but constitutionally intertwined with it, are Jersey, Guernsey (with its dependencies of Alderney and Sark) and the Isle of Man, each being a separate jurisdiction with its own legal system. Because of their peculiar constitutional relationship with the UK, their importance as offshore financial centres and the relative paucity of description of their sources of legal information elsewhere, the Channel Islands and the Isle of Man, notwithstanding their small size, are also treated fully in a separate section, for convenience alongside those on the jurisdictions of the UK proper.

This multiplicity of jurisdictions can present the seeker of information with problems. A question as to 'British' law is often not amenable to a single answer. The greatest practical problem is establishing the scope of particular sources. Despite the long and distinguished tradition of legal writing and publishing in Scotland and recent enterprise in Northern Ireland, it remains the case that the majority of legal sources emanating from the UK relate to English law for the English lawyer. This may be apparent, as with the two major reference works under the name of *Halsbury*, whose full titles are *Halsbury's Laws of England* and *Halsbury's Statutes of England and Wales*, yet it many other cases it is not. If it is indeed English law that is wanted, as will frequently be the case, well and good. But, if it is specifically the law of Scotland, Northern Ireland or one of the offshore jurisdictions that is wanted, care is required in ascertaining whether the law is indeed the same as that in England and if not how it differs. Unfortunately, it is not possible to give any hard and fast rules as to when the law will be the same and when it will differ. The legislation governing nationality and taxation, for example, is the same throughout the UK as might be expected. On the other hand, other areas, equally expected to be uniform, for example criminal law, are not. Even where provisions are the same, they may be physically contained in different pieces of legislation. Moreover, as explained further in the introduction to the chapter on England and Wales, much law derives not from any legislation but from the decisions of the courts and the courts in the different jurisdictions may develop the law in different directions. The only generalisation to be made is that the law of Northern Ireland, because of the nature of its legal system, is more likely to follow that in England, whereas Scots law is more likely to differ.

Although it comprises four countries with three jurisdictions, the UK is constitutionally a unitary state not a federal one. The unifying features are a single titular head of state in the person of the Sovereign, a single Parliament exercising ultimate sovereignty (subject to any qualification that membership of the European Union brings), and a single executive government. In this context, it is important to appreciate how the legislative process works in relation to the different jurisdictions. Parliament at Westminster may legislate for all or any part of the UK. The modern practice is for every Act of Parliament to carry a section, usually to be found at end at the end of the body of the Act but before any schedules, specifying the geographical extent of the Act. In the absence of such a section, the Act prima facie applies throughout the UK. It is also to be borne in mind when considering the commencement of statutes, that the relevant dates may vary between different jurisdictions. The chapter on Northern Ireland describes in more detail how, while retaining ultimate sovereignty, Westminster devolved law-making powers in certain areas to the Northern Ireland Assembly, and how those same powers are currently exercised at Westminster by means of delegated legislation.

The Parliament at Westminster, which passes Acts and which scrutinises to a greater or lesser extent Statutory Instruments (SIs) made by Ministers under powers delegated by Acts, is bicameral. The House of Commons is elected and the government is drawn from the party whose members form the majority. The membership of the House of Lords is made up of hereditary peers and those appointed for life. Although all bills generally have to pass through both Houses, the House of Commons by convention exercises exclusivity in relation to expenditure and taxation and by virtue of the Parliament Acts 1911 and 1949 retains ultimate power to pass any legislation without the consent of the Lords. Miers and Page (1990) gives an overview of the legislative process. The bible on the detail of Parliamentary procedure is Erskine May (1989), but Griffith and Ryle (1989), while also being detailed, gives a clearer picture of how Parliament functions in practice.

As well as a single sovereign legislature, a further unifying influence is that, except in criminal matters originating in Scotland, all three jurisdictions of the UK share a final court of appeal, namely the House of Lords. The judicial capacity of the House of Lords is now quite separate from its legislative and other capacities and is exercised through its Judicial Committee consisting of up to 13 senior judges appointed as 'Law Lords', Lords of Appeal in Ordinary to give them their formal title, who usually sit in panels of five to hear appeals. Their decisions are subsequently binding on all the courts in the jurisdiction from which the appeal originated, and in practice on all courts of the other jurisdictions where the law is the same.

An additional force towards homogeneity in UK law is now Europe. The UK became a member of what is now the European Union with effect from 1 January 1973, and European law applies in all its jurisdictions (see the chapter on the Channel Islands and the Isle of Man for their special position with regard to the EU). Implementation of directives is generally by means of SIs made under the European Communities Act 1972, though sometimes, for the most important directives, it has been expedient to implement by means of a separate Act. Most SIs will implement the directive throughout the UK, but sometimes there may be separate SIs, albeit in similar terms, for different jurisdictions because of the structure of existing legislation. Many SIs are also made in connection with the operation of EU regulations. Furthermore all UK courts, including the House of Lords, are subject to the decisions of the European Court of Justice at Luxembourg in matters of EU law. See in general the sources in the separate chapter on European Union law.

The UK is a party to the European Convention on Human Rights, but it has not incorporated the Convention into its domestic law by means of UK legislation. Without such incorporation, the provisions of the Convention, and the jurisprudence of the European Court of Human Rights at Strasbourg in interpreting them, cannot be applied directly by the UK courts. Nonetheless, European human rights law can, and increasingly does, play a part in UK law. It can be taken into account in statutory interpretation, where otherwise the result would be a breach of the UK's international obligations under the Convention. It may have persuasive value in reaching decisions relating to civil liberties where the law is otherwise unclear. And, because of the increasing interplay between the courts at Luxembourg and Strasbourg, it may be relevant when the UK courts are considering European Union law. An outstanding work on human rights in domestic law (ostensibly in England and Wales but of relevance throughout the UK in the context of the Convention) is Feldman (1993).

The constitution of the UK is said to be unwritten, in the sense that, in contrast to the majority of other states, there is no single charter or document with supreme status embodying the constitution. In the absence of a written constitution in that sense, there are no special constitutional courts to interpret its provisions. Furthermore, the courts cannot review the legality or legitimacy of Acts of Parliament. They may interpret statutes, and can rule that delegated legislation ostensibly made under statute is void if made outside the enabling powers in the parent Act. But the disability to overrule primary legislation is a consequence of the doctrine of the sovereignty of Parliament and a consequence of there being no written constitution against which to measure other legislation.

There are three main sources of constitutional law. First, there are statutes (subject to repeal like any other), stretching from Magna Carta (25 Edward I, confirming King John's agreement of 1215, still partly in force) through the Bill of Rights 1689, which represented the settlement of the English Revolution, to more recent enactments such as the Parliament Acts mentioned above and, of particular significance, the European Communities Act 1972. Secondly, there are the decisions of the courts, again with a large historic range, from the 17th century cases such as the *Case of Proclamations* (1611) 12 Co. Rep. 74, which curtailed the power of the Crown to legislate other than through Parliament, to the modern cases such as *Burmah Oil Co. v Lord Advocate* [1965] A.C. 75, which upheld the right of compensation for expropriation, and the cases defining the scope of European Community law, eg *H.P. Bulmer Ltd v J. Bollinger SA* [1974] Ch 401. Thirdly, there are constitutional conventions, which can be said to be binding in the political rather than the legal sense, for example that the Sovereign will not withhold Royal Assent to an Act of Parliament.

The leading textbooks on constitutional law are Wade and Bradley (1993) and De Smith and Brazier (1994), but also deserving special mention, for its distinguished contributors and for its attention to the constitution in the context of the European Union and the European Convention on Human Rights, is the recently re-written volume of *Halsbury's Laws* under the title 'Constitutional Law and Human Rights' (4th ed., vol.8(2), 1996 re-issue).

References for the sources cited in this section are given with the references for the England and Wales section that follows.

Editors' Note: Her Majesty's Stationery Office (HMSO) was the official government publisher for the UK for many years. On 1 October 1996 it was sold to a commercial company and, at the time of writing

(January 1997), its name is The Stationery Office. There is the possibility of a further change of name. In the circumstances, the Editors have decided to retain HMSO in the text and the citations for recent publications. In any case, many of the works mentioned were published before privatization. It will no doubt be some time before the full implications of the change of ownership become clear. At present, most of the channels of communication previously used to contact HMSO remain in place.

England and Wales

PETER CLINCH, HEATHER THRIFT AND DEREK WAY WITH AN INTRODUCTION BY GUY HOLBORN

Introduction to the legal system

Before the Norman conquest in 1066 there existed a rudimentary legal order through local custom and the written laws of the Anglo-Saxons, but there was no developed central legislature or system of courts. Though providing the traditional watershed for the founding of the English legal system, the impact of the arrival of the Normans was not immediate, the crucial development – the establishment of the mechanism to administer Royal Justice throughout the land – being generally credited to the reign of Henry II (1154–89). By both establishing Royal Courts centrally and sending the judges of those courts as itinerant justices out on assize, it was possible to impose a common law.

The expression the 'common law' now has a number of different meanings depending on the context. The establishment of a common law, as opposed to local law, provided its primary meaning. This in turn gave rise to 'common law' being the general description of the English legal system, with all its subsequent attributes. So the meaning of 'common law' in that context is in contradistinction to civil or Roman law, and is used to describe the family of legal systems throughout the English-speaking world to which it gave birth. The further usages, 'common law' as opposed to legislation and 'common law' as opposed to equity, are explained below.

The best introduction to English legal history is Baker (1990), but the most exhaustive general treatment, albeit superseded by modern scholarship is some areas, remains Holdsworth (1936–1972). The emphasis in Holdsworth is necessarily on the earlier periods. For the period 1750 to 1950 it can usefully be supplemented by Manchester (1980) and (1984) and by Cornish and Clark (1989). Hines (1990) provides a thorough bibliography of monographic literature on English legal history, made more useful by its introductory essays.

Subsequent chapters describe the union of England and Wales with first Scotland and then Ireland. The initial union of England with Wales was achieved by the conquest of Wales by Edward I in 1282. At first, English law did not extend to Wales, which continued to be administered by local custom, but by the statute of 1536 (27 Henry VIII c. 26) both legal and political union was formally imposed and the common law applied throughout. Nonetheless, there remain small differences in some areas, such as local government, and occasionally legislation is applied to Wales alone or applied to Wales differently on account of its separate regional, cultural, and historical identity.

The sources of law in England and Wales are twofold, legislation and the decisions of the courts. Customary law, while historically a source, is now almost wholly vestigial; and the works of legal writers have never been a formal source as in some other jurisdictions, though the classic authors such as Coke, Hale and Blackstone are regarded by the courts with the utmost respect and the views of some modern textbook writers may be highly persuasive and are sometimes cited in court. Legislation, whether in the form of primary legislation (statutes) or secondary legislation (Statutory Instruments), progressively encroaches so that more and more of the law is statute-based. Added to which, the machinery of modern government generates increasing quantities of administrative quasi-legislation, in the form of government circulars, codes of practice and so on, which, while having no direct legal effect, may have legal consequences. Nonetheless, there remain substantial areas of the law which are created and maintained by the judges without the intervention of legislation. Such law, resulting from the decisions of the courts, is described as 'common law' in another of its senses. In civil matters, tort and contract are examples of subjects which are almost wholly governed by common law, and in criminal law, there remain common law offences, most notably that of murder. Furthermore, the encroachment of statute law does not lessen the role of the judges since they are charged with interpreting it and the rules of statutory interpretation, on which see Cross (1995), are themselves largely judge-made.

The operation of the common law depends upon the doctrine of precedent, whereby like cases are decided alike and the decisions of the higher courts are binding on the lower courts. Cross and Harris (1991) is the standard monograph on the subject, which is also covered extensively in the general works on the English legal system mentioned later. An understanding of precedent and an understanding of the English legal system in general requires an overview of the court structure.

In criminal matters the lowest courts are the magistrates courts, where minor cases are heard either before a bench of lay magistrates (Justices of the Peace, which office is of ancient origin) advised by a legally qualified clerk, or before a single legally qualified stipendiary magistrate. Trial is said to be summary. The Crown Court, which superseded in 1971 the old system of assizes and Quarter Sessions, hears more serious cases and also appeals from magistrates courts. The trial is before a judge and jury and is said to be on indictment. The status of the presiding judge depends on the seriousness of the offence. The least serious are heard by barristers or solicitors sitting as part-time recorders, the more serious by Circuit Judges, and the most serious by High Court judges of the Queen's Bench Division. Appeal from the Crown Court lies to the Court of Appeal (Criminal Division).

In civil matters, the lowest courts are the County Courts, created by statute in 1846. Their jurisdiction is generally related to the size of the claim being made. Cases are heard by Circuit Judges (styled 'His Honour Judge Smith') or part-time recorders, though many preliminary and procedural matters are dealt with by District Judges (formerly called District Registrars). Appeal lies to the Court of Appeal (Civil Division).

The High Court derives from the original Royal Courts founded in the time of Henry II. By the end of the 14th century there had emerged two courts with distinct jurisdiction, the Court of King's Bench, which included criminal and other matters with which the Crown had an interest, and the Court of Common Pleas, which dealt largely with ordinary civil matters in which the King had no direct interest. In addition there was the Court of Exchequer, which from its origins in dealing with revenue, developed into a further civil court. Although having procedural differences, by the later part of the 17th century these three courts, which sat in Westminster Hall, had in many areas concurrent and rival jurisdiction.

Alongside these three courts, there developed the Court of Chancery with a parallel jurisdiction. The Court of Chancery had its origins in the King, initially in person, and then from the 14th century through his Lord Chancellor, dispensing justice in response to petitions in individual cases where the courts, which had become beset by the technicalities of forms of action, were unable to provide an equitable outcome. Thus at first the Court of Chancery was concerned with equity in its general meaning of fairness or justice. But by a gradual process, which was largely complete by the middle of the 17th century, the court became formalised, both in its procedure and its remedies, and equity had become hardened into its legal sense of the set of rules applied by the Court of Chancery. Equity also generated its own substantive legal doctrines, of which the trust is the most distinctive, and became associated with administering particular branches of the law, notably real property. (For the modern law of equity see Snell (1990) and Martin (1993).) Hence there arose the further distinct usage of the term 'common law'. The three courts other than the Court of Chancery – King's Bench, Common Pleas, and Exchequer – were said to administer common law as opposed to equity, and are described as the common law courts.

The Supreme Court of Judicature Acts 1873–75 radically reformed the court system, dispensing with the jurisdictional and procedural distinctions between common law and equity, and creating a single High Court organised in divisions. After some subsequent rationalisation the High Court now has three divisions, Queen's Bench, Chancery and Family, which each hear cases according to their subject matter. The 'Supreme Court' in the title of the 1873–75 legislation, and hence in the title of works such as the *Supreme Court Practice*, is something of a misnomer, or at any rate a source of confusion to those from other jurisdictions that do have Supreme Courts. For neither is it a court in its own right, nor is it supreme. It is simply the High Court and the Court of Appeal regarded collectively.

The High Court hears civil cases at first instance where, due to the size of the claim or for other reasons, the County Courts do not have jurisdiction. Cases are heard by a single High Court judge, styled 'Mr (or Mrs) Justice Smith' or 'Smith J.', and, except in defamation or one or two other exceptional categories of action, without a jury. As well as hearing cases at first instance, the Queen's Bench Division also has an important and separate supervisory role. It hears cases on points of law arising in magistrates courts by way of 'case stated', and it oversees by way of 'judicial review' the administrative decisions of ministers, government departments, inferior tribunals and other public bodies. Judicial review is not a method of appealing the merits of such decisions, but is a review of the legality and fairness of the decision-making process. In English law, the expression 'judicial review' hence means judicial review of administrative action, as opposed to its usual usage in the US and elsewhere as referring to the review by the courts of the constitutionality of legislation, which as explained in the introductory chapter is foreign to the UK constitution. In exercising its supervisory jurisdiction, the Queen's Bench sits as a 'Divisional Court' of two or three judges, at least one of whom is a judge of the Court of Appeal.

Within the divisions of the High Court there are a number of specialist courts. They are not jurisdictionally distinct, but simply convenient ways of organising particular types of business, usually before a judge with the requisite subject expertise. For example in the Chancery Division there is a Companies Court and a Patents Court, and within the Queen's Bench Division there is a Commercial Court and an Admiralty Court.

Appeal from the High Court is to the Court of Appeal (Civil Division). The Court of Appeal, in both its divisions, usually sits in panels of two or three. The judges of the Court of Appeal are called Lord Justices of Appeal (not Lords in the sense of peers, and not to be confused with Lords of Appeal in Ordinary, who are the judges of the House of Lords and peers). They are styled 'Lord Justice Smith' or 'Smith LJ'. Appeal thereafter is to the House of Lords as described in the introductory section on the UK.

A further forum to mention is the Judicial Committee of the Privy Council, whose principal role is to hear appeals from those Commonwealth countries, dwindling in number, who retain it as their final court of appeal. Its judges are usually drawn from the ranks of the Law Lords, so their decisions, in so far as they relate to English law, are in practice, if not theory, tantamount to a decision of the House of Lords. In this connection it may be mentioned that the decisions of the courts of other common law countries may, and frequently are, cited in the English courts. Though not binding, they are persuasive authority. Australian and New Zealand cases are probably the most common and highly regarded examples. The Privy Council also has a domestic jurisdiction for appeals arising from professional disciplinary proceedings, for example decisions of the General Medical Council to strike off doctors.

There are also quite a number of specialist tribunals, dealing with such matters as employment, immigration, social security and tax. The decisions of some tribunals are appealable to the courts; with others redress is only available by way of judicial review.

Some grasp of the structure of the legal profession is useful to give further understanding of the English legal system, of which it is a distinctive feature, and helpful for the practical purpose of using the sources described in the section later in the chapter on legal directories. The legal profession in England and Wales has two branches, barristers and solicitors, the division of labour between whom is as old as the legal system itself. There are about 8,500 practising barristers in England and Wales. They provide two main legal services, which, as is reflected in the relatively small size of the bar, are specialist in nature. First, they act as advocates before the courts: they are in US parlance trial lawyers. Traditionally, barristers have enjoyed exclusive rights of audience, save in magistrates courts and County Courts where solicitors may appear too. That monopoly was formally removed by the Courts and Legal Services Act 1990, but it remains the case that the vast majority of lawyers who appear before the higher courts are barristers. Their second function is to provide specialist advice in the form of written legal opinions. In performing both functions they act largely as a referral profession: with limited exceptions they can only act on the instructions of a solicitor, not directly on behalf of the ultimate client. Barristers are all self-employed (including those who prosecute on behalf of the Crown) and can form neither partnerships nor companies, but most for convenience practise from sets of ‘chambers’. All barristers have to belong to, and are ‘called to the bar’ (i.e. granted formal qualification) by, one of the four Inns of Court (Lincoln’s Inn, Inner Temple, Middle Temple and Gray’s Inn), which provide professional accommodation and collegiate facilities, but the official regulatory and professional body is the General Council of the Bar. Senior barristers may be appointed Queen’s Counsel (Q.C.s or ‘silks’). Apart from the method of their appointment,

Q.C.s have no particular connection with the Crown or government, and perform the same functions as other barristers. The title is simply a mark of their status in the profession, which means that they are likely to be instructed in the more difficult or important cases, with concomitantly greater remuneration. There are about 1000 Q.C.s. Traditionally (though no longer statutorily), High Court judges are almost exclusively appointed from the bar as are the majority of Circuit Judges.

In contrast to the size of the bar, there are about 67,000 solicitors in England and Wales. They perform all the legal functions except those reserved for barristers. They may be sole practitioners or employed by companies or government, but most practice in partnership, whether in small local firms or in the major international practices in the City of London. The Law Society is their professional body.

As well as barristers and solicitors, there are also a number of types of ancillary legal professional, of whom licensed conveyancers are notable newcomers. They now compete with solicitors in conveyancing of real property, particularly in domestic property sales, which area of business used to be the staple of the smaller firms of solicitors.

The works on the English legal system below explain further the workings of the legal profession. More detail will be found in Abel (1988): it pre-dates the changes that have taken place since the 1990 Act mentioned above, but it does bring together a very great deal of information, particularly statistical information, that remains of value.

Introductory works on the legal system and legal research

There are quite a number of works on the English legal system. Many of them are academic texts aimed at students studying the subject at the start of their degree courses. Probably the leading such text is Smith and Bailey (1996). A more traditional textbook and with a lot of detail is Walker and Walker (1994). In contrast, Zander (1993) and (1994) aims at a more contextual approach. Among the shorter textbooks is Kiralfy (1990), but in that category Eddey (1996) is particularly lucid and succinct.

Written for a more general audience, but nonetheless giving a very readable and fair portrayal of the system of administration of justice, is Berlins and Dyer (1994). The administration of justice in general is covered by White (1991), while reference might be made to Sanders and Young (1994) on the criminal justice system in particular and to Jacob (1987) for thoughtful background to the civil justice system. Griffith (1991) is a classic, if in some quarters controversial, account of the judiciary. Academic texts on legal method and reasoning, such as Farrar and Dugdale (1990) and Holland and Webb (1993), may also give insight into the operation of the common law.

Cornish (1987) provides a short but useful introductory guide to the legal system and how it relates to legal literature and was written with an audience of law librarians in mind. It forms the introductory chapter to the *Manual of law librarianship* (1987), which though now possibly a little dated with regard to current legal research sources, is a very substantial work containing much information of lasting value not only to the law librarian. The first English work aimed at law students on using law libraries and doing legal research was published in 1979; now in its third edition, Dane and Thomas (1996) is the well established text. It has been joined by a number of other works on legal research, with slightly differing emphases, including Clinch (1992), Tunkel (1992) and Holborn (1993). Holborn's guide provides a narrative introduction as well as a quick reference guide for those who have some basic knowledge but require a reminder for a particular problem in hand.

Legislation

Legislation in England and Wales is divided into two main parts: Primary Legislation, consisting of Acts (or Statutes) passed by Parliament; and Subordinate Legislation, made under powers delegated by Parliament. There is an official gazette, the *London Gazette* (1665–), but unlike the official gazettes of many countries, it is not the means of promulgating legislation. It is merely the means of formally publishing various government and legal notices. It is not generally a source of legal information and is consequently to be found in few law libraries.

All official legislation is published by HMSO (Her Majesty's Stationery Office) recently renamed The Stationery Office. Details of publications can be found in the *Daily List* which is cumulated (partly) into monthly and annual catalogues. The catalogues are available online from 1976 via BLAISE-LINE and on CD-ROM from 1980 via UKOP. Details of most HMSO and government department publications are available on the Internet from July 1995 via NUKOP. The online database, LAWTEL, indexes and provides summaries of a range of current legal sources, including legislation. Out of print HMSO publications can be obtained from HMSO Books (Photocopies Section).

Public General Acts

BILLS

Sources of information on parliamentary procedure are given in the general introduction to the United Kingdom. Every statute starts out as a parliamentary Bill. Bills are available only from HMSO and can be purchased either individually or on subscription. When a Bill is published it is given a serial number which is used for citation purposes. Each time a

Bill passes through a different stage in the parliamentary process, it is reissued and given a different number. Matters are further complicated by the fact that a Bill can be either a House of Commons Bill or a House of Lords Bill, depending on which House it is currently passing through. These numbers appear in round brackets if the current version of the Bill is being presented to the House of Lords and square brackets if being presented to the House of Commons. To cite a Bill correctly, the parliamentary session must be included, so, for example, the final version of the Disability Discrimination Bill for the 1994–95 session is cited: H.L. Bill 1994–95 (120).

The progress of Bills can be ascertained by referring to the Progress of Bills section of the latest *Current Law Monthly Digest*, or to appropriate journals such as the *Gazette* (of the Law Society), the *New Law Journal* and the *Solicitor's Journal*. However, the most useful source is the *Weekly Information Bulletin*. This provides details of all Bills for the current session of Parliament, together with the dates of the main debates and details of the relevant Standing Committee. A partial cumulation of the *Weekly Information Bulletin* is published at the end of the parliamentary session as the *Sessional Information Digest*. Both these publications are compiled by the House of Commons Library Public Information Office and are available on subscription from HMSO.

The best source of detailed information on draft legislation is the Parliamentary On-line Information Service, POLIS (also available on CD-ROM as the PARLIAMENT (database). It is an index to proceedings in the UK Parliament and contains references to all House of Commons Bills since May 1979, House of Lords Bills since November 1981 and all debates on legislation since 1982. Some Acts and Bills are now available on the Internet. For more information about parliamentary debates see page 530.

ACTS OF PARLIAMENT

Once a Bill has completed the parliamentary process it receives the Royal Assent and becomes an Act of Parliament. Acts of Parliament are sometimes collectively referred to as The Statute Book and individual Acts may be referred to as Statutes. When Acts are published they are given a Short Title, a Long Title and a number known as a Chapter Number (or just Number in the case of Church Assembly or General Synod Measures). They are issued individually as Queen's Printer's Copies. See page 519 below for further information about when the provisions of Acts may be brought into effect. This very rarely happens at the time of publication.

Prior to the end of 1962, Statutes were cited by regnal year and chapter number. The regnal year was always taken to be from the date of the monarch's accession and thus did not coincide with the parliamentary session, which generally runs from the beginning of November in each year. Since the beginning of 1963, Statutes have been cited by the calendar year and chapter number. However, in general, Acts are cited by their Short Title and Year, for example, the Disability Discrimination Act 1995.

COLLECTED EDITIONS

The individual issues are cumulated annually and have been published since 1831 as *Public General Acts and Measures.* Earlier legislation was published in various series including *Statutes of the Realm [1101–1713]* (1810–28) and *Statutes at Large from Magna Charta to* [various dates and editions]. A useful commercial series is *Current Law Statutes Annotated* (1948–), which reprints the full text of the Act with extensive annotations. There is also a useful general introductory section to most Acts giving historical details such as the names of any Law Commission, Royal Commission, Green or White Papers leading up to the Act. It will also give the details of the dates of the main debates, together with the principal *Hansard* references.

An Act may not come into force immediately it receives Royal Assent. The main drawback to the official series and to *Current Law Statutes Annotated* is that the texts of the Statutes are published as they first appeared when they received the Royal Assent.

Major Acts often make multiple changes, by amending and/or repealing sections of previous Statutes. Full-scale consolidating Acts are relatively rare. Attempts to produce an up-to-date definitive version of the Statutes have failed, including *The Statutes Revised*, the third edition of which was published in 1951. The latest attempt was *Statutes in Force* which was completed as a looseleaf between 1972 and 1981. This publication has now ceased in part and is due to be replaced by the STATUTE LAW DATABASE. However, at the time of writing, the Statutory Publications Office project is still under development.

Halsbury's Statutes of England and Wales is an extremely important collection, often used by lawyers as their first reference work for statutes. It appears as a multi-volume work, with each volume re-issued on a regular basis. It is arranged by subject and reprints the current version of the Act, together with extensive annotations. Details of any cases are given, plus any subordinate legislation made under delegated powers in the Act. In addition to the main volumes there are service binders containing additional texts and an annual cumulative supplement. A noter-up binder brings the work up to date to within a few months.

INDEXES AND TABLES

The official index to the Statutes is the *Chronological table of the Statutes*. It lists all Public General Acts from 1235 onwards and gives details of whether they are in force and all repeals or amendments. Although it is theoretically published annually, it is currently three years behind. The companion volume, listing the Acts by subject, is the *Index to the Statutes* and this is four years behind. The table of *Effect of Legislation*, in the 'Tables and Index' volume published as part of the *Public General Acts and Measures*, fills the gap to some extent but, generally speaking, the official indexes are woefully inadequate.

CURRENT INFORMATION

In addition to *Halsbury's Statutes* mentioned above, another useful source of current legislation is LEXIS. The STAT file in the ENGGEN library contains the full text of current Public General Acts from 1267, excluding Statutes enacted but not yet in force. All Acts covered by *Halsbury's Statutes* are included and the file contains the up-to-date, amended texts of the Statutes (indicating the statutory authority for amendments and commencement dates).

COMMENCEMENT DATES

As already stated, Acts do not come into effect automatically following Royal Assent. The 'commencement section' of an Act may contain provision for it to come into force at a later time, either specified in the Act or by means of a Commencement Order at an unspecified future date. Commencement Orders are one type of Statutory Instrument (see **Subordinate legislation**). Acts may be brought into effect in many stages by a series of SIs, over months or even years. There are various publications which can help determine whether the Act is in force or not. *Is it in force?* is published as part of *Halsbury's Statutes* and gives details of all commencement dates of sections of post-1970 Statutes in force as at 1 January of the year of publication. The noter-up binder of *Halsbury's Statutes* contains a supplement to *Is it in force?* for the current year. *Current Law Legislation Citator* is another useful publication. Although it will not actually give commencement dates, it refers to the relevant Statutory Instrument numbers for the Commencement Orders. The Dates of Commencement section of the most recent *Current Law Monthly Digest* covers the current year. LAWTEL probably provides the most recent information on commencement dates. Otherwise it may be necessary to contact the relevant government department, located using the *Civil Service yearbook* (available in print and CD-ROM format).

Local and Personal Acts

Local and Personal Acts (known prior to 1948 as Local and Private Acts) are Statutes that apply to a particular locality or individual. The distinction between Public and Local Acts is not always clear cut. Whether an Act is Public or Private depends on how the Bill was presented to Parliament.

Public Bills are presented either by the Government or by a Private Member. Local Bills are presented by the promoter, who may be a local authority, an organization, or an individual. Such Bills are not available from HMSO, as they are published by the promoter. The *Weekly Information Bulletin* contains a complete list of all such Bills, together with the address and telephone number details of the Agent depositing the document.

Once the Bill receives Royal Assent, the Act is given a Chapter Number in the usual way and is published by HMSO. In order to distinguish them from Public General Acts, the chapter number for a Local Act is expressed as a roman numeral, e.g. 'c.v' and the chapter number for a Personal Act is expressed as an italicized arabic numeral, e.g. '*c.5*'. Local and Personal Acts have been officially published only since 1922. Previously, some were published privately and in some instances only the printed Bill may exist, rather than the Act. Local Acts have been published since 1991 as part of *Current Law Statutes Annotated.*

INDEXES AND TABLES

The main tables and indexes are published annually. In addition, the House of Lords Private Bill Office has produced an *Alphabetical index to the Local and Personal Acts 1850–1995* (1996) which covers about 19,000 Private Acts, listed alphabetically, with names and places cross-referenced. The main retrospective published index is the *Index to Local and Personal Acts* (1948). There are also some older indexes and these include Vardon (1840) and Bramwell (1813–35).

AMENDMENT AND REPEAL

As with the Public Acts, a problem lies in establishing whether a particular Act is in force. The principal source of reference is the *Chronological table of local legislation 1797–1994* (1996).

Subordinate legislation

Subordinate or delegated legislation usually contains detailed provisions of the law. It is also normally used to implement European Union directives (see the general introduction to the U.K.). It is made under powers granted by Statute often by Minister and is not subject to the same parliamentary scrutiny as Acts. As with the Statutes there are two series; general and local. The key to identifying them is that they are usually referred to as Orders, Regulations, Rules, Warrants. Most subordinate legislation is published as *Statutory Instruments*, which before 1946 were known as *Statutory Rules and Orders*. SIs are usually referred to by their title and year, for example, the Disability Working Allowance (General) Regulations 1991 and cited by year and running number, for example,

SI 1991 No.2887 or SI 1991/2887. The individual SIs are cumulated into an annual bound volume edition and this is issued in several consecutive parts, each of which has an index and table of effects. The last part also contains a classified list of the local SIs. Local SIs may be printed individually but not reproduced in the annual bound volume edition or may not be printed at all.

Halsbury's Statutory Instruments is a very useful collection. As with *Halsbury's Statutes*, this is a multi-volume work arranged by subject and includes additional texts and service binders. The instruments themselves are not published in full text, except for a few of the more important ones.

The full text of SIs is also available on CD-ROM as SI-CD and the SI file in the ENGGEN library of LEXIS contains the full text of all SIs as currently in force from 1861 to the present. Local SIs which were not printed from 1922 onwards can be obtained from the Statutory Publications Office.

LIST OF STATUTORY INSTRUMENTS

HMSO publishes a monthly *List of Statutory Instruments*. This lists for the whole of the UK all general and local SIs for the particular month, whether the Instrument was published or not, and is arranged by broad subject headings. Each entry includes, among other things: the enabling power, the date when the Instrument was issued, made and comes into force, a short note of any effect, and the territorial extent and classification. It also includes a cumulative alphabetical list of SIs for the whole year and this information is also available in *Current Law Monthly Digest*. LAWTEL indexes SIs and is updated daily and they are also indexed in the BADGER database. SIs are now appearing on the Internet.

AMENDMENTS AND REVOCATIONS

In order to find out whether a particular general Statutory Instrument is in force by far the most useful publication is *Halsbury's Statutory Instruments*. Since 1994, Sweet & Maxwell have produced the *Current Law Statutory Instrument Citator* which indicates the current status of SIs affected in the years covered by the citator. Reference can be made to the *Table of Government Orders*, or to the *Index to Government Orders* for details of SIs on a given subject, or under a particular Act. Both of these are published by HMSO and as with the equivalent indexes to the Statutes, are very out of date.

ORDERS, PROCLAMATIONS, ETC.

Tracing subordinate legislation not published as *Statutory Instruments* is more problematic. Some, such as Proclamations and Royal Warrants, may be published in the *London Gazette*. Others may be published as House of Commons Papers, Bye-laws or as Traffic Regulation Orders. Quasi-legislation can also be problematic to trace. Codes of Practice, Circulars, rule books of the various Self-Regulatory Organizations, Standards, etc. are some of the publications which come under this category. The best place to start the search is probably HMSO as most of the important material is published by them. Alternatively, looseleaf subject encyclopedias reprint some, otherwise it will be necessary to contact the relevant body.

Treaties

The Foreign and Commonwealth Office is responsible for negotiating treaties, on behalf of the Government, which are finalised and signed by the Government under the Royal Prerogative. They are usually cited by their title, the place of signing and the date of signing. UK treaties generally appear first as Command Papers (see page 528) as part of the Foreign and Commonwealth Office 'Miscellaneous Series'. Since 1892, they have been published, after ratification, as the United Kingdom *Treaty Series*, the official series prepared by the Foreign Office. These are published as a sub-series to the Command Papers and therefore have both a Treaty Series and a Command Paper number. Between 1812 and 1968, treaties were also published as Command Papers in the *British and Foreign State Papers*, a series which was produced by the Foreign and Commonwealth Office Library and which includes other international materials in addition to treaties. If a Treaty is incorporated into domestic law, it sometimes appears as a schedule to the Statute or Statutory Instrument that enacted the Treaty. For older treaties, *Hertslet's Treaties, 1827–1925* may also be useful.

The text of important treaties may also be reprinted in practitioners' works in the relevant field, either as an appendix, or in looseleaf collections relating to a specific subject such as *Butterworths Tax Treaties* (1995) and Singh (1983).

Indexes to treaties

The most useful official index is Parry and Hopkins (1970). This was first published by HMSO in three volumes and covers all Treaties concluded by the UK between 1101 and 1968. A fourth volume was published in 1991 under the editorship of Harris and Shepherd and this covers the years 1969 to 1988. It also updates the previous three volumes.

HMSO also publishes *Indexes to Treaty Series* and this appears under three titles: *General Index to Treaty Series*, *Annual Index to Treaty Series* and *Supplementary List of Ratifications, Accessions, Withdrawals, etc*. These are published as both Command Papers and as part of the *Treaty Series*. The *General Index* is a three year cumulative index and was produced until 1983. The last volume covers the years 1977 to 1979. The *Supplementary List* is essentially a supplement to the *Annual Index* and is produced approximately four times per year. Because these indexes are not cumulative, it can be a very laborious task following them through. The safest way to establish the status of a Treaty is to telephone the Treaty Records Section of the Foreign and Commonwealth Office, which is a vital source of up-to-date information on Treaties.

In addition to the official indexes, there are various commercially published indexes, none of which is confined in scope to those Treaties to which the UK is a signatory. The most useful of these is Bowman and Harris (1984). The main work was published by Butterworths but a cumulative supplement is produced, the latest being in 1992, by the Treaty Centre at the University of Nottingham where indexes are held. The work covers over 1000 treaties and is the most comprehensive and up-to-date index available. Treaties are listed chronologically showing: the title of the Treaty in English, the date it was concluded, the locations of the Treaty, in both official and unofficial sources, the date of entry into force, the duration, any reservations, the language of the authentic text, who the Treaty is open to, the parties, the territorial scope, the signatories, denunciations, amendments and notes.

Law reports

Two basic characteristics have shaped the system of law reporting in England and Wales:

1. There is no system of official state reports, but report publishing is in the hands of over 20 different, often competing, private publishers;
2. The courts play no part in deciding which cases shall be published, or as lawyers say, reported – selection is in the hands of the editors of the law reports. Each report editor may employ a different policy, but Brown (1989) set out the selection criteria used by the editors of the *All England Law Reports*, one of the most widely used series of law reports. About 2500 cases are reported each year, which represents under 2 per cent of the cases heard. Research in 1985 (Clinch, 1989) on the number of cases from each level in the court hierarchy which are reported, indicated that virtually all decisions of the House of Lords are reported, a high percentage of the decisions of the Court of Appeal (Civil Division), in contrast with under 10 per cent of the decisions of the Court of Appeal (Criminal Division), a third or less of the decisions of the three divisions of the High Court, and very small numbers (under 5 per cent) of the decisions of lower courts and administrative tribunals are published.

Lists of law reports

Law reports may be divided into four types:

1. General advance series, covering all subjects and published as soon as possible after the decision was given. Examples include the newspaper law reports, such as *The Times* and *The Independent.*
2. General full-text services such as *The Law Reports*, the *All England Law Reports*, the *Weekly Law Reports*.
3. Special subject advance series, such as the cases appearing in *Criminal Law Review*.
4. Special subject full-text series such as *Criminal Appeal Reports*.

Unfortunately, it does not follow that a case reported briefly will be reported fully at a later date, nor that a case reported in full was originally reported as an advance report. Nevertheless the general series (advance and full text) form the basis of a good law library, supplemented by those specialist series appropriate to the needs of the users of the service.

A full list of the law reports covering the English jurisdiction and which are currently active was published in *Current Law Year Book* between 1991 and 1993. A revised list appeared in Clinch and McIlveen (1995).

Full text reports

The most authoritative series of law reports is *The Law Reports* (1865–). It cannot be termed official reports for it is not issued by the courts themselves, but the proofs are read by the judiciary before publication and the report of a case is usually the fullest, including, uniquely among English law reports, the skeleton arguments of counsel. Where a case is reported in two or more series including *The Law Reports*, the courts prefer citation from the latter publication. *The Law Reports* began publication in 1865 in eleven different sub-series. That number has been reduced in stages to the four which are current: *Appeal Cases, Chancery, Family* and *Queen's Bench*. During 1996 a CD-ROM entitled ELR containing the full text of the complete set of *The Law Reports* was published by Context Ltd. For commercial organizations the cost is £10,000 for the archive set. The disk is updated and is available either by subscription to the biannual updated CD-ROM or to ELR ONLINE UPDATES.

The *All England Law Reports* (1936–)appear in 48 weekly parts each year. Their subject coverage is wide and aimed at the general practitioner. The reports are available on a CD-ROM updated monthly, or on disk, updated weekly. The *Weekly Law Reports* (1953–) are prepared and published by the same organisation as *The Law Reports*. Each weekly issue contains cases which are allocated to either volume 1, 2 or 3 of the publication. Those cases in volumes 2 and 3 will eventually be published in fuller form in *The Law Reports*, while those in volume 1 will not. *WLR* is available electronically as a remote database: JUSTIS WEEKLY LAW, containing the full texts of *WLR* from 1984, and as a CD-ROM: JUSTIS WEEKLY LAW REPORTS, with a backfile to 1971. There is a high degree of duplication of cases reported in the *Weekly Law Reports* and the *All England Law Reports*.

LEXIS, the major legal database run on a computer in Dayton, Ohio, contains the widest selection of English case law searchable electronically. It includes the full text of virtually all reported cases published since 1945, plus the *All England Law Reports* from 1936, *Tax Cases* reports from 1875, and the full text of unreported cases since January 1980, of the House of Lords and Court of Appeal (Civil Division) plus a selection of High Court decisions.

LINK (Legal Information Network), an online information service primarily aimed at practising lawyers, has the full text of transcripts of House of Lords and Court of Appeal (Civil Division) cases.

A small number of special subject law report publications is now available electronically. JUSTIS INDUSTRIAL CASES on CD-ROM is the full text of *Industrial Cases Reports* (1972–) and *Restrictive Practices Cases* (1957–1972). JUSTIS FAMILY LAW CD-ROM contains the full text of *Family Law* from its inception in 1980. EIRLR is a CD-ROM of *Industrial Relations Law Reports* (1972–).

From November 1996 House of Lords judgments have appeared on the Internet on the same day that the judgment is delivered at http://www.parliament.the-stationery-office.co.uk/pa/ld/ldjudinf.htm MASON'S COMPUTER LAW REPORTS is available via Strathclyde University Law School site at http://www.strath.ac.uk/Departments/Law/diglib/mlr.html and through the legal information network LINK.

Reports in newspapers

National newspapers which carry brief law reports, such as *The Times* (see also http://www.the-times.co.uk), *Financial Times, Guardian* and *Independent* are also available on CD-ROM. The purchase of CD-ROMs of a few individual series may not be an attractive proposition for those libraries already with access to LEXIS. The width of coverage and currency of LEXIS outweigh the cost savings of inhouse as opposed to remote searching.

Administrative reports

An increasing number of administrative tribunals exercise quasi-judicial functions. Many tribunals publish their decisions only as duplicated copies circulated to interested parties. Some will provide standing order services for libraries. A few publish more formally: e.g. *Immigration Appeal Reports* (1972–) (a reprint of the first 22 years is now available from John Rees Rare Books), *Value Added Tax Tribunal Reports* (1973–) and selected *Social Security Commissioner's Decisions. Social Security*

Case Law, Digest of Commissioners' Decisions, a two volume looseleaf work compiled by Desmond Neligan and frequently referred to as Neligan's Digest, contains brief summaries of a large number of reported and some unreported decisions of the Commissioners.

Unreported cases

Transcripts of unreported cases for the higher courts and some administrative tribunals are available. A guide has been produced: Supreme Court Library (1996). A subscription service to all transcripts of House of Lords decisions is available by contacting the Judicial Office.

Older cases

Academics and students frequently need to refer to even older decisions. The medieval equivalent of the law reports are the Year Books. Modern reprints with English translations alongside were made in the 19th and 20th centuries by the Selden Society and the Ames Foundation. Practitioners are unlikely to need to consult these documents. From the mid 16th to the mid 19th centuries law reporting was in the hands of individual reporters and small firms of publishers. Over 500 different publications were produced during this period containing the reports of cases. Although some libraries will have original publications of the period, most will use one or more of the reprint series: *English Reports*, covering the whole period and including over 170 titles; the *Revised Reports*, covering the period 1785–1865 only and including about 140 titles; *All England Law Reports Reprint*, a selection of cases 1558–1935 which were considered by the editors in the 1950s still to be of value.

From 1822, when the *Law Journal* began to carry law reports regularly, journals became a source for reports and that trend continues. It should be noted that reports from journals are not included in the first two reprint collections.

Citations

A report of an individual, reported case may be referred to as follows:

Rolled Steel Products Ltd v BSC [1985] 3 All E R 52

which means that the case will be found in the *All England Law Reports* for 1985, volume 3 at page 52. Lists of the most frequently used legal abbreviations for law reports and other forms of legal publishing are given in several publications, the most comprehensive are Raistrick (1993) and Osborn (1993). See page 539, Dictionaries, for more information on abbreviations.

Indexes, digests and citators

Law reports are indexed in several different publications: one series of law reports, *The Law Reports*, publishes a set of red coloured volumes which index that series and about eight others. *Legal Journals Index* (1986–), indexes the contents of over 300 law journals published in the United Kingdom, including those carrying brief reports of cases, such as *Gazette* (formerly *Law Society's Gazette), New Law Journal* and *Solicitors Journal.* Three publications index cases and provide brief summaries: *Daily Law Reports Index* (1988–), *Current Law* (1947–) and *The Digest* (Green Band edition, 1971–). *DLRI* indexes the 1,500 or so cases which appear annually in the quality daily newspapers.

Current Law is published in several series, two of which are relevant to case law: *Current Law Monthly Digest* (1947–) and *Current Law Year Book* (1947–). The parts of the *Monthly Digest* are superseded annually, about six months after the December issue, by the *Year Book.* The annual volume consolidates the year's indexing but the sequence and layout of entries in the *Year Book* is not the same as in the monthly parts. Libraries usually discard the monthly parts and references to case summaries of past years are based on the *Year Book* entries. The *Year Book* and *Monthly Digest* are widely used by both practitioners and academics. They cover some of the journals listed in *LJI*, the newspaper reports of *DLRI* and index those publications which carry only the reports of cases, such as *All England Law Reports.* For many years they have also carried summaries submitted by solicitors and barristers of unreported cases involving damages for personal injuries. Since 1995 they have included summaries of House of Lords and Court of Appeal (Civil Division) reports, taken from the original transcripts. *Current Law Monthly Digest* and the *Year Books* back to 1986 are available on the electronic database: Current Legal Information.

LJI and *DLRI* are available in paper, CD-ROM and computer tape formats, the latter updated fortnightly. In their electronic form, they can be purchased on the same disk, along with *Current Law,* and by subscription only on the Internet.

The Digest indexes English as well as Commonwealth and European Union case law from earliest times to the present, with a brief headnote for every entry, but it does not cover specialist law reports comprehensively. It is available at present only in paper format, updated by quarterly and annual supplements.

The Digest is also a case citator but, for domestic English law, *Current Law Case Citator* (1947–) is to be preferred because it is more frequently updated, covers a wider range of active reports, is simpler to use and is becoming available on the Internet. Entries in the set of *Current Law Case Citators* link citations to the headnotes in the sister publication *Current Law Year Book* (1947–). Citations to cases during the present year may be traced using the cumulative table of cases at the back of the latest issue of *Current Law Monthly Digest.*

Alerting services

Alerting services for new case law include: *Current Law Monthly Digest* (see above), *Halsbury's Laws Monthly Review* (see page 537), *Busy Solicitors Digest*, a monthly publication aimed at practitioners, and the columns of: *Gazette* (the weekly journal of the Law Society), *New Law Journal* and *Solicitors Journal*. Three electronic alerting services are aimed at practitioners: LAWTEL, available by subscription over the Internet, contains summaries of over 10,000 reported and unreported cases from 1980 onwards, including a selection of personal injury and quantum reports, all updated daily. LINK (Legal Information Network) contains the full text of transcripts of Court of Appeal (Civil Division) and House of Lords cases since 1993. A new electronic service using fax and electronic mail, is NEW LAW PUBLISHING. Subscribers receive summaries or, if available, the full text of property, commercial and criminal decisions of the High Court, Court of Appeal, Privy Council and House of Lords.

Other important Government documents

Command papers

One of the most frequently sought types of parliamentary publication, apart from the text of legislation, is command papers. These are documents which originate outside Parliament and are presented to Parliament 'by command of' the Sovereign, usually by the Minister responsible. The Sovereign is never personally involved, for the procedure is merely a technical device used by Ministers to place documents before Parliament which have not been created through the business of Parliament. About 300 to 400 are presented each year; all are published by HMSO and are traceable through the *Annual* and *Monthly Catalogues* or the *Daily List* published by HMSO. There are several different types:

1. Statements of Government policy on a topic which may indicate the broad lines of future legislation, often referred to as 'White Papers'.
2. Reports of Royal Commissions: prestigious investigative bodies set up under Royal Warrant to examine a topic of public concern where legislation seems desirable.
3. Reports of Departmental Committees set up by a Minister to carry out investigations into a matter of public concern.
4. Reports of tribunals or commissions of inquiry set up to inquire into a matter of urgent public importance.
5. Reports of a number of permanent investigatory bodies such as the Law Commission.
6. Treaties and agreements with other countries and with international organisations. These form the largest single group of Command Papers and have their own series known as the *Treaty Series*. See page

522 for further details.

7. Annual accounts and statistics, such as the annual report of the Commissioner of Metropolitan Police, or the Home Office compilation published each year: *Criminal Statistics, England and Wales.*

NUMBERING

Command Papers were first published in 1833 and nearly 50,000 have been produced since then. The Papers are numbered sequentially in long series regardless of parliamentary session. There are six series, each with a prefix usually consisting of an abbreviation for the word 'Command' followed by a running number. The series and running number are frequently used as an abbreviated reference when citing an individual Paper. The two most recent series: Cmnd and Cm, which cover the period from 1956 to the present, are most in demand.

MICROFICHE EDITIONS

Command Papers are included in the microfiche reprint of the *House of Commons Parliamentary Papers 1801–*. A Readex Microprint edition of *British Parliamentary Papers* was completed in the 1960s but copies can only be made with special equipment which many libraries with the edition do not possess. A microfiche edition has been made available subsequently by the same publisher. Academic lawyers are more likely to require access to the historic papers though practitioners sometimes refer to them.

GREEN PAPERS

In 1967 the Government began publishing a new category of document: 'Green Papers'. These are consultation documents. At first they were published either by HMSO as a non-Parliamentary paper or by the relevant Government department. However, an increasing number is now published as part of the Command Paper series.

Law reform bodies

The reports of four important law reform bodies have been published by HMSO as Command Papers:

1. The Law Revision Committee (1934–1939), succeeded by
2. The Law Reform Committee (1952–)
3. The Criminal Law Revision Committee (1959–)
4. The Law Commission (1965–).

Of the four organizations, the publications of the Law Commission are the most frequently sought. It produces two different series of documents: *Law Commission Consultation Documents* (formerly, Working

Papers) set out options for changes in a particular area of law. *Law Commission Reports* contain the Commission's final recommendations and often also a draft bill setting out how the recommendations might be enacted. *Reports* are published by HMSO in the Command Paper series, *Consultation Papers* are also published by HMSO but as part of the large group of Non-Parliamentary Papers. *Consultation Documents* and *Reports* have been reprinted by Professional Books (part of Butterworths), and new volumes are added periodically. Full lists of all Reports and Consultation Papers published by HMSO were given at the back of each *Annual Report of the Law Commission* up to 1992.

Departments and QUANGOs

Government departments and the 500 or more organizations controlled or funded by the Government produce material of value to lawyers. The material is not published through HMSO but through individual outlets for each organization. The most important of the 500 organizations are the Quasi-Autonomous Non-Governmental Organizations (QUANGOs) such as the Equal Opportunities Commission or the Health and Safety Commission. Tracking down the publications of a particular government department or QUANGO can be difficult, but the *Catalogue of British Official Publications Not Published by HMSO* (1980–) and, better still, its CD-ROM equivalent: UNITED KINGDOM OFFICIAL PUBLICATIONS (UKOP), published four times a year, which lists HMSO publications in addition, are invaluable. Chadwyck-Healey also publish on microfiche the full text of a selection of non-HMSO documents included in the two catalogues.

HMSO DATABASE ONLINE is the HMSO bibliographic database from 1976 to date (updated monthly) and is available on the British Library's BLAISE-LINE online database. The University of Southampton's index is available at http://www.soton.ac.uk/~nukop/index.html

Committee reports

Other useful finding tools for official publications are: *Committee Reports Published by HMSO indexed by Chairman* (1982–), a quarterly list, and for historical research: *British Government Publications: an Index to Chairman of Committees and Commissions of Inquiry* (1969–1984), a four-volume work covering the period 1800–1982.

Parliamentary debates

It was not possible at all for the courts to look at the legislative history of a measure until the recent decision of the House of Lords in the case of *Pepper v Hart* [1993] A.C. 593 relaxed the so called exclusionary rule, to permit reference to parliamentary materials in specified and limited circumstances, when a court is attempting to construe the meaning of a Statute. The effect of this change has been to increase lawyers' interest in tracing what the Minister or promoter said about the meaning of a particular clause of a Bill. Hansard is the verbatim report of what was said in Parliament. There are three series: one each covering debates on the floor of the House of Commons and the House of Lords (both entitled *Official Reports of Parliamentary Debates*), and one, entitled *Official Report of Standing Committee Debates*, which reports committee scrutiny of Bills outside the chamber of the Commons. HANSARD ON CD-ROM comprises separate discs of the text of debates on the floor of the Commons (May 1988–) and Lords (session 1992/3–). Hansard has now become available at: http://www/parliament.the-stationery-office.co.uk/ on the Internet.

There is, as yet, no CD-ROM of Standing Committee debates. If a particular text cannot be found in the usual libraries, reference may be made to the House of Lords or House of Commons information services, as appropriate.

Encyclopedias, large collections and services

Halsbury's Laws of England is the major encyclopedia of English law and should be the first port of call for any legal enquiry, of which the precise subject matter is not immediately apparent. The fourth edition of Halsbury was completed in 1986 in 56 volumes and is updated by a process of continuous revision, involving the complete reissue of individual volumes. The updating machinery for Halsbury, which is described in the *User's guide* to the service, includes annual cumulative supplements published each March, bringing all volumes up to date to the end of the previous October. There is also a monthly current service, including two looseleaf binders, together with a *Monthly Review*. At the end of the year, the separate *Monthly Reviews* are replaced by an *Annual Abridgment*.

Forms and precedents

There are two encyclopedias in this category: *Encyclopaedia of forms and precedents other than court forms* 5th edn; and Atkin (1961) *Encyclopaedia of court forms in civil proceedings*, 2nd edn. Both are undergoing continuous revision by a process similar to that described above for Halsbury, with the use of reissue volumes and annual supplementary material. Each also has a *User's guide* and remains the most comprehensive collection of precedents in its field. It should be emphasized that many specialized precedents may also be found in the appropriate practitioners' textbooks.

Looseleaf encyclopedias

There is a growing number of looseleaf works on a whole range of legal subjects with the word 'Encyclopedia' in the title. A typical looseleaf encyclopedia will contain a narrative statement of its subject, and then separate sections containing the relevant statutes, statutory instruments, ministerial circulars, codes of practice, European Union directives, etc.

There are now too many looseleaf encyclopedias in existence for any titles of this nature to be mentioned here individually but particulars may be found in the catalogues of the leading law publishers.

Additional pages for looseleaf works are sent out several times a year to their subscribers, who have to file them and remove superseded pages. Because of this inconvenience, plans are in hand to convert many of these works to an electronic format, and these have now passed their initial stage. Particulars of these developments are available from both Butterworths and Sweet & Maxwell.

Directories

Courts

Courts of law are covered by *Shaw's directory of courts in the United Kingdom*. Part 1 covers the High Court of Justice, the Court of Appeal and the circuits, with details of circuit judges and of crown courts on each circuit. Part 2 gives details of county courts and Part 3 does the same for the courts of summary jurisdiction. *Shaw's directory of tribunals and regulatory bodies* provides similar information for tribunals.

Other courts directories include *London county courts directory* and *County court districts (England and Wales) index of place names*, specifying the county court appropriate for each location.

The courts guide so far covers only the South Eastern and Western Circuits. It gives particulars of facilities in each court in terms of robing rooms, how to get there by public transport or by car, parking and even the nearest eating places.

Judiciary

Hazell's guide to the judiciary and the courts, with the Holborn Law Society's Bar list gives details of the members of the Judicial Committee of the Privy Council, the judicial House of Lords and of the Supreme Court of Judicature, followed by the circuits, with lists of circuit judges, recorders and district judges. Also listed are tribunals, registries, Crown Court centres and magistrates' courts offices, coroners, county courts and petty sessional divisions.

Whitaker's almanack contains useful information on the senior judiciary, except the members of the Judicial Committee of the Privy Council, also lists of circuit judges, recorders and stipendiary magistrates. A list of tribunals is also provided, with details of the scope and work of each tribunal, their chairmen and (in some cases) other members.

Legal profession

The three most comprehensive directories are *Butterworths law directory*, *Waterlow's solicitors' and barristers' directory* and *The Law Society's directory of solicitors and barristers.* Each provides full alphabetical lists of individual solicitors and geographical lists of firms arranged under towns, alphabetical lists of individual barristers and geographical lists of chambers, with the usual details of address, telephone/fax numbers and partnerships. They contain varying amounts of information on groups or bodies ancillary to the legal profession and on legal services. Butterworths alone provides a separate *Legal services directory,* free with their *Law directory.*

Chambers and partners directory of the legal profession and *The legal 500* are both directed towards students hoping to enter the legal profession. Chambers aims to include the largest 1000 solicitors' firms in terms of numbers of partners and fee earners, together with all barristers' chambers in England and Wales containing two or more barristers and a clerk, while *The legal 500* aims to include only the largest 500 firms in the country. Both give descriptions of firms, with details as to partners and types of work undertaken.

SOLICITORS

Butterworths and Waterlow's directories give information on solicitors' specializations, while the Law Society's directory includes separate lists of solicitors and barristers employed in commerce, industry, central and local government and also local law society addresses.

The *Solicitors' regional directories* of the Law Society are each subtitled 'Your guide to choosing a solicitor' and claim to provide 'the most recent information known to the Law Society about the solicitors' practices in England and Wales at the time of going to press'. This information includes a summary of services provided by each firm and up to six main types of work undertaken by each solicitor within the firm. There are also indexes of solicitors within each area who are expert in foreign languages.

BARRISTERS

Information about the Bar is contained in the *Bar directory*, which has an alphabetical list of individual barristers and a geographical list of chambers under towns. It also includes a separate list of types of work undertaken by chambers and lists of Queen's Counsel and of barristers practising overseas. An additional detail in the chambers lists is a note on the languages spoken in each chambers. *Havers' companion to the Bar* covers much the same ground. A more specialized work is the *Commercial Bar Association directory*.

Government departments

Government departments and agencies are covered in great detail in the *Civil Service year book*, which lists over 7000 names in its index of individual officers. The section of *Whitaker's almanack* on 'Government departments and public offices' gives briefer information. There is also a useful *Guide to libraries and information units in government departments and other organisations*, published by the British Library.

Aldridge's *Directory of registers and records* covers a wide assortment of material including records of births, marriages and deaths, local land charges and companies registers, with details of how to get in touch with each body and the likely cost of the information.

Others

The Directory of grant-making trusts is likely to be of interest to solicitors engaged in charity work. It gives details of over 3000 trusts, with geographical and alphabetical indexes.

The Directory of British and Irish law libraries provides the most comprehensive list available of all types of law library in universities, government departments, law firms, etc.

The Commonwealth universities yearbook includes entries for all British universities, with lists of the membership of their law faculties. More detailed lists of law faculties, with particulars of the research interests of their members, may be found in SPTL (Annual) *Directory of members*, which is issued for private circulation but available to enquirers on request.

The Directory of expert witnesses (1995) lists experts and their special areas of expertise, with a subject index and an introduction on choosing an expert.

Shaw's directory of local authorities in the United Kingdom gives details of all the newly created local authorities, following the reorganization of local government.

Bibliographies

Monographs

GENERAL

The most comprehensive and up-to-date bibliography of English law is Raistrick (1997), which lists under each subject division not only the books relating to that subject, but also (in a separate subsection) the encyclopedias and periodicals. The lists of books contain, as well as current titles in their latest editions, established classics of continuing value.

The list of *Recommended holdings for law libraries* (BIALL, 1983), is applicable to all law libraries, while the lists in Appendix 1 of the *Statement of standards for university law library provision in England and Wales* (SPTL, 1995) are intended for academic law libraries only. They contain titles both of printed serials and of electronic databases.

The first two volumes of *Sweet and Maxwell's legal bibliography of the British Commonwealth of Nations* (1989) cover books on English law to 1954, together with the law of Wales, the Channel Islands and the Isle of Man. Chloros (1973) is a selective list compiled principally for academic lawyers, with commentaries added to each chapter.

LAW REPORTS AND LEGISLATION

For law reports only, Breem and Phillips (1991) is the leading authority. For England and Wales, it gives an initial list of general reports, together with lists of reports relating to particular courts and on particular subjects. The entries indicate whether the items listed have been reprinted, issued in micro format, or incorporated into a database such as LEXIS.

Statutes as well as law reports are dealt with in *Guide to law reports and statutes* (1962) which provides a full list of all the past editions of the English, Scottish and UK statutes, as well as regnal years. It provides an alphabetical list of English, Irish and Scottish law reports, with the periods covered by each, and a list of abbreviations used in referring to law reports and textbooks, together with a chronological list of the older English law reports, showing the volumes of the *English Reports* and the *Revised Reports* in which they have been reprinted.

PERIODICALS, THESES AND ESSAYS

The *Union list of legal periodicals* (1978) gives locations for all the legal periodicals held by the major law libraries in the UK in that year.

Legal theses and dissertations are listed in *Legal research in the UK 1905–1984* (1985). Limited reference for later years may be made to the *List of current legal research topics*, which ceased after 1988.

Tearle (1983) lists legal essays in about 340 collections, published during the five year period 1975 to 1979, under author, subject and jurisdiction.

PARTICULAR SUBJECTS

There are good, but rather out-of-date bibliographies of the legal profession and legal services by Campbell (1980), of jurisprudence by Dias (1979), of British and Irish labour law by Hepple and O'Higgins (1981) and of welfare law by Partington (1976).

Guides to legal research include Jeffries and Miskin (1990), Clinch (1992), Tunkel (1992), Holborn (1993), and Dane and Thomas (1996).

Serially published bibliographies

LEGAL

The most useful current legal bibliography is *Current Law Monthly Digest*, each issue of which includes details of the law books published during the month. The monthly lists are cumulated into the annual volumes of *Current Law year book*, where the titles are arranged under subject headings. Listing in *Current Law Monthly Digest* is often the first indication that a book has actually been published, as distinct from merely being announced.

Hammicks legal catalogue appears annually and supplies a separate list of looseleaf works with details of frequency and price, and has a separate section on CD-ROM and electronic products. It contains entries for books not yet published. It is now also available on CD-ROM.

Information about new or forthcoming titles may also be obtained in the lists issued by the major legal publishers, although the estimated dates of publication should always be treated with some scepticism. Surveys of new titles already published may be found in the special book issues of the *New Law Journal*, which appear three or four times a year.

GENERAL

The *British National Bibliography* appears weekly and is cumulated quarterly and then annually. It covers a large part of the publishing output of the country, therefore many of the items listed are of an ephemeral nature. Also, many books are listed twice, first as Cataloguing-in-Publication items, and again after publication.

Whitaker's books in print, which is published annually, is a combined author, title and keyword index to all UK and European English language titles still in print at the beginning of the current year. Its CD-ROM counterpart, BOOKBANK, includes in addition titles recently out of print and forthcoming. Similar information is given in BOOKFIND-CD together with its specialist service BOOKFIND-CD BUSINESS AND LAW.

CD-ROMs in the legal field are included in Worley (1995). The items listed are arranged under supplier, and some indication is given of future developments. A new service, WHITAKER-ROM (1996–), contains details of 10,000 CD-ROM and multimedia titles available worldwide and will appear twice a year.

GOVERNMENT PUBLICATIONS

Most Government publications are covered by the various lists issued by HMSO. The daily list is cumulated monthly and annually. There is also a sectional list on Law.

An increasing number of government publications is now published by the departments themselves, and are not included in the HMSO lists. They often do not appear in the BNB either. The *Catalogue of British official publications not published by HMSO* (1980–) lists the publications of over 500 organizations, including government departments, nationalized industries, research institutes and quangos. Issues appear every two months, and then cumulate into an annual volume the following year.

The *Catalogue of United Kingdom official publications on CD-ROM* combines all official publications both HMSO and non-HMSO. It also includes the publications of seventeen international organizations for which HMSO is the UK agent. It is published quarterly, covering the period since 1980.

The NEW UNITED KINGDOM OFFICIAL PUBLICATIONS ONLINE SERVICE (NUKOP ONLINE) gives enquirers using the World Wide Web access to information about UK official publications from July 1995 onwards.

Indexing and abstracting services

Legal Journals Index (1986–) is the best indexing service presently available for British legal journals. It aims to cover all journal titles published in the United Kingdom which are devoted to law or which frequently contain articles on legal topics. About 300 journals are indexed at present, and the comprehensive list of addresses of journals serves as a reference guide to current journal titles in law. The subject index headings are listed in Smith and Miskin (1990). Each issue also contains an author index, a case index, an index to legislation (both British and European) and a book review index. Document delivery of particular articles is also available on request, under a licence from the Copyright Licensing Agency. The issues of *Legal Journals Index* are published monthly, cumulated three-monthly and annually. They may also be obtained on a monthly CD-ROM as part of CURRENT LEGAL INFORMATION.

UK legal journals are also indexed in the *Current Law Monthly Digest*. A cumulated Index of Articles appears near the end of the *Current Law year book*. The subject headings employed by the *Current Law* service are much broader than those to be found in *Legal Journals Index*. Journal articles are indexed similarly under broad subject headings in *Halsbury's Laws Monthly Review*, with an annual cumulation in *Halsbury's abridgment*. The noter-up volume to *Halsbury's Laws of England* also contains a cumulated list of articles that have appeared in the *Monthly Reviews* for the current year.

FINANCIAL JOURNALS INDEX (1992–) provides summaries of relevant articles on insurance, pensions and banking. It is available on CD-ROM only as part of CURRENT LEGAL INFORMATION. The same applies to the BADGER

DATABASE OF SUPPLEMENTARY LEGAL MATERIALS. (BADGER stands for Broad All-purpose Database Geared for Easy Retrieval). This indexes and abstracts official press releases and consultative documents, practice directions and selected press comment, the HMSO *Daily List* and the *House of Commons Weekly Information Bulletin.*

Law under review: a quarterly bulletin of law reform projects (1987–) contains lists of current law reform projects, arranged under the government departments initiating them, and a list of projects previously reported and completed during the last quarter. There is also a section on current publications of Commonwealth law reform agencies.

The Index to Theses with abstracts (1950–) not only indexes theses accepted for higher degrees by the universities of Great Britain and Ireland, but also supplies short abstracts of the theses listed, starting from Volume 36 (1987). Theses in all subjects are covered, including law.

Dictionaries

English language

The *Oxford English dictionary* (1989) is the most authoritative dictionary of the English language, and it has often been referred to in court for the natural meanings of words under consideration. The *OED* defines over half a million words and includes over two million illustrative quotations. It is now available on CD-ROM and the hardback version consists of 20 volumes. The *New Shorter Oxford English Dictionary*, in two volumes, has been completely rewritten.

Law

The two most detailed legal dictionaries are *Stroud's judicial dictionary of words and phrases* (1986) and *Words and phrases legally defined* (1988). Both are primarily concerned with language which has been interpreted or defined by the judiciary, but have now added statutory definitions. Stroud tends to give more definitions of each word, and to refer to more cases. *Words and phrases* gives longer extracts from the cases. *Words and phrases* also refers back frequently to *Halsbury's Laws of England.*

Jowitt's dictionary of English law (1977) is a shorter work in two volumes, which aims to give more briefly a definition of every legal term, old and new, also including many Latin maxims, with their translations in modern English. The latest supplement was published in 1985. Smaller works, particularly suitable for students or lay persons, include the *Concise dictionary of law* (1994), Curzon (1993), Mozley & Whiteley (1993) and Osborn (1993).

There exists a number of more specialized law dictionaries. Broom

(1971), known as *Broom's legal maxims*, gives the most comprehensive collection of Latin maxims, with detailed explanations. These are also covered in a more recent work, *Latin words and phrases for lawyers* (1980).

James and Stebbings (1987) contains legal quotations arranged under 160 different subject headings. It provides indexes of authors and sources, and of key words.

For legal abbreviations, the new second edition of Raistrick (1993) contains more than 25 000 entries. The geographical coverage has been extended so as to include more entries from countries of the European union and from the world outside the common law countries. For those without access to Raistrick, shorter lists of abbreviations containing references to the principal UK law reports and legal journals may be found in *Current Law Monthly Digest* and in *Current Law year book.*

Other reference books

Practice books

The *Supreme Court practice*, often known familiarly as the 'White Book', is the principal authority on the working of the Supreme Court. It contains both the revised text of the Rules of the Supreme Court and also the prescribed forms and practice directions. A complete new edition now appears every two years, with updating by cumulative supplement and by newsletter during the period in between editions.

A briefer compendium, the *Annual practice* (1995–), contains the more important information in a more compact format and can be subscribed to separately.

The *County Court practice*, sometimes referred to as the 'Green Book', is the corresponding authority on the practice of the county courts. It contains the full text of the County Courts Act and County Court Rules, together with other relevant Acts and the prescribed forms. It appears annually.

Stone's Justices' manual contains a generous selection of the Acts and Statutory Instruments likely to be referred to in magistrates' courts, and this too appears annually.

Two practice books serve the needs of criminal law practitioners. The older established work is *Archbold's criminal pleading, evidence and practice*, which first appeared in 1822. It is kept up to date between the annual editions by two or three supplements a year. An alternative work is *Blackstone's criminal practice*, which aims to provide a single volume work completely renewed every year, so as to eliminate the need to refer to supplements.

Another specialized practice book, *Paterson's licensing acts*, meets the requirements of practitioners attending licensing sessions, and appears annually.

Legal aid is an important element in legal practice today, and the rules and regulations which govern it are set out in the annual *Legal Aid handbook.*

Professional codes of conduct

Special works deal with the codes of conduct of each branch of the profession.

The Code of Conduct of the Bar of England and Wales (1990) has superseded all previous disciplinary pronouncements, except in respect of anything done or omitted to be done before 31 March 1990. It is published in looseleaf format.

The Guide to the professional conduct of solicitors (1996) is the corresponding work for the solicitors' branch of the profession. It is republished about every three years. It is intended to publish any subsequent changes in issues of the *Professional Standards Bulletin.*

Qualification as a lawyer

Those seeking entry to the profession are advised to apply for details of courses and qualifications required to the General Council of the Bar or to the Law Society. Much additional information on both branches of the profession can be obtained from university careers and appointments offices.

Current information sources

Journals

ACADEMIC AND PRACTICE JOURNALS

The leading academic law journals include *Cambridge Law Journal* (1921–), *Law Quarterly Review* (1885–), *Modern Law Review* 1937–) and the *Oxford Journal of Legal Studies* (1981–). They contain lengthy analytical articles and thorough, but not especially current case notes. There is also a wide range of specialist journals covering particular areas of law, such as *Civil Justice Quarterly* (1982–), *Criminal Law Review* (1954–), *Family Law* (1971–), *Journal of Business Law* (1975–), *Journal of Legal History* (1980–), *Statute Law Review* (1980–). A fast expanding area is the publication of newsletters, often only a few pages long, issued frequently and mainly aimed at specialist practitioners.

Titles include *Environmental Law Brief, Intellectual Property Newsletter* (1986–), *Personal and Medical Injuries Law Letter* (1985–). Some of the larger law firms also produce their own newsletters, aimed at corporate clients, which are publicly available and provide authoritative commentary on the specialized areas of law handled by those firms. Titles include *Denton Hall Pensions Newsletter* (1992–), *Dibb Lupton Broomhead Business Brief* (1993–), *Herbert Smith Briefing* (1993–), *Linklater & Paines Property Law Now* (1994–).

Two English universities have created electronic journals which can be accessed over the Internet. The first to be developed was *Web Journal of Current Legal Issues* (1995–) located at the Law School of Newcastle University: http://www.ncl.ac.uk/~nlawwww/ on the Internet.

More recent is *JILT (The Journal of Law and Technology)* (1996–) run from the Law Technology Centre at the University of Warwick, at either: http://elj.warwick.ac.uk/elj/jilt or: http://jilt.law.strath.ac.uk/elj/jilt on the Internet.

Two paper listings provide details of the wide range of law journals available. Legal Information Resources produce a list of abbreviations for all the journals indexed in *Legal Journals Index* and its associated databases, which is arranged alphabetically by title and is biased towards the interests of practitioners, rather than academics. The indicative list of law library holdings, produced by the Society of Public Teachers of Law, SPTL (1995) is arranged by subject and selects not only journals but all sources of law. The indicative list is intended for academic law librarians.

CURRENT AWARENESS JOURNALS

The main current awareness journals, all weekly except where stated, are listed in alphabetical order:

Counsel: a bimonthly controlled circulation publication subtitled the Journal of the Bar of England and Wales. Contains news items and two or three-page articles on law and procedure aimed at barristers and the judiciary.

Gazette (formerly Law Society's Gazette): the journal of the Society representing solicitors, with news, short articles on practice law (some written by academics), procedure, administration and management, and 'Legal Update' containing short reports of cases, The whole journal is also available in full text on LEXIS.

The Lawyer: tabloid news magazine but with centre pages reviewing a single topic in more depth, also available in full text on the remote online database: LAWTEL.

Legal Business: ten times a year glossy magazine focusing on practice management and administration, featuring the people behind the business as much as the business itself.

Legal Times: weekly newspaper aimed at practitioners containing news and comment, and one or two lengthy case reports. Also supplements analysing topics or new legislation in depth.
New Law Journal: with news, two or three-page articles on practice matters, some written by academics and a section entitled 'Practitioner' containing extended reports of a few cases, short notes of others and lists of legislation. The whole journal is also available in full text on LEXIS.
Solicitors Journal: weekly, with news, two or three-page articles on matters of practice interest, and a regular insert: 'Lawbrief', printed on coloured paper, providing short notes on recent legal developments, the full text of practice directions, brief reports of cases and lists of new legislation with notes on those of interest to practising lawyers. In addition, several times a year subscribers receive substantial supplements on, for example, expert witnesses, practice management and charities.
LAWTEL: the remote online database (available over the Internet by subscription) carries Daily Update on the latest legal developments as well as the full text of the weekly journal: *The Lawyer* (see above).
London Gazette: official notices and information on legal matters, especially in connection with company and business law, published daily.

RESEARCH REPORTS

Apart from research reports produced as part of the investigations of official organizations such as Royal Commissions (see page 528), the most important series of research reports published which are relevant to the needs of lawyers, is the Home Office Research Unit's *Home Office Research Studies*. The responsibilities of the Home Office are wide ranging and only a proportion of the reports is relevant to law and criminology. Each report is on a different topic. In contrast, the Home Office Research and Statistics Department produces *Research Bulletin* twice a year, containing papers describing the results of research recently undertaken. The Unit also publishes an annual *Research Programme*. All these Home Office materials are of more interest to academics than practitioners.

The results of research undertaken by universities are published in academic and specialist journals, including those listed on page 540.

News information

The first news of legal developments is often found in the quality national newspapers: *The Times, Guardian, The Independent, Daily Telegraph* and *Financial Times*. The remote database, LAWTEL, includes a Daily Update of new legal developments. LINK carries the text of press releases of the Lord Chancellor's Department and the Central Office of Information, the Government's publicity department, all updated daily. Next come the weekly legal journals noted above. Some of this news is based on the press releases of Government Departments and QUANGOs.

Subscription services are available on application – addresses can be traced through *Civil Service year book*, available in paper and CD-ROM format. The UK Government Information service (http://www.open.gov.uk/) gives news summaries and uses other sites, for example: the Committee on Standards in Public Life (http://www.open.gov.uk/nolan/csplhome.htm).

A number of publishers, listed here in alphabetical order, including CCH Editions, FT Law and Tax, Industrial Relations Services and Monitor Press, produce newsletters, published at intervals up to monthly, each on a narrow practice area. New legislation, cases, procedural and other information is reported briefly, but in some instances the cases covered often remain unreported because of their narrow interest value, and the newsletter is the only source of information about the case, apart from obtaining the transcript. In the last few years, Sweet & Maxwell have published newsletters to update about a dozen of their most popular looseleaf works. These are available to non-subscribers.

Business and financial information

The Department of Trade and Industry is the Government department presently responsible for trade and commerce. In Wales, the Welsh Office has responsibilities or oversight of aspects of trade and commerce in the Principality. A useful annual publication which provides a factual review of Government policy and developments in Britain is *Britain: 1997 an official handbook* (published annually, with the appropriate year in the title). Companies in England, Wales and Scotland are registered by the Companies Registration Office, a Government agency now known as Companies House. It is based in Cardiff. The register of companies is published on microfilm but, in addition, subscribers to the Mercury Business Intelligence online service, can search the records electronically through the COMPANIES HOUSE DIRECT database.

A range of commercially published business directories is available, from the basic purchasing type directory such as *Kelly's*, listing names and addresses of companies under headings classified according to the product or service offered, through *Key British Enterprises*, better known simply as *KBE*, which contains summaries of balance sheets and brief personnel information, to *Major companies handbook* appearing twice a year, providing detailed financial information for a limited number of companies. *Kompass* provides facts and statistical data on products, services and company information. KOMPASS DATABASES provide comprehensive data in electronic format (online and CD-ROM) on 500,000 companies. Another electronic source, but without a paper counterpart, is DATASTREAM, providing company, financial market and economic data which can be downloaded into statistical software programmes.

A small proportion of all companies is registered on the London Stock

Exchange. *The Macmillan Stock Exchange Yearbook* provides mainly financial, loan and capital information about quoted companies.

The major business journals are *The Economist* and *Investors Chronicle*, both weekly. The scope of business information relevant to the lawyer is wide: handbooks such as *Croner's A–Z of Business Information Sources*, looseleaf and regularly updated, provides a more detailed review than is possible here.

Statistics

Official statistics of relevance to lawyers include: *Judicial statistics England and Wales*, an annual containing data on the civil and criminal business of the courts; the *Annual report of the Council on Tribunals*, giving the number of cases dealt with by tribunals; *Criminal statistics, England and Wales*, which has data and commentary on the number and type of cases dealt with and sentences. More detailed annual tables are released in five supplementary volumes: *Criminal statistics, England and Wales, supplementary tables*. More specialised statistics on the criminal process are contained in: *Offences of drunkenness, England and Wales; Statistics of the misuse of drugs in the United Kingdom; Statistics of breath tests, England and Wales; Offences relating to motor vehicles, England and Wales. The Report of the Commissioner of Police of the Metropolis* provides information about accidents and offences in London. Chief Constables of forces outside London also issue annual reports, published by the relevant Police Authority. Statistics on the treatment of offenders may be found in several sources: the *Report on the work of the Prison Department; Prison statistics, England and Wales; Probation statistics, England and Wales*. For statistical information on legal services, *Legal Aid Annual Reports (England and Wales)* provide data on assistance and costs, while the Law Society's *Annual statistical report* provides data about the solicitors' profession and trends and forecasts.

Guides to statistical sources include: *Guide to official statistics* which provides short notes on official and significant non-official sources. Walker (1981) is of more interest to the academic and those interested in historical data, since it has never been updated. Mort (1990) covers the statistical information available from trade associations, professional bodies, local authorities, banks, chambers of commerce etc.

Basic economic and trade indicators are published in several sources: *Employment Gazette*, published monthly, contains a statistical section on employment, retail prices, earnings and hours of work; *Business Briefing*, published weekly, carries news and the latest key business indicators from the Government's Central Statistical Office. The CSO's own publications carry the same data at a later date. A useful compilation of a wide range of Government statistics is *Monthly Digest of Statistics*.

Useful addresses

Associations

Association of Law Teachers (ALT), c/o Business Studies Department, Manchester College of Arts and Technology, Lower Hardman Street, Manchester M3 3ER, UK. Tel: +44 161 953 5995. Fax: +44 161 953 2259

British and Irish Association of Law Librarians (BIALL), 26 Myton Crescent, Warwick CV34 6QA, UK. Tel/Fax: +44 1926 491717. E-mail: 106033.52@compuserve.com Internet: http://www.swan.ac.uk/library/biallho.htm

British and Irish Legal Education Technology Association (BILETA), CTI-Law Technology Centre, University of Warwick, Coventry CV4 7AL, UK. Tel: +44 1203 523294. Fax: +44 1203 524105. Email: ctilaw@warwick.ac.uk. Internet: http://www.law.warwick.ac.uk

General Council of the Bar, 3 Bedford Row, London WC1R 4DB, UK. Tel: +44 171 242 0082. Fax: +44 171 831 9217

Honourable Society of Gray's Inn, London WC1R 5EU, UK. Tel: +44 171 405 8164. Fax: +44 171 831 8381

Honourable Society of Inner Temple, London WC4Y 7HL, UK. Tel: +44 171 797 8250. Fax: +44 171 797 8178

Honourable Society of Lincoln's Inn, London WC2A 3TL, UK. Tel: +44 171 405 1393. Fax: +44 171 831 1839

Honourable Society of Middle Temple, London EC4Y 9AT, UK. Tel: +44 171 353 4355. Fax: +44 171 583 3220

The Law Society of England & Wales, 113 Chancery Lane, London WC2A 1PL, UK. Tel: +44 171 242 1222. Fax: +44 171 831 0057. Internet: htttp://www.lawsoc.org.uk/

Magistrates' Association, 28 Fitzroy Square, London W1P 5HH, UK. Tel: +44 171 387 2353. Fax: +44 171 388 4020

Selden Society (legal history), c/o Mr V. Tunkel, Faculty of Laws, Queen Mary and Westfield College, University of London, Mile End Road, London E1 4NS Tel: +44 171 475 5555

Society of Public Teachers of Law (SPTL), c/o Professor D. J. Hayton, School of Law, King's College, London, Strand, London WC2R 2LS. Tel: +44 171 836 5654. Fax: +44 873 2465

Governmental organizations

Crown Prosecution Service, 50 Ludgate Hill, London EC4M 7EX, UK. Tel: +44 171 273 8000. Fax: +44 171 329 8002

Foreign and Commonwealth Office, King Charles Street, London SW1A 2AH, UK. Tel: +44 171 270 3000. Internet:http://www.fco.gov.uk/

Foreign and Commonwealth Office, Nationality, Treaty and Claims Dept, Clive House, Petty France, London SW1H 9HD, UK. Tel: +44 171 270 4079

Home Office, 50 Queen Anne's Gate, London SW1H 9AT, UK. Tel: +44 171 273 3000. Fax: +44 171 273 2190. Research and Statistics Department, Tel: +44 171 273 3000. Fax: +44 171–273 3674. Internet: http://www.open.gov.uk/home_off/rsdhome.htm

Lord Chancellor's Department, Trevelyan House, 30 Great Peter Street, London SW1P 2BU, UK. Tel:+44 171 210 8500. Internet: http://www/open.gov.uk/lcd/lcdhome.htm

Public Record Office, Chancery Lane, London WC2A 1LR, UK. Tel: +44 181 876 3444. Also at: Ruskin Avenue, Kew, Richmond, Surrey TW9 4DU, UK. Tel: +44 181 876 3444. Fax: +44 181 878 8905. Internet: http://www.open.gov.uk/pro/prohome.htm

Law reform bodies and pressure groups

Criminal Law Revision Committee, c/o Home Office (Legal Adviser's Branch), 50 Queen Anne's Gate, London SW1H 9AT, UK. Tel: +44 171 273 3000

Howard League for Penal Reform, 708 Holloway Road, London N19 3NL, UK. Tel: +44 171 281 7722. Fax: +44 171 281 7722

Justice, 95a Chancery Lane, London WC2A 1DT, UK. Tel: +44 171 405 6018. Fax: +44 171 831 1155

Law Commission, Conquest House, 37–38 John Street, Theobald's Road, London WC1N 2BQ, UK. Tel:+44 171 411 1220. Fax: +44 171 411 1297

Legal Action Group, 242–244 Pentonville Road, London N1 9UN, UK. Tel: +44 171 833 2931. Fax: +44 171 837 6094

Liberty, 21 Tabard Street, London SE1 4LA, UK. Tel: +44 171 403 3888. Fax: +44 171 407 5454

Lord Chancellor's Department, Advisory Committee on Statute Law, Statutory Publications Office, 6 Spring Gardens, London SW1A 2BP, UK. Tel: +44 171 389 3244. Fax: +44 171 389 7490

Courts and tribunals

Central Criminal Court, Old Bailey, London EC4M 7EH, UK. Tel: +44 171 248 3277

Copyright Tribunal, Room 4/6, Hazlitt House, 45 Southampton Buildings, London WC2A 1AR, UK. Tel: +44 171 438 4776

Central Office of the Industrial Tribunals, 19–21 Woburn Place, London WC1W 0LU, UK. Tel: +44 171 273 3000. Fax: +44 171 273 8677

Criminal Appeal Office, Room C301, Royal Courts of Justice, Strand, London WC2A 2LL, UK. Tel: +44 171 936 7344

Crown Office, Room C315, Royal Courts of Justice, Strand, London WC2A 2LL, UK. Tel: +44 171 936 6359

Employment Appeal Tribunal, 4 St James's Square, London SW1Y 4JU, UK. Tel: +44 171 270 3872

House of Lords, Judicial Office, London SW1A 0PW, UK. Tel: +44 171 219 3111

Immigration Appeal Tribunal, Thanet House, 231 Strand, London WC2R 1DA, UK. Tel: +44 171 353 8060

Independent Tribunal Service, City Gate House, 39–45 Finsbury Square, London EC2A 1PX, UK. Tel: +44 171 814 6500

Judicial Committee of the Privy Council, Whitehall, London SW1A 2AT, UK. Tel: +44 171 270 0485

Lands Tribunal, 48–49 Chancery Lane, London WC2A 1JR, UK. Tel: +44 171 936 7200. Fax: +44 171 404 0896

Royal Courts of Justice, Strand, London WC2A 2LL, UK. Tel: +44 171 936 6000. Fax: +44 171 936 6724

Special Commissioners of Income Tax, Combined Tax Tribunals Centre, 15–19 Bedford Avenue, London WC1B 3AS, UK. Tel: +44 171 631 4242

VAT Tribunal, Combined Tax Tribunals Centre, 15–19 Bedford Avenue, London WC1B 3AS, UK. Tel: +44 171 631 4242

Education and training

College of Law, Braboeuf Manor, Portsmouth Road, Guildford, Surrey GU3 1HA, UK. Tel: +44 1483 460200. Fax: +44 1483 460305

Inns of Court School of Law, 39 Eagle Street, London WC1R 4AP, UK. Tel: +44 171 404 5787. Fax: +44 171 831 4188

Lord Chancellor's Department, Advisory Committee on Legal Education and Conduct, 8th Floor, Millbank Tower, Millbank, London SW1P 4QU, UK. Tel: +44 171 217

4296. Fax: +44 171 217 4283. Judicial Studies Board, 14 Little St James's Street, London SW1A 1DP, UK. Tel: +44 171 925 0185. Fax: +44 171 321 0142. Magistrates Training, Southside, 105 Victoria Street, London SW1E 6QT, UK. Tel: +44 171 210 2191

There are Law Schools in most universities, each of which has its own research specialisms. For details consult *Commonwealth universities yearbook.*

Research institutions

See also note about university research above.

British Institute of International and Comparative Law, Charles Clore House, 17 Russell Square, London WC1B 5EA, UK. Tel: +44 171 636 5802. Fax: +44 171 323 2016

Institute of Advanced Legal Studies, School of Advanced Study, University of London, 17 Russell Square, London WC1B 5DR, UK. Tel: +44 171 637 1731. Fax: +44 171 580 9613. Internet: http://www.sas.ac.uk

Institute of Criminology, University of Cambridge, 7 West Street, Cambridge CB3 9DT, UK. Tel: +44 1223 335360. Fax: +44 1223 335356

Libraries and information services

Bodleian Law Library, University of Oxford, St Cross Building, Manor Road, Oxford OX1 3UR, UK. Tel: +44 1865–271463. Fax: +44 1865–271475. Internet: http://www/rsl.ox.ac.uk/boris/guides/law/law01.html

British Library, Official Publications and Social Sciences Service, Great Russell Street, London WC1B 3DG, UK. Tel: +44 171 412 7536. Internet: http://portico.bl.uk/. Science Reference and Information Service, 25 Southampton Buildings, London WC2A 1AW, UK. Tel: +44 171 323 7494. Fax: +44 171 323 7495. Internet: http://portico.bl.uk/

British Library of Political and Economic Science, London School of Economics and Political Science, 10 Portugal Street, London WC2A 2AE, UK. Tel: +44 171 405 7686

CCTA Government Information Service. Internet: http://www.open.gov.uk/

Companies House, Postal Search Section, Crown Way, Cardiff CF4 3UZ, UK. Tel: +44 1222 380801

Foreign and Commonwealth Office, Legal Library, King Charles Street, London SW1A 2AH, UK. Tel: +44 171 270 3050

Health and Safety Executive Information Centre, Health and Safety Laboratory, Broad Lane, Sheffield S3 7HQ, UK. Tel: +44 114 289 2345. Fax: +44 114 289 2333

House of Commons Library, Public Information Office, London SW1A 0AA, UK. Tel: +44 171 219 4272

House of Lords, Information Office, London SW1A 0PW, UK. Tel: +44 171 219 3107. Fax: +44 171 219 6396

Institute of Advanced Legal Studies Library, School of Advanced Study, University of London, 17 Russell Square, London WC1B 5DR. Tel: +44 171 637 1731. Fax: +44 171 436 8824. E-mail: ials.lib.@sas.ac.uk. Internet: http://www.sas.ac.uk

Lord Chancellor's Department, Library Services, Room 113, Trevelyan House, 30 Great Peter Street, London SW1P 2BP, UK. Tel: +44 171 210 8592. Fax: +44 171 210 8568

National Library of Wales, Aberystwyth, Dyfed SY23 3BU, UK. Tel: +44 1970 623816. Fax: +44 1970 615709

Squire Law Library, University of Cambridge, 10 West Road, Cambridge CB3 9DZ, UK. Tel: +44 1223 330077. Fax: +44 1223 330048. E-mail: sql1@ula.cam.ac.uk Internet: http://www.cam.ac.uk/libraries/

Supreme Court Library, Queen's Building, Royal Courts of Justice, Strand, London WC2A 2LL, UK. Tel: +44 171 936 6587. Fax: +44 171 936 6661

There are also law libraries in each university which has a law school. For details consult the *Directory of British and Irish law libraries.*

Publishers and booksellers

Blackstone Press, 9–15 Aldine Street, London W12 8AW. Tel: +44 181 740 1173. Fax: +44 181 743 2292

BLAISE-LINE, BLAISE Information Services, British Library National Bibiographic Service, Boston Spa, Wetherby, West Yorkshire LS23 7BQ, UK. Tel: +44 1937 546585

Butterworths, Halsbury House, 35 Chancery Lane, London WC2A 1EL, UK. Tel: +44 171 400 2500. Fax: +44 171 400 2842. Internet: http://www.butterworths.co.uk/

Cambridge University Press, Edinburgh Building, Shaftesbury Road, Cambridge CB2 2RU. Tel: +44 1223 312393. Fax: +44 1223 315052

CCH Editions Ltd., Telford Road, Bicester, Oxon., OX6 0XD. Tel: +44 1869 253300. Fax: +44 1869 245814

Chadwyck-Healey Ltd, The Quorum, Barnwell Road, Cambridge CB5 8RE, UK. Tel: +44 1223 215512. Fax: +44 1223 215513

Context Ltd, Grand Union House, 20 Kentish Town Road, London SW1 9NR, UK. Tel: +44 171 267 8989. Fax: +44 171 267 1133

Datastream International Ltd, Monmouth House, 58–64 City Road, London EC1Y 2AL, UK. Tel: +44 171 250 3000. Fax: +44 171 253 0171

The Economist Bookshop, Clare Market, London WC2A 2AA, UK. Tel: +44 171 405 5531

FT Law and Tax, 21–27 Lamb's Conduit Street, London WC1N 3NJ. Tel: +44 171 242 2548. Fax: +44 171 831 8119

Hammicks Legal Bookshop, 191–192 Fleet Street, London EC4A 2AH, UK. Tel: +44 171–405 5711. Fax: +44 171 831 9849. Also at: Trinity Court, 16 John Dalton Street, Manchester M2 6HY, UK. Tel: +44 161 832 5557. Fax: +44 161 832 2189

HMSO Books, Publications Centre, PO Box 276, London SW8 5DT, UK. Tel: +44 171 873 0011. Fax: +44 171 873 8463. Prestel: 50040. Internet: http://www.hmso.gov.uk/

Photocopies Section Tel: +44 171 873 8455. For details of other HMSO bookshops in Birmingham, Bristol, Cardiff, London, Manchester and Norwich, ask at the above Centre. Parliament site: http://www.parliament.the-stationery-office.co.uk/

Incorporated Council of Law Reporting for England and Wales, 3 Stone Buildings, Lincoln's Inn, London WC2A 3XN, UK. Tel: +44 171 242 6471

Jordan Publishing Ltd., 21 St Thomas Street, Bristol, BS1 8JS. Tel: +44 117 923 0600. Fax: +44 117 925 0486

Kluwer Law International, Sterling House, 66 Wilton Road, London SW1V 1DE. Tel: +44 171 821 1123. Fax: +44 171–630 5229

Law Society Publications, 50 Chancery Lane, London WC2A 1SX. Tel: +44 171 242 1222. Fax: +44 171 404 1124

Lawtel, Centaur Publishing Ltd, St Giles House, 50 Poland Street, London W1V 4AX, UK. Tel: +44 171 287 9800. Fax: +44 171 287 8483

Legal Information Resources Ltd, Elphin House, 1 New Road, Mytholmroyd, Hebden Bridge, West Yorkshire HX7 5DX, UK. Tel: +44 1422 886277. Fax: +44 1422 886250

Legal Library Services Ltd., Stationers Hall, 89 Sherborne Road, Yeovil, Somerset BA21 4HE. Tel: +44 1935 20807. Fax: +44 1935 20807. E-mail: elaine@legliby.demon.co.uk

LEXIS-NEXIS, See the addresses given on page 19 in the **General sources** chapter.

LINK, Legalease, 28–33 Cato Street, London W1H 5HS, UK. Tel: +44 171 396 9292. Fax: +44 171 396 9300. E-mail: legalease@link.org. Internet: http://www.link.org/

Oxford University Press, Walton Street, Oxford OX2 6DP. Tel: +44 1865 56767. Fax: +44 1865 56646

Parliamentary Bookshop, 12 Bridge Street, London SW1A 2JX, UK. Tel: +44 171 219 3890

Shaw and Sons Ltd., 21 Bourne Park, Bourne Road Crayford, Kent DA1 4BZ. Tel: +44 322 550676. Fax: +44 322 550553

Stationery Office *see under* HMSO (above).

Statutory Publications Office, America House, 6–8 Spring Gardens, London SW1A 2BP, UK. Tel: +44 171 389 3213

Sweet & Maxwell, 100 Avenue Road, London NW3 3PF, UK. Tel: +44 171 393 7000. Fax: +44 171 393 7010. DX 38861.

Tolley Publishing Company, 2 Addiscombe Road, Croydon, Surrey CR9 5AF. Tel: +44 181 686 9141. Fax: +44 181–686 3155

List of works cited

Note: Attention is drawn to the note at the end of the general introduction to the United Kingdom giving information about the changes affecting UK government publications.

Abel, R.L. (1988) *The legal profession in England and Wales.* Oxford: Blackwell.

Aldridge, T.N. (1993) *Directory of registers and records* 5th edn. London: Oyez Longman.

All England Law Reports. (1936–) London: Butterworths. Also available on CD-ROM.

Alphabetical index to the local and personal Acts, 1850–1988. (1991) (4 vols) London: House of Lords Private Bill Office.

Annual practice. (1883–1966; 1995–) London: Sweet & Maxwell. Title varies. Superseded by *Supreme Court Practice* in 1966, recommenced in new format 1995.

Annual report of the Council of Tribunals. London: HMSO.

Annual statistical report. London: Law Society.

Archbold's criminal pleading, evidence and practice. (1822–) London: Sweet & Maxwell. Annual volumes with supplements and newsletter.

Atkin, R.R. (1961–) *Encyclopaedia of court forms in civil proceedings* 2nd edn. London: Butterworths. Includes *User's guide.*

BADGER DATABASE OF SUPPLEMENTARY LEGAL MATERIALS (1994–) Hebden Bridge, Legal Information Resources. Available on CD-ROM as part of CURRENT LEGAL INFORMATION.

Baker, J.H. (1990) *An introduction to English legal history* 2nd edn. London: Butterworths.

Bar directory. (1991–) London: General Council of the Bar and FT Law and Tax.

Berlins, M. and Dyer, C. (1994) *The law machine* 4th edn. Harmondsworth: Penguin.

BIALL (1983) Recommended holdings for law libraries. (Appendices VI-XI of the *Standards for law libraries*). *Law Librarian,* special issue.

Blackstone's criminal practice. (1991–) London: Blackstone Press.

BLAISE-LINE (available from the British Library).

BOOKFIND-CD (1991–) Twickenham: Book Data.

BOOKFIND-CD BUSINESS & LAW (199?–) Twickenham: Book Data.

Bowman, M.J. and Harris, D.J. (1984) *Multilateral treaties: index and current status.* London: Butterworths.

Bramwell, G. (1813–35) *An analytical table of the private statutes, 1727–1834* (2 vols). London: T. Davison.

Breem, W.W.S. and Phillips, S. (1991) *Bibliography of Commonwealth law reports* London: Mansell.

Britain [year]: an official handbook. London: HMSO.

British and Foreign State Papers. (1812–1968) London: HMSO.

British Government Publications: an Index to Chairmen of Committees and Commission of Inquiry. (1969–1984) London: Library Association. 4 vols.

British Library (1996) *Guide to libraries and information units in government departments and other organisations* 32nd edn. London: British Library.

British national bibliography. (1950–) London: British Library. Also available on CD-ROM from Chadwyck-Healey.

British Parliamentary Papers [dates covered]. London: [original publisher]. Repr. 1960? Readex Microprint.

Broom, H. (1971) *A selection of legal maxims classified and illustrated.* Reprint of 10th edn. (1939). London: Sweet & Maxwell.

Brown, P. (1989) Law reporting: the inside story. *Law Librarian*, **20,** 15–18.

Business Briefing. London: Association of British Chambers of Commerce.

Busy Solicitors Digest. London: FT Law and Tax.

BUTTERWORTHS COMPANY LAW BOOKS ON SCREEN (1994–) London: Butterworths. Available as CD-ROM or floppy disk.

Butterworths law directory (1985–) London: Martindale-Hubbell.

Butterworths legal services directory (1988–) London: Martindale-Hubbell.

Butterworths tax treaties. (1985) London: Butterworths. Looseleaf.

Cambridge Law Journal. (1921–) Cambridge, CUP.

Campbell, D.J. (1980) *Annotated bibliography on the legal profession and legal services 1960–78.* Cardiff: University College of Cardiff Press.

Catalogue of British official publications not published by HMSO. (1980–) London: Chadwyck-Healey.

CATALOGUE OF UNITED KINGDOM OFFICIAL PUBLICATIONS (1980–) London: Chadwyck-Healey and HMSO. Available as CD-ROM.

Chambers & Partners (1990–) *Directory of the legal profession.* London: Chambers & Partners.

Chloros, A.G. (1973) *A bibliographical guide to the law of the United Kingdom, the Channel Islands and the Isle of Man* 2nd edn. London: Institute of Advanced Legal Studies.

Chronological table of local and personal and private Acts, 1539–1974. (1985) London: HMSO (available on request from the Law Commission).

Chronological table of the Statutes, 1235–. (1870–) London: HMSO.

Civil Justice Quarterly. (1982–) London: Sweet & Maxwell.

The Civil Service yearbook. (1974–) London: HMSO.

CIVIL SERVICE YEARBOOK (available from HMSO).

Clinch, P. (1989) *Systems of reporting judicial decision making.* Unpublished PhD thesis, University of Sheffield.

Clinch, P. (1992) *Using a law library: a student's guide to legal research skills.* London: Blackstone Press.

Clinch, P. and McIlveen, M. (1995) Help with citing English law reports correctly. *Law Librarian*, **26,** 543–546.

Code of conduct of the Bar of England and Wales (1990–) London: General Council of the Bar of England and Wales. Looseleaf.

Commercial Bar Association directory. (1995–) London: Blackstone Press.

Committee Reports published by HMSO indexed by Chairman (1983–) London: HMSO.

Commonwealth universities yearbook. (1958–) London: Association of Commonwealth Universities.

COMPANIES HOUSE DIRECT (available from Mercury Business Intelligence).

Concise dictionary of law. (1994) 3rd edn. Oxford: OUP.

Cornish, W.R. (1987) Legal systems and legal literature. In Manual of Law Librarianship (1987), pp. 39–72.

Cornish, W.R. and Clark, G. de N. (1989) *Law and society in England 1750–1950* London: Sweet & Maxwell.

Counsel. (1985–) London: Butterworths.

County Court districts (England and Wales) index of place names. (1992) 14th edn. London: HMSO.

County Court practice. (1945–) London: Butterworths. Available on CD-ROM from the end of 1996.
Courts guide. (1985–) London: Blackstone Press.
Criminal Appeal Reports. (1908–) London: Sweet & Maxwell.
Criminal Law Review. (1954–) London: Sweet & Maxwell.
Criminal statistics, England and Wales. (1857–) London: HMSO/*Supplementary Tables* (1980–).
Croner's A–Z of business information sources. Kingston upon Thames: Croner Publications Ltd.
Cross, R. (1995) *Statutory interpretation* 3rd edn. J. Bell and G. Engle. London: Butterworths.
Cross, R. and Harris, J.W. (1991) *Precedent in English law* 4th edn. Oxford: Clarendon Press.
Current Law Case Citator. (1947–) London: Sweet & Maxwell.
Current Law Legislation Citator, 1972–1988, 1989–. (1986–) London: Sweet & Maxwell.
Current Law Monthly Digest. (1947–) London: Sweet & Maxwell. Also available on CD-ROM from 1996 as part of CURRENT LEGAL INFORMATION.
Current Law Statutes Annotated, 1948–. (1948–) London: Sweet & Maxwell.
Current Law Statutory Instrument Citator, 1993–. (1994–) London: Sweet & Maxwell.
Current Law year book. (1947–) London: Sweet & Maxwell. Also available on CD-ROM from 1996 as part of CURRENT LEGAL INFORMATION.
CURRENT LEGAL INFORMATION (1996–) London: Sweet & Maxwell. Monthly CD-ROM service.
Curzon, L.B. (1993) *Dictionary of law* 4th edn. London: Pitman.
Daily Law Reports Index. (1988–) London: Sweet & Maxwell.
Daily list of government publications from Her Majesty's Stationery Office. London: HMSO.
Daily Telegraph (newspaper). London: Daily Telegraph plc.
Dane, J. and Thomas, P.A. (1996) *How to use a law library* 3rd edn. P.A. Thomas and C. Cope. London: Sweet & Maxwell.
DATASTREAM (available from Datastream International).
De Smith, S.A. and Brazier, R. (1994) *Constitutional and administrative law* 7th edn. R. Brazier. London: Penguin.
Denton Hall Pensions Newsletter. (1992–) London: Denton Hall.
Dias, P.W.M. (1979) *A bibliography of jurisprudence* 3rd edn. London: Butterworths.
Dibb Lupton Broomhead Business Brief. (1993–) London: Dibb Lupton Broomhead.
The Digest: annotated British, Commonwealth and European Cases 3rd edn. London: Butterworths. 51 volumes.
Directory of British and Irish law libraries (1995) 5th edn. Hebden Bridge: Legal Information Resources for BIALL.
Directory of expert witnesses (1995) London: FT Law and Tax for the Law Society. Also available on CD-ROM.
Directory of grant-making trusts. (1968–) Tonbridge: Charities Aid Foundation.
The Economist. (1843–) London: The Economist.
Eddey on the English legal system (1996) 6th edn. P. Darbyshire. London: Sweet & Maxwell.
EIRLR (available from Industrial Relations Services.
Employment Gazette. London: Employment Department Group.
Encyclopeadia of forms and precedents other than court forms. (1985–) 5th edn. London: Butterworths. Includes *User's guide.* Available as CD-ROM from the end of 1996.
English Reports, 1220–1865. (1900–1932) London: Stevens. Repr. 1974, Professional Books.

Environment Law Brief. London: IBC Publishing.
Erskine May's treatise on the law, privileges, proceedings and usage of Parliament. (1989) 21st edn. C.J. Boulton (ed.). London: Butterworths.
Family Law (1971–) Bristol: Family Law.
Farrar, J.H. and Dugdale, A.M. (1990) *Introduction to legal method* 3rd edn. London: Sweet & Maxwell.
Feldman, D. *Civil liberties and human rights in England and Wales* (1993) Oxford: Clarendon Press.
FINANCIAL JOURNALS INDEX (1992–) Hebden Bridge: Legal Information Resources. Also available on CD-ROM from 1996 as part of CURRENT LEGAL INFORMATION.
Financial Times. (1888–) London: Financial Times Ltd.
Gazette. (1903–) London: The Law Society.
Griffith, J.A.G. (1991) *The politics of the judiciary* 4th edn. London: Fontana Press.
Griffith, J.A.G. and Ryle, M. (1989) *Parliament: functions, practice and procedures* London: Sweet & Maxwell.
The Guardian. London: Guardian Newspapers.
Guide to law reports and statutes. (1962) 4th edn. London: Sweet & Maxwell; Edinburgh: Green.
Guide to official statistics. (1996) London: HMSO. Available on 2 disks for PCs.
Guide to the professional conduct of solicitors. (1996) 7th edn. London: Law Society.
Halsbury's Laws of England. (1973–) 4th edn. London: Butterworths. Includes *Annual abridgment; Monthly review; User's guide.*
Halsbury's Statutes of England and Wales. (1985–) 4th edn. London: Butterworths.
Halsbury's Statutory Instruments. (1988–) Grey vols. London: Butterworths.
Hammick's legal catalogue (Annual) London: Hammicks. Available on CD-ROM from 1996.
Hansard: Official Reports of Parliamentary Debates. London: HMSO.
Hansard: Official Reports of Standing Committee Debates. London: HMSO.
HANSARD ON CD-ROM (available from Chadwyck-Healey.
Harris, D.J. and Shepherd, J.A. (1991) (eds) *An index of British treaties, 1969–1988.* London: HMSO.
Havers' companion to the Bar (1991–) London: Sweet & Maxwell. Also available through LAWTEL.
Hazell's guide to the judiciary and the courts, with the Holborn Law Society's bar list. (1985–) London: Hazell.
Hepple, B.A. and O'Higgins, P. (1981) *A bibliography of the literature on British and Irish labour law to 1978.* London: Sweet & Maxwell.
Herbert Smith Briefing. (1993–) London: Herbert Smith.
Hertslet's Treaties, 1827–1925. (1910–1925) London: HMSO.
Hines, W.D. (1990) *English legal history: a bibliography and guide to the literature* New York; London: Garland.
HMSO Daily list of government publications. London: HMSO.
HMSO DATABASE ONLINE (1976–) (available from either HMSO Books or BLAISELINE).
HMSO Government Publications. (Monthly list). London: HMSO.
HMSO Government publications. (Annual catalogue) (1922–) London: HMSO.
HMSO (1996) *Law: section list no. 74.* London: HMSO.
Holborn, G. (1993) *Butterworths legal research guide.* London: Butterworths.
Holdsworth, W.S. (1936–72) *History of English law* (17 vols) various edns. London: Methuen, Sweet & Maxwell.
Holland, J.A. and Webb, J.S. (1993) *Learning legal rules: a student's guide to legal method and reasoning* 2nd edn. London: Blackstone Press.
Home Office Research Studies. London: HMSO. Irregular.
House of Commons Parliamentary Papers. (1801–) Cambridge: Chadwyck-Healey.
Immigration Appeal Reports. (1972–) London: HMSO. Volumes for 1972–1992 repr. by John Rees Rare Books.

The Independent Law Reports. (1986–) London: Newspaper Publishing plc.
Index to government orders in force on . . . (1891–) London: HMSO.
Index to local and personal acts, 1801–1947. (1948) London: HMSO.
Index to local and personal acts: supplementary index, 1948–1966. (1967) London: HMSO.
Index to the statutes covering the legislation in force on . . . (1870–) London: HMSO.
Index to theses with abstracts accepted for higher degrees of the universities of Great Britain and Ireland and the Council for National Academic Awards. (1950–) London: Aslib and Expert Information. From 1970– available as CD-ROM.
Industrial Cases Reports (1972–) London: Incorporated Council of Law Reporting.
Industrial Relations Law Reports. (1972–) London: Eclipse Publications.
Intellectual Property Newsletter. (1986–) Sudbury: Monitor Press.
Investors Chronicle. (1860–) London: Financial Times.
Is it in force?: a guide to the commencement of Statutes passed since 1st January 1970. (1985–) London: Butterworths.
Jacob, J.I.H. (1987) *The fabric of English civil justice.* The Hamlyn lectures, 38. London: Stevens.
James, S. and Stebbings, C. (1987) *A dictionary of legal quotations.* London: Croom Helm.
Jeffries, J. and Miskin, C. (1990) *Legal research in England and Wales.* Hebden Bridge: Legal Information Resources.
JILT: Journal of Law and Technology. (1996–) (available from either: http://elj.warwick.ac.uk/elj/jilt or: http://jilt.law.strath.ac.uk/elj/jilt.
Journal of Business Law. (1975–) London: Sweet & Maxwell.
Journal of Legal History. (1980–) London: Frank Cass.
Jowitt, W. (1977) *Dictionary of English law* 2nd edn. 2 vols. and supplement to 1985. London Sweet & Maxwell.
Judicial Statistics England and Wales. London: HMSO. Annual.
JUSTIS FAMILY LAW (CD-ROM) (available from Context Ltd).
JUSTIS INDUSTRIAL CASES (CD-ROM) (available from Context Ltd).
JUSTIS WEEKLY LAW (available from Context Ltd).
JUSTIS WEEKLY LAW REPORTS (available from Context Ltd).
Kelly's. London: Reed Information Services. Annual.
Key British Enterprises. London: Dunn & Bradstreet International.
Kiralfy, A.K.R. (1990) *The English legal system* 8th edn. London: Sweet & Maxwell.
KOMPASS DATABASES (available from Reed Information Services).
Kompass register of British industry and commerce. London: Reed Information Services. 5 vols. Annual.
Latin words and phrases for lawyers (1980) London: Law and Business Publications.
Law Commission Consultation Documents. London: HMSO. Volumes 1–18. Professional Books (1981–1996).
Law Commission Reports. London: HMSO. Volumes 1–29. Professional Books (1979–).
Law Journal. (1822–1949) London: E.B. Ince.
Law Quarterly Review. (1885–) London: Stevens.
The Law Reports. (1965–) London: Incorporated Council of Law Reporting.
Law Society (1991–) *Solicitors' regional directories* (8 vols). London: Law Society.
Law Society's directory of solicitors and barristers. (1991–) London: Law Society.
Law under review: a quarterly bulletin of law reform projects. (1987–) London: Law Commission.
LAWTEL (available from Centaur Publishing Ltd).
The Lawyer. (1987–) London: Centaur Communications Group.
Legal 500: the client's guide to UK law firms (1988–) London: Legalease. Available on disk. Internet: http://www.link.org
Legal aid annual reports (England and Wales). London: HMSO.

Legal Aid handbook. (1950–) London: Sweet & Maxwell.
Legal Business. (1990–) London: Legalease.
Legal journals index. (1986–) Hebden Bridge: Legal Information Resources. Also available on CD-ROM as part of CURRENT LEGAL INFORMATION.
Legal research in the United Kingdom 1905–1984: a classsified list of theses and dissertations successfully completed for postgraduate degrees awarded by universities and polytechnics in the United Kingdom from 1905–1984. (1985) London; Institute of Advanced Legal Studies.
Legal Studies. (1947–) London: Butterworths.
Legal Times. (1994–) London: Legalease.
LEXIS (available from LEXIS-NEXIS).
LINK (available from Legal Information Network).
Linklater & Paines Property Law Now. (1994–) London: Linklater & Paines.
List of current legal research topics. (1953–1988) London: Institute of Advanced Legal Studies.
List of statutory instruments: together with the list of statutory rules of Northern Ireland for the month of . . . (Monthly) London: HMSO.
London county courts directory. (1990) 12th edn. London: HMSO.
London Gazette (1665–) London: HMSO. Daily.
The Macmillan Stock Exchange yearbook. London: Macmillan Press.
Major companies handbook. London: Extel Financial.
Manchester, A.H. (1980) *A modern legal history of England and Wales, 1750–1950.* London: Butterworths.
Manchester, A.H. (1984) *Sources of English legal history: law, history and society in England and Wales, 1750–1950.* London: Butterworths.
Manual of law librarianship: the use and organization of legal literature. (1987) 2nd edn. Aldershot: Gower.
Martin, J.E. (1993) *Hanbury & Martin modern equity* 14th edn. London: Sweet & Maxwell.
Masons Computer Law Reports. (1995–) London Masons. Also available at: http://www.strath.ac.uk/Departments/Law/diglib/mlr.html
Miers, D.R. and Page, A.C. (1990) *Legislation* 2nd edn. London: Sweet & Maxwell.
Modern Law Review. (1937–) Oxford: Blackwell.
Monthly Digest of Statistics. London: HMSO.
Mort, D. (1990) *Sources of unofficial UK statistics.* London: Gower.
Mozley, H.N. and Whiteley, G.C. (1993) *Law dictionary* 11th edn. London: Butterworths
New Law Journal. (1965–) London: Butterworths.
NEW LAW PUBLISHING (available from New Law Publishing or Legal Publishing Section. OUP).
New shorter Oxford English dictionary on historical principles. (1993) (2 vols). Oxford: OUP.
NEW UNITED KINGDOM OFFICIAL PUBLICATIONS ONLINE SERVICE (NUKOP ONLINE) (1995–) Southampton: Ford Collection of British Official Publications, University of Southampton. Internet: http://www.soton.ac.uk/~nukop/index.html
Offences of drunkenness, England and Wales. London: HMSO. Annual.
Offences relating to motor vehicles, England and Wales. London: Home Office Statistical Department. Annual.
Official Reports of Parliamentary Debates. See Hansard.
Osborn, P.G. (1993) *Concise law dictionary* 8th edn. London: Sweet & Maxwell.
Oxford English dictionary (1989) 2nd edn. 20 vols. Oxford: OUP. Also available as CD-ROM.
Oxford Journal of Legal Studies. (1981–) Oxford: OUP.
PARLIAMENT (available from Context Ltd).

Parry, C. and Hopkins, C. (1970) (eds) *An index of British treaties, 1101–1968*. London: HMSO.
Partington, M. (1976) *Welfare rights: a bibliography on law and the poor.* London: Pinter.
Paterson's licensing acts. (1872–) London: Butterworths; Shaw.
Personal and Medical Injuries Law Letter. (1985–) London: IBC Publishing.
POLIS (available from Context Ltd).
Prison statistics, England and Wales. London: HMSO. Annual.
Probation statistics, England and Wales. London: HMSO. Annual.
Professional standards bulletin. (1989–) London: Law Society.
Public General Acts and Measures, [1831–]. London: HMSO. (Annual)
Raistrick, D. (1993) *Index to legal citations and abbreviations* 2nd edn. East Grinstead: Bowker-Saur.
Raistrick, D. (1997) *Lawyers' law books* 3rd edn. East Grinstead: Bowker-Saur.
Report of the Commissioner of Police of the Metropolis. London: HMSO. Annual.
Report on the work of the Prison Department. London: HMSO. Annual.
Research bulletin. London: Home Office Research and Planning Unit. Biannual.
Research programme. London: Home Office Research and Planning Unit. Annual.
Restrictive practices cases. (1957–1972) London: Incorporated Council of Law Reporting.
Revised reports 1785–1865. London: Sweet & Maxwell.
Sanders, A. and Young, R. (1994) *Criminal justice.* London: Butterworths.
Sessional Information Digest. (1983/84–) London: HMSO.
Shaw's directory of courts in the United Kingdom. (Annual) Crayford: Shaw.
Shaw's directory of local authorities in the United Kingdom (1996–) Crayford: Shaw.
Shaw's directory of tribunals and regulatory bodies. (1995–) Crayford: Shaw.
SI-CD (available from HMSO and Context Ltd).
Singh, M.N. (1983) (ed.) *International maritime law conventions.* London: Stevens. 4 vols.
Smith and Bailey on the modern English legal system (1996) 3rd edn. S.H. Bailey and M. Gunn. London: Sweet & Maxwell.
Smith, N. and Miskin, C. (1990–) 2nd edn. *A legal thesaurus.* Hebden Bridge: Legal Information Resources. Updated to summer 1994, both in print and on floppy disk.
Snell's equity (1990) 29th edn. P.V. Baker and P. St. J. Langan. London: Sweet & Maxwell.
Social Security case law: digest of Commissioners' decisions. (1979–) London: HMSO.
Social Security Commissioners' decisions (1948–) London: HMSO. Various series.
Solicitors Journal (1857–) London: Longman.
SPTL (Annual) *Directory of members.* London: Butterworths.
SPTL (1995) A library for the modern law school: statement of standards for university law library provision in England and Wales. *Legal studies*, December.
Statistics of breath tests, England and Wales. London: HMSO. Annual.
Statistics of the misuse of drugs in the United Kingdom. London: Home Office Statistical Department. Annual.
Statute Law Review. (1980–) Oxford: OUP.
Statutes at large from Magna Charta to [various dates and editions].
Statutes in force. (1972–) looseleaf official rev. edn. London: HMSO.
Statutes of the Realm [1101–1713] printed from original and authentic manuscripts. (1810–28) ed. A. Luders *et al.* London: Record Commission.
The statutes revised, 1235–1948. (1951) 3rd edn. London: HMSO.
Statutory Instruments. (1948–) London: HMSO.
Statutory Rules and Orders. (1891–1947) London: HMSO.
Statutory Rules and Orders and Statutory Instruments revised to December 31, 1948. (1949–52) London: HMSO.
Stone's justices manual. (1842–) (3 vols). London: Butterworths.

Stroud, F. (1986) *Judicial dictionary of words and phrases* 5th edn. 6 vols. with annual supplement. London: Sweet & Maxwell.

Supreme Court Library (1996) *Transcripts of judicial proceedings: how to obtain them.* 2nd ed. Hebden Bridge: Legal Information Resources.

Supreme Court practice (1966–) 2 vols. and supplement. London: Sweet & Maxwell. From 1995– available on CD-ROM.

Sweet and Maxwell's legal bibliography of the British Commonwealth of Nations (1989) (2 vols). Reprint of vols originally published in 1955 and 1957 London: Rees.

Table of government orders, 1671–. (1891–) London: HMSO.

Tax cases. (1875–) London: HMSO.

Tearle, B. (1983) *Index to legal essays: English language legal essays in Festschriften, memorial volumes, conference papers and other collections, 1975–1979* London: Mansell.

The Times. London: Times Newspapers. Available at http://www.the-times.co.uk

Treaty series. (1892–) London: HMSO.

Tunkel, V. (1992) *Legal research: law-finding and problem-solving.* London: Blackstone Press.

Union list of legal periodicals. (1978) 4th edn. London: Institute of Advanced Legal Studies.

UNITED KINGDOM OFFICIAL PUBLICATIONS (UKOP) (available from Chadwyck-Healey).

Value Added Tax Tribunal Reports. (1973–) London: HMSO.

Vardon, T. (1840) *Index to the local and personal and private acts, 1798–1839.* London: Printed by J.L.G. and L.J. Hansard.

Wade, E.C.S. and Bradley, A.W. (1993) *Constitutional and administrative law* 11th edn. by A.W. Bradley and K.D. Ewing, with T. St.J.N. Bates. London: Longman.

Walker, M. (1981) *Reviews of United Kingdom statistical sources, volume XV, crime* London: Pergamon.

Walker and Walker's English legal system (1994) 7th edn. R.J. Walker and R. Ward. London: Butterworths.

Waterlow's solicitors' and barristers' directory. (1984–) London: Waterlow. Also available through LAWTEL.

Web Journal of Current Legal Issues. (1995–) Available at: http://www.ncl.ac.uk/~nlawwww/

Weekly Information Bulletin. (1978–) London: HMSO.

Weekly Law Reports. (1953–) London: Incorporated Council of Law Reporting.

WHITAKER-ROM: THE TFPL INTERNATIONAL CD-ROM DIRECTORY (1996–) London: Whitaker; TFPL.

Whitaker's almanack. (1869–) London: Whitaker.

Whitaker's books in print. (1874–) London: Whitaker. Title varies. Available as CD-ROM BOOKBANK, monthly, bi-monthly or annual.

White, R. (1991) *The administration of justice* 2nd edn. Oxford: Blackwell.

Words and phrases judicially defined. (1988) 3rd edn. 4 vols with annual supplement. London: Butterworths.

Worley, L. (1995) CD-ROMs of interest to the legal profession. *Computers and law* **6**, 23–26.

Zander, M. (1993) *Cases and materials on the English legal system* 6th edn. London: Butterworths.

Zander, M. (1994) *The law-making process* 4th edn. London: Butterworths.

Northern Ireland

GEORGE WOODMAN

Introduction to the legal system

Northern Ireland is a part of the United Kingdom. It has its own legal system and there is constitutional provision for a devolved legislature and executive who would exercise considerable powers under the ultimate authority of Westminster.

Constitutional position

HISTORY 1800–1920

Until 1800 the whole of Ireland was a separate Kingdom under the same Crown as Great Britain with its own separate legislature and its own legal system. By the Act of Union in 1800 it became part of the United Kingdom returning members of Parliament to Westminster. The legal system continued as before.

In the latter part of the 19th century and the first part of the 20th the major issue of British domestic politics was whether Ireland should have an increased measure of legislative control or Home Rule. The main part of the island expressed in every general election from 1886 a preference for Home Rule and at the same time a majority in the North East corner of Ulster expressed an equally strong preference for remaining as an integral part of the United Kingdom. In an attempt to meet the growing conflicting demands for Home Rule and maintenance of the Union, the Government of Ireland Act 1920 was passed.

It made provision for two jurisdictions of Northern and Southern Ireland. Both would have bicameral parliaments with wide legislative and executive powers. Westminster would retain ultimate responsibility and both parts of Ireland would return members to it. There would be a

Council of Ireland with jurisdiction over certain areas common to the whole of Ireland and members would be nominated to it by both parliaments. In practice only the provisions relating to Northern Ireland were enacted.

HISTORY 1920 TO DATE

In 1921 Southern Ireland left the United Kingdom. Northern Ireland remained within it, having its own Government and bicameral parliament based on the Westminster model, although the Parliament at Westminster retained ultimate responsibility. The Council of Ireland was never formed and its functions within Northern Ireland were, after 1925, performed by the Government of Northern Ireland. The last Parliament of Northern Ireland was prorogued in 1972 and dissolved in 1973.

It was replaced by a unicameral Northern Ireland Assembly with an Executive drawn from its members. Provision was also made for a Secretary of State for Northern Ireland, who would be a Minister in the British Government and who would exercise Westminster's continuing responsibilities in the Province. In practice this structure only operated from January to May 1974. From March 1972 to December 1973 and since 1974 Northern Ireland has been governed directly from Westminster by the Secretary of State for Northern Ireland and his junior ministers.

The basic constitutional authority for the devolved administration described above and for the Constitution of Northern Ireland is the Northern Ireland Constitution Act 1973. This replaced most of the provisions of the Government of Ireland Act 1920. The present Direct Rule administration is governed by the Northern Ireland Act 1974. The 1973 and 1974 Acts together furnish the basis of the constitutional law of Northern Ireland. Parliament at Westminster, provides for two levels of government:

1. Those matters which are common to the whole of the United Kingdom and which, even with a devolved administration in existence, would remain the responsibility of the United Kingdom Government. These include foreign policy and the making of treaties, currency and the appointment and removal of judges. These are known as Excepted Matters and are listed in full in Sch. 2 of the 1973 Northern Ireland Constitution Act. The same legislation applies in most of these areas to the whole of the United Kingdom. There is another class, of Reserved Matters, which could be devolved to a local Assembly. These include taxation and policing and are listed in full in Sch. 3 of the 1973 Act.
2. All other matters which would be transferred to a local Assembly and Executive.

International position

As part of the United Kingdom Northern Ireland is a full member of the European Union and EC legislation applies as in the rest of the United Kingdom.

Introductory works on the legal system and legal research

The court system, set up in 1921, has continued to operate unchanged. The standard work is Dickson (1993). This 'simply describes in non-technical language what institutions and processes currently exist to put the law into operation in Northern Ireland'. A useful short summary is included in Central Office of Information (1995) pp. 103–107, which covers the structures of both government and the courts. The preliminary note to *Halsbury's Statutes* Vol.31 also contains useful descriptions of statute law, government and courts. Holborn (1993) has a useful short section on Northern Ireland (paras 7.27–7.33).

The most substantial discussion of legal literature is the chapter by Desmond Greer in Twining and Uglow (1981) even though it is now rather dated. The annual reports and catalogues of the SLS (Servicing the Legal System) publishing programme of Queen's University, Belfast are also a useful research tool. The chapter on Northern Ireland law by Elizabeth Madill in Dane and Thomas (1996) is a valuable introduction for students.

Constitution

Statutes in Force: Constitutional Law, section 29:3:1, brings together all constitutional legislation relating to Northern Ireland. *Halsbury's Statutes* Vol.31 on Northern Ireland provides valuable annotated texts of the 1973 and 1974 Acts. It contains very useful texts of other legislation relative to the Constitution, including some Acts of the Parliament of Northern Ireland and the pre-1800 Irish Parliament. It also includes an excellent short introduction setting out the constitutional history sketched above. This historical background receives a fuller treatment in Hadfield (1989).

Statutes

Relating to the United Kingdom as a whole

Acts of Parliament usually contain a section entitled 'extent' saying whether or how far they extend to Northern Ireland. If an Act does not include a section on 'extent' one can assume that it does extend to Northern Ireland in its entirety. An Act always says if it does not extend to Northern Ireland or if certain sections do. The annual volumes of *Northern Ireland Statutes* include a table listing all Acts of Parliament passed during the year which apply in whole or in part to Northern Ireland.

Relating exclusively to Northern Ireland

ORDERS IN COUNCIL

The bulk of Northern Ireland primary legislation appears as Orders in Council. These are mostly Statutory Instruments made under the Northern Ireland Act 1974. They are numbered as Statutory Instruments but also receive a second numbering as part of a sequence of Northern Ireland Orders in Council, e.g.

Children (Northern Ireland) Order 1995, SI.1995/755 (NI2)

They usually appear in their initial form as *Proposals for a Draft Order in Council*, published by HMSO in Belfast. On their appearance *Proposals* are accompanied by an *Explanatory Document* setting out the purposes of the legislation, which often mentions the corresponding legislation in Great Britain and are frequently the only places where this is done in detail. They are issued directly by the government department sponsoring the legislation. The best way of tracing both *Proposals* and *Explanatory Documents* is through the *House of Commons Weekly Information Bulletin.*

The next stage is for a Draft Order in Council to be laid before Parliament. Since Draft Orders can only be accepted or rejected in their entirety by Parliament, their text is exactly the same as that of the Order.

When the Order is made it finally appears, published in Belfast, in a looseleaf format which enables them to be collected for the annual volumes of *Northern Ireland Statutes.* This series started in 1921. Until 1972 it consisted of the Acts of the Parliament of Northern Ireland and since then Northern Ireland Orders in Council. The 1974 Volume also contained the few Measures passed by the Northern Ireland Assembly. Until 1967 the spine title was *Public General Acts: Northern Ireland.*

Although they are numbered as United Kingdom Statutory Instruments, Northern Ireland Orders in Council are not included in the annual set of bound volumes. They appear in HMSO *Daily Lists* under the heading 'Northern Ireland Statutory Instruments' and can be traced through the *Monthly* and *Annual Lists of Statutory Instruments* under the heading 'Northern Ireland'. The best source for tracing both the publication and parliamentary proceedings on the various stages of Orders in Council is the section on 'Northern Ireland Legislation in progress' in the *House of Commons Weekly Information Bulletin.* This information is collected in the *House of Commons Sessional Information Digest* which appears after the end of every session of Parliament.

ACTS OF THE PARLIAMENT OF NORTHERN IRELAND

Northern Ireland Acts had their own sequence of chapter numbering and can be recognized as Acts of the Parliament of Northern Ireland by the words 'Northern Ireland' appearing in brackets between the word 'Act' and the date, e.g.

Poultry Improvement Act (NI) 1968 ch.12

They can thus be distinguished from United Kingdom Acts relating to Northern Ireland, which have 'Northern Ireland' in brackets appearing before the word 'Act'.

UNITED KINGDOM ACTS RELATING EXCLUSIVELY TO NORTHERN IRELAND

A number of Acts relate exclusively to Northern Ireland which can be recognized and cited as, for example,

Pension Schemes (Northern Ireland) Act 1993 ch.48

These Acts are included in the *Public General Acts*, and not in *Northern Ireland Statutes*.

Legislation before 1921 still in force. Various Acts passed before Northern Ireland came into existence in 1921 are still in force. These are Acts passed by: the Irish Parliament up to 1800; the English Parliament until 1707; the Parliament of Great Britain from 1707 to 1800; the United Kingdom Parliament from 1800 to 1921. They can be found in the *Statutes revised (Northern Ireland)* 2nd edn, and traced through the *Index* and *Chronological tables* to the Statutes of Northern Ireland.

Statutes revised, Northern Ireland 2nd ed. (1982). This is the main cumulation of Statute Law applicable in Northern Ireland. It provides a definitive text of legislation in force in Northern Ireland as it stood on 31 May 1981. It consists of 13 looseleaf volumes arranged chronologically. There are four preliminary volumes, A–D, which cover Acts of the Irish and British Parliaments to 1800 and of the United Kingdom Parliament to 1921. Volumes 1–9 cover legislation enacted in Northern Ireland and Orders in Council to 1981.

An annual cumulative volume, in a similar format, lists amendments and is updated to 31 December of the year covered. It also gives amendments to post-1981 Orders in Council. Before using the cumulation it is advisable to read the editorial notes in its introduction. Changes in fines and certain other details like changes in government departments responsible for administering legislation are not included in the amendments.

Not included in *Statutes revised* are any post-1921 United Kingdom Public General Acts. These are all in *Statutes in force*, including those relating exclusively to Northern Ireland.

Halsbury's Statutes

Halsbury's Statutes includes at the beginning of each Statute a note on application to Northern Ireland. If an Act has been amended for Northern Ireland by different legislation from that operating in England and Wales, references will be given to the amending legislation without annotations. Sections of Acts which apply only to Northern Ireland are updated in the same way as the rest of the text, as are references to Northern Ireland within sections.

Volume 31 covers Northern Ireland constitutional law. It also has useful annotated texts of legislation relating to the police, courts and emergency provisions.

Indexes and chronological tables

An *Index to the Statutes: Northern Ireland* is published every three years, covering all primary legislation in force in Northern Ireland. Excluded are certain Statutes dealing with such matters as the status of foreign nationals, charges on the United Kingdom Consolidated Fund and functions exercised outside Northern Ireland by bodies whose jurisdiction covers the whole United Kingdom. Subject headings, while similar to those in the *Index to the Statutes* for Great Britain, are not identical. A *Chronological table of the Statutes: Northern Ireland* is published every two or three years. This again covers all Northern Ireland legislation and is arranged in sections covering pre-Union legislation, United Kingdom legislation in force in Northern Ireland, Acts of the Parliament of Northern Ireland, Assembly Measures and Northern Ireland Orders in Council.

The *Index to the Statutes* for Great Britain indexes only those Acts which relate to the constitutional position of Northern Ireland. References to the application of particular sections to Northern Ireland are also indexed. There is a heading 'Northern Ireland' under which constitutional matters are covered followed by very useful cross-references.

Local legislation

Until 1921 local legislation for Ireland was included in the series of *Local and Private Acts*. Law Commission (1996) and Devine (1996) are the essential tools in tracing these.

The Parliament of Northern Ireland passed its own Local Acts, which are cited in a similar manner to Westminster Local Acts, e.g.

Methodist Church in Ireland Act (NI) 1928 ch.v

They were bound in at the very end of the annual volumes of *Northern Ireland Statutes* and can be found by the simple expedient of opening them at the back. Local Acts at the Northern Ireland Parliament are not included in Law Commission (1996) but their amendments to pre-1921 Acts are noted.

Some Local Acts of the pre-1800 Irish Parliament are still in force. Not included in *Statutes revised*, these can be located through the 20-volume collection of *Irish Statutes* published by the King's Printer in Dublin between 1786 and 1800.

Subordinate legislation

Statutory Rules

These form the main collection of subordinate legislation in Northern Ireland, being the equivalent of Statutory Instruments in the rest of the United Kingdom. Northern Ireland government departments make them under powers conferred by an Act of the Northern Ireland Parliament, an Order in Council, an EC Directive or a Westminster Act. The third and fourth are much less common than the first two. They appear in an annual numbered sequence and contain the words 'Northern Ireland' in brackets after such words as 'Rules', 'Regulations' or 'Orders' unless the initial wording renders this superfluous. They should be cited as

> Public Service Vehicles (Construction) (Amendment) Regulations (Northern Ireland) 1994 SR.1994 No.435

They are collected in a set of annual volumes entitled *Northern Ireland Statutory Rules*. They first appeared in 1922. Until 1973 they were known as 'Statutory Rules and Orders' (abbreviated SR&O).

An *Index to the Statutory Rules: Northern Ireland* is published every three years. Indexed by subject it is subdivided by the statutory powers under which the Statutory Rules have been made. It also provides cross-references to the *Index to Statutory Instruments* and indexes certain Prerogative Orders which are not Statutory Rules, giving references to their appearance in the *Belfast Gazette*.

Statutory Rules are included in the HMSO *Daily Lists* under the heading 'Northern Ireland Statutory Rules'. Since 1983 they have been listed and cumulatively indexed in the *Monthly* and *Annual Lists of Statutory Instruments* in a special section after the main text. This is the best source for tracing recent Statutory Rules.

Statutory Instruments

As with the Public General Acts, a large number of Statutory Instruments applies to the United Kingdom as a whole. A statement of extent is normally included. It can generally be assumed that if a Statutory Instrument is made under a section of an Act which applies to Northern Ireland, it applies to Northern Ireland itself.

Apart from Orders in Council, each year some Statutory Instruments are made which apply exclusively to Northern Ireland. These are made by Westminster government departments and be traced and cited in the same way as other Statutory Instruments. Examples include:

Capital Allowances (Corresponding Northern Ireland Grants) Order 1993 SI 1993 No.2705

Unlike Orders in Council, they are included in the annual volumes of *Statutory Instruments* and can be traced through the *Index to Government Orders*. The Annual volumes of *Northern Ireland Statutory Rules* include a table of all Statutory Instruments made during the year which extend to Northern Ireland. Those exclusive to Northern Ireland are in a separate section.

A number of pre-1921 Statutory Rules and Orders, which are still in force in Northern Ireland, are indexed in the triennial indexes to Statutory Rules and are included in the annual volumes for that period. The 1903 edition of *Statutory Rules and Orders Revised* is still useful for older Irish Statutory Rules and Orders in force.

Halsbury's Statutory Instruments has a brief section on Northern Ireland in the part of Volume 4 devoted to Commonwealth and other territories. Statutory Instruments relating to Northern Ireland are listed and summarized. References to Northern Ireland in other Statutory Instruments are also noted and indexed.

Commentaries

Apart from the references in *Halsbury's Statutes*, little exists in the way of commentaries or annotated texts of Northern Ireland legislation. SLS have produced a few annotated editions of individual Orders in Council. All new legislation is noted on a monthly basis in the *Bulletin of Northern Ireland Law* with brief annotations.

The Consolidation of the Companies Acts (NI) 1960–1983: table of derivations, destinations and correspondences (1986) is one of the few sources to list clause-by-clause correspondences with the relevant Great Britain legislation.

Treaties

The Government of the United Kingdom is the treaty-making authority for Northern Ireland and there are no separate sources of information relating to Treaties in Northern Ireland. In a few instances separate Northern Ireland legislation has been required to enable Northern Ireland to fulfil its Treaty obligations. These can be traced through the sources listed above.

Law reports

The principal series is the *Northern Ireland Law Reports* (NILR), which appear quarterly. In practice, two quarterly sections frequently appear together and time lags are frequent. The *Northern Ireland Law Reports* contain cases from the High Court and Appeal Courts in Northern Ireland and cases referred from them to the House of Lords.

To supplement the *Northern Ireland Law Reports* and include some details of a wider range of cases than can be reported in them, the *Northern Ireland Judgments Bulletin* (NIJB) has been published since 1970. Circulation before 1985 was very limited. It comes out monthly in mimeographed format with blue covers (hence it is also referred to as The Blue Book). Cases from NIJB may be cited in court. They are rather more up-to-date than the NILR. The time lag is less than two years at present.

The *Bulletin of Northern Ireland Law* contains useful summaries of court and tribunal cases and is probably the most up-to-date source of information on case law.

Northern Ireland cases are also covered in *Criminal appeal reports, Tax cases* and *Taxation reports*. Greer and Childs (1976) covers cases reported during the period 1921 to 1970 in the *Northern Ireland Law Reports, Irish Jurist Reports, Irish Law Times Reports, Irish Reports, Law Reports, Criminal Appeal Cases and Tax Cases*. A supplement goes up to 1975. The Bar Library collects transcripts of Judgments as they are given.

Cases for the period 1921 to 1924 can be found in the *Irish Reports* and *Irish Law Times Reports*.

Precedents

The decisions of the House of Lords are binding on Courts in Northern Ireland. Where there is a conflict it is accepted that English or Scottish House of Lords decisions must be followed in preference to those of the Northern Ireland Court of Appeal. The Northern Ireland Courts post-1921 are the successor to the Irish Superior Courts before that date.

Tribunals

Several tribunals produce reports of cases which are issued with a limited circulation, such as *Reports of Industrial Tribunals*. They may be consulted by personal callers at the Central Office of Industrial Tribunals.

Decisions of the Lands Tribunal are also available, for which McCluskey *et al* (1992) is an essential adjunct. Cases are arranged under subject headings and briefly summarized. They can be traced through the Lands Tribunal's own system of numbering.

The Planning Appeals Commission produces an occasional bulletin which summarises judgments, and Reports of planning inquiries are also published. Cases of both the Lands Tribunal and the Planning Appeals

Commission are reported in the cases section of *The Property Journal (Northern Ireland).*

The decisions of the Social Security Commissioners are subdivided by the matter being considered, e.g. Income Support and appear as part of a numbered series. Decisions of the Fair Employment Tribunal are summarized in Rubinstein (1995). The Equal Opportunities Commission has published in looseleaf format *A casebook of decisions on sex discrimination and equal pay*, which gives case summaries July 1989 to March 1992, together with case and subject indexes and is regularly updated.

Decisions of all these tribunals are reported in the *Bulletin of Northern Ireland Law.*

Legal texts in electronic form

LEXIS covers the *Northern Ireland Law Reports* and the *Northern Ireland Judgment Bulletins* and some unreported judgments. This leads to a degree of duplication as the same cases are published by both series. The text of legislation is not available in machine readable form. The full text of the *Bulletin of Northern Ireland Law* since 1986 is available on JUSTIS.

Government documents

Annual Report (Lay Observer, 1972–) covers complaints against solicitors and briefly describes other activities of the Law Society of Northern Ireland. *Annual Report Standing Advisory Commission on Human Rights* (1975–) appears as a House of Commons Paper. The Commission was set up under the Northern Ireland Constitution Act 1973 to advise the Secretary of State on cases of discrimination on religious or other grounds. In practice this brief allows it to range widely. Its annual reports examine the human rights implications of the operation of the law over a wide range of issues. Of particular interest are the annexes to the Report which include specially commissioned research on a variety of topics. For example, the 1993–94 Report includes material on among other topics, on remand procedures, fair employment and abortion. Often these annexes become well known in their own right and it is frequently not appreciated that they appear as part of this *Annual Report.*

Ombudsman Northern Ireland *Annual Report* appears as a House of Commons Paper. The Ombudsman is a recently established name for the holder of two posts, the Northern Ireland Parliamentary Commissioner for Administration and the Northern Ireland Commissioner for Complaints. For many years these posts have been held by the same person, who deals with maladministration in government departments and other public bodies. Until 1988 separate annual reports were published for both the Parliamentary Commissioner and the Commissioner for Complaints. Since 1989 it has been the practice to issue the one annual report. Selected cases are summarized.

Reports of the *Examiner of Statutory Rules* scrutinise for technical defects secondary legislation which is not subject to affirmative or negative procedure in Parliament. Reports are issued every six months or so. No report appeared from 1989 to 1993 and the 32nd report was never published.

Law reform in Northern Ireland is spearheaded by the Law Reform Advisory Committee, a body which reports to the Secretary of State for Northern Ireland. It has existed since 1989 and publishes directly an annual report which includes a list of its publications. Its secretariat is provided by the Office of Law Reform, the government body which in practice acts as the Northern Ireland equivalent of the Law Commission. Details of law reform projects in Northern Ireland with contact addresses are given in *Law under review*.

Encyclopedias

The *Digest of Northern Ireland law* (1995) is essentially a popular introduction. It has chapters by expert contributors on all aspects of Northern Ireland law. These are issued as separate fascicles for insertion in a slipcase and can be purchased individually or as a complete work.

Directories

The Northern Ireland Section of *Hazell's guide to the judiciary and the courts with the Holborn Law Society's bar list* lists judges and senior court officials with addresses and telephone numbers of the Supreme Court, Crown and County and Magistrates Courts, with a complete list of barristers.

The Civil Service year book gives addresses and telephone numbers of all government departments and agencies with brief notes on functions. The Northern Ireland chapter includes Northern Ireland government departments, the Northern Ireland Office and the Northern Ireland Court Services. The book is well indexed.

Bibliographies and Indexes

The best and most recent general bibliography of Northern Ireland law is to be found in Dickson (1993), which is arranged by subject following the chapter headings of the main text and covers material up to the year of publication. It lists wider legal publications not directly related to Northern Ireland law but helpful to an understanding of it.

Northern Ireland is covered by Chloros (1973), which surveyed each area of law and compared the position with England and Wales. Each section is followed by a short bibliography. It was, however, produced just before a time of major constitutional and administrative change in Northern Ireland, with the result that certain sections were out of date by the time it appeared. With the passing of time most of the legislation in the surveys has been superseded. However, the bibliographies contain material not picked up by other sources and the whole chapter still serves as a model of what might be produced.

The standard older bibliography is *Sweet and Maxwell's legal bibliography of the British Commonwealth of Nations Vol. 4: Irish law to 1956* (1957), Vol.4: Irish law to 1956. Items are listed by author or title in an alphabetical sequence, with a subject index in which items relating to Northern Ireland are indicated by (NI) after them. Bibliographical details are sketchy but this compilation is still worth using as a starting-point for historical legal research. Twining and Uglow (1981) lists publications after 1957 and is clearly arranged, with a very useful, although now rather outdated, list of secondary sources.

There is a generous section devoted to Northern Ireland in Breem and Phillips (1991). Of specialized interest is Sullivan (1985).

Periodicals

Current periodical literature relating to Northern Ireland is covered by *Legal journals index*. Official publications and some periodical articles are also covered by the *Bulletin of Northern Ireland Law*.

O'Higgins (1966) covers articles from periodicals published all over the world and includes much Northern Ireland material. As the title suggests, it covers the whole island of Ireland and both pre- and post-1921 jurisdictions. It is arranged under subjects which are not divided jurisdictionally. To locate items relating to Northern Ireland it is necessary to search through the subjects looking for 'Northern Ireland' in the title. In spite of this slightly 'hit and miss' quality notably if Northern Ireland is not mentioned in the title, it is a very valuable bibliographical source. It has two supplements. The first published in 1973, lists articles up to 31 December 1972. The second published in 1983, goes up to 1981 but does include some later material.

Current information sources

Journals

The principal source of current legal information is the *Bulletin of Northern Ireland Law*. Arranged under subject headings, it covers all Northern Ireland legal developments, summarizes legislation and notes recent cases from all courts. It also includes recent appointments or changes of address. There are ten issues a year and it is cumulatively indexed.

Current Law also includes a section on Northern Ireland. The *Northern Ireland Legal Quarterly* is a long-established periodical centred on Queen's University but draws contributors from a much wider field. It prints extended articles, shorter notes on developments and book reviews. Its subject coverage extends over the full range of legal topics. It must be stressed that while the NILQ is an academic journal published in Northern Ireland, Northern Ireland is by no means its major topic. *Frontline* also has useful articles on welfare law.

Some journals published outside Northern Ireland include articles on developments there, e.g. *Public Law* and *New Law Journal*.

The *Property Journal (Northern Ireland)* was originally published simply as a series of case reports, but its scope has now expanded to include articles on property law and related fields and book reviews.

News information

Scope, the journal at the Northern Ireland Council for Voluntary Action, covers developments in the field of social law. *Fortnight*, Northern Ireland's only general periodical, which actually appears monthly, covers developments mostly in the area of human rights. The Government Information Service known as the Northern Ireland Information Service issues regular press releases. Of particular legal interest are those issued on the publication of new legislation, particularly *Proposals for Draft Orders in Council*. These provide useful summaries and background information and also give the addresses from which the *Explanatory Documents* issued with the *Proposals* (see page 560) may be obtained.

Business and financial information

Northern Ireland financial services are required to register with the United Kingdom regulatory bodies. The government department dealing with business is the Department of Economic Development for Northern Ireland. It maintains the Northern Ireland Companies Registry and exercises its responsibilities for the promotion of inward investment and the development of larger home industry through the Industrial Development Board.

The *Belfast Telegraph*, Northern Ireland's evening newspaper, includes *Business Telegraph* as a supplement every Tuesday. This is a useful source of business news.

The Business Library in Belfast Central Library is an invaluable source for local company and other business information.

Statistics

The main statistical source for the Northern Ireland legal system is *Judicial Statistics for Northern Ireland*, which includes statistics relating to the criminal and civil business conducted by the courts. Subdivided under the different courts, each section has tables of statistics and a commentary. Detailed figures are given in most cases for the current year only. The commentaries contain some comparative figures for a ten year period.

Basic statistics relating to the Northern Ireland justice system are included in Section 4 of the *Northern Ireland annual abstract of statistics*. These include the security situation and legal business generated by it, prison and crime statistics and statistics relating to the Courts. Most of these cover a ten-year period. The *Annual Abstract* also lists useful contact points for further information and refers to publications covering the same fields in greater detail. It also gives basic economic indicators. Trade statistics may be obtained from the Department of Economic Development Statistics Branch.

Useful addresses

Professional bodies

Bar of Northern Ireland, PO Box 414, Royal Courts of Justice, Chichester Street, Belfast BT1 3JP, UK. Tel: +44 1232 241523. Fax: 44 1232 231850. DX 002 NR Belfast

The Law Society of Northern Ireland, Law Society House, 98 Victoria Street, Belfast BT1 3JZ, UK. Tel: +44 1232 231614. Fax: +44 1232 232606.

Government organizations

Companies Registry, Department of Economic Development, IDB House, 64 Chichester Street, Belfast BT1 4JX, UK. Tel: +44 1232 233233. Fax: +44 1232 231328

Department of Economic Development, Netherleigh, Massey Avenue, Belfast BT4 2JP, UK. Tel: +44 1232-529900. Fax: +44 1232 529550. For trade statistics Tel: +44 1232 529505

Director of Public Prosecutions for Northern Ireland, Royal Courts of Justice, Chichester Street, Belfast BT1 3NX, UK. Tel: +44 1232 542422.

Industrial Development Board, IDB House, 64 Chichester Street, Belfast BT1 4JX, UK. Tel: +44 1232 233233. Fax: +44 1232 231328

Northern Ireland Court Service Headquarters, Windsor House, 9-15 Bedford Street, Belfast BT2 7LT, UK. Tel: +44 1232 328594. Fax: +44 1232 439110

Northern Ireland Court Service, Management Information Branch, Windsor House, 9–15 Bedford Street, Belfast BT2 7LT, UK. Tel: +44 1232 328594 ext. 216

Northern Ireland Information Service, Stormont Castle, Belfast BT4 3ST, UK. Tel: +44 1232 520700. Fax: +44 1232 528473, 528478, 528482.
Northern Ireland Information Service, Old Admiralty Building, Whitehall, London SW1A 2AZ, UK. Tel: +44 171 210 6471/2/3. Fax: +44 171 210 6283/3785
Northern Ireland Office, Whitehall, London SW1A 2AZ, UK. Tel: +44 171 210 3000
Northern Ireland Office, Stormont Castle, Belfast BT4 3ST, UK. Tel: +44 1232 520700
Northern Ireland Office, Statistics and Research Branch, Room G34, Massey House, Stoney Road, Belfast BT4 3SX, UK. Tel: +44 1232 527534
Standing Advisory Commission on Human Rights, 55 Royal Avenue, Belfast BT1 1TA, UK. Tel: +44 1232 243987. Fax: +44 1232 247844

Law reform

Office of Law Reform, First floor, Lancashire House, 5 Linenhall Street, Belfast BT2 8AA, UK. Tel: +44 1232 542900. Fax: +44 1232 542909
Law Reform Advisory Committee for Northern Ireland, Lancashire House, 5 Linenhall Street, Belfast BT2 8AA, UK

Courts

Supreme Courts of Judicature, Royal Courts of Justice, Chichester Street, Belfast BT1 3JF, UK. Tel: +44 1232 235111

Tribunals and related bodies

Central Office of Industrial Tribunals, Long Bridge House, 20–24 Waring Street, Belfast BT1 2EB, UK. Tel: +44 1232 327666
Equal Opportunities Commission for Northern Ireland, Chamber of Commerce House, 22 Great Victoria Street, Belfast BT2 2BA, UK. Tel: +44 1232 242752
Fair Employment Commission for Northern Ireland, Andras House, 60 Great Victoria Street, Belfast BT2 7BB, UK. Tel: +44 1232 240020. Fax: +44 1232 331544
Fair Employment Tribunal, Long Bridge House, 20–24 Waring Street, Belfast BT1 2EB, UK. Tel: +44 1232 327666.
Independent Tribunal Service (Northern Ireland), Cleaver House, 3 Donegall Square North, Belfast BT1 5GA, UK. Tel: +44 1232 539900
Lands Tribunal for Northern Ireland, Royal Courts of Justice, Chichester Street, Belfast BT1 3JJ, UK. Tel: +44 1232 327703. Fax: +44 1232 237451
Lay Observer for Northern Ireland, Room 409, Clarendon House, Adelaide Street, Belfast BT2 8NR, UK. Tel: +44 1232-541541, ext. 41540
Northern Ireland Parliamentary Commissioner for Administration/Northern Ireland Commissioner for Complaints, 33 Wellington Place, Belfast BT1 6HN, UK. Tel: +44 1232 233821. Fax: +44 1232 334912
Planning Appeals Commission, Park House, 87–91 Great Victoria Street, Belfast BT2 7AG, UK. Tel: +44 1232 244710. Fax: +44 1232 312536.

Legal education

Faculty of Law, The Queen's University of Belfast, 28 University Square, Belfast BT7 1NN, UK. Tel: +44 1232 245133, ext. 3451/3452. Fax: +44 1232 325590. Internet: http://www.law.qub.ac.uk/
Institute of Professional Legal Studies, The Queen's University of Belfast, 10 Lennoxvale, Belfast BT9 5BY, UK. Tel: +44 1232 245133, ext. 5566. Fax: +44 1232 661192
School of Public Policy, Economics and Law, University of Ulster at Jordanstown, Shore Road, Newtownabbey, Co Antrim, BT37 0QB, UK. Tel: +44 1232 366346/366339. Fax: +44 1232 366847

Libraries

The Bar Library, PO Box 414, Royal Courts of Justice, Chichester Street, Belfast BT1 3JP, UK. Tel: +44 1232 241523. Fax: +44 1232 231580. DX 002 NR Belfast

Business, Science and Technology Department, Belfast Public Library, Central Library, Royal Avenue, Belfast BT1 1EA, UK. Tel: +44 1232 243233. Fax: +44 1232 332819.

The Library, Law Society of Northern Ireland, Law Society House, 98 Victoria Street, Belfast BT1 3JZ, UK. Tel: +44 1232 231614, ext. 46. Fax: +44 1232 232606

Northern Ireland Assembly Library, Parliament Buildings, Stormont, Belfast BT4 3SY, UK. Tel: +44 1232 521250. Fax: +44 1232 521716.

Law Library, Main Library, The Queen's University of Belfast, Belfast BT7 1LS, UK. Tel: +44 1232 245133, ext. 3609/3640. Fax: +44 1232 242127. E-mail: M.dudley@qub.ac.uk

Publishers

Butterworths, 35 Chancery Lane, London WC2A 1EL, UK. Tel: +44 171 400 2500. Fax: +44 171 400 2842

Context Ltd, Grand Union House, 20 Kentish Town Road, London NW1 9NR, UK. Tel: +44 171 267 8989. Fax: +44 171 267 1133

Fortnight, 7 Lower Crescent, Belfast BT7 1NR, UK. Tel: +44 1232 311337. Fax: +44 1232 232650

Frontline, Law Centre (NI), 7 University Road, Belfast BT7 1NA, UK. Tel: +44 1232 321307

Gill and Macmillan, Goldenbridge, Inchicore, Dublin, Republic of Ireland. Tel: +353 1 453 1005. Fax: +353 1 454 1688

HMSO, 16 Arthur Street, Belfast BT1 4GD, UK. Tel: +44 1232 238451. Fax: +44 1232 235401

Incorporated Council for Law Reporting in Northern Ireland, Bar Library, Royal Courts of Justice, Chichester Street, Belfast BT1 3JF, UK.

Judicial Statistics for Northern Ireland, Management Information Branch, 18th floor, Windsor House, Bedford Street, Belfast BT2 7LT, UK. Tel: +44 1232 328594. Fax: +44 1232 439110

LEXIS-NEXIS, See the addresses given on page 19 in the **General sources** chapter.

Northern Ireland Annual Abstract of Statistics, Northern Ireland Statistics and Research Agency, 2nd floor, The Arches Centre, 11-13 Bloomfield Avenue, Belfast BT5 5HD, UK. Tel: +44 1232 526082

The Property Journal (Northern Ireland), William McCluskey, Department of Surveying, University of Ulster at Jordanstown, Newtownabbey, Co Antrim, BT37 0UB, UK. Tel: +44 1232 365131, ext. 2930

Scope, NICVA, 127 Ormeau Road, Belfast BT7 1SH, UK. Tel: +44 1232 321244. Fax: +44 1232 438350

SLS Legal Publications (NI), School of Law, The Queen's University of Belfast, 21 University Square, Belfast BT7 1NN, UK. Tel: +44 1232 245133, ext. 3857/3507 or 335224

List of works cited

Note: Attention is drawn to the note at the end of the general introduction to the United Kingdom chapter giving information about the changes affecting UK government publications.

Belfast Telegraph. (1870–) Belfast: Belfast Telegraph Newspapers.
Breem, Wallace and Phillips, Sally (1991) (eds) *Bibliography of Commonwealth law reports*. London: Mansell.
Bulletin of Northern Ireland Law. (1981–) Belfast: SLS.
Central Office of Information (1995) *Britain's legal system.* 2nd edn. London: HMSO.
Chloros, A.G. (1973). *Bibliographical guide to the law of the United Kingdom, the Channel Islands and the Isle of Man* 2nd edn. London: Institute of Advanced Legal Studies.
Chronological table of the Statutes: Northern Ireland. Belfast: HMSO.
Civil Service year book. London: HMSO.
Criminal appeal reports. (1908–) London: Stevens.
Current law. (1947–) London: Sweet and Maxwell.
Devine, R. (1996) *Index to the Local and Personal Acts 1850–1995.* London: HMSO.
Dickson, Brice (1993) *The legal system of Northern Ireland* 3rd edn. Belfast: SLS.
Digest of Northern Ireland Law (1995–) 2nd edn. Belfast: SLS.
Examiner of Statutory Rules (1974-) *Reports*. Belfast: HMSO.
Fortnight. (1970–). Belfast: Fortnight Publications.
Frontline. (1991–). Belfast: Law Centre (NI).
Government of Ireland Act, 1920 London: HMSO.
Greer, Desmond and Boyd, Frederick (1981) Northern Ireland. In Twining and Uglow (1981) *Law publishing and legal information*, pp. 83-116.
Greer, Desmond and Childs, Brian (1976) *Index to cases decided in the Courts of Northern Ireland and reported during the period 1921 to 1970.* Belfast: Incorporated Council for Law Reporting. Supplement to 1975.
Hadfield, Brigid (1989) *The Constitution of Northern Ireland.* Belfast: SLS.
Halsbury's Statutes. 4th edn. Vol.31: Northern Ireland (1994 re-issue) London: Butterworths.
Halsbury's Statutory Instruments. (1986–) London: Butterworths.
Hazell's guide to the judiciary and the courts with the Holborn Law Society's bar list. Henley-on-Thames: R. Hazell.
Holborn, Guy (1993) *Butterworths legal research guide.* London: Butterworths.
House of Commons Sessional Information Digest. London: HMSO.
House of Commons Weekly Information Bulletin. London: HMSO.
Index to Government Orders. London: HMSO.
Index to the Statutes. London: HMSO.
Index to the Statutes: Northern Ireland. Belfast: HMSO.
Index to the Statutory Rules: Northern Ireland. Belfast: HMSO.
Industrial Court, Northern Ireland (1963–). *Numbered decisions.* Belfast: HMSO.
Industrial Tribunals (1965–) *Reports.* Belfast: Central Office of Industrial Tribunals.
Irish Reports. (1894–) Dublin: Incorporated Council of Law Reporting for Ireland.
JUSTIS (available from Context Ltd).
Lands Tribunal, Northern Ireland (1965–) *Decisions.* Belfast: Lands Tribunal Office.
Law Commission (1986–) *Law under review.* London: Law Commission.
Law Commission (1996) *Chronological table of local legislation* [to 1994]. London: HMSO.
Lay Observer for Northern Ireland (1972–) *Annual report.* Belfast: HMSO.
Legal journals index. (1986–) Hebden Bridge: Legal Information Resources.
LEXIS. (available from LEXIS-NEXIS).
List of Statutory Instruments. (Annual) and (Monthly). London: HMSO.

McCluskey, W.J., Deddis, W.C., and Curry, M.R. (1992) *Lands tribunal index*. Jordanstown: University of Ulster Dept of Surveying.
Madill, Elizabeth (1996) Northern Ireland law. In Jean Dane and Philip A. Thomas *How to use a law library* 3rd edn. pp.169-178. London: Sweet and Maxwell.
New Law Journal. (1882–) London: Butterworths.
Northern Ireland Act 1974. London: HMSO.
Northern Ireland annual abstract of statistics. (1983–) Belfast: Northern Ireland Statistics and Research Agency.
Northern Ireland Constitution Act 1973. London: HMSO.
Northern Ireland Judgments Bulletin. (1970–) Belfast: Incorporated Council for Law Reporting for Northern Ireland. From 1994– published in London by Butterworths.
Northern Ireland Law Reports. (1925–) Belfast: Incorporated Council for Law Reporting in Northern Ireland. From 1992– published in London by Butterworths.
Northern Ireland Legal Quarterly. (1936–) Belfast: SLS.
Northern Ireland Statutes. (1921–) Belfast: HMSO.
Northern Ireland Statutory Rules. (1922–) Belfast: HMSO.
O'Higgins, Paul (1966) *A bibliography of periodical literature relating to Irish law*. Belfast: NI Legal Quarterly. (1973) First supplement. Belfast: NI Legal Quarterly. (1983) Second supplement. Belfast: SLS.
Ombudsman Northern Ireland (1970–) *Annual report*. London: HMSO.
Planning Appeals Commission *Bulletin*. Belfast: Planning Appeals Commission.
Property Journal (Northern Ireland). (1988–) Jordanstown: University of Ulster.
Public Law. (1954–) London: Sweet and Maxwell.
Rubinstein, Michael (1995) (ed.) *Fair employment case law* 2nd edn. Belfast: Fair Employment Commission for Northern Ireland.
Scope. (1976–) Belfast: NICVA.
Social Security Commissioners (1973–) *Decisions*. Belfast: HMSO.
Standing Advisory Commission on Human Rights (1975–) *Annual report*. London: HMSO.
Statutes revised, Northern Ireland. (1982) 2nd edn. Belfast: HMSO.
Sullivan, Mark G. (1985) A legal system responds to political violence: Northern Ireland, 1969–1984. A selected bibliography. *Legal Reference Services Quarterly* 5(1), 91–103.
Sweet & Maxwell's legal bibliography of the British Commonwealth of Nations Vol. 4: Irish law to 1956. London: Sweet and Maxwell.
Tax cases. (1884–) London: HMSO.
Taxation reports. (1939-1981) London: HMSO.
Twining, William and Uglow, Jennifer (1981) (eds) *Law publishing and legal information: small jurisdictions of the British Isles*. London: Sweet and Maxwell.

Acknowledgements

I would like to thank David Smith of the Northern Ireland Bar Library for advice with computer-based legal texts and Alison Lorrimer of the Library, Solicitor's Branch, Department of Finance and Personnel, for assistance with the business section.

I am especially grateful to Mandy McIlveen, Librarian of the Law Society of Northern Ireland, for her rigorous examination of an earlier draft of this chapter. In its present form it has benefited greatly from her comments and suggestions.

Scotland

DAVID R. HART

Introduction to legal system

Five historic peoples to whom names can be given occupied what we now know as Scotland. When Duncan I succeeded his grandfather in 1034, he sought to rule over Picts, Scots, Britons, Anglo-Saxons and Norsemen, but it was many years before a strong central government was established. Throughout the 11th and 12th centuries, Scotland developed into a feudal kingdom, with the king as the ultimate source of secular justice. Petitions from subjects seeking justice were dealt with according to the advice of the king's council, and the growing number of these led certain lords of council to specialize in judicial work. Their sessions became the most important civil court in Scotland, a situation formalized in 1532 when James V founded the College of Justice.

The Scots Parliament also developed from the king's council, emerging as a legislative body during the 15th century. From the 12th century, officers known as justiciars travelled throughout the country administering criminal justice, but this system was superseded in 1672 with the establishment of the High Court of Justiciary. At the local level, sheriffs exercised civil and criminal jurisdiction as they do to this day.

The evolving legal system was subject to many influences, including the Roman law taught in the European universities where many Scots studied. As a result, Scots law is usually described as a mixed or hybrid system with features of both the civil and common law families of legal system.

In 1603 James VI of Scotland ascended the English throne, an event known as the Union of the Crowns, though the two kingdoms remained separate entities. Just over a century later and after lengthy negotiations, a

Treaty of Union was ratified, the Scots Parliament was dissolved, and on 1 May 1707 the United Kingdom of Great Britain came into being. Article XVIII of the Treaty provided for the continuation of Scots law. Whilst 'the Laws which concern publick Right Policy and Civil Government' might be made the same throughout the United Kingdom, no alteration was to be made in 'Laws which concern private Right, except for evident utility of the subjects within Scotland'. Article XIX safeguarded the future of the Court of Session (or 'Colledge of Justice') and the Court of Justiciary.

Although over the intervening centuries the distinctiveness of Scots law has been somewhat eroded, Scotland retains an independent legal system and the law can be quite different from that elsewhere in the United Kingdom. This is particularly true of criminal law and areas of private law, e.g. contract, family, and property law.

The late 20th century finds Scotland part of the UK of Great Britain and Northern Ireland. There are 72 Scottish seats in the House of Commons and, when appropriate, separate legislative provisions applying to Scotland are enacted. The Secretary of State for Scotland is responsible for most matters affecting the country and his duties are discharged mainly through the five departments of the Scottish Office. The principal government law officer in Scotland is the Lord Advocate. The Lord Advocate's Department provides the government with legal advice and is responsible for drafting or adapting legislation, while the Crown Office controls prosecutions.

The issue of Scottish self-government was revived in the 1990s, with the main political parties each adopting a stance. In 1993 the government issued a policy document, *Scotland in the Union: a partnership for good*, 'prompted by a recognition that there is in Scotland a real concern that the Union may not have been functioning as effectively as it might' (Scottish Office, 1993: 7). There have been subsequent changes in the arrangements for handling Scottish business in Parliament, the role of the Scottish Grand Committee has been enhanced, and certain functions have been transferred from departments in Whitehall to the Scottish Office.

Introductory works on legal system and legal research

Central Office of Information publications provide a convenient introduction to various facets of British life. *Britain: an official handbook* (annual) includes a concise chapter which draws attention to differences in the legal systems of England and Wales, Scotland, and Northern Ireland in specific areas of justice and the law. More detail may be found in Central Office of Information (1993a) *Britain's legal systems* which forms part of the Aspects of Britain series. Titles in this useful series are published at reasonable cost and include *The British system of government* (1994a), *Criminal justice* (1995), *Parliament* (1994b), and *Scotland* (1993b). Another short book aimed at a wide readership is Manson-Smith (1995), which is very clearly written and makes helpful suggestions for further reading.

There are two textbooks on the Scottish legal system. Walker (1992) may be regarded as the standard work with valuable chapters on the development of Scots law and its sources. At half the length, White and Willock (1993) is more introductory in nature.

Zweigert and Kötz (1987: 211) assert that 'Scots law deserves particular attention from comparative lawyers as a special instance of the symbiosis of the English and Continental legal traditions' but at this level, and with the ready availability of the texts mentioned above, books which are fundamentally comparative add little. Simmonds (1976) deals with the three main legal systems of the United Kingdom in one narrative but is now so dated as to be of limited use. Sheridan and Cameron (1992) accords Scotland a chapter of its own.

Most books on legal research are written for the market south of the border, and Scotland may be treated briefly alongside other foreign jurisdictions, as in Holborn (1993). Although Scotland has its own legal literature, many sources are shared with the rest of the United Kingdom and the approach taken in Dane and Thomas (1996) is a valid one. The principal chapters deal with using law reports, legislation, journals and government publications, while in a separate chapter Hart (1996) highlights specifically Scottish sources, referring to earlier paragraphs for fuller treatment of common elements. Mackey (1992) is a serviceable guide, but its compactness precludes the level of detail to be found in Dane and Thomas; nor does it contain worked examples. Duffy (1992), though not without merit, is uncompetitively priced.

Legislation

Public General Acts

Parliament in London is the supreme legislative authority in the UK and can make laws for the country as a whole or for any part of it. Acts of Parliament (also known as statutes) may be either Public General or Local and Personal, the latter as the designation implies being restricted in application to a particular area, organization, or group of people and not of wider concern. Where appropriate, Acts include provisions which enable others, principally Ministers of the Crown (e.g. the Secretary of State for Scotland) and local government, to legislate under the authority of Parliament. The form of delegated legislation most frequently encountered is the statutory instrument.

Public General Acts are taken to apply throughout the United Kingdom unless the contrary is expressly indicated, usually in a section towards the end of the statute but before any schedules. For instance, 'Subject to subsection (4) below, this Act extends only to Scotland' (1995 c.39 s.53(3)) or 'This Act extends to England and Wales only' (1995 c.41 s.6(2)). According to Craies (1971: 470), in the absence of such a stipulation, an Act may be held inapplicable in Scotland if it can be inferred, from terminology and reference to legislation, institutions, and procedure, that the legislature only considered the law and practice of England. It is usually clear from the title of an Act that it pertains wholly or mostly to Scotland, e.g. Criminal Procedure (Scotland) Act 1995 or Education (Scotland) Act 1996. However, such Acts may still contain provisions extending to England and Wales or Northern Ireland and may amend or repeal legislation of general application.

Prior to the Union of 1707, Scotland had its own legislature and many Acts dating from that time are still extant. The Statute Law Revision (Scotland) Act 1964 assigned short titles to the enactments it did not repeal and citation thereafter generally follows modern practice, e.g. Leases Act 1449 (or 1449 c.6) or Registration Act 1617 (or 1617 c.16). The most convenient sources are the single-volume reprint of those still in force after the 1964 Act, *Acts of the Parliaments of Scotland 1424–1707* (1966), and *Statutes in Force* (1972–). The twelve-volume *Acts of the Parliaments of Scotland 1124–1707* (1814–1844) is known as the Record edition. Older books may cite Scots Acts by volume, page and chapter number of the Record edition, e.g. A.P.S. II, 35, c.6 or A.P.S. IV, 545, c.16, and this is still used for Acts which have been repealed.

Acts with provisions which related to Scotland were published annually as *Public General Statutes affecting Scotland* (1848–1947), known as Blackwood's Acts. In 1876 legislation dating from the period 1707–1847, and still in force, was published in three complementary volumes. A similar enterprise, *Scots Statutes Revised* (1899–1902), was undertaken later in the century with a ten volume compilation covering 1707–1900, followed by annual volumes of *Scots Statutes* (1902–1949). Both series gave the titles of Acts not reproduced in full and included Acts of Adjournal and Acts of Sederunt (which regulate procedure in the Scottish courts). Occasionally they differed as to whether an Act affected Scotland and it therefore appears in one series but not in the other. The Acts of 1901–1948 were also published as supplements to *Scots Law Times* (1893–).

Scottish Current Law Statutes [*1949–1990*] (1949–1991) published all Acts of Parliament, differentiated from its English cousin only by a green binding and the inclusion of Acts of Adjournal and Sederunt. In spite of a common misconception, found for example in Holborn (1993: 46 and 199), only the initial volume of the English *Current Law Statutes* [*1948–1990*] (1948–1991) excludes Scottish Acts. Annotations first appeared in 1950. In 1991 the two versions merged, though Acts of Adjournal and Sederunt are no longer reproduced. A very useful development was the addition of Local and Personal Acts, including those relating to Scotland, from 1992.

The official text of an Act is that printed by Her Majesty's Stationery Office (HMSO) and Scottish Acts are published first individually, and subsequently in both the annual volumes of *Public General Acts and Measures* (1831–) and *Statutes in Force* (1972–). The subject groups and subgroups of the latter include several specific to Scotland; otherwise Scottish Acts are integrated with English or legislation of general application. All Acts still in force on 31st December 1948, with the exception of Acts of the Parliaments of Scotland, were brought together in *Statutes Revised* (1950).

Exclusively Scottish Acts are also found in the *Law Reports Statutes* (1866–). Only those sections of Scottish Acts which have an effect in England and Wales or Northern Ireland are reproduced in *Halsbury's Statutes* (1985–) and sections of general Acts affecting only Scotland are generally omitted.

INDEXES

The *Index to the Statutes* (irregular) lists extant primary legislation, including pre- and post-1707 Scottish Acts, under subject headings and subheadings. Many headings include a territorial designation, e.g. Adjudication, S where S stands for Scotland. The *Chronological Table of the Statutes* (irregular) lists the Acts of the Parliaments of England 1235–1706, Great Britain 1707–1800, and the United Kingdom from 1801 in a single sequence. The Acts of the Parliaments of Scotland 1424–1706 appear separately, showing whether they are wholly or partly in force. Painstaking reference works such as the *Index* and *Chronological Table* take time to prepare and both are seriously out of date by the time they are published.

COMMENCEMENT

As is the case with all Public General Acts, Scottish Acts come into force either through a provision within the Act itself, known as the commencement section, or by means of a subsequent statutory instrument, known as a commencement order. *Is it in force?* (annual) is particularly useful for checking whether an Act passed during the previous 25 years has been brought into force, but must not be relied upon as regards subsequent amendments or repeals. Apart from the International Standard Book Number (ISBN) and the colour of the cover, the Scottish and English editions are identical. The current status of Acts can also be determined through use of the *Scottish Current Law Statute Citator 1948–1971* (1972), *Scottish Current Law Legislation Citator 1988* (1989) and *Current Law*

Legislation Citators (1996). Once again the two versions differ only in title and appearance, and coverage extends from 1947 as regards England and Wales but only from 1948 in respect of Scotland. The statute citator in *Current Law Monthly Digest* and the legislation citator in the service volumes for *Current Law Statutes* (1991–) update this information.

Local and Personal Acts

Local and Personal Acts once dominated the Statute Book, particularly throughout the Victorian era when the transport and public utilities infrastructure was being developed. Whereas in 1895 there were 44 Public General Acts and 173 Local and Personal Acts, in 1995 there were 54 public but only 11 local Acts. In most cases, a working knowledge of British place names should be sufficient to determine whether a given Act applies to someone or somewhere in Scotland, e.g. Harris Tweed Act 1993 or Edinburgh Assay Office Order Confirmation Act 1996. The official text of a local Act is that printed by HMSO but Acts are only published individually, with no annual volumes. This may go some way to explaining why major collections of Scottish local legislation are few and far between. *Current Law Statutes* (1991–) extended its coverage to Local and Personal Acts in 1992.

The *Index to Local and Personal Acts* (1949) lists legislation passed between 1801 and 1947 under fifteen broad subject headings and is updated by a *Supplementary Index to the Local and Personal Acts* (1967) and the *Local and Personal Acts: Tables and Index* (annual). The *Index to the Local and Personal Acts 1850–1995* (1996) lists Acts by short title with additional references from particular place names. A joint publication of the Law Commission and Scottish Law Commission, *Chronological Table of Local Legislation* (1985), attempted to record the effect of legislation passed between 1925 and 1974 upon any of the estimated 37,000 Local, Personal and Private Acts. From 1974 onwards this information was included in the *Chronological Table of the Statutes* (irregular). A revised version of part of the Law Commissions' table (1996) covers 1797–1994, listing all local Acts and providing details of repeals of and amendments to those Acts. It is possible to update this by means of the Effects of Legislation table which forms part of the final volume of the *Public General Acts and Measures* (1831–) each year. Local, Personal and Private Acts will not feature in future editions of the *Chronological Table of the Statutes.*

Subsidiary legislation

Like Acts, statutory instruments (SIs) are classified as either general or local in application. General statutory instruments, like Public General Acts, may apply throughout the UK or only to specified parts of it. They may contain a statement of extent, e.g. 'These Regulations shall extend to England only' (SI 1994/1729 reg.1(2)) or extent may be inferred from the title, e.g. The Environmentally Sensitive Areas Designation (Ynys Môn) (Welsh Language Provisions) Order 1994. However, all SIs detail the statutory authority and powers under which they were made in a preamble and in cases of doubt the territorial extent of the enabling provisions will clarify the territorial extent of the instrument. It is usually clear from the title of a statutory instrument that it pertains wholly to Scotland, e.g. The Spirit Drinks (Scotland) Amendment Regulations 1995 or The Fossil Fuel Levy (Scotland) Regulations 1996. In addition, there is a subsidiary numbering sequence for instruments extending only to Scotland, e.g. SI 1996/1012 (S.113). However, as instruments without such a number may well extend to Scotland, the only practical function of this appears to be to allow subscribers elsewhere to exclude purely Scottish material. The provisions regulating procedure in the Scottish courts, Acts of Adjournal and Acts of Sederunt, are issued as general statutory instruments.

The official text of a general statutory instrument is that printed by HMSO and Scottish SIs are published first individually, and subsequently in the annual volumes of *Statutory Instruments* (1949–) unless revoked or spent within the year in which they were registered. All instruments of a general and permanent character still in force on 31st December 1948 were brought together in *Statutory Rules & Orders and Statutory Instruments Revised* (1949–1952). As *Halsbury's Statutory Instruments* (1952–) excludes Scottish provisions, the principal alternative source is the CD-ROM version SI-CD.

INDEXES

The *Index to Government Orders* (irregular) lists statutory powers to make delegated legislation and the instruments exercising those powers under subject headings and subheadings. As with the *Index to the Statutes*, many headings include a territorial designation, e.g. Summary Jurisdiction, Scotland. The *Table of Government Orders* (irregular) lists instruments chronologically showing whether they are wholly or partly in force. The current status of SIs can also be determined through use of the *Scottish Current Law Legislation Citator 1988* (1989) and *Current Law Legislation Citators* (1996), updated by the SI citator in the service volumes for *Current Law Statutes* (1991–). Unfortunately both *Index* and *Table* are very out of date by the time they are published. The monthly issues and annual editions of *List of Statutory Instruments* are vital for tracing recent legislation, with helpful information (including territorial extent) arranged under subject headings accessed through alphabetical and numerical indexes.

LOCAL STATUTORY INSTRUMENTS

Whereas all general statutory instruments must be published by HMSO, this is not the case with all instruments classified as local. For instance, instruments imposing temporary restrictions on road traffic or affecting civil aviation in a particular area, though forming part of the numbered sequence of SIs, generally remain unpublished. However, should it prove necessary to obtain a copy of an unpublished local SI, the SI Registrar at HMSO would be able to oblige. Only a select few of those local instruments which are published by HMSO are included in the annual volumes of *Statutory Instruments*. Thus if, for example, The Angus and City of Dundee Tourist Board Scheme Order 1995 is likely to be required, the copy originally issued must be retained. Libraries in a given area may have a collection of such SIs of local concern, or it may be necessary to approach HMSO directly. With the unpublished, the published but omitted, and the revoked or spent to contend with, it is hardly surprising that the user of *Statutory Instruments* frequently encounters missing instruments. A straightforward way to explain most of these gaps is to consult the *List of Statutory Instruments* which indicates whether a particular SI is general or local, published or unpublished.

Codes and commentaries

Although its development was influenced by Roman law and the civil law systems of Europe, Scots law is not codified. While legislation and judicial precedent predominate, certain systematic expositions of Scots law dating from the mid 17th to the early 19th centuries have been accorded the status of formal sources. These are known as Institutional writings, the term deriving from the *Institutes* of the Emperor Justinian, and include Stair's *Institutions of the law of Scotland* first published in 1681, Erskine's *Institute of the law of Scotland* first published in 1773, Hume's *Commentaries on the law of Scotland respecting crimes* first published in 1797, and Bell's *Commentaries on the mercantile law of Scotland* first published in 1800. These may be regarded as potentially decisive in the absence of higher authority, but only in those areas of law where social change over the intervening period has not diminished their persuasiveness. There is some debate on certain aspects of Institutional writings: which works are to be included in the canon, their actual persuasiveness, and even whether they should properly be referred to as authoritative rather than Institutional writings. An appraisal of their current standing will be found in White and Willock (1993) along with a listing of those works generally accepted as Institutional.

Treaties

Her Majesty's Government exercises treaty-making power for all of the United Kingdom.

Law reports, judgments, digests

In Scotland, civil cases are heard in the Sheriff Courts, the Court of Session and, as a final court of appeal, in the House of Lords. The Outer House of the Court of Session determines cases at first instance, while the Inner House is mainly a court of appeal. Criminal cases are heard in the District Courts, the Sheriff Courts and the High Court of Justiciary. The High Court is both a court of first instance and the court of appeal.

Although there is no official series of law reports, that is to say reports produced by a court, *Session Cases* (1822–) is pre-eminent. The volumes for 1821 to 1906 appeared in five series, known by the names of five editors (Shaw, Dunlop, Macpherson, Rettie, and Fraser). It is essential to understand that, in addition to cases decided in the Court of Session itself, *Session Cases* includes decisions of the House of Lords and the High Court of Justiciary. As a consequence, there are three separately paginated sequences of law reports in each volume. An explanation of the method of citation is to be found in Walker (1992) or Hart (1996). *Session Cases* is published for the Scottish Council of Law Reporting, but the 1995 volume marks a change of publisher. It remains to be seen what effect this will have, especially on the title's reputation for being slow to appear.

Scots Law Times (1893–) is published weekly during session, the issues cumulating into annual volumes. There is a News section, which includes articles, but the bulk of the publication consists of law reports. Cases decided in the Court of Session, the High Court of Justiciary, and the House of Lords preponderate in the Reports section which, since 1989, appears in a volume on its own. Unlike their counterparts in *Session Cases*, these reports do not appear in separately paginated sequences. However *Scots Law Times* does place Sheriff Court reports, reports of cases decided in the Scottish Land Court and the Lands Tribunal for Scotland, and reports of cases decided in the Lyon Court in separate sequences, published in the volume containing the News section. Before 1982 there was also a section entitled Notes of recent decisions to which reference may still be made. Refer to Walker (1992) or Hart (1996) for the method of citation. Each volume has its own indexes and cumulative indexes cover cases reported from 1961 to date.

The Law Society of Scotland publishes *Scottish Criminal Case Reports* (1981–) and *Scottish Civil Law Reports* (1987–). Most cases are accompanied by a commentary varying in length and value. Hitherto unreported criminal cases from 1950–1980 were published as a supplement (1987). Indexes to both titles cumulate over a five year period.

Greens Weekly Digest (1986–) summarizes those decisions of the Scottish courts brought to the attention of the publishers, arranged by subject, with judgments of legal significance reported subsequently at length in the *Scots Law Times*. The full text of an opinion is to be preferred for use in court. A cumulative index covers 1986–1995 with future editions planned.

Specialized series

There are few specialized series in Scotland, e.g. *Greens Housing Law Reports* (1996–), *Greens Reparation Law Reports* (1996–), *Scottish Housing Law Reports* (1991–), *Scottish Land Court Reports* (1982–), and *Scottish Planning Appeal Decisions* (1976–). Depending upon the subject matter, reports of Scottish cases may appear in one of those which proliferate south of the border, e.g. *Industrial Relations Law Reports* (1972–). If the case is of significance for the law of England and Wales, appeals from the Court of Session to the House of Lords appear in *Appeal Cases* (1876–). Such a case may also be carried by *Weekly Law Reports* (1953–) and *All England Law Reports* (1936–). For many years the *Scotsman* newspaper published a weekly law report selected by Green's. However it is editorial policy at present to target the fortnightly coverage of Law and Justice at a lay audience, and law reports as such no longer feature. A handful of Scottish cases appear in the *Times Law Reports* (1990–).

Precedence of series

If a case has been reported in more than one series, it is the convention that *Session Cases* should be preferred to *Scots Law Times*, which in its turn should be preferred to *Scottish Civil Law Reports* or *Scottish Criminal Case Reports*. Failing a citation from one of the above, other sources including unreported opinions may be considered (McBryde, 1996). Transcripts of unreported cases are available on application to the Deputy Principal Clerk of Session, the Deputy Principal Clerk of Justiciary, or the appropriate Sheriff Clerk. There is a standard copying fee.

Older cases

Court of Session decisions for the 17th and 18th centuries were recorded in various private reports, based upon collections of notes made by advocates, clerks or judges, e.g. Stair's *Decisions* (1683–1687). In addition, the Faculty of Advocates appointed reporters and published in three series a *Faculty Collection* (1752–1808, 1811–1828, 1826–1841). The third series is contemporaneous with the early volumes of *Session Cases*, but includes decisions not reported therein. By the early 19th century, many of the older reports had become scarce and advocate William Maxwell Morison therefore gathered decisions from all sources available at the time, arranging them by subject.

Morison's *Decisions of the Court of Session* (1801–1807), known as his *Dictionary of decisions*, was published in 38 volumes. The *Dictionary* covers the period 1540–1808 and is continued to 1816 by Morison's *Synopsis* (1814–1816?), with cases Morison omitted appearing in Brown's *Supplement* (1826). With its appendices, supplements and synopses, it can be difficult to navigate but Walker (1985: 387) is probably correct to claim that 'Few lawyers now look further back than Morison for the older reports'. Tait's *Index* (1823) covers the printed collections and the *Dictionary*, listing cases alphabetically in a single sequence by name of the pursuer. The notes at pp. 499–533 cast light upon the constituent parts of the *Dictionary* and are an invaluable source for information on the history of law reporting in Scotland.

As noted above, *Session Cases* (1822–) includes House of Lords decisions in Scottish appeals from 1850 and criminal (Justiciary) cases from 1874. There are, in addition, various private reports of these known by the names of their editors. *Scots Revised Reports* (1898–1909) reprinted many pre-1873 decisions claimed to be still of practical utility. The *Scottish Law Reporter* (1865–1924) contains mainly decisions of the superior courts. *Sheriff Court Reports* (1885–1963) were published as part of the *Scottish Law Review* and may be bound with that set. Walker (1992: 470–475) provides a helpful summary of Scottish law reports old and modern.

Digests

Digests not only provide subject access to case law but their indexes may also supply the researcher, armed only with the names of parties, with the full citation for a dimly remembered case. The *Faculty Digest* (1924–) analyses cases reported since 1868 in *Session Cases*, the private Justiciary reports, *Scottish Law Reporter*, and *Scots Law Times* (excluding Sheriff Court decisions). As well as an index of the decisions digested, it includes tables of cases judicially referred to, legislation judicially commented on, and words judicially defined. The *Faculty Digest* was intended to continue Shaw (1869) who digested supreme court decisions from 1800 and House of Lords decisions from 1726 and provided indexes of parties by pursuer and by defender. The *Scots Digest* (1908–1948) covers the supreme courts from 1800 and the House of Lords from 1707. A table of cases judicially commented on first appears in the second series, and a table of statutes is found in the later continuations.

For older cases, Brown (1829) digests all the decisions in Morison's

Dictionary, Brown's *Supplement*, and certain of the private Court of Session reports, thus covering 1540–1827. There are no additional indexes.

Whereas there is little if any difference between the *Current Law* statutes published on either side of the border, the situation as regards the year book is more complex. Again distinctively bound in green, *Scottish Current Law Year Book* [*1948–1990*] (1949–1991) started a year later than its counterpart. The bulk of the text is identical to the English edition, digesting English cases, legislation applicable to England only, and legislation applicable throughout the UK. Scottish cases and legislation applicable to Scotland only appear in a separate sequence, summarized under subject headings adapted to reflect Scots terminology. However, significant differences in the provision of subject indexes, and minor differences in coverage, mean that Holborn (1993: 200) and Dane and Thomas (1996: 119) are mistaken in regarding *Scottish Current Law Year Book* as the English edition with a Scottish supplement. No equivalent to the *Current Law Consolidation* (1952) was published in Scotland. The treatment of information pertaining to Scotland only has differed little since *Current Law Year Book* [*1991–*] (1992–) became an amalgam of the two versions. *Current Law Monthly Digest* is consolidated to form the year book.

Citators

Alternative versions of reports of decisions, and information on how those decisions were viewed in later cases, may be traced by means of the *Current Law* case citators. The subsequent history of a case is of particular significance in a legal system which regards judicial precedent as a source of law. *Scottish Current Law* [*Case*] *Citator 1948–1976* (1977) lists cases reported in England during 1947–1976, and those (regardless of date or jurisdiction) judicially considered in the English courts, alphabetically by the names of the parties. This information is, in effect, the English edition of the case citator. It is followed by a separate section performing exactly the same function for cases reported in Scotland during 1948–1976 and those (regardless of date or jurisdiction) judicially considered in the Scottish courts. As with the monthly digests and year books, users in Scotland or those interested in Scottish developments must consult both sections. In *Scottish Current Law Case Citator 1988* (1989) both sections cover 1977–1988. *Current Law Case Citator 1989–1995* (1996), perhaps appropriately, sandwiches Scotland between England and Europe. The cumulative table of cases in *Current Law Monthly Digest* brings the citators up to date.

Scottish cases cited in English courts appear in the *Law Reports Consolidated Index* (1961–) and *Law Reports Index* (annual). Selected decisions are noted, beside Irish and Commonwealth cases, in *The Digest* (1971–). *Legal Journals Index* (1986–) and the tables of cases provided in most textbooks can also be used to trace decisions.

Computer-based systems of basic legal texts

The online LEXIS database is of little value for Scottish legislation as it includes only those provisions of Scottish Acts which affect British or UK legislation. Even provisions relating to Scotland in Acts of general application prior to 1980 are excluded. The position is much the same for statutory instruments. However, there is an important Scottish case law library containing the full text of cases reported in *Session Cases* and *Scots Law Times* from 1944, *Scottish Civil Law Reports*, *Scottish Criminal Case Reports*, and unreported decisions from the Court of Session (Outer House from 1985, Inner House from 1982).

The summaries of Acts, information on commencement dates, repeals and amendments, and bibliographic details of statutory instruments on LAWTEL encompass specifically Scottish legislation. While the case law database does not cover any native series of reports, Scottish cases reported in *All England Law Reports*, *Times Law Reports*, and *Weekly Law Reports* are summarized.

As previously mentioned, SI-CD includes the full text of Scottish statutory instruments from 1987. There is also a CD-ROM version of all the reports from *Scots Law Times*.

Other important government documents

Statements outlining policies that the government intends to put into effect are drawn up by the appropriate department and presented to Parliament, e.g. Scottish Office (1994a). These are known as White Papers and are often preceded by consultative documents or preliminary versions, known as Green Papers, e.g. Scottish Office (1994b) and Scottish Office (1994c). White papers are usually a prelude to legislation. Scottish Office (1993b), for example, led to the Children (Scotland) Act 1995. Whereas White papers are almost always made available as parliamentary papers published by HMSO, consultative documents may only be available from the issuing department. Newspaper reports rarely provide sufficient bibliographic detail to identify such publications and a few telephone calls may be required. HMSO publications may be traced through the *Daily List* and the monthly and annual catalogues. The *House of Commons Weekly Information Bulletin* is invaluable for tracing legislation before Parliament, and *Scots Law Times* and *Current Law Monthly Digest* both follow the progress of bills and other parliamentary proceedings.

Other official publications include the *Annual report* (1992–) of the Scottish Legal Services Ombudsman, appointed by the Secretary of State for Scotland to investigate the handling of complaints against solicitors and advocates. This post replaced that of the Lay Observer for Scotland whose *Annual report* (1977–1991) was also issued by HMSO. The

Commissioner for Local Administration in Scotland, popularly known as the Local Government Ombudsman, investigates complaints of injustice arising from maladministration by various bodies, including local authorities, and issues decisions (not published) and an *Annual report* (1976–). The Scottish Legal Aid Board assesses and, where appropriate, grants applications for legal aid in both civil and criminal court proceedings. Its *Annual report* (1988–) is packed with statistical information. The Scottish Committee of the Council on Tribunals has statutory powers to review the working of tribunals and inquiries in Scotland. Unlike the report of its parent organization, the committee's *Annual report* (1986–) is not submitted to Parliament but covers issues relevant to Scotland in more detail. The *Annual report* (1992–) of the Crown Office and Procurator Fiscal Service chronicles the performance of the public prosecutors and the investigation of sudden, suspicious and unexplained deaths. Improved availability and quality of information on the administration of justice was one of the aims of the *Justice charter for Scotland* issued by the Scottish Office (1991).

The Scottish Law Commission was established in 1965 to promote the reform of the law of Scotland. It consults widely through the dissemination of *Memoranda* (1966–1987) or *Discussion Papers* (1988–) and subsequently issues reports containing proposals as part of its series of *Publications* (1965–). The latter are published by HMSO as parliamentary papers. Annual reports and programmes of law reform also form part of the *Publications* and a useful appendix to the annual report lists documents issued since 1965, whether published or unpublished. From time to time, consultative documents or reports are produced jointly with the Law Commission for England and Wales.

Encyclopedias, large collections and services

The most recent endeavour to produce a comprehensive statement of Scots law in modern times is the *Laws of Scotland* (1987–), generally known as the *Stair memorial encyclopaedia*. The annotated narrative is contained in 25 volumes and organized alphabetically under 136 titles. Each title has its own index and each volume has its own tables of legislation and cases. A consolidated index, table of legislation, and table of cases in three further volumes cover the whole work. Reissued text volumes, incorporating revisions, are scheduled to appear from late 1997. An annual cumulative supplement and a looseleaf service update the individual titles and the various tables. The looseleaf service also updates *Is it in force?* and contains a glossary of Scots legal terms which has been published separately.

Greens Litigation styles (1994–) provides a modern compilation of styles for use in the Court of Session and the Sheriff Court, including diskettes containing the styles as data files. There is a companion *Greens Practice styles* (1995–).

In the fields of private law and court procedure, the *Parliament House book* (1982–) is an indispensable aid to the Scottish lawyer. It draws together in looseleaf format primary and delegated legislation, practice notes, solicitors' rules, and guidance notes issued by government departments and public offices. Division C contains the rules of the Court of Session annotated by Morrison *et al.* (1995) which, like other parts of this five volume work, is also available separately.

Directories

Although some of the directories noted in the chapter on England and Wales include sections on other jurisdictions in the British Isles, for comprehensive coverage of Scotland it is advisable to rely on one of the national publications. The *Blue book* (annual) and *Scottish law directory* (annual), known as the White Book, contain substantially the same information. They provide addresses for courts, tribunals, legal societies and organizations, central government departments, public offices, and local government authorities and, where appropriate, indicate key personnel. Authoritative lists of advocates and solicitors are provided and law firms are listed both alphabetically and by location. Perhaps of particular interest is the information on Scottish solicitors in practice abroad. Whereas previously the *Blue book* for a given year was published some months earlier than the apparently equivalent *Scottish law directory*, making the latter the more up-to-date, from 1997 both new editions should appear in March/April. Selected information from the *Scottish law directory* became available on CD-ROM in 1996.

The Faculty of Advocates *Directory* (1992) of practising members and their services is intended to be an annual publication from 1996. Further information on prominent individuals may be gleaned from *Who's Who in Scotland* (annual).

Bibliographies

Unfortunately, there is no modern comprehensive legal bibliography of Scotland. Volume 5 of Sweet & Maxwell's *Legal bibliography of the British Commonwealth of Nations* (1957) covers the period to 1956 in a single author/title alphabetical sequence with occasional groupings of material such as Local Courts and Records. Although there are few bibliographic details, this is still a reliable source and particularly useful for dates of editions. Chloros (1973: 216) mentions cumulative supplements, but there is no evidence that any were published. The select bibliography in Twining and Uglow (1981) sought to update it, though details of titles described as forthcoming are not always reliable.

A more considered listing in Chloros (1973) aimed to cover the standard works used by the legal profession, but both the law and legal publishing in Scotland have moved on since 1973.

It can be difficult to disentangle Scottish material from the otherwise convenient Raistrick (1985). Some subject headings are subdivided by jurisdiction, e.g. Criminal Law, others are not, e.g. Family Law. Titles listed under Scotland are of a general nature and do not represent the sum total of Scots legal texts included in the bibliography. This problem may be addressed in the projected third edition.

The alphabetical arrangement of Breem and Phillips (1991) does not lend itself to an understanding of the development of law reporting in Scotland, but all the necessary information is there and the defect is easily remedied by recourse to the helpful summary in Walker (1992: 470–475). Of great value for older material is Stair Society (1936), especially perhaps the chapter by Leadbetter on printed law reports. An index to the volume was published separately in 1939.

Scottish Current Law Year Book [*1948–1990*] (1949–1991) lists books and articles published during the year and, from 1955, these appear more conveniently in a distinct section. The 1956 volume indexes articles from 1948–1956. In the early years, bibliographic details of books are brief. Though *Scottish Current Law Year Book* is not just *Current Law Year Book* by another name, the coverage of books and articles in the English edition is usually identical. The merged version *Current Law Year Book* [*1991–*] (1992–) arranges information on books by jurisdiction subdivided by its standard subject headings. Articles, however, are integrated though specifically Scottish subject headings survive. Law features in the *Bibliography of Scotland* (1976–1987) continued by the National Library of Scotland's online version, printed out annually in microfiche format. Library of Congress subject headings are utilized, though slightly modified to reflect Scottish usage and terminology. Analytical entries make essays in collections more accessible and the bibliography is particularly useful for more elusive items such as published lectures. Some articles on Scots law are included, mostly those published in non-legal journals.

Indexing and abstracting services

Legal Journals Index (1986–) covers all Scottish titles including the surveys of current law and procedure such as *Greens Civil Practice Bulletin* (1995–). The indexing is exemplary and the components of the subject descriptor string, which includes an indication of jurisdiction when this is significant, are rotated so that a quick check under Scotland reveals all the entries in that issue or volume. In addition to the subject index, there are author, case, legislation, and book review indexes.

Whereas the appropriate sections of the *Current Law* year books may be regarded as bibliographies in so far as they are a permanent record of books and articles published, *Current Law Monthly Digest*'s inclusion of commentaries alongside legislation and case law may be regarded as an alerting service.

Legal research in the United Kingdom 1905–1984 (1985) is a classified list of postgraduate legal theses and dissertations accepted by United Kingdom institutions. Not all Scottish universities offering higher degrees in Law are covered by *Index to theses* (1950–).

Dictionaries

The classic dictionary is Bell (1890), but Beaton (1982) and Duncan (1992) both offer adequate if more concise definitions. The *Glossary* (1992) published by Butterworths in conjunction with the Law Society of Scotland, first appeared as part of the *Laws of Scotland* encyclopedia. The greater part of this slim volume deals with general Scottish legal terminology and Latin words and phrases which, since Roman law was an important source of Scots law, are still in frequent use. Terms used in European Community law appear in a separate section. Trayner (1894) goes into greater detail on Latin maxims and phrases, a useful form of shorthand.

The English language, so far as it has been interpreted in the Scottish courts, is the subject of Stewart (1995). The author restricts himself to words judicially considered since 1946 and thus complements his predecessors Dalrymple and Gibb (1946). However, unlike the earlier work which is confined to judgments of the supreme courts, interpretations from the Sheriff Court are admitted.

The most convenient single aid to deciphering legal citations and abbreviations is Raistrick (1993). The sheer number of entries, some quite bizarre, often requires the exercise of common sense assisted by any dates or indication of jurisdiction provided. Raistrick deliberately includes abbreviations which are not the recommended forms, so the index must not be taken as a guide to the construction of citations. Being annual publications, *Current Law Year Book [1991–]* (1992–) and the *Current Law Case Citator* (annual) are useful supplements. *Legal Journals Index* (1986–) is another up to date source for possible meanings of abbreviations, although these are not always the forms suggested by the publisher and this can mislead the unwary. Some abbreviations remain too new for published sources, while others unaccountably slip the net.

Occasional reference to either Robinson (1987) or Grant and Murison (1986) may be helpful.

Other reference books

Walker (1980) includes useful entries on Scots law. Though flawed, Walker (1985) is a serviceable source for information on those who made a noteworthy contribution to the legal literature of Scotland.

Law as a career in Scotland is covered by the Law Society of Scotland (1993) and the Faculty of Advocates (1988a). It is also an aspect of MacQueen (1993).

The titles of the practice rules and regulations governing solicitors in Scotland look misleadingly like the titles of statutory instruments, e.g. Admission as Solicitor (Scotland) Regulations 1986. In fact, they are promulgated by the Law Society of Scotland and published as Division F of the *Parliament House book* (1982–), conveniently reprinted as *Greens Solicitors compendium* (irregular). Here too may be found the profession's code of conduct, as schedule 1 to the Code of Conduct (Scotland) Rules 1992, and practice guidance notes as issued. Ryder (1995) and Smith and Barton (1995) deal with the professional conduct of solicitors. Guidance for advocates is provided by Faculty of Advocates (1988b).

Current information sources

Journals, research reports

The *Journal of the Law Society of Scotland* (1956–) is published monthly and carries articles as well as news of interest to the profession. The quarterly *Scottish Law Gazette* (1933–) also has contributed articles and regular columns on developments in specialist areas, e.g. alternative dispute resolution. The Scottish Legal Action Group, which seeks to promote equal access to justice in Scotland, publishes *SCOLAG* (1975–) to stimulate debate and disseminate legal knowledge. *Scottish Planning and Environmental Law* (1993–), formerly *Scottish Planning Law and Practice* (1980–1993), includes notes on the circulars issued by the Scottish Office Environment Department, Historic Scotland and other bodies, which give guidance on new legislation or administrative procedures. A regular feature reports on recent decisions of the Local Government Ombudsman. All of the above regularly carry book reviews, case and legislation notes.

For over 100 years the *Juridical Review* (1889–) has been Scotland's academic law journal. Closely associated with the faculties of law in the Scottish universities since 1956, it is 'committed to analysing and discussing the principles and practice of the law of Scotland, as defined broadly, and as seen in its historical, philosophical and comparative context' (1988 J.R. 133). It now appears six times a year, but the average article is shorter. A centenary index was published in 1988. *Juridical Review* faces competition from *Scottish Law and Practice Quarterly* (1995–), intended to provide in-depth coverage of substantive topics in both public and private law, and the *Edinburgh Law Review* (1996–) which aims to set the law of Scotland in an international and comparative context.

Scots Law Times (1893–) has been mentioned already in the context of case law reporting, but it is an important source for articles, book reviews, Acts of Adjournal and Acts of Sederunt, and news items. Bulletins targeted at practitioners provide surveys of current law and procedure in the fields of business, criminal, employment, family, and property law, reparation, and the civil courts, e.g. *Greens Business Law Bulletin* (1993–). The other titles in this series are listed at the end of the chapter.

The Central Research Unit in Edinburgh provides a social research service to all Scottish Office departments and related agencies, including the Crown Office, Scottish Courts Administration, Scottish Courts Service, Scottish Law Commission, and Scottish Prison Service. Results are usually published, either by the Scottish Office in the Central Research Unit Papers series or by HMSO, e.g. Cameron (1995). Central Research Unit (1995) lists work in progress, recently completed work, and published reports.

News information

Scots Law Times is published weekly during session and carries news of recent developments. The fortnightly *Bulletin of Legal Developments* (1966–) briefly notes Scotland.

The *Scotsman* and *Scotland on Sunday* are respectively the daily and weekly national newspapers. It is worth noting that the CD-ROM version of these only reproduces material for which the newspapers hold the copyright. Therefore, while news reports of cases appear, the law reports themselves do not.

The press office at the Scottish Office handles press releases for all departments, but each department issues its own circulars.

Business and financial information

All limited liability companies registered in Scotland are required to file annual accounts and returns with the Registrar of Companies in Edinburgh. Such documents may be inspected at the offices of Companies House in Edinburgh, Cardiff and London. The *Edinburgh Gazette* (twice weekly) provides official notification of company liquidations and receiverships.

There are several trade specific journals, but *Business and Finance in Scotland* (1974–), *Business Scotland* (1974–), and *Scottish Business Insider* 1984–) are general in coverage. The *Scotsman* publishes a daily business supplement. A useful article by Coll (1993) indicates further sources of interest to lawyers.

The Scottish Business Information Service was launched by the National Library of Scotland in 1989 and is the national resource for company and market data.

Statistics

The Scottish Office releases criminal statistics through the criminal justice series of its *Statistical Bulletin* (1991–). Individual issues focus on particular topics, e.g. criminal proceedings in Scottish courts, firearms, homicide, liquor licensing, motor vehicle offences, prisons, and recorded crime. Statistics relating to the children's hearings system are published annually in the companion social work series. The Scottish Courts Administration compiles statistics relating to the business of the civil courts, and legal and public departments, and HMSO publishes them as *Civil Judicial Statistics Scotland* (annual). Annual reports of bodies such as the Scottish Legal Aid Board are another source for statistical information on the legal system.

On a more general level, the *Scottish Abstract of Statistics* (annual) is 'designed to be the major reference volume for statistics of life in Scotland'. Information on the Scottish economy, including statistics, may be found in the *Scottish Economic Bulletin* (biannual).

Useful addresses

Associations of lawyers

Faculty of Advocates, Advocates' Library, Parliament House, Edinburgh EH1 1RF. Tel: +44 131 226 5071. Fax: +44 131 225 3642. DX: ED 302

Law Society of Scotland, The Law Society's Hall, 26 Drumsheugh Gardens, Edinburgh EH3 7YR. Tel: +44 131 226 7411. Fax: +44 131 225 2934. DX: ED 1

Law Society of Scotland, 141–142 avenue de Tevuren, B-1150 Brussels, Belgium. Tel: +32 2 743 8585. Fax: +32 2 743 8586. DX: 1065 BDE, Belgium

Government departments

Crown Office, 25 Chambers Street, Edinburgh EH1 1LA. Tel: +44 131 226 2626. Fax: +44 131 226 6564. DX: ED 310

Lord Advocate's Department, 2 Carlton Gardens, London SW1Y 5AA, UK. Tel: +44 171 210 1010. Fax: +44 171 210 1025

Registrar of Companies, Companies House (Scotland), 37 Castle Terrace, Edinburgh EH1 2EB. Tel: +44 131 535 5800. Fax: +44 131 535 5820. DX: ED 235

Scottish Office, St. Andrew's House, Edinburgh EH1 3DG. Tel: +44 131 556 8400. Fax: +44 131 244 2683

Law reform

Scottish Law Commission, 140 Causewayside, Edinburgh EH9 1PR. Tel: +44 131 668 2131. Fax: +44 131 662 4900

Courts

Court of Session, Parliament House, Parliament Square, Edinburgh EH1 1RQ. Tel: +44 131 225 2595. Fax: +44 131 225 8213. DX: ED 306

High Court of Justiciary, Justiciary Office, Parliament Square, Edinburgh EH1 1RQ. Tel: +44 131 225 2595. Fax: +44 131 220 6773. DX: ED 306

Education

University of Aberdeen, Faculty of Law, Taylor Building, Old Aberdeen AB9 2UB. Tel: +44 1224 272440. Fax: +44 1224 272442

University of Dundee, Department of Law, Scrymgeour Building, Park Place, Dundee DD1 4HN. Tel: +44 1382 344461. Fax: +44 1382 226905

University of Edinburgh, Faculty of Law, Old College, South Bridge, Edinburgh EH8 9YL. Tel: +44 131 650 2007. Fax: +44 131 662 4902

University of Glasgow, School of Law, Stair Building, Glasgow G12 8QQ. Tel: +44 141 330 6075. Fax: +44 141 330 5140

University of Strathclyde, Law School, Stenhouse Building, 173 Cathedral Street, Glasgow G4 0RQ. Tel: +44 141 552 4400. Fax: +44 141 553 1546. DX: GW 23

Libraries

National Library of Scotland, George IV Bridge, Edinburgh EH1 1EW. Tel: +44 131 226 4531. Fax: +44 131 220 6662

Scottish Business Information Service, Scottish Science Library, 33 Salisbury Place, Edinburgh EH9 1SL. Tel: +44 131 667 9554 . Fax: +44 131 662 0644

University of Aberdeen, Law Library, Taylor Building, Old Aberdeen AB9 2UB. Tel: +44 1224 272601. Fax: +44 1224 273893

University of Dundee, Law Library, Scrymgeour Building, Park Place, Dundee DD1 4HN. Tel: +44 1382 344100. Fax: +44 1382 228669

University of Edinburgh, Law Library, Old College, South Bridge, Edinburgh EH8 9YL. Tel: +44 131 650 2043. Fax: +44 131 650 6343

University of Glasgow, University Library, Hillhead Street, Glasgow G12 8QE. Tel: +44 141 330 6740. Fax: +44 141 330 4952

University of Strathclyde, Law Library, Stenhouse Building, 173 Cathedral Street, Glasgow G4 0RQ. Tel: +44 141 552 4400. Fax: +44 141 552 1546

Publishers and booksellers

Butterworths, 4 Hill Street, Edinburgh EH2 3JZ. Tel: +44 131 225 7828. Fax: +44 131 220 1833. DX: ED 211

T. & T. Clark, 59 George Street, Edinburgh EH2 2LQ. Tel: +44 131 225 4703. Fax: +44 131 220 4260. DX: ED 286

W. Green, 21 Alva Street, Edinburgh EH2 4PS. Tel: +44 131 225 4879. Fax: +44 131 225 2104. DX: ED 238

Her Majesty's Stationery Office, 71 Lothian Road, Edinburgh EH3 9AZ. Tel: +44 131 228 4181. Fax: +44 131 229 2734

LEXIS-NEXIS, Butterworths, 35 Chancery Lane, London WC2A 1EL, UK. Tel: +44 171 400 2500. Fax: +44 171 400 2842

SI Registrar, HMSO Publications Centre, 51 Nine Elms Lane, London SW8 5DR. Tel: +44 171 873 8240

List of works cited

Attention is drawn to the note at the end of the general introduction to the United Kingdom chapter giving information about the changes affecting UK government publications.

Acts of the Parliaments of Scotland 1124–1707. (1814–1844) Edinburgh: HMSO. 12v. Revised editions of volumes 5 and 6 were published 1870–1872 and an index was issued in 1875.

Acts of the Parliaments of Scotland 1424–1707. (1966) 2nd edn. Edinburgh: HMSO.

All England Law Reports. (1936–) London: Butterworths.

Appeal Cases. (1876–) The Law Reports. London: Incorporated Council of Law Reporting for England and Wales.

Beaton, J.A. (1982) *Scots law terms and expressions.* Edinburgh: Green.

Bell, G.J. (1870) *Commentaries on the law of Scotland and on the principles of mercantile jurisprudence* 7th edn. Edinburgh: T. & T. Clark. 2v. Reprinted (1990) Edinburgh: Law Society of Scotland.

Bell, W. (1890) *Bell's dictionary and digest of the law of Scotland* 7th edn. Edinburgh: Bell & Bradfute.

Bibliography of Scotland. (1976–1987) Edinburgh: National Library of Scotland.

BIBLIOGRAPHY OF SCOTLAND. (Internet: library.nls.uk or http://www.nls.uk).

Blue book: the Directory of the Law Society of Scotland. (Annual) Edinburgh: Butterworths.

Breem, W. and Phillips, S. (1991) (eds) *Bibliography of Commonwealth law reports.* London: Mansell.

Britain: an official handbook. (Annual) London: HMSO.

Brown, M.P. (1826) *Supplement to the Dictionary of the decisions of the Court of Session.* Edinburgh: Tait. 5v.

Brown, M.P. (1829) *General Synopsis of the decisions of the Court of Session.* Edinburgh: Tait. 4v.

Bulletin of Legal Developments. (1966–) London: British Institute of International and Comparative Law.

Business and Finance in Scotland. (1974–) Bonnyrigg: Scottish County Press.

Business Scotland. (1974–) Glasgow: Peebles Publishing.

Cameron, G.D.L. (1995) *Personal injury litigation in the Scottish courts: a descriptive analysis.* Central Research Unit Papers. Edinburgh: Scottish Office.

Central Office of Information (1993a) *Britain's legal systems.* Aspects of Britain. London: HMSO.

Central Office of Information (1993b) *Scotland.* Aspects of Britain. London: HMSO.

Central Office of Information (1994a) *The British system of government* 2nd edn. Aspects of Britain. London: HMSO.

Central Office of Information (1994b) *Parliament* 2nd edn. Aspects of Britain. London: HMSO.

Central Office of Information (1995) *Criminal justice* 2nd edn. Aspects of Britain. London: HMSO.

Central Research Unit (1995) *Register of research.* Edinburgh: Scottish Office.

Chloros, A.G. (1973) (ed.) *A bibliographical guide to the law of the United Kingdom, the Channel Islands and the Isle of Man* 2nd edn. London: Institute of Advanced Legal Studies.

Chronological table of local legislation. (1985) Edinburgh: Scottish Law Commission. 2v.

Chronological table of local legislation. (1996) London: HMSO. 4v. Covers 1797–1994.

Chronological Table of the Statutes. (Irregular) London: HMSO.

Civil Judicial Statistics Scotland. (Annual) Edinburgh: HMSO.

Coll, J. (1993) Business and law: a guide to sources for Scotland. *Law Librarian*, **24**, 112–115.

Commissioner for Local Administration in Scotland (1976–) *Annual report*. Edinburgh: HMSO.

Craies, W.F. (1971) *Craies on statute law* 7th edn. London: Sweet & Maxwell.

Crown Office and Procurator Fiscal Service (1992–) *Annual report*. Edinburgh: Crown Office.

Current Law Case Citator. (Annual) London: Sweet & Maxwell.

Current Law Case Citator 1989–1995. (1996) London: Sweet & Maxwell.

Current Law Consolidation. (1952) London: Sweet & Maxwell. Covers 1947–1951.

Current Law Legislation Citators. (Annual) London: Sweet & Maxwell.

Current Law Legislation Citators. (1996) London: Sweet & Maxwell. Covers statutes 1989–1995 and statutory instruments 1993–1995.

Current Law Monthly Digest. (Monthly) London: Sweet & Maxwell. Superseded by year book .

Current Law Statutes [1948–1990]. (1948–1991) London: Sweet & Maxwell.

Current Law Statutes. (1991–) London: Sweet & Maxwell.

Current Law Year Book [1947–1990]. (1948–1991) London: Sweet & Maxwell.

Current Law Year Book [1991–]. (1992–) London: Sweet & Maxwell. Also available on CD-ROM.

Daily List. (Daily) London: HMSO. Superseded by monthly and annual catalogues.

Dalrymple, A.W. and Gibb, A.D. (1946) *Dictionary of words and phrases judicially defined, and commented on, by the Scottish supreme courts*. Edinburgh: Green.

Dane, J. & Thomas, P.A. (1996) *How to use a law library: an introduction to legal skills* 3rd edn. London: Sweet & Maxwell.

The Digest: annotated British, Commonwealth and European cases. (1971–) 3rd edn. London: Butterworths.

Duffy, V. (1992) *Legal research in Scotland*. Guides to legal research, no.4. Hebden Bridge: Legal Information Resources.

Duncan, A.G.M. (1992) *Greens Glossary of Scottish legal terms* 3rd edn. Edinburgh: Green.

Edinburgh Gazette. (Twice weekly) Edinburgh: HMSO.

Edinburgh Law Review. (1996–) Edinburgh: T. & T. Clark.

Erskine, J. (1871) *An institute of the law of Scotland* 8th edn. Edinburgh: Bell & Bradfute. 2v. Reprinted (1989) Edinburgh: Law Society of Scotland.

[*Faculty Collection* 1st series]. (1752–1808) *Decisions of the Court of Session*. Edinburgh: Bell & Bradfute. 14v. Covers 1752–1808. Revised editions of the first 4 volumes were published 1787–1788. Publishers vary.

[*Faculty Collection* 2nd series]. (1811–1828) *Decisions of the first and second divisions of the Court of Session*. Edinburgh: Manners & Miller. 7v. Covers 1808–1825. Revised editions of the first 2 volumes were published 1815–1819.

[*Faculty Collection* 3rd series]. (1826–1841) *Decisions of the Court of Session*. Edinburgh: Anderson. 16v. Covers 1825–1841. Publishers vary.

[*Faculty Digest*]. (1924–) *An analytical digest of cases decided in the supreme courts of Scotland and, on appeal, in the House of Lords*. Edinburgh: T. & T. Clark. Covers 1868– . Publishers vary.

Faculty of Advocates (1988a) *A career in advocacy*. Edinburgh: Faculty of Advocates.

Faculty of Advocates (1988b) *Guide to the professional conduct of advocates*. Edinburgh: Faculty of Advocates.

Faculty of Advocates (1992) *Directory*. Edinburgh: Faculty of Advocates.

Glossary: Scottish legal terms and Latin maxims and European Community legal terms. (1992) Edinburgh: Butterworths.

Grant, W. and Murison, D.D. (1986) *The compact Scottish national dictionary*. Aberdeen: Aberdeen University Press.

Greens Business Law Bulletin. (1993–) Edinburgh: Green.

Greens Civil Practice Bulletin. (1995–) Edinburgh: Green.

Greens Criminal Law Bulletin. (1993–) Edinburgh: Green.

Greens Employment Law Bulletin. (1994–) Edinburgh: Green.
Greens Environmental Law Bulletin. (1994–1995) Edinburgh: Green.
Greens Family Law Bulletin. (1993–) Edinburgh: Green.
Greens Housing Law Reports. (1996–) Edinburgh: Green.
Greens Litigation styles. (1994–) Edinburgh: Green. Looseleaf.
Greens Practice styles. (1995–) Edinburgh: Green. Looseleaf.
Greens Property Law Bulletin. (1993–) Edinburgh: Green.
Greens Reparation Bulletin. (1995–) Edinburgh: Green.
Greens Reparation Law Reports. (1996–) Edinburgh: Green.
Greens Solicitors compendium. (Irregular) Edinburgh: Green.
Greens Weekly Digest. (1986–) Edinburgh: Green.
Greens Weekly Digest Index 1986–1995. (1996) Edinburgh: Green.
Halsbury's Statutes of England and Wales. (1985–) 4th edn. London: Butterworths.
Halsbury's Statutory Instruments. (1952–) London: Butterworths.
Hart, D.R. (1996) Scots law. In Dane and Thomas (1996), pp. 154–163.
Holborn, G. (1993) *Butterworths legal research guide*. London: Butterworths.
House of Commons Weekly Information Bulletin. (Weekly) London: HMSO.
HOUSE OF COMMONS WEEKLY INFORMATION BULLETIN. (Internet: http://www.parliament.uk).
Hume, D. (1844) *Commentaries on the law of Scotland, respecting crimes* 4th edn. Edinburgh: Bell & Bradfute. 2v. Reprinted (1986) Edinburgh: Law Society of Scotland.
Index to Government Orders. (Irregular) London: HMSO.
Index to Local and Personal Acts. (1949) London: HMSO. Covers 1801–1947.
Index to the Local and Personal Acts 1850–1995. (1996) London: HMSO. 4v.
Index to the Statutes. (Irregular) London: HMSO.
Index to theses accepted for higher degrees by the universities of Great Britain and Ireland. (1950–) London: Aslib.
Industrial Relations Law Reports. (1972–) London: IRS.
Is it in force?. (Annual) London: Butterworths.
Journal of the Law Society of Scotland. (1956–) Edinburgh: Law Society of Scotland.
Juridical Review. (1889–) Edinburgh: Green.
Juridical Review Centenary Index. (1988) Edinburgh: Green.
Law Reports Consolidated Index (1961–) London: Incorporated Council of Law Reporting for England and Wales. Covers 1951–.
Law Reports Index. (Annual). London: Incorporated Council of Law Reporting for England and Wales. Covers 1991– .
Law Reports Statutes. (1866–) London: Incorporated Council of Law Reporting for England and Wales.
Law Society of Scotland (1993) *So you want to be a lawyer?* Edinburgh: Law Society of Scotland.
Laws of Scotland: Stair memorial encyclopaedia. (1987–) Edinburgh: Butterworths.
LAWTEL (available from Centaur Publishing).
Lay Observer for Scotland (1977–1991) *Annual report*. Edinburgh: HMSO.
Leadbetter, J.S. (1936) The printed law reports 1540–1935. In Stair Society (1936), pp. 42–58.
Legal Journals Index. (1986–) Hebden Bridge: Legal Information Resources. Also available on CD-ROM.
Legal research in the United Kingdom 1905–1984. (1985) London: Institute of Advanced Legal Studies.
LEXIS (available from LEXIS-NEXIS).
List of Statutory Instruments together with the List of Statutory Rules for Northern Ireland. (Monthly) London: HMSO. Superseded by annual edition.
Local and Personal Acts: tables and index. (Annual) London: HMSO.
McBryde, W.W. (1996) The citation of cases in court. In *Scots law into the 21st century: essays in honour of W.A. Wilson*, ed. H.L. MacQueen, pp. 170–181. Edinburgh: Green.

Mackey, D.D. (1992) *How to use a Scottish law library*. Edinburgh: Green.
MacQueen, H.L. (1993) *Studying Scots law*. Edinburgh: Butterworths.
Manson-Smith, D. (1995) *The legal system of Scotland*. Edinburgh: HMSO.
Morison, W.M. (1801–1807) *The decisions of the Court of Session, from its institution to the present time, digested under proper heads, in the form of a dictionary*. Edinburgh: Bell & Bradfute. 38v.
Morison, W.M. (1814–1816?) *Synopsis of the decisions of the Court of Session, from the commencement of its sittings in two divisions, in continuation of the Dictionary of decisions*. Edinburgh: Anderson. 2v.
Morrison, N. *et al.* (1995) (eds) *Greens Annotated rules of the Court of Session*. Edinburgh: Green.
Parliament House book: statutes and regulations for Scottish lawyers. (1982–) Edinburgh: Green. Looseleaf.
Public General Acts and Measures. (1831–) London: HMSO. Title varies.
Public General Statutes affecting Scotland [1847–1947]. (1848–1947) Edinburgh: Blackwood.
Public General Statutes affecting Scotland. (1876) Edinburgh: Blackwood. 3v. Covers 1707–1847.
Raistrick, D. (1985) *Lawyers' law books: a practical index to legal literature* 2nd edn. Abingdon: Professional Books.
Raistrick, D. (1993) *Index to legal citations and abbreviations* 2nd edn. London: Bowker-Saur.
Robinson, M. (1987) *The concise Scots dictionary* New edn. Aberdeen: Aberdeen University Press.
Ryder, J. (1995) *Professional conduct for Scottish solicitors*. Edinburgh: Butterworths.
SCOLAG. (1975–) Glasgow: Scottish Legal Action Group.
Scotland on Sunday. (Weekly) Edinburgh: Scotsman Publications. Also available on CD-ROM.
Scots Digest. (1908–1948). Edinburgh: Green. Covers 1800–1947.
Scots Law Times. (1893–) Edinburgh: Green. Case reports also available on CD-ROM.
Scots Law Times Index 1961–1990. (1993) Edinburgh: Green. With supplements covering cases reported 1991–.
Scots Revised Reports. (1898–1909) Edinburgh: Green. 45v.
Scots Statutes [1901–1948]. (1902–1949) Edinburgh: Green.
Scots Statutes Revised. (1899–1902) Edinburgh: Green. 10v. Covers 1707–1900.
The Scotsman. (Daily) Edinburgh: Scotsman Publications. Also available on CD-ROM.
Scottish Abstract of Statistics. (Annual) Edinburgh: Scottish Office.
Scottish Business Insider. (1984–) Edinburgh: Insider Publications.
Scottish Civil Law Reports. (1987–) Edinburgh: Law Society of Scotland.
Scottish Committee of the Council on Tribunals (1986–) *Annual report*. Edinburgh: Scottish Committee of the Council on Tribunals.
Scottish Criminal Case Reports. (1981–) Edinburgh: Law Society of Scotland.
Scottish Criminal Case Reports Supplement (1950–80). (1987) Edinburgh: Law Society of Scotland.
Scottish Current Law [Case] Citator 1948–1976. (1977) Edinburgh: Green.
Scottish Current Law Case Citator 1988. (1989) Edinburgh: Green. Covers 1977–1988.
Scottish Current Law Legislation Citator 1988. (1989) Edinburgh: Green. Covers statutes 1972–1988 and statutory instruments 1947–1988.
Scottish Current Law Statute Citator 1948–1971. (1972) Edinburgh: Green.
Scottish Current Law Statutes [1949–1990]. (1949–1991) Edinburgh: Green.
Scottish Current Law Year Book [1948–1990]. (1949–1991) Edinburgh: Green.
Scottish Economic Bulletin. (Biannual) Edinburgh: HMSO.
Scottish Housing Law Reports. (1991–) Edinburgh: Shelter (Scotland).
Scottish Land Court Reports. (1982–) Edinburgh: Scottish Land Court.
Scottish Law and Practice Quarterly. (1995–) Edinburgh: T. & T. Clark.

Scottish Law Commission (1965–) *Publications*. Edinburgh: HMSO.
Scottish Law Commission (1966–1987) *Memoranda*. Edinburgh: Scottish Law Commission.
Scottish Law Commission (1988–) *Discussion papers*. Edinburgh: Scottish Law Commission.
Scottish Law Directory. (Annual) Edinburgh: T. & T. Clark. Also available on CD-ROM.
Scottish Law Gazette. (1933–) Edinburgh: Scottish Law Agents Society.
Scottish Law Reporter. (1865–1924) Edinburgh: Baxter.
Scottish Law Review. (1885–1963) Glasgow: Hodge.
Scottish Legal Aid Board (1988–) *Annual report*. Edinburgh: Scottish Legal Aid Board.
Scottish Legal Services Ombudsman (1992–) *Annual report*. Edinburgh: HMSO.
Scottish Office (1991) *The justice charter for Scotland*. Edinburgh: Scottish Office.
Scottish Office (1993a) *Scotland in the Union: a partnership for good*. Cm 2225. Edinburgh: HMSO.
Scottish Office (1993b) *Scotland's children: proposals for child care policy and law*. Cm 2286. Edinburgh: HMSO.
Scottish Office (1994a) *Firm and fair: improving the delivery of justice in Scotland*. Cm 2600. Edinburgh: HMSO.
Scottish Office (1994b) *Juries and verdicts*. Edinburgh: Scottish Office.
Scottish Office (1994c) *Sentencing and appeals*. Edinburgh: Scottish Office.
Scottish Planning and Environmental Law. (1993–) Glasgow: Planning Exchange.
Scottish Planning Appeal Decisions. (1976–) Glasgow: Planning Exchange.
Scottish Planning Law and Practice. (1980–1993) Glasgow: Planning Exchange.
[*Session Cases*]. (1822–) *Cases decided in the Court of Session*. Edinburgh: Green. Covers 1821– . Revised editions of the first 5 volumes were published 1834–1835. Publishers vary.
Shaw, P. (1869) *Digest of cases decided in the supreme courts of Scotland* 2nd edn. Edinburgh: T. & T. Clark. 3v.
Sheridan, M. and Cameron, J. (1992) *EC legal systems: an introductory guide*. London: Butterworths.
Sheriff Court Reports. (1885–1963) Glasgow: Hodge.
SI-CD (available from Context).
Simmonds, K.R. (1976) United Kingdom. In *International encyclopedia of comparative law* Vol.1. *National reports*, ed. V. Knapp, pp. U59–U102. Tübingen: Mohr.
Smith, I.S. and Barton, J.M. (1995) *Procedures and decisions of the Scottish Solicitors' Discipline Tribunal*. Edinburgh: T. & T. Clark.
Stair, Viscount (1683–1687) *Decisions of the Lords of Council and Session*. Edinburgh: the heir of Andrew Anderson. 2v. Covers 1661–1681.
Stair, Viscount (1981) *Institutions of the law of Scotland* 6th edn. Edinburgh: Edinburgh University Press.
Stair Society (1936) *An introductory survey of the sources and literature of Scots law*. Publications of the Stair Society, no.1. Edinburgh: Stair Society.
Stair Society (1939) *Index to An introductory survey of the sources and literature of Scots law*. Publications of the Stair Society, no.1a. Edinburgh: Stair Society.
Statistical Bulletin. Criminal Justice Series. (1991–) Edinburgh: Scottish Office.
Statutes in Force. (1972–) London: HMSO. Looseleaf.
Statutes Revised. (1950) 3rd edn. London: HMSO. 32v.
Statutory Instruments. (1949–) London: HMSO.
Statutory Rules & Orders and Statutory Instruments Revised to December 31, 1948. (1949–1952) London: HMSO. 25v.
Stewart, W.J. (1995) *Scottish contemporary judicial dictionary of words and phrases*. Edinburgh: Green.
Supplementary index to the Local and Personal Acts 1948–1966. (1967) London: HMSO
Sweet & Maxwell's *Legal bibliography of the British Commonwealth of Nations*. Vol.5. *Scottish law to 1956* 2nd edn. (1957) London: Sweet & Maxwell. Reprinted (1991)

London: John Rees.
Table of Government Orders. (Irregular) London: HMSO.
Tait, W. (1823) *Index to the decisions of the Court of Session, contained in all the original collections, and in Mr. Morison's Dictionary of decisions*. Edinburgh: Tait.
Times Law Reports. (1990–) Edinburgh: T. & T. Clark.
Trayner, J. (1894) *Latin maxims and phrases: collected from the Institutional writers on the law of Scotland and other sources* 4th edn. Edinburgh: Green. Reprinted (1993) Edinburgh: Green.
Twining, W. and Uglow, J. (1981) (eds) *Law publishing and legal information: small jurisdictions of the British Isles*. London: Sweet & Maxwell.
Walker, D.M. (1980) *The Oxford companion to law*. Oxford: Clarendon Press.
Walker, D.M. (1985) *The Scottish jurists*. Edinburgh: Green.
Walker, D.M. (1992) *The Scottish legal system: an introduction to the study of Scots law* 6th edn. Edinburgh: Green.
Weekly Law Reports. (1953–) London: Incorporated Council of Law Reporting for England and Wales.
White, R.M. and Willock, I.D. (1993) *The Scottish legal system*. Edinburgh: Butterworths.
Who's Who in Scotland. (Annual) Irvine: Carrick Media.
Zweigert, K. and Kötz, H. (1987) *Introduction to comparative law* 2nd edn. Vol.1. *The framework*. Oxford: Clarendon Press.

The Isle of Man and the Channel Islands

GEORGE WOODMAN

General position

The Isle of Man and the Channel Islands are dependencies of the British Crown. Although they acknowledge the sovereignty of the British monarch they are not part of the United Kingdom. They have considerable degrees of internal self-rule and contain a variety of jurisdictions and legal systems. Both have established themselves in recent years as important international financial centres.

Readers should note that the text and address lists for the Isle of Man precede those for the Channel Islands, and there is a single consolidated list of works cited at the end of the chapter.

International position

In both the Isle of Man and the Channel Islands the UK government is responsible for their external relations and defence. Their position in relation to treaties and international agreements is set out in a Foreign Office Circular of 16 October 1950, which is included in Tynwald Select Committee on Constitutional Issues (1980) as Appendix D and is further clarified in Foreign and Commonwealth Office Legal Advisers (1993).

They are not full members of the EU but belong to it for specific limited purposes such as trade and certain aspects of the rules relating to agricultural products. Protocol No.3 of the Act of Accession of the United Kingdom defines this relationship.

Treaties

International agreements made by the UK government are binding on the Islands. Unless the text of the agreement expressly or by implication provides that it shall not be so binding. In practice extensive consultation with their governments takes place and there is a requirement for treaties to be registered with the authorities. Solly (1994: 125–9) sets out the position clearly.

Isle of Man

Introduction to the legal system

Before 800 the Isle of Man was a Celtic island with strong links to Ireland. Early in the 9th century it was colonized by Norse settlers and for a long time control over the Island oscillated between the various political centres of the Norse world. In the late 970s the Kingdom of Man and the Sudreys consisting of Man and the Hebrides came into existence. At this period also, Tynwald, the Manx Parliament was established. It has existed ever since and is thus the oldest continuously meeting parliamentary institution. In 1098 the Kingdom of Man and the Sudreys came under the suzerainty of Norway.

The last King of the Sudreys died in 1265 and in 1266 the King of Norway ceded his rights over the Island to Alexander III of Scotland. After a period when control swung between Scotland and England it finally came under the English Crown in 1333. The feudal lordship of the Island was given by the Crown to the Stanley family in 1406. The Stanleys and their heirs the Dukes of Atholl governed it until the 18th century.

The vigorous contraband trade which developed by the mid-18th century led the British government to decide that a greater degree of control was necessary. In 1765 George III bought back his feudal rights under the Revestment Act. There now followed about a century when the Island was governed virtually as a crown colony.

This direct rule from Britain proved unpopular. Particularly resented was the spending of revenue raised in the Island in the United Kingdom. In 1866 Parliament passed the Isle of Man Customs, Harbours and Public Purposes Act which separated the finances of the Island from those of the United Kingdom allowing revenue raised there to be spent locally. In the same year Tynwald passed the House of Keys Election Act, providing for democratic elections, the first of which took place in 1867. Since 1866 the self-rule of the Isle of Man has continued to develop.

The Norse origins, together with feudal elements introduced under Scots law and further developments through English legislation and common law, have shaped the legal system. The courts, like Tynwald, trace their beginnings to the Norse period and the two Deemsters, the Isle of Man's High Court judges, hold an office which similarly dates back to the Kingdom of the Sudreys.

Introductory works on the legal system and legal research

There are several useful introductions to Manx legal practice. A short introduction is provided by Keenan (1993). Isle of Man Government (1987) provides a good description of the main points. Young (1983) reflects the author's background as a constitutional lawyer by covering much legal and parliamentary history. *The official Isle of Man yearbook* includes an outline of the Manx Constitution, which describes the Government, the court structure and the Island's international status. A shorter section describes recent constitutional changes and briefly summarizes relations with the United Kingdom and the European Community.

The most comprehensive treatment can be found in Solly (1994). This essential text covers all aspects of the Isle of Man's history, constitution, external relations and legal system. The best starting-point for research is the chapter by Jenny Uglow (1981) although it is now somewhat out of date. A useful short introduction to the literature is provided by Holborn (1993) paras 7.34–7.38.

Constitutional law

There is no written constitution for the Isle of Man and no published collection of Manx constitutional documents has been traced. The *Statutes in Force* volume on Constitutional Law 29.4 contains the texts of UK Statutes relating to the Isle of Man. Tynwald Select Committee on Constitutional Issues (1980) includes much useful material, notably the text of the Resolution outlining the constitutional objectives of Tynwald agreed on 14 July 1981 and restated on 15 April 1987. Quayle (1990) provides a valuable historical survey.

Legislation

Acts of Tynwald

These are subject to similar procedures as those for Bills at Westminster (they are set out in Solly (1994), *The official Isle of Man yearbook* and the *Tynwald companion* (1993). Acts are passed on the giving of Royal Assent, but they must be promulgated at the Tynwald Ceremony on Tynwald Day (5 July). Promulgation must take place within 18 months of the passing of the Act. Acts of Tynwald may be in force from the day they are passed or may be brought into force by an Executive (Appointed Day) order. Citation is similar to UK Acts of Parliament: Police Act 1983 c.11; Water Pollution Act 1993 c.14.

All legislation is available from the Central Reference Library. Acts are published individually and are available on annual subscription. An annual volume is not published. However, a legislation package is available on subscription which, in addition to Acts and Statutory Documents, includes a binder for the year's Acts. Details of forthcoming legislation is set out in Isle of Man Government and progress of legislation can be traced through the Agenda of Tynwald (available as part of the legislation package).

The *Manx Law Bulletin* (1983–) lists Acts recently passed by Tynwald and gives details of legislation in force. Summaries of forthcoming bills are also included.

The principal collection of Manx primary legislation is the *Statutes of the Isle of Man* (rev. ed.) (1974). There are 21 volumes covering the period from 1417 to 1970. They will be superseded with publication of the complete text of the Isle of Man Statutes both in hard copy and on CD-ROM as JUTA'S STATUTES OF THE ISLE OF MAN, the cut-off date being 31 December 1995. It is intended eventually to include Statutes judicially considered on the CD-ROM including the full text of the judgments, legislation pending and legislation considered. Juta also intend to upload the data on to their fileserver in Cape Town for access via the Internet.

Indexes

The main index to the Acts of Tynwald is the *Subject guide to Acts of Tynwald* published annually. In addition to the subject index itself, it includes alphabetical and chronological lists which refer back to the subject headings. References up to 1970 are to the volume and page numbers of the *Statutes of the Isle of Man* it is intended to continue using this form after the publication of JUTA'S STATUTES. From 1971 references are simply to the individual Acts by year and chapter number. References are not given to clauses within the Acts. It is indicated if any Statute is not yet in force.

Compilations

Sets of Isle of Man Statutes in Force have also been published. These cover various subject areas. The most recent is *Isle of Man companies legislation 1931–1993* (revised to April 1994). Also available are *Taxation Acts 1970–1991*.

A chronological listing of all shipping and harbours legislation applying in the Isle of Man is included in Marine Administration (1995a). Revocations and amendments are listed. Marine Administration (1995b) summarises shipping legislation.

Useful regulatory guides are published by the Financial Supervision Commission. These include texts of legislation and other documents in a looseleaf format. There are three available, on *Banks and banking* (1992a), *Collective investment schemes* (1992b) and *Investment businesses* (1992c). Bates (1992) is a rare annotated text of Manx legislation.

Statutory Documents

Until 1992 these were known as Government Circulars. They are similar to Statutory Instruments and are cited as follows: General Registry (Miscellaneous Fees) Order 1994 SD No 286/94; Petroleum (Royalties) Regulations 1995 SD No 261/95.

The Central Reference Library produces quarterly and annual lists of Statutory Documents, which are arranged chronologically. Dates of being laid before Tynwald and becoming effective are given.

UK legislation

A number of Acts of the UK parliament at Westminster extend to the Isle of Man either directly, if they cover foreign policy or other areas for which the UK government is responsible, or by extension through Order in Council taking the form of Statutory Instruments. These can be traced through Gumbley (1995) which also has a useful short introduction setting out the scope of Westminister legislation for the Island. It may be obtained through the Attorney General's Office. Fresh UK legislation extending to the Isle of Man is noted in the *Manx Law Bulletin.*

Both Acts and Statutory instruments relating to the Isle of Man are covered in their respective indexes under 'Isle of Man'. *Current Law* (1947–) also covers this legislation.

The Annual and Monthly Lists of Statutory Instruments also state whether a Statutory Instrument applies to the Isle of Man.

Law reports

Cases of the High Court (both the main civil court and the appeal court) and the High Bailiff's Court (the criminal court) are reported in *Manx Law Reports* (1961–) cited as MLR. They appear in annual parts with a bound volume every few years. The second part of 1993–95 has already appeared. Coverage is complete from 1961 and a volume covering 1952–1961 is in preparation. There is a cumulative index for 1961–1989 which it is intended to update shortly. It is hoped that the retrospective programme will be extended further.

Copies of recent and older unreported judgments are available from the General Registry. The most up-to-date source of case reports is in the case notes section of the *Manx Law Bulletin* (1983–) cited as *MLB*. These appear within a few months and are arranged by subject.

Also available are Prater's two indexes, covering cases 1884–1988 and subjects 1884–1971. These refer to cases using the case numbering systems designed for the collections of the Attorney-General's Office and the Isle of Man Law Society. Reports of selected cases are also included in Eason (1988). This work, written by a retired senior judge, consists of accounts of cases: 'within my personal knowledge arising when acting for one of the parties or dealt with by me either as High Bailiff [or] one of the Deemsters either on the first reading or as a member of the Court of Appeal'. The cases cover a wide variety of subjects, including agricultural holdings, family law and revenue.

English decisions are not binding in Manx courts but have strong persuasive force. In the absence of Manx precedent they will frequently be followed. There is a valuable discussion of precedent in Solly (1994) pp. 447–463. A very important source of precedents is *A list of constitutional and Privy Council judgments* . . . (1992). This lists all cases with either manuscript or printed sources. Especially useful is its coverage of appeals to the Judicial Committee of the Privy Council, the Isle of Man's final Court of Appeal.

The Rules of the High Court are published by the government and are available from the Central Reference Library.

Computer-based systems

Apart from the Juta Statutes already mentioned and the Manx material covered by *Legal Journals Index*, there are at present no other computer-based systems dealing with Manx law.

Government documents

Commission of Inquiry into Legal Services (1990) provides the most comprehensive description of the legal profession and the operation of the legal system. The Advocates' Scale of Fees 1963 updated to 1988 is included in an appendix. Isle of Man Government *Annual review of programmes and policies* includes much useful information about proposed legislation. Intended Bills are set out in an appendix. Other developments such as relations with the EU are also outlined.

Encyclopedias

There are no encyclopedic works dealing with law in the Isle of Man.

Directories

Isle of Man Government *General information fact file* is apparently designed for businesses setting up in the Isle of Man and bringing in personnel from outside the Island. These factsheets cover a variety of topics containing much financial and basic company information. Advocates and legal practitioners are listed with a brief outline of the basic legislation on legal services.

Hazell's guide to the judiciary and the courts gives addresses and phone numbers of Courts together with details of sittings. There is a complete list of law firms.

Manx Telecom *Telephone directory* combines both Directory and Yellow Pages. Government departments are listed in the Directory under the heading Isle of Man Government. There is also a helpful subject index. Lawyers appear in the Yellow Pages under 'Advocates' and 'Legal practitioners'. The Isle of Man Law Society has a useful listing in the section on Advocates.

The official Isle of Man yearbook is the most comprehensive Manx reference source. It covers all aspects of life on the Island. There are useful sections on the constitution and legal systems, as already indicated also sections on the organization of courts and court sittings. It lists addresses and phone numbers of government departments and other organizations and includes a list of advocates and much information on company formation and other business matters.

The Tynwald companion provides a guide to the procedure and membership of Tynwald and has useful lists of telephone numbers of government departments and courts There is a section on the European Union (including text of Protocol No.3 to the 1972 UK Act of Accession) and the European Convention on Human Rights.

Bibliographies and indexes

Comprehensive coverage of all Manx legal materials is again attempted in the bibliography of Twining and Uglow (1981). It records the position up to 1980, listing chronologically statutes, cases, texts and articles. Breem and Phillips (1991) has a section on the case law of the Isle of Man. A useful bibliography of records of court proceedings and collections of precedents, both printed and manuscript, is included in *A list of constitutional and Privy Council judgments* (1992). Solly (1994) does not include a bibliography but summarizes a number of official reports. The *Manx Law Bulletin* lists recent official and other publications in its subject guide under the heading 'Reports and publications'. Items relating to the Isle of Man can be traced through the *Legal Journals Index.*

Cubbon (1933) pp. 291–307 is useful for older materials, especially case reports. The most comprehensive older bibliography is *Sweet and Maxwell's legal bibliography of the British Commonwealth of Nations* (1989). Works are listed alphabetically with basic bibliographic details and there is a separate section for statutes. Chloros (1973) includes a useful chapter. There is a brief description of the main areas of law. Although written just before Britain entered the EC most of the internal law still applies and the text books mentioned in the bibliographical section are still of use.

Other sources

The *Advocates Admission Regulations* (1987, as amended in 1989) set out the qualifications required to practice. The syllabus for the Advocates' Examination of the Isle of Man Law Society is given in a schedule.

Current information sources

Journals

The *Manx Law Bulletin* (1983–) is the main source of current information on Manx law. In addition to the items already referred to and notices of developments in the local legal profession it includes longer articles and notes on legal topics.

News information

The main weekly paper is the *Isle of Man Examiner* (1880–) published weekly on Tuesdays. Proceedings of Tynwald and the Courts are well covered.

Business information

The *Isle of Man Examiner* has a useful business section. Its publishers also produces a business magazine *Focus* aimed at the international market. The Commercial Development Division of the Isle of Man Treasury is responsible for trade and company formation in the Isle of Man. The financial sector is under the oversight of the Financial Supervision Commission. For their addresses and that of the Companies Registry see the section on addresses at the end of the chapter.

Statistics

Crime statistics covering an eight-year period are included in the annual *Digest of economic and social statistics*. More detailed figures are given in the Isle of Man Constabulary *Annual report*, covering the current year with comparative figures for the previous year. The *Digest* also contains economic indicators and gives contact points for further information.

Useful addresses

Professional bodies

Isle of Man Law Society, Secretary: L. Keenan Esq, LLB, c/o Victoria Chambers, 51A Victoria Street, Douglas, Isle of Man IM1 2LD. Tel: +44 1624 611933. Fax: +44 1624 611893

Government departments

Attorney General, Attorney General's Chambers, Government Offices, Bucks Road, Douglas, Isle of Man IM1 2PP. Tel: +44 1624 685452

Commercial Development Division, Treasury, Illiam Dhone House, 2 Circular Road, Douglas, Isle of Man IM1 1PG. Tel: +44 1624 685755. Fax: +44 1624 685747

Companies Registry, Finch Road, Douglas, Isle of Man IM1 2SB. Tel: +44 1624 685233

Department of Home Affairs, Homefield, Woodbourne Road, Douglas, Isle of Man IM2 3NP. Tel: +44 1624 623355

Economic Affairs Division, Treasury, Illiam Dhone House, 2 Circular Road, Douglas, Isle of Man IM1 1PQ. Tel: +44 1624 685685, ext. 4261. Fax: +44 1624 685747

Financial Supervision Commission, PO Box 58, 1–4 Goldie Terrace, Upper Church Street, Douglas, Isle of Man IM99 1DT. Tel: +44 1624 624487. Fax: +44 1624 629342

Marine Administration, Department of Transport, Sea Terminal Building, Douglas, Isle of Man IM1 2RF. Tel: +44 1624 686643. Fax: +44 1624 627238

UK GOVERNMENT DEPARTMENTS

Foreign and Commonwealth Office, Downing Street, London SW1A 2AL, UK. Tel: +44 171 270 3000

Home Office, Criminal Justice and Constitutional Department, A Division, 50 Queen Anne's Gate, London SW1H 9AT, UK. Tel: +44 171 273 2575

Law reform

The responsible officer is HM Attorney General (see above).

Courts

General Registry, Finch Road, Douglas, Isle of Man IM1 2SB. Tel: +44 1624 685242. (Also address for High Court and Court of General Gaol Delivery).

High Bailiff's Court, Clerk to the High Bailiff, Government Offices, Buck's Road, Douglas, Isle of Man IM1 3PG. Tel: +44 1624 685471

Education and training

Enquiries about entrance requirements should be made to the Isle of Man Law Society at the address above. There are no law schools or research centres.

Libraries

Attorney General's Chambers, Library, Central Government Offices, Buck's Road, Douglas, Isle of Man IM1 3PP. Tel: +44 1624 685455. Fax: +44 1624 689162

Central Reference Library, Government Offices, Buck's Road, Douglas, Isle of Man IM1 3PW. Tel: +44 1624 685520. Fax: +44 1624 685522

Publishers and booksellers

The issue point for Isle of Man Government publications is the Central Reference Library (see above).

Executive Publications, Spring Valley Industrial Estate, Braddan, Isle of Man IM2 2QT. Tel: +44 1624 622066

Isle of Man Newspapers, Publishing House, Peel Road, Douglas, Isle of Man IM1 5PZ. Tel: +44 1624 623451. Fax: +44 1624 661041

Juta and Co Ltd, Mercury Crescent, Wetton 7780, Cape Town, Republic of South Africa. Tel: 021 797 5101. Fax: 021 762 7424. E-mail: Ciaran%jin@juta.co.za. (Enquiries about Juta Statutes should be addressed to Ciaran McGlinchey.)

Law Reports International, Trinity College, Oxford OX1 3BH. Tel: +44 1865 279893. Fax: +44 1865 279883

Lexicon Bookshop, 63 Strand Street, Douglas, Isle of Man IM1 2RL. Tel: +44 1624 673004. Fax: 01624 661959 (useful source of IOM publications).

Manx Telecom, Queen Victoria House, Victoria Street, Douglas, Isle of Man IM99 1HX. Tel: +44 1624 633633. Fax: +44 1624 636011

Parallel Books, 35 Malew Street, Castletown, Isle of Man IM9 1AE. Tel: +44 1624 822405

Channel Islands

Introduction to the legal system

The Channel Islands make up a geographical entity not a political one. There are, in fact, two main jurisdictions, the Bailiwicks of Jersey, the largest island, and of Guernsey, which also covers the smaller islands. Alderney and Sark have internal self-rule within the Bailiwick of Guernsey, whose legislature has ultimate responsibility in certain areas.

Geographically they are rather closer to France than to England. In around the year 933 they became part of the Duchy of Normandy. Their connection with the English Crown began in 1066 when William II, Duke of Normandy, conquered England. When in 1204, during the reign of King John, continental Normandy was lost, the Channel Islands remained under the English crown and continued to be governed as though the Kings of England were still Dukes of Normandy, even after the title was relinquished in 1259.

King John confirmed the traditional laws, customs and liberties of the Channel islanders. Subsequent Royal Charters, of which the most important was that granted by Elizabeth I on 15 March 1559, further upheld them. The customary law of Normandy was their source. As time passed legal practice started to diverge from that in Normandy itself and, as each island had its own courts, they developed individual characteristics. The tendency developed for judges to look to the principles of English common law, particularly after 1804 when the Code Napoléon replaced the local coutumes in France, so that the law of Normandy ceased to develop. Modern civil law is largely modelled on English statutes. However, in certain fields, especially property and inheritance, the law is substantially Norman in origin. Thus, the ancient customary law remains extremely important. Criminal law is based on English law with modifications to suit local conditions. This follows recommendations of a Royal Commission in 1847.

After the German occupation of 1940–45 various laws were passed reforming the structure of government.

In Jersey, Guernsey and Alderney, the legislature is known as the States. In Sark it is the Chief Pleas. In both Bailiwicks government is carried on through Committees of the States which take the place of government departments.

Sources of Norman law

The original codification of the Ancien Coutume was contained in Le Grand Coutumier du Pays et Duché de Normandie, which was written down in the 13th century. A printed text appeared in 1539 incorporating Le Rouillé's 1534 commentary.

When in 1581 the Governor and Royal Court of Guernsey were instructed by the Privy Council to examine the customary laws of both Guernsey and Normandy and to state where they agreed and disagreed, they adopted Terrien (1574) as their standard source of Norman law. They sent their notes of local differences to the Privy Council, who adopted this communication as the authoritative statement of Guernsey law and directed its publication. It was entitled the Approbation des Lois. Together with Terrien, it became the standard source of customary law in Guernsey.

The position in Jersey is more complex. Terrien, while respected, does not enjoy the same authority. *Ancien Coutume* (1539) is the text most often cited in Jersey courts. A Privy Council judgment in 1884 considered the works of P. Le Geyt the most authoritative on Jersey law. The first was published only in 1846, 150 years after the author's death, and 'Le Code Le Geyt' was not published until 1953.

Sheridan (1955) has a useful discussion on sources of Norman law, pp. 1141–1144 and Rowland (1992) has a valuable bibliography. The libraries included in the list of addresses all have substantial collections of texts on customary law.

Introduction to the legal system and legal research

For Guernsey, Loveridge (1975) and Ehmann and Le Pelley (1993) are useful. Especially valuable is Rowland (1992). Loveridge and Rowland also cover Alderney and Sark. Beaumont (1993) is the main source for

Sark. On Jersey, the account by Bois (1970) is the standard work. There is a brief outline and a discussion of Jersey's relationship to the European Union in the *Jersey financial services handbook.* Holborn (1993) paras 7.39–7.49 provides a good starting point for legal research.

The Constitutions

Statutes in Force section on Constitutional Law (29:4) contains the UK statutes at present applying to the Channel Islands. The Reform (Guernsey) Laws 1948 to 1993 provides a useful consolidation of constitutional and administrative law. Helpful summaries can be found in Loveridge (1975) and Ehmann and Le Pelley (1993).

The principal source of constitutional law for Alderney is the Government of Alderney Law (1987). Similar legislation for Sark is contained in the Reform (Sark) Law 1951. The text of this Law, with amendments, is included as an appendix to Beaumont (1993).

For Jersey the present main constitutional instrument is the *States of Jersey Law 1966.* This has been published in a looseleaf format with other legislation and Standing Orders relating to the States, public finance and land transactions, in effect creating a sourcebook of much constitutional and administrative law. Bois (1970) is the standard work.

The main piece of Guernsey legislation relating to the EU is the *European Communities (Bailiwick of Guernsey) Law 1973.* The *European Communities (Implementation) (Bailiwick of Guernsey) Law 1994* allows for the quick adoption of EC Directives. In Jersey the principal legislation is the *European Communities (Jersey) Law 1973.*

Legislation

All jurisdictions have two forms of legislation: one requires approval by the Privy Council, the other may be enacted directly without this approval. Frequently the former will be so drafted to allow for amendment by the latter. The locally enacted legislation should not be classed as subordinate, although forms of subordinate legislation exist. There is also United Kingdom legislation applying to the Islands. It should be noted that until the late 1940s legislation in both Bailiwicks was in French.

Guernsey, Alderney and Sark

The legislation requiring approval by the Privy Council takes the form of Laws. An excellent account of the process by which Guernsey legislation is made can be found in Lenfestey (1989). All draft legislation appears as a supplement inserted in the *Billet d'État* (see section on **Official publications** below). At the parliamentary stage a law is a Projet de Loi. If passed by the States it is sent to the Privy Council. Once ratified it is returned to Guernsey as an Order in Council for registration. Unless the Law itself makes provision for its commencement at some other time, it comes into force on the day it is registered. Publication follows registration.

The official in Guernsey responsible for registration is Her Majesty's Greffier. His department is the Greffe. The Greffe is the registry for legislation, judicial records, births, marriages and deaths, and companies. It also functions as a government bookshop. Similar functions are fulfilled by the Greffe in Sark and by the States Office in Alderney.

Officially Laws are styled 'Order in Council ratifying a Projet de Loi entitled . . .'. They are assigned a number in Roman numerals in an annual sequence, e.g. The Companies (Guernsey) Law 1994, XXXIII 1994.

Eventually bound volumes of *Ordres en Conseil* are published, covering one or more years. (There is a certain time lag. The latest available covers 1986–87.) These volumes are also numbered in a sequence of Roman numerals which are referred to in citations, e.g. The Tomato Marketing (Guernsey) Law 1952 is Ordres en Conseil Vol.XV p. 34. Certain other categories of material are also included (see below).

The main form of legislation directly enacted by the States of Guernsey consists of Ordinances. Laws are frequently so drafted that they can be amended by Ordinance. Like Projets de Loi, Ordinances are published at the draft stage in the *Billet d'État*. Once approved they are published and assigned a number in an annual sequence of Roman numerals, e.g. The Indirect Taxes, Duties and Imports (Increase of Rates) (Budget) Ordinance 1994, Ordinance No XXXIX of 1994. Bound volumes are also published. (The latest available is for 1991.) They are known as *Recueil d'Ordonnances* and are numbered and cited in a similar manner to the Ordres en Conseil, e.g. the Public Transport Ordinance 1986 is Recueil d'Ordonnances Tome XXIII, p. 351.

The Royal Court of Guernsey retains the right to legislate, mostly for its own procedures. These Orders of the Royal Court are numbered in their own separate annual sequence of Roman numerals, e.g. The Royal Court Civil Rules 1989, Order of the Royal Court No. VII of 1989.

Guernsey also issues its own Statutory Instruments (not to be confused with UK Statutory Instruments applying to Guernsey). These are numbered and cited in a similar fashion to SIs of the United Kingdom, e.g. The Wireless Telegraphy (Apparatus) Order 1994, SI No.17.

ALDERNEY AND SARK

The States of Alderney passes similar legislation to Guernsey. Laws are subject to approval by the Privy Council and should be cited similarly, e.g. The Companies (Alderney) Law 1994, XXXIV 1994.

It is important to note that while the States of Alderney is a totally separate legislature, its Laws and those of Sark are numbered as part of the sequence of Guernsey Laws. Laws of both Alderney and Sark appear in the bound volumes of *Ordres en Conseil.* The States of Alderney passes Ordinances numbered in a separate sequence, e.g. The Companies (Alderney) Law (Guarantee Companies) Ordinance 1995 Ordinance No.III of 1995.

Alderney also has its own sequence of Statutory Instruments, e.g. The Companies Articles (Standard Table) Regulations 1995 SI No.3. All Alderney legislation is available from the States Office. There are certain areas, such as Criminal law and Income Tax where legislation automatically has effect in Alderney. As a result the States of Guernsey create some legislation which applies exclusively there.

Similar legislative processes are followed on Sark. The Chief Pleas passes both Laws and Ordinances. Sark legislation is obtainable from the Greffe on the island.

INDEXES

Index of Orders in Council and other Matters of General Interest Registered on the Records of the Island of Guernsey (1990) was produced for internal use by the Royal Court, who hold on their computer a version updated to 30 June 1994. This is a very useful subject index as is the similar Index of Guernsey Ordinances covering up to early 1990. This index also covers Orders of the Royal Court. Printouts of both may be obtained on request. All legislation of Guernsey, Alderney and Sark is noted in the *Guernsey Law Journal.*

Robilliard (1985) is one of the very few modern texts on Channel Islands law. Useful texts of legislation in banking and related areas have been prepared by the Guernsey Financial Services Commission. KPMG Peat Marwick (1991) is a very useful introduction to legislation in banking, insurance and tax, although it is to some extent superseded by the Companies (Guernsey) Law 1994.

Jersey

As in Guernsey, the legislation requiring approval by the Privy Council takes the form of Laws, although publication and citation are rather different. Laws are numbered as part of an annual sequence prefixed by the letter L; e.g. Wills and Successions (Jersey) Law 1993 L18/93. All Laws are published in a suitable format for insertion in a ring binder and paginated as part of a two-year volume, to which citations refer. The example above is Volume 1992–1993, page 247.

These volumes continue the *Recueil des Lois* published in seven volumes and covering the period from 1771 to 1936. An eighth volume, in two parts, extends the series to 1960. Citations of older Laws refer to the *Recueil*, e.g. the Probate (Jersey) Law 1949 is at Tome VII, page 517.

Revised versions of certain Laws are published in a looseleaf format. These include income tax and road traffic.

Legislation passed by the States of Jersey which does not require approval by the Privy Council appears in the numbered series *Regulations and Orders* (R and O). This series also includes what should be classed as subordinate legislation. The numerical sequence is not annual but extends over many years. Examples are: Pilotage (Dues and Fees) (Amendment No.7) (Jersey) Order 1995 R&O/8888; Family Allowances (Jersey) Regulations 1995 R&O/8894.

Legislation at the draft stage appears in the *Propositions* (P) Series, numbered in an annual sequence, e.g. Draft Health and Safety at Work (Amendment No.2) (Jersey) Law 199 1995/p. 186.

The *General Index of Legislation* (spine title: Jersey Legislation in Force) is published annually in a ring binder. It is a subject index in two parts covering Laws and Regulations and Orders. References are given both to the Law number and to the volume and page number. (The column for the L number is, rather oddly, headed 'Pamphlet'.) With older laws the volume reference is of course to the *Receuil des Lois*. Current legislation can be traced through the monthly and annual lists of States of Jersey Publications.

Matthews and Sowden (1993) is a rare annotated text. KPMG Peat Marwick (1992b) covers Jersey.

All Jersey legislation is obtainable from the States Greffe Bookshop (see list of addresses). In Jersey there are separate Greffes. One, the States Greffe acts as a registry for the States. The other, the Judicial Greffe is a registry for the Courts.

United Kingdom legislation

Some UK legislation applies to the Channel Islands either by implication in that it concerns an area for which the UK government is responsible or else because it refers directly to them. It is now fairly unusual for an Act of Parliament to apply directly to the Channel Islands. The more usual procedure is for Acts to give powers to Her Majesty to extend their provisions to the Islands by Order in Council, normally through Statutory Instruments. Examples include: The Immigration (Guernsey) Order 1993 SI No.1796; The Weights and Measures (Jersey) Order 1992 SI No.1592.

Such legislation comes into force on being registered in the Islands or on an appointed day specified in the Order. The bound volumes of Guernsey *Ordres en Conseil* reprint UK legislation specifically for Guernsey in full. They note the registration of legislation that applies by implication but do not reprint it.

The *Index to the Statutes* and the *Index to Government Orders* cover all Channel Islands material under 'Channel Islands' and the names of the individual islands, with useful references to other subject headings. The *Lists of Statutory Instruments* are also good finding aids. Their indexes are in fact more useful for finding Channel Islands Statutory Instruments than the index to the sets of bound volumes which do not use 'Guernsey' or 'Jersey' as subject headings.

Current Law (1947–) also covers Statutory Instruments relating exclusively to one or more of the Channel Islands. It does not use 'Channel Islands' as an indexing term but only 'Guernsey' and 'Jersey'.

Law reports

There was no system of law reporting in Guernsey until the 1960s. Reports of individual cases of the Court of Appeal were issued from 1964 in the Criminal Division and from 1965 in the Civil Division. When the *Guernsey Law Journal* began to appear in 1985 cases were digested and in 1989 these law reports ceased to appear. In 1993 the *Guernsey Law Journal* claimed to include full case reports for the period covered by the particular issue, in effect reviving the *Guernsey Law Reports* (although this title is not formally used). It is intended to cover the period between 1989 and 1993 retrospectively. A Cumulative Index and Tables for the *Guernsey Law Journal* to the end of 1991 is available. The original texts of all judgments may be obtained from the Greffe.

The Guernsey Court of Appeal is also the Court of Appeal for Alderney and Sark. Cases originating there are covered by the law reports already mentioned.

Law reporting in Jersey started in 1950. An older publication, the *Table des Decisions* (1885–1863) digested unreported decisions which were filed at the Royal Court. (See below for a later volume of a rather different character.) As with legislation court proceedings in the Channel Islands were in French.

The first proper law reports were the *Jersey Judgments* (JJ) (1950–1984), which were published by the Royal Court. From 1985 they were succeeded by the *Jersey Law Reports* (JLR). They appear as an annual volume, within two years. The publishers have also issued an index and tables covering *Jersey Judgments* from 1970 to 1984 and the *Jersey Law Reports* from 1985 to 1989. In the next edition of this index it is intended to extend retrospective coverage back to 1950. Sets of *Jersey Judgments* are available from Law Reports International. Individual cases reported in the *Jersey Judgments* are available from the Judicial Greffe.

A further volume of the *Table des Decisions* was published in 1980 covering the period 1964–1978. It noted decisions not reported in the *Jersey Judgments*. There are no plans for any further volumes.

In addition to these printed judgments a Rapid Distribution Service has been available from the Judicial Greffe since 1988. Typescripts of Royal Court Judgments are sent out every week or so to subscribers. With each distribution an updated index is included.

The final Appeal Court for the Channel Islands is the Privy Council. In certain areas such as land law the Courts of the Islands and Norman customary law have precedence. With the more recent influences of English common law, judgments of the English High Court have the greater force.

Computer-based legal texts

Apart from *Legal Journals Index* in its machine-readable format (see below) there are no computer-based legal texts relating to the Channel Islands.

Government documents

The main purpose of the *Billet d'État* is to set out the business of the States. In addition to the legislation already covered it includes reports presented to the States and so forms Guernsey's principal official publication. The *Billet d'État* is paginated continuously throughout the year and individual issues appear as part of a Roman numeral sequence, e.g. XXIV 1995. An annual index is available.

The annual *States of Jersey Policy and Resources Committee Strategic Policy Review* indicates priorities for the coming year. An appendix sets out the States' legislation programme.

In addition to legislation the volumes of *Ordres en Conseil* contain 'other matters registered on the records of the Island of Guernsey'. These include the registration, but not the text of treaties, the appointment of judges and other officials, Prerogative Orders and notifications, but not details, of Privy Council Judgments.

Official notices appear in *La Gazette Officielle* in Guernsey or in the *Jersey Gazette*. Neither exists as a separate publication. They appear in the advertisements section of the *Guernsey Evening Press* and the *Jersey Evening Post* respectively. The *Alderney Official Gazette* is published separately.

International conventions and agreements: progress report provides a useful annual overview of Jersey's status as regards international agreements.

Encyclopedias

There are no encyclopaedic works dealing with law in the Channel Islands.

Directories

Hazell's Guide to the judiciary and courts gives addresses of courts and details of sittings in all four Channel Islands jurisdictions. Details of firms are also given, including for Guernsey but not for Jersey, the names of individual advocates.

Guernsey Telecoms *Telephone directory* combines directory and business directory. The opening pages include a section on States and Public Administration. Included are officials of the Royal Court, States' Committees and public services. The Yellow Pages under 'Advocates' lists all firms with complete membership. Fax numbers are also given. The main directory, in most cases, gives full address with post codes. Coverage extends to Alderney and Sark. English firms of solicitors are listed in the Yellow Pages under the heading 'Solicitors – English'.

The Jersey Telecoms *Jersey Telephone Directory* is similarly arranged with a similar opening section. The lists of firms again give names of individual advocates. There are headings for 'Advocates', 'Solicitors' and 'Solicitors – English'. Full postal addresses are given.

The *Jersey financial services handbook* includes useful summaries of legal and official information. The directory section includes States' Departments and a list of advocates. Similar volumes are planned for Guernsey, Alderney and the Channel Islands as a whole. They are successors to an earlier series of Channel Islands financial handbooks.

Bibliographies and indexes

Sweet and Maxwell's legal bibliography of the British Commonwealth of Nations (1989) forms the best bibliographical source for older material. It is arranged alphabetically subdivided into sections dealing with the Channel Islands as a whole and with the individual islands. Cross references are made to the chapter elsewhere in the bibliography on Anglo-Norman law. Coverage is up to 1954, with only basic bibliographical details. Chloros (1973) has a chapter on the Channel Islands. There are brief descriptions of the jurisdictions and summaries of the sources of law up to 1970. Bibliographical citations are reasonably full. Breem and Phillips (1991) is useful for sources of case law. By far the most recent comprehensive bibliography is provided by Rowland (1992).

Dictionaries

There are no dictionaries relating to the law of the Channel Islands.

Current information sources

Periodicals

The *Guernsey Law Journal* (*GLJ*) (1985–) is the only legal periodical published in the Channel Islands. There are two issues a year, each covering a period of six months. Its digest section is arranged by subject and summarises separate sections and court judgments. Separate sections are devoted to Alderney and Sark. It appears within 18 months of the period digested. It now carries Court of Appeal Reports. It also features occasional longer articles. It is the essential information source for law in the Bailiwick of Guernsey and an index and tables for the first six years is available.

News and business information

The *Guernsey Evening Press* and the *Jersey Evening Post* have extensive business sections. The *Jersey financial services handbook* is a useful source of business information.

Statistics

Statistics of criminal proceedings in Guernsey are contained in the *Annual Report* of the Chief Officer of Police (available on written application from Police Headquarters). Comparative figures are given for the previous year. The Chief Officer's *Annual Report* on the States of Jersey Police gives similar statistics for the year under review only. (The 1994 report does not present this information in the tabulated form of previous years.) It is available from the States Greffe Bookshop.

Basic economic indicators for Guernsey can be traced through the annual *Statistical Digest*, published by the States Advisory Committee. The equivalent publication for Jersey is the *States of Jersey Statistical Review*, obtainable from the States Greffe Bookshop.

Useful addresses

Professional bodies

Advocate Graham Hall, Secretary, Guernsey Bar, Carey, Langlois and Co., 7 New Street, St Peter Port, Guernsey GY1 4BZ. Tel: +44 1481 727272. Fax: +44 1481 711052

Law Society of Jersey, c/o Advocate Labesse, Bailhache Labesse, PO Box 513, Piermont House, 33 Pier Road, St Helier, Jersey. Tel: +44 1481 888777. Fax: +44 1481 888779

Government departments

Attorney General HM and Solicitor General HM, St James Chambers, St Peter Port, Guernsey GY1 2PA. Tel: +44 1481 723355. Fax: +44 1481 725439

Attorney General HM, Attorney General's Chambers, Solicitor General, Solicitor General's Chambers, Both at Royal Square, St Helier, Jersey JE1 1DD. Tel: +44 1534 502200. Fax: +44 1534 502299

Business Names and Companies Registry, Cyril Le Marquand House, The Parade, St Helier, Jersey JE4 8TZ. Tel: +44 1534 603000. Fax: +44 1534 603610

The Companies Registrar for Guernsey is HM Greffier; for Alderney, the Clerk of the Court; for Sark, the Greffier.

Clerk of the States, States Office, Queen Elizabeth II Street, St Anne, Alderney GY9 3AA. Tel: +44 1481 822816. Fax: +44 1481 822436

The Economics Unit, States Advisory and Finance Committee, Sir Charles Frossard House, PO Box 43, St Peter Port, Guernsey GY1 1FH. Tel: +44 1481 717006. Fax: +44 1481 712520

Financial Services Department, Cyril Le Marquand House, PO Box 267, The Parade, St Helier, Jersey JE4 8TP. Tel: +44 1534 603000. Fax: +44 1534 81955. Regulatory body for financial services.

Greffe, Royal Court House, St Peter Port, Guernsey GY1 2PA. Tel: +44 1481 725277. Fax: +44 1481 715097

The Greffier, La Chasse Marette, Sark GY9 0SF. Tel: +44 1481 832012. Fax: +44 1481 832622

Greffier of the States, States Offices, Royal Square, St Helier, Jersey JE1 1DD. Tel: +44 1534 502000. Fax: +44 1534 502098

Guernsey Financial Services Commission, Valley House, Hirzel Street, St Peter Port, Guernsey GY1 2NP. Tel: +44 1481 712706; (Insurance Division) +44 1481 712810. Fax: +44 1481 712016. Regulatory body for financial services. (For relevant UK Government Departments see Isle of Man list of addresses on page 00).

Law reform

In both Bailiwicks HM Attorney General is the responsible official.

Courts

The Bailiff, Bailiff's Chambers, The Royal Court House, St Peter Port, Guernsey GY1 2PB. Tel: +44 1481 726161. Fax: +44 1481 713861

The Bailiff, Bailiff's Chambers, Royal Court House, Royal Square, St Helier, Jersey JE1 1DD. Tel: +44 1534 502100. Fax: +44 1534 502199

The Court House, Queen Elizabeth II Street, St Anne, Alderney GY9 3AA. Tel: +44 1481 822817. Fax: +44 1481 823709

Judicial Greffier, Burrard House, Don Street, St Helier, Jersey JE2 4TR. Tel: +44 1534 502300. Fax: +44 01534 502399

In Sark the Greffier is Clerk of the Court.

Education and training

Enquiries about entrance requirements in Guernsey should be made to the Bailiff's Secretary at the Royal Court, from whom the Syllabus may be obtained. Similar enquiries should be made in Jersey to the Secretary of the Law Society (see addresses above). There are no law schools or research centres, but the following provides certificate courses in Norman–French law for Channel Islands lawyers:

U.E.R. Droit et Sciences Politiques, Université de Caen, Esplanade de la Paix, 14032 CAEN, France. Tel: +33 31–45–55–00. Fax: +33 31–45–66–00

Libraries

Priaulx Library, Candie Road, St Peter Port, Guernsey GY1 1UG. Tel: +44 1481 721998. Fax: +44 1481 713804

Reference Library, Halkett Place, St Helier, Jersey JE2 4WM. Tel: +44 1534 59992. Fax: +44 1534 69444

Royal Court Library, Royal Court House, St Peter Port, Guernsey GY1 2PB. Contact: Bailiff's Secretary.

Publishers and booksellers

Ashton and Denton Publishing Co (CI) Ltd., 5 Burlington House, St Saviour's Road, St Helier, Jersey JE2 4LA. Tel: +44 1534 35461. Fax: +44 1534 875805

Chief Officer of Police, Police Headquarters, Hospital Lane, St Peter Port, Guernsey GY1 2QN. Tel: +44 1481 725111. Fax: +44 1481 56432

Guernsey Evening Press and Star, Guernsey Press Co. Ltd, PO Box 57, Braye Road, Guernsey GY1 3BW. Tel: +44 1481 45866. Fax: +44 1481 49250

Guernsey Telecoms, Telecom Centre, PO Box 3, Upland Road, St Peter Port, Guernsey GY1 3AB. Tel: +44 1481 719927 (Directories). Fax: +44 1481 716952 (Directories)

Jersey Evening Post, PO Box 582, Five Oaks, St Saviour's, Jersey. Tel: +44 1534 611611. Fax: +44 1534 611622

Jersey Telecoms, PO Box 53, Telephone House, Minden Place, St Helier, Jersey JE4 8PB. Tel: +44 1534 882508 (Directory suppliers). Fax: +44 1534 882883

Jura Bookshop, 44 Don Street, St Helier, Jersey JE2 4TQ. Tel: +44 1534 36809. Fax: +441534 89093

KPMG Peat Marwick, PO Box 20, 20 New Street, St Peter Port, Guernsey GY1 4AN. Tel: +44 1481 721000. Fax: +44 1481 722373

KPMG Peat Marwick Mitchell, PO Box 453, 38/39 The Esplanade, St Helier, Jersey JE4 8WQ. Tel: +44 1534 888891. Fax: +44 1534 888892

Law Reports International, Trinity College, Oxford OX1 3BH, UK. Tel: +44 1865 279893. Fax: +441865 279883

The Press Shop, 8 Smith Street, St Peter Port, Guernsey GY1 3BW. Tel: +44 1481 724829. Fax: +44 1481 724829

States Greffe Bookshop, Royal Square, St Helier, Jersey JE1 1DD. Tel: +44 1534 502037. Fax: +44 1534 502098

The Greffe is the issue point for all Guernsey Government publications. In Alderney it is the Clerk of the States; in Sark the Greffe.

List of works cited

Attention is drawn to the note at the end of the general introduction to the United Kingdom chapter giving information about the changes affecting UK government publications.

Act of Accession to the European Communities 1972. London: HMSO.

Advocates Admission Regulations 1987. Douglas: Isle of Man Government. Issued with 1989 amendments.

Alderney Official Gazette (1994–) Alderney: States Office.

Approbation des Lois, Coutumes, etc, de l'Ile de Guernsey differents de Coutumier de Normande d'Ancionnette observé. (1583). Guernsey: Royal Court. Later editions 1817, 1822, 1897.

Bates, Jane D.N. (1992) *Isle of Man Companies Act 1992*. London: Sweet and Maxwell.

Beaumont, J.M. (1993) *The constitution and administration of Sark*. Guernsey: Guernsey Press.

Billet d'État. Guernsey: States of Guernsey. Published on sitting days. Annual index.

Bois, F. de L. (1970) *The constitutional history of Jersey*. Jersey: States Greffier.

Breem W. and Phillips S. (1991) (eds) *Bibliography of Commonwealth law reports*. London: Mansell.

Chloros, A.G. (1973) *Bibliographical guide to the law of the United Kingdom, the Channel Islands and the Isle of Man* 2nd edn. London: Institute of Advanced Legal Studies.

Commission of Inquiry into Legal Services (1990) *Report*. Douglas: Isle of Man Government.

Court of Appeal Civil Division [Guernsey] (1965–1989). *Reports of cases*. Guernsey: HM Greffier.

Court of Appeal Criminal Division [Guernsey] (1964–1989). *Reports of cases*. Guernsey: HM Greffier.

Cubbon, William (1933) *A bibliographical account of works relating to the Isle of Man*. London: Oxford University Press.

Current law (1947–). London: Sweet and Maxwell.

Digest of economic and social statistics. Douglas: Isle of Man Government. Annual.

Eason, R.K. (1988) *Reflections on the judicial process in the Isle of Man*. Douglas: Bridson and Horrox.

Ehmann, David and Le Pelley, Paul (1993) *A guide to the constitution of Guernsey (1994)*. Guernsey: Guernsey Press.

European Communities (Bailiwick of Guernsey) Law 1973. Guernsey: HM Greffier

European Communities (Implementation) (Bailiwick of Guernsey) Law 1994. Guernsey: HM Greffier.

European Communities (Jersey) Law 1973. Jersey: States Greffier.

Financial Supervision Commission (IOM) (1992a) *Regulatory guide for banks and building societies*. Douglas: The Commission. Looseleaf. Update service.

Financial Supervision Commission (IOM) (1992b) *Regulatory guide for collective investment schemes*. Douglas: The Commission. Looseleaf. Update service.

Financial Supervision Commission (IOM) (1992c) *Regulatory guide for investment businesses*. Douglas: The Commission. Looseleaf. Update service.

Focus. Douglas: Isle of Man Newspapers.

Foreign and Commonwealth Office Legal Advisers (1993) *Memorandum: the application of treaties to the Crown Dependencies*. London: FCO.

General index of legislation. Jersey: States Greffier. Annual. In ring binder. Spine title: Jersey legislation in force.

Government of Alderney Law, 1987. Guernsey: HM Greffier. (Issued with amendments).

Le grand coutumier du pays et duché de Normandie. [1539] Incorporates commentary by G.Le Rouillé, first published separately 1534. Rouen: Nicholas Le Roux.

Guernsey Evening Press. (1897–) Guernsey: Guernsey Press. Daily.

Guernsey Financial Services Commission (1990a) *Control of borrowing*. Guernsey: The Commission.

Guernsey Financial Services Commission (1990b) *Protection of investors*. Guernsey: The Commission.

Guernsey Financial Services Commission (1991) *Money laundering avoidance: guidance notes*. Guernsey: The Commission.

Guernsey Financial Services Commission (1993a) *A guide to the international company*. Guernsey: The Commission.

Guernsey Financial Services Commission (1993b) *The Protection of Investors (Bailiwick of Guernsey) Law 1987: Rules and Regulations*. Guernsey: The Commission.

Guernsey Financial Services Commission (1994) The Banking Supervision (Bailiwick of Guernsey) Law 1994 as amended and rules and regulations made thereunder. Guernsey: The Commission.

Guernsey Financial Services Commission (1995a) *Guernsey fund management guide*. Guernsey: The Commission.

Guernsey Financial Services Commission (1995b) *Guernsey insurance guide*. Guernsey: The Commission.

Guernsey Law Journal. (1985–) Guernsey: HM Attorney General. Twice yearly.

Guernsey Telecoms. *Telephone directory*. Annual.

Gumbley, K.F.W. (1995) *Chronological table of Acts of Parliament extending to the Isle of Man with subject guide* 3rd edn. Douglas: HM Attorney General.

Hazell's guide to the judiciary and courts with the Holborn Law society's bar list. Henley-on-Thames: R. Hazell. Annual.

Holborn, Guy (1993) *Butterworths legal research guide*. London: Butterworths.

Index of Guernsey Ordinances (1990). Guernsey: Royal Court. Updated version available from Royal Court.

Index of Orders in Council and other matters of general interest registered in the records of the Island of Guernsey. (1990) Guernsey: Royal Court. Updated version available from Royal Court.

Index to Government Orders. London: HMSO. Published every three years

Index to the Statutes. London: HMSO. Published every three years

International conventions and agreements: progress report. Jersey: States Greffe. Annual.

Isle of Man Constabulary. *Annual report*. Douglas: Isle of Man Government.

Isle of Man Examiner. (1880–) Douglas: Isle of Man Newspapers. Weekly.

Isle of Man Government. *Annual review of programmes and policies*. Douglas: Isle of Man Government.

Isle of Man Government. *General information fact file*. Douglas: Isle of Man Government. Updated regularly.

Isle of Man Government (1987) *The government and legal system of the Isle of Man*. Douglas: Isle of Man Government.

Isle of Man Statutes in force: Companies legislation 1991–1993. (1995) Douglas: Isle of Man Government.

Isle of Man Statutes in force: Taxation Acts 1970–1991. (1992) Douglas: Isle of Man Government.

Jersey Evening Post. (1890–). Jersey: Jersey Evening Post. Daily.

Jersey financial services handbook. Jersey: Ashton and Denton Publishing Co. (CI). Annual.

Jersey Judgments. (1950–1984) Jersey: Royal Court. Now distributed by Law Reports International

Jersey Law Reports (1985–) Oxford: Law Reports International.

Jersey Telecoms *Telephone directory*. Annual.

Juta's Statutes of the Isle of Man. Cape Town: Juta (1996–).

Keenan, Laurence (1993) The Isle of Man. *The Law Librarian*. 24(2) pp. 88–90.

Keeton, G.W. (1955) (ed.) *The United Kingdom: the development of its laws and constitutions*. London: Stevens.

KPMG Peat Marwick (1990) *Insurance in Guernsey*. Guernsey: KPMG Peat Marwick.

KPMG Peat Marwick (1991) *A guide to Guernsey Company Law requirements*. Guernsey: KPMG Peat Marwick.

KPMG Peat Marwick (1992a) *A guide to Guernsey personal tax*. Guernsey: KPMG Peat Marwick.

KPMG Peat Marwick (1992b) *Investment in the Channel Islands*. Guernsey: KPMG Peat Marwick.

KPMG Peat Marwick (1995) *Banking and finance in Guernsey*. Guernsey: KPMG Peat Marwick.

Legal Journals Index (1986–) Hebden Bridge: Legal Information Resources.

Le Geyt, P. (1848) *La Constitution, les Lois et usages de L'Isle de Jersey*. Jersey.

Le Geyt, P. (1953) *Privilèges, Lois et Coutumes de l'Ile de Jersey*. Jersey: Bigwoods. Known as 'Le Code Le Geyt'.

Lenfestey, J.G.T. (1989) Legislative drafting in a mini state. *Guernsey Law Journal*, 7, pp. 30–53.

Le Rouillé, G. *see* Le grand coutoumier.

A list of constitutional and Privy Council judgments affecting the Isle of Man from 1523 to 1991 and a complete list of written reasons for judgments of HM High Court of Justice of the Isle of Man and other Manx Courts from 1884 to 1991 (1992) 2nd edn. Douglas: HM Attorney General.

List of Statutory Instruments. (Annual) and (Monthly). London: HMSO.

Lists of Statutory Documents. Douglas: Central Reference Library. (quarterly and annual).

Loveridge, John (1975) *The constitution and law of Guernsey*. Guernsey: Guernsey Press.

Manx Law Bulletin. (1983–) Douglas: HM Attorney General. Twice yearly.

Manx law reports. (1961–) Oxford: Law Reports International.

Manx Telecom. *Telephone directory*. Douglas: Manx Telecom.

Marine Administration (IOM) (1995a) *Manx merchant shipping and harbours register*. Douglas: Marine Administration.

Marine Administration (IOM) (1995b) *Shipping fact file*. Douglas: Marine Administration. Sheets in folder.

Matthews, Paul and Sowden, Terry (1993) *The Jersey law of trusts*. 3rd edn. London: Key Haven Publications.

The official Isle of Man yearbook. Braddon: Executive Publications. Annual.

Orders in Council and other matters of general interest registered on the records of the island of Guernsey. (1803–) Guernsey: HM Greffier. Covers two- or three-year period. Spine title: Ordres en Conseil.

Orders in Council, Laws etc. (1771–) Jersey: States Greffier. In 7 volumes to 1936. 8th to 1960. Now looseleaf covering two years. Spine title: *Recueil des Lois*.

Ordinances of the States. (1800–) Guernsey: HM Greffier. Covers two- or three-year period. Spine title: *Recueil d'Ordonnances*.

Prater, David. *Manx Cases: index to cases 1884–1988*. Douglas: Isle of Man Law Society.

Prater, David. *Manx cases: subject index 1884–1971*. Douglas: Isle of Man Law Society.

Quayle, Robert (1990) The Isle of Man constitution. In Robinson and McCarroll (1990) *The Isle of Man* . . . pp. 123–132.

Reform (Guernsey) Laws, 1948 to 1993 (etc). Guernsey: HM Greffier.

Reform (Sark) Law 1951. Guernsey: HM Greffier.

Robilliard, St J.A. (1985) *Guernsey's housing control law*. Manchester: Manchester University Press.

Robinson, Vaughan and McCarroll, Danny (eds) (1990) *The Isle of Man: celebrating a sense of place*. Liverpool: Liverpool University Press.

Rowland G. (1992) The Bailiwick of Guernsey. *The Law Librarian*, 23(4), pp. 181–188.

Rules of the High Court. Douglas: Isle of Man Government.

Sheridan, L.A. (1955) The Channel Islands. In Keeton *The United Kingdom: the development of its laws and constitutions*. (1955) pp. 1141–53.

Solly, Mark (1994) *Government and law in the Isle of Man*. Castletown: Parallel Books.

States of Jersey Law 1966 [etc.] (1996) Jersey: States Greffe. Looseleaf, regularly updated.

States of Jersey Policy and Resources Committee *Strategic Policy Review*. St Helier: States of Jersey. Annual.

Statutes in Force (1972–). London: HMSO. Looseleaf. Updated.

Subject guide to Acts of Tynwald. Douglas: HM Attorney General. Annual.

Sweet and Maxwell's legal bibliography of the British Commonwealth of Nations (1989) (2 vols). Reprint of vols originally published in 1955 and 1957. London: Rees.

Table des Decisions de la Cour Royale de Jersey. (1885–1963) Jersey: Bigwoods. 7 Vols. Later Vol. (in English) covers 1964–1978.

Terrien, G. (1574) *Commentaires du Droit Civil et public que privé, observé au pays et Duché de Normandie*. Paris: Jacques du Pays. Another edition appeared in 1578.
Tynwald Select Committee on Constitutional Issues (1980) *2nd Interim Report*. Douglas: Tynwald.
The Tynwald companion (1993) Douglas: Tynwald. Published after each general election.
Twining, W. and Uglow, J. (1981) *Law publishing and legal information: jurisdictions of the British Isles*. London: Sweet and Maxwell.
Uglow, J. (1981) The Isle of Man. In Twining and Uglow (1981) *Law publishing and legal information: jurisdictions of the British Isles*. pp. 117–133.
Young, G.V.C. (1983) *A brief history of the Isle of Man*. Peel: Mansk-Svenska Pub. Co.

Acknowledgments

Very many people in Douglas, Guernsey and Jersey were outstandingly generous with time, information and gifts of legal materials, including: Mr. G.C. Rowland, HM Comptroller, Guernsey, who gave me invaluable lecture notes; Mr. G.H.C. Coppock, States Greffier, Jersey, provided useful leads; Mr. K.H. Tough, HM Greffier, Guernsey, with his infectious enthusiasm, gave me insights into the history of the Channel Islands, as well as much valuable legal guidance; Mr. G.H.C. Heywood, Central Reference Library, Miss J. Turley. H.M. Attorney-General's Secretary, and Mr. Lawrence Keenan, Advocate, guided me towards sources of Manx law.

I am especially grateful to Mrs. Sandra Greer, Northern Ireland Assembly Library, for her efficiency and exemplary patience in typing both this and the Northern Ireland chapter.

CHAPTER THIRTY-ONE

States of the former Yugoslavia

ANNE PRIES

Preamble

Because of the situation in former Yugoslavia, it was not possible to obtain all the relevant information from libraries there, several of which no longer even exist. Communication with the libraries which do still operate and with other agencies was rather difficult. It is regretted therefore that this chapter will have some lacunae. In an attempt to make the relevant aspects of the situation in Yugoslavia somewhat understandable, the introduction is more extensive than usual. This chapter will include the following sections:

- **General**
- **Serbia and Montenegro/Federal Republic of Yugoslavia**
- **Bosnia and Herzegovina**
- **Croatia**
- **Slovenia**
- **Macedonia**
- **List of works cited for the whole chapter**

General

This section describes materials relating to Yugoslavia up to about 1991 and also current comparative materials, often published in other countries, which will be of use for more than one of the present countries which are considered individually in the later sections of this chapter.

Introduction to the historical and constitutional background

After World War I Yugoslavia was formed from the territories of the independent kingdoms of Serbia and Montenegro and from several provinces of the Austro-Hungarian Empire: Croatia-Slavonia, Bosnia and Herzegovina, Slovenia, Vojvodina and Dalmatia. The formation of a new state was announced in Zagreb by a joint declaration of the National Council and Prince Alexander of Serbia on 1 December 1918. The first government of the United Kingdom of Serbia, Croatia and Slovenia was formed and a provisional National Assembly was installed in March 1919, consisting of 84 representatives for Serbia, 62 for Croatia, 42 for Bosnia-Herzegovina, 32 for Slovenia, 24 for South Serbia, 12 for Dalmatia and 4 for Vojvodina.

From the beginning the codes of law in Yugoslavia were not uniform for the entire country. Each part of the country retained the law which had been in force prior to the unification. When the kingdom was created, six different jurisdictions and six different systems of civil and criminal law and procedure and administrative law existed. Besides Serbian and Montenegrin law in the respective states, local provincial law in Croatia and Slavonia, Hungarian law and Austrian law were in force in the territory of the new kingdom. As soon as the government was in place, the authorities started to set up a uniform legal system. At first some Serbian laws were extended to the whole territory of Yugoslavia. By the Constitution of 1921 central government and local self-government were founded and a Legislative Committee was installed to prepare the unification of the legal system.

The period of the Kingdom of Yugoslavia started in 1929 when King Alexander suspended the constitution and declared himself the monarch of the country, and ended with the German invasion in 1941. By that time Yugoslavia was a monarchy under King Peter II and the Constitution of 1931 was in force which gave the King sweeping powers. By that time almost all major fields of law were covered by uniform laws.

The annexation of various segments of occupied Yugoslav territory was announced by the occupying powers: German, Hungarian, Italian and Bulgarian. One part of Yugoslavia was declared an independent country under the name of the Independent State of Croatia. Immediately after the invasion two guerrilla movements sprang up. The first was officially known as the Royal Yugoslav Army in the Fatherland and popularly as 'Chetnicks' under the command of Draža Mihalović ; the second was known as Partisans and Volunteers' Army of Yugoslavia for National Liberation or 'Partisans' under the command of Josip Broz Tito, Secretary General of the Communist Party of Yugoslavia. A more or less open civil war started between the Partisans and Chetnicks.

In 1942 the Communist Party created a central agency: the Anti-Fascist

Council of National Liberation of Yugoslavia, Antifašističko Vjeće Narodnog Oslobodjenja Jugoslavije, AVNOJ. In November 1943, the AVNOJ declared itself the supreme legislative and executive representative body, and its presidium representative of the state sovereignty. The Yugoslav government in exile was deprived of its rights as the legitimate government, particularly of the right to represent the peoples of Yugoslavia before foreign countries. King Peter II's return to Yugoslavia was prohibited.

When wartime hostilities ended, a new provisional government was nominated on 8 March 1945 and elections for the Constituent Assembly were held on 11 November. The People's Front, an umbrella organization of communists and collaborating parties, gained 90 per cent of the votes. The new assembly first met on 29 November. It was decided to organize Yugoslavia on federal principles. The name of the country changed to Federativna Narodna Republika Jugoslavije, FNRJ [Federal People's Republic of Yugoslavia], comprising six republics: Serbia (with the autonomous Vojvodina and Kosovo), Croatia, Bosnia/Herzegovina, Slovenia, Montenegro and Macedonia. So each of the major ethnic groups was given a separate political identity.

Tito was Prime Minister in the period 1945–1953 and President of the Republic from 1953 onwards until his death in 1980; he had been President/Secretary General of the Communist Party from 1937–1980.

By the Constitution of 1946, modelled on Stalin's Soviet Constitution of 1936, Yugoslavia was organized as a communist republic. Tito's break with Stalin and the rest of Eastern Europe was expressed in the new constitutions of 1953 and 1963. In the field of federal legislation, the individual republics could pass their own laws provided they were expressly authorized by a federal law (art.16). Amendments to the 1963 constitutions, made in 1967, 1968 and 1971 were part of a constitutional reform completed in 1974. An English translation of the communist constitution of the SFRY can be found in *The constitutions of the communist world* (Simons, 1980).

According to the 1974 Constitution, social self-government, exercised in all administrative levels, combined with social ownership formed the basis of the social and political system. The name of the country changed to Socijalistička Federativna Republika Jugoslavije, SFRJ [Socialist Federal Republic of Yugoslavia, SFRY]. The Assembly of the SFRY had two chambers: the Federal Chamber and the Chamber of the Republics and Provinces. The executive body of the Assembly was the Federal Executive Council, in which each republic and province was represented equally. The Presidency, consisting of 16 persons, elected the President. After the death of Tito, the function of President was replaced by the collective leadership of the Presidency.

Many factors led to the crisis, resulting in the disintegration of the country. It is far beyond the scope of this chapter to go into details. The emergency Congress of the League of Communists in February 1990 marked the beginning of the end. In June 1991 Croatia and Slovenia proclaimed independence and this meant the break-up of Yugoslavia. The separate republics adopted their own constitutions in the period between 1990 and 1991, see Vukadinović (1992) *The break-up of Yugoslavia: threats and challenges.*

Much of the legal system existing at the time of dissolution will of necessity still be relevant in the states of the former Yugoslavia. In particular the Savezna Republika Jugoslavija [Federal Republic of Yugoslavia (FRY)] was founded on 27 April 1992 and the same day the Constitution of the Federal Republic of Yugoslavia, formed by Serbia and Montenegro was adopted. The Federation of Serbia and Montenegro is the inheritor of the name Yugoslavia and continues many of the publications of the former Yugoslavia described below.

Introductory works on the legal system and legal research

The legal systems of the republics of former Yugoslavia have been changing very much during the last few years and the process of reform and reconstruction is still continuing. Introductory works to the current legal system have not yet been published.

The article by Reynolds (1992) on socialist legal systems in the *International Journal of Legal Information* gives useful background information, as does the chapter on Yugoslavia in Michta (1994). The chapters by Blagojević (1974) in the *International encyclopedia of comparative law* and by the same author in the *Modern legal systems cyclopedia* (Blagojević, 1991) mainly refer to the period of the SFRY, although the later has been supplemented by some pages on 'recent developments'; both remain important contributions. *Guide to the Yugoslav legal system*, a volume of over 200 pages, also by Blagojević, appeared in 1977. The book on *Yugoslav civil law* by Chloros (1970) is more dated but also remains valuable to an understanding of the Yugoslav legal system.

Good guides to earlier material are *Legal sources and bibliography of Yugoslavia* (Gjupanovich and Adamovich, 1964), the chapter on Yugoslavia in *Official publications of the Soviet Union and eastern Europe 1945–1980* (Terry, 1982) and the chapter on Yugoslavia in Gsovski and Grzybovski (1959).

Legislation

The source for laws in the Socialist Federative Republic of Yugoslavia was the *Službeni List Socijalističke Federativne Republike Jugoslavije.*

(Federativne Narodne Republike Jugoslavije) [Official Gazette of the Socialist Federal Republic (Federal People's Republic) of Yugoslavia] published in Belgrade 1945–1991, under slightly varying titles 1945–1963. In the period of the Kingdom, 1918–1944, it was entitled *Službene Novine* [Official News]. It contains texts of laws, decrees, regulations and executive orders issued by the government, the annual budget and other materials legally required to be published. It has an annual cumulative index arranged by subject.

The *Zbornik propisa Jugoslovenskog zakonodavstva: savezni, republiči i pokrajinski zakoni* [Collection of Yugoslav legislation: federal, republican and regional laws] (1988) was a compilation in three volumes which was probably the last statement of the laws of the 'old' Yugoslavia.

The Institut za uporedno pravo [Institute of Comparative Law] in Belgrade irregularly issues a monograph series containing English translations of Yugoslav legislation: *Collection of Yugoslav laws* (1962–); these include substantial works such as a translation of the Criminal Code in 1964. A useful collection of official documents of former Yugoslavia in English translations can be found in *Yugoslavia through documents: from its creation to its dissolution* (Trifunovska, 1994).

The daily journal of the Assembly of the SFRY, edited in several languages, *Stenografske Beleške* [Stenographic report] was published from 1945–1992; the English edition was named *Yugoslav Assembly*.

Codes and commentaries

An official monograph series with individual volumes devoted to particular laws on a subject is the *Zbirka saveznih propisa* [Collection of federal regulations] issued in Belgrade (1954–1990) after which the title was continued in the Federal Republic of Yugoslavia (see below).

Yugoslav criminal legislation, the Criminal Code [*Krivični zakon*] with annotations and an index and the Code of Criminal Procedure [*Zakon o krivičnom postupku*], has been published together with the criminal codes of the republics and autonomous provinces in 1978, edited by Perović. Commentary on the Code of Criminal Procedure can be found in Vasiljevič and Grubač (1987). The latest edition of the Criminal Code of the SFRY has been published as *Krivični zakon SFRJ* (Vuković, 1990).

The laws on economic reform in English, edited by Druker (1990), has been published in Belgrade.

Treaties

Since 1953 texts of international agreements and treaties concluded between Yugoslavia and foreign countries were published separately from the official gazette itself, in the *Službeni List. Međunarodni Ugovori. Federativne Narodne Republike Jugoslavije* until 1992. An annual list of international agreements concluded between Yugoslavia and other countries for the given year appears in *Jugoslovenski pregled* (1957–), that has an English edition: *Yugoslav Survey* (1960–) and in the German periodical *WGO: Monatshefte für Osteuropäisches Recht* (1959–).

The international documents concerning the Yugoslav civil war can be found in Trifunovska (1994) and generally in United Nations documentation and international law journals.

Law reports, judgments

The judicial system of the SFRY consisted of courts of general jurisdiction on various levels, of which the highest was the Supreme Court. There was also a Supreme Economic Arbitration Court. Similar courts existed at republic and province levels. Since the break-up of Yugoslavia the latter courts are the final courts of appeal for their respective jurisdictions.

Decisions of the Supreme Court of the SFRY were published in the *Bilten sudske prakse Saveznog suda* [Bulletin of the Federal Court's Practice] from 1975 to 1993 after which they were continued by a Serbian title (see below). The *Zbirka sudskih odluka* [Collection of court decisions] (1956–1983) covers the decisions of the Supreme, Supreme Military and Supreme Economic Courts. Decisions of the civil courts were published in the monthly periodical *Sudske prakse: stručno-informativni časopis* [Court practice: special informative periodical] (1981–?). A quarterly devoted to court and judicial practice in civil matters in the SFRY was: *Sudska i upravna praksa za organizacija udruženog rada, SIZ i radne zajednice* [Court and administrative practice on the organization of associated labour, self-management communities and workers' collectives] (?-1992). *Zakon o krivičnom postupku objašnjen sudskom praksom* [Law on criminal procedure with court practice] contains selected decisions (Petrić, 1983).

In the SFRY in 1963 Constitutional Courts were established on the federal level as well as in the six republics and two autonomous provinces. The performance of the Yugoslav Constitutional Courts was quite remarkable from the quantitative point of view but only infrequently acquired political importance according to Brunner (1992). The decisions of the Federal and Republican Constitutional Courts were published in the annual *Odluke i mišlenja Ustavnog suda Jugoslavije*

[Decisions and opinions of the Constitutional Court of Yugoslavia] (1972–1991), which has also been published in Slovenian and Macedonian. Decisions may also appear in *East European Case Reporter of Constitutional Law* (1994–).

Yugoslav legal journals (see below) usually contain selected decisions. The *OMRI Daily Digest* (1994–) published by the Open Media Research Institute gives English summaries of selected court decisions.

Bibliographies and indexing services

A recent general bibliography in English is *Yugoslavia: a comprehensive English-language bibliography* (Friedman, 1993).

The periodical *Arhiv za pravne i društvene nauke* [Archive of legal and social sciences] (1914–) gives an annual overview of legal publications edited by Radovanović and entitled 'Bibliografija knjiga iz oblasti prava i političkih nauka objavljenih na srpskohrvatskom jeziku . . . godine' [Bibliography of books on law and political sciences in Serbo-Croatian, published in . . .].

The *Bibliografija zvaničnih publikacija SFRJ. Knjige. Serijske publikacije* [Bibliography of official publications of the SFRY. Books and serial publications] (1971–1991) gives an overview of all government publications. It is arranged by subject according to the Universal Decimal Classification system. An annual cumulative index of authors and titles is provided.

Dictionaries

A recent edition the *Serbocroatian–English dictionary* by Benson, compiled in cooperation of the University of Pennsylvania, was published in 1994.

Current information sources

Journals, research reports

In the SFRY, and now the FRY, the Association of Yugoslav Jurists publishes the quarterly *Arhiv za Pravne i Društvene Nauke* (1914–) [Records on law and social sciences]. Its emphasis is on legal sciences and constitutional law and it has English summaries. Its annual bibliography of legal publications is particularly important.

The Union of Jurists' Associations in Belgrade has published the quarterly *Novo Jugoslovensko pravo = New Yugoslav law* (1950–1974), containing legal articles in English as well as current documentation and the text of new laws, decisions, resolutions. It was also published in French. It was succeeded by the bilingual periodical *Yugoslav law = Droit Yougoslave* (1975–1989?), published in cooperation with the Institute of Comparative Law in Belgrade. Besides articles on legal issues, it contained a survey of legislation in Yugoslavia, court practice and a bibliography of Yugoslav legal literature. The *Jugoslovenska revija za međunarodno pravo* [Yugoslav Review of International Law] (1954–) is issued three times a year, since 1994 by the Ministry of Science and Technology in cooperation with the Soros Foundation. Focused on criminal law is the *Jugoslovenska revija za kriminologiju i krivično pravo* [Yugoslav Review of Criminology and Criminal Law] (1963–).

Developments in 'Yugoslav law' and now the laws of the various countries which were part of Yugoslavia, are covered more and more frequently by journals published abroad devoted to Central and Eastern Europe. These include the *Review of Central and East European Law* (1992–) published in cooperation with the Institute of East European Law and Russian Studies of Leiden University, the *Parker School Journal of East European Law* (1994–) and the *BNA's Eastern Europe Reporter* (1991–). Other information on legal issues can be found in the publication of the Center for the Study of Constitutionalism in Eastern Europe in Chicago, *East European Constitutional Review* (1992–) as well as in the *Journal of Constitutional Law in Eastern and Central Europe* (1994–) and in the *Eastern European Forum Newsletter* (1993–), a publication of the London International Bar Association. Newsletters of law firms such as *Central Europe Newsletter* (1992–) and *Central European and CIS Legal Update* (1993–) among others can be extremely helpful. *Recht in Ost und West* (1957–) gives legal information in German as does *Osteuropa-Recht* (1955–). An overview of the legal changes can be found in the *Jahrbuch für Ostrecht* (1960–).

News information

A useful source for general information about the countries is the annual survey published in London by Economist Publications, *Country profile: annual survey of political and economic background.* In the period 1986–1991 the survey covered Yugoslavia; since 1992 the survey is published in two series: one on Bosnia-Herzegovina, Croatia, and Slovenia and the other on Macedonia and Serbia-Montenegro.

General information about the republics of former Yugoslavia is given on their home page on the Internet (addresses below for each country section). Besides the *OMRI Daily Digest,* OMRI in Prague publishes the weekly *Transition: Events and Issues in the Former Soviet Union and East Central and Southeastern Europe* (1995–), a journal of analysis and news on political, social, economic, legal and other affairs.

Business and financial information

Business information is given on the Internet home pages of the countries involved (addresses below for each country section). Many foreign periodicals are also focused on economic activities and business in the countries of former Yugoslavia such as KPMG's international newsletter, *Image on Central + Eastern Europe* (1991–), *Law in Transition* (1994–), a newsletter from the European Bank for Reconstruction and Development, *Doing business in Eastern Europe* (1992–) and in the *Parker School Journal of East European Law* (1994–). A German periodical devoted to legal aspects of commercial activities in eastern Europe is *WiRO: Wirtschaft und Recht in Osteuropa* (1992–).

The electronic periodical *OMRI Daily Digest* (1994–) gives political, economic and legal information; part II covers Central, Eastern and South-eastern Europe. Political and economic information on the country can also be found in part 2 of *SWB: Summary of World Broadcasts* (1993–) which covers Central Europe and the Balkans.

Statistics

Statistical data on the federal level were given in *Statistički godišnjak Jugoslavije = Statistical Yearbook of Yugoslavia* (1954–1991) which was published partly in English.

Federal Republic of Yugoslavia/Serbia and Montenegro

(Please also consult the **General** section above)

Introduction to the legal system

Serbia adopted its new constitution on 28 September 1990 and it was published in the *Službeni glasnik RS* 1990, no.1, item 1.

In a joint session of the SFRY Assembly, the National Assembly of the Republic of Serbia and the Assembly of the Republic of Montenegro on 27 April 1992, the participants adopted a 'Declaration on a new Yugoslavia'. The Savezna Republika Jugoslavija [Federal Republic of Yugoslavia (FRY)] was founded. On the same day the Constitution of the Federal Republic of Yugoslavia, formed by Serbia and Montenegro, was adopted. The provinces Kosovo and Vojvodina had already lost their autonomous status in 1990 with the adoption of the Constitution of Serbia on 28 September 1990.

The Federation of Serbia and Montenegro is the inheritor of the name Yugoslavia. According to article 1 of the Constitution, the Federal Republic shall be a sovereign federal state founded on the equality of citizens and the equality of its member republics. The two members of the federation are, however, considerably different in size and economic strength.

The Constitution of the FRY of April 1992 has been published together with related legislation as *Ustav Savezne Republika Jugoslavije; Ustavni zakon za sprovodenje Ustava; Zakon o izboru saveznih poslanika u Veće gradana Savezne skupštine; Zakon o izboru i razrešenju Predsednika Republika* [Constitution of the Republic of Jugoslavia; constitutional law for putting into effect the constitution; Law on the elections of the representatives of the Chamber of Citizens of the Federal Assembly; Law on the Election and Dismissal of the President of the Republic] (1992). *The Constitution of the Federal Republic of Yugoslavia* has been translated into English by Margot and Bosko Milosavljević (1992).

The federation has a bicameral parliament: *Savezna Skupština* [Federal Assembly], consisting of the first chamber: *Veće Republika* [Chamber of Republics] with 40 members, 20 for each republic, and the second chamber: *Veće Građana* [Chamber of Citizens], with 138 members. Federal deputies are elected for four-year terms. According to the Constitution, the President of the Federal Republic shall be elected by the Federal Assembly, for a four-year term, by secret ballot. He represents the Federal Republic at home and abroad, promulgates federal laws by decree, issues instruments of ratification of international treaties. He recommends to the Federal Assembly candidates for appointments as justices of the Federal Constitutional Court, the Federal Public Prosecutor and the Governor of the National Bank of Yugoslavia. As a rule, the President and the Federal Prime Minister may not be from the same member republic. The Federal Government, made up of a prime minister, deputy prime minister and federal ministers, adopts decrees, resolutions and other legislation for the enforcement of federal statutes and general enactments of the Federal Assembly.

The Federal Court (art.108 ff) is the court of the highest instance; the justices are appointed and dismissed by the Federal Assembly. The term is nine years. The Constitutional Court (art.124 ff) rules on the conformity of the constitutions of the member republics with the Federal Constitution. The Court is composed of seven justices, appointed for a nine-year term.

The Constitution of the Republic of Serbia has been translated into English by Margot and Bosko Milosavljević (1990). A German translation of the new constitution of Serbia has been published in Vienna, *Slowenien-Kroatien-Serbien: die neuen Verfassungen* (Marko and Boric, 1991). German translations of the constitution and other documents are to be found in the looseleaf *Wirtschaftsrecht der osteuropäischen Staaten* (Brunner, Schmidt and Westen, 1992–).

Legislation

The official gazette of the new Federation, FRY, has been published since 27 April 1992 as *Službeni List Savezne Republike Jugoslavije* [Official Gazette of the Federal Republic of Yugoslavia] containing all the legislation. Both partners of the FRY also have their own official gazettes: *Službeni glasnik Republike Srbije* [Official Gazette of the Republic of Serbia] (1945–); *Službeni list Republike Crne Gore* [Official Gazette of the Republic of Montenegro] (1945–).

The FRY publishes reports of debates in its Assembly under the same name used by the SFRY, *Stenografske Beleške* (1992–).

Codes and commentaries

A great part of the legislation of the SFRY (see above) has been adopted by the FRY. Yugoslav civil legislation was enacted in the form of separate statutes for every field of civil law, rather than as a single code. For civil procedure, the law of 24 December 1976, published in *Službeni list* 1977 no.4, *Zakon o paričnom postupku* [Law on civil procedure] was adopted by the FRY.

The official series of monographs, each volume devoted to laws on a particular subject, which was published by the SFRY, *Zbirka saveznih propisa* [Collection of federal regulations] (1954–1990) has been continued in the FRY.

The current Criminal Code of the FRY has been published in an annotated edition as *Krivični zakon Savezne Republike Jugoslavije* [Criminal Code of FRY] (Kokolj, 1993) and with a commentary (Stojanović, 1995). *Zakon o krivičnom postupku sa sudskom praksom i registrom pojmova* [Law on criminal procedure with court practice and index of legal concepts] is edited by Petaković (1990).

A new edition of laws on court practice in the FRY has been published, *Jugoslovenski procesni zakoni* (Srdić, 1994).

On the republican level in Serbia also by Petaković (1992) is *Krivični zakon Srbije* [Criminal law of Serbia]. More recent is *Krivično pravo u sudskoj praksi: KZ Srbije i KZ Crne Gore sa kommentarom i sudskom praksom* [Criminal law and court practice] which covers both Serbia and Montenegro with commentary and selected decisions (Zindović and Dragutinović, 1995). Also covering both Criminal Codes with commentary is Stojanović and Petrić (1996).

Treaties

Since 1993 the FRY has published its international treaties in the *Službeni List – Međunarodni Ugovori. Savezne Republike Jugoslavije.*

Law reports, judgments

Decisions of the Supreme Court of the FRY have been published under the title: *Bilten sudske prakse Vrhovnog suda Srbije* [Bulletin of the practice of the Supreme Court of Serbia] (1993–), edited by Milovan Deijer. Decisions of the civil courts are published in the monthly periodical published by the FRY, *Izbor sudske prakse: stručno-informativni časopis* [Selection of court practice: special informative periodical] (1993–). A quarterly devoted to judicial practice in civil matters in the FRY, *Sudske i upravna praksa: stalne, tematske publikacije* [Court and administrative practice . . .] (1993–) continues a similar SFRY title.

A retrospective compilation of decisions in Serbia is *Zbornik sudske prakse: 1975–1985* [Collection of court practice: 1975–1985] (Ivošević, 1995). The *Registar važećih propisa i sudske prakse* [Register of current regulations and court practice] cites court decisions interpreting legislation (Kitarović, 1992). There are several treatises which also compile selected decisions in a convenient format and these are listed under **Codes and commentaries** above.

Odluke i rešenja saveznog Ustavnog suda 1992 i 1993 [Decisions and resolutions of the Constitutional Court in 1992 and 1993] (1994) continues for the FRY the similar title of the SFRY.

Bibliographies

The *Bibliografija zvaničnih publikacija SRJ. Knjige. Serijske publikacije* [Bibliography of official publications of the FRY. Books and serial publications] (1992–) is edited by the Bibliographic Institute in Belgrade. The national libraries of both Serbia and Montenegro and the Biblioteka Matice Srpske (addresses below) produce regular general bibliographies.

Current information sources

Journals

The Association of Jurists in Serbia, in cooperation with the Faculty of Law in Belgrade issues a periodical devoted to the study of Yugoslav and comparative law, court practice in civil and criminal law and arbitration: *Pravni život* [Legal life] (1952–). Comments on legislation and court practice from both federal and Serbian courts, constitutional court practice and international commercial arbitration is given in *Pravo. Teorija i praksa* [Law, theory and practice] (1983–).

The Law Faculty in Belgrade publishes its own periodical: *Anali*

Pravnog Fakulteta u Belgradu [Annals of the Law Faculty in Belgrade] (1953–). Law faculties in other university cities have their own general legal periodicals too, for example, in Novi Sad the *Zbornik radova* (1966–), French edition entitled *Recueil des travaux.*

See also journals in the **General** section above.

News, business and financial information

The Ministry of Science, Technology and Development publishes *Ekonomski pregled: mesečni informativni pregled* [Economic Survey: monthly informative survey] (1994–). Another governmental publication is *Promene: poslovne informacije jugoslavenske vlade* [Changes: business information of the Yugoslav government] (1990–).

See also the **General** section above.

Statistics

The two main series of statistical yearbooks are *Statistički godišnjak Srbije* (1992–) previously entitled *Statistički godišnjak SR Srbije* (1951–1991) and *Statistički godišnjak Republike Crne Gore* (1991–) previously entitled *Statistički godišnjak SR Crne Gore.*

Useful addresses: FRY/Serbia and Montenegro

Associations of lawyers

Association of Jurists of Yugoslavia, Proleterskih brigada 74, POB 179, Belgrade, Serbia. Tel: +381 11 4448459

Savez Republiskih Pokrajinskih advokatskih Kamora Jugoslavije [Bar Association of the Federal Republic of Yugoslavia], Mose Pijade 13/1, 11000 Belgrade, Serbia. Tel: +381 11 339846

Government organizations

Ministry of Economic Affairs, Bulevar Avnoj-a 104, 11000 Belgrade, Serbia. Tel: +381 11 602555

Statistical Office, Knesa Milosa 20, 11000 Belgrade, Serbia. Tel: +381 11 1684951. Fax: +381 11 1681995

Education and training

Pravni Fakultet, Univerzitet u Beogradu [Law Faculty, University of Belgrade], Bulevar revolucije 67, 11000 Belgrade, Belgrade. Tel: +381 11 330116. Fax : +381 11 331313

Pravni Fakultet, Univerzitet Crne Gore, Podgorica [Law Faculty, University of Montenegro, Podgorica], 13 jali 1, 81000 Podgorica, Montenegro. Tel: +381 81 45237. Fax: +381 81 43587

Pravni Fakultet, Univerzitet u Novom Sadu [Law Faculty, University of Novi Sad], Trg. Dositeja Obradovica 1, 21000 Novi Sad, Serbia. Tel: +381 21 350377

Libraries

Biblioteka Matice Srpske [Yugoslav National Library], Ul. Matice srpske 1, 21000 Novi Sad, Serbia. Tel: +381 21 615599. Fax: +381 21 28574. Founded in 1826 in Budapest, transferred to Novi Sad in 1864. Copyright deposit library for Vojvodina and Yugoslavia.

Biblioteka Srpske akademije nauke i umetnosti [Library of the Serbian Academy of Sciences and Art] Knez Mihailova 35, 11001 Belgrade, Serbia. Tel: +381 11 637514. Fax: +381 11 182825. Founded in 1842.

Centralna narodna biblioteka Crne Gore [Central National Library of Montenegro], Pf.57, Bulevar Lenjina 163, 81250 Cetinje, Montenegro. Tel: +381 86 21143. Founded in 1946.

Narodna biblioteka Srbije [National Library of Serbia], Skerlićeva 1, 11000 Belgrade, Serbia. Tel: +381 11 451242. Fax: +381 11 452952. Founded in 1832. Federal copyright and deposit library.

Pravni Fakultet – Biblioteka [Library of the Law Faculty of the University of Belgrade], Bulevar revolucije 67, 11000 Belgrade, Serbia. Tel: +381 11 341501

Skupština SR Jugoslavije – Biblioteka [Parliamentary Library of the Federal Republic of Yugoslavia], Trg. Nikole Pašića 13, 11000 Belgrade, Serbia. Tel: +381 11 339651

Research institutes

Institut za uporedno pravo [Institute of Comparative Law], Terazije 41, 11000 Belgrade, Serbia. Tel: +381 11 333213

Others

Chamber of Commerce of Serbia, Generala Zdanova 13–15, 11000 Belgrade, Serbia. Tel: +381 11 340611. Fax: +381 11 330949

Bosnia and Herzegovina

Please also consult the **General** section above.

Historical and constitutional background

Republika Bosna i Hercegovina [Republic of Bosnia and Herzegovina] did not adopt a new constitution after the break-up of Yugoslavia; the Constitution of 1974 (see above) was kept in force with some changes. In the 1990 elections the separate ethnic groups voted for separate Muslim, Serb and Croat nationalist parties and this situation led to the partition of the country. In the framework of this chapter further details of the civil war and its causes must be neglected; for documents concerning the civil war in Bosnia, see Trifunovska (1994).

In February 1992 the Assembly of the Serbian nation of Bosnia-Herzegovina proclaimed an independent Bosnian Serb Republic which was later named 'Republika Srpska' (RS). The constitution of this Republic was published in the *Službeni glasnik srpskog naroda u Bosni i Hercegovini* of 16 March 1992.

In August 1993 the Bosnian Serbs and the Bosnian Croats accepted the Owen-Stoltenberg proposals on a union of three ethnic republics in Bosnia. The 1994 Washington (1 March) and Vienna (11 May) agreements established the so-called Bosnian (Muslim)/Croat Federation at 58 per cent of the Bosnian territory and determined the composition of an interim federal government. 'Bosnia and Herzegovina: Constitution of the Federation [8 March, 1994]' (1994) is to be found in *International Legal Materials*, 1994, **33**, pp. 740–784. There is a critical analysis of this constitution by Hayden (1994).

On 8 September 1995 the Bosnian, Croatian and FRY representatives reached an agreement on basic principles, the so called 'Geneva Agreement'. This agreement was followed by the 'New York Agreement' on further basic principles on 26 September 1995, and finally by the Dayton agreement.

The 1995 Constitution of Bosnia and Herzegovina, the so called Dayton Constitution, came into effect upon signature of Croatia and the Federal Republic of Yugoslavia and states that Bosnia and Herzegovina, henceforth the official name, shall continue its legal existence under international law as a state, with its present internationally recognized border. It shall contain two entities: the Federation of Bosnia and Herzegovina and the 'Republika Srpska'. Each entity may also enter into agreements with states and international organizations with the consent of the Parliamentary Assembly.

The Parliamentary Assembly has two chambers: the House of Peoples and the House of Representatives. The House of Peoples comprises five Croats, five Bosnians and five Serbs; the House of Representatives comprises 42 members, two-thirds elected from the territory of the Federation, one third from the territory of the 'Republika Srpska'. The Presidency of Bosnia and Herzegovina consists of three members: one Bosnian and one Croat, directly elected from the territory of the Federation, and one Serb, directly elected from the Srpska territory. The Council of Ministers is nominated by the Presidency. No more than two-thirds of all Ministers may be appointed from the territory of the Federation. The constitution may be amended by a decision of the Parliamentary Assembly (art.X,1). The Bosnia and Herzegovina Constitution 1995 has been published in English in the quarterly *Balkan Forum*, 1996, **4**, pp. 260–285 and examined in critical terms in Hayden (1995).

The Constitutional Court of Bosnia and Herzegovina has nine members: four shall be elected by the House of Representatives of the Federation, two by the Assembly of the Republika Srpska and three selected by the President of the European Court of Human Rights, after consultation with the Presidency. The term will be five years. The Constitutional Court has jurisdiction over issues referred by any other court in Bosnia and Herzegovina.

Introductory works on the legal system and legal research

See in the **General** section above.

Legislation

After World War II each of the Yugoslav federal republics had its own official gazette until the break-up of the country. In Bosnia/Herzegovina it was: *Službeni list . . . Republike Bosne i Hercegovine* (1944–). This is continued as one of the three official gazettes now published in Bosnia and Herzegovina. The other two are: *Službene novine Federacije Bosne i Hercegovine* [Official news of the Federation of B&H] (1995?–) and *Službeni glasnik Republike Srpske* [Official herald of the Republika Srbska], formerly *Službeni glasnik srpskog naroda u Bosni i Hercegovini* [Official herald of the Serbian people in Bosnia and Herzegovina].

Codes, commentaries and law reports

See in the **General** section above.

Bibliographies

A bibliography of Bosnia and Herzegovina has been published recently in Ankara: *Bosnia-Herzegovina bibliography* (1993).

Other reference works

A useful tool is the recent atlas of Croatia and Bosnia and Herzegovina, published by the Lexicographical Institute in Zagreb: *A concise atlas of the Republic of Croatia and of the Republic of Bosnia and Hercegovina* (1993).

Current information sources

See the general Internet addresses below and see also in the **General** section above.

Statistics

Statistical information can be found in the *Statistički godišnjak BiH* [1992–].

Useful addresses: Bosnia and Herzegovina

Associations of lawyers

Advokatsta Komoro SR BI [Bar Association of B & H], Saloma Albaharija 2, 71000 Sarajevo, Bosnia and Herzegovina. Tel: +387 71 216073

Savez Udruženja Pravnika BiH [Union of Jurists' Associations of B & H], Valtera Perića 11, 71000 Sarajevo, Bosnia and Herzegovina

Education and training

Univerzitet u Sarajevu [University of Sarajevo], Obala Vojvode Stepe 7/II, POB 186, 71000 Sarajevo, Bosnia and Herzegovina. Tel: +387 71 211216. Fax: +387 71 214289

Libraries

Narodna i universitetska biblioteka Bosne i Hercegovine [National and University Library of B & H], Obala Vojvose Stepe 42, POB 337, 71000 Sarajevo, Bosnia and Herzegovina. Tel: +387 71 537202. Founded in 1945. Copyright and deposit library. Building and collection badly damaged by war in 1992.

Others

Internet addresses for material related to Bosnia and Herzegovina:
http://www.cco.caltech.edu/bosnia/bosnia.html
http://www.x54all.nl/frankti/ondexeng.html

Chamber of Commerce, Marsala Tita 25, 71000 Sarajevo, Bosnia and Herzegovina. Tel: +387 71 537202

Croatia

Please also consult the **General** section above.

Historical and constitutional background

Republika Hrvatska [Republic of Croatia] adopted a new constitution on 22 December 1990 which was published in the *Narodne novine* 1990, No.56, item 1092. An English translation of the new constitution of Croatia can be found in *The rebirth of democracy: 12 constitutions of central and eastern Europe* (1995) and in the *Constitutions of central and eastern Europe* edited by Flanz (1995). A German translation of the new constitution of Croatia is *Slowenien-Kroatien-Serbien: die neuen Verfassungen* (Marko and Boric, 1991).

Croatia has a bicameral parliament, *Sabor Republike Hrvatske*. The first chamber consists of 68 members: *Županijski dom* [House of Countries]; the second chamber, *Zastupnički dom* [House of Representatives] has 138 members. *Županije* are units of local administration and self-government; large towns may be organized as *Županije*. The President of the Republic is the Head of State; he is elected for a five-year term by direct elections. He appoints and dismisses the prime minister. The government is responsible to the President and the Chamber of Representatives. The High Judicial Council has a president and 14 members, proposed by the *Županijski dom* and elected by the *Zastupnički dom* for a term of eight years, from notable judges, public prosecutors, lawyers and university professors of law. The regulations for the Constitutional Court can be found in arts.122–127. The 11 judges of the Court are elected in the same way and under the same conditions as the High Judicial Council.

Introductory works on the legal system and legal research

See in the **General** section above.

Legislation

The official gazette is the *Narodne novine: Službeni list Republike Hrvatske* [People's news: the official gazette of the Republic of Croatia] (1990–); previous edition *Narodne novine: Službeni list Socijalističke Republike Hrvatske* (1945–1990).

Parliamentary business was recorded in the Deputies Gazette of Croatia, the *Delegatski vjestnik* (1974–1990), now renamed *Izvješća Hrvatskogo Sabora* [Reports of the Croatian parliament] (1991–). An annual report, *Godišnjak*, contains reviews of the sessions of the House of Representatives and the House of Countries and important speeches and conclusions, adopted by the parliament.

Codes and commentaries

An official monograph series, similar to the *Zbirka* of the (S)FRY is the Croatian series *Zbirka pravnih propisa Narodnih novina* [Collection of legal rules published in the People's News] (1962–) published by the official publisher Narodne Novine. One of the most complete sources of Yugoslav civil law was available in this series.

In Croatia the current Civil Code has been published by Narodne Novine: *Građansko pravo: opći dio, obvezno i nasljedno pravo* [Civil Code: general part, law of obligations, inheritance law] (Vedriš, 1996). Current legislation in other subjects of civil law and family law has been published by the same publisher. In many cases Croatia adopted the former federal laws, for instance: Federal Law on Property of 1980 adopted by Croatia in 1991; Federal Law on Obligations of 1978 adopted by Croatia in 1991. The same can be said of the Law on Succession, the Law on Marriage and Family Relations, the Law on Marine and Inland Navigation and provisions of international private law.

For civil procedure, the federal law of 1977, *Zakon o paričnom postupku* [Law on Civil Procedure] was adopted by Croatia in 1991 as well as the federal law *Zakon o izvršnom postupku* [Law on Judicial Execution] (1978–1991).

Examples of new civil laws are: *Zakon o trgovačkim društvima* [Law on Trade Associations] (1995); *Pomorski zakonik* [Maritime Code] (1994) and the *Zakon o radu* [Labour Law] (1996).

Croatia made amendments to the old Croatian criminal code of 1977: *Krivični zakon Republike Hrvatske* in *Narodne Novine* 25/77, 50/78, 25/84, 52/87, 43/89, 8/90, 9/91, 33/92, 39/92 and 44/92. This Criminal Code was originally the former federal Criminal Code. The former federal Law on Criminal Procedure of 1977 was adopted by Croatia in 1991.

Examples of new legislation in the field of criminal law: *Zakon o kaznenim djelima podrivačke i terorističke djelatnosti protiv državnog suvereniteta i teritorijalne cjelovitosti Republike Hrvatske* [Law on subversive and terrorist criminal offences against state sovereignty and territorial integrity of the Republic of Croatia] (1992); *Zakon o amnestiji* (1990) [Amnesty Law] and *Zakon o oprostu od krivičnog progona i postupka za krivična djela počinjena u oružanim sukobima i u ratu protiv Republike Hrvatske* [Law on excuse for crimes committed during the armed conflicts and war against the Republic of Croatia] (1992).

Treaties

International treaties and agreements are published in the *Narodne novine – Međunarodni Ugovori* (1993–).

Law reports, judgments

The *Izbor odluka Vrhovnog suda Republike Hrvatske* [Selected judgments of the Supreme Court of the Republic of Croatia] (1993–) is published in Zagreb. *Pregled sudske prakse: Prilog (naše) Zakonitosti* (1972–) are officially published selected reports from various courts.

Before the break-up of Yugoslavia the decisions of the Croatian Constitutional Court were published annually in the *Odluke i mišlenja Ustavnog suda Jugoslavije* [Decisions and opinions of the Constitutional Court of Yugoslavia] (1972–1991).

Bibliographies

The national bibliography is the *Hrvatska Bibliografija,* published monthly and annually.

Other reference works

A useful tool is the recent atlas of Croatia and Bosnia and Herzegovina, published by the Lexicographical Institute in Zagreb: *A concise atlas of the Republic of Croatia and of the Republic of Bosnia and Hercegovina* (1993).

Current information sources

See the general Internet address below and see also in the **General** section above.

Journals, research reports

The Association of Croatian Jurists, in cooperation with other institutions, publishes *Zakonitost* (1990–). A periodical issued by the Association of Croatian Economic Jurists in Zagreb is *Pravo u gospodarstvu: časopis za gospodarsko-pravnu teoriju i praksu* [Journal for Business Law Theory and Practice] originally published from 1963. The Law Faculty in Zagreb issues the *Zbornik Pravnog Fakulteta u Zagrebu* [Zagreb Law Faculty Journal] (1948–). Under the title *Zbornik radova* (1963–) the journal of the Law Faculty of Split is published. A specialized journal devoted to maritime law is issued by the Croatian Academy of Sciences: *Uporedno pomorsko pravo = Comparative Maritime Law* (1960–).

Statistics

Statistical materials can be found in the *Statistički ljetopis Republike Hrvatske* (1993–) formerly *Statistički godišnjak SR Hrvatske* (1953–1991) and in the *Statistički ljetopis Hrvatskih županija* [Statistical yearbook of Croatian districts] (1994–).

Useful addresses: Croatia

Associations of lawyers

Odvjetniska Komora Hrvatske [Bar Association of Croatia], Zrinjevac 15, 41000 Zagreb, Croatia. Tel: +385 41 427710. Fax: +385 41 435251

Government organizations

Central Bureau of Statistics, Ilica 3, 41000 Zagreb, Croatia. Tel: +385 41 518070. Fax: +385 41 429413

Ministry of Industry, Avenija Vukovar 78, 41000 Zagreb, Croatia

Ministry of Justice, Ulica grada Vukovara 8, 1000 Zagreb, Croatia. Tel: +385 1 537622. Fax: +385 41 536321

Ministry of the Interior, Avenija Vukovar 33, 41000 Zagreb, Croatia

Education and training

Sveučilišna u Zagrebu [University of Zagreb], Trg Maršala Tita 14, 10000 Zagreb, Croatia. Tel: +385 41 464111/272411

Libraries

Biblioteka Pravnog Fakulteta u Zagrebu [Library of the Law Faculty in Zagreb], Trg Maršala Tita 14, 10000 Zagreb, Croatia. Tel: +385 41 564111 (switchboard); +385 41 564312 (Library). Fax: +385 41 564030. Founded in 1906.

Knjižnica Sabora Republike Hrvatske [Library of the Croatian Parliament], Trg Svetog Marka 6, 10000 Zagreb, Croatia. Tel: +385 41 569222; +385 41 126262 (switchboard); +385 41 569 590 (Library). Founded in 1861.

Nacionalna i sveučilišna biblioteka [National and University Library], Marulićev trg 21, 41000 Zagreb, Croatia. Tel: +385 41 446322 (switchboard); +385 41 445928 (information). Fax: +385 41 426676. Founded in the 17th century. Publishes the National Bibliography.

Others

Internet address for material on Croatia: http://www.tel.fer.hr/hrvatska/default.html

Chamber of Commerce in Croatia, Trg Franklin Roosvelta 2, 41000 Zagreb, Croatia. Tel: +385 41 443422

Slovenia

Please also consult the **General** section above.

Historical and constitutional background

Republika Slovenija [Republic of Slovenia] adopted a new constitution on 23 December 1991, which was published in the *Uradni list RS* 1991, no.33, item 1409. An English translation of the new constitution of Slovenia can be found in *The rebirth of democracy: 12 constitutions of central and eastern Europe* (1995) and in the *Constitutions of central and eastern Europe* edited by Flanz, published in 1995. A German translation of the new constitution of Slovenia is *Slowenien-Kroatien-Serbien: die neuen Verfassungen* (Marko and Boric, 1991). The constitution can also be found in Slovene, English and partly in French at http://www.sigor.si/us/eus-ds.html on the Internet.

Slovenia has a bicameral parliament: the *Drzavni Svet Republike Slovenije* [National Council of the Republic of Slovenia] with 40 members and the *Drzavni Zbor Republike Slovenije* [National Assembly of the Republic of Slovenia] with 90 members, elected for four years. The President represents the Republic; he is elected for five years by direct elections. He proposes to the National Assembly a candidate for the office of prime minister. The ministers are appointed and dismissed by the National Assembly, upon the proposal of the prime minister. The National Council (art.96 ff) represents social, economic, trade, professional and local interests. It is composed of 40 Councillors, representing employers, employees, farmers, small business persons and independent professionals. The National Council may require the establishment of a Parliamentary Inquiry, for a referendum and so on. The National Assembly may require the National Council to provide its opinions on specific matters.

The Supreme Court is the highest court in the state. The National Assembly elects judges upon the recommendation of the Judicial Council, a body composed of 11 members. The Constitutional Court consists of nine judges, elected by the National Assembly on the nomination of the President of the Republic. The new Law on the Constitutional Court, promulgated in *Uradni list RS* no.15/1994 is an important element in the judicial reforms; it is available in Slovene, English and French on the Court's extensive Internet site (http://www.sigov.si/us/eus-ds.html).

Introductory works on the legal system and legal research

See the **General** section above.

Legislation

The official gazette of Slovenia is the *Uradni list . . . Slovenije* published since 1945 in Ljubljana, with small variations in the title. Some important legislation is available in translation from an Internet site based at the Slovenian parliamentary library (http://www.sigov.si/cqi-bin/spl/dz). Parliamentary business is recorded in *Poročevalec Državnega zbora Republike Slovenije* (1975–).

Codes and commentaries

Yugoslav civil legislation was enacted in the form of separate statutes for every field of civil law. A handbook of civil and economic law (general part) in Slovenia has been written by Toplak (1990).

Slovenia issued the *Kazenski zakonik republike Slovenije* [Penal Code of the Republik Slovenia] in *Uradni list RS* of 13 October 1994, no.63, item 2167. It came into effect on 1 January 1995 replacing the old Criminal Code of the SFRY of 1977. The new criminal code is a modern and comprehensive one, consisting of a general part and a special part. A recent edition is by Bavcon (1995).

The new Code of Criminal Procedure, published in the *Uradni list RS* 1994, no.63, item 2168, also replaced the old code of the SFRY of 1977 and came into effect on 1 January 1995. The next item in the same *Uradni list RS* 1994, no.63 , item 2169, gives the new law on the public prosecutor, replacing the one of 1977.

Treaties

Treaties and international agreements concluded by Slovenia are published in *Uradni List Mednarodne pogodbe [MP].*

Law reports, judgments

At the time of writing there are no official publications of the Supreme Court, the civil court or the penal court. Decisions are reported in the general law journals.

Before the break-up of Yugoslavia the decisions of the Slovenian Constitutional Court were published annually in the *Odluke i mišlenja Ustavnog suda Jugoslavije* [Decisions and opinions of the Constitutional Court of Yugoslavia] (1972–1991). At present documents of the Constitutional court are published in the *Uradni list RS*. The Court's Internet site (address above) has many of the Court's decisions, many with full text English instructions.

Bibliographies

Official publications are included in the national bibliography of Slovenia, *Slovenska bibliografija*, published quarterly. *Slovenia: a bibliography in foreign languages* has been published in New York in two volumes (1990–1991).

Current information sources

See the general Internet address given below and in the **General** section above.

Journals, research reports

The Association of Jurists in Slovenia issues *Pravnik: Revija za pravno teorijo in prakso* [Lawyer: review of theory and practice] (1945–). The general legal journal of the faculty of law in Ljubljana is *Zbornik znanstvenih razprav* (1920/21–) which also has a table of contents in English.

Statistics

Statistical data can be found in the *Statistični letopis Slovenije* [Statistical chronicle of Slovenia] (1992–), formerly *Statistični letopis SR Slovenije* (1952–1991).

Useful addresses: Slovenia

Associations of lawyers

Odvelniska Zbornica Slovenije [Bar Association of Slovenia], Trdinova 8, 61000 Ljubljana, Slovenia. Tel: +386 61 312979

Society of Jurists of Slovenia, Dalmati-nova 4, Ljubljana, Slovenia

Government organizations

Government Information Office, Levstikova 10, Ljubljana, Slovenia. Tel: +386 2125 0111. Fax: +386 212312. Issues official government press releases

Ministry of Justice, Zupanciceva 3, 61000 Ljubljana, Slovenia. Tel: +386 61 1765271. Fax: +386 61 210200

Statistical Office of Slovenia, Vorzarski Pot 12, 61000 Ljubljana, Slovenia. Tel: +386 61 150141. Fax: +386 61 150134

Education and training

Univerza v Ljubljana, pravne fakultete [University of Ljubljana, Faculty of Law], Kongresni trg.12, 61000 Ljubljana, Slovenia. Tel: +386 61 125 4055. Fax: +386 61 125 4053

Libraries

Biblioteka Slovenske akademije znanosti i umetnosti [Library of the Slovenian Academy of Sciences and Art], Novi trg 4–5, 61001 Ljubljana, Slovenia. Tel: +386 61 125 6068. Fax: +386 61 125 5232

Drzavni Zbor RS, Dokumentacija s Knjižnjica [Parliament of Slovenia Library], Subičeva 4, 61000 Ljubljana, Slovenia. Tel: +386 61 125 30 60. Fax: +386 61 125 8160. Internet: http://www.sigov.si/cqi-bin/spl/dz for some important legislation in English translation. Attached to the National Assembly.

Knjižnica Pravne fakultete [Library of the Faculty of Law], Trg revolucije 11, Ljubljana, Slovenia. Founded in 1920.

Narodna in univerzitetna knjižnica [National and University Library], Turjaška 1, 61000 Ljubljana, Slovenia. Tel: +386 61 150 141. Fax: +386 61 150 134. Founded in 1774. Incorporates state copyright and deposit library. Publishes *Slovenska bibliografija* quarterly as well as other bibliographic periodicals.

University of Maribor Library, Gospejna 10, 62000 Maribor, Slovenia. Tel: +386 62 2581. Fax: +386 62 227558. The focus for computerized bibliographic services in Slovenia.

Publishers

Časopisni zavod Uradni list Republike Slovenije, Naročisniški oddelek, Slovenska 9 p.p. 379/VII, 1000 Ljubljana, Slovenia. Fax: +386 61 1251418. Official publisher, publishes the official gazette.

Others

Internet address for material on Slovenia: http://www.ij5.5i/slo.html
Centre for International Cooperation and Development, Kardeljeva Ploscad 1, 61000 Ljubljana, Slovenia. Tel: +386 61 183597. Fax: +386 61 343696
Chamber of Commerce of Slovenia, Slovenska 19, 61000 Ljubljana, Slovenia. Tel: +386 61 15122. Fax: +386 61 315944

Macedonia

Please also consult the **General** section above.

Historical and constitutional background

After a referendum held on 9 September 1991 Republika Makedonija [Republic of Macedonia] adopted a new constitution on 17 November 1991, which was published in the *Služben vesnik na RM* 1991, no.52, item 998. An English translation of the new constitution of Macedonia can be found in *The rebirth of democracy: 12 constitutions of central and eastern Europe* (1995) and in the looseleaf *Constitutions of central and eastern Europe* edited by Flanz (1995).

Greece objected to the use of the word 'Macedonia' in the constitutional name. The country was admitted to the membership of the UN but the dispute is the subject of continuing negotiations.

Macedonia has an unicameral Assembly [*Sobranie na Republika Makedonija*] with 120–140 members elected for four years. The President represents the Republic; he is elected for five years by direct elections. The executive branch of the government consists of the president, a prime minister, 15 ministries and several agencies. The judicial branch is independent. There are supreme, higher and lower courts. The Constitutional Court (art.108 ff) has nine judges, elected by the parliament for a single nine-year term. A special Judicial Council composed of seven members proposes the election, discipline and discharge of judges. The Public Attorney is elected by the Assembly (art.77). He protects the constitutional and legal rights of citizens when violated by bodies of state administration and by other bodies and organizations with public mandates. The Public Prosecutor's Office is a single and autonomous state body carrying out legal measures against persons who have committed criminal and other offences determined by law (art.106). The Public Prosecutor is appointed by the Assembly for six years and discharged by the Assembly.

Introductory works on the legal system and legal research

See the **General** section above.

Legislation

The official gazette of Macedonia *Služben vesnik na Republika Makedonija* has been published in Skopje since 1954, with slight variations in the title. The Assembly of Macedonia publishes the *Sobranski informator* [The Assembly's Informer] and the *Dneven informator* [Daily Informer] recording parliamentary business.

Codes and commentaries

The Macedonian Civil Code and the Code of Civil Procedure both date from 1977. In civil law, the basic ownership law of 1980 has been amended in 1990 (*Službeni list SFRY* no.36/1990). The Code of Civil Procedure has been amended in 1992 (*Služben Vesnik* no.24/1992).

Macedonia still uses the Criminal Code of 1977 (see above) although amended several times. The latest amendments have been published in the *Služben Vesnik* no.28/1991; 25/1992; 32/1993. The same is true of the Code of Criminal Procedure; the latest amendment has been published in the *Služben Vesnik* no.24/1992. New laws are expected in 1996, both in the field of criminal law and in criminal procedure.

Treaties

International treaties are published in the official gazette, *Služben Vesnik.*

Law reports, judgments

The Supreme Court prepares an annual bulletin, subdivided into three parts: penal, civil and administrative cases; no further information is available.

Before the break-up of Yugoslavia the decisions of the Macedonian Constitutional Court were published annually in the *Odluke i mišlenja Ustavnog suda Jugoslavije* [Decisions and opinions of the Constitutional Court of Yugoslavia] (1972–1991). Currently the decisions of the Constitutional Court of Macedonia are published in the official gazette. A retrospective collection of decisions of the Constitutional Court has been published recently: *Zbirka na odluki i rešenija na Ustavniot sud na Republika Makedonija 1991–1995* [Collection of decisions and resolutions of the Constitutional Court of the Republic of Macedonia 1991–1995] (1996).

Bibliographies

The *Makedonska bibliografija* (1951–) is published quarterly in three series and the yearbook *Bibliografija Makedonika* give general bibliographical information.

Dictionaries

Uzunov and Stevanović-Anćeska (1994) of the Faculty of Economics of the University of Skopje have compiled an *English–Macedonian and Macedonian–English Dictionary of economics and business.*

Current information sources

See the general Internet addresses below and also the **General** section above.

Journals, research reports

The Association of Macedonian Jurists, in cooperation with the Faculty of Law of Skopje, issues six times a year: *Pravna Misla: Spisanie za pravni i opštestveni prašanja* [Legal thought, writings in legal and social questions] (1953–). Starting with 1992 the monthly *Pravnik* [Lawyer] has been published by the Association of Macedonian jurists, working in the field of economic law.

Statistics

Statistical materials can be found in: *Statistički godišnjak na Makedonija* [Statistical Yearbook of Macedonia] (1992–), formerly *Statistički godišnjak SR Makedonija* (1945–1991).

Useful addresses: Macedonia

Associations of lawyers

Advokatska Komora na SR Makedonija [Bar Association of Macedonia], Pitu Guli 70, 91000 Skopje, Macedonia. Tel: +389 91 23455

Sojuz na Združenijata na Pravnicite na Makedonija [Union of Associations of Jurists of Macedonia], Ustaven sud na Makedonija XII udarna brigada 2, 91000 Skopje, Macedonia.

Education and training

Univerzitet 'Sv. Kiril i Metodij' [University of Skopje], POB 576, Bulevar Krste Misirkov b.b., 91000 Skopje, Macedonia. Tel: +389 91 116323. Fax: +38991 116 370

Research institutes

Open Media Research Institute (OMRI), 140 62 Prague 4. Motokov Building. Na Strzi 63., Prague, Czech Republic. Tel: +42-2-6114 2114; Fax: +42-2-6114 3323. Internet: http://www.omri.cz/Publications/Digests/DigestIndex.html

Libraries

Narodna i universitetska biblioteka 'Sv. Kliment Ohridski' [National and University Library `St. Kliment Ohridski'], Bul. Goce Delčev 6, 91000 Skopje, Macedonia. Tel: +389 91 115 177. Fax: +389 91 230 874. Founded in 1944. State copyright, central and deposit library, publishes the national bibliography

Others

Internet addresses for material on Macedonia:
http://enws121.eas.asu.edu/places/macedonia/republic/index.html
http://www.rit.edu/~bvs4997/macedonia/index1.html
http://www.auburn.edu/~mitrege/macedonia/

Chamber of Commerce for Macedonia, Ivo R. Lola 25, 91000 Skopje, Macedonia. Tel: +389 91 229211

List of works cited

This list contains the works cited in all the sections of this chapter.

Anali Pravnog Fakulteta u Beogradu. (1953–) Belgrade.

Arhiv za Pravne i Društvene Nauke [Records on law and social sciences]. (1914–) Belgrade: Association of Yugoslav Jurists. Quarterly.

Balkan Forum: an international journal of politics, economics and culture. (1993–) Skopje: Nova Makedonija.

Bavcon, Ljuba (1995) *Kazenski zakonik republike Slovenije* [Penal Code of the Republik Slovenia]. Ljubljana: Uradni list RS.

Benson, M. (1994) *Srpskohrvatsko–engleski re nik = Serbocroatian–English dictionary* 3rd edn. Cambridge: Cambridge University Press.

Bibliografija Makedonika. Skopje: Narodna i universitetska biblioteka 'Sv. Kliment Ohridski' [National and University Library `St. Kliment Ohridski'].

Bibliografija zvaničnih publikacija SFRJ. Knjige. Serijske publikacije (1971–1991) [Bibliography of official publications of the SFRY. Books and serial publications] Ed. R.

Glavički. Belgrade: Jugoslovenski bibliografsko-informacijski institut. Annual.

Bibliografija zvaničnih publikacija SRJ. Knjige. Serijske publikacije [Bibliography of official publications of the FRY. Books and serial publications] (1992–) Ed. R. Glavički. Belgrade: Jugoslovenski bibliografsko-informacijski institut. Annual.

Bilten sudske prakse Saveznog suda [Bulletin of the Federal Court's Practice]. (1975–1993) Belgrade: Službeni glasnik.

Bilten sudske prakse Vrhovnog suda Srbije [Bulletin of the Practice of the Supreme Court of Serbia]. (1993–) Belgrade: Službeni glasnik.

Blagojević, Borislav T. (1974) Yugoslavia. In *International encyclopedia of comparative law*, ed. V. Knapp, vol.1, pp. Y5–Y33. Tübingen: J.C.B. Mohr.

Blagojević, Borislav T. (1977) *Guide to the Yugoslav legal system*. Belgrade: Institute of Comparative Law.

Blagojević, Borislav T. (1991) The legal system of the Socialist Federal Republic of Yugoslavia (SFRY). In *Modern legal systems cyclopedia*, ed. K.R. Redden, vol.8, pp. 8.220.1–8.220.123. Buffalo, NY: Hein. Looseleaf; there has been some recent supplementation. Also a chapter preceding Blagojević by E.B. Ford Jr. entitled: The legal system of Yugoslavia: background, pp. 8.210.1–8.210.33.

BNA's Eastern Europe Reporter. (1991–) Washington, DC: Bureau of National Affairs.

Bosnia and Herzegovina: Constitution of the Federation [March 8, 1994]. (1994) *International Legal Materials*, **33**, pp. 740–784.

Bosnia and Herzegovina: Constitution 1995 (1996) *Balkan Forum*, **4**, pp. 260–285.

Bosnia-Herzegovina bibliography = Bosna-Herse bibliyografyasi. (1993) Dokmantasyon Daire Baskanligi, no.8. Ankara: T.C. Basbakanlik Devet Arsivleri Geral Mdrlg.

Brunner, G. (1992) Development of a constitutional judiciary in eastern Europe. *Review of Central and East European Law*, 1992, no.6, pp. 535–553.

Brunner, G., Schmidt, K. and Westen, K. (1992–) *Wirtschaftsrecht der osteuropäischen Staaten*. Baden-Baden: Nomos. Looseleaf.

Central Europe Newsletter. (1992–) London: Clifford Chance.

Central European and CIS Legal Update. (1993–) London: Baker & McKenzie.

Chloros, A.G. (1970) *Yugoslav civil law: history, family, property: commentary and texts*. Oxford: Clarendon Press.

Collection of Yugoslav Laws. (1962–) Belgrade: Institut za uporedno pravo [Institute of Comparative Law].

Concise atlas of the Republic of Croatia and of the Republic of Bosnia and Hercegovina. (1993) Zagreb: Miroslav Krleža Lexicographical Institute.

Country profile. annual survey of political and economic background [Yugoslavia]. (1992–) London: Economist Publications.

Delegatski vjestnik [Deputies Gazette]. (1974–1990) Zagreb.

Dneven Informator [Daily Informer]. Skopje. Records business of the Macedonian parliament.

Doing business in eastern Europe. (1992–) Bicester: CCH Editions Ltd.

Druker, J. (1990) (ed.) *The laws on economic reform*. Belgrade: Srboštampa.

East European Case Reporter of Constitutional Law. (1994–) Den Bosch: Bookworld.

East European Constitutional Review. (1992–) Chicago, Ill.: Center for the Study of Constitutionalism in Eastern Europe at the University of Chicago Law School in partnership with the Central European University.

Eastern European Forum Newsletter. (1993–) London: International Bar Association.

Ekonomski pregled: mesečni informativni pregled [Economic Survey: monthly informative survey]. (1994–) Belgrade: Savezno ministarstvo za nauku, tehnologiju i razvoj [Ministry of Science, Technology and Development].

Flanz, Gisbert H. (1995) *Constitutions of central and eastern Europe*. Dobbs Ferry, NY: Oceana. Looseleaf.

Friedman, Francine (1993) (ed.) *Yugoslavia: a comprehensive English-language bibliography*. Wilmington, Del.: Scholarly Resources.

Gjupanovich, F. and Adamovich, A. (1964) *Legal sources and bibliography of Yugosla-*

via. Praeger Publications in Russian History and World Communism, no.21. New York: Praeger.

Godišnjak [Yearbook (of the Croatian Parliament)]. (1993–) Zagreb.

Gsovski, V. and Grzybovski, K. (1959) (eds) *Government, law and courts in the Soviet Union and eastern Europe*. London: Stevens & Sons; The Hague: Mouton & Co. 2 vols.

Hayden, R.M. (1994) The Constitution of the Federation of Bosnia and Herzegovina: an imaginary constitution for an illusory 'federation'. *Balkan Forum*, **2**, pp. 77–91.

Hayden, R.M. (1995) The 1995 Agreements on Bosnia and Herzegovina and the Dayton Constitution: the political utility of a constitutional illusion. *East European Constitutional Review*, **4**, pp. 59–68.

Hrvatska Bibliografija. (1952?–) Zagreb. Monthly and annual.

Image on Central + Eastern Europe: the International KPMG Newsletter. (1991–) Brussels: KPMG.

Ivošević, Z. (1995) (ed.) *Zbornik sudske prakse: 1975–1985* [Collection of court practice: 1975–1985]. Belgrade: Sud udruženog rada Srbije.

Izbor odluka Vrhovnog suda Republike Hrvatske [Selection of decisions of the Supreme Court of the Republic of Croatia]. (1993–) Zagreb.

Izbor sudske prakse: stručno-informativni časopis [Selection of court practice: special informative periodical]. (1993–) Belgrade: 'Slobodan Jović'.

Izvješća Hrvatskogo Sabora [Reports of the Croatian Parliament]. (1991–) Zagreb.

Jahrbuch für Ostrecht. (1960–) Munich: Beck.

Journal of Constitutional Law in Eastern and Central Europe. (1994–) Den Bosch: Bookworld.

Jugoslovenska revija za kriminologiju i krivično pravo [Yugoslav Review of Criminology and Criminal Law]. (1963–) Belgrade.

Jugoslovenska revija za međunarodno pravo [Yugoslav Review of International Law]. (1954–) Belgrade: Ministry of Science and Technology in cooperation with the Soros Foundation.

Jugoslovenski pregled. (1957–) Belgrade. English edition: *Yugoslav Survey*.

Kitarović, I. (1992) (ed.) *Registar važećih propisa i sudske prakse* [Register of current regulations and court practice]. Belgrade: Savremena administracija.

Kokolj, M. (1993) (ed.) *Krivični zakon Savezne Republike Jugoslavije: sa objašnjenjima i uputstvima* [Criminal Code of the FRY: with interpretations and instructions]. Belgrade: Službeni glasnik.

Law in Transition: a Newsletter on Legal Cooperation & Training from the European Bank for Reconstruction and Development. (1994–) London: European Bank for Reconstruction and Development.

Makedonska bibliografija [Macedonian bibliography]. (1951–) Skopje: Narodna i universitetska biblioteka 'Sv. Kliment Ohridski [National and University Library `St. Kliment Ohridski']. Annual.

Marko, J. and Boric, T. (1991) *Slowenien-Kroatien-Serbien: die neuen Verfassungen*. Vienna: Böhlau Verlag.

Michta, A. (1994) *The government and politics of postcommunist Europe*. Westport, Conn.: Praeger.

Milosavljević, Margot and Milosavljević, Boško (1990) (trans.) *Constitution of the Republic of Serbia*. Belgrade: Srboštampa.

Milosavljević, Margot and Milosavljević, Boško (1992) (trans.) *Constitution of the Federal Republic of Yugoslavia*. Belgrade: Srboštampa for the Ministry of Information of the Republic of Serbia in Belgrade and the Secretariat for Information of the Republic of Montenegro in Podgorica.

Narodne novine – Međunarodni Ugovori [Peoples News – International Treaties]. (1993–) Zagreb: Narodne novine.

Narodne novine: Službeni list Republike Hrvatske [People's News: the official gazette of the Republic of Croatia]. (1990–) Zagreb: Narodne novine. Previous edition *Narodne novine: Službeni list Socijalističke Republike Hrvatske* (1945–1990).

Novo Jugoslovensko pravo = New Yugoslav Law. (1950–1974) Belgrade: Association of Jurists. French edition also published.

Odluke i mišlenja Ustavnog suda Jugoslavije [Decisions and opinions of the Constitutional Court of Yugoslavia]. (1972–1991) Belgrade: Ustavni sud. Annual.

Odluke i rešenja saveznog Ustavnog suda 1992 i 1993 [Decisions and resolutions of the Constitutional Court for 1992 and 1993]. (1994) Belgrade: Savezni ustavni sud.

OMRI Daily Digest. (1994–) Prague: Open Media Research Institute. Electronic periodical (available at Listserv@ubvm.cc.Buffalo.edu).

Osteuropa-Recht (1955–) Stuttgart: Gesellschaft für Osteuropakunde.

Parker School Journal of East European Law. (1994–) New York: Parker School of Foreign and Comparative Law, Columbia University School of Law.

Perović, M. (1978) (ed.) *Jugoslovensko krivično zakonodavstvo: Krivični zakon SFRJ sa napomenama i registrom pojmova, Zakon o krivičnom postupku, Krivići zakoni socijalističkih republika i socijalističkih autonomnih pokrajina* [Yugoslav criminal legislation. The Criminal Code of the SFRY with notes and index. The Code on Criminal Procedure. The criminal codes of the socialist republics and the socialist autonomous provinces]. Biblioteka 'Zbirke Propisa'. Belgrade: NIP Export Press.

Petaković, R. (1990) (ed.) *Zakon o krivičnom postupku sa sudskom praksom i registrom pojmova* [Law on criminal procedure with court practice and index of legal concepts]. Belgrade: Poslovni biro.

Petaković, R. (1992) (ed.) *Krivični zakon Srbije: sa sudskom praksom i registrom pojmova; Zakon o izvršenju krivičnih sankcija Srbije* [Criminal law of Serbia: with court practice and index of legal concepts; law on the execution of criminal sanctions in Serbia] 2nd edn. Belgrade: Poslovni biro.

Petrić, B. (1983) (ed.) *Zakon o krivičnom postupku objašnjen sudskom praksom* [Law on criminal procedure with court practice]. Belgrade: Službeni list SFRJ.

Poročevalec Državnega zbora Republike Slovenije [Gazette of the Deputies of the Republic of Slovenia]. (1975–) Ljubljana.

Pravna Misla: Spisanie za pravni i opštestveni prašanja. (1953–) Skopje: Association of Macedonian Jurists.

Pravni život: Časopis za pravnu teoriju i praksu [Legal life: periodical for legal theory and practice]. (1952–) Belgrade: Association of Jurists.

Pravnik. (1992–) Skopje: Association of Macedonian Jurists.

Pravnik: Revija za pravno teorijo in prakso. (1945–) Ljubljana: Association of Jurists in Slovenia.

Pravo. Teorija i praksa. (1983–) Novi Sad.

Pravo u gospodarstvu: časopis za gospodarsko-pravnu teoriju i praksu [Journal for Business Law Theory and Practice]. (1963–) Zagreb: Association for Economic Jurists. Title at first publication in 1963: *Privreda i pravo: časopis za gospodarsko-pravnu teoriju i praksu* [Economic law: . . .]. Date of change of title unknown.

Pregled sudske prakse: Prilog (naše) Zakonitosti. (1972–) Zagreb: Narodne novine. A co-publication of the Constitutional Court, the Supreme Court, the Economic Court and the Administrative Court of Croatia, the Ministry of Justice and Economy and the Republican Misdemeanour Chamber.

Promene: poslovne informacije jugoslavenske vlade [Changes: business information of the Yugoslav government]. (1990–) Belgrade: Savezno izvršno veće.

The rebirth of democracy: 12 constitutions of central and eastern Europe. (1995). Edited by The International Institute for Democracy. Strasbourg: Council of Europe. Croatia, pp. 67–113; Macedonia, pp. 331–378; Slovenia, pp. 553–616.

Recht in Ost und West. (1957–) Berlin: Arno Spitz.

Review of Central and East European Law. (1992–) Dordrecht: Kluwer. Published in cooperation with the Institute of East European Law and Russian Studies of Leiden University. Formerly *Review of Socialist Law.*

Review of Socialist Law. (1975–1991) Dordrecht: Nijhoff. Published in cooperation with the Institute of East European Law and Russian Studies of Leiden University. Superseded by *Review of Central and East European Law* (1992–).

Reynolds, T.H. (1992) Socialist legal systems: reflections on their emergence and demise. *International Journal of Legal Information*, **20**, pp. 215–237.

Simons, William B. (1980) *The constitutions of the communist world*. Alphen aan den Rijn: Sijthoff & Noordhoff.

Slovenia: a bibliography in foreign languages. (1990–1991) New York: Studia Slovenica. 2 vols.

Slovenska bibliografija [Slovene bibliography]. (1947–) Ljubljana: Narodna i universitetna knižnica.

Služben vesnik na Republika Makedonija [Official Herald of the Republic of Macedonia]. (1954–) Skopje.

Službene novine [Official news]. (1918–1944) Belgrade.

Službene novine Federacije Bosne i Hercegovine [Official News of the Federation of B&H]. (1995?–) Sarajevo.

Službeni glasnik Republike Srbije [Official Gazette of the Republic of Serbia]. (1945–) Belgrade.

Službeni glasnik Republike Srpske [Official Gazette of the 'Republika Srpske'. (199?–) Sarajevo.

Službeni glasnik srpskog naroda u Bosni i Hercegovini [Official Gazette of the Serbian people in B&H]. (199?–) Sarajevo.

Službeni list. Međunarodni Ugovori. (Federativne Narodne Republike Jugoslavije) [Official Gazette. International treaties]. (1953–1992) Belgrade: Štampa Državne Štamparije.

Službeni list. Međunarodni Ugovori. (Savezne Republike Jugoslavije) [Official Gazette. International treaties]. (1993–) Belgrade.

Službeni list Republike Bosne i Hercegovine [Official Gazette of the Republic B&H]. (1944–) Sarajevo.

Službeni list Republike Crne Gore [Official Gazette of the Republic of Montenegro]. (1945–) Titograd.

Službeni list Savezne Republike Jugoslavije [Official Gazette of the Federal Republic of Yugoslavia]. (1992–) Belgrade.

Službeni list Socijalističke Federativne Republike Jugoslavije (Federativne Narodne Republike Jugoslavije) [Official Gazette of the Socialist Federal Republic of Yugoslavia (Federal People's Republic)]. (1945–1991) Belgrade: Štampa Državne Štamparije. Earlier titles: *Službeni list Demoskratske Federativne Jugoslavije*, 1945; *Službeni list Federativne Narodne Republike Jugoslavije*, 1945–1963. Formerly *Službene Novine* [Official News], (1918–1941).

Sobranski informator [The Assembly's Informer]. Skopje.

Srdić, Milutin (1994) (ed.) *Jugoslovenski procesni zakoni* 5th edn. Belgrade: Službeni glasnik/Kosmos.

Statistički godišnjak BiH [Statistical yearbook of B&H]. (1992–) Sarajevo: Zavod za statistiku. Formerly *Statistički godišnjak SR BiH* (1945–1991).

Statistički godišnjak Jugoslavije = Statistical Yearbook of Yugoslavia. (1954–1991) Belgrade: Savezni zavod za statistiku. Partly in English.

Statistički godišnjak na Makedonija [Statistical yearbook of Macedonia]. (1992–) Skopje: Zavod za statistika. Formerly *Statistički godišnjak SR Makedonija* (1945–1991).

Statistički godišnjak Republike Crne Gore [Statistical yearbook of Montenegro]. (1991–) Titograd: Republički zavod za statistiku. Previously entitled: *Statistički godišnjak SR Crne Gore*.

Statistički godišnjak Srbije [Statistical yearbook of Serbia]. (1992–) Belgrade: Republički zavod za statistiku. Previously entitled: *Statistički godišnjak SR Srbije* (1951–1991).

Statistički ljetopis Hrvatskih županija [Statistical yearbook of Croatian Districts]. (1994–) Zagreb: Zavod za statistiku.

Statistički ljetopis Republike Hrvatske [Statistical yearbook of Croatia]. (1993–) Zagreb: Zavod za statistiku. Formerly *Statistički godišnjak SR Hrvatske* (1953–1991).

Statistički letopis Slovenije [Statistical yearbook of Slovenia]. [1992–] Ljubljana: Zavod Slovenije za statistiko. Formerly *Statisti ni letopis SR Slovenije* (1952–1991).

Stenografske Beleške/Skupština SFRJ, Savezno veće [Stenographic notes of the Assembly of the SFRY]. (1945–1992) Belgrade: Skupština SFRJ, Savezno veće. English edition: *Yugoslav Assembly*.

Stenografske Beleške/Skupština SR Srbije. (1992–) Belgrade: Narodna skupština RS.

Stojanović, Z. (1995) *Krivični zakon Savezne Republike Jugoslavije: sa komentarom i registrom pojmova* [Criminal Code of FRY with commentary and index]. Belgrade: Službeni list SRJ.

Stojanović, Z. and Petrić, O. (1996) *Komentar Krivičnog zakona Republike Srbije i Krivični zakon Republike Crne Gore s objašnjenjima* [Commentary on the Criminal Code of the Republic of Serbia and the Criminal Code of the Republic of Montenegro with explanations]. Belgrade: Službeni list SRJ.

Sudske i upravna praksa: stalne, tematske publikacije [Court and administrative practice: continuing, thematic publication]. (1993–) Belgrade: Savremena administracija. Quarterly.

Sudske prakse stručno-informativni časopis [Court practice: special informative periodical]. (1981–) Belgrade: Poslovna politica. Monthly.

Sudske i upravna praksa za organizacija udruženog rada, SIZ i radne zajednice [Court and administrative practice on the organization of associated labour, self-management communities and workers' collectives]. (?–1992) Belgrade: Savremena administracija.

SWB: Summary of World Broadcasts: part 2, Central Europe, the Balkans. (1993–) Reading: BBC Monitoring.

Terry, G.M. (1982) Yugoslavia. *Official publications of the Soviet Union and eastern Europe 1945–1980: a select annotated bibliography*, ed. G. Walker, pp. 151–185. London: Mansell.

Toplak, L. (1990) *Civilno pravo: Splošni del* [Civil law: general part] 3rd edn. Ljubljana: gospodarski vestnik.

Transition: Events and Issues in the Former Soviet Union and East Central and Southeastern Europe. (1995–) Prague: OMRI.

Trifunovska, S. (1994) (ed.) *Yugoslavia through documents: from its creation to its dissolution*. Dordrecht: Martinus Nijhoff

Uporedno pomorsko pravo = Comparative Maritime Law. (1960–) Zagreb: Croatian Academy of Sciences.

Uradni List. Mednarodne pogodbe [MP] [Official Gazette. International treaties]. (1993–) Ljubljana.

Uradni list . . . Slovenije [Official Gazette . . . Slovenia]. (1945–) Ljubljana.

Ustav Savezne Republika Jugoslavije; Ustavni zakon za sprovodenje Ustava; Zakon o izboru saveznih poslanika u Veće građana Savezne skupštine; Zakon o izboru i razrešenju Predsednika Republike. [Constitution of the Federal Republic of Yugoslavia; Constitutional Law for putting into effect of the Constitution; Law on the elections of the representatives of the Chamber of Citizens of the Federal Assembly; Law on the election and dismissal of the President of the Republic]. (1992) Belgrade: Savremena adminstratija/'Branko Donović'.

Uzunov, Nikola and Stevanović-Anćeska, Ljiljana (1994) *English–Macedonian and Macedonian–English Dictionary of economics and business*. Skopje: Ekonomski fakultet.

Vasiljević, T. and Grubač, M. (1987) *Komentar zakona o krivičnom postupku* [Commentary on the Code of Criminal Procedure] 3rd edn. Belgrade: Savremena Administracija.

Vedriš, M. (1996) *Građansko pravo: opći dio, obvezno i nasljedno pravo* [Civil Code: general part, law of obligations, inheritance law]. Zagreb: Narodne novine.

Vukadinović, R. (1992) *The break-up of Yugoslavia: threats and challenges*. The Hague: Clingendael.

Vuković, Š. (1990) (ed.) *Krivični zakon SFRJ* [Criminal Code SFRY] 9th edn. Belgrade: 'Branko Donović'.

WGO: Monatshefte für Osteuropäisches Recht. (1959–) Heidelberg: Müller.

WiRO: Wirtschaft und Recht in Osteuropa. (1992–) Munich: Beck.

Yugoslav law = Droit Yougoslave. (1975–1989?) Belgrade. Association of Jurists.

Yugoslav Survey. (1960–) Belgrade. English edition of *Jugoslovenski pregled.*

Zakonitost. (1990–) Zagreb: Association of Jurists in Croatia. Formerly *Naša zakonitost* (1947–1989).

Zbirka na odluki i rešenija na Ustavniot sud na Republika Makedonija 1991–1995 [Collection of decisions and resolutions of the Constitutional Court of the Republic of Macedonia 1991–1995]. (1996) Skopje.

Zbirka pravnih propisa Narodnih novina [Collections of legal rules published in the *People's News*]. (1962–) Zagreb: Narodne novina.

Zbirka saveznih propisa [Collection of federal regulations]. (1954–1990) Belgrade. Continued by *Zbirka saveznih propisa.* (1990–) eds D. Bogdanović, R. Čukić and M. Manasijević. Belgrade: Kosmos.

Zbirka sudskih odluka [Collection of court decisions]. (1956–1983) Belgrade: Službeni list SFRJ.

Zbornik Pravnog Fakulteta u Zagrebu. (1948–) Zagreb: Pravnog Fakulteta u Zagrebu.

Zbornik propisa Jugoslovenskog zakonodavstva: savezni, republiči i pokrajinski zakoni [Collection of Yugoslav legislation: federal, republican and regional laws]. (1988) Belgrade: Narodna Knjiga. 3 vols.

Zbornik radova. (1963–) Split: Pravni Fakultet u Splitu.

Zbornik radova. (1966–) Novi Sad: Pravni Fakultet u Novom Sadu. French edition entitled *Recueil des traveaux.*

Zbornik znanstvenih razprav. (1920/21–) Ljubljana: Univerza v Ljubljana, pravne fakultete [University of Ljubljana, Faculty of Law].

Zindović, I. and Dragutinović, O. ([1995]) *Krivično pravo i sudskoj praksi: KZ Srbije i KZ Crne Gore sa kommentarom i sudskom praksom* [Criminal law and court practice: Criminal law of Serbia and Criminal law of Montenegro with commentary and court practice] Belgrade: Litopapir.

Index

Note: The main sections only under each country are indexed, as are the names of the largest or multi-national databases. As considerably more information is given in the UK sections, that material is indexed in more detail than that for other countries.